INTEREST GROUPS
Policy and Politics in America

GRAHAM WOOTTON

Tufts University

Prentice-Hall, Inc., Englewood Cliffs, New Jersey 07632

Library of Congress Cataloging in Publication Data

Wootton, Graham.
  Interest groups.

  Includes bibliographical references and index.
    1. Pressure groups—United States. I. Title.
JK1118.W66 1985   322.4'3'0973   84-16023
ISBN 0-13-468877-5

To
Mary, Jini, and J.V.E.
and the memory of
Sarah and R.R.R.

Cover design: Lundgren Graphics, LTD.
Manufacturing buyer: Barbara Kittle

© 1985 by Prentice-Hall, Inc., Englewood Cliffs, New Jersey 07632

All rights reserved. No part of this book may be
reproduced, in any form or by any means,
without permission in writing from the publisher.

Printed in the United States of America

10 9 8 7 6 5 4 3 2 1

ISBN 0-13-468877-5 01

Prentice-Hall International, Inc., *London*
Prentice-Hall of Australia Pty. Limited, *Sydney*
Editora Prentice-Hall do Brasil, Ltda., *Rio de Janeiro*
Prentice-Hall Canada Inc., *Toronto*
Prentice-Hall of India Private Limited, *New Delhi*
Prentice-Hall of Japan, Inc., *Tokyo*
Prentice-Hall of Southeast Asia Pte. Ltd., *Singapore*
Whitehall Books Limited, *Wellington, New Zealand*

*(Acknowledgments begin on page 381, which constitutes a continuation of the
copyright page.)*

CONTENTS

PREFACE

This is a teaching book in more senses than one. To begin with, it provides a substantial amount of basic information about the whole range of interest groups that concern themselves with national domestic policy—from the occupationally-based to the ones derived from such categories as age, gender, and ethnicity, as well as those attempting to promote a cause, including some reflecting the "backyard revolution." Although each "entry" is necessarily brief, this picture of the American group universe may be the most comprehensive drawn in recent years (chapter 7). The book also contains a substantial amount of basic information about the methods and techniques used by interest groups in pursuing their objectives (chapter 8). In addition to the standard repertoire, this chapter has something to say about procedures that, arguably, ought always to be included: use of the "revolving door" between business and government to confer built-in-access; the favoring of some types of groups in the membership of federal advisory committees; and, more controversially as a characterization, the withholding of supplies from the market apparently for the purpose of inducing a change in government policy.

Such a map is as useful as any other map of its kind. But it is inherently "flat" and static. More rounded and dynamic are the complementary case studies in Part 3, including one touching on the pot lobby. There the methods and techniques actually adopted by interest groups in certain policy areas, mainly oil-and-gas but touching the environmental, are depicted in some depth. This enables me to introduce Time (the oil depletion issue had a different look in 1926–29, 1969–75, etc.), and to illustrate how American policy making works. The cases were chosen by policy type and mostly for their political significance or interest (energy, environment, taxation, which is also featured in chapter 1). As to policy type, I use the Lowi formulation as modified by others despite the continuing controversy it arouses (which is not concealed from the students to whom this book is addressed). In other words, I use the Lowi typology as a scaffolding for teaching purposes, but without commitment either to it or to *policies determine politics* or related propositions. Of course, distributive and regulatory policies as such have long been the warp and woof of American politics, not dependent on Professor Lowi's creative imagination. As to stages of policy making, the cases mainly focus on formulation, except that with Time inserted, the distinction stands out less clearly than it is made to appear in many case studies. The highway-beautification policy, however, does bring in implementation.

This is also a teaching book in the sense that it starts with the concrete (chapter 1) and proceeds to the abstract or conceptual, drawing on stimulating, even provocative, statements that gradually receive the proper qualification. Even at this early stage, I point students in the direction of more analytical thinking, for example, by suggesting the conditions under which an interest group, on the brink of success, may be brought down and defeated (cargo preference policy, chapter 1). The book also cultivates what literary critics have called "training for critical awareness," which I take to be fundamental to a liberal arts education. Here this means in part *not* glossing over questions, even of classification and typology, that are unsettled in the professional literature, and so *not* pretending even to undergraduates that everything is cut and dried. But, above all, "training for critical awareness" here means subjecting quotations from Authority and politically prominent persons to the indirect test of being related to a broader explanatory framework (chapters 2 through 6).

In searching out a structure of explanation of the pervasiveness, activities and general character of interest-group politics, I start with a working assumption that some may consider outmoded: that (using the nineteenth century terminology) society and state can be distinguished as separate realms or domains. Today, of course, there is overlapping at many points and even interpenetration. Still, the blurred line remains distinguishable, and even now the separation of social power (including interest groups) from political authority remains fundamental. In any case, this *inter*action of the social order and the political order constitutes the basic conceptual framework. It is first suggested that a certain kind of social structure, the "manner" in which society is "put together," tends toward a politics of special interests, and that this structural development is accompanied by appropriate changes in attitudes, reinforcing the tendency (chapter 2). This, however, runs up against the "free rider" or Olson problem (critically examined in chapter 3).

All this may be conceived as deriving from society. On the other, or state, side, the tendency toward a politics of special interests may be retarded or (as in the U.S.A.) greatly advanced by the political structure (chapters 4 and 5). The tendency will also be accelerated by the rise of the Positive State, i.e., in the number, scale, and range of functions assumed by government. The more "positive" the state, the greater its attraction for special interests and so the greater their stimulation (chapter 6).

If this explanatory structure stands up as a first approximation, then the clear blue sky of plausible commentary (in chapter 1) clouds over, simplicity turns into complexity, and to that extent the problem of America as a special-interest democracy becomes more intractable, at least in the short run. In any case, it is against this background of explanation that the descriptive material of chapters 7 and 8 is presented. This sequence may not suit every instructor in every teaching situation or circumstance. He or she might prefer to launch the course on a sea of description (as I used to do myself in the course on which this book is based). I changed my original sequence, having come to believe that neither the nature of contemporary interest groups nor their activities can be well understood, much less judged, except within a socio-political framework of interrelated parts, whose exposition I then brought forward to the beginning of the course and so to the front of this book. Even so, the work remains flexible enough for an instructor to open with part 2, and then, like a film director, to "flash-back" to part 1.

The retrospective Part 4, noting the significance of election results on interest group achievements between elections, and such successful initiatives as the abortion movement and (for a long period) the consumer movement, suggests that Mr. Macgruder was too pessimistic in saying that the individual cannot affect his or her situation—only "the big lobbies can do it." Moreover, there is reason to think that differentiated function (chapter 1) tends to determine a group's scope, and that scope tends to determine a group's influence. If so, then at least some "big lobbies" may be big only, so to speak, in a fairly limited way. Such brief reflections on influence lead into questions about the responsiveness of American government and so about its system of representation. This is seen (not for the first time) as dual: a functional system of representation, embodying interest groups, superimposed upon the traditional territorial system, and now tending to swamp it. Thus the question of a special-interest democracy turns out to be a special case or facet of a broader problem. On the other hand, some reforms would seem to be practicable even in the short run.

Retrospective in another sense, I wish to single out three research assistants who, in turn, fetched, carried, and "dug" specifically for this book: Robert Keough, Michael Tortorella, and Edward Chaiban. They combined cheerfulness with efficiency even when there was little to be cheerful about (which of course is when one needs it most). I am also grateful to Ms. Rebekah Herrick for compiling the index of names. But my greatest debts in the preparation of the manuscript are to my wife, Mary, and to Ms. Jini Kelly, who in turn typed and re-typed with great speed and accuracy. Embroiled much longer in the project than the three assistants, these two principals perhaps grew a shade less cheerful as time passed by. But their work and general support were indispensable, especially when I was discovering, too late, that a Departmental chairmanship is really a form of peonage. At Prentice-Hall, Ms. Audrey Marshall often smoothed my path. Some anonymous copy-editor served me well, as did the reviewers: Michael Baer, Office of the Dean, University of Kentucky; Guy Clifford, Department of Political Science, Bridgewater State College; James Christoph, Department of Political Science, Indiana University; T. Zane Reeves, Department of Political Science, University of New Mexico; William Thompson, Department of Public Administration, University of Nevada; Alan Clem, Department of Political Science, University of South Dakota; Richard Murray, Department of Political Science, University of Houston; Henry Turner, Department of Political Science, University of California; and Jack Treadway, Department of Political Science, Kutztown State College. Production editor Mr. Andrew Roney made it all seem easy. But I owe most to executive editor Mr. Stan Wakefield, who signed me up, reassured me when things went wrong, and displayed extraordinary patience at the many tiresome delays. He deserves to have a winner with this book (and I rather hope he gets it). Warm thanks, in any case, to all concerned at every stage.

Graham Wootton
Medford, Massachusetts

CHAPTER ONE
AMERICA:
"A Special-Interest Democracy"?

The subject for debate is:

> We don't have a democracy of the people now. We have a special-interest democracy. We have the auto lobby, the oil lobby. The individual has no way of appealing to the government.
> The true democracy is where the individual is able to affect his own situation. That is not true in this country anymore. The big lobbies can do it, but the individual can't.

The proposer was no radical, long-haired or short, but Mr. Jeb Stuart Magruder, ruefully reflecting in 1973 on his experience of the White House under President Nixon and then as no. 2 on the Committee to Reelect the President.[1] That it authored and directed the melodrama of the Watergate "break-in" (making the acronym CREEP unusually appropriate) is in itself no reason for brushing aside his characterization.

On the contrary, in the late seventies and early eighties, "all sorts and conditions" of men and women, far removed from Mr. Magruder in occupation and political outlook, were saying substantially the same thing, and so can now be summoned in support of that particular judgment. We first call expert witnesses and trained observers, then turn to elected and other public officials.

Looking back at the retreating summer from the vantage point of Labor Day, 1979, celebrated columnist (and confidant of presidents), James Reston feared that "the struggle for political advantage was getting out of hand," harming the Republic:

> It is the "special interest" groups that have been dominating the news this summer, with the help of newspapers and networks that have been dramatizing their strident claims. We have been "hearing it" for Big Business and Big Labor, for the blacks and the Jews, for Christ and Chrysler—all with some honest claims and grievances—but we have been hearing very little for compromise in defense of the nation or for the common defense of the West.[2]

Just before Christmas, Mr. Reston returned to the subject, citing Mr. Derek Bok, president of Harvard University. Thinking principally about the kind of education needed for the future, Mr. Bok had wondered whether we were preparing our children for it, "for a world of unlimited personal and group interests that is gone?" Nowadays, "America no longer seems diverse so much as it seems split asunder into innumerable special interests. We read daily of gray power, gay power, red power, black power; Sun Belt and Frost Belt; environmentalists and hardhats; industrial groups, professional groups, educational groups—all more conscious of their rights, all more aware of their claims on . . . society" (than, one is tempted to add, their duties or obligations). But President Bok's main point appears to have been:

> When so many groups organize to protect their special interests, the politics of activism can become a politics of immobility, and we find ourselves unable to reach effective solutions for inflation, energy shortages, environmental issues or other national problems.[3]

Early in 1980, President Bok's eminent colleague, Harvard Law School professor Archibald Cox, also (in effect) outlined the "harm" that was being done to the Republic, but also put the problem in perspective and drew out the implications for reform.

> Government has a new and very different role than when Tom Paine could say that the government which governs least governs best. Harnessing the power unlocked by science and technology required vast aggregations of wealth and human organization. To prevent abuse by the giant enterprises, and to protect those who could no longer help themselves, we expanded the activities of government and made it big and central. Washington has become the forum in which the special interests, business corporations and other organized groups contend for tax breaks, regulatory advantage, subsidies, rich government contracts and other advantages, with all the selfishness and ambition, and all too often with the ruthlessness and deceit, that once characterized the market place.

And so,

The problem is plain. The governmental institutions, processes and procedures that worked in a simpler day are not good enough for our big government and complex society. We cannot continue to allow dairy interests to dictate agricultural policy, truckers and teamsters to dictate transportation policy, the American Medical Association to block control of hospital costs, and other special interests to feather their nests at the expense of the progress of all. Nor is it good enough just to add more bureaus, more departments, more officials and more regulations. The challenge is to reshape the machinery of self-government so that the long-run progress of the whole enterprise is the center of attention, so that every citizen knows he can participate and that his participation counts, and so that decisions are taken, hard choices are made and problems are solved.[4]

That was how things seemed at the time to some well-placed observers. Public officials were also increasingly critical. Mr. Jody Powell, the White House press secretary under President Carter, asserted: "The voices of the special-interest lobbies have become so dominant that most Congressmen are afraid of any vote that might alienate them."[5] Some distinguished congresspersons agreed. Soon after Mr. Powell had spoken, Senator Edward Kennedy criticized his congressional colleagues for being too responsive to special-interest groups, whose growth "threatened" the very process of government. In October 1979 Representative David R. Obey (Dem.-Wisconsin) complained of special-interest "intimidation." In pressing for a Department of Education separate from the Department of Health, Education and Welfare (HEW), the National Education Association (according to Mr. Obey) had said "frankly" that if congresspersons "voted against it we wouldn't get any campaign funds." But the most lugubrious voice on Capitol Hill that year belonged to Speaker Thomas P. O'Neill, Jr., of Massachusetts. Sounding to Stephen V. Roberts of the *New York Times* "a bit like an Old Testament prophet," the Speaker remarked: "I fear for this Congress, believe me. Beware of the growth of these special-interests—it's staggering."[6]

That assessment was supported in January 1981 by Representative Michael L. Synar (Dem.-Oklahoma), looking back on his first term in the House. His encounters with lobbyists had been such that he concluded:

> Outside of the three big issues—energy, the economy and government regulation—the major issue of the 80s will be the impact of special interests on this country. They have become such a dominant force in politics, financially and informationwise. They have better grass-roots organizations than most congressmen.[7]

This, too, was how it looked from the White House, seen through Republican as well as Democrat eyes. In April 1979 President Carter, proposing a windfall profits tax to accompany the decontrol of oil prices, predicted that the congressional battle would be "a classic confrontation pitting the common and public good against the enormous power of a well-organized special interest." Three months later, asserting that government in America seemed too often incapable of action, he indicted the interests:

You see a Congress twisted and pulled in every direction by hundreds of well-financed and powerful special interests. You see every extreme position defended to the last vote, almost to the last breath, by one unyielding group or another.

You often see a balance and a fair approach that demands sacrifice, a little sacrifice from everyone, abandoned like an orphan, without support and without friends.

Often you see paralysis and stagnation and drift. You don't like it.

And neither do I.[8]

He returned to the theme in his farewell address. Drawing attention to the growth of "single-issue groups and special-interest organizations," he went on:

This is a disturbing factor in American political life. It tends to distort our purposes because the national interest is not always the sum of all our single or special interests.

We are all Americans together—and we must not forget that the common good is our common interest and our individual responsibility.[9]

That particular torch was picked up and carried by Mr. Carter's Republican conqueror, President Reagan. Already, on the eve of the election, he had toyed with the idea of "a new structuring of the presidential cabinet that will make the cabinet officers the managers of the national administration—not captives of the bureaucracy or the special interests in the departments they are supposed to direct."[10] Then, as Mr. Carter retreated to Georgia, President Reagan seemed almost to echo his predecessor's concern, pledging "loyalty to only one special interest group—'We, the people.' "[11] A few months later, his vice-president, George Bush, warned: "On and on they come, they're marching on Washington today, the special interests. And American people need to override these special interests. We have got to have your support now."[12] Then, in June, President Reagan, travelling West to drum up support for his economic plan, accused the House Democratic leadership of adopting a strategy that would "once again allow special-interest groups to triumph over the general economic interest of the nation."[13]

The following year, 1982, brought some of the sharpest criticisms ever, not overlooking the "muckraking" period before World War I. Thus, economist Barbara R. Bergmann, thinking of economic policy in general and fiscal policy (taxing and spending) in particular, asserted:

The growing hordes of lobbyists on Capitol Hill armed with campaign contributions for members of Congress is more than a political scandal. It is a serious threat to the conduct of United States economic policy.

"Our current budgetary disaster is in large part the result of activity by business PACs," or political action committees. These, as "formed by special interests" generally, not just business, were "multiplying as fast as cock-

roaches in a dirty kitchen." The headline for Professor Bergmann's article—
"Lobbying: Shakedown on Capitol Hill"—caught the "feeling tone" as well as
the substance of it.[14]

What are these political action committees? Not defined under exactly
that name in the 1970s legislation, a PAC has come to denote a committee,
other than a party or candidate committee, that accepts contributions or makes
expenditures for the purpose of influencing the nomination or election of one or
more individuals for public office. PACs may derive from corporations or labor
unions provided that the contributions are voluntary and the resulting funds
are kept separate. But others (about one in five in 1982) are "nonconnected,"
e.g., the National Conservative PAC. Generally, PACs, like rabbits if not
cockroaches, had multiplied from the end of 1975, when the total stood at 722.
Four years later the two thousand-mark was reached. By 1982 there were some
thirty-three hundred, two out of five of them corporate.

What also increased was the PAC share in the total campaign financing
of House and Senate elections. In 1982, for example, PACs provided the
winners of House elections with 35 percent of all the money they raised, as
against 28 percent in 1978 and 31 percent in 1980. This meant that, in 1983,
between one in five and one in four of the House (106 members) were
beholden to PACs, and so to special interests, for fifty percent or more of
their 1982 election campaign money. Exactly what that signifies is a controversial question, but it is surely cause for concern. This extends to conservative Republicans. It was Representative Guy VanderJagt (Michigan) who, in
1983, propounded a one-third "rule": when candidates get more than one-
third of their money from PACs, it "invites suspicion."[15] Earlier, Senator
Robert Dole (Kansas) had told the *Wall Street Journal*: "When these politi-
cal-action committees give money, they expect something in return other
than good government. It is making it much more difficult to legislate. We
may reach a point where if everybody is buying something with PAC
money, we can't get anything done."[16] On this subject, evidently, conservative midwesterners sounded very like the easterners quoted earlier, some of
whom were unmistakably liberal, suggesting that the issue is not necessarily
partisan.

In order to illustrate the difficulty of legislating, we may revert to fiscal
policy and the 1981–82 Budget (which Professor Bergmann had mainly in
mind).

FISCAL POLICY

Special interests came into President Reagan's calculations in 1981 for two
interrelated reasons. His historic initiative to make deep tax cuts in expenditures on social programs precipitated the usual vigorous opposition from their
beneficiaries and other defenders. Most unusually, however, President Rea-

gan overcame it. Actually achieving the proposed cuts was indeed what made the Reagan budget revolution (fiscal 1981–82) so revolutionary.[17]

The other side of the coin, of course, was the proposed cut of thirty percent over three years in the taxation of individual incomes combined with a larger and far more rapid depreciation of the plant and machinery used in business (so as to stimulate capital investment). That, too, was largely achieved by way of the Economic Recovery Tax Act of 1981, but this was an entirely different measure from the "clean bill" that the president had originally submitted to Congress. Interest groups, making the most of the "given" political situation, had much to do with bringing about the difference.

In sketching some aspects of the Economic Recovery Tax Act, we may first take note that not only was the original bill "clean" but that, up to a point, the president kept it so. Budget Director David A. Stockman discovered that when, in stage two ("Chapter II") of his strategy, he coolly set out to introduce equity (or fairness) into the administration's economic plan. Of his ten new proposals, calculated to save $20 billion, the most politically sensitive one was the elimination of or restriction upon some tax expenditures, commonly known as tax loopholes, i.e., selective tax relief for specific categories of taxpayers, worth to them (but by the same token lost to the revenue) about $150 billion in 1979.[18] Mr. Stockman did not flinch even from proposing an end to the controversial oil-depletion allowance, a special form of depreciation to be examined later in the book. This, in particular, the president promptly rejected. As Mr. Stockman recalled later: "He just jumped all over my tax proposals." Surprisingly philosophical about his rebuff, Mr. Stockman then characterized the proposals in this way: "Those were more like ornaments I was thinking of on the tax side. I call them equity ornaments. They're not really too good. They're not essential to the economics of the thing."[19]

As it turned out, the logic of the situation—the arithmetic—obliged the president to modify his original tax-cutting plan, mainly by reducing the thirty percent to twenty-five percent and making the new depreciation rules rather less favorable. In some business circles, that stimulated "a lot of telephoning and pounding on tables," spokesman for the National Association of Manufacturers recalled. Another business representative scoffed: "Supply-side economics without a supply-side tax cut."[20] Their indignation was premature. The new depreciation rules remained on balance remarkably generous, embodying a fundamental break with past practice and contributing to the greatest corporate tax cut in memory.

By now the once "clean" bill was being dirtied with what tax expert Joseph A. Pechman called "fiscal graffiti,"[21] the outward and visible signs that (as Karen W. Arenson would report) "all sorts of special interests had gotten into the act," including the trucking companies. Their case is particularly illuminating because it had nothing whatever to do with the great affairs of state in hand—i.e., the historic economic plan—and because it ended favorably to the interests despite the opposition of the White House. The background to it was the Motor Carrier Act of 1980 deregulating the industry. Before that the operating licenses granted by the government had changed hands for very large sums of money because they conferred quasi-monopolistic rights or franchises. Under the act licenses were distributed widely, which of course undermined the value of those already in existence.

The pain would have been eased if the IRS had been willing to accept the "loss" as a deduction against tax liability, but they declined, and a federal court supported them. So the American Trucking Associations, Inc. sought a special deal from Congress, hiring Mr. J. D. Williams, of Williams and Jensen, a star lobbyist who had learned his trade two decades earlier as assistant to Democratic Senator Robert S. Kerr, the millionaire oilman from Oklahoma, and went on to be a regional campaign manager for Hubert Humphrey's presidential run in 1968.[22] Mr. Williams had no difficulty in the House, where a friend, Representative Dan Rostenkowski, chaired the Ways and Means Committee. The Senate Finance Committee, with its Republican majority, presented more of an obstacle. But "J.D." worked quietly on, having trucking company executives flown to Washington to help their home-state senators to see the light. One way or another, in June 1981, he got two Republicans to join the Democrats for a favorable vote of 11-6. A Treasury official remarked ruefully: "We were blindsided." Thus the truckers were after all permitted to deduct, over five years, their so-called loss, at a real loss to the government and so to other taxpayers of more than $350 million.[23]

Another graffito that caught the eye, partly because it so obviously served the cause of the Super Rich, concerned tax write-offs for horse breeders, which President Reagan, perhaps sensitive to the symbolism of the issue, proposed to reduce although it had no other bearing upon his grand economic strategy. In the Ways and Means Committee, the New Jersey Democrat Frank Guarini got through an amendment enabling horse breeders to deduct the first $100,000 of their investment. That, financial journalist Robert Lenzner commented, would be well received by the Texas billionaire, Nelson Bunker Hunt, "the nation's single largest owner and breeder of thoroughbred horses," who stood to gain "a massive tax credit for his favorite pastime."[24] In the Senate, the lobbyist for the horse owners was Thomas "Tad" Davis, who squatted in the large room between the vice-president's office and the Senate floor when the tax bill was being discussed. When one of its moving spirits, Assistant Treasury Secretary John E. Chapoton, came out of the vice-president's office, "Tad" Davis would argue against the proposed reduction. In the end, the chairman of the Finance Committee (Robert Dole) and the administration relented, at an estimated cost to the revenue, by 1986, of $200 million.[25] A senior staff member of the highly professional Joint Taxation Committee of Congress commented that it was "a rich man's bill that amounts to a great raid on the Treasury."[26]

Such concessions, however, were no more than tidbits compared with what was handed on a platter to the oil interests. The crystallizing issue was, whose tax bill would prevail, the president's or the Democrats', specifically Mr. Rostenkowski's as chairman of Ways and Means? The president was determined to win. Acknowledging that the tax-cut battle would be more formidable than the earlier budget battle, he told reporters: "If we don't have the votes, we'll get them."[27] The House majority leader, Jim Wright of Texas, was no less candid, telling reporters: "Frankly, we'll put it in the bill if it will buy votes."[28]

At first, *it* meant continuing and increasing the tax credit allowed the two million oil-royalty owners (mostly, owners of the mineral rights) to reduce their liability under the windfall profits tax passed in 1980 as a *quid pro quo* for the decontrol of oil prices. The credit had been set at $1000 for one year; now it was to be continued and raised to $2500. Exactly who thought of this to begin with is not (at present) clear. Mr. Harold B. Scoggins, Jr., speaking for the Independent Petroleum Association of America (IPAA), the main lobbying arm of the independent producers, recalled that half-a-dozen bills to make the $1000 permanent had been introduced, and other bills contained variations on that theme. "But that $2500 credit, that's one thing I had never heard of before,"[29] by which he must have meant *before* June 4 (when Treasury Secretary Donald T. Regan mentioned it) or June 9 (when it appeared in the first version of the administration bill).[30]

In any case, the administration, abandoning the idea of a "clean" bill, was obviously setting out to retain the oil-state Democrats who had voted for the budget cuts, thus, ultimately, serving the cause of the special interests. About this time Richard Kline, Washington representative of the Domestic Wildcatters Association, appears to have approached Representative Charles Wilson, a Texas Democrat close to the independent producers, with much the same idea. Mr. Wilson spoke to Mr. Rostenkowski, and the poker game—(as a Democratic leader actually characterized it)—began. The plan was that if Mr. Wilson could recapture ten of the Democrats who had strayed from the fold (at the last big test, twenty-nine had voted with the Republicans), there would be relief for both royalty owners *and* independent producers in the Democratic bill.[31]

Although the concession to royalty owners had nothing whatever to do with incentives to production (a principal *motif* of the tax-cut program), its fate was probably never in doubt, especially since it was now pushed by a new lobby, the National Association of Royalty Owners, Inc., represented by attorney, Mr. L. L. ("Hank") Hankla. Besides, the total to be conceded would not be enormous. But would the Democrats really let the windfall profits tax be emasculated, that measure having been so recently passed (1980) as a matter of equity? Ways and Means (Dem., 23; Rep., 12) would and did, if only by a single vote (18-17) in the wee hours of July 22. With other such concessions to the oil interests, that was estimated to add up to a revenue loss of $9 billion (net) in the five fiscal years 1982 through 1986.[32]

The IPAA found that package much to their liking. They also feared that a suitable second package (a second tax bill as promised) might not be forthcoming. As their lobbyist, William C. Anderson, put it: "The train started to pull out of the station," and there was no second train in sight.[33] So some independent producers started a move toward the Ways and Means bill, threatening the Conable-Hance bill that was really President Reagan's. Representative Kent Hance (Dem.-Texas), fearing they would be "a good thirty votes" short of a majority, recommended raising the ante, i.e., giving the oil interests still more tax breaks. When Treasury Secretary Donald Regan demurred, Representative Jack Kemp (Rep.-New York) passed him a note saying: "Without Hance and those other Texans, we are going to lose big."[34] As a congressional staffer put it later: "Ways and Means made a bid and we had to match it." Otherwise "the word from Texas would have been, 'Screw the president's tax cut.' "[35]

Secretary Regan, perhaps reflecting that this was Washington, not Wall Street, gave way. Mr. Hance conferred then with another member of the Conservative Democratic Forum, Representative Charles W. Stenholm, and Republican Representative Thomas G. Loeffler (both Texans), as well as with three lobbyists for the IPAA. Such a team naturally served the oil interests well, drafting a bill that added about $7 billion to the value of the Ways and Means Committee's concessions. That other Texan, Representative Charles Wilson, the catalyst, commented ruefully: "I started the whole thing with the suggestion that the Democrats could pick up the votes of some southern Democrats by opening up the windfall profits tax. And then the Conable-Hance bill doubled us. I couldn't believe it. As usual, the oil folks came out ahead."[36]

The nominally Democratic-controlled House chose that revised version of Conable-Hance (238-195), the majority including forty-eight Democrats, twelve of them from the North. Twelve of the remainder (or one-third) were drawn from Texas, Oklahoma, and Louisiana. So the Kline-Wilson-Rostenkowski tactics failed, and the House went into conference with the Senate bearing gifts to the oil interests valued at more than $16 billion over the succeeding five (fiscal) years.

The Senate, however, had been far less generous or (some might say) extravagant, furnishing "only" $6 to $6.5 billion for the corresponding period. Yet the lobbyists, scores of whom kept vigil throughout the night in the hallways outside the small Ways and Means room where the conference was held, would not have despaired. As reporter David Rogers remarked, they had their "horses" (i.e., allies)[37] in the Senate delegation, including not only Republican Robert Dole (Kansas, an oil state) but also, on the nominal "other side," Democrats Russell Long (Louisiana) and Lloyd Bentsen (Texas), both proved friends of the industry. All three "were anxious to go higher," i.e., get nearer to the House total. And they did. "Prodded by" Senator Dole, the Ways and Means Democrats eventually agreed to a ballpark figure of $12 billion (in the end, $11.8 billion). That largesse was to be split three ways:

1. *reduction* of the windfall profits tax on *newly* discovered oil—from 30 percent to 15 percent—by 1986;
2. *extension* of the $1000 tax credit (due to end 1981) for oil-royalty owners as set off against 1980 windfall profits; its *increase* in 1981 from $1000 to $2500; then its "conversion" to two to three barrels a day from 1982;
3. *exemption* from windfall profits tax of "stripper" oil recovered by independent producers, a "stripper" well being one producing ten barrels a day or fewer.

That made for an intriguing policy "pattern," but alas, it had almost nothing to do with the president's economic plan for the nation, nor with common standards of equity. Admittedly, the provision for owners of "stripper" wells sounded as if something was to be done for the "little people." But more than half such wells were located in just three states—Texas, Oklahoma, and Kansas. The exemption meant, at current prices, $6 a barrel for his clients, estimated Richard Kline, wearing another hat as representative of the Council of Active Independent Oil and Gas Producers. That might not seem much, but it was "not uncommon" for an independent to pump 200 barrels a day from scores of small wells. Mr. Kline elaborated: "It's a real bonanza, there's no getting around it."[38]

Again, about half the total cost of the ultimate package would accrue to the royalty owners, for which there could be neither an energy-policy nor an incentives-to-production argument. Such arguments *could* be advanced for the reduction in windfall profits tax, but would have to confront the issue of fair play in government. The tax had been enacted, after all, as part of a bargain struck only the year before. By a stroke of the pen—deregulating the price of crude oil—the federal government had given the interests "instant" billions (thanks, ultimately, to OPEC), recovering some of it by the tax, part of the proceeds of which was intended to help low-income families defray the cost of what would inevitably be sharply increased heating bills.

Now, not only was the bargain being deliberately undermined but also the one opportunity to pass something of the kind actually failed at the very time when $11.8 billion was being handed over to the special interests. It took the form of a modest heating tax credit, the only item for energy consumers in the whole package. When the amendment came up in conference, Senator Dole asked (according to the transcript): "Do you have anything on this, Senator Long?" The distinguished senator from Louisiana replied: "I did not vote for it," to which Senator Dole responded: "I did not vote for it either." House Speaker "Tip" O'Neill wanted it. Representative Charles Rangel (Dem.-New York) fought for it in conference, but he was evidently isolated and the proposal "was killed without protest in the final minutes." Later the conference chairman himself, Representative Rostenkowski, would admit: "I like Tip but it wasn't something I was going to give my eyeteeth for."[39]

A House staffer who had worked on the Conable-Hance (i.e., the administration) bill in effect summed it all up. Savoring their victory, he mused:

"We only started out with $2500 for royalty owners and we came out with $11.8 billion over five years."[40] But the last word must be reserved for the budget director, David Stockman. The tax breaks for the oil interests were only the most startling of the concessions made to the interests generally. Journalist William Greider, in whom Mr. Stockman had been quietly confiding all along, reported later: "Again Stockman was not exhilarated by the victory. On the contrary, it seemed to leave a bad taste in his mouth, as though the democratic process had finally succeeded in shocking him by its intensity and its greed."[41] Closely observing and indeed participating "in the trading—special tax concessions for oil-lease holders and real-estate tax shelters, and generous loopholes that virtually eliminated the corporate income tax," Mr. Stockman asked his confidant: "Do you realize the greed that came to the forefront? The hogs were really feeding. The greed level, the level of opportunism, just got out of control."

POSTSCRIPT. In 1982, members of both tax committees were having second thoughts about their work in 1981. In the Senate, Finance Committee chairman Robert Dole, "pulled and tugged" conservatives and liberals to accept an increase in taxes amounting to almost $100 billion over three years. But, observed Robert Healy, "the one thing that Dole did not touch in his bill was the tax breaks given the oil industry in 1981."[42] Ways and Means chairman Dan Rostenkowski did make an attempt to recoup. In the Democratic caucus on July 21, he proposed, a "reform" package that some liberals, but hardly anyone else, found praiseworthy.[43] Remarking that the caucus discussion served to confirm his decision to retire from the House, the young Michigan Democrat William Brodhead commented: "They basically don't want to vote against the lobbyists, I'm so glad I'm leaving. . . . It is bad enough we have to go behind closed doors because we're afraid of the lobbyists but now they're afraid of voting behind closed doors because the lobbyists might find out what they did."

Despite a lukewarm reception in caucus, chairman Rostenkowski did attempt to move his Ways and Means Committee, "but the oil lobbyists descended on the committee like vultures," filling the offices of committee members for two days. The climax came at the committee meeting: "When Rostenkowski floated that paper on the oil stuff, everything hit the fan. They really went ape. The oil state Democrats said they would blow the Rostenkowski bill out of the water. They said there would be no bill if he went through with the oil amendments."

That was Representative Brodhead, a member of the committee.[44] So it came about that the Democrats simply accepted the Senate bill, which they took direct to the House-Senate conference. From this there came what was described as the largest tax increase in history. But the oil interests were left securely in possession of their winnings—all $11.8 billion—from the 1981 poker game.

For the interests, the great beauty of the 1981 deal (apart from the intrinsic appeal of $11.8 billion) was that a large part of the money was to go in tax credits and exemptions, i.e., *tax expenditures* that, in the ordinary course of events, do not come up for annual review and renewal but are virtually permanent. As the originator of the concept, Professor Stanley S. Surrey put it: "Most [of the tax-expenditure items] seem almost to live a life of their own, undisturbed and unexamined."[45] That may go some way to explaining why (by 1982) the grand total was approaching an annual cost of $330 billion, and why such expenditures had come to require 109 separate provisions of the tax code.[46]

In all this we must, of course, keep a sense of proportion: no one suggests that the special interests always prevail. This is worth illustrating, not for the fact itself (which is obvious) but in the hope of beginning to understand the conditions under which the interests may be held at bay on a policy issue. We turn to the maritime interests, particularly the labor unions, partly because they have played an influential role in maritime policy since at least 1910 and continued to do so in the 1980s, making use of a PAC.[47] The issue is cargo preference, embodied in a law requiring a certain proportion of government-generated cargoes to be carried in American ships. Its proposed extension constituted the great maritime lobbying battle of the period 1972–82.

REGULATORY POLICY

What the interests wanted to extend was the rule—a law—requiring that all Department of Defense shipments and fifty percent of all foreign-aid and subsidized-food-export shipments be carried in American ships. The goal in 1973–74 was to increase the proportion of imported oil and oil products in privately-owned American ships from a current four percent to twenty percent immediately, then rising by stages to thirty percent in June 1977. At the outset the odds on securing that did not seem at all favorable because, on paper at least, the opposition looked formidable:

1. eight cabinet departments, including Defense, State, Justice, and Treasury (openly in opposition from October 1973) as well as the White House Consumer Affairs Office and the Federal Energy Administration.

2. the American Petroleum Institute, which estimated that seventy-nine cents would be added to the cost of an imported barrel of oil, and the Federation of American Controlled Shipping. This delightfully ambiguous title apparently concealed p.r. or media activities, and it was against these activities, and against the organizers of the federation, that Senator Russell Long fulminated. Accusing Exxon of supplying the federation with material, he bitterly complained of "more misleading propaganda, more scurrilous propaganda, planted in editorials against this bill than any measure I have seen in my time here."[48]

3. Some journalists hit hard. In a characteristic passage, conservative columnist George Will wrote: "The bill's charm, limited but real, is that it involves no damned nonsense about merit, just straightforward theft, almost admirably brazen, like armed robbery compared with embezzlement."[49] (This was probably a conscious echo of something the English statesman, Lord Melbourne, said about the Order of the Garter, an honor bestowed by the Crown: "I like the Garter; there is no damned merit in it.")

The bill was indeed brazenly anticonsumer at a time of greatly heightened consumer self-consciousness and -confidence. Estimates of the increased cost of cargo preference to the consumer over the following decade varied from $60 billion down to a mere $20 billion. That would be *in addition to* the direct expenditures, estimated then at another $800 million by 1980. So there were grounds for the remark by a Republican from Oklahoma that the measure should be given a new title, the "Consumer and Taxpayer Ripoff Act of 1974."[50]

Yet the Energy Transportation Security Act of 1974 sailed through both Houses with the greatest of ease. In April it slipped out of the House Merchant Marine Committee after a voice vote, five Republicans filing dissenting views. Early in May it triumphed on the floor of the House (266-136). Virtually the same bill swept all before it in the Senate Commerce Committee in July (14-2), both dissenters, again, being Republicans. On the Senate floor in the week after the Labor Day recess, the bill also had an easy passage (42-28).

How, in a democracy, where consumers and common-or-garden taxpayers are everywhere and everybody, could that possibly happen? Certainly, the Committee of American Tanker Owners Inc. was busy on the other, insurgent side, hiring several lobbyists, of whom the most instantly recognizable was the Washington law firm of Smathers, Merrigen and Herlong.[51] But their registration as lobbyists for cargo preference appeared (of course, it might date back a while) only twelve days after the Senate vote. The key (one feels) was turned by the labor unions, the Marine Engineers' Benefit Association (MEBA), and the Seafarers' International Union (SIU), of which Senator Russell Long once said: "There's no one I'd rather have on my side than the Seafarers'."[52]

That is understandable if only because the SIU had been, to members of Congress, generous to a fault. Between 1964 and 1968 it had taken $750,000 from its general funds to credit, illegally, the accounts of its political action committee for disbursement to deserving candidates. Some $800,000 went to congressional candidates. Was that in any way related to the curious fact that, for fiscal 1970, the House Merchant Marine Committee authorized in *direct expenditures* (the shipbuilding and operating subsidies) $124.3 million *more* than President Nixon had asked for, *and* that nobody protested in the name of the general interest? It is even odder that, as signed by President Nixon in October 1969, the bill actually authorized not $124.3 million more but $130 million (fiscal 1970).

It is even more curious, almost bizarre, that although the SIU was indicted for its illegal diversion of general union funds, it was not prosecuted. In May 1972, a federal judge dismissed the case, pointing out that the Justice Department had failed for two years to pursue the matter. The Justice Department chose not to appeal. The treatment accorded two steamship companies stood out in sharp contrast. They, too, had lobbied by illegal methods. As one of their lobbyists confided: "I'd have a congressman to lunch and present him with a contribution."[53] But they were pursued under the Corrupt Practices Act and fined. For the 1972 election, Mr. George Steinbrenner III, principal owner of the Yankees, was also fined in his capacity as chairman of a shipbuilding company whose employees had ostensibly whipped up twenty-five thousand dollars for Mr. Nixon, which, however, had really come from the company itself.

For that famous (or notorious) election, the SIU gave no less than $100,000 to the Committee to Reelect the President. For one reason or another its victory in Congress in 1974 is no cause for surprise. But by then Mr. Nixon had departed in his helicopter; what position would President Ford take? In November he said he was "seriously concerned" about the inflationary impact of the bill and also its effect on foreign relations. But then came reports, denied by the White House, of a deal: President Ford would sign the bill if Congress cleared an administration trade-reform measure that had been languishing there for about a year. As if in line with that, the president took no position when the conference report came before the Senate on December 16. On December 30, however, he pocket-vetoed the cargo preference bill. To that decision, the young representative from Michigan, David Stockman, may have contributed. As if learning his future trade as budget director, he had been studying subcommittee reports in some detail. He found that: "Subcommittees dominated by special interests issued lopsided reports that hid their prejudices behind clouds of turgid prose [designed, he believed] to discourage understanding." For example, the cargo preference bill of 1974 "was a panegyric to the glories of forcing more oil imports into American ships."[54] He alerted his fellow Republicans, and the Republican (also from Michigan) in the White House kept the bill in his pocket.

That was defeat snatched from the jaws of victory. When the maritime interests returned to the attack in 1976–77, however, they must have felt very self-confident. Many of their old opponents lay in wait for them, such as Defense, State, and the Treasury (described as "not enamored"), and the American Petroleum Institute, but, these, after all, had been overcome in 1974. Secondly, they, management and unions, mobilized more fully than in 1974, and launched the U.S. Maritime Committee to Turn the Tide for an extensive p.r. campaign. To run it, the committee hired Rafshoon Communications. (Rafshoon had been media adviser to candidate Carter.) By the fall of 1977 it would spend over $1 million on TV spots and full-page advertisements in some fifty newspapers. Thirdly, *this* president would not be exercising a veto of any kind on the bill. On the contrary, he had been committed since the 1976 primaries to some cargo preference ("a fair share"), and had received a goodly share of their campaign contributions. Fourthly, $450,000 had been distributed in 1976 to 215 members of the House, with special attention of course to the Merchant Marine and Fisheries Committee, twenty-four of whose members (three out of five) had received in total some $82,000 for their 1976 campaigns. Its chairman, John M. Murphy (Dem.-New York), had come off particularly well: $46,000 in contributions over the previous five years, almost $10,000 (just from the maritime lobby) by way of a recent fund-raising party. A dozen members of the Senate Commerce Committee shared $129,000 between them. With all these assets, how could the maritime interests lose?

Yet lose they did, in 1977. To begin with, House proponents continued where they had left off in 1974, still seeking an ultimate 30 percent (by 1980). But, the administration disagreeing, they had to settle for a goal of 9.5 percent by 1982, and an immediate 4.5 percent. Even that slipped through their fingers, and they went away empty handed. Why? Under what conditions may such a special interest, so well endowed, so willing to convert its endowment into political currency and, for that and other reasons, so well connected to the highest ranks of American government, be defeated or just kept within tolerable bounds? If we knew the precise answer to that, and if the conditions were reproducible, we *might* be a shade less perturbed about the future (and the present state) of American democracy than the distinguished commentators quoted at the outset tended to make us.

Precision (on current knowledge) escapes us, but the elements that would enter into the answer seem fairly clear:

RAPID MOBILIZATION OF A COMPREHENSIVE OPPOSING COALITION. This one ranged from three public-interest groups (Common Cause, the Naderite Congress Watch, Environmental Policy Center[55]) and the League of Women Voters (which might also be so classified) to the American Petroleum Institute (API) and such companies as Getty Oil and Chevron (Standard Oil, California); the American Farm Bureau Federation, and National Council of Farmer Cooperatives; and the U.S. Chamber of Commerce.

SOUND DIVISION OF TACTICAL LOBBYING DUTIES, such that each component of the coalition pursued its own constituency under the watchful eye of a coordinator (the chamber, also responsible for going after Republicans and 1974 opponents).

Within that framework, letting the consumer/environmental groups play a more prominent role than the API and the oil companies was prudent. As Thomas Hennessy, who spoke for Getty Oil and the API put it: "I think Big Oil has been smart to let the environmentalists and consumer people carry the flag. I know because I represent an oil company and we're not that popular."[56]

"DEFINITION OF THE SITUATION." Mr. Hennessy was right, as far as he went. But there was a more "positive" reason for Big Oil's keeping in the background. Proponents of cargo preference were trying to make the issue: giants of the oil industry *v.* the downtrodden, almost defenseless maritime industry. Opponents, on the other hand, wanted the match to be perceived as: giants of the maritime industry (unions and management hand-in-glove) *v.* the downtrodden, almost defenseless consumers. It would seem that the opponents' "definition of the situation" came out on top, in part, presumably, because the administration's estimate of the increased cost (at current import levels, $110 million a year) was first more than doubled by the General Accounting Office ($240 million) and later quintupled ($610 million a year).

So far we have been taking the perspective of the opposing coalition. Now we look outside to their immediate environment:

DIVISIONS WITHIN THE ADMINISTRATION. Important departments remained opposed to cargo preference, as in 1974. The president's top economic advisers were opposed. Some of his political advisers were supportive but lukewarm, evidently trying to make the best of a bad job. Thus Stuart E. Eizenstat, chief adviser on domestic policy, confessing his view that the bill was conceptually "flawed," went on: "In light of your commitment to the industry and the likelihood that rejection of cargo preference will be seen as a broken promise, we support the limited cargo preference option outlined above."[57] "We" included Robert S. Strauss, special trade commissioner and Carter friend. Still, these (to the president) cross-pressures may have inhibited more vigorous action: the administration lobbying for the bill was not "heavy."

CRITICISM IN THE MEDIA. Among others, conservative columnist George Will had done his bit in 1974 ("straightforward theft"). The harshest criticism in 1977 came from the relatively liberal *Washington Post*. Under the headline, "How to Buy a Bill," an editorial writer, reflecting on the flood of campaign contributions, lashed out:

> The maritime lobby, with the help of its many friends in the White House and Congress, has invented a different kind of revenue sharing. The system has a certain scientific interest, since it's beginning to look like the political equivalent of the perpetual-motion machine. The maritime lobby—the unions, the ship operators and the shipyards—invests wisely in certain elections. The politicians express their gratitude by extending and augmenting the enormous subsidies that go to the U.S. merchant marine. That further enriches the maritime industry, enabling it to pour still larger contributions into political campaigns the next time around. It's a delightful system for everybody except, of course, the tax-

payers and consumers who supply the endless subsidies that keep the wheel turning.

The *Post* grimly concluded: "Public policy won't have much to do with this bill's steady progress toward passage. The maritime lobby takes the straightforward view that it bought the bill at the going price, and it is entitled to prompt delivery."

Cartoonist Herblock rubbed it in the following day. The good ship *Shipping Lobby* is racing by, swamping a small boat rowed by Consumer-Taxpayer. The cigar-smoking ship's captain is holding up "The Other America's Cup," which is overflowing with bags of money paid "For Outstanding Contributions to the Jimmy Carter Campaign and to Members of Congress."[58]

That was just one newspaper, although of course a very important one. Throughout the land, editorialists are said to have raised their voices in protest, stimulated mainly (it seems) by Common Cause, which sent out releases to 2200 papers listing the campaign contributions made by the maritime lobby to Congress as a whole and to committee members in particular. As a result, "You had to vote against this bill to prove you were not a whore," commented a professional, Stephan Lesher of Rafshoon Communications, propagandists for the other side.[59] That may well have been so when the vote was recorded in the House. But the remark glosses the fact that on the earlier voice vote (which has the great merit, for congresspersons, of going unrecorded) the bill was said, by Speaker "Tip" O'Neill, to have passed. The reversal after the House went from unrecorded to recorded suggests another variable in the conditions that made possible the 1977 defeat of the maritime interests—what Bruce Oppenheimer, in his study of the oil interests and Congress, called "rules, procedures, and processes."[60] For, despite the "heroic" efforts of the coalition, especially, perhaps, by Common Cause and by the Chamber of Commerce (which wrote to every member of Congress spelling out what the economic impact, including jobs, would be in every state of the Union), the bill *was going through*.

RULES, PROCEDURES, AND PROCESSES. Success was not only what Merchant Marine Committee chairman John M. Murphy expected: he announced publicly that he would win by thirty votes. In addition to other reasons for confidence, he must have known that Speaker "Tip" O'Neill was in his corner, as was the Speaker's Boston colleague and friend, Joseph Moakley (a member of the still-important Rules Committee).[61] Passage looked even more of "a sure thing" after the California Republican, Paul N. McCloskey, failed to head off the open rule (permitting amendments) that the Rules Committee had prescribed. Then came the approving voice vote, the Speaker determining that opponents had not asked *in time* for a roll call. Representative McCloskey expostulated to no avail. On the following day, he threw himself on the mercy of the House, apologizing for not having asked quickly enough for a roll call.

Chairman Murphy objected but then, curiously enough, relented, to the dismay of the maritime interests. Then, to the surprise of both sides, the bill was handsomely defeated, 165-257. Even on the roll call, a majority of Democrats voted *for* (148-132), including Representative Moakley. Republicans were solidly against (17-125). Mr. Lesher may be granted the last word from the protagonists: "Obviously, to not accept the victory "Tip" O'Neill had given them was a mistake. The furor, I think, would have been rather muted."[62]

The immediate point for us is that the publicity may well have put members on the defensive, but rules and procedures made it possible to convert that defensiveness into the required negative vote. The ultimate point is to qualify some of the remarks quoted at the outset: under some combination of conditions (sketched above as a first approximation, without any attempt at weighing their relative importance), the special interests can be defeated.

On the other hand, in 1981 the maritime interests were again tacking toward cargo preference, this time for dry cargo, not oil. The House Merchant Marine Committee approved a bill stipulating that about forty percent of American imports and exports of dry-cargo goods be carried in American ships. This, thundered the *New York Times,* "would be sheer, shameless protectionism," adding with some asperity:

> The American maritime industry priced itself out of the market decades ago. Building big ships costs two to three times as much in the United States as in Japan or Korea. American sailors are paid three to four times more than foreign crews. What remains of the industry depends on government patronage.

As the editorial writer explained, however, the effect would be to shift the subsidy from the government to the private sector, i.e., in the end, the consumers. "Moderate estimates suggest that the bill would raise the total cost of ocean transport in these commodities by at least a third."[63]

Nor was that all. In 1981–82 there was another drive by the maritime lobby to gain full exemption from the antitrust laws. The industry had enjoyed partial exemption since 1916, enabling shipping companies to agree among themselves on the rates (prices) to be charged (subject to review by the Federal Maritime Commission). Now they would be able to control capacity, i.e., limit the number of ships in the cartel, politely known as the North American Conference (America-Europe), and to share out the cargo, even, if need be, pool their revenues. Again, the *New York Times* thundered, "Beware of the Cargo Ship Cartel," and went on: "It is the bizarre proposition of the ocean shipping companies that they can increase their efficiency by further reducing their competition." They quoted Allen R. Ferguson, an economist specializing in maritime affairs, for the estimate that, if the companies raised their rates by a relatively modest twenty percent, America's cargo shipping costs would rise by $3 billion a year.[64]

All things considered, including other evidence that cannot be deployed here (some of which appears in part 3), one concludes that those who sounded a general alarm had reason to be perturbed, and that those who, like conservative columnist George Will, denounced specific policies had good grounds for their biting criticisms. But the very fact that the issue of special interests transcends party lines prompts the question: to what extent, if at all, could the situation be otherwise? Is there "something about" American society and government that tends to produce an exceptionally flourishing interest-group sector, making America in the eighties look less like a democracy of the people than "a special-interest democracy" (as Mr. Magruder remarked to author Studs Terkel)? Have the various distinguished commentators left some depths unplumbed?

It is important to attempt to answer such questions even before proceeding to describe contemporary groups and their methods because neither their nature nor their particular activities can be well understood, much less judged, except within a "social framework" of interrelated parts that is, in the short run, "given." To search out a structure of explanation, we shall start with a working assumption that some scholars will consider old-fashioned: that (using the nineteenth-century terminology) *society* and *state* can be distinguished as separate realms or domains. Today, obviously, there is overlapping at many points, and even interpenetration, exemplified in the *iron triangles* (interest group on one side; agency plus congressional committee on the others), and in the relatively new rival to that concept, *networks* (more extensive than mere triangles),[65] and also in the "revolving door" between industry and government. Still, the blurred line remains distinguishable, and even now the separation of social power (including interest groups) from political authority remains fundamental.

The explanatory structure will take the following form:

I. A certain kind of *social structure*, the "manner" in which society is "put together" (as historian Samuel P. Hays expressed it), *tends* toward a politics of special interests.

II. That structural development is accompanied by appropriate, or "matching," *attitudes*—inquiring, measuring, weighing, bargaining, etc., which is consistent with what academic lawyer Arthur Selwyn Miller said about one subclass of organizations, the voluntary associations—that their rise seemed to be related to "the application of scientific concepts to human activity."[66] Such attitudes, usually treated by political scientists under the heading of political culture (values, beliefs, and feelings), reinforce the tendency toward a politics of special interests.

Other components of political culture, developed independently of changes in the social structure (or the organizational revolution), sustain the tendency. The legitimacy accorded interest groups may be cited as an example.

Both I and II are for convenience dealt with in chapter 2, "The Organizational Revolution."

III. The tendency, however, runs up against the *free-rider*, or Olsonian, problem, named for economist Mancur Olson. Roughly: why join and make the effort, which, if successful, will benefit you anyway, if you are qualified, i.e., belong to the right category? As against that, it will be suggested that the problem is not as acute in practice as logic appears to predict (chapter 3).

Note that I, II, and III may be conceived as deriving from society. Then, as from the side of the state:

IV. The tendency may be retarded or (as in the United States) greatly advanced by the political structure. This is examined in two parts: constitutional rules and arrangements (chapter 4), and Congress, that unique legislative body (chapter 5), including some indication of how they color the American party system.

V. The tendency will be accelerated by the rise of the *positive state,* i.e., the number, scale, and range of functions assumed by government, and with that the number, size, and variety of authoritative organizations, or bureaucracies. The more positive the state, the greater its attraction for the special interests (chapter 6).

Note, finally, that this mode of analysis is a teaching device: the enormously difficult problem of the interaction between the variables is entirely neglected. The question of the actual historical sequence is likewise left open. It would appear that autonomous stirrings within the socioeconomic order (society), common to the advanced industrial societies with market economies, mark the relevant beginning. Even so, the state exercises "reverse impact" on society, intentionally (as with tax policies) but also unintentionally.

So the issue is complex. But chapters 2 through 6 would seem to constitute a useful first approximation. At least you will have been forced to think about a conceptual framework for the more detailed study that starts in chapter 7.

CHAPTER TWO
THE ORGANIZATIONAL
REVOLUTION:
Values and Beliefs

GROUPS DEFINED

So far the terms *special interests* and *interest groups* have been used inter-changeably and defined only by drawing attention to what they did. That, technically, *is* a kind of definition. The name for it is *ostensive*,[1] which derives from a Latin word meaning "to show." One showed the oil companies, the maritime unions and others on the (political) job, influencing public policy, and left you to infer the meaning of whichever term happened to be used in context. But now one had better pause to propitiate the gods with some definitions of a more familiar kind. In academic writing, *interest group* is by far the commoner term.

Commissioned to review the interest-group literature, Robert Salisbury reported: "in the empirical literature deviation is rare from the following usage: *An interest group is an organized association which engages in activity relative to government decisions*."[2] A difficulty is that *organized association* and similar terms, such as Alfred de Grazia's *privately organized aggregation*,[3] tend to drive a wedge between an entity specially created for specific purposes, exclu-sively political or a mixture of the political and the "domestic" (e.g., services to a sector of industry), and an entity (or interest) "in position" for some other purpose or function, such as exploring for, drilling, refining, and distributing crude oil. The reason is that, since the seventeenth century, *association* has denoted "a body of persons who have combined to execute a common purpose or advance a common cause; the whole organization which they form to effect their purpose." Correspondingly, the verb *to associate* has since then meant "to combine for a common purpose, or to join or form an association." This is also what the words mean in contemporary American-English.[4] Now we would not call Mobil an association in that three-hundred-year-old sense. Yet it works hard at influencing public policy from its base as America's number three industrial company (1982). Apart from keeping its own corps of lobbyists busy, it mounts a sustained and costly public relations campaign on national issues (as will be touched upon in a later chapter). In short, the term *organized association* tends not only to exclude (as all definitions do) but also to exclude politically significant activity.

For that reason alone, while accepting for this book the general verdict of the political-science profession (subject to amendment and clarification), one wishes to replace *organized association* by *organization*, which applies without argument to Mobil, Exxon, Getty Oil, and other corporations or producing units. Thus we reach: "An interest group is an organization which engages in activity relative to governmental decisions," although a personal preference would be to substitute *public policy* for the last two words.

Even now we are not quite ready to proceed. Writing mainly for a professional audience, Robert Salisbury did not need to explain that, although the common formulation seemed to include political parties ("organized association which engages in . . . "), these are in fact *not* covered by the umbrella of *interest group*, which essentially denotes a nonparty body. The two are commonly set apart by two variables at least: the parties put up candidates for election and otherwise engage in the biennial rites and ceremonies in hope of getting their eager hands on the levers of governmental authority; and in principle they encompass a wider range of public policies. In practice, their reach exceeds their grasp (not counting their grasp of public office), but they remain somewhat broader than the interest groups. Some of these, as on the abortion question, tend indeed to be single-issue, which perturbed many analysts as the nation entered the 1980s. In any event, an interest group is nonparty.

Should public bodies—Federal Trade Commission, U.S. Department of Justice, and especially those representing states, cities and counties, since they, too, converge on Washington for the purpose of influencing policy—count as interest groups? Not in this book at least. The fundamental framework here is the interaction of the social order and the political order (or of social power and political authority). This requires the traditional private/public distinction, which, although blurred in the 1980s, is still discernible. As Robert Presthus has put it, public bodies (or rather the officials) "have formal authority and responsibility for running the government . . . they assume an official obligation to control the formal political apparatus."[5]

Thus the definition, in our hands, becomes: "An interest group is a private, nonparty organization which engages in activity relative to *governmental decisions*" (or, according to taste, *public policy*).

Be sensitive, finally, to the unavoidable awkwardness of referring to *any* more-than-one-purpose organization (it might be called *several-purpose*, since *multi-purpose* suggests too much) as an interest group (in the sense now established). If you go looking, you will find only one entity or body, not two (organization/interest group). Take the Marine Engineers' Benefit Association. It certainly qualifies as an interest group, but not every day of the week. A high proportion of its time, one presumes, is devoted to collective bargaining, services to members, and otherwise securing benefits for them. Can it be an interest group on Wednesday but something else for the rest of the week? The same problem arises with Exxon, Mobil, Getty Oil, and hundreds of other corporations. What it boils down to is this: in such contexts, *interest group* does not refer to a discrete, separable or distinguishable entity but rather to a distinguishable class of behavior, or activity. For the several-purpose organization, the attempt to influence public policy is simply *one* of its purposes or functions, or, alternatively put, one of *the ways of pursuing or discharging* its basic function.

In order to make that abstract statement concrete, consider Robert Presthus's study of (fundamentally) nonpolitical organizations in the United States and Canada in the late sixties and early seventies. (*Nonpolitical* is *not* a distinction that Professor Presthus himself made in context. Using a very broad conception of *political*, he treated all interest groups as such.) He found that in the United States, almost sixty percent of such organizations used lobbyists to influence public policy; in Canada, about a third. The Canadian figure in particular would be substantially raised if help of a legal nature were counted as lobbying, for example the drafting of a brief to put before government. In both countries about two out of three of the professional directors of such organizations disclosed that they had "participated directly in an important policy issue involving government" at the federal or state (or equivalent) level. All told, between one-quarter and one-third of the organizations in the two countries were "intensely active politically," judging this both by the proportion using lobbyists, and by high placing on a scale of political activism (based on the percentage of directors who interacted twice a week or more with legislators and senior bureaucrats).[6]

Such elasticity of concept is hard to pin down in words. David Truman, author of a landmark book in this field, attempted it by distinguishing between *interest group* and *political interest group*. But, as Robert Salisbury reported in his review of the literature, that goes against the grain of the profession, the great majority of whom would agree with another leading specialist, Joseph LaPalombara in reserving *interest group*, without adjective, for that which impinges on public policy.[7] In any case, to this writer's way of thinking, resorting to two terms perpetuates the ambiguity by implying that there are two entities where in reality, except for the pure political specialization, there is only one (for example, Mobil Oil, possessed, you might say, of two faces but a single body). This awkwardness, evidently, is something we have to live with.

CLASSIFICATION

These considerations have a direct bearing on the way one sets about the job of classification (or of making a typology, which is a multidimensional classification). For it follows that what is needed is a classification or typology of private (nonparty) organizations, not just of the "pure" interest groups, those that have no other reason for being than to "engage in activity relative to government decisions." That was explicitly recognized in 1935 by Harwood Childs of Princeton, author of the first such classification, when he wrote that to confine the concept "to a few organizations that for the moment appear to be exerting influence upon public officials is to ignore the fact that potentially any group may at times exert such an influence."[8] He did not himself build upon that insight, simply distinguishing for the particular purpose in hand between groups "based on such differentials as age, sex, occupation, and race" and those created "to further special ideas." That corresponds to what group leaders themselves have been known to identify as groups-*of* and groups-*for*, and to political scientist Allen Potter's *whom one stands for* in contradistinction to *what one stands for*,[9] e.g., the Marine Engineers as against the National Right to Life Committee; the National Organization of Women in contrast to the American Arts Alliance, formed in 1977 to influence Congress, the White House, and government agencies as well as the general public. (This group was to provide an "assertive voice" in favor of legislation for the arts, including "such seemingly unrelated matters as energy, tax reform, social security and the postal system."[10])

Ideally, however, one ought also to distinguish between degrees of politicization, the extent to which organizations attempt (severally) to secure their objectives via the political authorities. In principle, that could be done by way of some such scale of political activism as that employed by Robert Presthus. Doing the usual violence to reality, one could then "cut" politicization into two or three (or more) parts ("dichotomize," "trichotomize," etc.), which with the -*of* and -*for* distinction, would provide a 2×2 or 2×3 (etc.) division of political space.

Given that array, one could further divide the organizations-*of* as Harwood Childs did, possibly adding religion to age, sex, occupation, and race on the assumption that like sex and race, it is in reality more ascribed than achieved (that is, more inherited than truly chosen). Occupation could be subdivided in the traditional way into business, labor, professional-education, and the like. At present, however, political space cannot be mapped in that way. So one is driven back to the traditional categories as in the work of Harwood Childs, V. O. Key, Jr., and even the more "theoretical" David Truman.[11] That means falling back on categories denoting dominant substantive interests such as business-industrial, labor, agricultural, professional, ethnic, religious, women's issues, and the like, categories which obviously overlap to a disturbing degree. It also means identifying groups created, as Harwood Childs remarked, "to further special ideas." Among these one includes the public-interest groups and environmental groups which surged forward in the 1970s.

Still, the discussion above will have been worthwhile if it drives home the point that the interaction of organizations with government constitutes our real subject, or alternatively put, it is the influence of that part of the social order upon public policy. The matrix for the interest-group activity and the lobbying is in fact the organizational society. This is nothing less than a new social structure. To a bird's eye view of its development we now turn. This should help us on the way to discovering to what extent President Wilson's famous 1912 pronouncement still holds good in the 1980s: "The government of the United States at present is a foster child of the special interests." For the special interests (it should now be clear) are to a high degree the basic organizations of society wearing, so to speak, fancy dress.

The phrase *the organizational revolution* has become a little threadbare since it was used in 1953, apparently for the first time, by economist and social philosopher Kenneth Boulding.[12] Even so it is worth reusing for the purpose of stressing the comparative newness of what so many of us take for granted (because always part of the furniture of our lives), and in particular because it underlies the whole interest-group phenomenon. No organizational revolution, no question of the special interests being the foster parent of the government of the United States (to turn President Wilson's remark inside out). Indeed, no organizational revolution, no interest-group politics worth writing about.

The organizational revolution is itself but one facet of something broader still: modernization, "the process of change toward those kinds of social, economic, and political systems that developed in western Europe from the seventeenth century to the nineteenth and then spread to other European countries, to North America, and in the nineteenth and twentieth centuries to the South American, Asian, and African countries."[13] That formulation, from S. N. Eisenstadt, is obviously general; when it comes to singling out particular parts, authors have made modernization a coat of many colors. Nevertheless, everyone identifies structural change as a crucial aspect of it. The fundamental concept is differentiation. As a first approach this may be thought of in a (relatively) "micro" way, as in sociologist Neil Smelser's version: "the evolution from a multifunctional role structure to several more specialized structures."[14] A stock example is the building of a formal educational system, in which schools and colleges absorb much or most of the educational-*cum*-socialization functions previously discharged by families and churches. For a broader sweep (more suitable here) we turn again to Professor Eisenstadt, for whom differentiation is the process through which the main social functions or the major institutional spheres become dissociated from one another.[15] Thus, the religious sphere becomes dissociated from the political, the political from the economic, and so on.

What is immediately relevant for us is that embedded in this new matrix is what the French scholar Raymond Aron has called "one specific trait of modern societies, the separation of social power and political authority, the differentiation of functions, in particular, of political functions."[16] This separation, so characteristic of the nineteenth century (if not of the twentieth, a point to which we shall return) provides the foundation for interest-group politics. For the characteristic offspring of modern society (insofar as the workaday world is concerned) is the formal organization. Some wear the mantle and carry the burden of authority for the nation as a whole (executives, bureaucracies, legislatures); most stand apart from that magic circle, busy with their own work (as defined by society), but drawn into the circle from time to time as a means of grappling or coping with that work. Their interaction (the "most" with the "some") gives rise, under certain conditions, to class politics, but in the United States, for reasons long debated, it crystallized essentially as the politics of interest groups.

That drawing into, or at least toward, the circle was unavoidable if only because the size of the circle increased. For one specifically political component of modernization was the growing extension of the territorial range of government, a broad tendency identified in particular as the encroachment of the center upon the periphery, accompanied by an intensification of the power of the political, administrative, and legal agencies of that center.[17] In the wake of such developments, the organizations also came to demand more *of* government, the rising tide of democracy accomplishing its own form of encroachment upon the traditional institutions (another specifically political component of modernization).

So far our focus has been morphological, or anatomical. But, as historian Samuel Hays has pointed out, the new forms embodied "new ways of ordering social relationships." Ultimately derived from science as applied to social affairs in the broad sense, these new forms themselves became "carriers" of the scientific ethos. In other words, the organizations, especially as their scale of operations increased, came to approach problems in a cool, scientific (or rationalist) spirit, analyzing, calculating, demonstrating, reasoning, arguing, in the course of which ends would be defined, means identified, and the necessary resources gathered and applied. But *that* could not be executed without differential authority: in such "technical systems" (as Professor Hays calls them) "some men organize and control the lives of other men according to their particular conceptions as to what is preferable."[18] This obviously lies at the heart of interest-group politics, these organizations being not only technical systems but systems of power, able to advance their conceptions of what is preferable as against each other but above all as against government, which of course harbors many of its own. The interaction of the business corporation and government represents the type-case.

DIFFERENTIATION AND INTEGRATION

Up to a point, differentiation entails divisiveness; certainly, in creating greater diversity (or heterogeneity), it threatens integration, thus putting the social whole at risk. This explains why, as French sociologist Emile Durkheim (a founding father of the discipline) noted in the 1880s, increasing differentiation (or division of labor) is actually accompanied by the invention of new coordinating devices, or, in other words, by increasing integration. It follows, as Professor Smelser has pointed out, that differentiation "is not by itself sufficient for modernization [which] proceeds as a contrapuntal interplay" between differentiation and integration.

The apparent paradox does not end there: integration itself entails still more differentiation. Thus, for example, when differentiated working or operational units, such as business corporations within a particular industry or sector, set out to advance "the interests of the trade," they may do so through a new instrument, a trade association. This, from the standpoint of the social whole (or society), is a step toward integration. "City centrals" of trade unions embody another such tendency. The end product of this "dialectic" of forms is the creation of a second tier in social space made up of organizations of organizations (or, to make that perhaps easier to grasp, associations of organizations). Evidently, the "units" have changed their nature: trade unions bring together flesh-and-blood persons, but city centrals bring together trade unions as if they were homogeneous entities.

This "dialectic of forms" does not end there but leads on to *peaks* such as the National Association of Manufacturers (NAM) and the AFL-CIO. In a perfectly symmetrical world, these peaks would be simply associations of associations of organizations, manufacturing corporations (for example) being wholly "contained" within the appropriate sectoral trade associations, which would in turn form the building blocks for the NAM. Outside the Federal Republic of Germany, however, such symmetry is hard to discern. Thus the building blocks—members—of the NAM have always included flesh-and-blood persons as well as firms and corporations.

However untidily organized, peaks presumptively serve integration. Hence the point and counterpoint (Professor Smelser's "contrapuntal interplay") of differentiation, integration, differentiation. *Both* processes precipitate private organizations that are integral parts of the social structure and, as such, perennially "available" for influencing the public authorities.

These considerations apply to the fundamental division of labor in society—as far as this analysis is concerned, the workaday world. Beyond its walls and fortresses, differentiation may also be discerned in organizations of ethnics, the elderly, the youthful, women, and so on—social categories into which "agitators" have breathed organizational life by using various combinations of rhetorical appeal and practical incentives. But that represents a late stage of the organizational revolution in America: what might be termed the pure voluntary associations made their appearance much earlier. These are the organizations-*for:* philosophic or scientific discussion; walking or climbing mountains; playing chess; the prosecution of great causes, such as the abolition of slavery. In this realm, obviously, *different* social categories converge on *something:* what is *in common* lies at the end of the rainbow, not at the beginning. In other words, what binds, or from another perspective, energizes is not a sociological characteristic (job, "race," age, sex, etc.) but an activity to enjoy, a goal to achieve, even a yearning.

Put it all together and you will see that the change in the very texture of our lives has been profound: "new forms of social organization . . . new ways of ordering human relationships"—a transformation in the "manner" in which society is "put together," as Samuel Hays pointed out in his illuminating discussion.[19] It is against that backcloth that any worthwhile inquiry into contemporary interest-group politics must be placed.

POLITICAL CULTURE

The culture concept had its origin in anthropology, which, as a dicipline, for long enjoyed unity under its aegis, as the distinguished anthropologist Eric Wolf recalled in 1980.[20] Kroeber and Kluckhohn (both eminent) defined it as

> patterned ways of thinking, feeling, and reacting, acquired and transmitted mainly by symbols, constituting the distinctive achievements of human groups, including their embodiment in artifacts; the essential core of culture consists of traditional (i.e., historically derived and selected) ideas and especially their attached values.[21]

That, married to concepts from psychoanalysis and psychology, produced psychoanthropology, or the psychocultural approach, which, augmented by other social sciences, especially a particular brand of sociology, gave rise in the midfifties to the concept of *political* culture. This was given content and currency by Samuel Beer and his Harvard colleagues, but its incorporation into "mainstream" political science was essentially the handiwork of Gabriel Almond and associates at Stanford.[22] Denoting "orientations to political action" (values, beliefs, and feelings), it imputed "some explanatory power to the psychological or subjective dimension of politics."[23]

Where the political culture "comes from," especially its general relationship to political structure (say, government), has been the subject of some controversy. The charge was that the Almondians had been guilty of *uni-directionalism*, of teaching that the "causal arrow" pointed only one way—from culture to structure. Into this one need not enter except to agree with Arend Lijphart that the "political culturists" *had* allowed for the impact of structure on culture, making the "system of causality" complex and "multidirectional."[24] By 1980, in any case, the Almondian view was clear beyond doubt—that culture and structure act and react on each other, so that culture is caused as well as causing.[25]

That "two-way" mode of thinking (more accurately expressed by saying that, within another framework, an independent variable may be presented as dependent) is something we all have to come to terms with in the social sciences. In this instance, it means reminding ourselves that the organizational revolution was accompanied by a revolution in values, said by historian Robert H. Wiebe to include *efficiency*, *continuity*, and *regularity*, ("the natural values of the trade associations and somewhat later of the craft unions as well"), and *group* (or collective) *action*.[26] That of course is consonant with fellow historian Samuel Hays's remark about organizations as bearers of a scientific ethos. Here both the structural (or organizational) and cultural may be seen as deriving from something else—modernization.

Similarly, political scientists Nie, Powell, and Prewitt, developing the work of Almond and Verba, explored the interconnections between economic development (a major component of modernization) and political participation. That economic development is associated with marked increases in the general level of political participation was already well known. But what was the nature of the causal chain? This was their theory:[27]

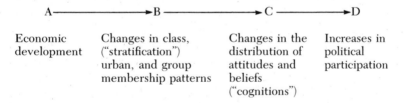

A	B	C	D
Economic development	Changes in class, ("stratification") urban, and group membership patterns	Changes in the distribution of attitudes and beliefs ("cognitions")	Increases in political participation

This reads:

"Economic development alters the social structure of a nation. As nations become more economically developed, three major changes occur: (1) the relative size of the upper and middle classes becomes greater; (2) larger numbers of citizens are concentrated in the urban areas; and (3) the density and complexity of economic and secondary organizations increases. These social changes imply political changes. Greater proportions of the population find themselves in life situations which lead to increased political information, political awareness, sense of personal political efficacy, and other relevant attitudes. These attitude changes, in turn, lead to increases in political participation," i.e., activities such as talking politics, contacting local and national officials, joining formal political parties or organizations—but (in this research) excluding voting.

What matters for the purpose in hand is mainly link, or phase, C, with which political culture may be equated. Technically, it stands out as an intervening variable between (in their causal model) independent variable A and dependent variable D.

How exactly B "moves" to D—the extent to which the path that B actually follows "passes through" C (changing attitudes), or, bypassing C, "goes direct" to D (meaning that an attitudinal change is *not* entailed)—need not be pursued here. It is enough to understand that in our framework, we are focusing on the explanatory variables "closest" to *what has to be examined*, i.e., on B (where the organizational revolution would be placed) and on C (identified as components of the political culture). Thus the "remoter" variables are neglected. Since the reciprocal interaction between B and C is also neglected, we shall in effect treat each one as an independent variable. This is only a first approximation but easy to correct and refine if you proceed to more advanced study in political science. Here the essential purpose is to build a structure of explanation, ultimately of why America has indeed become something like a special-interest state; immediately, to enable you to get your bearings before you start grappling with the voluminous details about interest groups and their activities in the 1980s.

This brings us back on track to political culture as an independent variable that accounts, in part, for the "shape" or pattern of interest-group politics. In this context, a crucial component of the political culture is widely acknowledged to be what Almond and Verba termed "subjective competence" but which Nie et al., reverting to an earlier practice, called "political efficacy." Later, in another change of cast, Verba and Nie explicitly equated political efficacy with subjective competence.[28] (However, two authorities on political participation, Milbrath and Goel, drew a line between these two concepts.[29])

To elicit the sense of *subjective competence*, Almond and Verba asked (in their sample survey of 5000 people in five countries) whether respondents could "do something about" an unjust local or national regulation. Some three out of four Americans thought they could, i.e., expressed local *and* national competence; about two out of three of the British did so. Germans matched the British in local competence, but not many more than one out of three of them felt competent nationally, which was also the Mexican level. Nationally, fewer than one out of three Italians felt subjectively competent, whereas about half of the Mexicans and the Italians felt competent locally.[30]

The significance of this for our purpose is that competent citizens "perceive themselves as able to affect governmental decisions through political influence: by forming groups, by threatening the withdrawal of their vote or other reprisals."[31] To what extent would such groups be formed? Of the "local competents" (those feeling competent in local affairs), three out of four in the U.S. would work through a (primary) group; rather more than four out of ten in Britain. But in West Germany it would be only about two out of ten. That particular contrast is all the more interesting knowing that the proportion of local competents in Britain and Germany was about the same.[32] But our immediate intention here is to illustrate the "carry-over" from political culture to group formation, groups that did "not exist, at least in a politically relevant sense, before the political stress situation" arose,[33] and with that its contribution to interest-group politics.

Of course, *political efficacy*, defined more recently (1979) by Dale C. Nelson "as a belief in one's ability to influence political authorities and other political actors,"[34] is but one component of political culture. Another in the now-classic Almondian literature is a sense of *civic obligation* and with that a propensity to be politically active. In the U.S. over half of those questioned said they felt such an obligation. If the proportion fails to impress, compare British respondents (39 percent), German (22 percent), and Italian (a rather dismal 10 percent).[35] Much of the expected activity would (it was said) take the form of participation in civic bodies, suggesting another link between political culture and interest-group politics. So one could go on. But it must be sufficient to say that, adding more and more ingredients, one could end up (as Almond and Verba did) by identifying a *participant political culture*, with direct and indirect significance for the pattern of interest-group politics. At the time of the research, the U.S. was the outstanding embodiment of such a culture.

There are other ways of employing political culture in partial explanation of interest-group patterns. Samuel Beer's (or the Beer-Ulam) formulation remains illuminating. It invites us to "apply" political culture to authority and purpose in government, to conceptions of means and ends.[36] That can lead us to consider, for example, variations in the legitimacy accorded interest groups. These, for instance, have been found (by Robert Presthus, an American scholar teaching in Canada) to be more legitimate there than in the United States.[37] The general idea was summed up by Michael T. Hayes in 1981: political culture shapes "prevailing conceptions of what politics should be about, who should be allowed to participate, and what kinds of tactics will be accepted as legitimate."[38] That obviously bears not merely on the tactics used by interest groups but on their fundamental freedom of action and general place in the political system. One way or another, even this brief and incomplete treatment should be enough to convince you that political culture deserves its place in our structure of explanation.

CHAPTER THREE
ORGANIZATIONS INTO INTEREST GROUPS

In tracing the outline of the organizational revolution, one pointed out that most of the resulting organizations—building blocks of contemporary social structure—discharge functions that are essentially nonpolitical. Yet to a marked degree such organizations have been politicized, i.e., they have ventured or been drawn into the authoritative realm of government. One must now acknowledge what was deliberately glossed over earlier: there is nothing automatic about the "transition" from organization to interest group, nor indeed from social category to organization (including the wholly political bodies such as those *pro* and *con* the law on abortion). At each stage, apparently, there is a hurdle to be jumped. It was an economist, Mancur Olson, Jr., who alerted the political-science profession both to the existence of the obstacle and to the conditions under which it could be surmounted.

THE FREE-RIDER PROBLEM

Professor Olson went straight to the heart of the matter: the proliferation of organizations (he argued) is not inescapable, nor is the succeeding stage—that is, the carry-over of organizations into the sphere of government—inevitable, not even almost inevitable. The reasons he gave in the chapter now being paraphrased—chapter 5—were partly derived from the history of Britain, but he soon reverted to the logical argument already set out in the introduction and opening chapter. Formation/proliferation are not inevitable because rational individuals who would stand to gain from organizing in pursuit of common interests will not actually set about doing so except under certain conditions. The reason is partly that each individual will receive "only a minuscule share" of the benefits of any action he or she takes in the group interest, whereas organizing or even being organized entails some cost in time and/or money that is individually borne. Besides, the benefits gained will come their way in any case so long as they are "qualified" (belong to the proper category).[1] So rational individuals will sit back expectantly, crying, "Let George (or Georgina) do it!" This, in effect, is the free-rider problem. In other but perhaps more "dignified" words, it is the problem of public goods. Keeping America inviolable—the defense of the nation—is a public good which you naturally wish to see provided but for which, if you are rational (in the economist's sense), you would prefer not to pay. Of course, the government gives you no choice: Pay up or else—that is, in the last resort, it resorts to coercion. That points to one of the conditions under which a presumed tendency to group formation/proliferation in pursuit of a collective good—which is like a public good but limited to some collectivity or "constituency"—will be actualized: You, the calculating individual and therefore reluctant joiner, are coerced into joining. The stock example, much favored by Mr. Olson, concerns the labor union, "The single most important type of organized interest group in the private sector," or at least the "single best known type."[2] Join the union or else! Hence the well-known pattern of closed, union, or agency shop. Of course "muscle " may in some situations achieve the required result.

The only other way around the obstacle (the argument continues) is to offer the calculating individual individual benefits, or selective incentives, over and above the collective benefits (derived from the exertions of the group) that will drop like ripe plums into all "qualified" laps whether or not these belong to fully paid-up members of the organization. Now the appeal becomes: Join our association, and receive this valuable journal, become eligible for insurance coverage at these uniquely favorable rates, and receive many other concessions. This may of course be combined with coercion: In addition, unless you join you will be unable to practice in this state, county, or city.

None of this, it should be noted, is held to apply to small groups. Here rational individuals can be expected to act because each will get a substantial proportion of the gain from the collective (or public) good (there being relatively few to share in it). Also, the gain will be more perceptible to the calculating individual, whose contribution, furthermore, will be more publicly acknowledged. Even so, members will not provide as much of the collective good as they ideally could because even in a small group they do have to share with the free riders. Still, it remains true—the "most important single point about small groups in the present context"—that "they may very well be able to provide themselves with a collective good. . . . In this, small groups differ from larger ones." The rule is that "the larger the group, the less will it further its common interests."[3] If so, there is nothing automatic about formation/proliferation, despite the tendencies apparently induced by the division of labor.

If the small (presumably, primary) group constitutes an exception to the general rule, this also tends (the author concedes) to be incomplete or inadequate in the realms of religion, philanthropy, and "lost causes." These are areas in which the individual appears to be less rational (in the economist's sense) and the theory accordingly less useful. It comes into its own principally in the sphere of economics, in application to economic organizations.[4]

No serious evaluation of this important work will be attempted here: one must strictly limit oneself to a few points in relation to the theme of this chapter. First, since the theory does not really account for the emergence of groups devoted to good causes, whether lost or not, it is rather limited.[5] No doubt the economic organizations are thick on the ground, enjoy long life, and, in virtue of the work they do, are well endowed. Even so the pure specializations have greater political significance in American (as in British) history than Mr. Olson seems willing to acknowledge. How different the course of American history would have been without the Anti-Slavery Society and the Anti-Saloon League. Or think back to the environmental-ecological movement of the 1970s hotly pursuing several public goods. Reflect, too, on the emergence (and success) of Common Cause in the same decade, also in pursuit of public goods, but without the advantage of either coercion or selective benefits.[6] Recall, too, the exertions of many in behalf of or against abortion, a grave issue carried over into the 1980s. If less numerous than economic organizations, these cause groups—organizations-*for*—confront issues that bear upon the quality of life, even of civilization. Yet to borrow critic Matthew Arnold's characterization of the poet Shelley, none of the protagonists is "a beautiful and ineffectual angel, beating in the void, his luminous wings in vain." On the contrary, such protagonists often play "rough" and pack a political "wallop," so they cannot be discounted.

At bottom what is at stake here is nothing less than rival "models of man" (including woman) and in particular rival beliefs about the place or even the possibility of *dis*interested behavior—not, of course, to be confused with *un*interested behavior—or the relative standing of what the English eighteenth-century moralists posed as self-love v. benevolence. Basic as the issue is, it cannot be pursued here, much less resolved. But in reading the history of groups and movements, one would have to try very hard to avoid perceiving the fairly swift emergence of groups pursuing public goods without coercion or selective benefits. A foreign example that bears upon another dimension of the Olson theory—that class-oriented action will not occur if the individuals in that class act rationally—is provided by the London Working Men's Association, founded in 1836. The celebrated Six Points of their charter (or proposed legislative bill) included several public goods, among them equal electoral districts, the secret ballot, and removal of the property qualifications for election as a member of Parliament. In pursuit of the Six Points, members of the working class (in the North of England and the Midlands as well as London) joined forces: no coercion, no selective benefits, much sacrifice. Think of George Shell, writing to his parents on the eve of a Chartist demonstration: "I shall this night be engaged in a glorious struggle for freedom, and should it please God to spare my life I shall see you soon; but, if not, grieve not for me, I shall have fallen in a noble cause. Farewell! . . . Yours truly . . ." That Chartist contingent set off with pikes and sticks and muskets, proving no match for the soldiers, who killed fourteen and wounded fifty, ten of whom succumbed later. George Shell was not spared: he was eighteen years old.[7]

It is profitable to recall the Chartist experience for another reason. The main movement did not last beyond midcentury, so it might be argued that the lack of coercion and of selective incentives proved fatal. (Five of the Six Points were eventually enacted, although it took until 1918.) But then the argument would be about the survival and proliferation of groups rather than their launching, which is often taken to be the basic point, as for example in Salisbury's saying that Olson's work "quite fundamentally undermines all extant theories of group formation,"[8] and David Greenstone's reference, in his discussion of that work, to the "large costs of developing effective organizations."[9] In fact, in the Olson house there are many mansions, including at least the following "transitions":

1. sociological or occupational category to a group (presumably small, or primary, such as a circle of friends at work);
2. primary group to secondary group, or organization;
3. secondary group "spilling over" as interest group (political in the Trumanite language).

These distinctions are analytical: the "natural history" of it all is hardly developed. Presumably, especially in the economic sphere, the small-group stage is crucial, the buckle that binds, the way station from category to a secondary group. However, the place of the small group in the Olson schema is doubtful conceptually, quite apart from historically, as the James Bill and Robert Hardgrave, among others, have pointed out.[10] The small group is supposed to be an exception to the general rule because the advantages of belonging to one stand out more: proportionally greater share of the public good, greater awareness as well as greater public acknowledgment of a person's contribution. Even so, the small group (Mr. Olson admits) does not escape the free-rider handicap: even in the smallest group, "group-oriented action is problematic because each member has an incentive to pay as small a share of the cost of the public good as possible."[11] If so, the really rational or calculating individual would surely hold back even at this level. For him or her the golden rule in groups of all sizes logically should still be: Let George or Georgina do it!

One wonders, in passing, whether organizational costs are really as severe a "deterrent" as the model and, it would seem, virtually all commentators have assumed. It was not always thought so. Thus the famous Kansas editor, William Allen White, advocating participation in "the invisible government" of groups, believed (back in 1924) "it takes time and intelligence, and a little money, but not much."[12]

That topic, in any case, leads into what David Greenstone has called "repression costs," which in turn brings in the postulated role of small group historically rather than conceptually considered. Take labor unions as, at one time, a species of small groups: according to the Olson schema, the transition (number 2 above) was accomplished mainly by compulsion of the closed/union shop variety and/or in coming out on strike (intimidation, presumably). But, of course, as James Q. Wilson remarks, unions must exist before they can impose or bargain for a closed or union shop: how do they "get there" and keep going? Besides, some unions flourish without ever making any such imposition.[13] For example, some Indiana locals of the Communication Workers of America were found (by H.C. Roberts, Jr.) to have recruited extremely well—but they had no union-security agreements. Selective incentives, then? No, or none of any significance. The local with no benefits recruited about two-thirds of its potential membership. Only a tiny proportion of the members in three locals said that they joined to get the benefits or would leave if these were withdrawn.[14]

It is undoubtedly true that, at a certain (but not yet clearly defined) stage, many unions do come to offer selective incentives, such as the death and disability benefits provided by the Carpenters and Joiners. When that is done, recruitment may well increase. But, asks English social scientist Brian Barry, can one really hope to explain the higher recruitments in Britain compared with the U.S. by pointing to selective incentives, or the variations in union recruitment over time or within different industries in any single country? Other variables, surely, would have to be conjured up.

So one could go on, but it is hardly worth it, for this is a game that any number of people can play. Illustration from history is better than nothing but it is not conclusive. Brian Barry cuts through to the heart of the matter in his reproach to Mr. Olson: "I think one has to say that he tends to pick the cases which support his thesis rather than by sampling the universe of organizations of a certain type within certain spatio-temporal boundaries."[15] In other words, the proper procedure would be to take a representative sample. Of course, the critics who have simply offered counter-illustrations have to be pronounced guilty on the same charge.

One of the few in this Olsonian context who have used a sampling procedure is William A. Gamson. He studied challenging groups, some of which were occupationally based; others, socialistic, "nativist," or broadly reformist (such as the Anti-Slavery Society) but united (so far as concerns us) in the pursuit of a collective good. To what extent did these groups resort to the use of selective incentives? Mr. Gamson drew a probability sample of the five to six hundred of these identified in the period 1800 to 1945. That yielded fifty-three, of which eleven had resorted to selective incentives in one form or another. Since it was also established that groups may grow large without selective incentives, it seemed that Mr. Gamson would not be able to bear "glad tidings" to the Olsonians. But that would be in terms of "transitions" 1 and 2 above, whereas he himself, William Gamson, in fact had his eye on the comparative rate of success. Groups may grow large without selective incentives but they will have difficulty, he found, in converting size into success, judged by winning recognition or acceptance or by new advantages. Whether large or moderate in size, the eleven offering selective incentives achieved at least one form of success.

On that basis, Mr. Gamson concluded that his research lent support to the Olson hypothesis. But that came from focusing on the "achievement test" rather than on the closely related but apparently not identical issue of formation/proliferation. Even so it was found "not impossible" for groups to achieve success relying on nothing more than loyalty or solidarity (which, reverting to our earlier discussion, might be not so distantly related to altruism).[16]

Another test of the Olson hypothesis bears upon number 3 of the "transitions" mentioned earlier, in which a secondary group "spills over" as an interest group (*political*, in the Truman terminology). It was undertaken by British social scientist, David Marsh. Just as Brian Barry had asked whether variations in union membership (in Britain) could really be explained by variations in selective incentives, so Professor Marsh wondered whether that would work for variations in the membership of the Confederation of British Industry (CBI), the peak (taller and wider than the National Association of Manufacturers in the U.S.). On the basis of interviews with representatives of member-firms, he concluded that the loss of membership in 1974 was principally due to "perceived variations in the supply of the collective good"—what the CBI was judged to be getting from the government as a (political) interest group. That was congruent with his general finding that, although some firms—essentially the small ones—joined for the services (selective benefits), many firms apparently joined in pursuit of the collective good.[17]

Mr. Marsh's general view is that the Olson analysis tends toward an undue concentration upon selective incentives, which up to a point fits the Gamson finding that challenging groups *can* grow large without selective incentives (or coercion). Whether that holds generally with groups is at present impossible to say. But if there *can* be growth without those two "crutches" or "facilities," how would that be explained? Among the answers explored in the literature, two will be touched upon here—sponsorship and leadership—thus in effect refining or modifying the Olson theory. But before attempting that, a refinement at "the other end"—among the hindrances to be overcome—will be disposed of.

REPRESSION COSTS

Commentators have done well to point out that the costs hindering group formation/proliferation are not only organizational: repression costs may also be imposed, providing a very different explanation of aborted or thwarted or stunted development. Mancur Olson reveals some awareness of this in one of his many criticisms of the Truman model, according to which prolonged social dislocation or disturbance of a serious nature will produce new patterns of social interaction, including the formation of new groups. Drawing as Mr. Olson often does on British history, he argues that, according to the model, labor unions should have appeared when the dislocation/disturbance did, with the Industrial Revolution, that is, late eighteenth century, not after the middle of the nineteenth century. He goes on: "Admittedly, the legal environment was possibly also a factor; British unions were outlawed during part of the Industrial Revolution."[18]

That is far too tentative. During the course of the eighteenth century, some forty acts of Parliament were passed outlawing specific "combinations" of workers, who were also retarded by prosecutions under the conspiracy laws. The acts of 1799 and 1800 made a general attack through blanket prohibitions that lasted about a quarter of a century. Unions were not stamped out but they were held back, some going "underground" (with clandestine meetings, secret oaths and rituals, etc.). Others brazened it out, but some members paid the price from time to time by being sent to jail for fourteen days' hard labor. That being a criminal penalty reminds one that all members were criminals in the eyes of the law. Even after the law had been repealed (1824, 1825), six farmers' laborers in the notorious Dorchester case were sentenced to seven years' transportation, on the face of it for administering an illegal oath (the method of "the underground"), but in reality for attempting to organize a union. "Transportation" meant that prisoners were bundled off to a penal colony overseas. The two who were dumped in Tasmania were put to work with a chain gang, and the others were taken to New South Wales (Australia).

So one could go on at least to the 1870s because, in the intervening half-century or so, unions, although legal, were hit by the doctrine of restraint of trade. In other words, the lawyers attacked the methods, not the thing itself—fundamentally strike action and picketing. Parliament did not provide relief until the period 1871–76. Were one to continue, one would also deal specifically with Mr. Olson's related criticism of David Truman that the major national unions in Britain did not develop until after 1850. Several of the points made above bear on that, and many other factors would have to be taken into account. Thus the (first) Industrial Revolution did not just "happen" in 1760 or even 1760–1800, but was a process extending gradually, in fact, to about 1850. After that time, too, the experience of prosperity was significant: substantial bodies of (skilled) workers became reconciled to the new industrial system and the market economy. And the revolution in communications was also crucial to the building of *national* organizations, especially of course the coming of the railroads. But enough has been recalled to make the point—Mancur Olson's appeal to British history against David Truman does not work.[19] Also, David Greenstone and the authors he cites are correct: there may be repression costs as well as organizational costs (and in the history of labor unions, there is no "may be" about it—there were such costs in virtually every industrializing society in the West). As to organizations in general, this means that slow growth or no growth (in this context) cannot be simply explained by reference to the problem of providing collective or public goods. Race relations in America have been cited as another kind of illustration of this.[20]

Sponsorship is William Gamson's term for a helping hand, either from a wealthy individual or from a well-established organization. About a quarter of the challenging groups in his sample had received some help of the kind. Its significance for group formation or proliferation will be clear to you: in Mr. Gamson's image, the presence of a few dedicated, well-paying passengers makes it possible to carry more free riders "out there." As you would expect, there is some reason to think that this was more important in the early days when the organizations were still rather small.[21]

LEADERSHIP

Such terms as *leader* and *leadership* are conspicuous in Mr. Olson's classic essay by their absence (they do not appear at all in the index). Even leadership roles are seldom differentiated and analyzed. It is true that the existence of ruch roles is implied throughout, as in the discussion of selective incentives. But even then it is the organization, not some organizer, that is said to offer the inducement.

Yet leadership surely has a claim to being considered a distinct variable. In 1969 Robert Salisbury sought to make it so by proposing a theory of interest groups as "benefit exchanges." Entrepreneurs were said to "invest some form of capital resources in a set of selective benefits to be made available to those who join the organization."[22] From that investment they would expect a return—a job, salary with expenses, status, power, and the like. This is an exchange relationship, in which potential members are tantamount to a market. The entrepreneur tries to put together a saleable package.

This explicit recognition of the role of entrepreneur, particularly in getting people to join an organization as distinct from retaining them after they have joined, may be read as an improvement on the Olson model. But exchange theory remained constricted by the same rationalist (or rational-calculating) assumptions from which beliefs about the indispensability of selective benefits (or coercion) may be logically derived. In the real world of socio-political movements and groups there have always been leaders as well as entrepreneurs, i.e., those demonstrably able to persuade others to join and act without any such inducements. At one end of the leadership spectrum we might place what editor William Allen White long ago identified as "the paid organizer—the salesman [who] generally sells with the idea of a ritual, a grip and a password, and a vast lot of flubdubbery of suspicion, bigotry, and fear."[23] From the "salesman" who recruits by "merchandizing the byproducts of ignorance" we might pass on to the agitator and the demagogue, ultimately reaching those endowed with charisma, the gift of grace. Initially at least, the leadership they exercise often seems to have little to do with anything as mundane as selective benefits. In other words, a theory of group formation should incorporate charisma, rhetoric, and even flubdubbery.

On this question as on the larger debate, you will have to make up your own mind, no bad thing because the effort should contribute to intellectual growth. There is in any case no generally acceptable way of summarizing a debate that, in desultory fashion, has already extended over a generation. In other words, there is no orthodoxy to present to you. In thinking things out for yourself, bear in mind that, although the discussion has often been conducted in historical terms, the real issue is the working of the contemporary political system. One aspect of it clearly is: to what extent, in practice as distinct from social and constitutional theory, *can* sociological categories mobilize in pursuit of their interests, *can* small groups develop into larger and presumably more effective ones as the need arises? Are some elements in society more or less permanently disadvantaged?

On such questions as those you will of course bring to bear your judgment of the logic of collective action as formulated by Mancur Olson. Remember that it *is* logic, and that, as Charles Hagan remarked in 1966, Mr. Olson does glide rather easily from logical expectation to factual existence "as if the logical outcomes were empirically based."[24] Some empirical material is presented, but (as Brian Barry pointed out) it does not derive from a scientific sampling of the universe and so amounts to illustration rather than validation of the hypothesis.

As to the logic itself, it all turns on the postulate of rationality. As Robert Golembiewski remarked also in 1966, Mr. Olson presents "delicate formal statements of what logically follows if man is rational" in the *economist's* sense, which does indeed tend to cut off substantial parts of the argument from the "*realities* of collective action."[25] In other words, the postulate appears to be at variance with "group dynamics" and with much that is known to have happened in the realm of socio-political movements and groups. The historical record reveals fairly clearly and consistently that men and women are much more than desiccated computers.

Moreover, as David Marsh added in 1978, the postulate of the carefully calculating individual tends to serve as a self-fulfilling prophecy.[26] Assume (as a derivation, conscious or not, from psychological egoism) that the individual must act in this calculating, self-interested way, and you will research for evidence of that presumed characteristic and even be inclined to find it or to explain away the failure. Never forget that the postulates of one discipline may be hotly debated in another. What professors of economics postulate so that they can have a subject to profess may be questioned or even actively disputed by historians, moral and political philosophers, and others who have learned to detect not only the postulates but also the "inarticulate major premises," at least in the other person's discipline if not their own. Unity of knowledge is a luxury that the modern world does not enjoy. Models of the Individual, in particular, are not identical even in the social sciences.

None of this should be read, in the final summing up, as disparaging the work of Mancur Olson. He gave political scientists a not wholly undeserved black eye for their too-easy assumptions about group formation and growth, and subsequent interaction with government. The sharp blow made the profession think again, as revealed in the very considerable discussion that followed and still continued as the seventies drew to a close. It would not have happened had he not had something important to say and said it well.

CHAPTER FOUR
THE CONSTITUTION

So far one has been attempting to explain the pervasiveness of interest-group activity in terms of these variables:

1. (a) a certain type of *social structure*, and (b) *appropriate attitudes* to go with (a)—learned dispositions to inquire and research, measure and calculate, bargain and negotiate, etc. (the organizational revolution);
2. *political culture:* if 1(b) were "torn away" from 1(a), it could be fitted in here with such broader considerations as legitimacy;
3. granted that 1 and 2 "blend" to create a potential for interest-group action: *leadership, entrepreneurship,* and possibly *sponsorship* to convert that potential into active political form, overcoming the Olsonian handicaps where these are, in practice as distinct from logic, significant.

What accentuates such tendencies in the United States is clearly its political structure, which may be resolved here for convenience into two parts: first, some broad constitutional features and provisions, and second, those that bear upon the Congress, together with some of its own rules and customs. The latter will be dealt with in the next chapter.

To set the constitutional scene for the interplay of organizations and government in the United States is rather a daunting task.[1] In searching for a principle of selection, the most relevant concept may be the classical Greek idea about the ethical influence of institutions. Apply this to a constitution, that "ordering of the magistracies [public offices] of a state, and especially of the supreme authority," as the Oxford classicist, W. L. Newman, discussing Aristotle, put it in the 1880s. A constitution embodies an ethos that tends to be absorbed by its citizens, indirectly as well as directly: its central provisions incline citizens in a certain direction. In other words, constitution, laws, etc., not only "enforce certain outward acts, but they create dispositions,"[2] or, as we should say a century after Newman, tend to induce attitudinal as well as behavioral change.

Raising one's sights from "micro" to "macro," one may attempt to limit this investigation by asking simply: what is there about the American Constitution that stimulates organizational life and tends, perhaps, to induce a certain kind of interplay between organizations and government—in short, a politics of interest groups? Even this is far from being an easy question. According to the conventional wisdom, and even unaided common sense, one should be quick to weigh the contribution of the First Amendment: "Congress shall make no law respecting an establishment of religion, or prohibiting the free exercise thereof; or abridging the freedom of speech, or of the press; or the right of the people peaceably to assemble, and to petition the Government for a redress of grievances."

That this must have been of *some* importance in associational growth is doubtless true. One way to grasp that is by resorting to the comparative method. Passed in 1789, the First Amendment was ratified (with the other nine articles of the Bill of Rights) just before Christmas 1791. In France in that very year the legislative attack on the corporations (guilds), with (as we should now say) their "closed shop" ethos, reached a dramatic climax. It had been mounted partly in accordance with the trend toward economic liberalism, but the Swiss political theorist Jean-Jacques Rousseau had also supplied ammunition by distinguishing between individual interest and the general interest and recommending nothing "in between"—no intermediaries to get in the way. That, in fact, was exactly the language used by the Breton lawyer-legislator Le Chapelier in his speech to the French Constituent Assembly in June 1791 in support of his bill. In future there was to be only the particular interest of each individual and the general interest: no one would be allowed to stir up in the citizens any "intermediary interest" (*un intérêt intermédiaire*) and so detach them from the commonweal. His bill prohibiting all industrial associations was passed without discussion.[3] The law was later incorporated in the penal code.

In succeeding years the prohibition was extended to cover "any association for dealing with political questions." This, too, was carried over into the penal code: no association of more than twenty persons having a religious, literary, political, or other object could be formed unless the government approved on terms that it was free to impose. In 1834 a new act went after even the smaller groups. Altogether, as Professor Louis Rolland has concluded, no group of any consequence could be formed without government authorization, and even that did not confer legal status. On that issue the government would have to make another determination according to the test of public usefulness.[4]

Principle and practice never coincided exactly. As in Britain, employers were favored. The organizational growth of workers could not be completely uprooted, as Professor Jean-Daniel Reynaud has remarked.[5] Still, the French authorities, while at times displaying the tolerance for which they have such great talent (when it pleases them), also knew how to strike hard. Thus between 1848 (the revolutionary year, supposedly marking a new beginning) and 1864, they started proceedings against some eleven-hundred workers' groups, involving about sixty-eight hundred persons, of whom two out of three were sentenced to prison terms. Many more were fined.[6]

By 1834, the year of the legislation directed at even the minnows, de Tocqueville had made his American visit and was writing the first volume of his celebrated work. So its backcloth was a society—his homeland—that had been "atomized" in political and economic relations insofar as this was attainable by legislative act. That, of course, was a major reason why he was so intrigued by the lively associational life which he found in the United States (not that he disagreed with the policy back home). The contrast between the two countries remained through his lifetime (he died in 1859). He would have had to live another five years or so (to 1864) to see the workers get some relief, and to 1884 to see their being granted freedom of association. He would have had to survive into this century (1901) to see general freedom of association established.

From this thumbnail exercise in the comparative method it would seem reasonable to conclude, provisionally, that the rules of the game do make a difference—they partly explain the well-attested weakness of French associational life. But how far do they go in explaining the relative strength of American associational life? Note first that the First Amendment says nothing in so many words about freedom (or a right) of association. Speech, embracing the press; peaceable assembly; petition—but not association as such. Why not? Was this an oversight, or a deliberate omission, or did the Founding Fathers assume that the freedoms (or rights) they specified added up to a freedom of association?

This is hallowed ground and, for that reason alone, has to be traversed circumspectly. All the same, one cannot suppress doubts about the interpretation offered by the distinguished judge, Charles E. Wyzanski, Jr., who implied that freedom of association was omitted because the Fathers "plainly did not believe in such a wide freedom." According to him, the Founding Fathers

> were not deceived by the verbal kinship of the phrases *freedom of speech, freedom of assembly* and *freedom of association*. They observed that the triad represented an ascending order of complexity. Or, to use the legal catchword of the day, they represent successively closer approaches to 'clear and present danger.'[7]

One admires the symmetry, but is the judgment sound? Psychologically, could they have gone so far in the First Amendment (farther than any nation in recorded history)—and then reined themselves in? Two hypotheses suggest themselves, not necessarily mutually exclusive:

1. freedom of association was implied in the religious clauses, especially "free exercise." In this view, freedom of association was already there, part of the normal expectation and practice. This need not have implied any strong commitment to religious freedom, into which America may really have "stumbled," as Perry Miller, celebrated historian of the New England religious experience, once put it: "We got a variety of sects as we got a college catalogue: the denominations . . . multiplied until there was nothing anybody could do about them. Wherefore we gave them permission to exist, and called the result freedom of the mind."[8]

Even so, once religious pluralism was accepted, however reluctantly, it would have tended to carry over into the secular sphere. In other words, the religious association would have tended to become a standing model for associations of many other kinds.

2. For what it's worth, the second hypothesis is less derivative, perhaps even original: freedom of association does not, probably cannot, become "an issue" in law and practice until the organizational revolution has occurred or is well under way. We have to recall that originally *association* was a verb-noun (or gerund), denoting the act of associating. This was consistent with the fairly simple physical or symbolic "units of behavior," such as presenting a petition, speaking freely, and peaceably assembling, that constituted the traditional forms of (acceptable) political expression of the relevant kind. But as groups "harden" into organizations with full-time officials, resources, a continuing existence, etc., the word *association* comes to be a straightforward noun denoting a legal or at least a recognizable *entity* that, sooner or later, has to be accommodated within the legal as well as the political system.

From this hypothesis we would expect to observe, more or less keeping step with the growing organizational complexity of the social structure, a gradual elucidation, happily combined with confirmation, of the specified First Amendment rights (neglecting here the religious clauses), and then an enlargement of them, or perhaps rediscovery, so as to find a place for a right of association in a sense more relevant or appropriate to the new milieu. Something like this does seem to have happened. The drift or current may be identified, as a minimum, from the following markers:

1868—CRANDALL V. NEVADA.[9] In striking down a Nevada tax on persons leaving the state, the U.S. Supreme Court gave this as one of its reasons: a citizen of the United States had the right "to come to the seat of government to assert any claim he may have upon that government, to transact any business he may have with it, to seek its protection, to share its offices, to engage

in administering its functions."[10] But the celebrated case in this period came
up eight years later:

1876—UNITED STATES V. CRUIKSHANK.[11]   Usually counted as the first case
in which the right of assembly was at issue before the Supreme Court, this
had come out of some activities of the Ku Klux Klan. For reasons that need
not for the moment concern us, the indictment on charges of having deprived
certain citizens of *their* right of peaceable assembly, etc., failed. But in its
decision the Court asserted as dicta—pronouncements or assertions that are
not part of the Court's decision—these principles:

> The right of the people peaceably to assemble for the purpose of petitioning
> Congress for a redress of grievances, or for anything else connected with the
> powers or the duties of the national government, is an attribute of national
> citizenship, and, as such, under the protection of, and guaranteed by, the
> United States. The very idea of a government, republican in form, implies a
> right on the part of its citizens to meet peaceably for consultation in respect of
> public affairs and to petition for redress of grievances.

Two points may be noted for the purpose in hand. The reference to national
citizenship was in line with the dual-citizenship concept developed in a famous (or notorious) series of cases (*Slaughter-House*) three years before.[12] It
meant that the clause in the Fourteenth Amendment to the effect that no
state shall abridge the privileges and immunities of "citizens of the United
States" applied only to them, very narrowly defined, and not to a category
now conjured up in the minds of the justices for the first time, citizens of a
state. As applied in the *Cruikshank* case this meant that those persons
"merely" pursuing some "peaceful and lawful purpose" not connected with
the federal government were just acting as citizens of a state, not as citizens of
the United States. As such they did not enjoy the protection of the Fourteenth Amendment.

But, you may well object, how is it that we have shifted gear from the
First Amendment (or Bill of Rights) to the Fourteenth? Part of the answer is
that the Bill of Rights applied only to ("against") the federal government,
Madison's attempt to direct it toward the states (as with freedom of speech
and of the press) having failed in the Senate. In a series of decisions from 1833
onward[13] the Supreme Court had kept up the restriction. Now, clutching the
Fourteenth Amendment, resourceful litigants tried "end runs" around that
obstacle. Many years would pass, however, before the play worked.

The other point of interest in that quotation from *Cruikshank* is more
directly linked to the First Amendment. It concerns the relationship between
petitioning and assembling. On the face of it, the Court seemed inclined to
construe the right of assembly as instrumental to the right to petition Congress. It was as if the First Amendment had been written (as an authoritative
commentary well says): "the right of the people peaceably to assemble" *in*

order to "petition the government for a redress of grievances," and not "the right of the people peaceably to assemble, and to petition the government for a redress of grievances."[14]

The hypothesis proposed here is that as the organizational society developed, neither this "dependent" status for the right of assembly nor the several limitations and ambiguities surrounding the relevant clauses of the First Amendment could be indefinitely sustained. What happened, in any case, is well established even if the terminology is in dispute: some parts of the First Amendment have been drawn into, assimilated to, absorbed by, the Fourteenth (if we were to use "incorporated," the shade of the late Justice Frankfurter would return to haunt us, for he believed that the term denoted "instant" development instead of the slow process it undoubtedly was). Thus:

1925—GITLOW V. NEW YORK.[15] This arose out of one of several state attacks on radicalism, Benjamin Gitlow and others having called for a proletarian revolution and a Communist reconstruction of society. In sustaining the conviction, the Court just happened to say in its written opinion ("casually" is how a number of authorities put it):

> For present purposes we may and do assume that freedom of speech and of the press—which are protected by the First Amendment from abridgment by Congress—are among the fundamental personal rights and "liberties" protected by the due process clause of the Fourteenth Amendment from impairment by the states.

Without argument, they simply added—and here the tone certainly strikes one as casual—that "the incidental statement" in a Supreme Court case three years earlier to the effect that the Fourteenth Amendment imposes no restrictions on the states as to free speech was not "determinative."[16]

1931—NEAR V. MINNESOTA.[17] So far as concerns this book, freedom of the press is so close to freedom of speech that we may simply note the Supreme Court case that (as some say) "nationalized" it, that is, held it guaranteed by the Fourteenth Amendment.

1937—DE JONGE V. OREGON.[18] The penumbra of ambiguity surrounding the status of the right of assembly was dispelled in the same decade in another of the "radical" cases. Speaking this time for a unanimous Court (the Minnesota case cited above was decided only five to four), Chief Justice Hughes remarked in his written opinion:

> Freedom of speech and of the press are fundamental rights which are safeguarded by the due process clause of the Fourteenth Amendment in the Federal Constitution. . . . The right of peaceable assembly is a right cognate to those of free speech and free press and is equally fundamental.

The Chief Justice proceeded to cite with warm approval the *Cruikshank* dictum quoted above, starting with "The very idea of a government, republican in form. . . ." There, as so often, seeds sown by the Court in one epoch flourish in another.

Here, then, the Fourteenth Amendment's cloak has been cast over parts of the First. In the course of that, the right to assembly has been, so to speak, upgraded. But that is not all. Consistently with the advance of the organizational society, the historic right of petition has been broadened. From "a redress of grievances" it has come to include inputs for a more positive use of governmental power in behalf of the "interest and prosperity of the petitioners." In line with that, it includes the right, by groups as well as individuals, to petition the administrative agencies and the courts as well as the traditional targets (subject of course to the special nature of courts compared with other institutions).[19]

All this is congruent with the hypothesis of an "intensification" and expansion of First Amendment rights in harmony with the maturing of the organizational society. However, in terms of such a society, one surprising omission remained: acknowledgement of a right of association as such. On the contrary, for a brief moment in the 1920s, the tide seemed almost to be on the ebb. Thus, in 1923, New York State legislated against one category of oath-bound association, virtually the Ku Klux Klan, making exceptions for such bodies as student fraternities and labor unions. Perhaps taking its cue from the early French legislation noted above, New York established strict requirements for those organizations with more than twenty members: they had to register annually, and they had to provide a copy of the constitution and rules together with a list of the officers and members. Seeing this as a reasonable exertion of the state police power to which the liberty of association had to yield, the Court) in 1928 sustained the constitutionality of the law.[20] They omitted, as David Fellman has remarked, to consider the argument that exposure is repressive, as the New York statute doubtless intended.[21]

1958—NATIONAL ASSOCIATION FOR THE ADVANCEMENT OF COLORED PEOPLE V. ALABAMA.[22] That exposure is repressive was acknowledged just thirty years later by Mr. Justice Harlan (speaking for the whole Court) in a landmark case: "It is hardly a novel perception that compelled disclosure of affiliation with groups engaged in advocacy may constitute [an] . . . effective . . . restraint on freedom of association."

Alabama had tried to stop the work of the NAACP and to get it out of the state (it had been chartered in New York). A state court required it to produce various records, including names and addresses of its agents and members in Alabama. Putting aside that requirement as having no substantial bearing on the case, Mr. Justice Harlan reaffirmed that "effective advocacy of both public and private points of view, particularly controversial ones, is undeniably enhanced by group association," which we might take as a sentiment well attuned to the organizational society. So, too, with the following much quoted sentence:

> It is beyond debate that freedom to engage in association for the advancement of beliefs and ideas is an inseparable aspect of the "liberty" assured by the due process clause of the Fourteenth Amendment, which embraces freedom of speech.[23]

The Court agreed that due process had been violated, in effect finding for the NAACP. Was this, recalling the 1928 case from New York, *simply* because the Court and the times had changed? No; in 1928 the Klan made no effort to comply, whereas the NAACP did comply to a considerable degree—holding back, in the last resort, only its membership lists. And of course the Klan was a horse of a very different color, at least as seen through northern eyes. One way or another the Court put the 1928 case behind it.

So one could go on, following the "line of descent" through the cases. It is more profitable for us to note and reflect on two things. First, this is the case in which the Supreme Court used the phrase "the right of association" for the first time "in a forthright constitutional holding," David Fellman reports,[24] as distinct (one supposes) from incidental references and *dicta*. The phrase apparently comes up again in the similar case from Arkansas (*Bates v. City of Little Rock*, 1960).[25] There is even one instance (at least)—a follow-on from the 1958 Alabama decision, which by no means settled the situation there—of the curious formulation, "the right to freedom of association."[26] That was 1964. So, from about the midfifties to the midsixties, a right of association in so many words is catching up with the relevant rights of the First Amendment.

But where had it come *from* (apart from behind)? One authority, Robert F. Cushman, says that all such decisions (1958, 1964, and the related ones) "rested on a freedom of association held to be protected by the First Amendment and made applicable to the states by the Fourteenth."[27] Does that mean that it is *derivative* from speech (and press), assembly, and petition (the question once asked about assembly)? From their reading of the cases, some authorities have gained that impression.[28] One of the cases cited is *Healy v. James* (1972). The administration at the Central Connecticut State College had refused in 1969 to allow students to form a chapter of the Students for a Democratic Society. The Supreme Court held that this violated the students' right of association conceived of (according to a commentator) as "a construct of First Amendment liberties."[29]

Possibly on the same wavelength is the view once expressed by Mr. Justice Douglas: the right of association, although "not expressly included in the First Amendment," was necessary to make "the express guarantees fully meaningful." It was "contained in the penumbra of the First Amendment."[30] Whether being within the penumbra makes the right derivative may be safely

left to lawyers (and, perhaps, metaphysicians). In any case, an altogether
different view is that the right of association is separate and autonomous, to
illustrate which *NAACP v. Alabama* (1958) has been cited.[31]

This issue has to be left to other hands. It is enough for our purpose to
note one further stage in the evolving story:

1973—KUSPER V. PONTIKES:[32] "There can no longer be any doubt that
freedom to associate with others for the common advancement of political
beliefs and ideas is a form of 'orderly group activity' protected by the First
and Fourteenth Amendments." That was in the context of political parties,
but free choice there was said to be "an integral part of this basic constitutional freedom." Thus, we may conclude that sometime between the late
1950s and early 1970s (depending on the exact context and what we might
wish to emphasize), the organizational society reached a certain kind of matu-
rity. From another vantage point, the organizations then became, in legal
terms, fully "equipped" for their interchanges with government, or at least
more fully equipped than they are in any other comparable nation.

That discussion arose out of the question: what is there about the American Constitution (broadly conceived) that stimulates organizational growth and
with it a politics of interest groups? Noting that such growth, especially in the
field of religion, had already started before the First Amendment was ratified
in 1791, we seem to have detected a powerful "forcing" effect from that
famous constitutional provision. And although the evidence for it is not direct,
the "Greek hypothesis" about the power of a constitution to shape expecta-
tions and dispositions, in particular perhaps *in* the Supreme Court Justices
themselves, does seem to gain considerable support.

In venturing to carry the analysis a bit further, one will be able to offer
only a minimal treatment (because a comprehensive or merely a more thorough treatment worthy of the subject would consume far too much space).
The general feature to which everyone has pointed goes under various names:
decentralization, deconcentration, dispersal, devolution, diffusion, fragmenta-
tion, and "centrifugal tendencies."

Of these notions, which just represent a sampling that happens to be
easily recalled, the last is probably the least apt. Anyone who knows anything
about American history knows that state and local government did not fly off
from some swirling center: in a way like the religious denominations, the
states were there first. The same objection holds against a number of the
other commonly used terms, although resort to any such, often so convenient
for an author, is only a venial, not a mortal, sin. In any case, nobody doubts
that the Constitution tended to produce what one would like to call a weak
state (in the European sense of *state*) but, to avoid confusion, one had better
refer to as a fragmented political system, or a system characterized by an
unusually wide diffusion of political authority.

FEDERALISM

The groundwork for such diffusion was originally the existence of the thirteen independent entities, although the construction upon the given base was actuated and guided by certain values and beliefs about political authority. What the Founders (or enough of them) wanted was "to hold the central authority to a minimum," as Martin Diamond put it.[33] Hence, of course (in the words of Arthur W. MacMahon) that "division of activities between the autonomous parts and the common or central organs of a composite whole"[34] which came to be called "federal," although the word itself does not appear in the document.

Since most of the thirteen states had no intention of "abdicating," that division was done in such a way as to retain them as viable units of government. As James Madison put it:

> The powers delegated by the proposed Constitution to the federal government are few and defined. Those which are to remain in the state governments are numerous and indefinite . . . [and] will extend to all the objects which, in the ordinary course of affairs, concern the lives, liberties, and properties of the people, and the internal order, improvement, and prosperity of the state.[35]

Although he and his collaborators on the *Federalist* papers were out to persuade (this was the "selling," in 1788, of ratification of the Constitution), Madison's emphasis was no doubt justifiable. From it alone one could anticipate that as the twig is bent, so does the branch grow—that the political system as a whole would tend to exhibit the characteristics of "localism." This would be fostered by much else, including of course the single-member electoral district—arrangements so rooted in the states that these would play a leading role in the very selection of the central government. Beyond all that one could anticipate the "Greek effect" which Madison came close to identifying in his discussion of the "prepossessions," favorable to the states, of both the people and their representatives; in particular, the "local spirit" with which members of Congress would be infused. Already they had "but too frequently displayed the character, rather of partisans of their respective states than of impartial guardians of a common interest."[36] From that it would not have been difficult for someone who knew the classics (as Madison did) to predict that the very institutions born of the existing "local spirit" would foster and reinforce it as the decades passed, adding to a presumption in favor of local action and what Herbert Wechsler called "local sensitivity to central intervention."[37]

SEPARATION OF POWERS

The diffusion of authority inherent in the federal principle was augmented by the separation of powers not only at the center but in state government as well. In establishing the strategic principle, the Founders were once again moved by practical experience and current needs with some yeasty infusion of values and beliefs derived, immediately, from the French philosopher, Baron de Montesquieu. A major question to which he had sought an answer was: what kind of institutions would conduce toward political liberty, meaning "peace of mind" (*la "tranquillité d'espirit"*) about one's security (or safety)? To enjoy liberty in that sense, the system of government would have to be such that citizens need not be afraid of one another. How could that be arranged? Like another French aristocrat, de Tocqueville, almost exactly a hundred years later, Montesquieu went overseas to find the (empirical) answer—to England as the one country in the world "which had political liberty as the direct object of its constitution." And by what means did the English secure that end? By (in shorthand) the separation of powers (or so Montesquieu thought). Thus his general proposition: when legislative and executive power are united in the same person or the same body of magistrates—roughly, public officials—there is no liberty. So, too, if the judicial power is not separated from the legislative and the executive.[38]

According to the French scholar, Joseph Dedieu, the book in which that was published (in 1748) was known to the American colonists from 1755 and was "passionately discussed."[39] Certainly, Madison did write early in 1788:

> The oracle who is always consulted and cited on this subject is the celebrated Montesquieu. If he be not the author of this invaluable precept in the science of politics, he has the merit at least of displaying and recommending it most effectually to the attention of mankind.[40]

Yet the principle (Madison continued) had been misunderstood. Montesquieu did not mean that the legislative, executive, and judicial "departments ought to have no *partial agency* in, or no *control* over, the acts of each other." His meaning could "amount to no more than this, that where the *whole* power of one department is exercised by the same hands which possess the *whole* power of another department, the fundamental principles of a free constitution are subverted."[41]

If so, the so-called separation of powers would of course entail some sharing of powers, the separation turning out to be essentially a separation of persons/roles/institutions. This, as everyone knows, is what was actually arranged by the Founding Fathers, the president given a veto power over legislation, Senate "advising and consenting" and "confirming," and so on. It may well be true, as Martin Diamond argued, that there was more to this than a Montesquieu-type concern for liberty, and a concomitant concern for checks and balances—that the Founders were also trying to give the president room to breathe and act, to create the strongest executive possible in the circumstances.[42] It is no doubt true that the separation of powers is "usable" by a unitary system (France since 1958, for example). But it is hard to believe that, in the total American context, the separation of powers did not entail weak, as well as limited, government, and impossible to believe that this is not how it all turned out, whatever the intention.

It is, however, enough to agree that, one way or another, the American political system is characterized by an exceptionally wide diffusion of authority with some well-planned arrangements whereby some parts can effectively "resist and frustrate" (Madison's own term)[43] some of the other parts, for at least some of the time. What does this mean for organizations as interest groups? At the very least it provides an unusually large number of points of entry into the political system, including the judicial "department," notably the U.S. Supreme Court. The entry points may also serve as easy exits, so that groups rebuffed or repulsed *here* can quickly re-form and press their luck *there*. That "can" is practicable, too, thanks to the exceptionally favored position of the groups in law, as sketched in the first section of this chapter.

Secondly, and consistent with the "Greek hypothesis," the whole "set" of the system favors a certain political style—bargaining, compromising, "wheeling" if not exactly "dealing," a politics of temporary liaisons and ephemeral coalitions, of camaraderie by the month, of favors given at a price and with every expectation of a return. Put differently, the Constitution in the broad sense has ethical influence—it tends to shape the personalities of those who play roles *not* of their defining. In general the climate created (or reinforced, acknowledging the influence of sociological and geographical factors) seems to be one in which interest groups would flourish.

And political parties too? you may well ask. And if so, why do these *not* counteract the diffusion of authority, help override the checks and balances? Yes, the parties flourish too—but on terms strongly influenced by the Constitution (resting in a sociogeographic matrix of continental size). What happens is that the centrifugal tendencies (allowing oneself the luxury of calling them that) carry the parties as well as other entities from the center toward the circumference. The federal principle itself entailed such an outward thrust—state responsibility for the electoral rules of the game, later assisted by the direct primary, as well as the sheer existence of the states themselves. And the local spirit of which Madison wrote (originally in some measure the source of the federal principle) sustains the outward momentum. One manifestation of it is that congresspersons are "good ol' local boys" (some girls) with roots in their territories.

For these reasons alone the parties naturally have a state-and-local frame of reference. Other influences were at work at the other end, inhibiting the emergence of strong national parties on the European model: heterogeneity, for example, and continentality with eventually a population to match. It is just possible that one or other of the modern ideologies and movements, such as those of the Left that moved so many European nations between, say, 1860 and 1960, producing mass political parties with full-time bureaucracies and so on, might have provided some unifying influence. But for all sorts of reasons America was indeed "exceptional."

Even at the center the separation of powers inhibits party growth and discipline: the separated institutions develop a life of their own to which party tends to be subordinated. This is what a Democratic member of the House Rules Committee had to say in the early 1970s:

> Even if the president is of our own party, I would still think that we are a 'House-first' institution. Legislatively speaking, we have to assert our independence, I think you can forget loyalty to the president because I think party and leadership ought to cover that as the case might be.

The case might be a little more lucid, but the general drift can be discerned, and Republicans on the Rules Committee appear to be part of it.[44]

Add that institutional ethos to the prevalent "localism" at the base, and party discipline and loyalty are hardly to be expected. Consider, for example, the Carter administration gasoline rationing bill that reached the House floor in July 1979. It would have given the president authority to draw up a rationing plan for a national emergency, subject to guidelines and the ultimate check of rejection if the president decided to put it into effect. But by a vote of 232 to 187 the House passed a Republican amendment according *each* house of Congress a right to veto the plan immediately after it had been drafted and so *before* it had been put into effect. It cannot be doubted, as New York Democrat Richard L. Ottinger remarked, that "the special interests" were at work. But localism/parochialism was also at work. Of the 232, 76 were Democrats, voting against not only a Democratic president but also their own party leaders in the House. Acknowledging a defeat for the leadership, House Speaker Thomas P. O'Neill asserted that "a lot of people" among the seventy-six did not understand the amendment. But some "considered loyal to the Democratic leadership" told a Washington reporter that "they knew exactly what they were doing when they voted for" the amendment. Said a New Hampshire Democrat: "I intended to vote for it. I knew what I was voting for. There is nothing wrong with reviewing the president's actions, especially when it directly affects my constituency."[45] Even more dramatic examples of that occurred in the battle of the budget in 1981, as recorded in the opening chapter.

This brings us back to the localism underlying congressional politics. A high proportion of the candidates fight the good fight with little or no help from their party, which they would get automatically in many Western European countries. Without effective party organization, they *have* to fend for themselves, collecting a team of campaign workers and supporters, and raising the money to pay bills that will range all the way from substantial to intolerably large. To a high and increasing degree, as also noted earlier, the money comes in from the interest groups.

To sum up: a "chain of connection"—a Madisonian phrase, from *Federalist* paper 47—leading all the way back to 1787 has, with sociogeographic forces, produced decentralized political parties to match the other decentralized (or localized) features of the system. Such parties bear so little resemblance to European political parties that Morton Grodzins called them "anti-parties."[46] Except for a brief burst of glory during the nominating and electing of a president, and for arranging the work of Congress, they "rarely coalesce power at all," but serve rather "as a canopy under which special and local interests are represented with little regard for anything that can be called a party program."[47] This provides both encouragement and opportunities for interest groups, whose influence (all other things being equal) may be expected to vary inversely with the strength of the parties.

CHAPTER FIVE
CONGRESS

The "legislature is the natural habitat" of interest groups, as William J. Keefe and Morris S. Ogul remarked.[1] That was in the American context, but the generalization holds good for England as far back as the fifteenth century, when the City of London (the great merchants) were drawn toward the House of Commons, prudently supplying some of the speakers with such gifts as one pipe of red wine, a cask containing 105 gallons, and two barrels of *vini dulcis* for services to be rendered. Late in the sixteenth century, the City was drawn to Parliament in order to get a river diverted to the north of its own "domain." This took a private bill, for which the City paid all the fees, but then added something for the Clerk of the Upper House (or House of Lords). As a result that measure "has always appeared in the collections of printed statutes with chapter number as though it were a public bill."[2] In the same period the City of Westminster gave dinners to members of the committees considering its legislation, and the clothiers are on record as having written to members of Parliament "humbly" seeking "your honourable presence and assistance by two of the clock at the committee of the bill," also that "you will be well pleased to consider the equity therein desired,"[3]

This was happening in the age of the first Queen Elizabeth, when "the lobbying and organized intervention of outside private interests" crystallized as a distinctive practice. "The pioneer in this business of lobbying"—the City of London—even worked out a "whole procedure" for it, such that, for example, bills originated by City companies or crafts or even by individual citizens were to be first "cleared" with the City hierarchy before submission to Parliament.[4] Leap forward now to the late nineteenth century (when another queen—Victoria—was reaching the end of an even longer reign), and observe the extent to which the Commons was still the "natural habitat" of the interest groups:

> It is undeniable that during the session just ended there has been an atmosphere of money in the lobby and precincts of the House of Commons scarcely known before. All manner of "interests" have gathered there as they gather in Washington and in the various state legislatures in America. More attempts to influence the votes of members have been made than has been known before, or, at any rate, than members can recollect since the days of railway construction. Incidents connected with the Telephone Bill, the Petroleum Bill and the Clerical Rates Bill point to closer connection between finance and legislation than is desirable or safe.[5]

The point of these historical touches is not simply to support, tending to universalize, the Keefe/Ogul proposition, but also to bring out the special, almost "privileged," position occupied by Congress. For Parliament is no longer the "natural habitat" of interest groups except in the perhaps irreducible sense that a representative assembly based on universal suffrage is always likely to be a focus for interest-group activity. But that, in the British Parliament, is now more symbolic than real if one is thinking of the determination of legislative policy, for such power has ebbed away from Parliament toward the government, including the bureaucracy.[6] By contrast, Congress remains "the natural habitat" in the more interesting sense. The reasons are obvious: although an ebb-and-flow between Congress and the presidency is discernible over the years, it is kept within the bounds by the Constitution.

The formal powers granted Congress constitute only the beginning of the story, but they remain formidable to this day, including power to tax and to spend, not only for "the common defense" but also for the "general welfare" of the nation; to regulate foreign and interstate commerce; to declare war; and to propose amendments to the Constitution. Note that the general welfare concept harbors a "sleeper": it enables Congress to spend money, for example, on education which it is not specifically authorized to do elsewhere in the Constitution.

That is not the only "sleeper": another may be found in clause 18 at the very end of article 1, section 8: "To make all laws which shall be necessary and proper for carrying into effect the foregoing powers, and all other powers vested by this Constitution in the government of the United States, or in any department or officer thereof." In other words, authority for Congress to "choose its own means of converting the powers granted to it into effective national policy."[7]

Thus Richard H. Leach, a modern authority. Alexander Hamilton had put it differently in the controversy that erupted when he proposed to create a national bank, which on the face of it was not authorized by the Constitution. In opposing the proposal, Jefferson said it was not "necessary" in the sense of clause 18, that is, the enumerated powers in clauses 1 through 17 *could* be "carried into effect" without a national bank. In rebuttal, Hamilton argued for a broad interpretation of congressional powers, of that clause 18 in particular: Congress had the right to use "all the means requisite and fairly applicable to the attainment of the ends of such power," unless specifically forbidden, immoral, or contrary to the "essential ends of political society."[8] President Washington agreed, and Hamilton got his way and his bank.

The issue came up again, however, after the War of 1812 in circumstances that need not be recalled here, and reached the Supreme Court in 1819. The Court held unanimously that the act incorporating the bank was constitutional. In delivering the celebrated opinion (which is still a delight to read), Chief Justice Marshall subjected what he called "the peculiar language of this clause" (18) to a cool analysis, especially as to the meaning of "necessary." The upshot was this: "We think the sound construction of the Constitution must allow to the national legislature that discretion, with respect to the means by which the powers it confers are to be carried into execution, which will enable that body to perform the high duties assigned to it, in the manner most beneficial to the people."[9]

Such "discretionary" powers have come to be known as "implied": evidently, they greatly augment the delegated powers (not to mention those enjoyed concurrently with the states, or the inherent ones, conjured up to enable the national government to cope with a world of sovereign states).

It is of course true, as Richard Leach remarks, that "the mere lodgment of power in Congress has not been equivalent to the full exercise thereof."[10] Congress has "surrendered" (i.e., delegated) some power to various agencies. It has to operate within the general separating-and-checking system, which entails compromise, getting along, accepting and making oneself believe that half-a-loaf is better than none. Congress itself, of course, is not a unified body: it was deliberately cut in two as yet another move within the great strategic plan of separating-and-checking.[11]

What this means is that the *de facto* power of Congress is less than the *de jure*, a common feature but unusually marked in the American case. Even so, when the last qualification has been made, Congress still stands out as a major power center, toward which the interest groups naturally gravitate. It does indeed provide their "natural habitat."

Think now of Congress's own rules and customs[12] and the extent to which these work with the grain of the Constitution to "encourage" interest-groups activity. One would not dispute the common view that the decentralization flowing from the Constitution tends to find its way into the nooks and crannies of the political structure, producing, among other things, a loosely organized Congress, manifested in part in the standing committee system.[13] (Select committees, including conference committees, and joint committees will be ignored here.) But it is historically (and logically) false to assume that the "progression" from the general to *this* particular is inevitable. In fact, the decentralization (or centralization) of Congress, the House in particular, has varied within fairly wide limits. A powerful standing committee system, superficially a bench mark of decentralization, *can* be made to work in a relatively centralized way. And, of course, it has—from 1890 to about 1910. What had happened (in 1889, when Thomas B. Reed of Maine became Speaker) was a *change of the rules of the House,* (the Reed Rules), which meant, relatively, a centralization of power.[14] In other words, decentralization in the House is *not* just a matter of symmetry (a kind of "strain toward consistency," as sociologists say), but the result of identifiable political decisions; at one stage, party-political decisions. Those representatives who built up the pressure that, in 1910, broke the power of Speaker Joseph G. Cannon (Reed's successor but one),[15] were clearer in the head than some of today's political scientists. In 1906, in a debate in which many strong criticisms of the rules were expressed by representatives, one of them hit the right nail hard on the head: "We can change of the rules of the House. We can if we will. . . . The majority party can, if it will, make a few simple changes in the rules that will go a great way to restore the ancient capacities and prestige of the House."[16]

In 1909–10 the rules were changed (thanks to a bipartisan coalition). If the immediate beneficiaries were the party caucuses, the ultimate ones were the standing committees, which "won solid institutionalized independence from party leaders both inside and outside Congress."[17] This meant more decentralization of power, congruent with the general tendency of the total system but clearly not an inevitable consequence of it. So too with the custom, strengthened by the same reform, of allocating committee chairmanships according to seniority, which also pointed in the direction of decentralized power (and of conservatism as long, at least, as the old one-party South survived).

At this stage, you might well object: are not all legislatures in liberal democracies equipped with standing committees, and, if so, what's so special about the American Congress? The most obvious contrast is with the British Parliament: After a first, purely formal "reading" of the Bill—a copy is simply left on the Clerk's desk—it is then considered and approved in principle in the second reading debate; next, it is scrutinized by a part (a standing committee); finally, it passes back, possibly somewhat amended, to the whole. In the earliest Congresses the whole did come before the part, although the committees "raised" were *ad hoc,* or temporary. But gradually the standing-committee system was established *and* (what does not necessarily follow) made the starting point of the procedure. Thus today the part (normally) comes before the whole, and, as everyone knows, the whole may never be reached. As the young Woodrow Wilson, referring to a bill, wrote so well (the hyperbole still charms, and even makes the point stick in one's memory): "When it goes from the clerk's desk to a committee-room it crosses a parliamentary bridge of sighs to dim dungeons of silence whence it will never return. The means and time of its death are unknown, but its friends never see it again."[18]

Of course, even in Wilson's day some "culling"was essential. As late as the 40th Congress (during the post-Civil War period, 1867–69) the total number of bills *introduced* was only 2000-plus. By the 51st Congress, which opened in 1889, not long after he was writing, the total exceeded 19,000 (compared with 268 in the first Congress one hundred years earlier, 1789–91).[19] Besides, many bills probably deserved to be sent to the dungeons, especially those private ones drawn up to bend the existing law in favor of individual beneficiaries (the alleged purpose behind the ABSCAM scandals of 1980).

In any case, for the purpose of this inquiry, the point is the remarkable growth of the standing-committee system and the remarkable place it occupies in the legislative process and so in the policy-making process as a whole. Following an early period of luxuriant growth, then some "die back," the committees were pruned after World War II and again, in the Senate, in 1977. This left the House with twenty-two, and the Senate with fifteen of these committees in the 95th Congress. The acquisition of power along the way has been even more remarkable:

> Over the passing years the standing committees of Congress have acquired power to hold hearings; to sit and act when and where they deem it advisable during sessions, recesses, and adjourned periods; to send for persons and papers; to take testimony and make expenditures; to investigate and report upon any matter within their jurisdiction; to oversee the execution of the laws; to certify contumacious witnesses for contempt; to adopt rules and appoint subcommittees; to report in certain cases at any time or not to report.[20]

This was not planned: it grew like a coral reef. So one could not assert that it was done by stealth. Nevertheless one *can* safely assert that it was done without the knowledge or, therefore, the consent of the American electorate. Would they have agreed to giving the standing committees what a distinguished authority on Congress, Nelson W. Polsby, once characterized as "independent sovereignty of their own, subject only to the infrequent reversals and modifications of their powers by House party leaders backed by large and insistent 'majorities' "?[21] Nor has it ever been demonstrated by the apologists for Congress that this great accretion of power to the standing committees has been no more than proportional to the increase in the work to be done (some of it self-imposed), or in any case that it represents the most democratic or even the most efficient way of carrying it out. If, as implied in chapter 1, we are wondering about the responsiveness of the American political system, the domain of the standing committee may be a good place to start looking. For "independent sovereignty" is an attribute that the special interests naturally find immensely attractive, especially when exercised on a small scale (relatively easy to "touch") and in comparative obscurity.

Of course, the attribution of sovereignty to standing committees was not meant to be taken too seriously. Nor does anyone suppose that all such committees are equally well endowed. Since the "power of the purse" is crucial, so are the relevant committees: Ways and Means, in the House; Finance, in the Senate. The money they raise (mostly from individual and corporation income taxes) is "spoken for" by the subject (standing) committees and, all being well, allocated to the manifold purposes of government by Congress as a whole. But between that *authorization* and the actual expenditures stand the hard-faced members of the two Appropriations Committees, more desiccated calculators than dedicated partisans. Since they have to *appropriate* before an agency, etc., can lawfully spend, they obviously have the importance of gatekeepers.

The House (but not the Senate) has another gatekeeper—the Rules Committee. Originally a select committee, it has been standing since 1880, after which it "worked for" the party leadership, notably the Speaker,[22] in determining *what* measures coming up from the committees should be presented to the House, *and how* these should be debated (e.g., with or without amendments; within what limits of time, etc.). Escaping from his clutches during the 1909–10 revolt, it became what some are pleased to call "independent." Independent of the party leadership is what they mean, but there have been times when, dominated by an unrepresentative alliance of Republicans and Southern Democrats, it seemed rather to be independent of the nation. Even as late as 1970, the committee blocked two bills—to buttress the working of the Equal Employment Opportunity Commission, and to set up an independent agency for consumer protection—that had passed the Senate and attracted general support in the House itself.

Since the midseventies, however, the pendulum has swung back more than a little. On the Democratic side (and the House remained Democratic even after the party's great setback in 1980), the Speaker has not only chaired the Steering and Policy Committee (formed in 1973 to make committee assignments), but has also made nominations to the Rules Committee (subject, ultimately, to the approval of the Democratic caucus). President-elect Reagan showed his awareness of this when paying Speaker "Tip" O'Neill a courtesy call a few weeks after the 1980 election. After chatting about the Notre Dame football team, Mr. Reagan got down to business, asking the Speaker to let Republicans have more seats on the Rules Committee (as well as on the Ways and Means Committee). The Speaker declined to attempt to modify the existing (Rules Committee) ratio of 11:5.

Taken by themselves, those reforms of the midseventies evidently embodied a centralizing tendency, but the tide did not run very strongly. As we shall see, there was a countertendency in the form of a great increase in subcommittees. Even at the level of parent committees, it remains true that some of these act almost as agents of the special interests. As a representative remarked when a select committee was discussing the committee organization of the House in the early 1970s: "It has generally been regarded . . . that the members of the committees should almost be partisans for the legislation that goes through the committee *and for the special interest groups that are affected by it.*"[23] What is striking is that the part in italics (added here) does not necessarily follow from the part of the sentence just before the conjunction "and." That committee members might be or become partisans for their "own" bills is one thing: that they should be partisans for the relevant special interests is quite another. However, no one doubts the reality, which is still as Roger Davidson described it in 1974: "Biased policy makers tend to act as lobbyists for the interests supposedly under their purview."[24] Hence of course a fundamental reason why it is so hard to reform the committee system. As a Common Cause observer put it: "Special interests view the present committee system as holy writ. They have mastered it. They have a stake in it."[25]

But then, you might well ask, why are these committee policy makers so biased? The proximate (and approximate) answer is that committee assignments are made largely in accordance with House members' own wishes, which are compounded of many elements, including an intellectual interest married to a desire to influence public policy within that range, but commonly reflecting above all one master wish—to be reelected. This prompts many actions, including of course the cultivation of one's home base, more of a problem for the young members than the old, as Richard F. Fenno, Jr., reports, but something that concerns even the experienced, whose constituency contacts may degenerate into something "like a one-night stand in a singles bar."[26] That is hard to evaluate, but it is clear that another way of preparing for reelection is to get on the right committees: "These include the so-called pork and interest committees—most notably, Agriculture, Interior, Merchant Marine and Fisheries, and Public Works."[27]

These committees (one of which featured in a case dealt with in chapter 1) are "accessible" even to "junior members" seeking "direct constituency payoffs," i.e., electoral rewards.[28] This is "the electoral connection" made familiar by David R. Mayhew. The basic premise here is that "the modern Congress" is "an assembly of professional politicians spinning out political careers."[29] This implies that they seek committee assignments mainly to serve their careers, which makes for biased representation: proportionately too many from the farming constituencies on the Agriculture Committee, from the coastal areas on Merchant Marine and Fisheries, etc., implying in each case proportionately too few from the great urban and suburban environments. That this deliberately built-in bias does not always "carry over" into favorable policies is evidenced by the outcome of the cargo-preference case touched upon in the opening chapter. But it goes some way to explain the level of subsidy granted the maritime industry for both construction and operation. The construction subsidy (to make up the difference in the cost of building in American, as compared with foreign, shipyards) amounted to $3.16 *billion* from 1936 to the midseventies. The operating subsidy (to make up for higher American shipping costs, mainly wages) was of the order of $5.56 *billion* in the same period.[30] That's quite a bit of subsidy for a market economy, also known as free enterprise. Free from what, exactly? Only from government interventions other than paying out subsidies? Only from irksome government regulations? There *are* arguments for these subsidies (cast usually in terms of national defense); the point is rather that such departures from the official philosophy of the American politico-economic system have been made by the standing committees without little public debate or knowledge. This is a meaningful sense in which the standing committees could be called "little legislatures," Woodrow Wilson's characterization of a hundred years ago.[31] As Professor Davidson has pointed out, they are hardly that in another possible sense of the term—composed so as to mirror, more or less, the nation, or even the big legislature, Congress.[32]

Underlying this discussion is of course the question of responsiveness implied in chapter 1. According to an old tradition in democratic theory, responsiveness tends to be a function of representation, a "hypothesis" brought to vivid life in American experience and perhaps even validated by it. Drawing on that, we should *expect* the "little legislatures" to be mainly responsible to the special interests for it is these, in practice, that are represented in them.

Here we come to a complication that can no longer be kept from view: the "little legislatures" have given birth to what George F. Goodwin, Jr. called "miniature legislatures," i.e., subcommittees.[33] Congressional subcommittees are of several kinds, and of increasing importance generally. But in this context one has in mind those that are in "line of descent" from the standing committees.

SUBCOMMITTEES

For many moons after Woodrow Wilson wrote, in fact up to the period of his presidency, the standing committees kept on increasing. In 1946, however, having already been cut back, they underwent more serious surgery and emerged truncated (55 percent lopped off in the Senate; 60 percent in the House). But, contrary to nature if not to government, those truncated limbs grew new parts, or subcommittees. By the seventies, the House total had grown to 112; the Senate's to 107.[34] Relate that 219 to the nominal parents, the standing subjects committees, whose total stood then (1970) at 37, of which 21 served the House. One writes "nominal" for at least two reasons. To some degree, the increase was less the result of a "loving" decision to reproduce than of "adoption," a policy forced on the standing committees by the hundreds of new Democrats elected to the House after 1958.[35] Younger and more liberal than the apparently "extinct volcanoes" who had dominated many of the key standing committees, they pressed for "a piece of the action," for policy as well as personal reasons. In 1969, in response to their pressure, the moribund House Democratic Caucus was revived in order to serve as an instrument of internal reform. But still Speaker John McCormack, they believed, stood in their way. As a young liberal, Representative Richard Bolling (Dem.-Missouri) put it in 1969:

> The real reason for being against John McCormack as Speaker is that at every point he's opposed all of the changes that anybody suggested in the institution. His allies are the worst Democrats in the House of Representatives. They are the southern racist reactionaries and those who represent the remnants of the big city machines.[36]

No doubt his relationship with southern Democrats would be worth studying.[37] In any event, as the reformers were warming up, they had a stroke of luck in the form of two *exposés,* one in the New York *Daily News* and more importantly, one in *Life* magazine, of a well-known lawyer-lobbyist, a close friend of the Speaker's for two decades who had, in fact, enjoyed the use of the Speaker's office for some of his many "interventions" in the administrative and judicial process. The lobbyist was convicted (of improper influence), and so was the Speaker's chief legislative aide (perjury). Although *Life* argued that the Speaker was "more than naively involved," nothing was proved, but he retired precipitately, the first House Speaker to retire voluntarily since 1858.[38]

  With Mr. McCormack safely back in his native South Boston, the "young Turks" among the House Democrats were able to press on with their reforms—notably the "end run" around the committee chairmen, who had formerly dominated the subcommittees, seeing to it that the "right people" were appointed, what tasks the subcommittees should be allocated, when these should meet, and so on.[39] Thus fortuitously assisted, the quantitative changes of a decade and a half tended to introduce a qualitative one—an era of subcommittee rule, or policy making. That was already true of several fields, notably the House Appropriations Committee, divided (Richard Fenno reported) "among a dozen or so subcommittees, ranging in size between five and eleven members. Each subcommittee has jurisdiction over a cluster of executive agencies, *and each produces a separate appropriation bill.*"[40] (Emphasis added). By the midsixties, 96 percent of all House Appropriations Committee meetings were, in fact, Lilliputian, i.e., meetings of subcommittees. Moreover, neither Education and Labor (90 percent) nor Interior (82 percent) was far behind.[41]

  In the first half of the seventies, however, the tendency was carried much further by way of the Subcommittee Bill of Rights.[42] Approved by the Democratic Caucus in 1973, this required (among other things) that all committees of more than fifteen members establish a minimum of four sub-committees; that committee chairmen refer bills to subcommittees within two weeks (so that they could no longer "sit" on legislation); that the Democratic caucus on the committees choose the subcommittee chairman, and clearly demarcate the jurisdictions of subcommittees (provisions obviously designed to weaken the power of full-committee chairmen). The results were startling. Ways and Means, for example, was opened up, its territory being divided into several provinces, even though tax legislation remained with the parent body. Thanks to a later attack, House Appropriations was opened up in another sense by way of a general rule limiting senior Democrats to membership in not more than two subcommittees of a given committee. This change in the composition of the existing subcommittees, bringing in younger members, was to be reinforced by having the House Democratic Caucus approve the chairmen of Appropriations subcommittees. By the midseventies, a spokesman for the Rules Committee (which was left intact) could disclose just how far the reformist wave had taken the House: "We're now in the position where we're getting more and more legislation by subcommittee. . . . We've been having more and more subcommittee chairmen coming before the committee . . . requesting a rule on a bill they're handling."

That was the House: what of the Senate? Its use of subcommittees was already marked, so by the end of the seventies the golden age of committee government in Congress seemed to be drawing to a close, apparently supplanted by subcommittee government. In preparing to assess what this means for interest-group politics, one must recall at least one other fundamental reform of the midseventies—the opening up of congressional proceedings to public scrutiny to an unheard-of degree. It had started with the Legislative Reorganization Act of 1970, which penetrated the veil of secrecy covering the legislators' voting records, revealing a good deal of what went on not only on the House floor but even in committee. This "sunshine" grew stronger in 1973, when the House resolved to open committee and subcommittee meetings to the public, even the "mark-up" sessions—the final amending of the draft and write-up of the measure—previously conducted behind closed doors. Two years later the Senate more or less followed suit. Some meetings may still be closed but there is a presumption of openness. As Leroy N. Rieselbach summed it up: "The burden of proof now falls on those who want to meet in secret; they must persuade their colleagues to keep the public out."[43] The effect was dramatic even in that reforming year, 1975, itself (see Table 5-1).[44]

But such figures include committee hearings, traditionally wide open. (They do not include joint committees, although the trend was also discernible there: from 15 percent closed in 1974 to 7 percent in 1975). More significant are the figures for mark-up sessions, still largely closed in the Senate as late as the previous year (see Table 5-2).

TABLE 5–1   Full and Subcommittee meetings
closed, 1973–1975 (in percentages)

YEAR	SENATE	HOUSE
1973	25	10
1974	25	8
1974	15	3

This meant that in 1975 slightly more sunshine was being let into House mark-ups than even into House hearings (2.8 percent closed). In that year, for the first time, *all* Ways and Means mark-ups were held in public. But the change derived essentially from House Appropriations, which opened *all* such sessions of its full committee, a lead followed by three of its thirteen subcommittees. Altogether only 4 percent of its mark-up sessions were closed in 1975, as against 47 percent the previous year. For the first time since *Congressional Quarterly* started keeping score in 1953, the Senate opened most of its mark-up sessions. Even the Finance Committee, analogue of Ways and Means, closed no more than 8 percent of its mark-ups, compared to 100 percent in 1974.[45]

That by no means exhausts the "revolution" of the seventies within Congress: House-Senate conference committees, the occasion for some skulduggery in the past, also allowed some sunshine to filter in; above all, subcommittees were endowed with their own permanent staffs. However, one must draw a line here in order to pursue the question of what the changes signified for interest-group politics, admitting in advance that little in the way of detailed research findings has yet been published. The most general point is almost tautological: the flow of power toward the subcommittees (taken by itself) adds to that decentralization of the American political system identified in chapter 4, providing many more points of access. This is something commonly believed to favor interest groups, which is in fact the lesson drawn by two specialists, Keefe and Ogul: "An extensive subcommittee system is likely to be advantageous because it offers additional points of access in the legislative process."[46] Support for that may be extracted from the work of another specialist, Roger Davidson, discussing the setting up in Congress of "advocacy

TABLE 5–2   Closed mark-up sessions, 1974–75
(in percentages)

YEAR	SENATE	HOUSE
1974	72	4.6
1975	29	2.2

committees" as a strategy of reform.[47] He meant "a large number of narrow jurisdiction committees" frankly intended to "become advocates of the interests and programs within their purview. This would maximize the chances for any interest to grasp control of a committee and get its viewpoint articulated and would encourage policy entrepreneurship on the part of individual legislators or groups of like-minded members." The proliferation of subcommittees would seem to be a development of that kind,[48] in which case interest groups should be among its beneficiaries.

Apart from political scientists, some professional observers read the changes in much the same way. Thus, a spokesman for the American Bar Association said in 1973, even before reform had run its course, that there were then "over 200 subcommittee chairmen" with a hand in "fiscal-monetary-credit policy matters," and went on to draw this rather daunting conclusion: "The resulting congressional environment invites pressure tactics—of either the carrot or stick variety—by lobbying forces representing all manner of private-interest groups, since action may be stopped or modified at any one of many legislative stages."[49]

On the other hand, political scientists Norman Ornstein and Shirley Elder heard a seemingly different story from the lobbyists they interviewed. As a corporation representative explained: "It's not like the old days when you could see one or two people and your job was done. You have to work harder now, see more people."[50] They identified the "one or two people" as a "chairman and a handful of powerful senior members." As a result of the reforms (these two Congressional experts agreed), "there were many more people to be contacted and persuaded to support a lobbyist's point of view," which "made life rather more difficult for traditional lobbyists in many ways."

What we could deduce from that is not necessarily inconsistent with the other judgments: *some* kinds of interest *groups* have been put at a disadvantage. This might be true (a) specifically, such as in relation to a key committee, or (b) for some generally applicable reason, such as the loss, to some groups, of more or less exclusive information. Point (a) is represented in the literature by Catherine Rudder, a political scientist who also served as administrative assistant to a southern representative; point (b), by Walter J. Oleszek, another political scientist drawn to Washington (the Congressional Reference Service, specializing in American national government).

Discussing the effect of letting in "sunshine" rather than of the structural changes, Dr. Oleszek noted that whereas unions and corporations had usually enjoyed "inside" information "about the actions of individual members of Congress," that had become available to others—"citizens and less powerful organizations."[51] What these will make of their opportunities remains to be seen. But the "pressures on members of Congress" are indeed likely to be less one-sided than in the past. If so, then some established groups will have lost some ground for this informational reason alone.

Dr. Rudder studied the House Ways and Means Committee in the light of the reforms. She reported in 1978 that several special interests "such as oil, big business, and the American Medical Association are perceived, especially by senior members, Republicans and southern Democrats, to have lost support on the committee."[52] This was not a function of its increase in size as such (almost 50 percent, as noted above) but of the political outlook of the new arrivals (which, of course, might have been different). As a long-serving member said about the new members of the enlarged committee, they "are suspicious, more so than I've ever seen before. They go to the Caucus and challenge on the floor. I feel sorry for business. Every proposal is seen as a rip-off, even though it may provide jobs." (The word *Caucus* alone points to a Democratic informant, since Republicans meet under the sweeter-sounding *Conference*.)

What, then, should we conclude? You must make up your own mind, but the following appears to be warranted: the committee, etc., reforms of the midseventies incommoded, inconvenienced, or disadvantaged some kinds of interest groups while strengthening interest-group politics as a general feature of the American political system.

CAVEATS AND RIDERS

Since one cannot say everything at once, some *caveats* have now to be entered, and some riders attached to the general propositions. So far only decentralizing (or dispersing-of-authority) tendencies have been remarked upon: it is time to acknowledge the appearance, in the very same period, of countertendencies, which, if not exactly centralizing, must be presumed to have put the brakes on the decentralizing:

A. Party became more important, at least among the Democrats controlling the House. *Party* here means (a) the Caucus, (b) the Speaker, and (c) the Steering and Policy Committee, each of which gained more power as a result of the reforms. Which of these had come off best by the end of the seventies, we need not attempt to determine. It is enough here to note that political scientists have always equated stronger party leadership and "connection" in Congress with greater centralization and, presumptively, greater coherence in policy making.

The question then arises: which of the two tendencies has prevailed? Discussing (implicitly) this very issue, although when the tide of reform was still running, another congressional authority, Charles O. Jones, concluded that the reforms of the previous five years might well bring about "greater decentralization" than even the existing "strong committee system" had provided.[53] That was said in 1975 but it seemed to hold at the beginning of the eighties.

B. The Budget reform of 1974 (the Budget and Impoundment Control Act) was at least designed to centralize. The previous arrangements[54] were decentralized in the sense that authorization to spend, revenue raising, and appropriation to spend were each handled by different committees, even by subcommittees, without reference to the overall result in even the simple arithmetical sense of the *net* result of the policies adopted—on taxes, programs (etc.), and actual spending—being a deficit (say) of $20 billion in some fiscal year. It naturally followed that the effect on the economy (inflationary in this example) could not be gauged either. Obviously, Congress (and the nation) needed a "point" at which the "lines" converged, so that expenditure could be considered in relation to income (or revenue).

The 1974 reform was comprehensive, including a new and stricter timetable for the whole fiscal operation. What principally matters here is the superimposition of a House and a Senate Budget Committee on the existing pattern of committees and subcommittees in general and on the money committees in particular. Helped by a Congressional Budget Office, they were charged with balancing revenues and expenditures, or at least with drawing attention to the failure to balance and what that implied for the economy. In asking what this reform signified for interest groups, one might answer either obliquely, *via* the concept of decentralization, or more directly, from what has been specifically observed or otherwise researched.

As to the former, Richard Fenno's view (in 1975) of the consequences of the change as a whole was: "The new budget system has produced a wider dispersion of influence *by adding a new set of participants to budgetary decision making* within each chamber."[55] The phrase in italics (not in the original) is literally true, but it may prove more profitable to think rather of a new set of roles, since ten participants in the House Budget Committee (HBC) were drawn from the two money committees—five from Ways and Means and five from Appropriations, in practice divided in each case 3:2 in favor of the Democrats. Moreover, the Democratic Caucus elected all their side of the HBC. The Republican side of it was arranged by the minority leader, John J. Rhodes. In addition, the two leaderships were each afforded one representative.[56] Such a combination of Caucus and leadership influence would usually be read as a centralizing force.

Some evidence on this has been provided by another close observer of Congress, James A. Thurber, writing in 1978:

> House Democratic leaders are forced through the budget process to mobilize members behind budget resolutions that do not always please committee and subcommittee chairpersons, interest groups, agencies of the executive branch, or the president. They must build coalitions and centralize decision making in a House that is highly decentralized.[57]

Vacating the House temporarily, we may explore the Senate in search of clues to the effectiveness of the new budget process in terms of the centralization of authority—ultimately, what that implies for interest-group politics. Undoubtedly the Senate Budget Committee (SBC) started off with a bang. In August 1975 Senator John C. Stennis took the annual military procurement bill to the Senate floor for final approval. Brought back from the House, the bill was only $750 million in excess of what the Senate had approved earlier, i.e., some $25 billion (out of a total budget of $400 billion). But, *ipso facto*, that was also in excess of what the SBC had approved, and its chairman, Senator Muskie, put his foot down even on Senator Stennis, chairman not only of the Armed Services Committee but also of the Defense Subcommittee of the Appropriations Committee. Collecting enough Republican feet on the SBC to protect the new budget procedure, Senator Muskie persuaded the Senate to defeat the measure by six votes. Of course, the issue was not the amount of money but the authority. As Washington journalist, Joel Havemann commented: "What mattered was that Muskie had used the budget process to challenge one of the most powerful committee chairmen in the Senate—and had won."[58]

The centralizing tendency also won—on that occasion. But would it continue? Wasn't there a hint of retribution in a budget-committee staffer's remark: "We'll remember our friends"? Certainly from 1976 onward, as Aaron Wildavsky, an authority on budgetary processes in more than one country, reported, the Budget Committees found the going more difficult. These (he concluded in 1979)

> saw they were entering an already established congressional arena with prearranged power structures. . . . The budget committees sense the realities of Capitol Hill; they know that other committees will not accept budget directives that change priorities radically. What the committees can do, however, is try to create a sense of limits.[59]

That became abundantly, and, for many observers, painfully clear during the course of 1979. Caught on the House floor (in May) in a crossfire of amendments to the fiscal 1980 budget (i.e., for the year starting October 1, 1980), the HBC survived as "walking wounded." But the House not only failed to keep to the new timetable but also roundly criticized the new budget process itself. The central argument was that the HBC (chaired by Representative Robert N. Giaimo, Dem.-Connecticut) was encroaching upon the work of other standing committees, e.g., by proposing to eliminate the oil companies' foreign tax credits.[60] This was a matter for Ways and Means, complained its chairman (Representative Al Ullman, Dem.-Oregon). There were other complaints of the kind.[61]

It was, however, the revenue-sharing issue (in May–June) that revealed most clearly the way the wind was blowing. The HBC wanted to cut by $2.3 billion the amount of general revenue sharing allocated to state governments, most of whose budgets were said to be in surplus, half enjoying "surpluses greater than what they now receive in revenue-sharing funds."[62] The Committee got its way on the floor, beating off four attempts at restoration, the closest vote being 190-195. But the figure of $2.3 billion came up again in a Housing and Urban Development (HUD) appropriations bill in late June. Representative Bill Nelson (Dem.-Florida), a freshman but a member of the HBC, tried to get the total reduced by some $680,000 (presumably hoping to save something). The recorded vote rejecting his amendment went down by 102-302. What had happened? As Common Cause pointed out, some ninety of those members who had voted *against* in May voted *for* (virtually) in June. So where did that leave the budget process introduced in 1974? One answer, not necessarily conclusive but by no means unwarranted, came from an appropriations staffer. During the budget process "it is very easy to vote against large spending. But when it comes down to the appropriations bill, where the real money is [legislators] have to think again."[63]

Where is this line of thought leading us? Having first emphasized decentralization (believed to be, in some sense, "good for" interest groups), we set out to explore some possible countertendencies. One of these had to do with the new budget process introduced in 1974. Wouldn't this go against the tide, constitute a centralizing force? If it did, would it have enough impetus to override, or neutralize, the other tendency, thus tending to "discipline" the special interests and even to diminish them?

The first part of the answer to that question has been roundabout: without specific reference to interest groups as actors (although doubtless they were in the wings and even onstage), one tried to discover how the 1974 budget process was working out *vis-à-vis* the "traditional" committees and subcommittees. The tentative conclusion is: at the end of the seventies, not very well. At least, that reform seems unlikely to cancel out or seriously check the decentralizing tendencies earlier remarked upon.

Turning now to the more specific part of the answer, one notes that Joel Havemann, who monitored the changes very carefully for the *National Journal* and wrote a detailed book on the subject, did address this very issue. Writing of the new budget process, he said: "Its mere existence created a counterpoint to the demands of special interest groups and permitted the enactment of economy measures in government pensions and highway construction. It changed the shape of the 1976 tax bill."[64] He was referring to the HBC's check on outlays for highway construction for fiscal 1977, and on increases in federal pay (beyond 5 percent) the previous year. In these and a few other cases the two budget committees did indeed serve "as counterweights to the special interests that sought federal benefits." As a result the "cozy relationships" that the interests had enjoyed "with the committee responsible for their legislation"[65] were undermined (on those occasions).

Even in those early postreform days, there was at least one striking contrary instance, as Mr. Havemann himself recalled. The issue was postal subsidies for second-, third-, and fourth-class mail; the amount, $307 million; the beneficiaries, sundry mailers, including magazines and newspapers. The Post Office and Civil Service Committee wanted the subsidy to continue, but

President Ford requested no funding, and the ranking Republican on the HBC, Representative Delbert L. Latta (Ohio), moved to delete, which passed, 11-6. Representative Butler Derrick (Dem.-South Carolina), a member of the HBC, must have spoken for some of his colleagues (and millions of Americans): "When I throw out 80 percent of my mail before leaving the post office, it's time to do something" about subsidies on other than first-class mail.[66]

Then came the deluge: Representative Latta called it "the heaviest two-day lobbying effort" he had ever experienced.[67] It was of course mounted by "the firms and publications" that would have lost the subsidy.[68] The Ohio Republican held his ground, remarking that the subsidy mainly benefited "large publications that could afford higher mailing costs." Other members bent to the wind. On the last day of the HBC meetings, Representative Giaimo moved to restore the subsidy, saying that the HBC should not set itself against the Post Office and Civil Service Committee.[69] His amendment was carried by voice vote, and so went conveniently unrecorded. There followed a moving scene, proving that not everyone is an ingrate: "When the committee's vote was complete, a delegation of satisfied lobbyists stood up and left the committee room. One of them, from the Magazine Publishers Association of America, looked in Giaimo's direction and said, 'Thank you.' "[70] Representative Giaimo, you will recall, was chairman of the House Budget Committee.

As part of the juggling with the figures in the budget inherited from President Ford for fiscal 1978, but also in line with his campaign promises, President Carter proposed (February 1977) to save $300 million by dropping 10 of 320 projects for developing water resources. Some of these, but by no means all, had had funds appropriated. In any case, under the Budget and Impoundment Control Act of 1974, a president is entitled to defer projects for a while and even to ask Congress to rescind. President Carter did not entirely lack support. One courageous member, George Miller (Dem.-California), risked saying that some of the projects, even in his own district, "read like a horror story." But generally, of course, the congressional air was rent with cries of anguish. One of the angriest voices belonged to Senator Edmund S. Muskie of Maine, where the plan was to build not one dam but two (the Dickey and Lincoln School Dams project) over the opposition of wildlife preservationists. It had been authorized in 1965 but work had not started, nor indeed had funds been appropriated. As already noted, Senator Muskie was chairman of the SBC.

On the merits of these projects, we must suspend judgment, except to note that one, a classic Army Corps of Engineers navigation project in Louisiana, had been denounced as a special-interest project, the purpose being to facilitate the movement of large oil rigs built inland to the Gulf and elsewhere.[71] It must be enough here to record that on March 28 the HBC voted 13-11 to make cuts to the extent of $280 million. That member of the HBC, Representative Butler Derrick, pulled together the nine Democrats and four Republicans.

On March 30, however, no less a person than the majority leader, Jim Wright (Texas) set about undoing the work of the HBC. He got the vote of a fellow Texas Democrat who had been absent, two days earlier, and of two liberal Democrats, David Obey (Wisconsin) and Thomas Ashley (Ohio), who both switched votes to overturn the HBC, of which they were members.[72] The result was a 14-11 defeat for the HBC: the water projects survived intact.

The point of this report is not simply that, as the *Congressional Quarterly* writer James R. Wagner (with Harrison H. Donnelly) put it, "Public works have long been controversial because there is a tendency for one member to support another's project in return for support for his own."[73] Nor is it simply that this pork barrel legislation, a species of logrolling, can withstand the new budget process even to the extent of "recruiting" some members of both budget committees. The main point for this discussion is to mark the limits of the 1974 budget process as an effective counterweight to the special interests.

Of course, it would be premature to write off the process in that sense: it may work better in the eighties. At present, however, it is reasonable to conclude that whichever way we approach the issue, roundabout or direct, it seems that the decentralizing tendencies of subcommittee proliferation have not been seriously impeded either by the 1974 budget process or by the revival of the mainly Democratic leadership. This means that the particular structural conditions favoring interest-group politics continue substantially unchanged.

Continuing the *caveats* and riders, the conclusion reached above is reinforced if we turn from the structural to the normative. What that cryptic statement means is that we have been considering committees and subcommittees only as structures in a rather simple sense. But they are of course groups. A group has not only a structure but a set of norms regulating the behavior of individual members (at least in matters of consequence to it). It is impossible to generalize with confidence about Congress as a whole, having learned from Richard Fenno and others that committees, etc., differ and that the differences matter. But the following are among the norms usually identified and most relevant to our theme here:

1. *specialization:* make yourself an expert within a specific range of public policy, meanwhile being content to
2. *serve an apprenticeship:* be respectful, even deferential, to those who have "been around" many years and become experts; show
3. *courtesy*, in Parliamentary style but also to some degree in substance, not treading on the toes of others, which merges into
4. *reciprocity:* from keeping out of one another's way to mutual help, logrolling, and bargaining.

The reforms of the first half of the seventies weakened (2) in at least two senses. First, there was the successful "palace revolution" of the younger members against the seniors, which badly dented if it did not destroy the seniority rule for the allocating of chairmanships and of memberships in important committees. Secondly, the proliferation of subcommittees obviated the need for long apprenticeships: now the younger member could "plunge right in," even collect a chairmanship at a surprisingly early stage in his or her congressional career. But that of course entailed more of (1), and more of (1) entailed more of (4), and perhaps of its near relation, (3). At least the need for courtesy, usually identified more with the Senate than the House, would not have been reduced.

Much more would have to be said about these (and related) norms if the focus of inquiry were Congress as such. Even the bare outline just completed, however, enables us to observe that the norms *go with* the grain of the structures, i.e., the "physical" proliferation, to reinforce the (net) decentralization of decision-making power in Congress.

Committee and subcommittee structure, including biased composition, combine, then, with the norms to sustain and even advance decentralization, and decentralization favors interest-group politics. On the other hand, decentralization is not equally conducive to all forms of it, or, in other words, to all kinds of public policy. It is, in fact, associated with a particular species of policy commonly called *distributive*,[74] and with a special sort of interest-group politics, exemplified above in the cases of subsidies for some classes of mail and the water resources projects.

That classification of public policies in which the distributive has its being, or place, derives from an influential article by Theodore J. Lowi published in 1964.[75] With its fellows—regulatory policy and *re*distributive policy (later augmented)—we need not concern ourselves at present. It is enough to note, first of all, what Professor Lowi meant by distributive, and secondly the connection between such policies, the committee system in Congress, and interest-group politics:

> Distributive policies are characterized by the ease with which they can be disaggregated and dispensed unit by small unit, each unit more or less in isolation from other units and from any general rule. . . . They are policies in which the indulged and the deprived, the loser and the recipient, need never come into direct confrontation.

In ordinary English, *can be disaggregated* means "capable of being divided up into small parts or items": building a dam here, deepening a harbor there, straightening a river somewhere else (work, evidently, that is never done); subsidies; tax loopholes, defense contracts, and the like. Ultimately, resources are, as always, scarce (otherwise economists would be out of a job), but, to the participants in the policymaking, it does not seem so. Similarly, if you follow the trail far enough, you will find losers (also known as taxpayers, consumers), but these are not the sort of groups (categories, really) that rush in as rivals.

This implies that little or no conflict is generated about the wisdom of going ahead, only perhaps about the size of the relative shares. Such grave disputations can be settled by rolling logs: at its simplest, "I'll support your dam if you'll support my flood-wall." Logrolling might be taken as a special case of reciprocity, oiled by courtesy.

Now, distributive politics (Professor Lowi continued) "tends to stabilize around an institutional unit." There are no prizes for guessing *where:* "In most cases, it is the congressional committee (or subcommittee)."[76] No prizes because the previous discussion has led up to the answer, and in any case there obviously is a kind of symmetry between disaggregated politics and what might be called disaggregated structures: "bits" of things to be decided *matching*[77] "bits" of the decision-making apparatus.

That many an interest group may find this scene attractive is also obvious. An interest group might also be regarded as itself disaggregated (thus extending the symmetry), or as an organizational "bit," such as a farm-commodity organization. Even if it is more considerable, it may be pursuing a policy "bit" (e.g., an increment to an existing law), or one that can be passed off as such, the more plausibly because the relevant "bit" of the decision-making apparatus (e.g., a subcommittee) tends to be obscured from general view. In any case, there is little doubt that some interest groups, distributive policies, and the committee/subcommittee structure do *match*.

CHAPTER SIX
THE POSITIVE STATE

Given the variables so far identified in chapters 2 through 5, the interest-group pattern will depend upon the "reach" of government, i.e., the functions discharged. The greater the reach (range, or scope), the greater the "pull" exerted by government on organizations, or in other words, the greater is the attraction for them.

The state in America was never as limited (or "negative") as many would have us believe. The American tradition has really been one of *empirical collectivism*, as political theorist Francis W. Coker named it back in 1934.[1] *Empirical* in that context means guided by practical experience and necessity rather than by some general "philosophy of history" or guide to social action and change (such as Marxism). *Collectivism* may be read as government intervention in socioeconomic affairs, entailing a tendency to enlarge the public domain in the political sense.

That practical collectivism is part of the American tradition may be readily illustrated from historian Carter Goodrich's reconstruction of the economic functions undertaken by early American governments (1783–1861). Even the headings for the primary documents he tracked down and arranged are almost enough for our purposes: promotion of transport (canals, roads, bridges, railways, shipping, etc.), whose development contemporaries summed up as "internal improvements"; encouragement of western settlement (as by the disposal of public land on easy terms); encouragement of manufactures (by raising tariff barriers); protection of commerce; provision of money and credit; facilitation of corporate enterprise; the development of human capacities (through education, or at least literacy), and the like.[2] In order to promote those developments and achievements, the federal government, by 1871, had granted private corporations and the states something like one-eighth of the present land area of the nation.[3]

The 1870s and 1880s were, even more than usual, a period of transition. Much of what government had promoted, notably the "internal improvements," had been for the benefit of an agrarian society. Now one of those improvements, the railroads, had come back in corporate form to haunt the farmers in more than one region of the country but especially the Middle West, who complained loudly of, and organized vigorously against, the exactions of oligopolistic, and even—over great stretches of territory—monopolistic power. Since the railroad executives did indeed have the farmers where they wanted them when it came to fixing charges for carrying freight, governments were compelled to intervene.

Even more, however, in the long view of history, government promotion in those years really amounted to the creation of what some like to call the *infrastructure* of a modern, industrially based market economy. After the Civil War the building went up rapidly despite the two great setbacks, the depressions of 1873 and 1893. By then the federal government had "faced off Big Business with direct regulation and general control powers,"[4] thinking of the Interstate Commerce Act of 1887 (regulating the railroads, which embodied the greatest corporate power of the age), and the Sherman Act (antitrust) of 1890.

Thus the emphasis in public policy toward the economy began to change from *promotion* to *regulation*, a trend sustained in the Theodore Roosevelt-Woodrow Wilson era by another antitrust measure (the Clayton Act) and a mechanism for nipping monopolistic tendencies in the bud; another for saving the consumer from adulterated and falsely labeled food and drugs; and yet another creating a kind of central, but still privately owned, bank with supervision of the banking industry. In other words, the state was getting distinctly more "positive," the federal government imposing some nonmarket controls upon the economy.

Promotion, of course, had not come to an end. But it might be said to have been undergoing a mutation—the promoting of particular clienteles, starting perhaps with the much earlier administrative recognition of native Americans, or American Indians.[5] But the clearest cases come out of the organizational revolution: the departments of Labor and of Commerce, separated in 1913 after having been formed as one ten years before. Agriculture provides another, if ultimately more ambiguous, case. The interests of farmers had been promoted by the three celebrated acts of 1862, including the establishment of a Department of Agriculture under a commissioner who attained cabinet rank about a quarter of a century later, in 1889. (The other 1862 measures were the Homestead Act, memorable for its virtual gift of 160 acres to farmers or would-be farmers, and the first Morrill Act, which gave the states 30,000 acres [per each of their members of Congress] for colleges to teach subjects "related to agriculture and the mechanic arts.") But in federal policy during the agricultural depression after World War I, and of course during the New Deal era precipitated by the Great Depression, one finds it much harder to separate promotion from regulation because a fundamental feature throughout was restriction (or regulation) of agricultural output. There the useful working distinction tends to have outlived its usefulness.

The New Deal, as everyone knows, was so "positive" that it incurred the opposition, even the wrath, of a majority of the Supreme Court. In the end, the federal intervention in the labor market did confer collective-bargaining rights on labor unions that now included the semiskilled workers in the new mass-production industries as well as the craftsmen who had, as usual, been organized first. Above all, perhaps, the "positivism" revealed itself in social policy, in which the American tradition had indeed been deficient by compar-ison with most other advanced industrial societies. Relief of the poor and needy still rested on a base derived from Elizabethan England and "carried over" as a purely local responsibility, which President Hoover was still de-fending as late as 1931 in the face of eight million unemployed (25 percent of the nonfarm employees). Even after that rate had reached 37 percent as it did in 1933 (representing a staggering 12,800,000 out of work), the national re-sponse was not all that quick in coming. So powerful was the resistance both to "federalization" and "socialization" of the risks that workers ran in the industrially based market economies that such provision probably could not have been made without a change of government in the national admin-istration.[6] In any event, after the incoming Roosevelt administration had tried various emergency measures, it pressed for and obtained provision in the form of the Social Security Act of 1935, covering both insurance (unem-ployment, retirement, survivors', and disability) as well as "public assistance" as the last resort (which is the component that has come to be popularly known as "welfare").

This was the great breakthrough, giving American public policy a new dimension that was soon extended by the first federal provision of public housing. Here, again, however, lines get crossed. The federal underwriting (1934) of relatively cheap mortgages for home purchase, etc., was designed to get the housing industry back on its feet, i.e., to promote. But of course it would also help the would-be home owner of modest means, i.e., it provided a social service.

As you would expect from the record of economic collapse, the regula-tory thread remained easy to discern. It appeared in the form of the Securities and Exchange Commission (SEC) of 1934. The federal insurance of bank accounts combined with some regulation of banking procedures constituted another new function of the kind. But the thread is also easily discernible because regulation stimulated by technological change was also gaining momentum. "Power" in "Federal Power Commission" originally (1920) meant water power; in 1935 its scope was extended to cover electric power and the public utilities (as the scope of the SEC was extended at the same time to cover their financial dealings). Three years later another mutation brought in natural gas. The development of radio broadcasting with its limited frequencies promoted the Federal Radio Commission (1927), transformed into the Federal Communications Commission in 1934. The invention of the flying machine led to commercial aviation, requiring governmental supervision of safety standards at least. In these and some other instances, however, one must acknowledge yet another crossing of the policy lines. As James Q. Wilson has pointed out, with radio and aviation the impulse to *regulate* was mixed up with the desire to *promote*.[7] One might identify a hybrid type of policy—to promote by regulating (or promotion by way of regulation). Here again the simplicity of the categories has vanished.

Then came another war, as usual a great forcing-ground for government as nations bent their energies to one overriding objective. Out of that particular war came nuclear energy and, ultimately, travel into outer space, made possible by government as entrepreneur but entailing regulation as well. After the uneasy peace turned into cold war, briefly hot in Korea, the defense function not only recovered its importance but also turned into an exceptionally prominent feature of the settled landscape. At the same time technology was transforming the weapons that could be made available, at a price. The result was that government became a buyer of weapons and related goods on an unprecedented scale. This (and other purchasing) has prompted some writers to treat government-as-buyer as a distinct function, a practice which is defensible although not deemed necessary for the simpler purpose in hand.[8] The main point in any case is that toward the end of the 1960s, the Department of Defense (or the Pentagon) was signing agreements, annually, with some 22,000 prime contractors and 100,000 subcontractors, although among the former, the top one hundred corporations naturally got the lion's share— over two-thirds of the money being spent through contracts of $10,000 or more.[9] In 1978 total military procurement exceeded $65 billion of the $105 billion that went for national defense as a whole (itself some 23 percent of the total federal outlay for *all* functions). About $52 billion's worth of work was actually put out to business firms in the United States that year, most of it (92 percent) by way of negotiated (i.e., not publicly advertised) contracts.

Despite that burden, the social service state was extended (as, in the end, with Medicare and Medicaid in the midsixties). The most striking aspect of the positive state in this period, however, was the sharp rise of the curve of regulation. Up to a point, the federal government accepted responsibility for the protection of consumers as well as for safety in workshops; for the enforcements of civil rights, notably of blacks and women; for protection of the environment and conservation of energy use and resources; and much else. In 1970–75 there occurred a "quiet explosion in the scope and pervasiveness of federal regulation." In that period of six years the number of pages published annually in the *Federal Register* tripled, reaching 60,000 pages. It had been 20,000 in 1970 (and 2400 in 1936).[10]

The "cost" of function being structure, the direct consequence of these developments has been a burgeoning bureaucracy (with implications, of course, for interest-group politics). The general story has often been told. At the beginning of the nineteenth century, there was just the president and a personal secretary, the three classical departments (State, Treasury, War) recently augmented by one for the navy ("War" had implied "army"), and the attorney general, still in solitary splendor (he worked out of his own home). The whole total came to only 132. Adding in the other two branches makes it 291 for the Washington establishment. Around the country and abroad, there were another 2500 or so wearing civilian clothes, mainly postmasters and revenue collectors.[11]

Between that period and the Civil War, only one department was created (Interior, 1849), and, even after the wartime expansion, the total number of civilian employees in the executive branch in 1871 stood at only some 50,000, three out of four of whom worked for the Post Office. This was translated into a department in 1872, preceded by Justice (1870) and followed by Agriculture (1889), which had had a commissioner since 1862. (The postmaster general himself had been of cabinet rank since President Jackson's day.) These by now eight departments bore the burden until the beginning of this century, when the total in the executive branch reached 231,000. Most of them, although a smaller proportion (say, six out of ten), were still to be found in the Post Office. To one side, so to speak, stood the sole regulatory body, the Interstate Commerce Commission (ICC) established in 1887.

The contrast with the situation as the 1980s opened could hardly be more pronounced. The president enjoyed the services of about two dozen immediate personal assistants, the inner core of a White House team of 382 (1979). This in turn occupied the center of a circle (in all) 1675, making up his executive office, or, thinking more objectively, the "institutionalized presidency." Among its more significant components were the Office of Management and Budget, the Council of Economic Advisers, the National Security Council, the Office of Science and Technology, and the Council on Environmental Quality.

By 1980 the eight cabinet departments of a hundred years earlier had grown to thirteen, counting the fighting services as one under the Defense Department, and Aid for International Development under the State Department. Education had been torn from the clutches of Health, Education and Welfare the previous year. Each of course had "swollen" beyond recognition. Just two of the eight put together (Treasury plus Agriculture) now employed more than the whole of the executive branch at the beginning of the century—130,873 (Treasury) + 115,078 = 245,951 (1979) as against 231,056 (1901). That was also true of one of the service departments alone, the air force, smallest of the three (238,190 in 1979) and of course nonexistent in the earlier period. That is counting only *civilians*, of whom there were some 971,000 in the Department of Defense as a whole, over a third of those employed in the executive branch.

Still with an eye to the significance of all this for interest-group politics, we should also remind ourselves that, in "swelling," the departments naturally developed subsystems, in particular the operating units for which the generic name is bureaus (the actual titles vary). Thus by 1980 the Agriculture Department had seven operational divisions, further subdivided into 21 bureaus (commonly called *agencies*), which naturally act as magnets to the various elements that make up the agricultural community. Many of these elements may be identified as *clienteles*, immediately of the relevant bureau; more broadly, of the department. Such other departments as Labor and Commerce also have their clienteles, which, undressed, are of course none other than special interests.

This, it is discouraging to realize, is only the end of the beginning, not the beginning of the end (to adapt the Churchillian phrase from a graver context). What has been touched upon just reflects government in traditional forms. Beyond their ken were fifty to sixty less traditional units, the independent agencies. The precise total depends on the definition and the purpose of the inquiry: here we shall settle for fifty-two, the number listed by name in the 1981 edition of the *Statistical Abstract*. The list starts with ACTION (more easily recognized as the Peace Corps, which became an independent agency in 1971); passes by way of the International Communications Agency (which replaced the United States Information Agency in 1978) and the Tennessee Valley Authority (TVA); and ends with the U.S. Postal Service, which was translated from an executive department with effect from 1971, and the Veterans Administration (VA).[12] Obviously, this is a mixed bag. The VA serves a clientele that has never lost its importance since the Civil War. The TVA is public enterprise, invented in 1933 to control flooding by the Tennessee River, improve navigation on it, and supply low-cost electricity. But, for our purpose at least, the independent regulatory commissions stand out as the crucial category. In addition to those inherited from earlier periods, the post-World War era saw the establishment of the Atomic Energy Commission, from which the Nuclear Regulatory Commission was carved out, with effect from 1975, to supervise the plants and to license the export of radioactive material, the Environmental Protection Agency (1970), and the Consumer Product Safety Commission (1972). Clearly, the regulatory tide was still running, although some dikes would soon be built against it in some sectors.

In reflecting upon the regulatory policy of the positive state, still with special reference to interest groups, do not make the elementary error of assuming that all of it is concentrated in the independent commissions. In

1977 Peter Woll calculated that thirty-five "units" (to avoid a specification by name) *within* traditional departments were exercising regulatory functions. An example is furnished by the Food and Drug Administration (FDA), derived from the Pure Food and Drug Act (1906). The act was originally administered in the Bureau of Chemistry within the Department of Agriculture. Twenty or so years later that bureau was replaced by the newly created FDA, which found its way into the newly created Health, Education and Welfare Department in the 1950s. Several bureaus with regulatory authority remain within Agriculture. The Federal Aviation Administration, responsible for air safety and much else, is a distinct legal entity within the Department of Transportation (having been an independent agency). The Occupational Safety and Health Administration is located within the Department of Labor, and so on. All told, there is probably nothing more positive about the positive state than its regulatory side: perhaps eighty agencies in all (1977), according to Professor Woll. Earlier, journalist Louis M. Kohlmeier, Jr., had estimated that, even within the realm of economic affairs alone, there were one hundred "federal administrative agencies and offices" with "authority to write regulations which apply with the force of law to private obligations and privileges." This may have been a wider concept than Professor Woll was using. In any case, no one doubts that regulation looms large in the positive state.[13]

As to the total number of functionaries, or public officials, working in these structures, that stood at 2,900,000 in 1980, and we can add on fifty to sixty thousand more for the legislative and judicial branches. It was, you may recall, 231,000 at the beginning of the century. But didn't the resident population increase? Of course it did, but "only" from 77 million or so (1901) to about 226 million (1980). You do not need a calculator to see at once the disproportion. The staggering difference is the cumulative consequence of political decisions to be positive, i.e., to assume this or that function. The "cost" of function was said earlier (in shorthand) to be structure. It could also be expressed as the number of persons required to make the structures work.

To say that is to be reminded of an important aspect of the subject so far neglected here, and still to be neglected except for the following brief remarks. Great as the number of federal employees may appear to be, it is dwarfed by the number employed in state and local government (see Table 6-1).[14]

TABLE 6-1   Governmental Employment: Selected Years

	1950	1970	1980
Federal (civilian)	2,117,000	2,881,000	2,907,000
State	1,057,000	2,755,000	3,753,000
Local	3,228,000	7,392,000	9,562,000
Total	6,402,000	13,028,000	16,222,000

TABLE 6-2   State of California: Functional Growth, 1850–1935

YEAR	NUMBER OF FUNCTIONS CURRENTLY UNDERTAKEN
1850	20
1900	109
1910	159
1920	260
1935	420*

*452 functions had been assumed in the period, but some had not been retained.

Clearly the federal share (civilian) has fallen from about a third of the grand total in 1950 to well under a fifth in 1980. Putting aside local government, we may simply draw out the implication of the figures—that the positive state is not confined to the federal government, as many appear to believe, but (to say the least) includes state government as well. California will serve as illustration. In 1850 its state government carried out twenty functions, including support of common schools; maintaining a militia, legislature, and state courts; housing prisoners, and caring for the insane. From 1879 to the mid-1930s, no legislature adjourned without adding one or more functions to the existing crop,[15] with the result, shown in Table 6-2.

Examination of the list reveals a very large regulatory component, but with some social-service provision, which today, of course, has increased enormously throughout the state system under the stimulus of federal aid. The general point is that in thinking about the rise of the positive state, we must not suppose that it has been manifest only in the national government. All government has become more positive, in other liberal-democracies as well as the United States.

What has it all signified for interest-group politics? Several considerations may be adduced at this stage, leaving a more rounded answer to emerge in due course. As a first approximation, one says that the assumption of so many functions by government draws groups into its realm whether they like it or not. Be it ever so humble, government has always something to give or concede. But a government that takes on a hundred functions (promotional, regulatory, social service, etc.,) must surely expect to be courted, harangued, threatened, and occasionally besieged by those who are affected in process or result. In the nourishing soil of the positive state, the species *interest group* spreads (borrowing from the Psalms) "like a green bay tree."

The refinement of the approximation has to do with the aptness of the term *drawn* in some instances that have proved to be politically important. Just before World War I, President Taft ostensibly precipitated the U.S. Chamber of Commerce, having stressed the need for such a central association (or peak). His secretary for Commerce then brought the local chambers together. But representation to that end had also come from the private sector, including the National Association of Manufacturers, a peak already in position.

Another instance, both clearer and more significant in the end, is furnished by the creation of the Department of Agriculture. Initially, farmers were not *drawn* by it—they *pushed* for it through the United States Agricultural Society (formed in Washington, D.C., in 1852), saw it established in 1862, and then turned it in their direction. Remarks made in 1889 when the department, headed by a commissioner, was being upgraded to cabinet level, are most illuminating about interest-group politics in general. In the congressional debate, a critic asserted that "the creation of a cabinet office at the head of a great department with numerous clerks will not increase the agricultural productiveness of the country to the extent of a single hill of beans, it will merely create additional offices for politicians to fill." That carries the ring of truth. But it is a representative's answer that illuminates most: "Mr. Speaker, I am in favor of the passage of this bill, in the first place because the farmers of my state want it; and, in the second place, because it is right."[16] For whatever combination of reasons, Congress agreed with him. The point was reinforced by Secretary Jeremiah Rusk in the first of his annual reports:

> There had been a demand on the part of a large majority of the farmers of the country that *that Department at the seat of government which was organized to represent their interests* should be clothed with the same dignity and power that other executive departments had, and that it should have its influence in national affairs and be recognized in the councils of the nation.[17]

Generally, however, the assumption by the federal government of a very wide range of functions has been in response less to the demands of specific associations or interests than, in part, to the efforts of individual reformers but principally to war and preparation for war, the growth of population, and to influences so diffuse, or inchoate, that one retreats into calling them "societal." On that basis, one can reasonably assert that the functional development of government "draws groups into its realm."

With the functions come the structures, naturally revealing the characteristics of the organizational revolution sketched in chapter 2. The broad effect has been to modify the Constitution (so some of the statements made about it in chapter 4 turn out to have been first approximations). One common way of characterizing the general effect is to say that it has produced a fourth branch of government, undreamed of by the Founding Fathers. This is clearly true, but in more senses than one. The conventional sense turns on the sheer size of the new establishment, the 2.9 million laborers in this pleasant vineyard. How many decision-making points that entails is anybody's guess, but the number will obviously be very large. Moreover, in this context, federal is local or at least regional, some 87 percent of the employees (1979) *not* being in Washington, D.C., at all, but spread out from sea to shining sea, some even beyond. For some interests, that distribution matters: farming is the obvious but not the only one.

At least two features other than sheer size make this great structure both formidable and yet attractive to the interests. One is the modern method of "filling" it—by merit rather than patronage. Conceived in 1871 but not funded by Congress, this system got under way in earnest in 1883. Today probably nine out of ten federal workers are so covered. This, again, is not what the Founding Fathers intended. As Robert S. Page reminded us: "They put their faith in periodic elections, legislatures, and an elected chief executive, rather than in a bureaucracy, however pure and efficient."[18]

But if nine out of ten employees hold tenure on merit, they, or at least the more important of them, are going to "outlive" chief executives and all but the very senior congresspersons, traditionally hailing from what was for so long the one-party South. (Apart of course from Supreme Court justices, who do not come into this particular picture). If all goes well, a chief executive presides for eight years; an assistant secretary (the political rank immediately above the permanent civil servants) lasts a couple of years or so. But the higher civil servants eke out something like seventeen to twenty-five years.[19] They may not survive unscathed, but they are not easily moved even by the arrival of a vigorous chief executive determined to disturb them. The problem was implicitly acknowledged by President Reagan on the eve of his dramatic win in 1980. He said that he would strengthen the cabinet in order to make its members "managers of the national administration—not captives of the bureaucracy or special interests in the departments they are supposed to direct."[20]

The other feature is interrelated, although separable in principle. What some call the positive (and others the administrative, or bureaucratic) state could also, by focusing upon another facet, be designated *the professional state*. Extending the work of Don K. Price and others, Frederic C. Mosher used the phrase in 1968, pointing out that about a third of all *government* employees, including teachers, were engaged in professional or technical work; one fifth, if teachers were excluded. He had in mind foresters and geologists; doctors and lawyers; civil engineers and scientists. Even the one-fifth was twice the relevant proportion employed in the private sector.[21] In certain personnel grades, separate salary schedules have been established for professionals in engineering and architecture, medicine and nursing, veterinary medicine, metallurgy and printing management, and petroleum engineering.[22]

What this means for interest-group politics is a large question to which one offers here a minimum answer. First, professionalism in practice[23] reinforces the point about the merit system. What opens up tends to be a life-long career. Secondly, that noun is as significant as the adjective: as George J. Gordon shrewdly remarked, professionalism implies a career within government service, not just a job. Ideas about organization (or bureaucracy) after the introduction of the merit system in 1883 had turned upon job (or role, or position), and how one was related to another in a hierarchy.[24] This does not mean, thirdly, that professionals "only" constitute *staff* (advisers) rather than *line* (decision makers). On the contrary, according to Professor Mosher, professionals make up the *core* of an agency (centering on the bureau) as well as its *corps* (implying a professional ethos). They control "the key line positions" in the agency, providing "the main, perhaps the exclusive source of its leadership."[25] Fourthly, professionals in government tend to look askance at politically prompted, in contradistinction to professionally sound, policies, and may even be averse to politicians as a breed or class. By the same token they will reach out to fellow professionals, some of whom may be on Capitol Hill, but many more of whom will be out in the field, often working for interest groups. Fellow feeling among fellow professionals provides some basis for interest-group access to the bureau, although the result in the end is less likely to be one-way influence than a mutually beneficial reciprocity.

The discussion so far has simply taken the phrase *fourth branch* of government at its face value, and then drawn out some of the implications for interest-group politics. Now one has to acknowledge that the convenient label may also mislead for at least two closely related reasons. As you know, the word *execute* as it comes down to us from Latin through French, means to carry something into effect: a plan, law, or judicial sentence. As it stands, it admits of no modification, grants no room for maneuver. Now, historically, the fourth branch *appeared* to be an extension of the executive, and its members today are all subordinates of the chief executive (or of the heads of departments, who, however, are *his* subordinates). So newcomers to the subject could be pardoned for assuming that civil servants *execute* what the president, or Congress, has ordained. In fact, the rise of the positive state has given civil servants a great deal of discretionary power. This development is clearest in the distinctive regulatory area, which is to say outside the regular executive departments. Authorities differ on when the process really started. James Q. Wilson dates it (essentially) from the Interstate Commerce Act of 1887. In creating the commission, Congress created problems "caused by the need to make binding choices without any clear standards for choice."[26] For Theodore J. Lowi the rot set in a generation later, with the Clayton Act of 1914 and the setting up of the Federal Trade Commission, which received "an enormous grant of discretion" because Congress failed to define competition in markets, leaving others to decide at what point it could be deemed to have been breached.[27]

Although every educated person needs to know *what* has changed—how today differs from yesterday, a form of comparative study—in this particular inquiry we are less interested in the *exact* moment than in the present-day reality. Today the discretionary power of civil servants properly so called (that is, in the executive branch as such rather than the regulatory commissions) is great. Civil servants *can* decide, within a range not too rigidly prescribed. If the standard of reference is the public sector as a whole, the range will not be wide, but that will apply to most interest groups most of the time. Since civil servants *can* "deliver" on some things, their bureaus act as beacons on a moonless night for groups within their territory.

A closely related point is the confusion about the character of *the administrative process*. This, too, is not an "intensification" of the executive. Far from being identical with execution, the administrative process incorporates the whole spread of governmental functions traditionally identified: legislative and judicial (or quasi-judicial) as well as executive. It is legislative in that rules are promulgated, judicial or quasi-judicial in that adjudication on specific cases is practiced. So the phrase fourth branch of government may easily mislead the uninitiated: within limits, it is not a *branch* at all but a whole. Or, one might say that, like the Trinity, it is three-in-one (transcending the separation of powers). The reality, in any case, is that this part of the permanent government, so professionalized and so largely "blanketed in" by the merit system, has much to offer the interests, which naturally gravitate toward such a world within a world.

Notice that, insofar as professionals (in interest groups) speak to professionals (in government), the decentralization of the total system is in a sense reinforced. But the main conclusion here is that, as Francis E. Rourke put it in 1965, the bureaucrats (in government) "have now become a central factor in the policy process: in the initiation of proposals, the weighing of alternatives, and the resolution of conflict."[28] By 1978 Professor Rourke was expressing it even more confidently:

> The power of executive agencies and officials over the direction and development of public policy in the United States has grown remarkably in recent years . . . the center of decision making in American politics now lies within the executive branch, where political and career officials meet to hammer out the policies by which the lives of Americans are governed.

The American political system had become increasingly "executive centered" (a term he put in quotes, not for citation but to emphasize its novelty).

Where does that leave Congress? Professor Rourke's view emerged only obliquely. Because the American political system is now (he argued) executive centered, the attention given to elections by the press, and to voters' attitudes and behavior by scholars, has been a bit misplaced or at least disproportionate.[29] From that we might deduce a belief that Congress, too, had received disproportionate attention. By contrast, or at least in modification, John Bibby and Roger Davidson have argued: "While this may be what some have called an 'executive-centered' age, one can excessively depreciate the role of Congress."[30] With that we can all agree: the question is how to strike a balance. It is not, however, a question that need be pursued here. This much is obvious:

Congress's fundamental role is, under the Constitution, unassailable. But we should also keep reminding ourselves that, even in legislative policy, power, *de facto* when not *de jure*, is shared. It is not simply that the chief executive is part of the legislative process. It is also that, in the words of Randall B. Ripley, "the bureaucratic-congressional relationship is at the center of public policy development in the United States."[31] On the other hand, Congress oversees significant "stretches" of the administrative process. In these senses (and others) the lines drawn in this chapter and the two previous ones touch even if they do not quite converge.

Subject to such qualifications, one would conclude that the rise of the positive state has indeed made the American political system executive centered. Lobbyists were probably among the first to notice it. From his research in the early sixties, based on long personal interviews, Lester W. Milbrath found: "Usually people think that members of Congress are the only targets of lobbying. In actual fact, however, most lobbyists are as concerned with decisions made in the executive branch as with those made in the legislative branch."

Later in the book Professor Milbrath became, in one context, more emphatic, reporting that "for many trade associations, more governmental decisions crucial to them are made in the executive branch than in the legislative branch."[32] The pioneering Milbrath report on Washington lobbyists prompts the thought that we observers of the scene might find it useful to treat lobbyists as pointers, those highly trained hunting dogs that stand rigid, muzzle stretched, often with one foot raised, when they pick up a scent. In other words, they might well be used for pointing to changes in the distribution of authoritative power.

In conclusion, a warning: this chapter must be considered in the context of chapters 4 and 5. It is only too easy to assume that the rise of the positive state portends or already has produced a strong, centralized state, even a corporate state, as argued by economist Donald R. Fusfeld in 1971.[33] That the rise of the positive state entails some centralization is clear enough. But it remains true that the new or expanded functions were imposed on an antiquated (or, if you prefer, not modernized) political structure. As we have learned in particular from Louis Hartz and Samuel Huntington, because American society was "born modern" (i.e., did not have feudal or other traditional institutions to get rid of), the political structure did not need to be modernized, or centralized,[34] to achieve that end (the reverse of the European experience). Thus America could continue to enjoy the luxury of *divided power*, which it retains to this day. Such diffusion of power was traced in the earlier chapters mainly under the rubric of decentralization. At the same time the *functions*, new and old, have continued to be shared (only the institutions, or "personnel," being in fact kept separated).[35]

All this, it has been commonly believed, makes for inefficiency in governance. But the main point for us is: while the rise of the positive state has naturally attracted the interest groups more than ever, that has not been accompanied by a strengthening of its own power, or sovereignty. On balance, the American state remains relatively decentralized, permeable, and weak. To place the increased functional responsibilities of the twentieth century on that eighteenth-century political structure seems an excellent design for accentuating the already marked tendency toward a flourishing interest-group regime.

CHAPTER SEVEN
THE UNIVERSE
OF GROUPS

The drift of the argument so far is that the strategic variables identified and analyzed (chapters 2 through 6) combine and interact, in ways as yet best known to providence, to "precipitate" a great array of (formal) organizations, or secondary groups, which tend either to be interest groups exclusively (NORML, National Abortion Rights Action League, etc.) or to assume the role of interest groups as occasion demands. Once that is understood, *some* of the remarks and events reported in the opening chapter lose their capacity to surprise. Given the strategic variables (or sociopolitical forces at work), we must expect to observe in America a powerful tendency toward a special-interest democracy (Mr. Jeb Magruder) or special-interest state (the characterization favored by Common Cause). This is not historicism, meaning here the notion that we are the victims of processes that we can do little or nothing to modify. Nor does realistic assessment demand approval or even acceptance. On the contrary, those of us still perturbed, if no longer surprised, by that tendency need to grasp how and why one kind of social structure turned into another and what political consequences were entailed (without neglecting the "reverse flow" of the political on the social order itself, i.e., the reciprocal action of society and state). Only then can we discern more clearly the parameters (or limits) of reform in the *short* run.

Our immediate task, however, is to discover some "numbers" for the

organizations precipitated by the historical processes outlined, and to identify the most prominent of the politically interesting ones. It is quite a task.
Firm numbers are disagreeably difficult to come by, and a collection of
documents about organizations (charters, constitutions, policy statements,
and the like), such as exists for Britain, is altogether lacking for America at ⌣
the present time.[1] So what follows is somewhat sketchy and certainly incomplete. Even so, this descriptive material is ampler than in most books, so
you may wish to read lightly at first and then return to focus upon particular
areas.

Recalling first the theme of differentiation (chapter 2), you may find it
easy to digest two numbers: over 16 million business units in three legal forms
(1979), and some 15,800 national organizations of a (more or less) voluntary or
membership kind (1982). Such associations in communities and states were
said to have "greatly" exceeded 200,000 at the beginning of the sixties, when
8000 national associations were actually counted (the true total was estimated
to have been more like 12,000; but the 8000/12,000 would not be comparable
with the 15,000.[2] Just ten years earlier, the editors of *Fortune* (with Russell
Davenport) had also arrived at a figure of 200,000 but believed that to be the
grand total in the United States, including clubs, lodges, and fraternities.[3]

The total given for national organizations in 1980 is firm enough for our
purpose. A breakdown is available, too, in the standard source (Gale's *Encyclopedia*), but it may be more profitable to change focus to interest groups and
their frequency distribution. In 1968–72 Robert Presthus subjected eight sites
in the United States and Canada to intensive analysis. The eight were Washington, D.C./Ottawa; Michigan/Ontario; Lousiana/Quebec; Washington State/
British Columbia. The three Canadian provinces had three-quarters of the
Canadian population and four-fifths of the gross national product. Taking random samples (about 25 percent) of private groups, he identified "nine types of
groups, based upon their major substantive interest," acknowledging, however, "the overlapping functions and multiple objectives which characterize
most groups." (Table 7-1 shows his admittedly "conventional, straightforward
taxonomy of groups." As you see, in both countries, the leading five types
account for about three-quarters of all such private groups. They could be
reduced to four by combining educational with professional.[4])

In this book our focus is mainly on one of Professor Presthus's eight
sites, Washington, D.C. There of course the flora and fauna are thick on the
ground. One indication of it is the listing of Washington organizations with
the prefix *National* in their titles. They totalled about fifteen hundred in May
1980. (This figure is based on the number of listings which appear in the
Washington Metropolitan Area White Pages, 467 through 473; 468 through
472 carried about a thousand entries; 467 and 473 about 300 all told.) Some of
these, however, were not interest groups as such, and, conversely, some
interest groups were not in that list, having other titles. So we turn to the
work of Kay Lehman Schlozman and John T. Tierney in 1982. They took a

TABLE 7–1 Frequency distribution of organizations in the United States and Canada: proportion in each category (in percentages)

	UNITED STATES	CANADA
Business-industrial	23	20
Labor	18	14
Professional	17	12
Educational	10	11
Welfare	9	16
Religious	3	6
Fraternal-service	5	5
Social-recreational	3	11
Agricultural	1	1
Ethnic	1	1
Other	9	4
	(n=765)	(n=640)

sample of two hundred Washington-based interest groups, *not* for the purpose of sampling Washington lobbyists as such "or even the universe of organizations represented," but rather to focus upon interest-group *activity* in the capital. Unlike Professor Presthus (and most other American specialists on interest groups), they included business corporations. They found the organizations to be distributed as shown in Table 7-2.[5]

TABLE 7–2 Frequency distribution of interest groups based in Washington, D.C. (in percentages)

	NUMBER	PERCENT	CUMULATIVE (%)
Business Corporations	61	30	
Trade Associations	37	18	
Other Business	11	6	
			54
Labor Unions	23	12	
			66
Professional Associations	15	8	
			74
Public Interest Groups	25	12	
Civil Rights & the Poor	8	4	
Ideological Groups	5	2	
Other	15	8	
	n=200	100	

Obviously the coverage here is quite different from that in Table 7–1. Yet the importance of business again stands out, with labor and the professions well represented. Together these account for some three out of four of the interest groups.

To sum up in slightly different terms, we may draw on the research of Jack L. Walker into the origin and maintenance of voluntary associations open to members and concerned with public policy at the national level. Professor Walker reported in 1981 that "the great majority of interest groups grow up around discrete occupational roles, industrial sectors, or bureaucratic specialties," a conclusion also implied in a paper he coauthored with Thomas L. Gais and Mark A. Peterson in 1982.[6] This finding is just what we would expect as a consequence of the processes of differentiation to which the "division of labor" is, of course, fundamental.

Such statistics are not infallible guides to political significance. Farm groups, for example, did not earn separate mention in the Schlozman-Tierney list and reached only 1 percent in Presthus's although constituting about 5 percent of "Gale's nationals." As we shall see, at least some farm groups remain politically important. Even so, such frequency distributions provide useful rough maps of the shape of the group universe and by the same token suggest the appropriate layout for concrete material about the groups themselves.

BUSINESS

Using the term *business* as convenient shorthand for industry as well as commerce, we could approach this world within a world through the operating units (oil well, factory, office), but the most relevant concept here is the business firm, i.e., business organization under a single management, the person or persons who would decide whether to "activate" the firm as an interest group. "Person" is accurate for 12.3 million firms (76 percent) since these are proprietorships, some of which (e.g., office-based physicians) are politically interesting but fit elsewhere in our map. Active partnerships account for 1.3 million (8 percent), some of which are also politically interesting, notably the Washington law firms, but these, too, fit elsewhere. That leaves the 2.5 million active corporations (15 percent). Of course most of these are small. Potentially, the most politically interesting could be expected to be found among the 15 percent of active corporations with receipts of $1 million or more, accounting for 92 percent of total corporate receipts (all 1979).[7]

Even within that range there are fish so big that they make the rest seem like minnows. Variously known as the giant corporations, megacorporations, or, more prosaically, very large firms, they may be identified by name in *Fortune's* annual list (the May issue) of the 500 largest U.S. industrial corporations. At the pinnacle in 1980 stood Exxon, measured by both sales (over $103 billion) and assets ($56.6 billion). (The sales figure "controls"; e.g., Mobil was no. 2 in 1980, though no. 3—after General Motors—in assets.) In the language of Shakespeare, Exxon "bestrides" America, and indeed the world, "like a colossus." It extends to almost one hundred countries (partly under its old name, Esso), and so, clearly, earns its unofficial title, "the United Nations of Oil." As business reporter Anthony J. Parisi put it, Exxon "is almost incomprehensibly big." One way, used by Mark Nadel, to make it more comprehensible is to rank Exxon (and other megacorporations) in terms of the states of the Union. Even in 1973, Exxon outranked California and New York. By 1980 Exxon's $103 billion was almost three times California's total revenue of $36 billion. In fact, it fractionally exceeded the combined revenues of California, New York, Pennsylvania, Texas, and Illinois. Another way is to relate Exxon to states in the United Nations sense. Mr. Parisi calculated that in 1979 Exxon's revenues were a shade higher than the gross national product (GNP) of Sweden, and not much less than Spain's.[8] Comparisons of this kind are somewhat forced but they do translate the billions into a scale with which we are more familiar.

If Exxon is the colossus, it is flanked by giants. Despite the difficulties experienced by the car industry, General Motors remained in the top five in 1980. Ford Motor was then no. 6 (with sales about a billion dollars in excess of California's revenue). IBM was no. 8 (its sales not far off the revenue of the state in which it has its HQ, New York). General Electric was also in the top ten. ITT, a conglomerate, came in no 13. (AT&T did not appear in the list because it was not classified as industrial.)

Most of the giants of 1980, however, were in the same business as Exxon. Whereas in 1974, seven oil companies had been "scattered among the top twenty," with only Exxon in the top five, for 1980 Ford S. Worthy could report (in *Fortune*) that "thirteen of the top twenty, and four of the top five, are oils." (Historically, it is interesting that three of the four are in line of descent from the Standard Oil Trust broken up by the Supreme Court in 1911. Another four, i.e., a total of seven, appear within the top twenty of the *Fortune* 500.) Even the no. 2 position was then occupied by an oil company, the Mobil Corporation, which had pushed General Motors a little further down the ladder. In 1980 the top eighteen oil companies had assets equal to about a quarter of the total assets of the *Fortune* 500.[9]

Once again the device of comparing American corporations to foreign states has the capacity to "instruct by startling," as this method might be called. Taking eighteen leading oil companies, economist and consultant Walter S. Measday found that in 1979 they had a cash flow of over $40 billion. And that was "within shouting distance" of the GNP of Norway ($45 billion) and Venezuela ($42 billion), and far more than the GNP of such countries as Greece, Portugal, New Zealand, Chile, and Peru.[10]

It is of course true that the very large firm (defined as one with assets of $250 million or more) does not flourish in every sector of the economy. But (in 1975) such firms controlled more than half the assets in four sectors: manufacturing, mining, transport and utilities, and banking and finance. In manufacturing (responsible for 25 percent of the national income), 448 such firms (out of some 217,000 in that sector) then controlled over 72 percent of the assets. The two-hundred largest accounted for 43 percent of the value added to manufacturing and 31 percent of employment in manufacturing, all according to the computations of Edward S. Herman, professor of finance at the Wharton School.[11]

In bringing together such statistics, one is not reproducing the error attributed (rightly or wrongly) to political economist Charles E. Lindblom (of Yale) by political scientist, James Q. Wilson (of Harvard).[12] Accusing Professor Lindblom of perpetuating a fallacy "well known to every student of politics," Professor Wilson charged him with imputing

> power to an institution or class on the basis of the resources it possesses. . . . One cannot *assume* that the disproportionate possession of certain resources (money, organization, status) leads to the disproportionate exercise of political power. Everything depends on whether a resource can be converted into power, and at what rate and at what price. That, in turn, can only be learned by finding out who wins and who loses.

There is a third theory of power, much favored in recent years. It neglects winners and losers in specific policy contests in favor of the question: "Who really benefits from the whole set of arrangements now in use?" But the immediate point is to disavow any belief that prodigious revenues and marked control over assets, etc., necessarily "carry over" into interest-group politics.

On the other hand, one does wish to resist the curious notion, evidently cherished by many interest-group specialists, that a corporation as such should not be accounted an interest group. On that one need not *assume* anything: one need only examine the evidence. It is perfectly clear from the work of Edwin M. Epstein and others that corporations have acted as interest groups for at least 150 years. (Business influence, before the corporate form developed, is of course as old as the Republic. In 1800 only six manufacturing concerns were incorporated. Professor Epstein made 1820 his benchmark.) In his book on the corporation in American politics, Professor Epstein has a chapter heading that evokes the truth: "Corporate Political Involvement: A Long-Standing Fact."[13] Leaping over the years, one observes that in the late seventies about five-hundred corporations maintained offices in Washington. The Ford Motor Company employed forty full-time representatives; Gulf Oil, a dozen. Among those corporations that bothered to register their lobbyists in 1980—the 1946 Act requiring registration of lobbyists is so loose that to register is almost a matter of taste—were Exxon, Mobil, Texaco (in the top five of *Fortune's* 500); ITT; General Dynamics (no. 79, in 1980); and the Crane Packing Company of Illinois, which recorded a lobbying interest in taxation. Obviously, corporate resources were being spent in the hope of exercising political influence, which is sufficient to earn classification as an interest group (success being a desideratum but not always attainable). So too with Mobil's well-known public relations campaign, which uses up real resources ($3 million on promotion and advertising in 1981) to influence public policy as well as the public. Corporate political action committees constitute a special case. Certainly they shot up from fewer than a hundred as late as 1974 to fourteen hundred in July 1982. In the year and a half preceding the 1982 election, they contributed $23.1 million (surpassing labor, which once had the PAC field to itself) by $5.4 million.[14] On the other hand, whether that should be attributed to the corporations as distinct from management and employees, who are said to give "freely," is a highly controversial question. On that, one need not take a position at this stage since it is perfectly obvious on other grounds that corporations are interest groups. Bernadette Budde, director of political education for the Business Industry Political Action Committee (BIPAC) put it simply in 1981: "All corporations lobby but not every company has a PAC"[15]

Raising our sights from the "operating" or working level occupied by business firms (and their establishments, or plants), we perceive an array of close to thirty-five hundred organizations making up a second tier in sociopolitical space. These are business entities in the narrower sense. The proprietorships in the total of business firms include individually owned farms and office-based physicians, and the partnerships include law firms, so many of which, in Washington at least, act as interest groups. If these were "projected" to the second tier, the number given above would obviously be greater than thirty-five hundred. Their turn will of course come later.

To survey even thirty-five hundred is impossible here. What authors commonly provide is an *ad hoc* sampling. Rather than supplying the usual catalogue, however, it may be more profitable to take (from chapter 2) Neil Smelser's "contrapuntal interplay" (differentiation and integration) and use it as a guide to the second-tier business structure, all of course with an eye to interest-group activity.

Following that tack, one may identify two principal modes or forms of integration at this level. But first a warning: integration is often in the eye of the beholder, historian or social scientist, who judges the meaning for the nation of a whole series of complicated social processes. (The exceptions occur in times of crisis, notably war, which make for a certain clarity of mind.) Contemporary actors talk, at least, in different, more immediately practical terms. Consider, for example, the American Paper and Pulp Association formed at Saratoga Springs in 1878. The minutes of the first five annual meetings disclose that the main preoccupations were "overproduction, the continued building of new machines, and the failure of the manufacturers to live up to the understanding or agreement that production should be cut."[16] But to us standing back from the scene and observing the broader consequences, the new association marks or embodies a stage on the road to integration.

The two main integrative forms at this second-order level are the trade association and the employers' organization. The latter is familiar to everyone but may as well be defined formally as "a group which is composed of or fostered by employers and which seeks to promote the employers' interests in labor matters." The trade association is a voluntary, nonprofit organization of enterprises in the same industry or trade. "Such enterprises may be individuals, partnerships, or corporations," in "nearly all" instances competitors.[17]

As national bodies, both types are essentially products of the first stage of the organizational revolution, which, in America as in Britain, may be identified (for our purpose here) as occurring between 1860 and 1914. Businessmen had long attempted to protect themselves from the rigors of competition by gentlemen's agreements, since written ones to restrict output or fix prices were prohibited at common law. For an obvious reason, they tended to be ineffective, hence the gentle reproach against those who had failed "to live up to the understanding or agreement." Many other restrictive devices were thought up, including the pool, the cartel (an import from Germany), and the trust (a brilliant American adaptation of a concept peculiar to English law),[18] each of which represents (to us) a mode of integration. To the disappointment of the entrepreneurs and their lawyers, the modes all suffered from various defects, including, in the end, disabling legal ones. In contrast, the trade association was successfully developed as a partial "answer" to the problem—of market uncertainty and capriciousness—and, in our terms, as an alternative mode of integration.

As an institution, it has certainly flourished. Only a few associations existed in the 1860s.[19] More sprang up during the two following decades, when they focused "almost exclusively" on securing "market control."[20] But as the states and even the federal government set their faces against price and output agreements, the emphasis apparently changed from market control to more positive or "constructive" goals, such as product standardization and the exchange of "recent and accurate information," tending, according to one economist, to convert the trade association into an "educational institution."[21] The tendency of trade associations to widen their scope and increase their numbers was fostered in various ways, especially by the Supreme Court's adoption in 1911, during the famous case that broke up Standard Oil, of a "rule of reason" (the Court stated that not every elimination of competition is unlawful), and then by the need for government-industry cooperation in World War I.[22] Between 1914 and 1919 the total increased from 800 to at least 1500,[23] perhaps as many as 2000.[24]

Of the many things that might be singled out within the developments so far touched upon, three must suffice here. First, the integration achieved, in principle, by trade associations was really of two kinds even apart from the geographical. The first has already been noticed except for the name—*horizontal*, an association bringing together producers at the same stage of production, i.e., competitors. But other associations embodied the *vertical* principle, covering successive stages of production or distribution. Some were hybrids, both vertical and horizontal.[25] This was one way of managing industrial complexity, an aspect of historian Robert Wiebe's thesis that the period 1877–1920 is to be characterized as a "search for order."[26]

Secondly, the fairly distinct line that had separated society from state in the nineteenth century was beginning, in important areas, to get blurred. That is one meaning of the First World War. Another is that the "drive" was *from* the state and its imperious wartime requirements *to* society, tending to erode the conception, adequate for the previous century, of the social order's *determining* the political order. With that, the first-approximation idea of an interest-group's "reaching out" to government also suffers a setback, demanding some modification in context. After the war, in any case, the scene permanently changed. Some of the wartime arrangements crystallized as institutions, bringing into play such important trade associations as the American Petroleum Institute. As secretary of commerce, Herbert Hoover encouraged trade associations, seeing in them instruments for self-regulation. They got their chance, to an extent he could not have dreamed of, after the market economy collapsed in the first year of his administration as president. For central to his successor FDR's plan for rebuilding the system was the National Industrial Recovery Act (NIRA). Its core component was the use of trade associations to draft codes of fair competition for their industries that, once approved by the president, would be enforceable at law. That naturally sent an electric shock through the trade-association body. Existing associations secured a measure of that market control which, overtly or covertly, they had been seeking for a generation or more. But even at that date coverage was not complete, or universal. So NIRA "forced" growth (in the hothouse gardener's sense), cultivating through its agent the NRA (National Recovery Administration) about eight hundred new trade associations.[27]

Evidently, in such a system, trade associations were ceasing to be purely private bodies (thus putting the definition of interest-groups—chapter 2— under strain). In fact, this whole "deal" within the New Deal tended toward the corporatism then being practiced (or at least talked about) in Italy, and which has been rediscovered in the late 1970s and early 1980s, in America as elsewhere, as neocorporatism. As it turned out at the time, of course, the whole drift was too much for the Supreme Court, which in 1935 declared the NIRA to be unconstitutional. Probably most of those trade associations so recently "invigorated," "aroused," "consolidated," and indeed "called into life" (phrases used by Clair Wilcox)[28] would not have faded away. But that was never put to the test because the outbreak of World War II again cast trade associations for a quasi-public role.

Of course, the concept of a quasi- or semi-public role in crises or emergencies still leaves room for trade associations to act "privately" in the long run, i.e., like an interest group as defined in chapter 2. Certainly by the early sixties many were well positioned for the exercise of influence. In his sample of 101 lobbyists in Washington, Lester Milbrath found that 43 represented small trade associations, and 9 spoke for larger ones, enough to make up a luncheon group—the Washington Trade Association Executive Club. But Professor Milbrath also spotted a trend for trade associations to set up their headquarters in the capital.[29] By 1979 when the grand total may have reached 5100 nationwide, at least 1350 (26 percent) were located in the Washington metropolitan area.[30] In the two preceding years, 176 had emerged within the District of Columbia alone, an increase of 21 percent. (One writes "emerged" to gloss over one's ignorance of the proportion that *migrated* to Washington as distinct from being *launched* there.) According to another calculation, there were, in early 1983, in the Washington metropolitan area, 2666 trade associations *and* professional societies, but that figure could hardly have been comparable with the 1350. However, the same person—Debra J. Stratton, speaking for the American Society of Association Executives[31]—reported a 65 percent increase in that (combined) category from 1971, and this is consistent with what we expect from other sources. Specifically on trade associations alone, metropolitan New York was then reported to have lost ground in the same period by 15 percent (dropping to 2568)[32] although Chicago, with 868, stayed about the same. All in all, these is good reason to expect that trade associations are busying themselves as interest groups.

EMPLOYERS' ORGANIZATIONS

These, embodying the other mode of integration at this second-order level, have to be treated summarily here. Although such organizations go back a long way,[33] the modern "movement" (the term was used) dates from the mid-1880s. The Stove Founders' National Defense Association (later the National Founders' Association) has often been given pride of place.[34] What concerns us now is that, like the United Typothetae at the same time (employers in book, job, and magazine printing), it was the offshoot of a trade association,[35] suggesting that the tendency to differentiation was being carried a stage further. This in turn can be represented as a response to the differentiation brought about by laboring men, who, by 1866, had created thirty to forty "national trade organizations,"[36] at the base of which were arrayed about three hundred locals when the war ended, a total that rose to more than a thousand before the decade was out.

Thus the stage was being set for integration at a higher level within the world of the worker as of the entrepreneur. Workers made their move early, with "city centrals, cooperatives, regional associations, and, encompassing all of them, the National Labor Union" by the late 1860s.[37] More of a broad interest group than a union peak, the National Labor Union (1866) embodied a measure of centralization,[38] i.e., vertical integration. So did its *de facto* successor, the Knights of Labor, launched in 1869 but "going national" only about ten years later. Setting out to recruit all sorts, unskilled as well as skilled, black as well as white, and even, in the end, women, the Knights embodied a greater measure of vertical integration than the National Labor Union, in achievement as well as aspiration. For, as Albert Fried has recalled, the executive board of the general assembly (delegates representing the entire membership) had considerable control over local bodies.[39]

All this is not an extended "aside" from the nominal subject. For in the first half of the eighties, the Knights shot ahead at an unprecedented speed, from 52,000 in 1883 to some 702,000 in 1886. *Most* of that increase (some 590,000) had in fact been secured in the eighteen months after 1885, following its triumphant strike against Jay Gould's Wabash railroad. Little wonder that the distinguished economist, Richard T. Ely could call it "the most powerful and the most remarkable labor organization of modern times."[40]

As it happened, for reasons not to be examined here, the Knights soon went into a decline. But employers could not then see that the outcome would be its virtual collapse before the century was out. Besides, the decade was marked by union militancy and by the "riot" in Haymarket Square, Chicago (May, 1886), for which no unions were responsible but from which their reputation suffered. The decade also saw the launching (1881) of the Federation of Organized Trades and Labor Unions (FOTLU). Modelled on the Trades Union Congress in Britain (1868), it brought together such crafts-men as typographers, carpenters, and glassworkers for the purpose of playing an independent, essentially interest-group role. Many were already in the Knights of Labor but felt themselves neglected. In organizing the trades—craftsmen—the new body was instituting a form of horizontal integration. This was perpetuated in late 1886 when the FOTLU reorganized and re-named itself the American Federation of Labor. But we should not exaggerate the degree of integration it embodied. Dual unionism now prevailed: two rival peaks. Even after one was left in command of the field, it organized only craftsmen. Moreover, the individual craft unions were deliberately left with a high degree of autonomy, so much so that the basic arrangement has been likened, by Professor Fried, to a confederation rather than a federation.[41]

Even so, the house of labor now had a third "storey" for skilled workers at least. That alone would surely have stimulated industrialists to go and do likewise. Merchants had already shown the way, having mounted a commer-cial convention in Detroit in 1865, "the first occasion on which the merchants of the nation assembled together, to consult in reference to those great indus-trial and financial questions in which they have a common interest." At the second such convention, in Boston, three years later, merchants had launched a National Board of Trade (by which they meant a National Chamber of Commerce, titles that they used interchangeably).[42] But when the first indus-trial peak was created in 1895, it was not in "dialectical" response to the labor peaks but rather to the disastrous business conditions. The five years 1893–97 saw the first of the "great depressions" in American experience. Manufacturing firms went over like bowling pins in such leading manufacturing states as New York, Pennsylvania, Illinois, and Massachusetts. The number of unemployed workers almost reached 4 million (14–15 percent of the civilian labor force) in 1897. At the same time the systematic search for export markets was just getting under way, manufacturers in particular lifting their eyes toward southern horizons (Central and South America). Out of such immediate concerns the National Association of Manufacturers (NAM) was born in January 1895 at Cincinnati, Ohio, where more than six hundred manufacturers had assembled. They were welcomed by the governor (the ill-starred William McKinley), whose rousing theme was the need for "foreign markets for our surplus products," in agriculture as well as manufacturing.

So preoccupied, the NAM did not touch "the question of labor" until the turn of the century when (at its 1901 convention) the "relations of capital and labor" were brought to the forefront.[43] By then unions had 1.1 million members, some 70 percent of whom belonged (paid up) to the American Federation of Labor.[44] As the NAM president in 1901 foresaw and feared, "organized capital" was coming to be "confronted by organized labor." The NAM had the backing of over a thousand manufacturers (at that time, individuals as well as "firms and corporations" could belong, according to the revised constitution, 1896, article 1); 87 unions were affiliated to the AF of L. But the day-to-day confrontation took place of course at the place of work, or establishment. In 1898, a thousand or so strikes had affected about 3800 establishments; by 1901, the totals were 2900 and close to 11,000, respectively.[45] The inevitable counterattack was launched in 1903 under a new and more aggressive NAM president, David M. Parry, of Indianapolis. In that year strikes numbered almost 3500; over 20,000 establishments were affected. Led by the NAM, the employers fought back through such bodies as the Citizens' Industrial Associations of America (whose first president was the current president of the NAM) and the National Council for Industrial Defense (1907). This was so close to the legislative committee of the NAM that the two were (officially) said to be "for all the world like Siamese twins—you cannot separate them." Why, then, create two bodies? The NAM's own answer would seem to have been that "the council has focused many forces which were not available through direct membership of the association."[46] In other words, the council was a device for mobilizing a wide range of groups in pursuit of certain goals in the field of industrial, mainly labor, relations.

That was essentially interest-group work (in the states as well as Washington). Labor policy in the other, collective bargaining sense still devolved upon the second-order associations. Some of these, like the National Metal Trades Association (in 1921: about 1000 firms; 600,000 highly skilled workers) covered the nation, although the center of gravity appears to have been in the eastern United States and Canada.[47] Others bargained within a narrower range, e.g., the Building Trades Employers' Association of the City of New York, and the Building Construction Employers' Association of Chicago.[48]

So, from an early stage, the NAM embodied or sought two modes of integration: of firms and corporations as producers and sellers but also as employers of labor, representing an extension of the original design. The greatest single initiative under the latter was the "open shop" campaign. Assisted by scores of *ad hoc* "open shop" organizations, the NAM was so successful, admittedly in changed circumstances, that the immediate postwar period has been called the "open shop decade." That turning back of the tide of history (as it seems in retrospect) was reversed only by FDR's New Deal (not counting the herculean efforts of workers in the mass production industries, mobilized by what came to be a rival "peak" to the AF of L, the Congress of Industrial Organizations).

Today the NAM still supports its affiliate, the National Industrial Council, which encompasses some 300 national, state, and local manufacturing and commercial organizations that "connect" about 100,000 firms. But the association also speaks for some 12,000 corporate members (individual membership being no longer permitted). No doubt that exaggerates the degree of integration in its sector not only because (in the early seventies) three eligible corporations refrained from joining for every one that made the effort (and paid the dues), but also because of the startling turnover in membership. At the time 1300 to 1400 members a year were recruited—but as many lapsed. Even so, the NAM brought some order into a complex if not chaotic scene. Nearly 3000 of the 12,000 or so corporate members had places on one or more of the sixteen standing committees. It also secured a measure of geographical integration: each of the fifty states supplied two persons to the 175-member board, the policy-approving (if not exactly policy-making) body.[49] There can be little doubt that if a peak of this kind did not exist today, it would have to be invented. In large-scale, complex societies, governance itself (the act or process of governing) requires such "grand simplifications." By the same token, the existence of such a network facilitates, perhaps even encourages interest-group representations through its most prominent "nodule," the central body.

U.S. CHAMBER OF COMMERCE

Obviously, no association of manufacturers, however comprehensive, could integrate the sprawling world of business. Surprisingly, the really effective integration of merchants and traders took a very long time to arrange. The New York Chamber of Commerce saw light of day in 1768. Two years later it received a royal charter from King George III, thus earning that splendid title, "The Corporation of the Chamber of Commerce in the City of New York, in America."[50] By the Civil War, there were perhaps thirty such bodies (counting twenty boards of trade). When the first attempt at integration came in 1868 (the National Board of Trade), the foundations of today's

Association of British Chambers of Commerce had been laid for about eight years, although chambers of commerce in the British Isles dated only from the mid-1780s.[51]

Around about the turn of the century, the pressure of numbers, and accordingly the "strain toward" integration, was growing. In 1898 someone well placed to make an accurate count reached a total of 2944 locally, about one hundred nationally, but many of these seem not to have been chambers of commerce. An official count at the end of 1912 produced a total of 3356, but, again, these were "all sorts": not more than six out of ten (1772) carried one or other of the appropriate names (chambers of commerce, boards of trade, and the like. Of course, the names used are not infallible guides to function, but we have little else to go on.) Seven or eight months later, a trade journal reported that there were more than "4500 commercial organizations in the United States, and over 1000 of sufficient importance to justify membership in the National Chamber of Commerce."[52]

By that the writer meant the Chamber of Commerce of the United States of America, which had been created—at last—in April 1912. The need for an effective "association of associations" (as a Ford Motor Company officer expressed it) had long been apparent, the National Board of Trade having become "helpless as a lobbyist."[53] But no third-order (nor indeed second-order) organization can be explained simply by felt need, the "strain toward." Someone has to exercise leadership, and even then may not fully succeed, which proved to be the fate of the National Council of Commerce (born 1907, lingered on until 1912). Meanwhile the Boston Chamber and the Chicago Association of Commerce had taken up the running, eventually persuading the secretary of commerce and labor to give the project his blessing and support. He in turn won over President Taft, who, in a message to Congress on foreign affairs (December 1911), commended "the coordination of effort" by "certain unofficial associations" to promote commerce, but regretted that "the great number of such associations and the comparative lack of cooperation between them fail to secure an efficiency commensurate with the public interest. Some central organization in touch with associations and chambers of commerce throughout the country would, I believe, be of great value."[54]

After a secret meeting in February 1912 between federal government officials and a small business group from across the nation selected by the Boston Chamber, President Taft invited about a thousand business associations to a founding convention. Held at a Washington hotel in April, it was attended by 700–750 delegates (depending on which source one follows).[55] This new ship was then successfully launched. The National Council scuttled itself (but not before it had generously handed over its remaining funds). The National Board of Trade said it would stay in service until the new vessel got well under way, which it succeeded in doing. By the following year (1913) it had more than "six-hundred commercial organizations" on board as well as over seventeen hundred individuals (themselves members of the six hundred). Any risk of entering the doldrums was averted by the entry of the U.S. (1917) into World War I. There is nothing quite like a good war for stimulating business organizations (and labor unions, too).

Thus a third-order structure for integration in the realm of business was at last rounded out if not completed, with the chamber as "a horizontal organization," and the NAM as "a vertical organization." It had taken about two generations (1868 to 1913). Since that period had also seen the rooting and rapid growth of the AF of L, all on top of the development of a great second-order network (national unions, trade associations, and employers' organizations, many dedicated to restoring or preventing "open shop" rule), capital and labor now had their champions drawn up against each other. But these were champions who would fight as interest groups, i.e., through Congress and the White House (as well as in the states). The NAM deplored the trend, denouncing attempts to "create class distinctions in the community and to sow the seeds of class hatred," bravely declaring that "we have no classes in this country," and endlessly complaining about "class legislation" in Congress.[56] In its perception, evidently, interest-group politics tended to be an expression (or perpetuation) of class struggle by other means. Even if true, that might well be regarded as preferable to the contemporary class war fought between owners and workers on such battlefields as Michigan, West Virginia, and Colorado.[57] The six years 1911–16 (reported labor specialists Philip Taft and Philip Ross) "rank among the most violent in American history, except for the Civil War." That in a country with the "bloodiest and most violent labor history of any industrial nation in the world."[58]

For most of the years between that war and its successor, the third-order structure so laboriously built up in the other interwar period remained intact. Yet, in retrospect at least, the structure was not immaculate: it did not specifically integrate the smaller enterprises as such, nor—by the same token—facilitate their activity as interest groups. In contrast, the second great merger movement was well under way in the 1920s, especially the latter half. Much of it proceeded by way of acquisition, in which big business gobbled up small business. As Robert Sobel explained: "Usually, the small firm was forced to submit, either through lack of capital, personnel, or ability to adapt to new circumstances, or through the destructive competition from the giants."[59]

A start on what turned out to be a specialized structure for small business, and so the foundation for a small business lobby of considerable complexity in the 1980s, was made in 1937 with the establishment of the NSB, the National Small Business Association. (This should not be confused with the Small Business Administration, a federal agency set up in 1953 to "aid, counsel, assist, and protect the interests of small business.") The NSB (a peak) is interesting in part because its creation does not follow what one half-expects to be the natural sequence: ascending levels of integration, i.e., from first-order to second-order, thence to third-order. Such intermediate bodies as the Smaller Business Association of New England appeared (1938) only after the peak had been reached. So, too, with the Council of Smaller Enterprises (Cleveland, Ohio), and the Independent Business Association of Wisconsin (Madison).[60]

The NSB filled a gap, how adequately it is hard to judge. We do know that in 1941 a Conference of American Small Business Organizations put in an appearance, followed two years later, in California, by the National Federation of Independent Business (NFIB), which proved to be the more enduring rival. By 1980 it had some 600,000 members, described (by the organization itself) as typically "a retailer grossing $100,000 to $200,000 a year." Three out of four of them employed fewer than ten persons. But the NSB had about fifty thousand "small-business executives" in membership. Between the two bodies some "tension" has been reported.[61] Indeed, one outside but well-placed observer claimed (in 1977) that "until recently, the federation and the association spent as much time competing for members as working on issues."[62]

To the academic observer, the obvious solution would have been a merger, but although, apparently, talked about at one time, it had not been achieved by the early 1980s, probably, in part, because the obvious is not obvious, or not palatable, to the insiders with jobs and prospects at stake (the common difficulty). So that measure of integration was still lacking in 1983. However, from the midseventies two other routes were followed. In 1977 the NSB launched a Small Business Legislative Council (SBLC), embracing about twenty trade associations, to discuss policy and coordinate lobbying. That may be called integrative because it replaced *ad hoc* coalitions with a standing arrangement. In 1982 the SBLC aligned seventy-five national, and a number of state, trade associations, claiming to speak for four million small businesses.

The more comprehensive and ambitious attempt at integration crystallized in 1975 as the Council of Small and Independent Business Associations. This brought together for some purposes both the federation and the association (the context for the qualification, "until recently," in the penultimate paragraph). It also included the National Association of Small Business Investment Companies, then numbering 320. This was a body stimulated by government, being a product of the Small Business Investment Act of 1958, which enabled the Small Business Administration (1953) to guarantee the loans the companies actually made. In the early eighties the council still had the original three: the regional bodies mentioned earlier and several others,— the Mid-Continent Small Business United (Kansas City, Mo.) and the Smaller Manufacturers Council (Pittsburg)—and such relative newcomers as the National Business League (minorities) and the National Association of Women Business Owners. However, this fell short of real integration because the council was not a distinct entity but remained what it had been from the start:

"an informal mechanism with no separate staff."[63] In 1980 it "tackled few legislative issues because a consensus of members often was difficult to achieve."[64] On the other hand, it was accorded access to policy makers at high points in the government, which is of course a necessary if not sufficient condition for effective direct lobbying over a certain range of issues.

Complicating one's assessment of such third-order integration from the late seventies was the establishment of a small-business center within the U.S. Chamber of Commerce. Described by its director as essentially a service department for its smaller companies, "targeting their concerns," interpreting relevant issues and mobilizing support, it promoted local specialization through its chambers across the nation (the integrated body thus bringing about differentiation). By early 1979, some five hundred of the Chamber's twenty-five hundred affiliates had set up small business task forces or separate small business councils, and the Center for Small Business no longer had to "prod" the periphery.[65] By 1980 the total had risen to about seven hundred. Insofar as the Chamber itself already had a very large clientele of small businesses (in 1982, nine out of ten chamber members employed fewer than one hundred persons), its policy tended to erode that form of integration brought about by the other organizations from 1937.

Whether that erosion would persist seemed to depend, in the early eighties, on a number of variables, including:

1. *The Chamber's real motivation* in taking that particular initiative at that particular time. Was it trying to modify its image as being representative, essentially, of Big Business? And if so, was it doing so for p.r. reasons (as the term *image* suggests), or to please its own small-business clientele, the source of seventy-five percent of its revenue from dues (1982)? Or was it a cool calculation to "piggy-back on the ride" (as Dave Kromarsky, of NSB, suggested), since Small Business had become "a force to be reckoned with"?[66]

2. *Government's perception of the Chamber* in this new-found, or newly declared, role as a spokesman for small business. For instance: the administration invited representation from the chamber's Center for Small Business at a White House conference to be held in March 1977. Apparently, Small Business protested. In any case, the invitation was withdrawn. There may have been poetic justice in that, for earlier the chamber had attended a White House meeting for officers of Big Business.

3. *Small Business's own morale, self-confidence, and strategy.* On that a well-placed observer within the Small Business Administration detected in 1979 a transition from "organizations to a movement. It may take two, five, or ten years to get there, but we're on the way."[67] If so, then, for that reason alone, one would expect the high-level integration to come, and, increasingly, via Small Business itself.

All that lies in the future. For the present, there can be little doubt that, in the words of *National Journal's* James W. Singer in 1979: "In an era when small is beautiful, the country's small business lobby is reaching for the big time."[68]

BUSINESS INTEGRATION: THE 1980s

Reverting now to integration for business as a whole, one draws attention to three remarkable features, embodying incompatible or at least not readily reconcilable trends: attempts to build what would have to be called a fourth-order structure; the rapid development and broadening of the U.S. Chamber, tending to make it the major force at the current third-order level; the creation of the Business Roundtable from the body of the Business Council, both of which, being directly representative of the giant corporations through their very top officers, short-circuit the chamber as well as the NAM on major issues.

In the postwar era, two tendencies were discernible that pointed toward a fourth-order structure: their outward and visible signs were the Conference of National Organizations (CNO) and the Greenbrier Conference. Started toward the end of World War II under another, more ephemeral name, the CNO originally brought together sixteen national organizations, but doubled that number in its most fruitful phase (twenty-nine members were reported for 1972). Three meetings a year were to be held, providing "a unique opportunity for labor and management, agriculture, education, and other elements of our society to get to know each other."[69] Labor in the form of the Brotherhood of Railroad Trainmen soon retreated, but what was left was remarkable enough, including trade associations, the Chamber of Commerce, NAM; veterans; consumers; women's clubs; Farmer Cooperatives and the American Farm Bureau Federation; the National Education Association; the American Medical Association; even Lions and Kiwanis. If these organizations could be said to speak for their members in this CNO context, the total covered would indeed be very large. An honorary official once estimated in 1955: "It would be my guess that what goes on at our meetings in one way or another could affect the thinking and lives of 30 to 40 million Americans."

Whether they could ever find the "common ground upon which we all may stand" in relation to "certain fundamental, national problems . . . which reach far and beyond the scope and purview of any one national organization," is of course improbable. We can hardly judge because the proceedings were conducted in secret and the papers presented, even the list of members, were kept from the press (but not, evidently, from political scientist Donald Roots Hall).[70] The main point for this analysis is that, in the early sixties, delegates perceived the CNO as having "tremendous potential . . . in the development of a more unified approach toward the solution of many of our national problems." Well founded or not, that sentiment embodied an aspiration toward a still higher level of integration.

Named for the Greenbrier Hotel in West Virginia where the meetings were held, the Greenbrier Conference belonged to the same era as the CNO and attracted some of the same clientele. War, this time the Korean, was again the catalyst: informal talks in 1950 between the American Farm

Bureau Federation and the NAM, perturbed by the imposition of stabilization controls, led to an organization broader in membership and policy concerns. After two meetings in Philadelphia in 1951, the Greenbrier Hotel became the venue for annual miniconventions, to which an extra meeting was occasionally added, as in both 1958 and 1959, to coordinate strategy over the Labor-Management Reporting and Disclosure Act (best remembered under the name of its sponsors, Landrum-Griffin), an attempt to guarantee due process for individual members of unions and generally to promote their democratic working. Like the CNO gatherings, these were intended to be kept secret, but reporter James Deakin and farm economist Wesley McCune among others pierced the veil, as did Professor Hall somewhat later.[71]

That the conference was not simply a pleasant occasion inaugurated by cocktails in the West Virginia Room and dinner in the Crystal Dining Room is attested by the caliber of those in attendance, who, indeed, were far from being "association hacks" (as Donald Hall pointed out). Among those who came in 1963, for example, were the presidents of the American Bankers Association, American Medical Association, American Retail Federation, Farm Bureau Federation, National Association of Real Estate Boards, and Pharmaceutical Manufacturers Association; the chairman and managing director of the International Monetary Fund; past presidents of the national chamber and the Investment Bankers Association; and many a vice-president, including one from the NAM, supported by general counsel and by a vice-president of Republic Steel who was also a director of NAM. Standard Oil was represented by a man of undetermined rank; the First National City Bank of New York by a senior vice-president. A former undersecretary of the Interior Department and a former assistant director of the Budget brought some government experience to the deliberations.

What were the deliberations about? The federal budget and of course that perennial topic, tax reduction; the unsettling drive for consumer protection; unemployment; "labor union power." Of this the fight for the Landrum-Griffin Act of 1959 provides an illustration:

> The core of their technique, as spelled out by its practitioners, was to focus on uncommitted House members, particularly those in marginal districts. There a deliberate effort was made to translate public anger at the disclosure of union corruption by the McClellan Committee into a barrage of letters urging the congressmen to vote for a tougher labor bill.[72]

That was supported by a media campaign, including a one-hour TV program exhibiting union violence (put out by local stations under business sponsorship or even under the name of "public service"). The program was pushed by heavy advertising and by almost five million mailings.

In this chapter, however, one is less concerned with such efforts (conveniently "worked in" here) than with tracing the continued upward momentum of business (and indeed other) groups that had started a hundred years or so earlier. It does seem to be true that neither this nor the related tendency got very far toward a fourth-order structure. If either had, America would have acquired some of the necessary elements of a neocorporate state. But the tide rose high and then receded. What the developments perhaps reveal, then, is that the upward organizational thrust from American society is strong enough to "lift" above the third-order level only *ad hoc*, for limited purposes and periods of time. In this context, society's reach may be said to exceed its grasp. In other words, the third-order "line" marks the practical limit of the upward organizational thrust.

The form of third-order business integration underwent a distinct change in the 1980s. In 1972 economist Herbert Stein had said that the NAM was really "Pittsburgh business" and the national chamber "Main Street business."[73] Even then the Chamber already harbored many manufacturing firms. These, by 1980, included General Motors, General Electric, AMAX, Owens-Corning, and Caterpillar Tractors, apart from Exxon and Conoco.[74] Moreover, as the decade advanced, the chamber itself was advancing at astonishing speed. In 1982 membership reached 250,000, having been 50,000 in 1975 (when a new president, Richard L. Lesher, took over). About 5000 of the new total were "organization members," that is, (a) state, regional, and local chambers of commerce, including some overseas, and (b) trade and professional associations. At their base (the chamber liked to claim) stood a great army of five million persons. The rest of the total was made up of "business and professional members," ranging from sole proprietors through the smaller companies (86 percent of the membership comprises firms employing fifty workers or fewer) to the giant corporation. Thus, by the early 1980s, if not before, the chamber had broken the bounds of "Main Steet." It could even claim, not unreasonably, to be the premier business peak in the country, bringing to America a greater measure of integration in the business world than ever before, despite the independent course charted by the *smaller companies*, particularly in the 1970s.

Meanwhile, however, a teasing fate had been busy preparing (in effect) a more serious challenge to all such third-order integration: the independent mobilization of the *greater companies*. This was not new: it had started in 1933 with the Business Advisory Council, set up by Secretary of Commerce Daniel C. Roper, "to make available to the Department of Commerce seasoned judgment and experience on matters affecting the relation of the department and business." The initiative seems to have come from him (i.e., thinking back to the question of the origins of groups, *from* state *to* society). Confronting the Great Depression, Roosevelt's new secretary asked himself "what changes in the practices and policies" of the department should be made. He proceeded to consult some leading businessmen whom he knew personally. Their "cordial"[75] response produced the Business Advisory and

Planning Council (to evoke the fuller, New Deal-ish title seldom used in the postwar political-science literature. In fact, most of the standard works specifically on interest groups have little or nothing to say about the council under either title).

Whether both sides really had the same thing in mind is, as usual in this context, unclear: one says "as usual" mainly because all these direct interchanges between corporations and government (CNO, Greenbrier, and, as we shall learn, the Business Roundtable) have been conducted in secrecy (within "an aura of secrecy," a congressional committee would say *à propos* the Business Advisory Committee but of general application).[76] At his most ambitious, Secretary Roper seems to have hoped that the meeting of minds he arranged would be (as historian Kim McQuaid put it in 1982) "the germ of a national economic parliament that would one day include 'representatives of all groups in the economic and social structure of the country,' and bring them into 'constant relationships' with one another,"[77] which sounds very much like neocorporatism. What members of the council sought, on the other hand, may have rested on fear, a diffused apprehension: "If industry does not organize and govern itself, either the state or federal government will—with the consequent paralyzing effects on intitiative and progress."[78] Expressed somewhat more positively, their aim was to bring about "self-regulation of industry with government approval." The council, in their perception, "would first marry corporate expertise to federal power, and then serve as a long-range economic planning council with primary responsibility for formulating industrial recovery strategy."[79]

Evidently, these were not your "average" business tycoons: they supported the National Recovery Administration and helped to draw up its industry codes (mentioned earlier as precipitants of trade associations).[80] They included some of the most "intellectual" business leaders America has ever produced, such as Gerard Swope, who not only put General Electric on its feet but recognized, and tried to overcome, worker alienation on the job, a complement perhaps to his service for the famous Settlement Houses of Chicago and New York.[81] He was cut from the same cloth as Ralph Nader, in the judgment of historian Forrest McDonald.[82]

The other founding fathers were not quite like Swope (or Nader): Henry Harriman (national chamber), Walter Teagle (Standard Oil, N.J., now Exxon), and Louis Kirstein (Federated Department Stores). Even so, they and the men they chose for the council,[83] which would range from between forty and sixty-five chief executive officers, were clearly "different" from their kind, making one wonder to what extent the council should be regarded as a form of integration. Structurally, such varied industries as steel and textiles, different regions of the country, small as well as large manufacturers,[84] were "covered" by the initial invitations. Some representation of "small and middle-sized business" there has always been, but the "predominant membership" (Grant McConnell would write in 1966) "has been drawn from the world of large corporations."[85] As Emanuel Celler's House subcommittee studying antitrust issues put it, the current or former members of the council had come from

> 2 of the 4 largest rubber manufacturers, 3 of the 5 largest automobile manufac-
> turers, 3 of the 10 largest steel producers, 4 of the 10 largest companies in the
> chemical field, 2 of the 3 largest manufacturers of electrical equipment, 2 of
> the 3 largest manufacturers of textiles, 4 of the 16 largest oil companies and 3
> of the largest glass manufacturers.[86]

Moreover, the "constitutional" status of the council was so peculiar as to throw doubt upon its character and, accordingly, its true role. "No executive order formally establishing the council was ever drawn up," although it was attached to the Department of Commerce, where its staff were provided with free accommodation. Its composition and the agenda for its meetings were determined by the corporate leaders.[87] By 1960 two "work-and-play"[88] sessions a year were being held (at such salubrious resorts at Sea Island, Georgia; Pebble Beach, California; and Hot Springs, Virginia). To these, high government officials were invited. In addition, four "real" meetings a year took place in Washington. These seem to be the ones historian Kim McQuaid had in mind in writing that council meetings were attended by "high Commerce Department bureaucrats" only when "specifically invited. Such invitations were rare indeed."[89] Obviously, the council was a hybrid form.

So it remained for twenty-eight years, touching many issues of public policy, including foreign affairs, *de facto* advising the Department of State as well as the Department of Commerce, and proposing suitable names for periods of government service.[90] Among them were three prominent council members selected by President Eisenhower in 1952, "all political novices": George Humphrey for the Treasury, Charles Wilson for Defense, and Robert T. Stevens for the army.[91] Others recruited through this channel included W. Averell Harriman, and Douglas Dillon, the New York investment banker (recalled financial journalist, Beatson Wallace from Hot Springs, Va., in May 1982, during the spring "work-and-play" meeting of the council). In some ways, things had not changed at all: the press contingent (twenty-five to thirty) was still kept at bay, barred from the working sessions and reduced essentially to spending "days and nights scouring the hotel in search of newsy tidbits,"[92] which, on the evidence of the stories filed, were hard to come by. The council still had captains at the helm: the chairman, four vice-chairmen, and most members of the executive committee of fourteen were also chairmen of the boards of their companies.

On the other hand, the council was no longer a quasi-public body, i.e., one in which the "distinction" between "public and private had been hopelessly lost" (Grant McConnell), that had been *in* government but not *of* it (Kim McQuaid). For early in 1961, led by Roger Blough of United States Steel, the council cut loose from the department, having already been deprived of its office space there and generally reduced in status. Professor McConnell advanced two reasons in explanation. One was the accidental fact that in 1960 General Electric had been indicted with twenty-eight other corporations for price-fixing, bid-rigging, and division of the market for switch-gear equipment, and its chairman happened to be chairman of the Business Advisory Council that year. Some company officials were jailed, "although through his ignorance of what was going on in his company" (as Professor McConnell drily remarked), the GE chairman was not among them. Even so, the episode was embarrassing: however hybrid its character, the council was certainly in the business of advising a federal government department. Secondly, some public criticism of the council following the Celler antitrust investigation prompted President Kennedy's secretary of commerce, Luther Hartwell Hodges, to propose various changes, notably better representation for small businessmen and an end to the exclusion of the press from the meetings of the council.[93]

That account is incomplete. It ignores the impact of Hobart Rowen's prize-winning article in *Harper's* (September 1960) about the "most powerful private club" in America, which attracted the attention of candidate Kennedy and his "insurgents." Moreover, Secretary Hodges had strong views of his own. Although a successful practitioner of business, he told the National Press Club that he would not be "its tool and not its automatic spokesman." In marked contrast to Charles E. Wilson, who had moved from GM and the Business Council to Defense under President Eisenhower, he believed (as he publicly said) that "what is good for General Motors may, or may not, be good for the country,"[94] referring to the celebrated identification that Mr. Wilson had once incautiously presented. Secretary Hodges also believed (but did *not* say so publicly) that "no group ought to have the special channel to government thinking available to [the council]," which of course goes to the heart of the democratic problem of access. Nor, unlike his predecessors, was he prepared to appoint to the council whomever the council's executive committee selected. True, he also sought the two reforms Professor McConnell mentioned, but it was his basic philosophy that set him on a collision course with the council (as Mr. Rowen, interviewing him for *Newsweek*, realized at the time).[95] In fact, after initial resistance, those reform proposals were accepted in April 1961 (the luncheon meeting at which the director of the Bureau of the Budget addressed the council was opened, on the record, to the press). But Secretary Hodges went much further, imposing himself as a virtual chairman of proceedings and ejecting the council's staff director and secretaries from the two rooms they had enjoyed in the Department of Commerce. In other words, the secretary was determined to make the council fit the general pattern of federal advisory committees. What happened, however, is that the group decided to "disaffiliate" from the Commerce Department, which promptly claimed and retained the official title, forcing the departing body to choose another. Meeting at the University Club in New York, they made a rather clever choice: Business Council.

Under whatever title, their future could not have seemed auspicious. Amazingly, their fortunes almost immediately revived, because President Kennedy decided that he now needed to woo the business community even if it cost him a somersault. In September he gave the whole council a cocktail party at the White House: it was (an aide conceded) "kiss-and-make-up." At the usual fall meeting the following month, a council member remarked with a smile: "Only the name has changed."[96] That was prompted by the sight of an "all-star team of seven cabinet or near-cabinet officials" dancing attendance on the meeting (only Secretary Hodges had put in an appearance in the previous spring). It is also true that the main Hodges reforms were abandoned (no government official need be invited, the council to control the agenda and to continue to meet behind closed doors). Secretary Hodges himself (who failed to show up for that fall meeting) was left "twisting slowly in the wind." Even so, the bottom line was that the council was no longer adviser to one or two departments but to the whole administration. When President Johnson, after the assassination, wanted to reach out to the business community, he called the chairman of the Business Council, not the head of the NAM or of the Chamber of Commerce of the United States.[97] In that we may discern one of the political meanings of high-level integration.

The Business Council has survived into the very different world of the eighties with 215 members, a budget put at $250–500,000, and a staff (in Washington) of two to five (all 1983). It was then meeting four times a year, twice in the capital and twice at Hot Springs, Virginia. For the May 1982 meeting 115 members registered, accompanied by 93 wives—presumably their own. Featured speakers included Secretary of State Alexander Haig; Edwin L. Harper, assistant to President Reagan; William J. Casey, director of the CIA; General David C. Jones, chairman of the Joint Chiefs of Staff; and A. W. Clausen, president of the World Bank (formerly chairman of the Bank of America). Even allowing for the Victorian charm of the Homestead Hotel, with its columned Great Hall lobby where tea and pastries would be served at the proper time of 4 P.M. to the background of a string quartet,[98] the Business Council evidently still enjoyed great prestige in Washington circles. It hardly qualifies as "America's House of Lords."[99] But one sees why the analogy was drawn.

BUSINESS ROUNDTABLE

If the Business Council was "America's House of Lords," what would that make the Business Roundtable? Hardly the House of Commons if only because some people are members of both bodies, which cannot be true of the two chambers of the British Parliament. Besides, the roundtable is itself all gold and glitter, bringing together the chief executive officers (CEOs) of nearly two hundred of the major corporations of America, including the ten leaders of the *Fortune* 500 list (1980); 70 of the top 100; 113 of the top 200. From outside *Fortune's* (industrial) list, there were the four largest public utilities in the land; three of the leading commercial banks; two of the largest life insurance companies;[100] and five of the largest transportation companies. The roundtable even touched a privately owned, but very large, corporation with worldwide interests: Bechtel.[101] Its man on the roundtable's policy committee in 1979 was George P. Shultz, destined only a few years later to replace Alexander Haig as secretary of state. (A Bechtel executive had already joined the Reagan administration: Caspar Weinberger, secretary of defense.)

Mark Green and Arnold Buchsbaum have calculated the $-trillions that the member companies of the roundtable control in assets and revenues, concluding that "if the Business Roundtable were a country, its GNP would be second only to that of the United States." There is something unreal about such an analogy: the "collective gross revenues" of the member companies, said by them to be "equal to one-half" of the GNP of the United States, are simply not at the roundtable's disposal.[102] The more valid point, surely, is that the member companies are assessed on a sliding scale constructed from annual revenues and stockholders' equities, which assures the roundtable a handsome income. Its budget in 1979 was of the order of $2.5 million. (Compare the Business Council's budget of not more than $500,000 even in the early 1980s.) It is also true that the organization is indirectly subsidized by member companies in at least two ways: companies bear the costs of attending roundtable meetings and "frequently" pay for special projects carried out by roundtable task forces.[103]

In any case, what the member companies mainly contribute is surely the talent of its CEOs. To understand that, we have to understand the origin of the roundtable in the early seventies and how it is organized for action in the middle-eighties. It starts out as the confluence of three streams:

  I.   the Labor Law Study Committee (1965),
 II.   the Construction Users Anti-Inflation Roundtable (1969), and
III.   the March Group (1973), an emanation of the Business Council.

Both (I) and (II) were counters to the unions, the first to prevent repeal of section 14(b) of the Taft-Hartley Act (prohibiting the closed shop, etc.); the second, the handiwork of Roger Blough, designed to hold down wages in the construction industry. Having fought shoulder-to-shoulder against the unions during President Nixon's first term, enlisting his aid, (I) and (II) joined forces in the fall of 1972, taking the name of Business Roundtable.

During the course of the year, several men prominent in public life had shared their apprehensions about the "drift" of federal government, probably bemoaning (*inter alia*) the regulatory explosion that had started in the midsixties: John Connally, about to give up the Treasury to return to Texas; two members of the Business Council, John Harper (Alcoa) and Frederich Borch (General Electric); and Arthur Burns (chairman of the Federal Reserve Board). After discussions, the two Business Council men convened, in March 1973, a meeting of about a dozen CEOs and their principal Washington representatives. At bottom they were, as a participant would say later, the "action-oriented members of the Business Council."[104]

True to that characterization, the March Group took at the outset two crucially important strategic decisions: they alone, from "the field," would attend the meetings—no substitutes or stand-ins would be permitted. They would be joined by their leading Washington lobbyists, the better to carry out the other fundamental decision—that they, the CEOs, would lobby in person, not only on Capitol Hill but also in the executive departments. In short, the member companies would be contributing the talent of their CEOs in person for this essentially political work.

What happened next is fairly clear: the March Group gradually "infiltrated" the Business Roundtable and ended up controlling it by the classic corporate route of a merger. This cannot have been particularly difficult to accomplish. Alcoa and General Electric not only provided two leaders of the March Group but had also been represented in the two founding organizations, as had U.S. Steel, whose Roger Blough, only recently retired, was now running the Business Roundtable. All three had of course worked together on the Business Council. *Why* the March Group chose that route is far from clear. The principal authority on the subject (up to 1983) suggests that leaders of the March Group wished to broaden their corporate base at a time when the institutionalized presidency was slowly sinking (it was of course the Watergate period) and not really attending to the affairs of the nation.[105] In itself that explanation is unconvincing because the March Group could have broadened out from the base they already had. Why bother to take over a second-order association essentially geared to labor relations and then fill it with CEOs, many of whom were active in the Business Council (and accordingly quite easy to recruit)? Why not, in other words, follow the shortest distance between two points? One's own hypothesis is that the comparative obscurity and unimportance of the Roundtable at that time *was* the attraction. After all, as already noted, the Business (Advisory) Council had always done its good work by stealth. Even after some years of operation, Commerce Secretary Roper's reply to an inquisitive reporter who wondered what his advisory council really did answered only: "Still waters run deep."[106] Thus a tradition was established, as a later generation of reporters would discover. It was a tradition that the roundtable proved ready and willing to sustain. Even today it discloses not only relatively little about itself (except for its policy committee, even its membership is kept secret), which may be defensible, but also about its easy access and possibly disproportionate role in the shaping of public policy, in which the public—the Republic—has a legitimate interest. In short, reverting to the early seventies, one wonders whether Big Business may not have made a third strategic decision—to work through a little known organization, the original roundtable, rather than sail then under its own colors. Even in 1975 the new roundtable was still being called "a low-profile outfit" (by Ronald Soble of the *Los Angeles Times*). Late in 1976 *Business Week* would report: "Formed in 1972, the roundtable worked behind the scenes for years."[107]

In any event, it is known that by 1974 one of the founders of the March Group, John Harper, was presiding over the Business Roundtable, which could boast about one hundred top executives. The original leaders took a back seat or "were gradually eased out."[108] The insurgents brought with them the policy of personal commitment on the part of the CEOs, a policy still practiced in the 1980s. There seems little reason to doubt the judgment of William Whyte, the well known lobbyist for U.S. Steel and personal friend of President Ford's, that "chief executive involvement" is the Roundtable's most important contribution. For as Mr. Harper expressed it: "No organization can hire the talent we can put together. It would be impossible."[109] Certainly, the personal commitment explains why the roundtable can manage with such a small permanent staff: an executive director, with his own small team, including three lobbyists, in Washington; and a president, with two executive directors (public information and construction) in New York. The executive director and the president were, at the beginning of the eighties, Mr. John Post, a former lawyer and businessman, and Mr. G. Wallace Bates, respectively.

Apart from the plain meaning of these developments, what did they signify for integration? No doubt, as Thomas Ferguson and Joel Rogers summed it up in 1979, "the roundtable represents an extraordinary consolidation of corporate political power."[110] Moreover, true to its origins, it embodies a keen interest in labor relations and collective bargaining, judging by the specification of the role *executive director—construction*, and through the network of "local user" groups that derives from the 1969 forerunner ("users" being those executives who commission, or employ, the construction contractors).[111] Judging by the complaints of the unions in 1979, "local users" are effective. It appears that these "local user" roundtables have no institutional ties to *the* roundtable.[112] So the arrangement is not as close as the one between the NAM and its affiliated national industrial councils. On the other hand, "local users" and the national body "march to the same drummer" (in the judgment of a *Fortune* writer, Gilbert Burck).[113] Since the probability of informal collaboration is surely high, and since *the* roundtable has taken a strong antiunion line in Washington, one may conclude that it does cater to management as employer as well as interest group—a kind of integration for the larger companies.

The roundtable even "corrals" elements of the Federal Reserve System—the twelve regional banks governed by a presidentially appointed board of seven and embracing the main commercial banks across the nation. The congressional antitrust investigation mentioned earlier found that 23 of the 108 directors of the twelve district banks had links with the roundtable. In the late seventies, five of the nine directors of the New York "Fed" were in the roundtable, including David Rockefeller (Chase Manhattan), a member of the policy committee. In fact, more than a quarter of the members of that committee were also members of the "Fed." As the late Wright Patman (Dem.-Texas), a chairman of the House Banking Committee but no admirer of the banking industry, said in 1978: "In many instances the roundtable and the Federal Reserve are one and the same—honeycombed with interlocking personnel."[114]

The survival into the eighties of the Business Council as an ostensible rival does not appear in fact to derogate from the integration sought by the roundtable. For, as reported in 1982, "today's roundtable essentially includes Business Council members."[115] In 1977, certainly, 37 of the 45 members of the roundtable's policy committee were members of the council.[116] More significantly, there has been much overlapping at the top of the two organizations, for example, *in and around*[117] 1981–82 (see Table 7-3).

TABLE 7–3   Business Roundtable and Business Council: Interlocking Leadership

ROUNDTABLE	COUNCIL
Clifton C. *Garvin,* Jr. (Exxon) chairman	executive committee
Walter B. *Wriston* (Citicorp) vice-chairman, executive & policy committees	chairman
Theodore F. *Brophy* (General Telephone & Electronics) vice-chairman	executive committee
James H. *Evans* (Union Pacific) vice-chairman	executive committee
In the late seventies/early eighties *(see note 117) such interlocks had included:*	
John D. *deButts* (AT&T) vice-chairman	chairman
Irving S. *Shapiro* (Du Pont) chairman	vice-chairman
Thomas A. *Murphy* (GM) chairman	vice-chairman
Charles L. *Brown* (AT&T) policy committee	vice-chairman
James L. *Ferguson* (General Foods) policy committee	executive committee
Robert S. *Hatfield* (Continental Group) policy committee	executive committee
Donald V. *Seibert* (J.C. Penney) policy committee	vice-chairman

TABLE 7–4   Roundtable, National Chamber, NAM: Interlocking Leadership

Business Roundtable policy committee	U.C. Chamber's Board	NAM Board
John W. *Hanley* chairman & CEO Monsanto	John W. *Hanley*	John W. *Hanley*
Charles J. *Pilliod*, Jr. Chairman, Goodyear Tire & Rubber (also cochairman, Roundtable)	Charles J. *Pilliod*, Jr.	Charles J. *Pilliod*, Jr.
W. H. Krome *George* chairman & CEO Alcoa		W. H. Krome *George*

If the Business Council is to a considerable degree the shadow of the Business Roundtable, integration, presumably, is the better served (although, by the same token, one wonders why two organizations continued to be needed). But where does all this leave the integrative role of the two older peaks, the NAM and the U.S. Chamber of Commerce, for the 1980s? This is very difficult to answer realistically. We know that the roundtable speaks for the great corporations, but many of these are members of the NAM and, nowadays, of the national chamber, which, as noted earlier, is no longer just "Main Street business." On the other hand, of course, the chamber still stands at the center of a great network of Main Streets, which it has learned to mobilize through a field force of thirty-three, based in six offices (1979). They sponsor congressional action committees for the study of legislative issues and for generating mail to Congress and the federal government.

Here again one observes, in the early eighties, substantial interlocking, remembering that the roundtable's policy committee hooks into the Business Council (again, see note 117. See also Table 7-4. The items in column 1 are correct for 1979; in both columns 2 and 3, for 1983).

In some such instances the representation is of the company rather than the CEO personally, e.g., Monsanto on the boards of the chamber and the NAM. Thinking of company rather than personal representation, one recalls the long service of Du Pont's Irving Shapiro on the roundtable: chairman and, by virtue of that, continuing with "emeritus" or "senior" status; vice-chairman/executive committee, Business Council; also Du Pont's representation on the board of the NAM (in the person—1983—of Edward G. Jefferson, chairman and CEO).[118]

All this may be thought of as superimposed upon the special relationship of the roundtable to the Business Council, of which some illustrations have been provided. Taken as a whole, these structures so far outlined ought to bring about a very considerable measure of integration, over the long haul. At least, they create a presumption of it, allowing for short-run differences, dissension, and possibly serious conflict (since no one supposes that Business is monolithic). Certainly, we are entitled to conclude that Business has created a comprehensive network, well staffed and richly endowed. Its very existence probably affords a substantial degree of influence, since, even if poorly utilized, it is something that government has to take into consideration. If that is correct, then one notes with interest the continued expansion of the network in this decade. Big Business had been "taken care of" over the years, in various ways. Eventually, Small Business followed suit. What about Medium Business (assuming one could distinguish)? In 1980 the American Business Conference was inaugurated. It was designed to bring together a hundred medium-size growth companies on the roundtable principle of representation *via* the CEOs. By 1983 it had apparently recruited some eighty to ninety such companies and had a staff of about ten working in Washington. It is too early to say whether the conference has been successful in demarcating new ground. A survey of high-level officials of major corporations in early 1983 seemed to imply that the Business Conference had yet to carve out a niche for itself (in the perception of these interviewed, of course).[119] But, on balance, we may surely conclude that, so far as we can tell from structure, Business, by the early 1980s, had positioned itself well for political representation and the exercise of political influence.

Taking one's clue from the frequency distribution of groups based in Washington (e.g., Table 7–2), one has given Business pride of place and extensive treatment. The other types of groups have their importance, but cannot here be treated as fully. Labor unions (rather than professional associations) are taken next in order to round out the industrial picture, i.e., in the belief that what goes on in this sector of the interest-group world is, not exclusively but to a significant degree, a continuation of industrial conflict by other means.

LABOR UNIONS

Their earlier attempts at integration were touched upon in the section on employers' organizations, to whose own development the union moves were "dialectically" related. The story was taken to the point where the AF of L was left virtually in command of the field as a union peak. Its range, of course, was limited. To say that it was confined to craft unions is not exact because it did include, for example, the United Mine Workers. In general, it is true that the integration pursued was horizontal, cutting across industries. Its rapid growth at the turn of the century (quadrupling membership in a five-year period) helped to concentrate the mind of the NAM on labor and industrial relations. "Organized capital," as the NAM president said, was coming to be "confronted by organized labor."

At that very point, however, "American trade unionism became the victim of a historical irony" (the distinguished labor historian, David Brody has written).[120] Along with of the AF of L, it was really organized for the mid- and late nineteenth century. But the early years of this century saw the accelerated development of very large corporations as a result, immediately, of the first great merger movement (chapter 2), coming on top of the internal growth of firms in 1880s. In these the "visible hand of managerial direction" was replacing "the invisible hand of market forces" (business historian Alfred Chandler would eventually write).[121] That visible hand was quickly raised to strike the unions a series of heavy blows. Much of the great corporate upsurge had at its base the marriage of mass production, then rapidly increasing, to the mass-distribution system already developed in the later decades of the previous century. Mass production means, of course, the elimination or reduction of skill and the "celebration" of the unskilled and the semiskilled workers, whom the AF of L failed to organize.[122] That changed only after a titanic struggle within the federation in the mid-1930s. Impaled on Labor's "rock of ages"—the craft principle—the reformers within the federation set up a committee "to encourage and promote organization of workers in the mass-production industries." They did not make it. But, having been thrown out of the federation, they—ten unions—did succeed in organizing the mass-production industries on industrial lines (e.g., the United Automobile Workers, and the United Steelworkers). By 1938 the membership of the new peak—renamed Congress of Industrial Organizations (CIO)—exceeded the AF of L's by some four hundred thousand although the older body soon recovered ground and outdistanced the new body from 1942 onward.

That was not the only flaw in the integrative structure. A substantial number of unions (with a membership of over a million in 1942) kept apart from both peaks and went their own way. After 1941 these independents included the United Mine Workers (UMWA), which John L. Lewis withdrew first from the AF of L and then from the CIO. Apart from a brief period of reaffiliation (to the AF of L) after World War II, the UMWA has been on the outside ever since.

In 1955 there were still 1.6 million unionists on the outside. But the cause of integration was then advanced by the merger of the two peaks, the newer one contributing about thirty unions (and more than five million members); the older one, well over a hundred unions and not far short of eleven million members. Thus the marriage produced 139 unions and sixteen million members. But the new structure suffered a severe jolt in 1957, when the AFL-CIO expelled the International Brotherhood of Teamsters for the corruption that seems to have plagued this union almost from its beginning at the turn of the century. Then, in 1968, Walter Reuther withdrew his Auto Workers after a dispute with George Meany, president of the central organization, which thus lost its two largest building blocks.

The Auto Workers returned to the fold in 1981, but the Teamsters remained outside. By then it was claiming 2.3 million members. No one doubted that it was a giant, although clearly still a flawed giant. More interesting, however, for the theme of integration was its changing composition. Originally for team drivers, it naturally took in the truckers, but these, by 1981, constituted only a quarter of the total membership. The rest were in warehousing (another traditional strength), but also in food processing, manufacturing, and the service industries (public as well as private). That is what labor reporter, Wilfrid C. Rodgers, meant by saying that the Teamsters "has evolved from a truckdrivers' union into a massive industrial union."[123] The characterization is common and understandable. But there seems to be advantage in reserving *industrial* for coverage of a whole industry, and using *general* to denote unions that spread themselves widely but without being confined to a craft or skill: for example, the Teamsters organizes workers in breweries, on farms and in canneries, in Safeway Supermarkets and A&P stores; clerks and technicians at Blue Cross/Blue Shield; sanitation men, especially in New York; airline employees; even policemen as well as a few tugboat captains, zoo-keepers, and teachers.[124]

Such "outreach" tendencies are not confined to the Teamsters. Within the AFL-CIO, even the Auto Workers, a classic industrial union, had (1983) "most of its dues-paying members in plants other than auto assembly plants," according to its president, Douglas Fraser. It had even spread into the nursing field and colleges.[125] Such an old craft union as the International Brotherhood of Electrical Workers (IBEW) has extended itself into "high tech" (e.g., in New England, Raytheon). In fact, it has become increasingly difficult to determine just *what* or *who* is being integrated by the major unions (of which, with over a million members in 1980, the IBEW is clearly one).[126]

As for integration at the top, the AFL-CIO advanced into the eighties with one prodigal son, the Auto Workers, returned home, but still lacking 66 unions (in 1978) that chose to keep their distance, including several that had once been in the CIO or the AFL-CIO. That meant there were 4.5 million unionists outside the AFL-CIO. Its own 108 unions brought together 15.5 million persons. Eight could each claim more than 250,000 women members.[127] It follows that the AFL-CIO integrated, in principle, rather more than three out of four of the American union members, within the framework of six out of ten of the national unions.

Having said that, one might well be challenged by the question: how much integration (in principle) are you really talking about? It is true that the density even of unions as a whole, not just AFL-CIO, is rather dismal (density equals union membership as a proportion of total labor force, or some other such denominator). The total labor force density was over 24 percent in 1955, but less than 20 percent in 1978.

Of course, to make "total labor force" the denominator is ill-advised (except for those who take pleasure in the unions' discomfiture). Obviously, substantial numbers of people within the total labor force (e.g., middle managers, supervisors, etc.) are simply not available, by role or attitude, for recruitment into unions. Subtracted, they reduce the denominator, and so increase the density, very considerably. Even so, if we replace *total* labor by *nonagricultural* labor, whose sphere "most closely approximates the area of potential organization,"[128] then we still find numbers that are perturbing for the world of Labor. Density in that more limited sense was over 33 percent in 1955 but barely 24 percent in 1978. Here again the denominator should be reduced, increasing density. But it has to be admitted that less and less was being integrated, even in principle.

The AFL-CIO itself exhibited the same tendency, with obvious implications for its role as an interest group. But this was also being gradually shaped by the profound change in its composition. Its increase in the late seventies (1976–78) came from the five unions,[129] three of which derived from what Australian economist Colin Clark called the tertiary (or services) sector:[130]

1. American Federation of State, County and Municipal Employees (AFSCME) (1936)
2. American Federation of Government Employees (AFGE) (1932). In fact, between 1960 and 1978, these two "at least tripled in size,"[131] although during the seventies the AFGE was losing some of the ground gained earlier. These of course are public-sector unions. By 1980 the AFGE had about a quarter of a million members; the AFSCME, more than a million. By 1983 it would be ranked second in the AFL-CIO.[132]
3. The Service Employees International Union (SEIU) (1932) was the third of the growing trio (1976–78) within the tertiary sector. By 1980 it had collected 650,000 members, an increase of 67 percent over 1968, and stood then in seventh place in the hierarchy. Here again, obviously, is another union very different in kind from the traditional leaders, craft or industrial.

And who was then no. 1, AFL-CIO? The United Food and Commercial Workers Union, which many of us had only just heard of. Some of the growth (1976–78) noted above had come through merger, notably the absorption into the AFSCME of the Civil Service Employees Association, an accession of strength of 207,000 (in our terms, a furthering of integration, since what had been *associational* now became *unionist*). But the most spectacular of mergers in the late seventies/early eighties was the one that brought together (1979) the Retail Clerks International Union (736,000), which could trace its history to the early years of the AF of L, and the Amalgamated Meat Cutters and Butcher Workmen (500,000), which belonged to the same era, and whose roots, locally extended as far as the Knights of Labor. From that marriage came the Food and Commercial Workers. In 1983, even after the return of the Auto Workers, it was the largest union in the AFL-CIO. How surprised the retail clerks, butchers, and slaughterers of a century ago would be if they returned to the scene today to find their union at the top of the ladder.

Add in the Communications Workers (650,000), the Hotel Employees and Restaurant Employees International Union (400,000),[133] the rapidly growing American Federation of Teachers (up to 500,000 by 1980), etc., and we see very clearly that, once again, the very foundation of the central body has shifted. What exactly this means for the AFL-CIO as an interest group is difficult, and perhaps too early, to determine. But already, it appears to a close observer, these unions rooted in the service industries "often become the swing vote that dictates power between the old line craft unions and industrial unions within the AFL-CIO hierarchy."[134] Given the trend toward the tertiary, one may predict that, before the century is out, unions deriving from the service industries will no longer be simply "the swing vote" but predominant, even commanding, within the central body. But how much they, and so the AFL-CIO, will have to command—how many troops—is at present uncertain.

PROFESSIONAL ASSOCIATIONS

Central to the growth of the tertiary sector are the professions, which may indeed constitute its most significant component. As with the Hotel and Restaurant Employees and other such unions, professional associations reflect the provision of a service, but one embodying "the application of special knowledge requiring long training, the exercise of discretion, and a commitment to some kind of standard to which the pursuit of self-interest is subordinated."[135] That statement, its author (Corinne Lathrop Gilb) would probably agree, expresses the professional ideal, not necessarily the practice.

Part of the political significance of the professionals derives from the leadership roles they have assumed, but what mainly matters here is that, as S. M. Lipset and Mildred Schwartz summed it up long ago, they "are among the best organized occupational groups. As such, they have the capacity to serve as major interest groups which channel political communication and affect political decisions."[136] A list would of course be endless, but this is not so much a problem of counting as such as of identifying the professions with certainty. In this context, the long-term trend has been to turn "mere" occupations into professions. It is often impossible to tell from the published record whether the threshold has been reached and passed. For example, what of the National Association of Social Workers (former 1945, re-formed 1955)? Dr. Gilb put it in the "major national professional" category. "Major, national" it is (ninety thousand in 1983). But is social work a profession in the same sense as law and medicine? What of the American Chiropractic Association (originally 1930, re-formed 1963)? The therapy seems to have helped people of one's acquaintance, but is regarded with scepticism by the American Medical Association. The case of schoolteachers is of particular interest. The "first afoot," the National Education Association (NEA), whose roots extend to 1857, stressed teaching as a profession. The self-perception of those Chicago teachers who launched the AFT in World War I may well have been different. We know, at least, that they promptly threw in their lot with organized labor by affiliating to the AF of L, to whose successor they still cling. The NEA stands aloof, but with 1.7 million members (1983), it is not only larger than any AFL-CIO union but has also been forced by competition into collective bargaining, i.e., *de facto* to be more like a "regular" labor union.

Of more immediate significance for us is the extent to which these associations have been politicized. The NEA, AFT, and Social Workers, for example, all have or support political action committees. Even the Chiropractors have joined in the PAC fun. They had long been an active interest group, e.g., opposing (1972) the legalization of abortion and of marijuana and other drugs,[137] but more persistently in pursuit of professional acceptance and recognition, notably by the American Medical Association. Challenged in the courts, the AMA retreated a little in 1980, its new code of ethics leaving individual physicians free to decide whether "to associate with chiropractors or other practitioners." That concession was enough to keep the American College of Surgeons from sending a fraternal delegate to the AMA's 1980 convention.[138]

Evidently, the subject is a very large one. Even narrowed to the professions-as-interest groups (as defined in chapter 2), it is worthy of a book that has yet to be written. Here all one can do is erect a few signposts to some features of three professions that "project" major interest groups: medicine, law, and education. The NEA has already crossed our path. For about two generations (counting from its rebirth in 1870 under its present name), it contributed less to the integration of public school teachers than might have been expected, since it was dominated by college professors and school superintendents. But "by 1925 the classroom teacher had been made a first-class NEA citizen,"[139] meaning that she (or he) could attend the representative assembly as a delegate from the local/state affiliates and make her (or his) voice heard. Even so, as late as 1968 (according to an independent critic, James D. Koerner), density—for the teachers—was only 52 percent[140] in the NEA as such, i.e., as distinct from the state and local affiliates, which are, with regional variations, well patronized.

By 1975 the NEA had circumnavigated that problem, completing what Marshall Donley called "its unification of affiliates."[141] From then on, if you—a public school teacher—joined the state or local association, you were also deemed to have joined the NEA, which automatically raised the density as well as the "mere" total, impressive as that was (and is). No wonder that presidential candidate Jimmy Carter was pleased in 1976 to receive the NEA endorsement. The price, it became increasingly clear, was the detachment of Education from Health, Education and Welfare. To many detached observers, HEW was an administrative monstrosity dating from the Eisenhower era. But that did not make its demolition any the easier even though President Carter played his part as promised. What opponents feared was that an independent department of education would not be all that independent of the NEA. So they put together a Committee Against a Separate Department of Education to counter the NEA-led coalition of about one hundred interest groups from the field. The committee included the AFT, the AFL-CIO itself, famous universities ranging from Harvard and Columbia to Michigan and California, and the Association of American Colleges, representing (since 1915) the liberal-arts colleges. Despite that, the legislation passed in the fall of 1979 and a secretary of education was installed before Christmas.[142] More than any other organization, the NEA could take credit for having "pulled it off." The election of President Reagan in 1980 threatened to undo its handiwork, but in 1983 the department was still surviving. By then, in any case, with a membership exceeded only by the Teamsters, and integrating fifty-three state, and perhaps ten thousand local, groups, the NEA could face the future with equanimity.

The NEA's organizational success was not achieved directly at the expense of the rival AFT, which, apart from its own sources of energy, had the help of a friend. This was the Industrial Union Department (IUD) of the AFL-CIO, which Walter Reuther of the Auto Workers (that classic industrial union) had seen as a power base (only to be ultimately disappointed) after the two peaks had been reunited in 1955. It was he (reported Joseph Monsen and Mark Cannon) who had the IUD (a) provide two part-time organizers for the AFT recruiting drive in the late fifties/early sixties and (b) subsidize three of the AFT's own organizers, full-time, for the same purpose, not to mention generous financial support.[143] One result was that in 1961 the AFT local in New York City (United Federation of Teachers) knocked out the NEA as the bargaining unit there—a famous victory. That in turn greatly stimulated successful organizing drives in large school systems across the nation, and put some writing on the wall for the NEA. The latter learned another lesson, proceeding to forge an unofficial link to the AFL-CIO through the AFSCME,[144] then run by (the late) Jerry Wurf, a champion worthy of the AFT's president, Albert Shanker.

The AFT's organizing drive *was* achieved at some other body's expense, that of the American Association of University Professors (AAUP), formed in 1915, essentially to protect academic freedom. By the midseventies the AFT had already recruited some 40,000 college teachers, at a time when the AAUP itself could boast of only about 90,000 such; the NEA had also collected some college teachers. Since there were, perhaps, 600,000 college faculty "available," the AAUP's density was made to seem even less impressive. By 1983 its total had fallen below 70,000.

Of course, the forty thousand college teachers did not constitute the AFT's staple diet, being only some 9 percent of the total membership at that time. The K–12 teachers made up the 91 percent, or 410,000, concentrated "largely in the urban centers of the predominantly urban states," as Stephen K. Bailey put it.[145] By 1983 the grand total reached 580,000 on the basis of some 2000 locals. All in all, schoolteachers are well provided for. The degree of integration would be greater still if the NEA and AFT merged, which seemed on the cards in 1973–74, but did not happen. Even so, the total achievement is remarkable.

Of course, the integration of the teachers is only a part of the story. In telling the rest of it, one could vividly illustrate the general theme of differentiation-integration. Thus, to manage the schools there were (in 1977) some 87,000 elected officials ensconced in about 15,000 school districts. To integrate the school board members (sometimes known as "school trustees"), other structures had been developed, the state associations. These in turn were to be integrated by what used in fact to be called the National Council of State School Boards Associations, a title now shortened to National School Boards Association (whose roots extend to 1940). This joined hands with many others in the NEA. With some 1600 other organizations (such as the National Catholic Educational Association, 1904, and the American Library Association, 1876), the NEA was a cog in a very big wheel, the American Council on Education (ACE, 1918).

The story, however, cannot be continued here, essentially for lack of space. But, on present knowledge, it would not in any case be very profitable to continue further because there is a limit to what we can learn from form, or "anatomy," without the monographic (or detailed) studies of the "physiology," which we generally lack. We see that the NEA, which was always a stock example in textbooks of a great educational peak, has very largely turned into a teachers' union. We may also learn that the ACE has always tilted toward higher education. It was a vice-president of the ACE who pointed out in 1975 that all chairpersons had been college or university presidents, and that half of the previous thirteen had been drawn from the Ivy Leagues and the land-grant universities of high esteem.[146]

Besides, our principal concern in the end is with political physiology, or working, i.e., political significance. One list of Washington-based associations reputed[147] to rank high in "representational effectiveness" in education policy, 1973–74, contained twenty names. Some specialists thought then that "any list of twenty is too long by two-thirds."[148] Such critics would have done better to point out that a list containing the NEA, the National Catholic Educational Association, the AFT, the American Library Association, the National Audio-Visual Association (a trade body), as well as the ACE and the National Association of State Universities and Land-Grant Colleges (1887), was employing too broad a concept of education policy. The question always is: *effective* over *what range of* education (or any other form of public) policy? Thus the AFT did not count in the making of higher-education policy, nor the State Universities and Land-Grant Colleges in elementary and secondary, so they should not be mentioned in the same breath. The latter occupied a central position in higher education, as did the more "junior" American Association of State Colleges and Universities (1961), the Association of American Universities (1900), representing the fifty or so "majors," as did some others, including of course the peak, the ACE. In the midseventies, the ACE was bringing together about a dozen such bodies for a monthly meeting in Washington of their leading officials. Like the Business Roundtable, no substitutes or surrogates were permitted.

Also writing in 1975, Norman C. Thomas followed the correct procedure in distinguishing between policy *ranges*. Thus, for *elementary and secondary* education, he reported the existence of a "big six," including the first five listed above in the sentence starting "Such critics . . ." The sixth came as a surprise: the U.S. Chamber of Commerce. But an official of one of the five confided that the chamber was "the only effective opposition to us." Professor Thomas seemed to accept that assessment, or at least he did not dispute the chamber's place among the six.[149]

Whether, in the mideighties, the educational "establishment" still has *that* "big six" at its core is not altogether clear as one writes. But no doubt *an* establishment[150] persists, for each policy range. That, in a way, is what *interest-group politics* means.

If *Medicine* were interpreted broadly, hundreds of organizations would be on parade. One would see, toward the front, the American Dental Association (1859): 140,000 members and a political action committee ($628,000 for the 1982 election). Then there would be the endodontists (1969), those who bore the root canals, and many others, including the dental hygienists, also supporters of a PAC. The American Veterinary Medical Association (1863), with some thirty-five thousand members and a PAC, would also be on parade. Approaching Medicine in the narrower sense, one would alight upon the American Nurses Association (1869), which speaks for about 170,000 registered nurses. The ANA is clearly integrative: nine hundred district associations drawn together by fifty-three state and territorial associations whose lines converge in the peak itself. Such is the way of the world in the 1980s that the ANA maintains both a PAC and a Washington office. Even the far smaller National Federation of Licensed Practical Nurses (1949) has deemed it prudent to sponsor a PAC and retain a Washington representative.

Organizations of physicians and surgeons are dazzlingly varied, corresponding to the seemingly endless specialisms and subspecialisms. There is even American Holistic Medical Association (1978) to encourage treating the patient in the round, or as a whole person instead of a "slice" or bit of one. Some are essentially technical and scientific, like those resembling England's two highly esteemed royal colleges: the American College of Surgeons (1913) and the American College of Physicians (1915). The National Medical Association (1895) caters for black physicians.

More political are the American Academy of Family Physicians (1947), with a membership of some fifty thousand and a PAC, and of course the American Medical Association, founded a hundred years earlier. Based on close to two thousand state and regional medical societies, the AMA is integrative in that territorial sense, but its hold on the profession weakened during the 1970s. Some statistics, using the concept of full dues-paying membership, may be considered too "constraining." More favorable to the association is the concept of "active private-practice physicians on the AMA rolls," which yielded a total of some 170,000 for 1979 (apart from the 40,000 students and residents). Even so, that was little advance on 1965 (165,000 or so), and the denominator had increased to 427,000 (1978) as against 292,000 doctors in 1965. It followed that density had dropped from almost 57 percent in 1965 to under 39 percent in 1978, when some 164,000 such physicians had been in membership.[151] That reflected in some degree "disenchantment with its past policies," as association officials admitted to journalist Robert Reinhold in 1980.[152] They were referring to the AMA's denunciation of such policies as Medicare in the midsixties. From about that time, indeed, "most of the major health programs" enacted had been passed over the strong opposition of the AMA.[153]

That, however, should not be taken as indicative of its influence on public policy. The association stopped compulsory national health insurance, even though President Truman wanted it. That was due more than anything to the brilliant campaign waged, 1949–52, by the association's hired gun, the husband-and-wife p.r. team of Whitaker and Baxter.[154] Its help to the hospital associations in the 1979 defeat of President Carter's proposal for mandatory cost containment was called, by one of their officials, "absolutely critical."[155]

What this all means, in any case, is that the AMA, although it does have its scientific side, is an intensely political body. Its Washington office included five full-time lobbyists in 1979. Its political instrument, AMPAC, drawing from the PACs of the state associations, had just disbursed (1977–78) more than $1.6 million to congressional candidates. In addition, AMPAC had spent some $47,000 independently on regional magazine advertising for the benefit of seventeen candidates. Even counting only the acknowledged PAC expenditure, the AMA was clearly no. 1. For the 1982 elections it had to yield pride of place to the realtors ($2.2 million) in the rank order of most generous PAC contributors to congressional candidates. But its $1.7 million was still enormous.[156]

That number rings a bell: it is just about what AMA political action committees in ten states spent for the *1980* state legislative elections. That actually exceeded, by some $391,000, what AMPAC had contributed to federal candidates for 1980. For 1982 the California Medical PAC was on top for at least three-quarters of its cycle (January 1981 to June 1982): some $442,000.[157] Clearly, if we consistently put it all together instead of limiting ourselves to the federal, we would reach some rather staggering sums of money spent by doctors for political influence, year in, year out. Obviously only a very rich profession could afford it. Whether, as was said in 1971, "thirty to forty percent of doctors were making a financial killing in medicine" and "unnecessary surgery (was) being performed,"[158] is hardly for the outside layman to judge. For saying it, Dr. John H. Knowles, director of the famous Massachusetts General Hospital (when appointed at age thirty-five, the youngest ever), was censured by the AMA's Committee on Ethics and

Discipline.[159] But the late Dr. Knowles was right to point (in effect) to what makes possible the AMA's outstanding interest-group role: "It doesn't take any great insight to observe that in a profession where the median income now stands at nearly $50,000 a year a substantial percentage of doctors are making a killing."[160]

A decade or so later (1981 through November 1982), the AMA would raise, but not entirely disburse for that election, some $2.4 million. Among the associational PACs, only the National Association of Realtors raised more ($2.98 million), and it then had 620,000 in membership.

In touching upon the legal profession in the context of interest groups, one cannot limit oneself to the representative bodies. The broadest of these is the American Bar Association (1878). It is *the* integrative organization (280,000 in 1982, making for a density of rather more than 50 percent, which, by American standards, is considerable). On the other hand, although it lobbies hard and effectively, it has not (1983) established a PAC, which sets it off from the NEA, AMA, and many others at that level. The Association of Trial Lawyers of America (1946) does sponsor a PAC, particularly to oppose "no fault" car insurance (a cause the ABA once embraced but thought better of, since, at its best, it had striven to transcend the mere self-interest of the profession). The Association of Trial Lawyers is a substantial body (forty-to-fifty thousand members) but clearly limited in range.

In any case, in law, unlike, for the most part, medicine and education, the "working units" at the base are often enough important interest groups in their own right. To begin with there were, in 1982, about fifty law firms in the U.S. each employing more than two hundred lawyers. The top dozen may be said to have each employed three hundred or more—although, strictly, no. 12 (O'Melveny & Myers, Los Angeles) had 298—with "a supporting cast of thousands" (as journalist Tamar Lewin put it) and yearly billings of $40 million *plus*.[161] Not one of these, nor indeed any of the top two dozen, was located in Washington, D.C., yet they and other such leading firms impinged upon public policy in their own special way. Antitrust lawsuits provide a ready example. These kept Donovan, Newton & Irvine (New York) busy for about two decades. Another New York firm, Weil, Gotshal & Manges grew rapidly in part by specializing in antitrust. In 1951 it employed 13 lawyers. By 1982 it had 259 lawyers and ranked no. 16 in the nation. Presumably some of the $14.8 million paid by AT & T in 1981 to Sidley & Austin, Chicago (then ranked no. 5 nationally), and some of the $4.1 million so disbursed in 1979 had to do with the Justice Department's suit, started in 1974, to break up the Bell system. So, too, with the $7.8 million the corporation paid Dewey, Ballantine, Bushby, Palmer & Wood (New York) in 1981.[162]

The Washington law firms are smaller (only ten in the top two hundred in 1982) but tend of course to be more directly and persistently engaged as interest groups. Indeed, in the judgment of a close observer of the Washington scene (Bryce Nelson, *Los Angeles Times*) writing in 1980:

Washington lawyers are not only among the wealthiest in the world but are also among the most important players in the game of determining national policy. . . . The increase in firms that openly specialize in lobbying Congress and in firms that form political action committees to give money directly to political candidates has been substantial.[163]

This "small world of big Washington lawyers"[164] will be elaborated upon a little (it has not been studied in depth by political scientists) when we turn to the subject of lobbyists and lobbying within the context of the methods employed by interest groups to achieve their objectives.

AGRICULTURE

Agriculture and agricultural organization are so much a part of the American epic that it is hard *not* to delve into the past. Here the temptation must be resisted. One must confine oneself to a few analytical points, although placed within their historical contexts (as, ideally, they always should be in the social sciences, at least to begin with).

Think first about the origins of groups (chapter 2). The catalyst for the first national body—the Grange—was someone working then for the U.S. Department of Agriculture (USDA), Oliver Hudson Kelley. Travelling through the South in 1866 on official business, he perceived the poverty, ignorance, and lack of social amenities in the farming areas. With others he launched in 1867 the National Order of the Patrons of Husbandry, built on the Masonic model (Kelley and some of the other initiators had been "made"). The "units" to be thus integrated were the *granges*, meaning farmhouses, but that was the name that caught on for the whole. Again, some two generations later, the ground for the American Farm Bureau Federation was prepared by Binghamton Chamber of Commerce in Broome County, New York, whose secretary in particular perceived the need to rejuvenate local agriculture and so keep a proper balance, economic and social, between town and country, urban and rural. Out of the chamber's concern came a county agent, appointed by USDA as early as 1911, who would work with local groups (or bureaus) to spread knowledge of new and improved farming methods. In part, the county agent proceeded to create local organizations by getting help from the existing networks, notably the Grange's, which bears upon the Olson problem discussed in chapter 3. Even more relevant to that is the launching of the agricultural extension service in 1914 (the Smith-Lever Act) to carry the good scientific news far and wide. The farm bureau movement "piggy backed" across the East and Middle West on the extension service, and eventually (1919–20) crystallized as the American Farm Bureau Federation. Once again private interests had been developed "under public initiative" (as a contemporary historian expressed it).[165] Once again, accordingly, we observe some blurring of the line between private and public, society and state.

This manifestation of it has both interesting aspects and ironic over-
tones. Why did the public authorities encourage and stimulate a new organization rather than build upon an existing one? Having suffered a great fall
(in membership) in the last quarter of the nineteenth century, the Grange
had gradually recovered in the twentieth. By 1910 it had about 223,000
family memberships. From 1902 the Farmers (Educational and Cooperative)
Union had also been available. This, known nowadays as the National
Farmers Union, had originally filled the gap left in the South by the
Farmers' Alliance, which earlier, in the 1880s, had filled the gap left there
by the decline of the Grange and grown also in the North. By 1910 the
Farmers Union was also considerable: about 116,000 families. But, like the
Grange, it was, at the time, a "secret" ritualized organization and in that
(and perhaps other senses) an exclusive one. As a USDA official explained,
the public authorities wanted a "nonsecret . . . permanent institution open
to all the farmers in the county." Besides, among other reasons, how jealous
(he went on) the others[166] would be "by apparent favoritism in the selection
of one organization in preference to another."[167]

The irony is that the very organization set up (among other reasons) to
ward off charges of favoritism quickly came to be seen by the older bodies as
very much the favorite of the public authorities, specifically the Agricultural
Extension Service of the USDA. No doubt, this way of expressing it is legalis-
tic. The county agent did not look to Washington but to county government
and to the local farm bureaus. Thus the Farm Bureau Federation (wrote
historian Donald Holley) "assumed a quasi-public status, developing close ties
with the extension service system and monopolizing the machinery of agricultural administration."[168] Yet the county agent remained (and remains) a public
official. Such a symbiotic relationship, in which of course the private/public
distinction tended to be submerged, must largely account for the astonishing
organizational success of the federation, which "flashed" from nothing much at
all, and in no time at all, to a total larger than the Grange's. The exact figure
is not cited because different sources give different totals; but the hothouse
growth in two or three years is a fact.

Thus, in agriculture as in industry and commerce as well as, up to a
point, the world of Labor, the basic shape of the representational structure
was drawn in the period between the Civil War and the First World War, or
its immediate aftermath. But no peak had emerged. Even during the more
recent war, when government wanted sectors or industries to speak with a
single voice, two representative bodies had sprung up—one, the Farmer's
National War Council, from the "progressive state granges,"[169] some State
Farmers Unions, and the American Society of Equity; the other, the National
Board of Farm Organizations, which seems to have faded away by the end of
the twenties, revealing some overlap but taking in the organized dairymen
and resting essentially on the National Farmers Union. After the Farm Bureau Federation had shot up as if from a launching pad, some may have

expected it to become *the* peak. But, as historian Gilbert Fite would recall, writing in 1956:

> if the sons of toil expected that they would now have a single, unified voice in Washington, they were doomed to disappointment. From the early 1920s to the present time there has been a weakening lack of unity among the organizations which are supposed to speak for the nation's farmers.[170]

Even as he wrote, those who, in the Farm Bureau heartland out West, were forming what came to be called the National Farmers Organization (Corning, Iowa, 1955) were compounding the disunity. Its original purpose was specialized: to bargain on behalf of farmer-members with dealers or processors or any others on the chain of their supply-and-demand. The obvious inference is correct: this was indeed a protest movement well within the tradition of agrarian radicalism. Any doubt on that score would have been dispelled when, in the 1960s, the NFO attempted "withholding," the hayseed equivalent of a workingmen's strike, instances of which produced some violence (as in Britain).[171] For all sorts of reasons, "withholding" did not work (in either country). From the midseventies, direct selling (farmer-consumer) seems to have paid off a little. But gradually the NFO turned into a more "orthodox" interest group. By 1982 it had thirty to forty thousand members, concentrated in Iowa and Missouri. If its heart still belonged to Corning, Iowa, it was prudent enough to maintain an office in Washington, D.C. and the—by then—almost inevitable PAC.

By this time the other three general bodies had been "regular" interest groups for about two generations, i.e., since about the end of World War I. As in so many other ways, those wartime years were truly years of profound transition. Having started out fraternal or "expressive," the Grange soon embraced politics. When that attachment cooled, other groups (Farmers' Alliances, Populist party) carried the torch along other routes. By 1900 it had burned out. Just after the turn of the century, the Farmers Union appeared (again in Texas, where, from the organizational evidence alone, people must have been "hurting" for quite a long time). There followed a period of two happy decades, part of it blissful: the golden age of agriculture, in which farmers prospered but their organizations correspondingly languished. The bubble burst in 1920, wiping the organizational slate clean; in effect, the modern history of the farmers' movement starts about then, or a littler earlier. Some farmers were already taking the other road, as through the Nonpartisan League of North Dakota (1915), which, spreading out a little, especially into Minnesota, was a political party in all but name. Otherwise farmers settled down as interest groups rather than parties. Thus, the Grange had maintained legislative committees ever since 1885 but "had considered that the maintenance of a paid representative in Washington smacked too much of 'lobbying'."[172] In 1919 it bent before the wind and appointed such a person: T.C.

Atkeson, farmer, lawyer, professor, college president, who stayed until 1927. The Farm Bureau followed suit in 1920, but in what turned out to be a portent for the future, it went one better by taking on a professional p.r. man: Gray Silver, from West Virginia (like Atkeson). The Farmers Union also had representation in Washington from about this time.

Exactly how these lined up organizationally in the 1980s is difficult to determine. The basic problem has always been that they do not count members in the same way. Thus in 1960 the Grange counted individuals; the Farm Bureau, families. Some state farm bureaus, the actual membership "units," stipulated that 50 percent of an applicant's income must come from farming, which still left the door wide open. Similarly, the Farmers Union included businesspersons, those who kept farms supplied with essentials or marketed farm products. The NFO took those farmers or farm owners who had agreed to the basic strategy.[173]

In a rare attempt at securing comparability, Robert L. Tontz painstakingly worked his way through the organizations' records, discussed the question with their officials, and made various adjustments—particularly by "deflating" the Grange's individual memberships to a family basis—to produce this result.[174] As you see, even this material is not fully satisfactory, but it does appear to quantify the trends correctly and on a comparable foundation. The choice of years (see Table 7-5) was partly governed by the wish to bring out turning-points.

It follows that membership totals claimed for the 1980s (or any time) should be received with great caution. For 1982 the Farm Bureau claimed to integrate nearly three thousand bureaus and 3.2 million farm families. The Grange (according to its information director, Judy Massabny) had 430,000, stabilized during the seventies after an acknowledged decline. Northern New England even reported the first membership gains in years: in Maine, since the 1950s (an increase of 34 in 1981 over 1980); New Hampshire, since the 1930s (102 in 1982 over 1981).[175] The Farmers Union counted 300,000 farm families. As noted earlier, the NFO was far smaller.

What density these numbers imply is anybody's guess. When, in 1958, Samuel Beer wrote his landmark article comparing group representation in Britain and the United States, he put the density for the American farmers

TABLE 7–5 Family Memberships of general farmers' organizations

	1930	1933	1950	MID-1950s	1960
Farm Bureau	321,000	163,000	1,450,000	1,623,000[1]	1,600,000
The Grange	316,000		442,000		394,000
Farmers Union		77,900		278,000[2]	

1. 1955
2. 1956

organized at "no more than 30 percent" and that was spread out among three general organizations and some minor ones, as against the 90 percent density concentrated in one organization (the National Farmers' Union) in Britain. In the 1980s the presence of the NFO (only just formed when Professor Beer was writing) widens the spread somewhat. More seriously, it is impossible to be sure of the numerator because memberships are still counted in different ways. The denominator (expressing the total number available to be recruited as members) is easy to determine if the appropriate concept is total agricultural employment. This "sole or primary agricultural employment of persons sixteen years old and older" amounted to just under 3.3 million in 1979. But what did that mean, politically? Something like a half of them did not live on the farms. The farm operators—persons self-employed in agriculture— amounted to 1.6 million, but only an even 1.1 million of them actually lived on farms. The remaining third lived in nonfarm homes in the open country or even in towns. Again, only one farm family in twelve relied solely on farming for their income: most of the others brought in wages or salaries.[176] These cross-cutting affiliations (or overlapping memberships) seem likely to have political significance, but what it is, one is at present in no position to say. If one had to guess the density (as an index of potential power), one would put it at about 40 percent in the early 1980s.

As to integration, some sectors did integrate to a remarkable degree, providing a firm foundation for interest-group roles. The dairy industry affords a striking example. Politically, it had been served from 1916 by the National Milk Producers Federation. But the industry suffered from a "lack of coordination," as the federation itself told the Senate Agriculture Committee in 1933.[177] That weakness was redressed in the most direct possible way in the late 1960s by the creation of dairy cooperatives on a grand scale. Between 1967 and 1970 more than 170 local cooperatives carrying seventy thousand members merged into four "mega-cooperatives" (echoing "mega-corporations," for industrial giants like Exxon and General Electric):

ASSOCIATED MILK PRODUCERS, INC. (AMPI), 1969.   Rooted in Texas and Arkansas through Milk Producers Inc. (1967), this had extended itself as far north as Minnesota, then joining with fourteen co-ops in the Chicago area to bring about the AMPI. In 1971 it added a large Wisconsin co-op to the team. By 1974 it had forty thousand members in twenty states and controlled 75 percent of the milk supplies in many major markets, such as Chicago; Houston, Dallas, San Antonio; Indianapolis; and Oklahoma City. That meant "big money. Sales totalled $1.1 billion" in the year ended June 30, 1973, reported Robert A. Wright from San Antonio.[178] It also meant big political money, potentially almost $4 million a year (based on a voluntary contribution of $99.90 per member, an amount chosen to escape the reporting requirement that starts ten cents higher). As will be touched upon, AMPI through its political instrument, TAPE, was one of those cooperatives that actualized its potential power to great and startling effect during the Nixon administration. In 1972 TAPE turned into CTAPE, Committe for Thorough Agricultural Political Education. It was not quite clear who was to be thoroughly politically educated. Certainly, on its track record up to that time, the AMPI did not need any political education.

MID-AMERICA DAIRYMEN, INC. (MID-AM), 1968.   This was an amalgamation of thirty-one cooperatives in Iowa, Kansas, Illinois, and Missouri (where, in Springfield, it placed its headquarters). It settled down at about half the size of AMPI, which it emulated by soon adopting (1970) an interest-group role. Its instrument was ADEPT (Agricultural and Dairy Educational Political Trust).

DAIRYMEN, INC., 1968.   Originally eight cooperatives in the South (Virginia to Louisiana), Dairymen later emerged with others, extending as far as Indiana but remaining essentially southern. It settled down at about ten thousand members, and quickly adopted an interest-group role, if mainly a supportive one, *via* SPACE (Special Political Agricultural Community Education).[179]

The fourth "mega-cooperative" (Milk Marketing Inc., 1970, whose center of gravity was originally Ohio) seems to have been less interesting politically. But eventually organizing ten thousand members, it contributed to integration. Altogether, these (with three other) mergers meant that by 1971 seven cooperatives could "speak . . . for one-half of the U.S. milk supply . . . in contrast to more than one hundred co-ops speaking for the same volume of milk in the same number of markets five years ago."

That is integration. The political meaning of such integration is that it provided the financial and administrative basis for a political machine. Every month the parent cooperative would be mailing out the checks due for milk to their member-farmers. A check-off of rather more than $8 per head would yield the fraction less than $100 a year set for each contributor. Even John Connally at the Treasury was impressed. As he explained it to President Nixon and the others at the March 23 (1971) meeting:

> These dairymen are organized; they're adamant; they're militant. This particular group, AMPT, which is the American Milk Producers Institute or something, I uh, represents about forty thousand people. Frankly, they tap these fellows—I believe it's one-third of one percent of their total sales or $99 a year whichever is . . .

(President Nixon, interjecting: Like a union)

> Oh, it's a checkoff. No question about it. And they're meeting, and they're having meetings . . . they're amassing an enormous amount of money that they're going to put into political activities, very frankly. . . . They've got . . . a

legitimate cause. I wouldn't recommend that . . . you do that if it didn't have any merit to it. . . . They're doing some things that I think are a little strong-armed tactics, perhaps, in . . . the organizing . . . but . . . I don't criticize that unless we are prepared to take on business and labor and all at the same time. There's no point denying the farmer what's a practice for the labor; and . . . so . . . I wouldn't judge it on a moral basis.[180]

Certainly, the arithmetic was correct. The potential "interest-group" income for the three giant co-ops was very nearly $7 million a year. That potential must have been substantially actualized since they could promise President Nixon a cool $2 million for his reelection campaign. Of course that was an investment, not a gift of charity. And the first installment of the return was received with gratifying speed: an increase in the support price of milk of $500–700 million (presumably in a full year, perhaps $300 million in the 1971 milk checks from the federal government). Even so, not every group has such an enviable cash flow as to permit so profitable a political investment.

However, the dairy co-ops and their interest-group *alter egos* were brilliant exceptions to the general finding that the "cause" of integration was not advanced in the seventies and early eighties but remained essentially as it was in the midsixties, when agricultural economist Don Paarlberg characterized it as "a babel of voices." The noise would be sharply increased if one introduced the commodity organization so far neglected except for dairy products. Professor Paarlberg noted that "American agriculture produces and sells some 250 farm products," from a(vocados) to z(innias), and that "many" of their producers had also produced associations.[181] These, no doubt, run into hundreds. But how many are politically interesting? Another authority, Ross Talbot, once endorsed the view that an "estimated fifty to sixty special commodity groups are more or less active on the political scene."[182] These would include the National Wool Growers Association (1865), the Cotton Council of America (1938), the National Association of Wheat Growers (1950), the National Corn Growers Association (1957), the Tobacco Institute (1958), and the National Cattlemen's Association (1977). In principle, these were in themselves integrative, e.g., the Wheat Growers (sixteen state associations, with a claimed membership of seventy-nine thousand, in 1982). But generally the separatist organization along commodity lines pointed the other way, a tendency not arrested by the launching of a National Conference of Commodity Organizations. And, politically, each one cut its own swathe: the Wool Growers, with a Washington office and a PAC, the delightfully named RAMS, (Responsible Action to Maintain Sheep); the Cotton Council, maintaining a Washington presence, and the Committee for the Advancement of Cotton, apparently a PAC; the Wheat Growers, based in Washington and supporting a PAC; the Corn Growers, sporting a Washington lobbyist; the Cattlemen, with a Washington office and a Cattle PAC. The Tobacco Institute is essentially a lobbying and p.r. instrument for the large growers. It supports the Tobacco People's Public Affairs Committee (a p.r. device) and sponsors a PAC.

Moreover, surveying the whole agricultural scene, one observes "disintegrative" tendencies during the 1970s. Some of these were *ad hoc*. Thus, in 1978, a group of about two hundred farmers at Hidalgo, Texas intercepted a truckload of watermelons being imported from Mexico, blocking traffic on both sides of the Rio Grande. They were dispersed with the aid of nightsticks and tear gas, which also dislodged the one thousand spectators.[183] But the principal sustained manifestation of such militancy, which has been on the scene since the fall of 1977, was the AAM, i.e., the American Agriculture Movement. It was a real movement in its "spontaneity, with separate groups springing up in rapid succession across major farming regions," although Colorado was in the eye of the storm. It was also a movement in having "no officers, no membership lists, and no dues," operating expenses being borne mainly by individuals. But it was already an interest group in seeking to change public policy. The background to this was "large surpluses of grain, which have led to the price declines. The farmers' bins and the grain elevators are filled with more wheat and corn than the farmers can sell."[184] When the harvest of the 1977 crop began, there were already 1.2 billion bushels in hand, about two years' domestic consumption. Despite that, *and* the 1977 crop, in the "Alice-in-Wonderland" economics of the agricultural world, farmers busied themselves planting winter wheat to come up in spring and summer 1978, cumulatively inducing more chaos in the market. Even so, they wanted, in effect, far more support from the federal government (or taxpayer), mainly for wheat and corn.

Starting off with rallies and tractor motorcades that fall, the AAM proceeded near Christmas to advocate not only withholding (the NFO—and thirties—method) but also a buying boycott, as of farm machinery and the like. From that the AAM gravitated to Washington. The most spectacular invasion occurred in February 1979, when some two thousand tractors and trucks bore down on Capitol Hill bearing such billboards as: "The tractors are here! AAM is for *real!!!*" No one doubted it, least of all the car drivers and cabbies, or indeed the public at large after it was learned that the Mall between the Washington Monument and the Capitol had suffered damage from the tractors to the extent of $3.6 million.[185]

In 1983 the AAM was still a loosely organized movement of thirty-four state associations. It was then "fighting the system" in other ways, as by trying to prevent a foreclosure sale in Colorado. This failed (in January). A state leader explained: "The mace you could stand, but the tear gas you couldn't." Other bodies were springing up, nearer to movements than to regular interest groups. The Farmer's Liberation Army, in Kansas, was one. Its founder—Mr. Keith Shive, a Kansas wheat and milo farmer—characterized it as "halfway between an army and the Salvation Army." Ohio had its Family Farm Movement; South Dakota, its Famine.[186] Evidently, this was, up to a point, part of what Harry Boyte called in 1980 "the backyard revolution."[187] Bearing in mind the creation in 1955 of the NFO, which clearly belongs to the movement end of the continuum (movement–orthodox interest group), one wondered whether some major realignment of agricultural forces was not under way.

The immediate point for us, however, is that in the early 1980s the goal of integration was still proving elusive, and may even have receded somewhat, especially if one also took into account the mobilization of agribusiness through, e.g., the Agriculture Council of America, which did not even exist until the early seventies.

Perhaps the time has come to suggest that, after all, the emperor has no clothes, i.e., that an autonomous, overall peak for agriculture has hardly ever been attained. The so-called Farm Bloc (the term started as a journalistic joke) was certainly not such a peak. Even as it was taking shape (spring 1920), rivals, including elements of the Farmers' National Council (continuation of the wartime body), were holding their own conference. True, the Farm Bloc did include the leading three (with some *ad hoc* bodies such as the Corn Belt Committee of 22), and "within a year or two" of its formation enjoyed remarkable success.[188] But the roots of the bloc were in the Senate, so it was not autonomous, i.e., did not belong wholly or even mainly to the "private sector," or society. Besides, when the bill[189] that prepared the way, eventually, for price supports during the New Deal was "first introduced in 1924, the major farm organizations were sharply divided over it."[190]

The Farm Bloc was succeeded by the American Council of Agriculture, launched in 1924 "to make it possible for the existing agricultural organizations of whatever character to speak with voice through a united leadership wherever and whenever the general well-being of agriculture is concerned." With offices in Chicago and Washington, and a (claimed) base of 2.5 million farmers, it apparently was autonomous and a genuine peak. This was the instrument used to pass the bill against the fervent opposition of the White House. As a congressman explained in 1928, he was voting for the bill against his better judgment "because the crowd at home are on my trail." The Wichita *Beacon* believed that a majority had been obtained "under the bludgeoning of one of the most persistent and skillful lobbies ever seen in Washington."[191] But President Coolidge's second veto put the American Council of Agriculture out of business, so in its four years it cannot have put down deep roots.

Thrown back on their own resources again, the three general organizations did meet as a National Agricultural Conference in 1932 and did reach accord on an important issue.[192] According to one observer, "it was the first time in the history of organized agriculture that the 'big three' have ever reached unanimous agreement on a project of such momentous significance to the industry."[193] No doubt the Depression helped to bring this about.

Since World War II, the nearest thing to an autonomous peak seems to have been the National Farm Coalition of 1969–1979. Founded on the initiative of the Farmers Union and the National Grange, the coalition wanted to prevent certain fundamental changes in farm policy, notably price supports.

In due course, thirty-two farm groups joined in the fight. Even so, the Farm Bureau was a notable absentee, having been converted over the years to a "free market" philosophy. In any case, the coalition appears not to have survived into the 1980s. Even the more narrowly based National Conference of Commodity Organizations, which brought together thirty-six of the fifty to sixty politically active ones in the late 1950s, had little success.[194]

Thus the evidence of over sixty years suggests, even against the authority of Professor Paarlberg, that agriculture cannot be expected (except in crises) to "speak with one voice," politically.[195] *Is* there an industry *to be spoken for*, or only the thirteen major farm types of the Census of Agriculture? Politically, at least, many of these *are* different. Dairy farms have constituted the only livestock category with a direct price-support program. Cash grain and cotton farms are the only ones for which major crop commodity programs have been maintained for more than half a century.

Even more telling, perhaps, is the extraordinary fact that so many of what are defined as farms are really hobby farms and rural residences (annual sales of up to $5000): they account for 44 percent of all farms but only 2 percent of all sales. Were the owners *in farming*? At the other end of the scale, the 81,300 largest farms, some 3.3 percent of the whole, account for 44 percent of gross sales. Over six thousand of these each grossed $1 million or more in 1978: 0.26 percent of all farms accounting for very nearly 20 percent of all sales.[196] From that range, which is presumably reflected to some extent in the composition of the general organizations—which, like true total numbers, seems not to be available to independent scholars—how could one expect a single voice? Perhaps it is time to recall that in the Bible (Genesis) the babel—confusion of voices—was caused by a structure: the tower that was to reach to heaven, deemed an impious aspiration. The analogy is not in the first instance with tower as peak but rather with the structure of what is officially defined as farming. From the outside, at least, the "babel" appears to be precipitated by that structure.

To what extent *the babel of voices* has made a difference to the effectiveness of American, as compared with British, farm organizations, is one of the central questions raised by English political scientist Graham Wilson for an earlier period;[197] but it cannot be pursued here. One may simply recall that such disunity—lack of integrations at the top—has, at least, *not prevented*, over the years, very favorable government treatment of large components of agriculture, including corn, hogs, wheat, cotton, tobacco, rice, peanuts, milk, and the concomitant dairy products. Even the methods variously employed represented a victory over the American tradition, or philosophy: production controls (the so-called adjustments) marketing agreements, price fixing, and the like. Moreover, *parity*—that concept unique even in the exotic, sometimes bizarre, world of American interest groups—was secured. On the surface, parity simply meant restoring to the farmers, in terms of industrial products, the purchasing power they had enjoyed in their best years ever since the development of commercialized agriculture: the five years ending in 1914. At a deeper level, as economist John D. Black in effect remarked at the time (in relation to the McNary-Haugen bill, but his point is just as illuminating for the parity concept itself), the agricultural world was trying to look the newer industrial/commercial world in the eye and to keep on equal terms with it (as Labor had, by then, failed to do, as that perceptive economist also noted).[198] According to the official free-market philosophy, agricultural America could not hold back the tide. But that was economics. Politically, it succeeded in doing so in considerable measure by brandishing the device of parity. Despite disunity at the top, farm organizations played some now hard-to-evaluate part in that *tour de force*. Nor is all this "just history," not touching contemporary lives. On the contrary, the link between milk price supports and parity was broken only from 1982. The American taxpayer was then paying $250,000 *an hour* to buy up "surplus" dairy products, *surplus* meaning that quantity which that taxpayer, wearing her or his other hat as so-called sovereign consumer, chose *not* to buy at the going price. And of course such price supports were not eliminated in 1982, just continued on a different basis. The "of course" does not reflect cynicism, merely awareness that federal government programs, once they have reached the years of discretion, tend to enjoy the gift of eternal life.

Way back in chapter 2 we stood on the shoulders of Harwood Childs in order to distinguish groups "based on such differentials as age, sex, occupation, and race" from those created "to further special ideas," which corresponds to Allen Potter's *whom one stands for* as against *what one stands for*, or (as we may say) organizations-*of* as distinct from organizations-*for*. So far this chapter has been given over entirely to occupationally derived organizations. Such extended treatment is appropriate because they constitute the core of the economic function, or, thinking institutionally, of the economy. Thanks to the organizational revolution, they might well be regarded nowadays as a kind of Establishment, as permanent structurally and even in composition (allowing for size) as components of the federal government. Still, the other organizations-*of* do matter politically, as do the organizations-*for*, or cause groups (to use the more familiar name). So their place on the map must be sketched in, and their "representative actors" identified.

OTHER ORGANIZATIONS-*OF*

It is convenient to pick up the threads from the three remaining differentials mentioned by Harwood Childs: (a) age, sex, and race. In this context, *sex* is often denoted by *gender*, and *race* by *ethnicity*—a broader tendency because there the challenge is to the concept of race rather than to the word for it. What all three have in common is that they are "given" (or natural) social categories and may thus be distinguished from (b), organizations derived from some common experience, such as the shared perils of wartime military service and the shared deprivations of living in poverty or at its uncomfortable edge. Tending to defy classification in either of these two broad subclasses are (c), religious experience and practice and the corresponding institutions. These might be treated as reflecting shared experience, especially by evangelicals and those who have been "born again." On the other hand, for millions of people, religion is something one is virtually born with, part of a family tradition, which tends to require placement under (a). Does this question matter? Up to a point, yes. Subclass (b) tends to be made up of "transients" in comparison with (a), since age (or aging), gender, and ethnicity (as well as occupation) provide perennial lines of cleavage. In that light, religious or denominational allegiance deserves, politically at least, to find a place under (a).

GENDER: WOMEN'S GROUPS

Such bodies as Rotary International (1905), Kiwanis International (1915), and Lions Club International (1917) were still surviving as male bastions in the early 1980s, despite some challenge to their authority. It is not altogether clear, however, whether these should count as projections of *business*men rather than of men as such (and so belong to the earlier category). More specifically male and political were the Men's Rights Association (1971), attempting (in effect) to hold back the rising tide of women's liberation, and the organization touted in Boston in the early 1980s to promote sensual relations between men and boys, which would have required some changes in the existing law.

   In this context, however, the long-running drama has been mounted by women, off and on since at least the 1840s. In that decade of "rampant woman," the two streams of activity—for abolition and temperance—combined in the demand for women's suffrage. Unlike the anti-slavery movement, however, the temperance stream did not lose its identity after the Civil War but ran on first into the Prohibition Party and then into the Anti-Saloon League, which actually achieved the impossible—it made America (officially) dry. By a curious coincidence, Prohibition was effective in the very same year (1920) that women became entitled to vote.

   In the organization society, a major victory commonly (if paradoxically) poses problems for the successful organization, which may well have residual resources to deploy and to which some of those in leadership roles will be "indebted" for their careers (as a necessary consequence of the organizational revolution). One such problem is that of goal succession: roughly, what next? One answer came: after the entitlement to vote, actual participation. To pursue that goal, the National American Woman Suffrage Association was allowed

The problems they
    may in counter.

to expire in 1920 in order to rise immediately from the ashes as the League of Women Voters.

As in Britain, the movement developed a militant Left, known by 1920 as the National Woman's Party. Formerly, it had been the Congressional Union for Woman Suffrage, founded in 1913 by Alice Paul, who had served her apprenticeship to militancy in the English suffragette movement. Its answer to the question *what next?* proved to be quite different from its rival's since it "focused solely on the goal of total equality for women" (as Janet Boles would one day record).[199] That translated from 1923 onward into the Equal Rights Amendment (ERA) to the Constitution. Nearly half a century later, it was passed by Congress but not ratified despite an extension of time.

While these were fighting on a broad front, others were choosing their ground more circumspectly, e.g., the National Federation of Business and Professional Women's Clubs (1919), whose goal of elevating "the standards for women in business and the professions" readily translated into conditions of employment on equal terms with men, specifically equal pay. This meant that the federation (whose members were, and are, individuals) was never "merely" expressive (say, relished for itself) but political, so it does not come as a surprise to find that in the early 1980s the federation would maintain a PAC.

Women's clubs formed one side of a tripartite structure that a contemporary writer (in 1922) called "the most powerful lobby in Washington."[200] The other two components were derivatives of the suffragists and of the temperance workers, whom the clubwomen had at first regarded "as fanatics and not quite in the same social set." But "today the clubs and the causes are very much the same thing. The merging of the three forces was inevitable." Possibly, but what actually brought them together, according to the same author's own account, was that their representatives "had ample time, while waiting together in the lobbies of Senate and House, to compare notes and to learn that they were there for the same fundamental purpose."

Out of that shared experience came the Women's Joint Congressional Committee, self-described as "the outcome of a movement on the part of the great national organizations of women to pool their resources and cooperate for the support of federal legislation which affects the interest of women in particular and makes for good government in general." The "great organizations" numbered fourteen,[201] said to represent seven million women. But the totals cited add up to nearer six than seven million (6.3), and some, in any case, are unreal, e.g., the League of Women Voters was credited with two million. That is .the measure of the mailing list inherited in 1920 from its predecessor, but by 1923 the League had shrunk to about 100,000.[202] No doubt, women had created a great wave, but now the tide was on the ebb. It took the Left with it: the Woman's Party went down from fifty thousand in 1920 to about eight thousand three years later.

There followed, according to Barbara Decker, "forty years in the wilderness," 1920–60, the second half of which was particularly galling for the younger, livelier women. It was given short shrift by Professor Decker as follows: "The Women's Liberation Movement: 1940–1960. None!"[203] If that is a debatable one-word proposition, it cannot be debated here. It must be enough to note the rising of another great wave, starting with the National Organization for Women in 1966. It took over the principal unfinished business of the Woman's Party—the ERA—and added other things, one of which ("the right of women to control their reproductive lives") proved to be divisive. Its adoption led to a splinter movement. Even so, the parent body reached about thirty thousand in 1973.

Meanwhile, women's groups to suit all tastes had been springing up, many in line of descent from NOW and largely concentrating on sex discrimination in particular settings or in general: WEAL (Women's Equity Action League), a 1968 breakaway from NOW; the Women's Law Fund, a 1972 breakaway from WEAL; Human Rights for Women, Inc. (another breakaway from NOW or perhaps from its Legal Defense and Education Fund); the Women's Lobby (1972); FEW (Federally Employed Women) (1968); and, in a rather special category, the Women's Rights Project, a 1973 emanation of the American Civil Liberties Union. If these belonged to the Center, several others emerged on the Left in this organizationally fertile period of the late sixties and early seventies. They could be categorized as radical feminists and socialist feminists.

The need for integration was obvious but seldom met. The 1969 Congress to Unite Women brought together all sorts, and reached agreement on many things (at least on paper). The Women's Strike for Equality (1970) was an effective day of protest nationwide. But integration of that kind and at that level proved virtually impossible to sustain. However, the National Women's Political Caucus (1971) set out "to awaken, organize, and assert the vast political power represented by women—53 percent of the population.[204] More or less in conjunction with NOW, the caucus enjoyed considerable, although not complete, success in platform building at the 1972 Democratic Convention. The Republican Convention, on the other hand, was less accommodating.

From 1972 to 1982, however, virtually all the leading women's organizations already established at the outset did support the most significant single policy initiative of the period, the ERA. Proponents included most of the groups that had constituted the Women's Joint Congressional Committee in the early 1920s, (perhaps nine out of the fourteen went along; the most notable dissenter, perhaps predictably, was the DAR); and of course the National Woman's Party (which had set the ball rolling back in 1923);[205] as well as the mushrooming creations of the 1960s. The amendment had passed Congress with (deceptive) ease: 354-23 in the House, 84-4 in the Senate, but for the ratification struggle (as it turned out to be), two peaks were formed: the ERA Ratification Council (1972–75) and ERAmerica, launched in 1976. How effective these were is hard to assess. Here it must suffice to recall that in 1972 alone, twenty-two states had ratified, but in the five years, 1973 through 1977, only thirteen followed suit, producing the much-quoted figure of thirty-five[206] (as against the constitutionally required total of thirty-eight). This despite the emergence, from mid-1974, of vigorous "pro-ERA coalitions containing up to a hundred groups" in the unratified states, i.e., despite considerable integration at that level. The national centerpiece may have been the Equal Rights Amendment Ratification Council, based in Washington.[207] Then, in February 1981, three thousand women representing about eighty organizations converged on Congress for a Women's Rights Day, which brought out not only such "regulars" as NOW, the American Association of University Women, and the National Council of Jewish Women but also Mormons for ERA, Catholics for a Free Choice, the National Conference of Puerto Rico Women as well as the United States Auto Workers and the National Education Association.[208]

Even so, the movement ran out of time in June 1982, failing to capture the elusive three additional states before the thirty-nine-month extension expired. *Why* the whole initiative 1972–82 failed is a large and complicated question that can barely be touched upon here. It is all the more intriguing because "the ERA won—at least in the opinion polls" (as Daniels, Darcy, and Westphal have made plain to anyone who prefers truth to propaganda).[209] From the Gallup and other unimpeachable polls, they properly concluded: "In 1974, three Americans favored the ERA for every one who opposed it. Support for the ERA continued at a ratio of about two to one throughout the early ratification years."

The proportion fell during the presidential election year of 1980 (for, surely, partisan reasons). Even then, over half the population remained in favor. When time ran out in 1982, the proportion in favor was back to about two to one.[210] Once again, evidently, the political system was being responsive to special interests that had never been, since 1974 at least, anything but a minority. This would have been no surprise to the chastened Jeb Magruder, whose characterization of American democracy served as a peg for this discussion. But he had had economic interests in mind. Here we begin to see that the problem is broader and accordingly more complex (and, presumably, more difficult to resolve).

Discussion of causes must be limited to the minimum called for by our conceptual framework (the interaction of the social order and the political order, i.e., political sociology). Unlike occupation, or economic function, gender as such does not provide a "secure" basis for a movement or interest group. What the National Women's Political Caucus called "the vast political power represented by women—53 percent of the population" is obviously a myth. So, in this very context of ERA, is Claire Booth Luce's pronouncement in early 1982: "Women are the most powerful single interest group, and if they want something, all they have to do is organize. They don't want it that badly. It's had it."[211] All such remarks take it for granted that women can be politically united on specifically women's issues. Even if that were true, the Olsonian problem (chapter 3) would have to be overcome, a problem ERA proponents hardly addressed, not even the academics among them (Anne Costain seems to have been one of the select few).[212] In any case, women are obviously not united even on women's rights. They were far from united (in Britain or America) even on something as fundamental as women's suffrage. On ERA, women divided along several lines, including religion and education (as Conover, Coombs, and Gray summed up the literature in 1980).[213] Thus in Colorado, Kathleen Beatty disclosed that the anti-ERA women typified the religious Right, which was congruent with the Brady-Tedin finding in Texas: "fundamentalist religion was a principal source of the political attitudes of the anti-ERA women. Their political beliefs may be viewed as extensions of their religious beliefs."[214] (This is not to say that *all* religious fundamentalists were opposed to ERA. On the contrary, a plurality of both sexes favored ERA even as late as 1982. Source: See note 209. One is simply touching upon attributes of particular anti-ERA women.) In any case, all this could have been anticipated if only from the history of the women's movement. Yet, as Professor Janet Boles acknowledged in retrospect, "ERA supporters were admittedly caught by surprise by the emergence of effective *ad hoc* organizations in opposition." Reviewing the debacle of June 1982, *Time* alleged that proponents in general, and one leader in particular, were "inept" at practical politics. But anybody can learn "how to find a precinct list or run a phone bank,"[215] at which women as such—i.e., as distinct from say, women trade unionists—have for obvious reasons usually had less practice than men. Much more fundamental was the ostensible failure to think in terms of political sociology—that the conversion of such an "inert" category as gender into a political force is always contingent, or problematic.

There were signs in late 1982 that the leading organization, NOW, whose membership was reported to have shot up to 210,000,[216] had learned that lesson. By early October some $2 million had been collected through NOWPAC (for federal elections) and NOW Equality PAC (for state and local elections). And in a training session on the working of PACs, the outgoing president, Eleanor Smeal, was saying: "I worry about the purist notion that we can look at a candidate only on the basis of our issues."[217] Altogether it seemed that NOW, at least, was becoming more like an orthodox interest group.

ETHNICITY

That the "melting pot" did not, after all, really melt is not universally accepted. Sociologist Herbert Gans believes the implied identification (among whites, the "classical" immigrants) to be essentially expressive rather than purposive, and even in late 1981 historian Stephan Thernstrom doubted that "there has been, as yet, much of an ethnic revival at the grass roots."[218] But the revisionist view that the "melting pot" did not melt is widely held. Social philosopher Michael Novak has even declared some ethnics, as least, to be "unmeltable." In 1982 Mark Stolarik, executive director of the Balch Institute for Ethnic Studies in Philadelphia, would tell a *Wall Street Journal* reporter (Doron P. Levin): "All this proves is the failure of the melting pot. These groups never really melted."[219]

Certainly, some of the organizations arising from the ethnic line of cleavage have been more than expressive. The Chicago-based Polish National Alliance (1880) pressed the White House strongly in and after both world wars for a genuinely independent Poland. The German-American Bund (1936) identified itself as a distinctly political organization, and expected its members, in America, to "remain worthy of our Germanic blood." More recently, the Italian American Civil Rights League fought against the common equation: Mafia (or organized crime) equals Italians in general and Sicilians in particular. Native Americans have produced a good crop of groups, from the Association on American Indian Affairs (one of whose parents was the American Indian Defense Association) to the newer and more aggressive American Indian Movement, which sought (and fought) to recover the original tribal lands. Similarly, those who used to be known as Mexican-Americans had their League of United Latin American Citizens (LULAC), essentially to counter discrimination, but in the fifties and sixties they developed a whole new set of groups to speak for those now called Spanish-Americans, or Hispanics. These were virtually all *politically purposive*, not merely *expressive*. Characteristically, even the older, "respectable" body (LULAC) moved toward the Left. At its fiftieth anniversary convention in 1979, it set about discarding "its Establishment image," its president-elect (Ruben Bonilla) telling the nearly five thousand delegates: "I see a new era of activism that will make Hispanic Americans a truly visible political force."[220] Similarly, among those of Japanese descent, the *Nisei* (second generation, born here) had formed in 1930 the Japanese-American Citizens League. But this, in the eyes of the third (*Sansei*) and fourth (*Yonsei*) generation, has been compromised by its ostensible passivity during the "relocation" of 1942, when their parents and grandparents had been placed in camps away from the West Coast as a security measure after the Japanese attack on Pearl Harbor. *Sansei* and *Yonsei* began to speak in the sixties and seventies of "yellow pride" and "yellow power."[221] In 1983, John J. McCloy, lawyer and distinguished public servant, would argue against the revised claim of "the Japanese-American lobby" for "additional large-scale damage-claim payments" for the wartime relocation. He argued: "If we bow to this lobby, we will perpetuate injustice."[222]

To the uninstructed *goy*, it is not entirely clear whether "projections" from the Jewish community should be treated here or under the rubric of religious groups. But, in 1977, discussing "the limits of ethnicity," the New York man-of-letters Irving Howe had much to say about "the Jewish turn to ethnicity," encouraging the outsider to treat Jewish groups as ethnic.[223] However conceived, the field has been fertile. The earlier crop included the American Jewish Conference, pressing for a Jewish state in Palestine; when that was achieved, the American Zionist Council (financial aid to Israel from the federal government); and its successor, the American Israel Public Affairs Committee (AIPAC). These worked well. As a leading official recalled: "I had organized 36 Senators and 150 House Members behind a grant for Israel. The State Department didn't want to put Israel into the aid program; we had to fight in Congress for it."[224] From an earlier period still but very much alive are the American Jewish Committee (1906) and the Anti-Defamation League of the B'nai B'rith (1913), on whose behalf the lobbyist David A. Brody registered in 1978.

For integration there are two bodies, the National Jewish Community Relations Advisory Council and the Conference of Presidents of Major Jewish Organizations. In 1978 the former bound together over a hundred local chapters and nine national gorups. But for the most part it set its sights below Washington, which it did not lobby. The conference is interesting in part because it bears upon the question of origins (chapter 3). The stimulus seems to have come from the government, wanting to speak to one more or less representative body (or person) rather than a dozen or so. In this instance (William J. Lanouette reported) the then president of the World Jewish Congress "called Secretary of State John Foster Dulles to request an interview. Dulles opened his calendar, saw the names of umpteen presidents of Jewish organizations, and said he was too busy, suggesting that we all get together and just send one representative to Washington." That produced, in 1955, the conference which, by 1978, covered thirty-two organizations,[225] whose heads took turns as its president. By 1982 the total had reached thirty-six, prompting author Mark Helprin to liken the "structure of the Jewish communal organization in the United States" to a "weak" system of government: "There are so many groupings . . . that coalitions are fragile and must be assembled according to the lowest common denominator, especially if the goal is unanimity in what is perceived to be a hostile world."[226]

Since 1972 Americans of Arab descent have also been mobilized, particularly through the National Association of Arab Americans. Its efforts have been obliquely supplemented by lobbyists registered to work for Saudi Arabia. One, in the late seventies, was Crawford Cook, a p.r. specialist; another was Frederick G. Dutton. In 1983 he apparently went beyond the call of duty by writing, not as a lobbyist but as "a private U.S. citizen," to every member of Congress, urging a thorough review of all American aid to Israel. This, he argued, amounted to $10.3 billion a year, not the $2.5 billion usually quoted. Mr. Dutton reached that total by counting in "charitable donations, sale of Israeli bonds, Israeli bank borrowing, and American purchases from Israel."[227]

In this book, which focuses on domestic policy, the great story under this subheading has of course to do with blacks. It embodies what the Swedish sociologist, Gunnar Myrdal (later a Nobel prize-winner) classically posed as *an*

American dilemma: the commitment to equality *v.* the unequal, indeed brutal, treatment of Negroes (in a sense, the story since he wrote in 1944 is about the transformation of *Negroes* into *blacks*). The whole thing adds up to what journalist Lerone Bennett (of *Ebony*) has aptly called "the greatest moral struggle of this century."[228]

Here, clearly, one cannot even begin to do it justice. One simply recalls that for obvious reasons (even free blacks suffered legal disabilities as well as political handicaps) the conversion of sociological category into interest group suffered from fits and starts over a very long period. Putting aside the courageous efforts from at least the closing years of the eighteenth century to the early years of the twentieth, one observes the creation of the modern structure in 1909 with the National Association for the Advancement of Colored People (NAACP) as the foundation stone. It was bi- (or multi-) racial. Indeed, the initial conference in 1909 was precipitated by Oswald Garrison Villard, publisher of the *New York Evening Post,* who was partly of German descent,[229] and the first president in 1910 was a distinguished Boston lawyer, Moorfield Storey. This is not to underrate the role of the black sociologist, W.E.B. Du Bois, either then or over the following quarter of a century. But to the white leaders, the organization was of course *-for* not *-of.* That applied also to the (National) Urban League, which emerged under that title in 1916 as an amalgamation of three other bodies, whose roots extended almost as far as the NAACP's. One of the three, the National League on Urban Conditions Among Negroes, had been founded in New York by George E. Haynes (a black). But the Urban League got going with white help, which it continues to receive, with the principal aim of providing opportunities and jobs. Essentially "a professional community services agency" as distinct from a membership organization, its philosophy was interracial. That holds also for the two Second World War creations. The Congress of Racial Equality (CORE), launched by James Farmer in Chicago (1942), was firmly interracial, being in a sense an offspring of the pacifist body, the Fellowship of Reconciliation (by which Mr. Farmer was employed). Even as late as 1961, two out of three of the members and most of the national officers were white.[230] The Southern Regional Council was also firmly interracial, as the title of its predecessor (Commission on Interracial Cooperation, 1919) reminds us. Formed in Atlanta in 1944 by whites and blacks of distinction, it inherited several state groups from the former commission and was in that sense a membership organization. This changed in 1954, the membership passing to Councils on Human Relations in the various states.[231]

In the beginning, then, the distinction *-of* and *-for* serves only as a first approximation. Even so, it brings out an important point regarding group origins and the Olson problem (chapter 3): the significant use of an "external force" (whites) to convert sociological category into interest groups.

The story of the sixties is the gradual squeezing out of the whites from leadership and even membership, bringing *-of* closer to reality. Fighting for voting-rights reforms in the mid-sixties, the Leadership Conference on Civil Rights was a wide-ranging coalition of seventy-nine organizations. But Martin Luther King's Southern Christian Leadership Conference, integrating about a hundred churches and civic bodies in thirty states, was "from the start Negro-led and Negro-dominated" (as the Kerner report expressed it).[232] So was SNCC (Student Non-Violent Coordinating Committee), started by black and white students in 1960 (under the auspices of Dr. King himself but they soon left him far behind). In the small membership ranks, the black:white proportion was once about four to one. But in 1966 its new leader, Trinidadian Stokely Carmichael turned his back on integration, ejected the white minority, and aggressively proclaimed "black power."

Contemporaneously, CORE went the same way. In 1966, under a new leader (Floyd McKissick), CORE also proclaimed "black power." By 1968 the national officers were black (including, that year, a new leader, Roy Innis) and the white component of the membership was being eliminated.

It will not be forgotten that this was also the period of the Black Panther Party (Oakland, 1966), and when the Black Muslims (dating from 1930) took on a new lease of life, in part thanks to the conversion of boxer Muhammad Ali (born Cassius Marcellus Clay in the year when CORE was founded). It was also the period of much else congruent with our theme, including the formation (1968) of the League of Revolutionary Black Workers in Detroit. This gravitated from doing battle with the automobile manufacturers and even more fiercely with the United Auto Workers to attempting to organize the black community in the city (where it was instrumental in forming a branch of the Panthers).[233] But the general proposition is well enough supported: by, say, 1970 (i.e., sixty years after the NAACP had got under way with the help and indeed leadership of white liberals), black interest groups tended more and more to "coincide" with the sociological (or racial) category.

What has happened since then to black interest groups as such is not as clear as one would wish (since detailed monographs for the more recent period have yet to be published). But the general position is clear. As the black mayor of Atlanta explained: "Anyone looking for the civil-rights movement in the streets is fooling himself. Politics is the civil-rights movement of the 1970s. Politics is our first hurrah. It's where things are today."[234] By *politics* he essentially meant the electoral kind, often referred to as "the new black politics." The results have been remarkable. In 1965 the number of black elected officials may have been under five hundred. By 1970, it was approaching fifteen hundred (1469), and in July 1980 it was close to five thousand (4912).[235] This included 182 mayors, installed in several of the great cities, such as Los Angeles, Detroit, and Cleveland (Chicago was captured in 1983). Against that backcloth, the black interest groups as such appear to be somewhat less flourishing and effective. SNCC as SCC (*Non-Violent* has long since been dropped) faded early. CORE (based in New York) survived but suffered both internal and external attack. Internally, Roy Innis, who had taken over from Floyd McKissick in 1968, was challenged by him and James Farmer for all sorts of alleged irregularites. The Attorney General of the State of New York was also in hot pursuit of CORE from 1978. Late in 1981 CORE reached an agreement with the attorney general's office settling charges that it had misused almost $500,000 in charitable contributions. As a part of the settlement, Mr. Innis was required to "contribute $35,000 to the organization over the next three years." The agreement did not require CORE "to admit any wrong-doing in its handling of funds," but no doubt it was true (as Richard J. Meislin reported) that the three-year investigation "had seriously limited" CORE's ability to raise funds and conduct its affairs."[236]

The third of the activist triumvirate, from the years of excitement and struggle, the Southern Christian Leadership Conference (Atlanta) lingered on, mainly in the South, naturally. It marched in Alabama in 1979 to draw attention to the criminal conviction of a mentally-retarded black, a worthy cause (one need not doubt) but lacking the epic quality of the years 1957–68 (when its leader fell to an assassin's bullet).

Thus the black movement entered the eighties effectively shorn of its activist wing and returned, more or less, to "regular" interest-group politics. The Southern Regional Council (Atlanta), still helped by whites of distinction, studied rural development in the South and published a report. The Urban League, based in New York, kept up its traditional work but with a bureau in Washington to monitor legislation and regulations as these impinged upon minorities. Also based in New York, and still maintaining a Washington Bureau, the NAACP, oldest of all, and still the only true membership organization of its kind, went quietly on despite some difficulties, internal and external.

Whether, this time around, "regular" interest-group activity will satisfy the black constituency, particularly its younger component, remains to be seen. Much, perhaps everything, will depend upon the achievements of the new black politics, that conversion of sociological potential into electoral, as well as interest-group, power.

AGE: OLDER AMERICANS

When, in 1935, Harwood Childs drew the contours of group cleavage, he mentioned age, but did not stop to make finer distinctions. Under this rubric, obviously, young as well as old could be placed, e.g., the Massachusetts Independent Student Congress lobbying for a legal drinking age of nineteen instead of the proposed twenty-one (at the time, 1979, it was eighteen). National candidates for treatment would include, on the Left, Students for a Democratic Society, and, on the Right, Young Americans for Freedom. But Professor Childs might well have been thinking of the elderly. Only two years earlier in California, Dr. Francis Everett Townsend, a physician, had proposed his celebrated plan to rescue the elderly poor: up to $200 a month for those citizens sixty years old or above who were not gainfully employed, the cost to be financed by a 2 percent federal sales tax. Congress declined, but did pass the landmark Social Security Act in 1935.

Certainly, a generation or so later (the sixties and seventies), *old* age was *the* thing, politically. Forty years after the Townsend Plan was inaugurated a *Boston Globe* team would write: "Not since the 1930s . . . have the elderly been such a political force to be reckoned with nationally and on the local and state level."[237] They quoted a former Massachusetts state legislator for the view that the elderly are "among the two or three most powerful lobbies at the State House. They're more powerful than insurance, the banks or the environmentalists" (a sobering thought for any Bay State resident). Nationally, no doubt, old age had by then been well mobilized, including, among the broader organizations:

1. National Committee on the Aging (1950), "the first to be deeply affected by the modern senior movement" (wrote an authority, Henry Pratt),[238]

2. American Association of Retired Persons (1958), to which the National Retired Teachers Association (1947) gave birth. But the umbilical cord was not broken. The two shared staff, leadership and facilities (in 1981 they still had the same Washington address), although the AARP had its own board of directors and national network. From time to time, in policy initiatives, they walk hand-in-hand. Thus, in 1978, they called on retirees to send copies of their medical bills to President Carter in the hope of bringing about national health insurance.[239]

3. National Council of Senior Citizens (1961), formed specifically to do battle for Medicare. Having attained that, it lived on in pursuit of national health insurance and a great many other policies. This was the body (according to a deposition filed in Washington in 1973) that special counsel to President Nixon, Charles W. Colson, grumbled about: "This outfit is giving us trouble." It was his way of explaining to the Internal Revenue Service why he wanted a list of contributors.[240]

4. Gray Panthers (1970), formed by Margaret E. ("Maggie") Kuhn and a handful of friends who found themselves on the brink of mandatory retirement and did not fancy it. How sweet the taste of victory must have been when, in 1977, they helped persuade Congress to put back mandatory retirement from sixty-five to seventy years of age. They continue to lobby. December 1981 found them outside the White House demonstrating against the administration's policy affecting the elderly. The sign one (man) carried read: "H-ousing NOT H-bombs." Housing was evidently on Ms. Kuhn's mind. In January she had opened in Philadelphia a Shared Housing Resource Center to promote "intergenerational housing alternatives for older people," or shared housing. This she was already practicing in the Germantown section of Philadelphia, where she shared her two adjoining "three-storey stone and stucco houses" with seven others of both sexes and varying ages, supported by household pets, including a dog "who is predominantly a poodle" (as Judy Klemesrud reported).[241]

Many other groups, hard to keep track of, have emerged as champions of the elderly, or "older Americans" (the term they are said to prefer). The National Association of Mature People, based in Oklahoma, is one of the relatively new ones (100,000 in 1982). Its executive director then disclosed a particular concern for the startling increase in health care costs. Although represented in a lobbying coalition for the aging, the association was not itself (he went on) a lobby: "We don't have a lot of money to put into lobbying."[242] But, one noticed later, the association did manage to maintain a director of government relations in Washington.

Some idea of the scale of operations in the 1980s may be gleaned from Save Our Security, or SOS, the coalition put together in 1979 by Robert M. Ball, commissioner of social security 1962–73, and Wilbur Cohen, former secretary of HEW (Health, Education and Welfare) to beat off (as they did) the Carter administration's proposed reductions in benefits. After President Reagan returned to the attack, SOS was again mobilized in 1981, "made up of about one hundred organizations claiming 35 to 40 million contributors to and beneficiaries of the system."[243] Of course, many, like the AFL-CIO, did not belong to the category. Even so it was a formidable array, and (as Warren Weaver would recall) it "dealt President Reagan his only major legislative defeat" that year, "forcing him to withdraw from congressional consideration his proposals to reduce social security benefits." Mr. Warren judged that 1981 might prove to be "a watershed year for the elderly and their political apparatus."[244]

That was a reasonable judgment, although, in the end, after the coast was clear (i.e., after the 1982 elections), the powers-that-be did extract some concessions from the elderly, e.g., a delay of half-a-year in the usual cost-of-living adjustment. What remained remarkable, however, was that the elderly were able to exert as much influence as they did. Many were those who had thought that it would be difficult to convert such an "involuntary association" (as Carol Greenwald called it) into an interest group.[245] As late as 1969 the American Gerontological Society took the view that the conditions were lacking for "the formation and maintenance" of such interest groups, so old-age political movements were, and presumably would continue to be, "handicapped from their very inception."[246] Even Angus Campbell, an outstanding social scientist, judged that the elderly had not become, and were not likely to become "a self-conscious political group with a sense of common interest and a capacity to move as a group."[247]

Of course, grounds for skepticism existed. But there were leaders who knew "instinctively," very likely without ever having read or even heard of Mancur Olson, what needed to be done: offer "selective benefits at attractive prices to members," such services as "travel, drugs, legal aid and so forth," including, perhaps above all, insurance on favorable terms.[248] Had the Townsend Movement of the 1930s introduced its selective benefits in time (toilet soap; vitamins and minerals; and the intriguingly-named old fashioned hore-hound drops), it might have survived (judging by the work of Abraham Holtzman).[249] A generation later, in any case, the corresponding organizations not only survived but flourished. Additionally, one of these more or less piggy-backed. This was the National Council of Senior Citizens, helped along its arduous road by Labor, notably the Industrial Union Department of the AFL-CIO (Walter Reuther's "baby"); the auto workers, steelworkers, electrical workers, and machinists.[250]

One way or another, as journalist Steven Roberts summed it up in the fall, 1977: "Old people have come of age as a political force in Washington. The influence of "gray power" was demonstrated last week when the Senate overwhelmingly passed legislation prohibiting mandatory retirement before the age of seventy for most workers."[251] The House had already passed "an even tougher bill last month with little dissent." All this "despite the opposition of such powerful organizations as the Chamber of Commerce and the National Association of Manufacturers." Said a lobbyist for the chamber, with (one feels) a sigh: "It's such an emotional issue. It's very difficult for any congressman to vote against the elderly."

That rounds off our treatment of the principal groups derived from Harwood Child's three "given" or natural differentials: sex (translated for our time as gender); "race" (extended in principle to ethnicity but focused mainly on blacks); and age (restricted to "older Americans"). The addition here of religious affiliation as another kind of "given" tends to lead us into another large domain, but we cannot follow far.

RELIGIOUS OR DENOMINATIONAL GROUPS

Historically, of course, Protestant groups or denominations made an immense impact on public policy if only through the abolition movement and especially through the Anti-Saloon League that brought about Prohibition. Looking back from the eighties, however, one could agree that the modern "church lobby" may be dated from the civil-rights debates in Congress in 1963 and 1964, when "rabbis, ministers and priests—along with laity—descended on Washington by the thousands."[252] There they lobbied so hard for civil rights that (on June 30, 1964) Senator Richard B. Russell (Georgia) looked up at the packed galleries where many wore their clerical garb and said:

> During the course of this debate, we have seen cardinals, bishops, elders, stated clerks, common preachers, priests and rabbis come to Washington to press for the passage of this bill. They have sought to make its passage a moral issue. Day after day men of the cloth have been standing on the Mall urging a favorable vote on the bill. They have encouraged and prompted thousands of good citizens to sign petitions supporting the bill.[253]

These were "visiting firemen." There already existed a permanent establishment, one that included:

1.   the Friends (or Quakers);
2.   Congregationalists;

3. Presbyterians and Northern Baptists, on whose behalf lobbyists had registered from time to time;
4. the Methodists, who had not registered but who maintained a strategic base near the Capitol (other groups similarly established a presence in the D.C. area—for example, the Women's Christian Temperance Union, whose legislative department made use of a part-time lobbyist even though its HQ was still at Evanston, Ill.);
5. and the National Catholic Welfare Conference, which is now the U.S. Catholic Conference.

Its lobbying instrument was its legal department, one of whose members registered as a lobbyist.[254] By the end of the decade, just the major Protestant bodies plus the Catholic ones were believed to be costing $1 million a year to keep on the job—of lobbying, whether acknowledged or not.[255]

As to integration, the Catholic Conference was in itself a kind of peak, whose effectiveness impressed such well-placed observers as Murray Stedman and James Adams, who characterized it as "undoubtedly . . . the most formidable religious agency in Washington."[256] Protestants and a few Orthodox churches had their Federal Council of the Churches of Christ in America (Philadelphia, 1908, which made it about nine years older than the Conference). It had opened a Washington office in 1945—but then kept it on a very short leash. In 1950, church activists threw the federal council overboard and replaced it with the National Council of the Churches of Christ in the U.S., based in New York but with an office in Washington. But, even after almost a decade and a half, Professor Stedman judged it to be "far less effective than its Catholic counterpart." A principal reason was Protestant pluralism—that the Washington office was "only one of scores of Protestant 'offices' in the nation's capital, which means that the problem of coordination is always difficult and sometimes impossible."[257]

Certainly, the U.S. Catholic Conference went on from strength to strength, producing a full-time Office of Government Liaison, worked by three laymen with 125 others (clergy and lay) on hand for information, advice, and congressional appearances. In the early 1980s, the Protestant "offices" amounted to about a score in Washington alone, including, apart from "Main Line," the Mennonite Central Committee and the General Conference of Seventh-Day Adventists. If you count others such as the National Association of Evangelicals (supporting voluntary prayers in the public schools), and half a dozen or more Jewish groups, like the Reformed Church in America, the Synagogue Council of America, and the Union of American Hebrew Congregations (treating these as religious rather than ethnic, as some clearly deserve), then you get some sense of the fertility of this field. (There were also specialisms: Impact, an "interfaith organization" that monitored the progress of U.S. food policy and health care; and Bread for the World, "interdenominational Christian," part of the anti-hunger lobby.)

Here we turn from the organizations derived from occupational and "natural" attributes (choosing to include religious affiliation) to those derived from common experience of a more haphazard kind. Three species will be briefly identified.

THE UNEMPLOYED

Mass unemployment unprecedented in scale and only skimpily relieved pre-cipitated unemployed leagues in the early 1930s. Out of these came the Federation of Unemployed Workers Leagues of America which, with many other such bodies, led, in 1935, to the Workers' Alliance of America, which sociologists Piven and Cloward characterized as "perhaps the most formidable organization of the able-bodied unemployed in American history." Its second convention in April 1936 attracted nine hundred delegates representing or-ganizations from thirty-six states. By the end of the year the alliance extended to forty-three states, with an estimated membership, dues-paying despite the grim situation, of 300,000. Congressional lobbying was its fundamental method. As with the Old People's Movement (the Townsend Plan), however, the New Deal reforms of the mid- and late-thirties took the wind out of its sails. It dissolved in 1941.[258]

THE POOR

Of course, the unemployed in the 1930s were poor. But, as organized in the alliance, they were primarily able-bodied white men. In the 1960s, the socio-logical category underlying the National Welfare Rights Organization was made up "mostly of black women who are, practically speaking, unemployable in today's market."[259] Local groups of them (and some men) were integrated nationally by Dr. George A. Wiley, who had stopped professing chemistry in order to take part in the civil rights movement. Leaving CORE in the spring of 1966, he opened in Washington, D.C., the Poverty/Rights Action Center. This "became the organizing vehicle" for the National Welfare Rights Orga-nization (NWRO). By 1969 it would claim over 100,000 dues-paying members in about 350 local groups.[260] Its basic method was to confront the public authorities locally with specific demands and to mount demonstrations across the nation, some simultaneously. For having made existing recipients more aware of their entitlements and for having encouraged the eligible to apply, NWRO, with other components of the movement, has been credited with having greatly increased the welfare rolls.[261]

Guided by the conceptual framework, one may add two observations. First, as to the conversion of a sociological category into a movement/interest group, particularly when, as James Q. Wilson has argued in exactly this context of NWRO, the category is made up of lower-class people, one wonders how the Olson problem was overcome. Part of the answer seems to have been that potential members were *at the outset* offered the functional equivalent of a *selective benefit*. Thus, as Lawrence Bailis disclosed about the Massachusetts chapter, potential members were advised: We can help you gain this or that benefit, but you have to attend our next meeting.[262]

Another part of the answer is that NWRO piggybacked on various institutions, such as the Council of Churches in Cleveland and especially the National Council of Churches, which "has been extremely helpful to Wiley in a number of ways; indeed, without its assistance the center might not have survived,"[263] from which it follows that the NWRO might not have been born.

Secondly, the NWRO was at bottom an organization-*of*: of welfare recipients. But it included Dr. Wiley, a professor of chemistry by trade, and others who were middle-class or at least nonrecipients. To the extent that persons outside the category joined in and contributed, NWRO was an organization-*for*. Moreover, some of the most important of these "outsiders" came from the public side (or state) not from the private side (or society), e.g., the Office of Economic Opportunity and VISTA, originally an emanation of OEO, later incorporated in ACTION.

What this points to, once again, is that the benchmark of a fairly clear separation between society and state (accurate enough for the nineteenth and early twentieth century) had been, in part, engulfed. And not only as to origins. For, in the early seventies, the NWRO was gradually "transformed from a protest organization to a negotiating and lobbying organization,"[264] or, in the terminology here used, from movement to "regular" interest group.

Then, as the seventies advanced, NWRO went into a decline, partly because movements generally lost their steam, and partly, perhaps, because it failed to solve the recurring problem of goal succession. Now "the poor lobby" changed its character. Its main component in the 1930s had been unemployed able-bodied whites; in the 1960s, largely unemployable black women. Either way, organizations-*of*. In the late seventies and early eighties, the poor lobby suffered a mutation and became essentially -*for*. Moreover, looking back in 1982 over the ground they had done so much to illuminate, Piven and Cloward placed the new poor lobby at one corner of an "iron triangle."[265] In particular, they were focusing upon "a structure of agencies (staffed, they said, by "millions")

> that is mandated to act on the rights of large population groups, that is more or less accessible to these groups, and that is ultimately dependent on them for survival. The result is not the well-organized and well-articulated interest-group politics that characterizes the relations between business and government. But the result nevertheless is an institutionalized structure that tends to articulate and focus popular demands on state entities that are susceptible to these demands.[266]

The emphasis in that passage is less trilateral (no congressional unit is specified) than bilateral: the "institutionalized interdependence" of those who run the "benefit service, and regulatory programs" and their beneficiaries, or "constituencies." In any case, in the 1980s, the relevant interactions can hardly be contained within the concept of a triangle. This concept generally has been under fire since at least 1977–78 when Hugh Heclo, actually mentioning welfare policies, argued for its replacement by *issue networks* to denote the "webs of influence" that "provoke and guide the exercise of power."[267]

The general argument cannot be dissected here. One simply notes that *issue network* provided a better fit than *iron triangle* for "the poor lobby" of the early 1980s. For in addition to the *professionals* (embedded in "institutionalized interdependence"), *organized labor* played a leadership role, and *philanthropic bodies* (convenient shorthand for churches, charities, civil rights groups, foundations, and the like) were well mobilized and resourceful. Under those broad headings, many permutations could be discerned, including (as well reported by *Congressional Quarterly*):[268]

ISSUES	NETWORKS
Food Stamps	National Anti-Hunger Coalition (late 1979), launched by the Food Research and Action Center (FRAC), a nonprofit public interest law firm and advocacy unit. Six other groups joined in later, including the Community Nutrition Institute (CNI), an advocacy training and research organization (located, like FRAC, in N.W. Washington). Both had substantial budgets, from foundations but also from the government (thus blurring the private/public distinction). In 1980 funding came from the Catholic Church's Campaign for Human Development. March 1981: Coalition conveyed some 400 local advocates and (NB) recipients to Capitol Hill (the -*ofs* brought in by the -*fors*, almost as a resource).
Child Nutrition (breakfast and lunch subsidies at school, and WIC, supplemental feeding program for women, infants, and children)	Child Nutrition Coalition: CNI, FRAC, National Congress of Parents and Teachers, the Children's Foundation, but also two trade associations (National Milk Producers Federation, American School Food Service Association) and some turkey, chicken, and egg producers. Note the combination of organizations-*of* (economic, or functional) with organizations-*for*, both private and quasi-public.

Other networks extended to education, low-income housing, Medicaid, and legal services (for which even the American Bar Association fought hard and successfully). But, as against Professors Piven and Cloward, who, in the fourth of their relevant books (1982), exuded confidence and optimism perhaps for the first time, in this context there remained a gap in coverage. As *Congressional Quarterly* reported:

> At the other end of the soup line was Aid to Families with Dependent Children (AFDC), the benefit most people mean when they say 'welfare'. . . . There had been no lead group for welfare lobbyists since the National Welfare Rights Organization dissolved in the mid-1970s. . . .

According to lobbyists and congressional aides, one obstacle in the way was that, unlike food stamps and other programs, AFDC "had very few participants among the *working* poor" (emphasis added): "Most of its constituents were children in the poorest and most powerless niche of society."[269]

Perhaps, once again, as in 1966, they needed to be mobilized by the right sort of leadership. In 1983, in any case, their cause was championed from the outside by yet another network: the Coalition on Block Grants and Human Needs, which had been launched in 1981. Two years later it embraced a hundred groups, from Gray Panthers and Planned Parenthood (odd bedfellows) to the League of Women Voters and the U.S. Catholic Conference. It worked well on at least one occasion. The Reagan administration proposed to cut $1.8 billion from entitlement programs, including AFDC to the tune of $750 million (the same for food stamps). The coalition's "quiet lobbying" (reported *Business Week*) killed the proposal in the Senate Budget Committee, which voted to maintain the funding.[270] The House even voted to increase it.

VETERANS

The sequence in the last section tended to be from -*of* to -*for*. With veterans, setting aside the Society of the Cincinnati (a group of Revolutionary army officers which caused concern in 1783 because it was perceived as the nucleus of a hereditary aristocracy), the sequence was from -*for* to -*of*, i.e., *from* a number of charitable bodies formed during the Civil War *to* the Grand Army of the Republic after it was over. The most important was probably the Ladies' Association for Soldiers' Relief (Philadelphia, 1862). They took in money and "sanitary stores," visited the hospitals and even the battlefield. To their "considerable consternation" they had to spend one night in a tent "in the midst of a camp of eleven thousand eight hundred and thirty-five soldiers, on a bleak common, in midwinter!"[271]

Of course, once America had turned itself into a nation-in-arms,[272] organizations-*of* became inevitable. In the six months or so after the victories of

April 1865, about 800,000 men were demobilized, i.e., just dumped on the market to fend for themselves, swamping the charitable employment bureaus and "protective societies." The unemployed veterans demonstrated and occasionally rioted. Clubs and leagues sprang up, but among the "entrepreneurs" responsible for converting potential into actual were practicing politicians who knew a good thing when they saw it. Democratic politicians had already made a start for the 1864 presidential election with clubs throughout the North for discharged soldiers or those on leave. These made up the "McClellan Legion," backing General McClellan against Lincoln. Republicans counterattacked, as with the Union War Eagles of New York and (in the city) the "active working 'Veteran Union Club.' " But the great breakthrough came in Illinois in 1866, when a former Union army surgeon and other veterans founded the Grand Army of the Republic. But he was close to, and perhaps acting for, the Republican governor, and he was aided by a Republican congressman (both former Union army officers).[273] In due course the Grand Army became almost the *alter ego* of the Republican Party. The connection paid off handsomely, e.g., pensions for disabilities whether or not war-related. (These were for Union veterans, of course. The losing side was not organized until the United Confederate Veterans was formed in 1889. Like the South in general, its surviving soldiers returned to ruin and destitution.)

Members of the Grand Army lived on until after World War II, but in the meantime every "American war" (except the Korean) produced its own distinctive organization-*of* (see Table 7-6).

Of course, there were many other associations, some specialized (Paralyzed Veterans of America, Blinded Veterans Association, Military Order of the Purple Heart), and some more general that appeared to duplicate others, e.g., United Spanish War Veterans; Veterans of World War One of the U.S.A., "the Wonnies"; and the Combined National Veterans' Association of America. And if one researched the *military lobby* as distinct from veterans, one would take account of the National Guard, a powerful interest group (as Martha Derthick has shown). One would also bring in Vincent Davis's "admirals lobby," and several others.[274] But even without any of these the ones listed in Table 7-6 make up a formidable force. Not counting auxiliaries (such as spouses, who are not -*ofs*), the total in 1980 (from numbers provided by Bill Keller)[275] was over 5,250,000: American Legion (2.7 million), VFW (1.8 million), Disabled American Veterans (666,000), AMVETS (150,000), Vietnam Veterans of America (1400; most Vietnam veterans who joined were apparently to be found in the traditional associations). To which one might add 25,000 or so for AVC.

With perhaps the exception of AVC, which was regarded as harboring "dangerous thoughts" (such as "citizens first, veterans second"),[276] veterans have been treated by congressmen with an "astonishing tenderness" accorded few other organized interests (wrote journalist Douglass Cater in 1959; for comparison, he mentioned "Irish patriotism" and agriculture).[277] But the most

TABLE 7–6   Veterans' Organizations

1 The Spanish-American War of 1898, which an American diplomat dubbed "a splendid little war" because it cost America "only" 400 battle deaths (but about 5000 deaths in all).	American Veterans of Foreign Service (Cuba) + National Society of the Army of the Philippines = Army Veterans of the Philippines, Cuba, and Puerto Rico (1903) 1914: renamed Veterans of Foreign Wars of the United States (VFW)
2 World War I (1917–18) (America lost about 116,000, all causes.)	American Legion (Paris, 1919) Disabled American Veterans (1921)
3 World War II (1941–46) (America lost about 300,000)	American Veterans Committee (1943), (AVC, which is accounted a little left of center); American Veterans of World War II (1944), later called AMVETs.
4 Korean War (1950–53)	
5 Vietnam "War" (? 1962*–1973)	American Indo-China Veterans Legion (1971), Vietnam Veterans of America (1979)

*"The United States is now involved in an undeclared war in South Vietnam." James Reston, *New York Times*, Feb. 13, 1962.

powerful, unquestionably, has been the American Legion, which "greatly overshadowed" even the Grand Army of the Republic in extracting money from the federal Treasury (in the judgment of the late V.O. Key, Jr.).[278] One of the main policies he had in mind was the bonus bill (so many dollars a month for each year of military service). The Legion got one through in 1922 ($50 a month), only to have it vetoed by President Harding. But a less generous (some might say, extravagant) version survived President Coolidge's veto in 1924. Payment ($1000 per head, on average, for about 3.5 million) was to be made in 1945. Over the veto of two other presidents (Hoover and Roosevelt), veterans secured first a loan on, and then prepayment of, the bonus (in 1936). More than any other organization, the Legion is credited with having "beaten" those four presidents in a row. In ten years its principal lobbyist, John Thomas Taylor, calculated that he had personally written between fifteen hundred and two thousand of the Legion bills, a "goodly percentage" of which (judged Marcus Duffield) had got into the statute book "word for word."[279]

World War II naturally gave the older bodies a blood transfusion and precipitated new ones. They settled down with the VA (Veterans Administration) and the two congressional committees on Veterans' Affairs in a distinctly circumscribed relationship for which (Professor Heclo notwithstanding) "iron triangle" remains the most appropriate concept. As Bill Keller of *Congres-*

sional Quarterly reported, veterans' programs (costing $21 billion annually in the early 1980s) "are born and bred in an unusually closed system." The congressional committees are essentially advocates, especially in the House, where veterans' bills even get extra-special procedural treatment and pass with only a handful of *No's*. The leading organizations are given free space, with free access to the federal telephone system, in VA installations. The "triangle" is insulated from review by the courts, VA decisions being exempted from lawsuits. In the internal appeals system, the organizations play a prominent role. The whole "set" is reinforced by "exchanges" of staff: an organizational lobbyist crosses over to a veterans' affairs committee; a "staffer" for the veterans' affairs committee becomes chief counsel to the VA (the celebrated "revolving door"). It has been hard for "outsiders" to penetrate the circle. That applies to the Vietnam Veterans of America, as its lobbyist, Steve Champlin, remarked: "It's a $21 billion world that nobody pays any attention to," which captures a great deal of the political significance of the traditional "iron triangle" concept.[280] Moreover, even if an incoming administration (perhaps prodded by such a budget director as David Stockman) begins to pay some attention, it tends to find that this subgovernment has excellent perimeter defenses. This makes it unusually resistant to change.

If not the "triangle" as such, then veterans' organizations as a whole have also been exceptionally well placed for mounting attacks. Groups organized for religious, charitable, and educational purposes are tax exempt so long as "no substantial part" of their activities entails "carrying on propaganda or otherwise attempting to influence legislation," i.e., they must not lobby. Being charitable, the veterans' organizations are tax exempt. But, as a most special of special privileges, they are also permitted to lobby. That IRS provision was challenged in court in 1982 by Taxation With Representation, a public-interest law firm, but the wonder is that it existed at all. In May 1983 the U.S. Supreme Court unanimously reversed a ruling of the U.S. Court of Appeals (7-3), holding that the veterans, by "longstanding policy," constituted a special case. The holding applied to thirty-five thousand tax-exempt veterans' groups, including local posts of the leading ones.[281]

ORGANIZATIONS-*FOR* (OR CAUSE GROUPS)

Here we should pause to remind ourselves (again) that the categories we are using represent only a first approximation, enabling us to produce a rough sketch map and so get our bearings. Some organizations-*of* promote causes beyond themselves (so to speak), e.g., the League of Women Voters. Even some organizations-*of* (or at least what underlies them) provide the matrix for organizations-*for*. If churches/religious groups are accepted as falling within the latter, then they can be seen as furnishing two classic cases: *for* abolition, both of slavery and the saloon (essentially a Protestant campaign). The

Friends Peace Committee (1892), comprising devout Quakers, affords another example. In other policy areas, the AFL-CIO has fairly consistently distinguished itself by going beyond the call of duty, at least as narrowly defined.

In political science, such "hybridization" is unavoidable, sociopolitical reality being more complex, many-sided, and accordingly more elusive than the formal or logical categories would seem to suggest. Even so, the big distinction stays true: the cause groups bring together persons from many different occupations and functional roles, of different ages and "races," both sexes, and with no necessary shared experience (of being unemployed, on welfare, or wearing uniform in time of war). What unites them, making them (in the right circumstances) a social group, is essentially what they stand *for*.

Many of these groups are woven into the rich fabric of American history, e.g., the New England Anti-Slavery Society (1832) and the American Anti-Slavery Society (1833), which disbanded in 1865, and its less militant rival, the American and Foreign Anti-Slavery Society (1840), which seems to have passed ultimately into the Republican Party. Well-known names in this century, and surviving, include the American Civil Liberties Union (1920), Americans for Democratic Action (which emerged in 1947 from the wartime Union for Democratic Action), and, at the Right end of the political spectrum, the John Birch Society (1958), American Conservative Union (1964), and Conservative Caucus Inc. (1974), which has a mass following. Distinguished also is the Committee for Economic Development, started by progressive businessmen (1942) to plan for the postwar period but evolving into a research-oriented institution that draws fruitfully on the intellectual resources of academia.

Most if not all of those may be regarded as "here to stay." Some others are obviously ephemeral, e.g., the Committee of Americans for the Canal Treaties (Panama), which promptly disbanded after ratification, and, a decade earlier, the Campaign to Stop Government Spying (the CIA's—illegal—surveillance of students' organizations and meetings). Still others perhaps fall in between, with a past but an uncertain future: The National Organization for the Reform of Marijuana Laws (NORML), Action for Children's Television, American Arts Alliance (an "assertive voice" *for* legislation for the arts but also impinging on energy, tax, social security, etc., policy),[282] National Gun Control Center, Committee for Freedom of Choice in Cancer Therapy (for legalizing use of laetrile), International Institute for Preserving and Protecting Weights and Measures (i.e., the Anglo-Saxon System), Project DETEST (surely the cleverest acronym for many a year, standing for Demystify the Established Standardized Tests), the National Association for Neighborhood Schools, National Coalition for the Homeless, and National Committee to Preserve Social Security.

The last-named is particularly interesting for its bearing upon the Olson problem. According to the Postal Service, the National Committee in 1983 dispatched 400,000 letters inviting membership (at $10) and offering a "free personal confidential computer printout" of an individual's social security record. The invitation added: "This free service is available only to those joining the National Committee."[283] In Olsonian terms, that translates into an offer of a selective benefit. In fact, however, anyone can easily check on one's record of contributions (the "quarters") by simply calling the relevant social security office. (The Postal Service was reported to have found acceptable the measures proposed by the committee to clear up the misunderstanding.)

Unless social security is properly funded, the issue, if not necessarily the same organizations, will remain with us throughout the eighties and beyond. The other exceptionally important policy questions of the mideighties (and, concomitantly significant, organizations-*for*) included the following:

ABORTION LAW AND RIGHTS.   This deeply divisive issue may be traced to the 1960s and especially to the Supreme Court's ruling in 1973. In the mideighties it engaged at least ten associations, above all these specialized ones: National Abortion Rights Action League and the Religious Coalition for Abortion Rights, confronted by the National Right to Life Committee, and the National Committee for Human Rights Amendment,

CONSERVATION/THE ENVIRONMENT.   Private concern and public policy extend back at least a hundred years. The concern began to find expression in the Sierra Club (1892), founded by Scottish-born naturalist John Muir. The National Audubon Society was formed in 1905. But the conservation movement is usually dated from 1908, when President Theodore Roosevelt put his authority behind it through a famous conference in the East Room of the White House. The contemporary story starts in the 1960s, when Congress passed one major piece of environmental legislation after another, and at least three important interest groups appeared in quick succession: Environmental Defense Fund (1967) (research and litigation, not lobbying as such); then, in 1969, Friends of the Earth (for vigorous lobbying) and Natural Resources Defense Council (which seemed not unlike the Defense Fund but with a focus at the time on enforcement and implementation).[284] Earth Day, 1970, saw the birth of Environmental Action, which had, and a decade later retained, a particular concern for solid waste disposal. Two years later the Environmental Policy Center sprang into life. This, not a membership organization, revealed a keen interest in federal energy policy, federal strip-mining law, offshore oil development, and the monitoring of nuclear energy plants.

So it is not surprising that the Council on Environmental Quality should have reported in 1973:

> There are now about twice as many environmental organizations as before Earth Day. One-half of the groups from which the council heard did not exist before 1969. The newer groups appear to be as firmly established as the older ones. Most of the weaker organizations have disappeared, and the number of organizations is beginning to stabilize.[285]

That number was put at about sixty in 1982.[286] It would have included those set up in the interwar years, such as the National Parks and Conservation Association (1919), Isaak Walton League of America (1922), the Wilderness Society (1935), and the National Wildlife Federation (1936), which enjoys a following in the millions. A staff of five hundred in Washington put it on a par with the American Petroleum Institute (as *Congressional Quarterly* remarked).[287]

Numbers in the sense of "individual environmentalists" also seem to have been growing at that time. Over half of those groups responding to the council's survey reported an increase in membership after Earth Day. Above a quarter had stayed at about the same level, the remainder reporting some losses.[288] During the course of the seventies, the growth curve for the movement as a whole probably flattened out and may even have fallen a little. Moreover, from the middle of the decade, the shadow of energy was falling over environment. By 1979 some leaders in the field were already looking back to the seventies as "the golden age of environmentalism," fearing it was over.[289]

Growth, at least, was not over. In 1980 the new (Reagan) administration in general and the new interior secretary (James Watt) in particular stung some members of the public (lapsed or novitiate) into signing on. Membership rolls and contributions rose "sharply."[290] In 1982, the Sierra Club alone added ninety-five thousand new members, reawakened (its executive director, Michael McCloskey, would write) by "the anti-environmental stance of James Watt, Anne Gorsuch, and other administration officials."[291] That would seem to have given the Sierra Club a membership total of the order of 200,000. When W. Lloyd Tupping opened its Washington office in 1967 (with one assistant), the total had been "only" 48,000. By 1982, also, the no. 2, historically—the Audubon Society—was up to 422,000 members (with 457 local chapters), enabling its president, Russell W. Peterson, to claim that "power is with the people, and we are potentially one of the most powerful citizens' groups." National Wildlife had by then climbed to 4.6 million "members," perhaps more realistically thought of as supporters and contributors. So many of its members were hunting-and-shooting "types" that it has been well called "the General Motors of the environmentalist movement."[292]

Still, it is part of the essence of the *gesellschaft* development that the resulting organizations are always open to being politicized, given the right conditions. That had started, in the sense of having a lobbyist who registered, in 1954 (the Council on Environmental Quality reported).[293] This was almost certainly a reference to former economics professor, Spencer M. Smith, Jr., who registered then for the Citizens Committee on Natural Resources, which set out, as a nonmembership organization, to do battle on several environmental issues. For some years he was the "only professional lobbyist for a private conservation organization."[294] But by 1973 over thirty registered environmental lobbyists were stalking the halls of Congress[295] (and, no doubt, the anterooms, at least, of the agencies).

The movement has also been politicized in the other sense—the elector-al. This may perhaps be dated from the League of Conservation Voters, a very early "branch" of the Friends of the Earth. Marion Edey explained the plan in terms that are perfectly in tune with this book:

> The traditional conservation groups are afraid to be openly political, because they have a tax-exempt status to protect. Their official purpose is educational. They are forced to rely almost entirely upon persuasion. They have never really aroused their sleeping majority, because they never take sides where numbers count the most—in elections. . . . They are acting almost like a small special interest, but they cannot compete with the real special interests because they can't lobby openly, and they have far less money.[296]

So the movement edged toward an electoral role. That very year (1970) the league collected and disbursed $50,000 in campaign contributions and two years later raised the ante to $60,000. In 1980 the league spent some $460,000, much of it independently so as not to count against the candidates' official expenditures. Its characteristic method was to publish the environ-mental record of candidates.

In 1980, too, the Sierra Club came out with a PAC. Thus even a hiking club (1892) becomes something of a political machine in the end.

From the subject of environment one could make an easy transition to other broad *policy areas* of a closely related kind (energy, consumerism), or to the *actual groups* (public interest; public-interest law firms) that venture into such areas, hoping to slay dragons (which they have from time to time suc-ceeded in doing, to everybody's amazement at first except perhaps their own). For several reasons it is convenient to turn to energy.

ENERGY.   This is of course another big subject attracting a proportionate gathering of interest groups. Back in 1976 Andrew McFarland found that the number of *public*-interest groups alone in this policy area was about twenty.[297] Two years later the Citizen/Labor/Energy Coalition was stitched together in "opposition to constantly rising energy prices" (wrote Merrill Sheils et al. of *Newsweek*).[298] By 1979, on a base representing, theoretically, 15 million Americans, some two hundred organizations belonged, including ADA; the Machinists and the Steelworkers; Gray Panthers and the National Council of Senior Citizens; the Players' Association of the National Football League; and that team from a different league, the United Presbyterian Church.

Meeting in Washington in April 1979 the coalition agreed on strategies designed to stop "oil-company ripoffs." In October a national day of protest was mounted: it included "call-ins" (White House, Congress); and church "pray-ins" (*for* whom was not entirely clear); and demonstrations (at the American Petroleum Institute, the headquarters of Standard Oil of Indiana, and elsewhere). Senator Howard Metzenbaum and Representative Toby Mof-fett also introduced the Citizens Energy Act of 1979, intended to convert the strategies into legislation.[299] Attempting to swim against the tide of decontrol, they and the coalition made little progress. But the work continued into the early eighties, embracing energy prices, supplies, and conservation as well as studying competitiveness within the industry.

Of course, the line of cleavage does not always stand out so starkly. President Reagan's proposal in January 1983 for an oil-import tax of $5 a barrel, estimated to yield $8 billion a year, precipitated a wide-ranging coalition to prevent its passage. In the van were Texaco and the Edison Electric Institute, followed by the Petrochemicals Energy Group, the National Council of Farmer Cooperatives, and various trade associations such as Air Transport and those speaking for the utilities. New England interests were particularly apprehensive, for obvious reasons. There was the industry lobbyist who expostulated: "We're 100%, rip-snorting, wild-eyed against the idea." But Senator Edward Kennedy and Speaker "Tip" O'Neill were also concerned. The coalition also extended as far as two groups that speak for consumers.[300] One was the Consumer Energy Council of America (consumer groups, labor and farm unions, senior citizens' organizations with an admixture of public power systems, and rural electric cooperatives). The other was more firmly rooted—the Consumer Federation of America, which started in 1967 with about fifty groups and by 1983 had risen to some 225, mostly local but with not far off a quarter of them national (essentially labor unions). To that extent it appears to integrate the lobbying efforts of its member organizations. In the early eighties, it employed three lobbyists and sported a political action fund.

Interest groups have been actively resisting nuclear-power development for about a generation now. An early classic case arose out of the 1958 proposal of the Pacific Gas and Electric Company (PGE) to site a nuclear reactor at Bodega Head, "a magnificent granite promontory" some forty miles north of San Francisco. For PGE the omens seemed favorable. It had itself long been a force in California politics. The California Public Utilities Commission was supportive, as were the county authorities. Enthusiastic businessmen set up a Committee to Develop Bodega Bay.[301]

The opposition was not impressive. It contained one proven champion— the Sierra Club. The rest were the organizational equivalent of raw recruits, mustered for the occasion, initially the small local Committee to Preserve Bodega Head, later the Northern California Association to Preserve Bodega Bay and Harbor, supported by an untried troop with particular targets (e.g., Parents and Others for Pure Milk). They found it hard to get off the ground because the county supervisors were evidently determined to stifle public debate. Yet in late 1964, PGE gave up the ghost, withdrawing its application for a permit, having little to show for its effort except a seventy-foot hole on the Head (which, since it cost $4 million to bore, must have felt like a hole *in* the head).

In reviewing these events and the outcome, the celebrated environmentalist, Lynton Caldwell, and his colleague Lynton Hayes (the actual author) concluded: "Due to the relentless pressure of citizens' groups, the PGE eventually withdrew its plan for the reactor at the site." That, their own analysis reveals, is too compressed a statement. At least one intervention by the federal government was "crucial": the U.S. Geological Survey (USGS) hired a seismologist to determine whether or not the proximity of the proposed reactor to the San Andreas Fault entailed risk of a nuclear accident. The USGS later warned that development on that site was risky, and the regulatory staff of the Atomic Energy Commission agreed.[302] That is believed to be the point at which PGE "surrendered."

On the other hand, the citizens' groups certainly deserve great credit for preventing "early closure" (which almost happened) and for keeping the issue alive by fighting at the state level and by securing national publicity. It was some combination of publicity and also a request from such a group that apparently led Secretary of the Interior Stewart Udall to offer the services of the USGS.[303] Thus a judicious conclusion might be that the groups' "relentless pressure" was a necessary, but not a sufficient, condition of success.

There followed (late sixties/midseventies) another such battle fought out in Oregon, where the Eugene Future Power Committee delayed the project by using the ballot initiative (a portent for the future). But it must be enough to note that by October 1976, despite the early opposition, sixty-one reactors had been licensed nationwide.[304] In New England, however, interest groups had already mobilized (i.e., pre-Seabrook). The New England Coalition Against Nuclear Pollution (NECNP) had been formed in the midsixties by Vermonters anxious to stop the Vermont Yankee nuclear development near Brattleboro. Legal intervention and publicity were its methods then and as it expanded to cover the six-state region.[305] Even civil disobedience was being practiced pre-Seabrook. In 1975 a group of militants toppled a weather-testing tower at a proposed reactor site in Montague, western Massachusetts.[306]

Elsewhere, in the West and old Northwest (Ohio), activists were limbering up for a fight by means of the initiative, as already successfully used, up to the point of imposing delay, at Eugene, Oregon. The assault opened in California but ran up against the "well-financed nuclear industry," including the Atomic Industrial Forum.[307] Founded in 1953, the Washington-based forum serves as a peak for the industry.[308] But since this is itself a mixture of public/private, the forum may be regarded as a hybrid, integrating not only the makers of electrical generating equipment and the utilities but also educational bodies and government agencies as well as labor and research organizations. Confronted by the formidable array, the "loose and poorly financed coalition of environmentalists" lost the day: the initiative was defeated by a two-to-one margin. In six other states (Oregon, Washington, Arizona, Colorado, Montana, and Ohio) that year—1976—similar initiatives went down to similar defeats. These victories for the industry had cost money, for political advertising and for a circular to over half-a-million registered voters in California advocating a *no* vote. According to Harry Boyte, "business around the country poured in millions to defeat the measure—utilities in western Pennsylvania alone contributed over two million dollars."[309] The Sierra Club put the cost at $6 million (presumably a grand total for all seven initiatives).[310] Still, the industry had saved the day.

Back east, opponents of nuclear power were starting to tack in another direction, quite possibly (David Howard Davis has speculated) "in response to the initiatives' failure."[311] But the driving wind of civil disobedience had already come up, not only at Montague, Massachusetts, but in the demonstration by the Greenleaf Harvesters Guild against the Seabrook project. Modelled on the medieval crafts guilds, but also inspired by Gandhi, the guild apparently eked out a frugal living by harvesting fruit and pruning apple trees. In April 1976 forty guildsmen marched from Manchester to Seabrook, New Hampshire, where one of them climbed a weather tower and sat there (like Diogenes) for several days.[312]

In any case, the Clamshell Alliance came onstage that year. Its methods certainly contrasted sharply with NECNP's. As one leader (who had helped to topple the weather-testing tower at Montague) put it: "There's a real role for NECNP's legal action, but no nuke has ever been defeated by law. There has to be some solution beyond letting a court mess you around. The Clamshell Alliance takes a further, nonviolent step in resisting."[313] It drew together local groups, or "clams," including some individuals from the Seacoast Anti-Pollution League[314] who had been trying to make use of the law only to become disenchanted with that method. A year later the Clamshell would have (depending on definitions) thirty to fifty local groups throughout the region but with concentrations near the proposed sites. At that time—1977—the NECNP claimed twenty-five to thirty groups, with six hundred and fifty members and several thousand participants.[315]

By then the Clamshell had impinged on the national consciousness by two striking acts of civil disobedience. In July 1976 construction started at Seabrook. In August, eight hundred "Clamshellers" marched to the site, and ignoring an injunction, tried to close down the job. One hundred and seventy-nine of them were arrested and charged. That was just a trial run. By the end of April 1977, the Clamshell had *trained* about eighteen hundred persons in the method of nonviolent civil disobedience. This force, perhaps as many as two thousand, was directed at the construction site on May 1, again in defiance of an injunction. As a result state troopers arrested the easily remembered total of 1414, most of whom played their aces by declining to post bail. The attorney general had anticipated neither that refusal nor indeed the mass arrests,[316] (the orders for which, one is left to infer, may have come from the hardline governor, Meldrim Thomson). In any case, the refusal of bail overwhelmed the jails, forcing the authorities to open up the armories. Before "normal procedure" was resumed, the state of New Hampshire was "out" by well over half-a-million dollars. Some demonstrators paid their own price, however, later drawing sentences that were not only "relatively severe" but (according to Donald Stever, an assistant attorney-general at the time) in excess of the "general recommendations made by then attorney general, David Souter."[317]

Despite that reception, the Clamshell in due course planned to return to Seabrook in still greater force on June 24, 1978: an expected five thousand would descend on the site to "occupy and restore" it. But at least two factors served to change the nature of this demonstration. One illustrates the internal constraints upon interest-group methods. The mass arrests in 1977 and the "relative severity" of some sentences had had their effect. "Many" of those in Clamshell's (required) nonviolence training sessions asked to "serve on support teams rather than participate in the occupation." A training session leader explained: "They were willing to spend four days but didn't want to take the chance of spending the summer in jail." Others, of course, remained implacable, so by the summer of 1978 the movement was losing its cohesion as well as its drive (e.g., Boston Clamshell was divided, the enragés—recalling the French Revolution—wanting to cut through the fence surrounding the site, if need be).[318]

The other factor illustrates the external constraints upon interest-group methods: the Clamshell was probably not going to be able in 1978 to "live off the countryside." As reporters Michael Kennedy and Richard Higgins explained: "The Clamshell Alliance has always made a point of emphasizing its local base, and for the June 24 demonstration it was counting on local people for camping areas, loan of vehicles, and other logistical support."[319] But "local people," remembering 1977, were apprehensive and unwilling or less willing to provide such support. Many "Clams," local themselves, were aware of their neighbors' views.

So, meeting at Portsmouth about two weeks before the day, the leadership decided to accept the offer of the new attorney general, Thomas Rath: to hold a three-day rally, "lawful and peaceful," on a designated tract outside the fence. That is what happened, a vast crowd of nine to ten thousand turning out for a weekend of speeches and music. It was fun, but it may or may not have been politics.

The change of strategy decided at Portsmouth and the resulting jamboree evidently divided the Clamshell Alliance. The militants marched on to their own drummer. In early August a representative could even be heard saying, at a congressional hearing, that the Clamshell planned a marine blockade, one using boats and canoes to stop a barge carrying a vital part of the reactor pressure vessel—a 427-ton structure to house the plant's radioactive fuel—from arriving from Somerset, Massachusetts.[320] Later in the month a group actually occupied a triangular traffic island outside the main entrance to the plant, setting up an information booth and displaying signs. Refusing to move, nine were arrested for disorderly conduct.[321] Then, over the Memorial Day weekend, 1980, eleven hundred protestors made another foray to

Seabrook,[322] but, after 1977, the movement seems to have lost something on the way.

Meanwhile, however, Clamshell-type regional alliances had made appearances elsewhere: the Abalone (California), Crabshell (Washington), and others, several of them in the South, including the Palmetto (South Carolina), Catfish and Conchshell (Florida), Oyster Shell (Louisianna), and Sunflower (Kansas). These demonstrated at the Barnwell reprocessing facility in South Carolina in the summer of 1978. In 1981 the Abalone Alliance of supporters attacked the Diablo Canyon plant in California which had been licensed and constructed despite closeness to a major geological fault (contrast the Bodega Head issue case from which we started). Thousands turned out, many arriving on the beach by boat, and attempted to scale the fence.[323] Extended over twelve days, the demonstration precipitated 1637 arrests, which exceeded the Seabrook total. It also precipitated a lawsuit by the Pacific Legal Foundation representing pronuclear groups. They asked for $1 million to cover the police expense.[324]

This tumult and commotion across the land, and even the echoes of the more orderly procedures, were doubtless heard and pondered in the nation's capital. Some "messages" were delivered more directly. Thus, in May 1979, a few months after the malfunction at the Three Mile Island plant, "the largest antinuclear protest rally in U.S. history"[325] took place on the Washington Mall. By then the formidable Ralph Nader had taken the plunge into nuclear policy, launching (1974–75) Critical Mass as a vehicle for opposition. Other national groups resorted to the courts, as the Natural Resources Defense Council and the Sierra Club sued successfully in federal court in 1976 to "prevent the interim use of plutonium in power reactors in the United States."[326] But this is a trail we dare not attempt to follow. We must be content with a sketch of the role of citizens' groups up and down the country in this crucial policy area (one form of Harry Boyte's "backyard revolution").[327]

One cannot find space here even to sketch the analogue of the popular movement against nuclear power—that against nuclear weapons, important as this came to be in the late seventies and early eighties, especially from 1982. But a few points may be ventured. Specialists had long coordinated (so to speak) their apprehensions: the Washington-based Federation of American Scientists (essentially a lobbying group formed in 1945 to work for the civilian control of atomic energy); the National Committee for a Sane Nuclear Policy (1957), later known as SANE; and the Union of Concerned Scientists (1969), based in Cambridge, Massachusetts. In the SALT II[328] discussions, agreement and drive for ratification, gaining momentum 1977–79, specialists (not necessarily scientists) lined up against specialists. New Directions was launched in 1977 specifically to fight for SALT II. By 1979 it had fourteen thousand members. Already occupying some part of the field were the Council for a Livable World (1962), which served the cause of arms reduction and control, and had twelve thousand supporters in 1969; and the American Committee on East-

West Accord (1974), with two hundred members (1969), persons of distinction. These, with the Federation of American Scientists, put together Americans for SALT, men and women of distinction and moderation. On its executive committee the organized scientists were represented as well as the Auto Workers, the Machinists, ADA, and religious bodies—the Friends Committeee on National Legislation, the U.S. Catholic Conference, and the National Council of Churches—including the *ad hoc* Religious Committee on SALT, an emanation of the National Council of Churches.

What corresponded, among opponents, to Americans for SALT was the Coalition for Peace Through Strength, an emanation of the American Security Council. The council had been started in 1955 by high-ranking retired officers of the armed services, although they opened their ranks to such distinguished civilians as Dr. Edward Teller, commonly designated the "father" of the hydrogen bomb. Financed by corporations, universities, and research institutions, the ASC sought security through increased defense spending. Accordingly, it has been much exercised by what its president, John M. Fisher (a former FBI official) characterized in 1978 as "a massive, highly organized anti-defense lobby," to which he attributed a great deal. In that article he called for "prodefense coalitions willing to take a stand for American military superiority and peace through strength."[329] Hence the Coalition for Peace Through Strength, which he chaired. In 1979 it had in membership about fifty conservative groups, including the top two, the American Conservative Union (1964) and the Conservative Caucus (1974), one of whose leaders, Governor Meldrim Thomson of New Hampshire, jousted with Clamshell on Seabrook field. More specialized was the Committee on the Present Danger, founded in 1976 by Paul H. Nitze, a member of the SALT negotiating team until 1974, and Yale law professor Eugene V. Rostow, to educate the public about the need for increased defense spending.

The national debate and tug-of-war cannot be pursued here except to illustrate the interaction of (a) national and local levels, and (b) policy issues that, although closely related in principle, had been defined and certainly developed as separate causes. The purpose is to bring out the "artificial" simplicity of the analytical method in contrast to the complexity of the real world. By 1978, as the Clamshell Alliance and supporters were besieging a commercial nuclear undertaking, others were blockading or invading nuclear-weapons installations. That summer a group straddled the railroad tracks leading to the Rocky Flats plant, near Golden, Colorado. They sat there for at least a month despite fifty or more arrests. To the northwest, in Washington, several hundred scaled a 6-foot metal fence to "claim" a piece of ground inside the U.S. naval base at Bangor where Trident nuclear-missile submarines were expected. Peacefully dispersed, a contingent returned the following day, when three thousand were arrested. Survival Sunday at the Hollywood Bowl attracted ten thousand people, who were addressed by (among others) former senator Eugene McCarthy and Daniel Ellsberg (of the Pentagon Papers and, more recently, Rocky Flats). At the end of the rally, the audience held hands as Peter, Paul and Mary sang "Blowin' in the Wind."[330] Back east, protesters "sat in" at the UN special session on disarmament, hoping perhaps to speed things up. Nearly three thousand were themselves slowed down by being arrested.

Some individuals epitomized in themselves the tendency of the two movements to mingle if not exactly merge at that time. Thus, a retired school teacher from California, Bob Schneider, who had learned the theory (i.e., political science) at Wesleyan, Middletown, Connecticut, drove his 1953 Plymouth to Seattle to demonstrate against the Trident missile submarines, then returned south to Rocky Flats to join the "blockade," after which he drove right across country to New York for the protest at the UN (where he was arrested). He then headed north again to Seabrook in New Hampshire, "an odyssey" (as he called it) of about five thousand miles.[331] Had he stayed around for six or seven weeks, he could have participated with Clamshell in a different mission from the Seabrook one. On the anniversary of the dropping of the Hiroshima bomb in early August, Clamshell marched to the Portsmouth Naval Shipyard (nuclear "sub" maintenance facility, actually in Maine), thence south again to the Pease Air Force base in New Hampshire. The base was significant because it was home to the 509th Bomb Wing, said by the demonstrators to be "the group responsible for the atomic bombing" of the Japanese cities.[332]

The organizational link then forged between the two movements was Mobilization for Survival, its title echoing the anti-Vietnam War association. The connection between the two, in the minds of militants, was well brought out when (in 1978) the Boston chapter mounted a three-day vigil at historic Faneuil Hall[333] against both manifestations of the nuclear issue. Poet Denise Levertov told the 250 demonstrators: "Nuclear power is as much a weapon as bombs. Unless we stop nuclear bombs and nuclear energy, we will be committing not only murder, but suicide."[334]

Meanwhile (it will be recalled) the national struggle over SALT II was already under way. Unable here to chart its course, one makes merely the following observations. The "tumult and the shouting" in the localities had the effect that, in 1979, to a greater extent than usual in such campaigns, the center had to reach out to the periphery, tending to fuse, for the time being and on this issue, the national with the local. The administration itself made an extraordinary effort, dispatching a team of State Department officials to win over opinion leaders in nineteen major cities, a "push" which cost altogether over $600,000. Many of these were later invited to the White House for further briefings. The record of endorsements was passed on to senators. Interest-group opponents of SALT II used a variety of methods, many of which cost money: film for TV; direct mail running into millions of pieces; political advertising; speaking tours, one with a petition drive; and the like. In comparison, the (underfunded) proponents of SALT II made no great showing, relying mainly on film, aired on relatively few TV stations, and on a team of speakers.[335]

All that touches only part of a remarkable campaign, whose outcome was inconclusive. In December, a Senate committee adopted a report to the effect that the SALT treaty, in its current form, did not serve American security interests. But, soon afterward, the Soviets invaded Afghanistan, putting paid to the treaty and the drive for its ratification. That set the scene for another variation on the theme of interaction national and local. The shelving of SALT II meant that the nuclear-arms competition between the U.S. and the Soviet Union would probably accelerate. That probability became a certainty after President Reagan took over the White House in January 1981. This in turn stirred various national groups "working on arms control or peace issues," of which there were reported to be as many as ninety. As so often, however, their funding for this purpose presented a serious problem. The Coalition for Peace Through Strength had apparently been funded by the American Security Council, which rested on the solid foundation of what President Eisenhower chose to call "the military-industrial complex." But Americans for SALT had had to rely on the generosity of a few of its founders. In any case, the ninety leading groups were able to "raise no more than $20 million from all sources in 1981." As late as December 1982, a conference on the very subject of "funding for the prevention of nuclear war" had to be funded from outside the groups—by the Field Foundation, Jay Harris, the Levinson Foundation (Boston), the New World Foundation, and both the Rockefeller Family Associates and the Rockefeller Family Fund.[336]

Meanwhile, the cause had taken fire up and down the country. During 1982, by "an overall 60 to 40 percent margin," voters in "nine states, several dozen cities, and more than five hundred small towns" endorsed nuclear-freeze propositions. By the fall, some fifteen hundred local peace groups were of the same mind.[337] That spring and summer, in metropolitan New York, the movement had "infiltrated" the professions as such: Nurses for a Non-Nuclear Future, Social Workers for Nuclear Disarmament, Architects for Social Responsibility, the Life Insurance Committee for a Nuclear Weapons Freeze, Dancers for Disarmament, Performing Artists for Nuclear Disarmament, and the youthful Future Generations for Nuclear Disarmament. It had also revived some of the earlier hybrids (*fors* embedded in *ofs*, i.e., occupations), e.g., the New York chapter of Physicians for Social Responsibility.[338] Others of the kind in this era included: Lawyers Alliance for Nuclear Arms Control, Educators for Social Responsibility, and Business Alert to Nuclear War. These and other stirrings in the area (and beyond) produced a great rally in Central Park, attended by at least 750,000 (some reported nearly a million).

In 1982–83 the spotlight again picked out the national stage. The movement acquired a peak, the Nuclear Weapons Freeze Campaign, with a national coordinator. In a pastoral letter, the National Conference of Catholic

Bishops came out for nuclear disarmament. With the American Conservative Union and Peace Through Strength raising their voices in opposition, something like a national debate began to be heard. It was heard in both the White House and in Congress. In resuming arms-control talks with the Soviets, President Reagan may well have taken into consideration the Western European peace movement so vociferously opposed to the deployment of American missiles in their territory. But America's own nuclear-freeze groups believed that they had contributed substantially to the administration's change of policy.[339]

Another phase of the national lobbying of Congress started in March 1983. It culminated in the House of Representatives in early May with the passing of a nonbinding resolution calling on President Reagan to negotiate a "mutual and verifiable freeze and reductions in nuclear weapons" with the Soviet Union.[340] Although the Senate was unlikely to follow suit in 1983[341] and President Reagan remained adamantly opposed, the passing of the resolution marked a significant stage in the development of the policy. Perceived by its backers "primarily as a political tool" (Susan Trausch reported), it was intended to "let the administration know that a large chunk of the American people want to see an end to the arms race."[342] That is what a small chunk of them had been saying, in words and by what some European anarchists used to call the "propaganda of the deed"—in this context, civil disobedience, of course, not assassination—since at least the latter part of the seventies.

Prominent within the energy policy arena, as indeed within the environmental, were two species of cause group (or organization-*for*): those that came in the late sixties and early seventies to be called "public interest groups" and "public interest law firms." The Pacific Legal Foundation was one such. Among others that cropped up were the Environmental Defense Fund and the National Resources Defense Council, both equipped with legal talent to go off to court in pursuit of public policy. Examples of the other kind included Environmental Action, Environmental Policy Center, and Critical Mass. The most prominent of these in the early eighties was still Common Cause, "a citizen's movement" that got under way in September 1970. Consumers groups also belong here, being more *-for* than *-of*. Note in particular that the main tradition within consumerism since the first organization appeared in 1899 (the National Consumers League) has been to range quite widely in what, since the late sixties, could be termed the "public interest" style. Child labor and woman suffrage were among the characteristic issues preoccupying the league before World War I. Indeed, historian Arthur S. Link (an authority on the period and on the president, Woodrow Wilson) placed the league on his list of "several important organized groups dedicated to social justice."[343] In our time the league has taken up the cause of migrant farm workers and of safety at the place of work. Think, too, of organizational structure. The Consumer Federation (1967) has labor unions in membership as well as rural electric co-ops, so it is not simply an organization of consumers *as such*. Several of Ralph Nader's pro-consumer creations were not even membership organizations and so essentially -*for*.

What has this long chapter attempted to accomplish? Immediately, it constitutes a sketch map of the territory occupied by interest groups in America, drawing attention to the basic types encountered, their approximate dimensions and locations. Like any other map, it is confined to external features, but should at least enable you to find your way around. Beyond that, the very detail depicts the extent to which America is indeed inclined to be a special-interest democracy. But our judgment on that turns in part on understanding the methods used by the groups in pursuit of their policy objectives. To the analysis of such methods we now turn.

CHAPTER EIGHT
METHODS
AND TECHNIQUES
OF INFLUENCE

How interest groups proceed in pursuit of their policy objectives has already been touched upon here and there. The approaches recalled in the last chapter ranged from face-to-face representations, legal advocacy and the making of campaign contributions, to the "withholding" of essential supplies, demonstrations and even civil disobedience. In the opening chapter lobbyists in 1982 were seen descending on one House committee "like vultures." But those and other such references were made *en passant* in order to put a little flesh on the bone. Now we stand in need of a more systematic treatment.

Many lists of interest-group methods have been compiled. But since this book is intended to suggest one coherent way of thinking about the subject (rather than to be encyclopedic), the idea and so the treatment of methods ought to be derived from the conceptual framework set out in part 1. Recall first the *gemeinschaft-gesellschaft* tendency and the change in the structural mix," or proportions, that it entailed (chapter 2). In the predominantly *gemeinschaft* phase, granted the characteristics of the American Constitution (chapters 4 and 5), and the relative "autonomy" or independence of society and state (before the drawing-together sketched in chapter 6), the idea of method was unambiguous. Within the federal government, there was really only one place to go (Capitol Hill), reachable by only a few practicable routes. The interaction between spokesperson or petitioner and policy maker was essentially face-to-face. Take the classic case of the Tariff Acts (*classic* because so central to the American political experience and specifically because, many would agree, the "history of the American tariffs records the triumph of special interests over the general welfare").[1] Thus, in the 1820s, "the manufacturers and producers who suffered competition from imports" clamored for protective tariffs. Their lobbyists insinuated themselves *de facto* into the various stages of the congressional proceedings from House Ways and Means to the final House-Senate conference. Local groups submitted memorials, or petitions, particularly for the 1824 Act, which built the high tariff wall. Although the woolen interests had come off well (high duties on both raw wool and finished woolen goods), their spokespersons were "back in Washington" three years later trying to raise the level still higher. The Act of 1828 embodies the first great "Christmas tree," although uncharitable critics dubbed it the "tariff of abominations."

In such circumstances the concept of method is obviously a simple one. By contrast, in a predominantly *gesellschaft* society the question becomes more complicated. The rise of the positive state (chapter 6) entailed the growth of government, producing an array of new targets: departments, agencies, and the presidency, increasingly institutionalized as time went on. For the same (but also other) reasons, the U.S. Supreme Court (as well as lesser courts) tended to assume continuous policy-making roles whether so named and acknowledged or not. Accordingly the courts, too, turned into inviting targets for some kinds of interest groups in certain situations.

Now the very notion of methods clouds over. It is not only that there are three potential targets, each of which may be approached in different ways (counting the writs used to activate the U.S. Supreme Court and friend-of-the-court briefs as, up to a point, the functional equivalent of, say, giving evidence at congressional hearings or making representations to an agency). It is also that, under a constitution in which the separation of powers is also a sharing of powers (chapter 4), an institution marginal to a particular policy determination may be used, in principle, to influence the one that is central to the determination. For example: an interest group may persuade a congressional committee to stimulate a bureau or agency. The lines would cross still more if federal district courts were included, not to mention state courts, from which the Judicial Everest—the U.S. Supreme Court—may also be climbed.

Within the private domain, the organizational revolution opened up many new ways of reaching a given center of authority in Washington. A medium-size company might make its own representations, but then supplement that by moving through its sectoral trade association and/or that association of associations, a peak. It also opened up, almost necessitated, cooperative arrangements between otherwise distinct organizations in pursuit of public-policy goals, at least in the form of *ad hoc* coalitions. Since these moves would not preclude "working through" some other center of federal authority, marginal "on the day," the permutations tended to increase markedly.

These developments alone make it necessary to separate out what was unified ("self-contained," you might say) in the predominantly *gemeinschaft* phase (the earlier part of the last century). As long as there was virtually only one authoritative target, "methods" could denote little more than what people did to hit that target: appeal in person, either individually or as a delegation; memorialize, or petition, from distant constituencies; hire someone to buttonhole legislators and make a case; and so (not very far) on. Once there is more than one target and more than a pathway to each, a pattern of advance to the appropriate target will be discernible. It may be neither well planned nor well executed, but it will exist . . . the end product of the interest-group moves, or actions. But if thought out at all (and surely some rational calculation must be imputed), the pattern itself has a claim to be denoted by the term *method*.

Exactly which labels, or terms, we choose to use is far less important than to recognize that, in a predominantly *gesellschaft* society, there are, in this context, two "movements," not one: first, from interest group to any one institution, particularly governmental, treated *as if* set apart, more or less, from the relevant complex; and second, the group's overall pattern of approach to the (primary) policy-making center. As for labels, the former will be here denoted by *technique*; the latter by *method*. Thus, techniques permuted or combined make up a method.

Despite some fine case studies, it is at present impossible to generalize even about which methods (including sequences) are regularly employed, much less predict which methods promise success (although one might propose that certain techniques, notably campaign contributions, work only too well). The broadest generalization one can make about methods is that, with the transition from the relatively *gemeinschaft* to the relatively *gesellschaft* stage, they take longer to reach the target, i.e., become more and more roundabout. That, as noted above, is implied in the virtual widening of available targets and in the unprecedented growth of private organizations. But at least two other features of the organizational revolution were of crucial importance. The key to both is communications, in more senses than one. First, not necessarily historically, comes a more systematic mobilization of constituents' opinions, finding classic expression in telegrams as well as letters and postal cards to congresspersons. When the interests were grappling with Congress over tariffs in the 1820s, mail was being carried by stage coach over the 104,000 miles of post roads then in operation. But in the following decade official mail began to be carried by the new railroads, of which thirty thousand miles had been constructed by 1860. Two years later the railway mail service was inaugurated, followed by free delivery to addressees—instead of to a post office, or, earlier still, the county courthouse—which the introduction of stamps (1847) had made practicable. By 1871 some fifty cities had carrier service. Two years later the postal card, a European innovation, was made available for one cent (a domestic letter then cost three cents *per* half-ounce).

Bulk mailings at special low rates would follow. Meanwhile (1861) the tele-graphic message, or telegram, had been made available for transmission coast-to-coast. The other celebrated transcontinental link—the meeting of the Central Pacific and Union Pacific railroads near Salt Lake City—had been forged in 1869.[2]   *The Beginnings of Lobbying.*

With the telephone's use spreading in the eighties and nineties, such technical developments and service offerings seemed almost custom-built for the mobilization of interests at the periphery, thus tending to make methods more and more roundabout. It is somehow fitting that this should have been perceived by one of the great railroad promoters of the period, Collis Huntington, president of Central Pacific. In the seventies, when "lobbying for the first time became a vital element in government," Huntington could see beyond that intensification of the traditional direct approach. As historian David Rothman would explain: Huntington, "convinced that elected officials were attentive to constituents' telegrams and letters, detailed men to ar-range writing campaigns."[3] Like his rival Ted Scott, of the Texas & Pacific, he also sought the endorsement of local groups, including counties, for his bills before Congress. Thus the ground was being prepared for some aston-ishing ploys of this kind. In 1917, for example, one Anti-Saloon League official "boasted that he had personally seen to the sending of nine hundred" telegrams in a single day. These were sent to representatives "demanding that they vote in a particular way," no doubt in the cause of Prohibition. In 1913 well over nine thousand organizations had presented petitions, one of which bore six million signatures. The classic contemporary case occurred in 1983 on the issue of the 10 percent withholding of bank interest and divi-dends scheduled to start on July 1. In a very late run, the banks, led by the American Bankers Association (1875), buried Congress with protests from customer-constituents, who had been suitably excited and supplied with materials. And so it came about that, for example, Republican Senator Dave Durenberger (Minn.) received nearly 175,000 "pieces of mail"; Democratic Senator Paul Tsongas (Mass.), "almost 200,000 letters and postcards." As late as mid-May, Congress succumbed, throwing the car into reverse.[4]

With that revolution in communications went another one in the same era, or perhaps it should count as two closely related revolutions: the rise of the popular press and of public relations as a concern and practice, with pretensions ultimately to being acknowleded a profession. Various technical inventions (including the linotype machine in the 1880s as well as the tele-graph), combined with the rapidly increasing population to lay the foundation for the first mass medium. It was *mass* in the number of dailies published, of which there were some twenty-two hundred at the turn of the century (up from fewer than six hundred in 1870). Mass, too, in circulation: a sevenfold increase in that same period (population did not quite double). By 1900 two of the dailies each enjoyed a circulation of over a million. The political signifi-cance of these and related changes was profound, but must here be limited strictly to what it meant for interest-group methods. It now became possible for some groups to penetrate some parts of the press, passing off propaganda as objective news and even as independent comment. With about $28 million a year to spend on advertising, the public utilities, mainly the electric power companies, showed how the press could be used. Their Ohio committee, for example, claimed that in 1926 "over 20,000 column inches of news and 150 editorials *written by utility press agents* were printed in Ohio newspapers" (italics added). Thirty-five thousand column inches of "utility news" were placed in Indiana papers (in a year, presumably). An Oregon agency, apparently independent but subsidized by the utilities, had 14,000 newspaper clients: in four years, it placed the equivalent of over 65,000 *pages* of utility "news."[5] "Canned" news and other such materials are still supplied and used (by radio stations, too) without attribution to the interest-group source. But the point now is to observe the increasing "obliqueness" of interest-group methods.

The other facet of the communications revolution particularly relevant here for its impact on the character of interest-group methods was the growth of public relations. The use of the words, revealing an awareness of the public as a force to be considered, goes back to at least 1882. But the term in its recognizable modern sense seems to date from 1906: "The public relations problem of the railroads." That was indeed the context of the new activity: to create a favorable image for certain corporate enterprises, such as the railroads, AT&T, and perhaps above all Standard Oil. It was not for nothing that one of the early press agents, Ivy Lee, whom Standard Oil hired, was dubbed a "physician to corporate bodies." By 1909 New York City alone was reported to have ten thousand press agents, new ones being "born every minute." By 1913 several enterprises, including the public utilities, had established their own internal "departments of public relations." Others followed suit in the thirties and forties.[6]

That was part of an extremely important development politically because, somewhere along the line, corporate p.r. ceased to be defensive in the pre-1914 sense and began to lay down a more "positive" groundwork for the celebration of the socioeconomic system, which political scientist Norton Long likened (in 1937) to insuring against fundamental change. But the general point here is that interest-group methods were tending to become ever more circuitous. This had been noted, in different words, back in 1888, when the former librarian of Congress, A. R. Spofford, distinguished between the older type of lobbyists ("the harpies and vultures of politics"), and those who "seek to organize a public opinion favorable to their measures, by the industrious collection and publication of facts. . . . No lobby scheme can succeed unless supported by a strong outside public sentiment."[7] As one would expect, however, the tendency became more marked (or at least remarked upon) in the decade or so before World War I. What a senator said in relation to his own chamber may be applied more broadly. Identifying "powerful and concerted lobbying" (over tariffs, 1913), he went on: "It is not the personal appeal to senators, but the newer form of organized activity to mold public sentiment, and to influence senators by means of public pressure from various sources."[8]

IDEA AND NAME

That senator's apparent willingness to squeeze the newer idea of molding public sentiment into the traditional idea of lobbying, but also Spofford's rejection of both *lobbyist* and *lobbying* in application to the newer art of influencing public opinion, confront us with the problem of terminology. In the predominantly *gemeinschaft* phase, when the activity—essentially the face-to-face persuasion of legislators—became noticeable, observers evidently needed a name for it and its practitioners. Resorting to a well-known figure of speech,[9] they (or someone) introduced words derived from the anteroom or hall of a legislative building that is open to the public and so available for interviews between members and nonmembers. From it—the lobby—came the needed nouns and verbs, perhaps starting with *lobby-agent* (1829) and eventually including *lobby-member* and *lobbyist; lobby* and *to lobby;* and the verb-noun, *lobbying*. By 1847 when Chauncey Goodrich of Yale revised Webster's famous dictionary, the nation had a formal definition of *lobby member:* "a person who frequents the lobby of a house of legislation." In the 1860s the lexicographers were more explicit, rounding off the sentence just quoted with: "in order to influence the action of the members" (1860), and "for the purpose of influencing measures" (1864).

But just as the lexicographers were beginning to tie down the terms and so catch up with the activity, this itself, as we have seen, was beginning to change. Not only were interest groups blazing more roundabout trails leading to Congress: they were also beginning to discover, as the state became more positive, that some of the decisions they wished to influence were lodged in the executive, or bureaucracy. Yet neither of these extensions of the original idea was ever given a new name by the political-science profession. Someone making representations to an agency or bureau came to be known, by default, as a lobbyist (although, if practicing law, he or she may still resist the appellation), while the activity itself is commonly called *lobbying*. But this term would not usually be applied to the most roundabout of the roundabout methods—the appeal to, or manipulation of, public opinion, in a very broad, or diffuse, sense. Nor would the specialist in that line of work be called a lobbyist. Yet the other principal strand of the roundabout skein—the activation of specific constituencies—is very frequently denoted by *grassroots lobbying*, although, perversely, the person who plans or undertakes it is seldom if ever designated *grassroots lobbyist* or even *lobbyist*.

Reading that paragraph, you are entitled (but not obligated) to feel a little confused. You would find yourself in good company. In 1954 the U.S. Supreme Court wrestled with this very issue and divided five-to-three, Mr. Justice Clark taking no part in the deliberations or decision, over both concept and terminology. One of the three dissenters differed from the other two as well as from the majority. At issue was the constitutionality of the Federal Regulation of Lobbying Act of 1946, which, on the face of it, was intended to make lobbyists register and supply certain financial details about their activities. But Congress, while providing several of the needed definitions, had neglected *lobbyist* and *lobbying*. The latter term appears only in the short title of the act (cited above); the former does not appear in the act at all (although it is in the Senate and House reports, where "three classes of so-called lobbyists" are characterized).

It is clear, however, that Congress had meant to capture in its registering and reporting net both the roundabout and the direct approaches (to Congress itself, i.e., in respect of legislation).[10] That stands out in the act, as in #307(b): "To influence, directly or indirectly, the passage or defeat of any legislation by the Congress of the United States."[11] But we also have the evidence (as to intentions) of the Senate and House reports, saying that the act covered: "First. Those who do not visit the Capitol but initiate propaganda from all over the country, in the form of letters and telegrams, many of which have been based entirely upon misinformation as to the facts."

But starting in 1953, the Supreme Court went out of its way to restrict the concept of lobbying to direct approaches only. According to Mr. Justice Frankfurter, speaking for the Court (two of the justices took no part), lobbying "in its commonly accepted sense" meant "representations made directly to the Congress, its members, or its committees" and did not include what a congressman had called attempts "to saturate the thinking of the community."[12] In 1954 the Court (now divided) kept to the same virtual definition: lobbying meant "direct communication with members of Congress on pending or proposed federal legislation."[13]

That virtual definition may indeed have "saved the act" (i.e., removed doubts about its constitutionality), as Chief Justice Warren remarked in finding (in effect) for the government. But it was at the intellectual cost of making confusion worse confounded (for political science). For the Court did not simply exclude one whole class of activities (indirect, or roundabout, methods) from the reach of registration and reporting. It also conjured up a phrase that is not in the act (as Mr. Justice Douglas, dissenting, pointed out): "direct communication with Congress." And this, he further objected, was being interpreted too narrowly, becoming "a new concept."

Alas! His own concept (Mr. Justice Black concurring) only added to the confusion (from the standpoint, still, of political science): "To influence 'directly' the passage or defeat of legislation includes any number of methods—

for example, nationwide radio, television or advertising programs promoting a particular measure, as well as the 'buttonholing' of Congress. To include the latter while excluding the former is to rewrite the act."

With that last sentence, one happens to agree. But the points to be grasped in this context of methods are the following. First, in the Court's deliberations, even contortions, we may see refracted the *gemeinschaft-gesell-schaft* tendency as it works itself out within a unique and vibrant constitutional tradition—that crystallized in the First Amendment, particularly the right of the people "to petition the government for a redress of grievances." Up to a point, Mr. Justice Douglas and Mr. Justice Black seemed willing to extend the *concept* of lobbying to make it "symmetrical" or congruent with the realities, technical and sociological, of a predominantly *gesellschaft* social order. On the other hand, the prevailing majority held on firmly to a concept of lobbying more congruent with a predominantly *gemeinschaft* social order, or at least one which had flourished in that era. But their purpose was not anachronistic—they were looking back in order to rescue something for the present, i.e., to give the government (or Congress) part of what it wanted while steering everybody away from the forbidden waters of the First Amendment. The Douglas-Black line, on the other hand, was to suggest that the majority was playing fast and loose with concepts and definitions merely to save an act that was not worth saving.

In any case, since the majority's opinion naturally prevailed, it follows that the lawyer's (or Supreme Court's) conception of lobbying and so of inter-est-group methods does not (at present) coincide with the political scientist's. For if lobbying is defined as simply making direct contacts, there obviously can be no such thing as indirect lobbying—a distinction commonly drawn in so many words in the textbooks. Yet, for reasons suggested earlier in the chapter, the distinction between direct and roundabout is well founded. So what is one to do? The solution adopted here is to sustain the distinction established earlier in the chapter but to refrain from using the word *lobbying* to denote the roundabout, or indirect. This means giving up such handy (if now hackneyed) terms as *grassroots lobbying* and instead referring either to roundabout meth-ods of influence or to the concrete behavior (e.g., propaganda, mobilizing the constituencies, and the like).

LOBBYING AND LOBBYISTS

Thinking of lobbying and lobbyists within the context of the social order's interaction with political authority, one would like to be able to reproduce a definitive listing with numbers in relation to policies and institutional targets. But all we have is a list derived from the Regulation of Lobbying Act, 1946, which, as noted, excluded (or failed to include) policy making within the executive branch. Then of course the U.S. Supreme Court set to work on the act, finding in summary that there were "three prerequisites to coverage" (and, accordingly, to registration, the basis for a list):[14]

1. The *person*[15] must have solicited, collected, or received contributions;
2. one of the main purposes of such *person*, or one of the main purposes of such contributions, must have been to influence the passage or defeat of legislation by Congress;
3. the intended method of accomplishing this purpose must have been through direct communication with members of Congress.

It follows that any list so derived is seriously incomplete. But it may convey a sense of which elements in the social order (at a given time) "project" toward Congress in respect of what kinds of legislative policies (see Table 8–1).[16]

That is no more than a (nonstatistical) sampling of a list whose own foundation is glaringly weak. Even so, the table gives us some inkling of the forces arrayed in the congressional domain, in 1980, what they were seeking then, and who was *registered* as trying to get it for them. This prompts the question: how many such intermediaries—lobbyists—were *registered* at the time? It is surprisingly difficult to be sure. Only a year or two earlier (1977–78), totals ranging from about two thousand to thirty-seven hundred had been reported. These figures came from specialists ranging from political scientist Carol S. Greenwald to Common Cause investigator, Tamar Lewin, who, apparently after studying the original sources—the House of Representatives' Office of Records and Registration, and the Senate's Office of Public Records—wrote: "Four times a year, some 3700 of the Washington lobbyists fill out 2-page reports intended to show their receipts and expenditures."[17] But by mid-1980, Bill Keller, of the authoritative *Congressional Quarterly*, was "conveying" a total of "5500 individuals" registered with both House and Senate. ("Conveying" because it is not absolutely clear in context whether he had made his own count or was relying on Edward Zuckerman, author of a newsletter on lobbying.)[18] Of course, one expects registrations to vary over time as the legislative issues vary, but such great variation within a short period makes one wonder if the counters were not using different definitions. Mr. Keller himself drew attention to the question of "multiple filings by individuals who lobby for several clients."

With such reservations in mind, one notes that the total for the last quarter of 1982 was reported to be sixty-five hundred,[19] an ostensible increase of about one thousand since mid-1980. That, in any case, included only those who bothered to register. As Ms. Lewin reminded us, neither the House Office nor the Senate's has power to act against "lobbyists who fail to register, do not disclose fully, or consistently miss the filing deadlines." As someone else well said, the 1946 act is "more loophole than law." How many practising but unregistered lobbyists congregate in Washington is a subject for speculation

TABLE 8-1 Lobby Registrations Made During 1980

ORGANIZATIONS	ISSUES/TOPICS	LOBBYISTS (REGISTERED)
Corporations and businesses:		
Crane Packing Co., Ill.	General tax legislation including the pending Windfall Profits Tax Act	1 (D.C. law firm)
Energol Corp., Wash.	Windfall profits tax, etc.	1 (D.C. law firm)
Exxon Corp., N.Y.	Legislation dealing with environmental issues, synthetic fuels, solar energy and R & D	1
General Dynamics Corp., Mo.	Maritime legislation, etc.	1 (D.C. law firm)
Gulf Oil Corp., Pa.	Legislative matters pertaining to oil, gas, windfall profits, hazardous waste, synfuels and marketing	1
International Telephone and Telegraph Corp., N.Y.	Telecommunications—for; windfall profits tax—for some portions, opposed to others; Chrysler loan guarantees—for; etc.	1
Mobil Oil Corp., N.Y.	Legislation affecting the production of oil and gas	1 (D.C. law firm)
Rocky Mountain Energy Corp., N.Y.	Crude oil windfall profits tax of 1979	1 (D.C. law firm)
Shell Oil Corp., Texas	Maritime legislation generally	1 (D.C. law firm)
Texaco Inc., N.Y.	Production, refining, marketing, & transportation of oil, gas & other minerals	1

TABLE 8–1 (cont.)

ORGANIZATIONS	ISSUES/TOPICS	LOBBYISTS (REGISTERED)
Individual:		
W. H. Bates, Kansas City, Mo. (filing for self)	Principal interest is in Natural Gas Policy Act . . . with specific interest in respect to incremental pricing of natural gas.	
Trade Associations:		
American Gas Association, Arlington, Va.	Synthetic fuels and conservation, etc., crude oil windfall profits tax	1
American Medical Association, Chicago, Ill.	All federal legislation of a health or medical nature	1
American Petroleum Institute, D.C.	Divestiture and any other legislation of concern to the petroleum industry	1
Independent Petroleum Association of America, D.C.	All tax bills dealing with taxation of natural resources, land use legislation	1
National Association of Realtors, D.C.	Legislation affecting real estate generally; and Truth in Lending Act amendments. Condominium legislation, etc.	1
National Education Association, D.C.	Public Education	1
Tobacco Tax Council, Richmond, Va.	Matters that pertain to the federal aspects of tobacco products	1
Western Oil and Gas Association, L.A.	All legislation concerning the petroleum industry	1

ORGANIZATIONS	ISSUES/TOPICS	LOBBYISTS (REGISTERED)
Peaks:		
Business Roundtable, N.Y.	All regulatory reform legislation	1
Chamber of Commerce of the United States, D.C.	Matters of interest to the business community about which the chamber may wish to make recommendations or comments	1
National Association of Manufacturers, D.C.	General energy legislation, including, but not limited to, oil control, synthetic fuels, energy taxes, coal conversion, etc.	2
National Small Business Association, D.C.	Trucking deregulation—oppose provisions therein, etc.	1
Agriculture:		
American Farm Bureau Federation, Ill.	Transportation	1
Dairymen Inc., Ky.	Agricultural co-ops and the dairy industry	1 (D.C. law firm)
Florida Tomato Exchange, Fla.	Legislation affecting agricultural industries, in particular, the tomato industry	1 (D.C. law firm)
National Association of Wheat Growers, D.C.	Agricultural and food policy, including grain standards & inspection, tax policy, etc.	1
National Farmers Organization, Inc., Iowa	Legislation (not yet introduced) to clarify tax-exempt status of agricultural organizations under Internal Revenue Code Section 501(c)(5)	1 (D.C. law firm)

TABLE 8–1 (cont.)

ORGANIZATIONS	ISSUES/TOPICS	LOBBYISTS (REGISTERED)
The Sugar Association, D.C.	All legislation concerning sugar	2
Labor:		
Amalgamated Clothing and Textile Workers Union, N.Y.	Legislation affecting working people	1
Industrial Union Department, AFL-CIO, D.C.	All bills affecting the welfare of the country generally, and specifically bills affecting working people, etc.	1
Consumer:		
Consumer Federation of America, D.C.	Drug Regulation Reform Act of 1978; appropriations to FTC for effect of advertisements on children	1
Consumers Union of the United States, Inc., N.Y.	Issues affecting consumers	1
Energy:		
Solar Lobby, D.C.	Renewable energy and energy conservation legislation	2
Environmental:		
Environmental Policy Center, D.C.	All legislation affecting coal development and utilization, etc.	1
Friends of the Earth, D.C.	Legislation to preserve, restore, and insure rational use of the ecosphere	1

ORGANIZATIONS	ISSUES/TOPICS	LOBBYISTS (REGISTERED)
Sierra Club, Calif.	(Acts detailed)	2
Zero Population Growth, Inc., D.C.	A national population policy, refugee & immigration policy	1
Ethnic:		
The Confederated Tribes of Warm Springs, Ore.	Legislation relating to Indian Affairs; Bureau of Indian Affairs; Department of the Interior and other agencies	1
National Black Media Coalition, D.C.	Increased participation of minorities, ownership, management in communications	1 (D.C. law firm)
Public interest:		
American Civil Liberties Union, New York, N.Y.	Continuing interest in congressional as well as other action in any way affecting civil liberties	4
Common Cause, D.C.	Promotion of social welfare in the United States	2
League of Women Voters of the United States, D.C.	Human resources, international relations, natural resources, representative government	1
Public Relations:		
Hill and Knowlton Inc., New York, N.Y.	Business interests of firms employing Hill and Knowlton	2

TABLE 8–1 (cont.)

ORGANIZATIONS	ISSUES/TOPICS	LOBBYISTS (REGISTERED)
Reform:		
Congressional District Action Committee, Del. (also Md.)	A constitutional amendment that would provide legal protection for all human persons from the time of conception until natural death; legislation that will prohibit federal dollars from being used for abortions	-
Right to Life Crusade, Okla.	Any amendments to funding bills that will prohibit the use of federal funds for abortion	1
Gay Rights National Lobby, Inc., D.C.	In favor of civil rights for lesbians and gay men	1
National Coalition to Ban Handguns	Favors strong legislative controls on handgun sales and possession	1
National Organization for the Reform of Marijuana Laws, D.C.	The elimination of criminal penalties for marijuana smoking under the Controlled Substances Act of 1970	1

as well as definition. Estimates made within a few months of each other by qualified observers (e.g., Tamar Lewin and *Time* in mid-1978) were very far apart.[20] Here one will settle for a number to match up with date (1980) and concept (lobbying *Congress*). Edward Zuckerman estimated that, altogether, about 20,000 people in Washington earned *at least part of their living* by lobbying Congress. If so, there may have been some 14–15,000 unregistered lobbyists of the relevant kind (20,000 minus 5500).

Whatever the exact total, everybody agrees about the trend—since the late 1960s, *upward*. For reasons implied above, this, too, is hard to quantify. We may proceed from a logical expectation (chapter 6): the more positive the state, the greater the number and concentration of interest groups/lobbies in Washington (all other things being equal, including relatively weak political parties). One index of that greater "positive-ness" was the regulatory explosion of the seventies: 1970–79, twenty new regulatory agencies (compared with eleven for the whole New Deal era), a *Federal Register* up to 77,000 pages (from 20,000 in 1970), and so on. Most of it was so-called social environmental protection, industrial safety, product safety and specification, affirmative action, and the like. But, inevitably, it impinged heavily on the business world. So we may expect corporations and trade associations to strengthen their lobbying teams in Washington (under whatever titles) and even increasingly to relocate there themselves, or at least set up a new establishment. Both these things did happen. In the early seventies (a Washington-based professor, Jimmy D. Johnson, observed) companies were "opening at least a dozen new offices each year in Washington—some costing $200,000 annually to operate." By 1972, he judged, about 80 percent of the one thousand leading U.S. companies either (a) had offices in the capital or (b) made use of law firms, agencies or consultants "to represent them full time."[21]

At the second-order level, it has been calculated that, of the six thousand or so national trade and professional associations, over fifteen hundred (27 percent) "are now headquartered for lobbying effect in Washington,"[22] and about fifty labor unions maintain a Washington office, apart from the AFL-CIO. Although we lack a firm comparable benchmark for an earlier date, that is widely believed to represent a substantial increase over the recent past.

As to (a), whereas in the late sixties about one hundred corporations had maintained Washington lobbies, over five hundred did so by the late seventies. Thus, the Ford Motor Company, which had managed with three Washington representatives in the early sixties, had forty full-timers on the payroll there in the late seventies.[23] By then Gulf Oil's team of four (1973) had expanded to a dozen. On the other hand, B. F. Goodrich (chemicals as well as tires) had relied essentially on its legal staff and its trade association. But in 1972 it engaged its first full-time lobbyist. A vice-president explained: "My feeling was that so many regulatory activities were burgeoning in Washington, and the whole matter of relations with government becoming so complex . . . that we needed somebody who knew Washington well."[24]

To some undetermined extent, these trends converged and overlapped. For example, take the American Petroleum Institute. It moved to Washington from N.Y.C. in 1971. Reorganized in 1973–74, it increased its lobbying team to ten (from three to five, registered, before that), formed a new policy analysis committee to keep an eye on legislation, and plunged more vigorously into p.r. By 1980, the API had a dozen lobbyists, a p.r. department of twenty-five and a policy analysis team of fifteen, over and above some three hundred employees in Washington, and perhaps the same number elsewhere, financed from a budget of some $30 million (derived from 350 firms, including the big seven or eight, and seven thousand individual members).[25]

Casting one's net more widely, one notes what former *Life* correspondent, David Sheridan noted in 1972: "The number of lobbyists is growing steadily." He used a broad definition: "Men and women who work more or less full-time at trying to influence government actions and decisions in favor of their clients."[26] On that basis, he put the Washington total at about five thousand. Looking back over the period 1973–78, other journalistic observers judged that the total number of lobbyists (undefined but evidently broadly conceived) had "soared from about eight thousand to over fifteen thousand."[27]

Here again discrepancies obtrude: the eight thousand of 1973 can hardly have been counted on the same basis of five thousand of 1972. Still, no one doubts that the decade saw a very substantial increase. And beyond the imperfect statistics was the evidence of one's eyes, of lobbyists as a physical presence: "Their mass arrival has transformed Washington's downtown K Street into a virtual hall of lobbies. New office buildings springing up west of the White House along Pennsylvania Avenue fill up with lobbyists as soon as the painters walk out."[28] With that went the growth of expensive restaurants "around K Street to cater for the expense account tastes of a new branch of government: lawyers, lobbyists, consultants and news media executives, all eager to buy long, tax-deductible lunches for their government clients and sources."[29]

WASHINGTON LOBBY: CHANGING COMPOSITION

That last quotation prompts the question: with the migration of many organizations to Washington, the establishment there of others *de novo*, and the interrelated increase in the number of practicing lobbyists, what changes in the composition of the "lobbying force" have been taking place? There is no Milbrath for the early eighties as there was for the late fifties, so one simply draws attention to four features.

One is that women have entered fully into what was principally a man's preserve. They had been "used" from an early stage. Thus, about a century ago, A. R. Spofford listed "the charms of feminine attraction" among the techniques employed by lobbyists to get "the public man . . . to look favorably upon the measures which interested parties seek to have enacted." Even today a lobbyist has been known to provide facilities (e.g., an apartment) if not the "feminine attraction."[30] But gradually women came into lobbying proper, not only on behalf of their "own" organizations-*of* and -*for* (chapter 7) but also in labor unions. But a further stage was passed in the latter half of the seventies. In 1979–80, women were registered to lobby for Chevron, U.S.A. (owned by Standard Oil of California), Gulf Oil, Firestone Tire & Rubber, and the Air Transport Association of America, among others. In late 1975 there were only a dozen of them lobbying for corporations or trade associations, little more than a good quorum for the association—Women in Government Relations—that they boldly formed. By May 1979, their organization could boast almost two hundred members and a monthly recruitment of about ten. "Ms. Lobbyist goes to Washington," indeed.[31]

An even more significant "mutation" has already come to our attention: the entry into the lobbying field of the public-interest lobbyist. Whatever the difficulty of defining "the public interest," such representatives certainly speak for a broader public than the traditional lobbyist. Of course, the phenomenon was not entirely novel: the National Consumers League dates from 1899; the American Civil Liberties Union (ACLU) from 1920. But now came a great surge forward. In 1973–74 Jeffrey Berry counted eighty-three in Washington alone. Some of these (e.g., Committee for a Free China) will not be accounted public-interest groups in this book. But, even allowing for some exclusions here, a great advance no doubt occurred after 1960 (almost two out of three on Professor Berry's list were that recent).[32] The public-interest law firm may be taken as a subspecies of the public interest lobby. A conference of "public-interest advocates" mounted in 1976 brought together over one hundred, "most of which had either been established or significantly revitalized since the mid-sixties." Others counted 150, in the very same year. Again, "litigation as a form of pressure group activity," was not novel.[33] The National Consumers League resorted to it from 1908, soon followed by the NAACP and the ACLU among others. But the generous funding, scale of operations, specialization and skill of these post-1960 public-interest law firms set them apart from what had gone before. Altogether, these developments seemed to constitute a profoundly important change in the composition of the lobbying force.

The third feature was related to the second: the increasing tendency of two Washington roles to merge, producing the lawyer-lobbyist. One is not thinking here of counsel on the staff of an organization but rather of (a) the freelance lawyer and (b) the member, probably a partner, of a law firm, nowadays essentially in Washington. This is part of a wider question about the relationship of lobbyist to organization: hired hand or member of the staff; self-employed or employee (using this term to include vice-presidents for governmental relations, and the like)? The position when Professor Milbrath published his standard work in 1963 was as shown in Table 8-2 (somewhat rearranged for the purpose in hand).[34]

TABLE 8–2   Lobbyists: Members of Initiating Organizations or Self-employed

Organizational members			
trade association executives		19	
officers of organizations		9	
staff		33	
general counsel		6	67 (59%)
Self-employed ("outsiders")			
Washington representatives		18	
Lawyers: freelance	14		
in large law firms	10	24	
P.R. consultants		2	
Lobbyist entrepreneurs		3	47 (41%)
			114

So the ratio of (a) to (b) above was then fourteen to ten. In the early eighties, one does not know the ratio but cannot doubt that, as lobbying entities, the large law firms have greatly increased in numbers and significance. For example, take Wilmer, Cutler and Pickering, interesting in part because Mr. Lloyd Cutler has long been a major figure in the overlapping terrains of Washington law and government. Writing in 1978, Mark Green reported that, "in the past few years," the firm had "represented the following interests on Capitol Hill":[35]

> J. P. Morgan and Company and the American Express Company on bills amending the Bank Holding Company Act; J. C. Penney on a variety of consumer legislation; Kaiser Industries; the National Corporation for Housing Partnerships; Yale, Stanford, and the Massachusetts Institute of Technology on tax matters; the American Basketball Association on its effort to merge with the National Basketball Association; the Dealer Bank Association, the Jonathan Development Corporation and Oil Investment Institute on various financial issues—as well as American Airlines, the Chronicle Publishing Company, the Automobile Manufacturers Association, the Pharmaceutical Manufacturers Association, and the American Iron and Steel Institute.

Table 8-3, a partial list for 1980, was chosen to illustrate the range, or because a name is familiar (e.g., former senator George Smathers), or because the firm will cross our path later in the case studies.[36]

Do not read too much into this list. Like Professor Milbrath's of 1963, it is based on registrations. The names of some famous lawyer practioners of the lobbying art (as defined by political scientists) did not appear: neither the Clifford (Clark M.) of Clifford and Miller, for example, nor the Corcoran (Thomas G.) of Corcoran, Foley, Youngman and Rowe, so celebrated in Washington circles that he bore a nickname, "Tommy the Cork." Even so, the list illustrates how far the traditional concept of a lobbyist has changed.

The fourth feature is the growing prominence, at least, of another self-employed "outsider," the policy entrepreneur (see Table 8–2). He or she, as

TABLE 8–3   Washington Law Firms Registering as Lobbyists and Their Clients (1980)

LAW FIRMS	CLIENTS
Patton, Boggs & Blow	American Pharmaceutical Association, Business Roundtable, California Westside Farmers, Chemical Manufacturers Association, Council to Protect Earned Employment Rights, Dillingham Corp., International Cogeneration Society, Karf Industries Inc., Merchants National Bank of Mobil, Multi Minerals Corp., National Association of Chain Drug Stores, Wilshire Oil Co., of Texas, and others
Arent, Fox, Kinter, Plotkin & Kahn	Nissho-Iawai American Corp.
Arnold & Porter	American Invsco Corp., Morgan Stanley & Co., Inc., Securities Industry Association, Table Grape Growers Association
Caplin & Drysdale	Aetna Life & Casualty Co., American Family Life Assurance Co., of Georgia, Public Broadcasting Communications, Inc.
Covington & Burling	Hugo Neu & Sons Inc., International Business Machines Corp.
Foley, Lardner, Hollabaugh & Jacobs	First National Wisconsin Bank of Milwaukee, Phosphate Rock Export Association, Smith Barney, Harris Upham & Co.
Groom & Nordberg	American President Lines, John Hancock Mutual Life Insurance Co., Matson Navigation, Phoenix Mutual Life Insurance Co., The Travelers Insurance Co., Western Conference of Teamsters Pension Trust Fund
Hogan & Hartson	National Farmers Organization Inc., Semiconductor Industry Association, Vinland National Center
Hydeman, Mason & Goodell	States Line
Miller & Chevalier	The Association of Private Pension and Welfare Plans Inc., Investors Diversified Services Inc., National Automobile Dealers Association, Redwood Lincoln Mercury Leasing Inc.
Smathers, Symington & Herlong	Filmways Inc.; Kansas City, Missouri
Wilmer & Pickering	C.P.C. International Inc.

defined by Professor Milbrath, is a policy specialist, in contrast to the Washington representative—an envoy for an organization with headquarters out-of-town—who is essentially a jack-of-all-trades. One of the best known of the species in the late seventies and early eighties was Charls E. Walker, a specialist in taxation. Formerly on the staff of the American Bankers Association, Mr. Walker served as deputy secretary at the Treasury in the Nixon administration. Leaving in 1973, he set up Charls E. Walker Associates Inc. Within a year or two his clients included Ford Motor Co., General Electric Co., General Motors Corp., Goodyear Tire and Rubber Co., International Paper Co., U.S. Steel Corp., and Weyerhaueser Co.,[37] (a giant in lumber). By late 1980 he was reported to represent no fewer than fifty major corporations, including Procter and Gamble and Union Carbide.[38] Certainly his firm[39] was registered in 1980 in the service of more than two dozen large corporations, including American Telephone and Telegraph, Kaiser Aluminum and Chemical, and Owens Corning Fiberglass.

Within the self-employed category, the lobbying firm of Timmons and Company was also making a name for itself in the late seventies and early eighties. It does not fit readily into the Milbrathian schema, not being notable for skill in a particular policy area (lobbyist entrepreneur), but on the other hand appearing to be much more than an envoy for out-of-town corporations (Washington representative). Given all the changes, the latter concept may well be less apt than it was, or perhaps Timmons and Company will prove to be a mutation. In any event, after six years as administrative assistant to Representative Bill Brock (Rep.-Tennessee), William E. Timmons left in 1968 to serve as Mr. Nixon's convention director. His reward was a job in the Nixon White House, where he was head of the Office of Congressional Relations for about five years. At the end of 1974 he left to launch his own lobbying firm. In October 1977 it had a staff of ten, including four partners, of whom Tom C. Korologos was probably the best known,[40] and as many rich clients as it needed. They would have to be rich: "It costs a company about $100,000 a year to hire the wit and wisdom of Mr. Korologos and his partners in Timmons and Company, one of those institutions that play a large but almost invisible role in the way Washington works."[41] And that was in 1977 dollars. Clients then included Standard Oil of Indiana, the American Petroleum Institute, Genesco (a clothing manufacturer), G. D. Searle Pharmaceuticals, the National Rifle Association, Business Roundtable, and the Trial Lawyers Association. New names that surfaced in 1980 included H. J. Heinz Company and Chrysler Corporation (for its bail-out loan).[42] The firm also registered then for Filmways Inc. But it had to get along part of the year without the services of its principal. For Mr. Timmons was back again at managing the Republican National Convention, this time for Ronald Reagan, the man who became president. After that triumph, he took charge of "the transition teams sent into every significant federal agency to lay the groundwork for the new president and administration." As a White House official remarked to Rudy Abramson of the *Los Angeles Times:* "In effect, Bill Timmons set up the government. That's exactly what it amounts to. There isn't anyone of importance here that he doesn't know. He wrote the book for the Reagan administration."[43] It took time. The day after President Reagan was sworn in, Mr. Timmons returned to his office for only the third time in seven months. But there seemed likely to be compensations. As "one of his lobbyist colleagues" put it: "The only thing Timmons needs to do now is to call all of his clients and tell them his fee is being doubled."[44]

Here we may observe another "mutation": the p.r. lobbyist (on the lines of the lawyer-lobbyist). Hill and Knowlton, Inc., constitutes a remarkable example, as we shall see when we come to study the deregulation of natural gas. In 1980 it was registered to lobby for the Distilled Spirits Council of the U.S.; Florists Transworld Delivery Association; Health Insurance Association of America; Hide Action Program; RKO General; Seattle First National Bank; and Uniroyal.

In direct line of descent in the early eighties was Gray and Company, named for Robert Keith Gray, who had directed Hill and Knowlton's Washington office for two decades before serving as Mr. Reagan's communications director in the 1980 campaign and then as codirector of Mr. Reagan's inauguration, obviously a very happy and profitable conjunction. He then decided to "grab the brass ring" (as he told Robert M. Kaus), i.e., go into business for himself. He set up shop in the charming Georgetown section of Washington (so like a section of Chelsea in London). By 1982 Gray and Company was the "second largest independent p.r. firm in the nation, with annual billings of $9 million." There were others of the kind, including the Hannaford Company, one of whose principals, Peter Hannaford, had served Mr. Reagan in California. The other principal, Michael K. Deaver, actually followed President Reagan to the White House. These happen to be Republican examples. It should not be assumed that Democrats have lacked ambition of this kind. Ms. Anne Wexler, who dealt with interest groups for President Carter, had already put out her own p.r. shingle. More tellingly, Gray and Company took on as chief lobbyist Gary Hymel, who had been administrative assistant to the Speaker of the House, Democrat "Tip" O'Neill. One of Mr. Hymel's first assignments was to defeat President Reagan's proposal for a minimum corporate tax. He explained for the benefit of the uninitiated: "It's not a party thing, it's a technical thing. A lot of Democrats are against the minimum tax. And it's not something Tip O'Neill's going to break his pick over."[45]

More self-consciously partisan was the Kamber Group, a p.r. and lobbying firm founded by Victor S. Kamber in the summer of 1980. A former AFL-CIO publicist, Mr. Kamber observed (early in 1981): "Under Carter, we saw a tremendous growth in the business-oriented firms: Hill and Knowlton, Walker, Timmons. Well, I think we'll get a burst of growth under Reagan." Recruiting Ray Marshall, President Carter's labor secretary, and Mr. Marshall's special assistant for public affairs (Frank Greer), Mr. Kamber set out to serve "left-of-center, liberal interests," labor unions particularly. During his first year, his declared goal was to become the "Hill and Knowlton of the Left." After three years, however, he was noting that his group is "often referred to as the 'Bob Gray and Company of the left.' "[46]

P.r. work, evidently, is infectious.

So much for some of the characteristics of the contemporary lobbying "cadre." Next: how do they go about their business?

LOBBYING

Immediately, lobbyists seek access. On this the professional political scientists and the journalists are, for once, agreed. David Truman set the scene more than a generation ago: "Toward whatever institution of government we observe interest groups operating, the common feature of all their efforts is the attempt to achieve effective access to points of decision." Access is their "intermediate facilitating objective." Almost thirty years later journalist Charles Peters, from his close observation of the Washington habitat, its flora and fauna, would write: "Very often the key to effective lobbying is simply *access*."[47] In a way, of course, one hardly needs to quote authority: the point seems obvious enough. Yet there may be more to it than one at first realizes. Why, exactly, is access so important? Professor Truman provides no direct answer, probably taking it for granted, but Mr. Peters summons up a part of one:[48]

> Why is access so vital? If the other side can't get similar access, a lobbyist's views may be all the official ever hears. Especially on smaller issues, where a decision either way won't rock the ship of state too much, whichever side gets to the congressman usually wins. This also can be true on larger and more controversial issues in nonelection years, when officials care less about public opinion. Even when the congressman hears other views, the voice of a friend is likely to stand out in the cacophony of opinions.

This "psychology of access" counts in all branches of government (the argument continues) because, according to Mr. Peters,

> most government officials are basically decent people who want to be nice and want to be liked. Faced with a living, breathing fellow human being who wants something very much, with perhaps only an abstract argument on the other side, the natural reaction is to be obliging. That's why if you are a lobbyist, just getting through to a high official and presenting your case, using facts, figures, and persuasion—no favors involved—gives you a good chance for success. In fact, this is the way most lobbying victories are won.

That juxtaposition of "getting through to a high official" with "the way most lobbying victories are won" marks the point at which the path taken by (at least) some political scientists would diverge from the one marked out by the journalist. As Abraham Holtzman put it back in the midsixties in the context of lobbyists and legislative lobbying: "To provide a group with an opportunity for presenting its case is to afford it only the shallowest form of access."[49] That, for the mid-eighties, would have to be restated less emphatically since the number of lobbyists has markedly increased, and so, presumably, the "demand" for access, while its "supply," by legislators at least if not by their aides, has tended to decline with the decrease in the net working time that legislators, senators particularly, have available for "distribution." Even so, the implication of Professor Holtzman's remark surely survives: access is a necessary, but hardly a sufficient, condition of success, contrary to what Mr. Peters appears to imply in the last sentence of the second quotation from him.

Everyone, however, agrees that access is important, so the next question is either: (a) how do lobbyists go about securing it? or (b) how is access secured? These questions "look alike" but are not identical: (a) directs inquiry more toward the discrete (or distinguishable) acts, the concrete steps taken, here and now; (b), more toward certain attributes of the "underlying" interest group, intrinsic or in the perceptions of others (essentially decision makers), on which the "attached" lobbyists build, and of which they take advantage. If so, (b) is the correct question at this stage, "correct" meaning only that the research it prompts is likely to be the more productive, certainly the more comprehensive.

As to (b), the *locus classicus* remains David Truman's *The Governmental Process* even though his ground plan entails a treatment (of the variables conducive to access) that is scattered over several chapters (as may be readily confirmed from the index). To begin with, he identified three variables:

1. position of the organization in the social structure
2. effective organization in terms of the issue at stake
3. skills and other qualities of leadership.

Professor Truman considered no.1 to be "the most basic factor" governing access.[50] It is, however, far from clear how he would respond if asked: how do you really know that? Probably he was making a judgment finely honed by reading, reflection and discussion, exercising educated common sense, as most of us in the profession are still obliged to do over a wide range of politically significant but unsettled questions (unless we choose to remain mute).

Following his lead but without specific commitment to the order of importance, one recalls that the first variable turns upon the prestige enjoyed by some organizations more than others and upon the deference accorded them in consequence. He cited the American Bar Association, the U.S. Chamber of Commerce, and major corporations, such as (one may extrapolate) AT & T, Exxon, ITT, and General Motors, all giants and all household names. Their presidents and chief executive officers enjoy virtually automatic access at the highest level. But the esteem if not exactly the deference extends, up to a point, to their workaday lobbyists as well.

Variable 2 conjures up not just organization but organization for the issue at stake, "the problem at hand." It means "knowing the ropes" and being sufficiently cohesive as an organization to enable its weight to be brought to bear. It includes institutionalized ways (as, extrapolating, through membership of an advisory committee) of learning what changes are in the wind.

Variable 3 is close to no. 2 since it takes a person to know the ropes and to gather intelligence about changes in the wind. Perhaps the main analytical distinction is that variable 2 turns upon the properties of organizations; no.3, upon the attributes of persons. Here, in any case, Professor Truman singled out former congresspersons turned lobbyists. They know how to get things done in Washington: "Their stock-in-trade is access."[51]

Are you puzzled by the absence of any reference to financial strength as a variable conducive to access? The explanation is that it is "contained" within variable 1. For in the immediately preceding chapter, Professor Truman had written: "In most societies status and prestige are closely correlated with income. That is, both prestige and money are among the rewards for persons and groups occupying high position."[52] This he did not specifically repeat in the following chapter when he came to the subject of access.

That point prepares the way for a deepening of the preliminary Trumanite analysis encompassing the three variables. The first of these, generating money as well as prestige, will tend to be self-sustaining. Money can be and is used for p.r. campaigns, muted as well as loud, sustained as well as brief, that tend to augment prestige and reinforce position. In the Trumanite language: "Other things being equal, position is a determinant of financial strength, and affluence facilitates propaganda activities."[53]

Money is also used, probably now more than ever, to make electoral-campaign contributions. What that less-than-charitable giving achieves in total is the subject of controversy, but the minimum is surely access, provided of course that the amount is noticeable. By the 96th Congress (1978–80), it took about $1000 for a senator and $500 for a representative, except in the larger states, where one had to give more in order to stand out from the crowd. That was "the accepted price of access" at the time, according to Washington journalist Charles Peters.[54]

With that one is tending to cross over from (b) to (a), from broad predisposing variables to the more specific, discrete activities by lobbyists. For whereas both p.r. and campaign-giving constitute "backcloth" for day-to-day lobbying, the contributions are commonly made or arranged by lobbyists. That apparently remained true in the early eighties despite the great growth of political action committees (PACs), on which lobbyists (under various names) were still prominent, even to the extent, in some instances, of controlling disbursements. In any case, even in 1980, most of the money, judging for example by contributions to congressional leaders and committee chairmen, still moved outside the PAC circle (see Table 8–4).[55]

TABLE 8–4   PAC Contributions to House and Senate Leaders and Committee Chairmen, 1980

	AVERAGE PAC CONTRIBUTIONS ($)	AVERAGE TOTAL CONTRIBUTIONS ($)	PAC CONTRIBUTIONS AS PROPORTION OF TOTAL CONTRIBUTIONS (%)
Senate	283,608	1,419,508	20.0
House	66,476	169,085	39.3

The implication is that, quite apart from the PACs, lobbyists in a more traditional sense continued to be bearers of gold, if not frankincense and myrrh, to members or would-be members of Congress. However, one focuses upon PACs because these appear in the 1980s to provide the main channel for *interest-group* contributions.

Exactly what these mean in terms of public policy has been and remains a controversial question. Some observers (e.g., Jack Newfield of the *Village Voice* in New York City) believe and say out loud that Congress can be "bought,"[56] by the oil lobby, among others. One can immediately agree that substantial campaign contributions must afford access. Take Senator Robert Dole (Rep.-Kansas), a strong supporter of the oil and gas interests, and chairman of the Senate Finance Committee from 1980. In 1980, he received PAC contributions totalling about $43,000 from forty-six enterprises in the closely related fields of energy and utilities, equal to about 17 percent of all (close to $255,000) he received from Business. According to the Peters rule noted above, the contributors shown in Table 8–5, among others, must be presumed to have gained (or retained) access to him or at least his senior aides.[57]

Recalling the issue of cargo preference (chapter 1), we next move over to the House and check out contributions to Representative Walter Jones (Dem.-North Carolina), who was reelected unopposed in 1980, having squashed his Republican opponent (80 percent of the vote) two years earlier. (Rep. Jones was chairman of the Merchant Marine & Fisheries Committee in the 96th Congress—more precisely, Jan. 1, 1979 to November 24, 1980.) We find that *via* PACs, Labor contributed $6650, nearly 95 percent of it from four maritime unions. Applying the Peters rule, the following at least would have secured (or retained) access to him:

	$
Marine Engineers Beneficial Association (MEBA)	5000
Masters, Mates, and Pilots International	500
Seafarers' International Union of North America	500

Evidently the Marine Engineers deserved not merely access but a red carpet leading to it.

TABLE 8–5   PAC Contributions of $1000 and Above to Senator Robert Dole by Energy Companies and Utilities for his 1980 Reelection Campaign

DONORS	AMOUNTS $
Ashland Oil Inc.	5000
Enserch Corporation	2500
Fluor Corporation	2500
Sun Company Inc.	2500
American Petroleum Refiners Association	2000
Koch Industries Inc.	2000
Standard Oil Company of Indiana	2000
Union Oil Company of California	2000
MAPCO Inc.	1500
Panhandle Eastern Pipeline Inc.	1500
Cities Service Company	1000
Coastal Corporation	1000
Louisiana Energy National PAC	1000
Mid-Continent Oil & Gas Association	1000
Mobil Corporation	1000
Pennzoil Company	1000
Petrolane Inc.	1000
Superior Oil Company	1000
Tenneco Inc.	1000
Tosco Corporation	1000

An even more royal treatment could have been expected from Representative Jim Wright, the House Majority Leader, to whom the MEBA gave no less than $6000 (in the stated period). Since the Seafarers also provided Mr. Wright with $2500 and found $3000 for Representative Tom Foley, the House majority whip, and the Maritime Union of America contributed $1000 to the Speaker himself, Representative "Tip" O'Neill, all three leadership bases in the House seemed to have been well loaded.

What that suggests is that the Peters rule may need a rider attached— that the sums mentioned as conferring access are higher for congressional leaders as well as for (his own qualification) those from the larger states. Both points may be illustrated from maritime contributions to Senator Alan Cranston of California, Senate majority whip until 1980, when the wind of change turned *majority* in his title into *minority*. The MEBA provided $10,000 and the Seafarers $10,600 (for 1980 elections).

That, in pursuit of access, the maritime (and economic other) interests tend to ignore party labels may be illustrated from their treatment of Oregon's two Republican senators. High up on the Appropriations Committee (and chairman from 1980), Senator Mark Hatfield received $5000—for 1978 elections—from the MEBA. Senator Robert Packwood came off even better at their hands ($9000)—for 1980 elections—but then he was high up on the

Commerce Committee (and chairman from 1980). This was Democratic Senator Magnuson's old committee, which has jurisdiction over maritime policy in the Senate.

Access for lobbyists may also be thought of in a more "macro" way, bringing into focus corporations that form an industry or a sector within an industry. Take, for example, the defense contractors to the Pentagon. Here again, as journalist Michael R. Gordon has written, "the first step in influencing Congress is to gain access, which is one important rationale for defense contractor political action committee (PAC) contributions." A "macro" view of that was compiled by him for the *National Journal* in 1981 (see Table 8–6).[58]

Backed, almost "propelled," by such contributions, the lobbyists, and perhaps even some of the "defense-related" specialists, seem likely not just to get a foot in the door but even to cross the threshold.

More "macro" still would be a focus upon a whole industry's PAC contributions. During the 1979–80 electoral cycle, 190 oil and gas PACs[59] disbursed over $6 million to House and Senate candidates. As Russell D. Hemenway remarked, that total exceeded the spending of the national Democratic party committee.[60] Two hundred forty-one of the candidates received $5000 or more. One hundred six of the House candidates received $10,000 or more, a guarantee of access to those who were elected, as 73 (69 percent) of them were. Twenty-eight of the senatorial candidates received a bountiful $20,000 or more. Of the twenty-eight, no fewer than twenty (71 percent) were elected.

Need one go on? Trade, European empire builders used to say, follows the flag. In American politics (a kind of empire building), access follows the campaign contribution—provided it's a large enough signal to catch the eye.

HONORARIA

There is another financial way to the heart of congresspersons—along the primrose path of honoraria. An honorarium is of course a payment for services rendered, less (in principle) than a commercial fee but more memorable than a kiss on the wrist. All the congressman or -woman has to do is show up at the appointed place and hour, utter a few well-chosen words, and, if he or she does not collect there and then, depart. The Seafarers' breakfasts have been exceptionally agreeable occasions for such exercises: they provided not only the cereal and juices but also the text for the speeches. Read; collect, sooner or later, your $1000; and depart in peace.

To carry that side of the story further, one notes that in 1979, Representative "Tip" O'Neill, in addition to the $1000 contributed by the National Maritime Union, received the same amount as an honorarium from the MEBA. Whether they demanded more from him than the Seafarers once required of the anointed is unclear. Perhaps, in any case, the point (as we discovered earlier) is that he had proved very sympathetic to the cargo-preference policy

TABLE 8–6 PAC Contributions (1979–80) and Defense-related Registered Lobbyists: The Top Ten Defense Contractors

	DEFENSE CONTRACTS, FISCAL 1980 ($ BILLIONS)	DEFENSE-RELATED PERSONNEL IN WASHINGTON	DEFENSE-RELATED REGISTERED LOBBYISTS	PAC CONTRIBUTIONS (1979–80) ($)
General Dynamics Corp.	3.5	40	0	279,741
McDonnell Douglas Corp.	3.2	5	3	73,750
United Technologies Corp.	3.1	12–15	1	173,525
Boeing Co.	2.4	24	5	152,372
General Electric Co.	2.2	50	5	231,935
Lockheed Aircraft Corp.	2.1	15	2	129,520
Hughes Aircraft Co.	1.8	45	0	138,478
Raytheon Co.	1.7	20	0	30,750
Tenneco Inc.*	1.5	?	?	216,600
Grumman Corp.	1.3	7	1	282,680

*Declined to supply information to *National Journal*

even before he became the Speaker of the House. Had he had his way, in fact, that policy would have been legislated.

Naturally, Business does not allow the devil to have all the best tunes. The U.S. Chamber of Commerce, for instance, disburses honoraria fairly widely. In 1979 they were not as generous as the Seafarers had been earlier: $500 each for Senators Dole, Domenici, and Stevens and for Representatives Jim Wright, James Jones, and Trent Lott; only $300 for Representative Dan Rostenkowski, and a mere $250 for not only Representative Robert Michel but also Senator Charles Percy. Nevertheless, such relatively small sums are distinctive and so memorable either because they originate outside the context of campaign contributions or because they reinforce what has been given in the other form.

So much for what former senator James Abourezk once characterized as "the honorarium game" (which he, among others, had learned to play effectively). Exactly how it relates to the big game of campaign contributions seems not to have been researched. Some honoraria may well be linked to specific policy issues of current concern. But, restricting oneself for the moment to the question of access, one is inclined to expect a pattern in which the honorarium proves to be consistently supplementary to the campaign contribution. Of course, the donor need not be the same group. The $1000 honorarium to Speaker "Tip" O'Neill came from the MEBA and the $1000 campaign contribution from the Maritime Union of America. But that was two thousand dollars' worth of access, at least, for the maritime unions.

GIFTS IN KIND

Of course, gifts may be made in kind as well as cash. At this point the question, *access to whom?*, can no longer be avoided. By implication, the answer so far has been: to members of Congress. That still applies to gifts in kind. Rockwell International once entertained then Senator Herman Talmadge and Representative Olin E. Teague, as chairman of the House Committee on Science and Technology, at a fishing lodge in Florida. But specific departmental rules notwithstanding, gifts in kind are also proferred to, and have been accepted by, appointed (including career) officials. Defense contractors have shown themselves particularly adept at dispensing hospitality to bureaucrats, none more so than Rockwell, manufacturers of the B-1 Bomber. A goose-hunting lodge in Maryland and a fishing lodge in the Bahamas were royally placed at the disposal of assorted public officials. One of them was the then director of research and development at the Pentagon, distinguished for his "influential involvement" (Defense Secretary Donald H. Rumsfeld would say) in the B-1 program, so crucial to Rockwell's future. In late 1981, the Reagan administration was proposing to revive the B-1 program.

Of course, the defense contractors did not have a monopoly of the technique. In 1976, for instance, the Southern Railway entertained the then secretary of agriculture, Earl L. Butz, at its "place" near Charleston, South Carolina, where one could shoot, swim or golf. The Agriculture Department has much to say before the Interstate Commerce Commission in rail rate cases, and Southern is one of the great carriers in the South of agricultural products.

To mention golf is to be reminded that those seeking access do not neglect the great American sport. Between 1964 and 1973, United States Steel entertained Representative Gerald Ford, the future president, for "golfing weekends." The first of the billion dollar corporations (at the turn of the century) had one lodge near the Pine Valley Country Club in Clementon, N. J., and another place near Disney World in Florida, convenient for the Bay Hill Country Club.[61] Its lobbyist made the arrangements. Can anyone doubt that he enjoyed easy access to Mr. Ford? Not, of course, exclusively: other corporations were kind to the then House minority leader. The principal lobbyist for the Ford Motor Company was another of his frequent golfing companions.[62] In fact, Mr. Ford was the recognized friend of Big Business lobbyists in Washington, and everyone knew it. They were the ones who enjoyed intimate access to him.[63] Some undetermined part of it was secured by gifts in kind.

Free entertainment of that kind spills over easily into free hospitality and other provisions. At Dublin in April 1979, a fourteen-member U.S. congressional delegation was given dinner by Mr. James Dineen, of Milton, Massachusetts, one of Raytheon's lobbyists. His daughter, Margaret, legislative counsel for a pipeline company, flew over from Washington for the occasion.[64] Giving dinner to a large congressional delegation overseas may be uncommon. But a lobbyist's paying for a congressperson's dinner and even an entire hotel bill is common enough. Such modest gifts as imported liquors, French perfume, and theater tickets are not uncommon. Investigative reporter Jack Anderson has even recorded that some lobbyists have solved the familiar problem of what to give by passing along a credit card (how one wishes one could afford to do that at Christmas).[65]

Free transportation has been part of the pattern. A *New York Times* team once discovered that U.S. Steel, Lockheed Aircraft, and Tenneco (in oil and much else) were giving congresspersons and bureaucrats free lifts. A subsidiary of Standard Oil, Indiana, flew the then secretary of commerce, Peter G. Peterson, to Chicago, free of charge. Clayton Enterprises evidently found it advantageous for its motel business to fly Senator Robert Dole to a distant dinner engagement. Earlier the American Railroad Association had provided a special train to carry congresspersons to the Kentucky Derby. As a variation on the theme, the Ford Motor Company leased Lincoln Continentals to important senators and representatives for $750 a year, about a fifth of what it was then charging the common people.[66]

Money and favors . . . even sexual favors have been alleged. In March

1981 it was learned that a thirty-year old woman lobbyist, "of great charm if dubious expertise," had in January 1980 briefly shared a Florida vacation home with three congressmen. Later that year she had posed for *Playboy* wearing a scarf and garter belt, clasping a briefcase. On the art of lobbying, she commented: "The advantage of being a pretty woman is that you have a slightly better chance of getting into a congressman's office."[67] That would seem to underrate the odds even allowing for less informality in dress. Discussing the increase in women lobbyists using conventional techniques, the Washington vice-president of a defense contractor told *Business Week* in 1979: "In the Washington scene the most important thing is to open office doors, and men always welcome the opportunity to chat with an attractive gal."[68] The tone will not endear him to feminists, but physical attractiveness as another resource for gaining access need not be denied.

There is of course no reason to suppose that women lobbyists generally are any the less professional in their approach than men. There is indeed another side to the topic—the provision by men lobbyists of broadminded women for the delectation of congressmen, or at least of suitable accommodation with opportunities for "pressing the flesh" in other than the usual campaigning sense. Lobbyist Charles ("Chuck") Lipsen has revealed how, as a beginner, he acted as a go-between and "cover" for one senator, and rented an apartment in his name as a place of assignation for three other senators, who reimbursed him and took turns to visit suitable companions. He also demonstrated his sense of fair play between the sexes by providing "cover" for two (married) congresswomen who were kicking over the traces.[69] Ask yourself: would Mr. Lipsen, still registered as a lobbyist in 1980, have had a problem of access to those congresspersons at least? It seems unlikely.

How common are favors of that sort? One hardly knows. The standard works on Washington lobbyists by political scientists rarely give the slightest hint of any such impropriety, and say little even about gifts in kind in general. This may be because their sources were the lobbyists themselves.[70] It was the print journalists not the political scientists who discovered and reported the scandals of the past several decades and prepared us, up to a point, for Watergate and ABSCAM. On the other hand, it is not certain that Jack Anderson was justified, after ABSCAM had broken, in writing even about the relatively legitimate techniques that: "Virtually every member of Congress openly accepts money and favors from special-interest moneymen trying to influence legislation."[71] As to the illegitimate techniques, these, for obvious reasons, are not fully known. What is clear is that they deserve to be mentioned as part of the pattern of favors made to secure or maintain access. Otherwise the picture presented is really out of focus.

However, one's corrective to the conventional accounts, so heavily dependent upon what lobbyists choose to tell inquirers from the groves of Academe, must not be allowed to produce an imbalance of its own. Certainly there are two other important access-creating and -sustaining techniques. One of these is friendship, professional if not personal, or, less charitably, *crony-ism*. Its roots are as manifold as the modes of social interaction, but the thickest is marked "revolving doors" (a term much favored in Washington) or "musical chairs." The latter seems the more apt, conveying the notion of helter-skelter movement after the music abruptly stops (i.e., especially after an election).

MUSICAL CHAIRS

The root idea has often been exposed. As set out in 1972 by journalist Michael C. Jensen, it took this form:

> Hundreds of generals, high-level civil servants, commissioners and congressmen each year switch from government jobs to closely related careers in private industry.
>
> Some of them live in two worlds, moving easily back and forth between government and industry—a pool of skilled professionals who alternate between sensitive political posts and high-salaried positions in business.[72]

In context, *business* included business schools and law practices, but the concept is here extended beyond business and government—Mr. Jensen's subject on that occasion—to cover the whole of the private sector. In other words, the term is here applied to interchanges between the public and private sectors, with business and government as the special case.

That makes the subject rather broad. Not inappropriately so: if X leaves the White House for a high position in Y, then Y's lobbyist(s) will surely gain vicariously, securing easier access. It is a cardinal, but common, error in the study of interest-group influence to focus too much on the foreground, to the comparative neglect of the background. However, to keep the topic within manageable bounds in this book, one had better confine oneself to the lower-level, or more "up-front," interchanges, i.e., to lobbyists. The type-case from an earlier period is embodied in the peripatetic career of Bryce N. Harlow. From "close personal aide" to President Eisenhower, he graduated, as a dedicated Republican, to counselor to President Nixon, earning a not unacceptable $42,500. For a reported six-figure salary, he then embraced another form of "soap" as vice-president of governmental relations and principal lobbyist of Procter and Gamble. While occupying that role, he had much to do with writing three Republican party platforms.[73]

Clark MacGregor took the same not-so-lonely road from the Nixon White House to the Washington office of United Technologies Corporation, one of the leading defense contractors. He was followed in 1977 by Hugh E. Witt, formerly of the Defense Department, but then in charge of federal procurement policy at the Office of Management and Budget. Not surprisingly, he took on the duties of director of legislative liaison, for which he was evidently well prepared. In 1980, room at the top was found for General Alexander M. Haig, immediately from the Supreme Command of NATO but earlier a special adviser to President Nixon. Apart from his own contribution, he would without necessarily lifting a finger help any UT lobbyist secure access (as suggested in the previous paragraph); by 1981 General Haig was back in government as President Reagan's secretary of state.

These are not isolated instances. After "the Georgians" went down to defeat in 1980, Hubert L. Harris, brought into the White House from Atlanta, stayed on to lobby for the Associated Builders and Contractors. Just after the election, Ron Ziegler, President Nixon's press secretary, was appointed president of the National Association of Truck Stop Operators.

From the departments many a path has been beaten. Choosing examples from areas touched upon in this book, one may note that two of the heads of the Oil and Gas Office of the Department of the Interior were transformed into lobbyists for oil companies (Sinclair; Lone Star Gas). A third found a niche at the American Petroleum Institute (API).[74] There Massachusetts-born Charles J. DiBona would eventually arrive, having been a White House energy adviser and deputy director of the Federal Energy Administration. In due season, he succeeded Frank Ikard as director of the API. The regulatory agencies have not been barren. Thus Carl E. Bagge, a commissioner of the Federal Power Commission, moved over to the presidency of the Washington-based National Coal Association, doubling his salary of $38,000 a year.[75]

Texas-born Frank Ikard reportedly had done rather better in making his move to the top of API: $200,000 a year (so one can well understand that he moved by choice). He exemplifies that other source of lobbyists—Congress. An experienced member of the House, he had served on Ways and Means as a friend of its legendary chairman, Wilbur Mills. A far more experienced member, Wayne Aspinall (Dem.-Colorado), first elected in 1948, and chairman of the Interior Committee, had no choice, having gone down to defeat in 1972. He was saved from hardship (discounting the excellent congressional pensions) by a retainer from American Metal Climax for lobbying duties. Since it had a keen interest in strip-mining legislation, who could be more useful than a long-serving chairman of Interior? In 1978 the Pennsylvania Democrat, Representative Fred B. Rooney, suffered a surprising defeat. First elected in 1963, he had won easily in 1976 and was Chairman of the Transportation Subcommittee of the Commerce Committee, which was significant for his district. Had he been perceived as too solicitous of the railroads, less caring of the trucking industry? In any case, his first client as a consultant was the Association of American Railroads.[76] In 1980, but in the primary, another such specialist, Oregon Democrat Robert Duncan, chairman of the Transportation Subcommittee of Appropriations, a role significant for his district (Portland), was knocked out. But a local law firm set him up in Washington, from which base he would, among other things, lobby on—of course—transportation issues.[77]

Congressional staffs constitute another important component of musical chairs, or institutionalized interchange, facilitating access. Their growth is one of the staggering facts of American federal government in the post-World War II period. Here only two species, committee staff and personal staff, need be considered (see Table 8–7).[78]

These developments, which clearly reflect the changes outlined in chapter 5 (such as the great increase in subcommittees), have made available a large pool of politically skilled men and women, most of whom do not stay on such jobs for any length of time.[79] Some of them become lobbyists. The examples of Tom C. Korologos and William E. Timmons, both congressional aides originally, have already come our way (another partner in their lobbying firm, Michael Reed, served on the House leadership staff). An example of a committee-staff move "outside" is provided by Frank Slatinshek, once staff director of the House Armed Services Committee. F. Slatinshek and Associates Inc. were registered in 1980 in the cause of General Dynamics, Grumman Aerospace, and United Technologies. Their declared interest was in "defense authorizations and appropriations." Charles B. Curtis was legal counsel to the House Commerce Committee from 1971 to 1976, working closely with Representative John D. Dingell, who, by 1981, had risen to the chairmanship. During the Carter administration, Mr. Curtis had become chairman of the Federal Energy Regulatory Commission. In 1981 he was taken on as a consultant by, with the possibility of being asked to lobby for, the General Public Utilities Corporation, which was seeking federal aid for the clean-up of its Three-Mile Island disaster. It was a sound choice if only because the House Commerce Committee would have had to authorize the clean-up. The principal lobbyist, however, would be Charls E. Walker, an even sounder choice in view of his proved capacity in general and, in particular, his close relationship with the Reagan administration.[80]

So much for the principal players in this form of "musical chairs" insofar as it concerns access for lobbyists. Where most of the players come from is the subject of some dispute. That many lobbyists are former congresspersons has been characterized as a myth. "Only a handful," say congressional experts William Keefe and Morris Ogul.[81] Only a third of the Washington lobbying corps, says interest-group specialist Carol S. Greenwald.[82] Evidently, their

TABLE 8–7   Committee Staff and Personal Staff, U.S. Congress, 1947, 1972, and 1979

YEAR	COMMITTEE STAFF		PERSONAL STAFF	
	HOUSE	SENATE	HOUSE	SENATE
1947	167	232	1440	590
1972	817	844	5280	2426
1979	1959	1098	7067	3612
Totals (1979)	3057		10,679	

ostensible agreement as to a myth conceals great disagreement about the numbers. By contrast, close Washington observer, Charles Peters, arguing that "the most effective legal way of influencing a public official" is to have "something in common, being a member of the same 'club'," added: "That is why so many former congressmen work as lobbyists on Capitol Hill."[83]

Whether that qualifies him as one of the mythmakers (who are rarely identified) is not clear. But the source for the Keefe-Ogul view is Lester Milbrath's work. He found that only three out of 114 lobbyists (2.6 percent) had previously held elective office. Of those who had ever worked on Capitol Hill, at least eight had served as committee staff and at least nine as personal staff, say 15 percent. But well over a third (36 percent) had come from the executive branch, the greatest single source.

However, as you would surely guess from the totals even if you did not remember, Professor Milbrath's record was limited to registered lobbyists and undertaken in the late 1950s. In 1980 *Congressional Quarterly* compiled a list, which it acknowledged to be "certainly incomplete," of over sixty former members of Congress "currently earning a living as counselors, strategists or persuaders for special interests in Washington,"[84] i.e., as lobbyists in the broad sense. Do congresspersons enjoy any special advantages over other lobbyists from a different background?

The answer from the literature is a qualified *yes*, but the reasons given are different. Remarking upon the "considerable proportion of former members of Congress" who become lobbyists, David Truman concluded that they were "of great use" but not because they enjoy floor privileges and other lobbyists do not. Such privileges, in his view, are essentially symbolic of the former members' connections and knowledge of how things get done. In other words, floor privileges count mainly because they tell the world: this person enjoys access.[85] On the other hand, ex-senatorial lobbyists have been observed "circulating while the Senate considered legislation of interest to their clients." Since they (and former representatives) are also allowed into the members' gymnasium and dining room "and other sanctuaries closed to civilian lobbyists,"[86] ex-members would on balance seem to enjoy a distinct advantage over others, *ceteris paribus*.

However, that *other things being equal* reservation prompts at least one rider to the general statement. Some former congressional aides, especially from the Senate, may well have connections only a little less valuable than a former member of Congress's. They will probably have been around long enough to have given much help and dispensed some favors. Moreover, when they were employed on the Hill, they were probably better informed on many important issues than most representatives and senators. It does not necessarily follow that they will continue to enjoy that (presumed) advantage *vis-à-vis* ex-congresspersons who are now concentrating on lobbying. But that seems likely, bearing in mind that a congressperson's skills lie less in research than in communication (to use a shorthand term understandable in this context).

This leads into the second of the access-creating and -sustaining techniques introduced above as counters to what risked being too much of an emphasis on certain other modes. This second technique is the supply of information by lobbyists to both legislators and bureaucrats.

THE INFORMATION NEXUS

David Truman long ago remarked that one of "the informal determinants of access" was "the legislator-politician's need of information and the ability of a group to supply it." The general proposition advanced was: "Access is likely to be available to groups *somewhat* in proportion to their ability to meet this need."[87] *Somewhat* has been italicized here as a warning that the suggestion of proportionality ought not to be taken too seriously. For Professor Truman in his introduction of the topic had already singled out three classes of variables governing access, notably the position of the group or organization in the social structure (see the passage above on direct lobbying). That was being taken for granted in his later discussion specifically of the legislator-politician. In any case, no one doubts the significance of a lobbyist's ability to supply information.

As to the range, several types of information have been distinguished. Norman J. Ornstein and Shirley Elder identified three: (a) substantive (e.g., Rockwell International on the capability of the B-1); (b) strategic (e.g., what the building of the B-1 would mean in terms of jobs in certain constituencies); (c) political (extending from the rebuttal of arguments to precise knowledge of legislative procedure).[88] Others make do with two categories: (a) technical and (b) political (as in David Truman), and (a) "factual and legal" and (b) "about influence relationships or influence potentialities in a given situation" (Lewis Anthony Dexter).[89] There seems little to choose between these schemas. For our purposes the more parsimonious version—using two categories—will suffice.

Wondering about the importance of (a) relative to (b), one notes that Professor Dexter, writing in 1969 on how organizations are represented in Washington, confidently dismissed (b) as generally "marginal." "Some people," he asserted,

> exaggerate the role of power and pull in U.S. governmental decisions, or simply have a passion for the "inside dope," the "real reason." They can and do waste a good deal of time in focusing on influence relationships rather than on the merits of the case—or in trying to cultivate influence of their own through contacts, rather than dealing with the issues. The latter type is dismissed by some sophisticated Washington hands with a phrase about "those guys who think government relations is playing golf out at Burning Tree."[90]

That there may have been far more to such beliefs among lobbyists than the scoffers allowed is suggested by "corporate Watergate," many of whose practices, unmasked in the midseventies, extended back to the sixties, from which the passage quoted in fact dates. That very golf club was cited as a place where lobbyists plied their trade by "entertaining" decision makers, even a president. Of course, it would be absurd to make too much of this and the other forms of "entertainment." It is one string to the lobbyist's bow. Often forcefully criticized, it has nonetheless been used in one form or another for at least a century. Moreover, it would be imprudent to assume that a lobbyist merely argues cases on their merits as if no other inducements are brought to bear quite apart from "entertainment." That goes against the grain of the evidence built up for a century or more as well as of contemporary knowledge.

Whether, on the other hand, one should conclude, with Professor Truman, that his (b) is "of at least equal importance" with (a), is uncertain. One can hardly say *a priori* what "mix" is practiced or likely to be decisive under what conditions in respect of what kinds of issues. In other words, one hardly knows what "mix" of *reason* and *power* (or *influence*) lobbyists resort to or find most effective.

To mention reason, or the merits of the case, leads into the other aspect of the supply of information by lobbyists, its accuracy. At the extreme, the position is crystal clear: lobbyists cannot afford to offer up outright lies. These, sooner or later, will boomerang, destroying access to the justifiably outraged decision makers. As someone who had fought the good fight said to Ornstein and Elder: "You can't ever afford to lie to a member of Congress because if you lose access to him, you've had it."[91]

However, the concept of a lie or falsehood is more complicated than it seems. In 1980–81 the New York Clearing House Association, representing the twelve leading New York banks, lobbied both the state legislature and the Federal Reserve authorities to permit IBFs (international banking facilities) in New York City, making it possible for them to deal there in Eurodollars. In the course of their lobbying bankers claimed that the IBFs would create fifty thousand jobs in New York City. After they got their way, they admitted that "about five thousand might be created within a few years,"[92] or, as it was later put, "eventually."[93] Was that deception or miscalculation? Bankers themselves admitted to having made "wild assertions" on the subject.[94]

Such a gross discrepancy may be uncommon (the admission of it is certainly rare). Whoever invented the phrase "lies, damned lies, and statistics," probably had something subtler in mind, such as the "convenient" choice of a base year, the "clever" use of percentages, or some gloss in presentation. Certainly there is an art (some would say, black) as well as a science of statistics. Above all, short of a direct lie, there may be misrepresentation in the sense of concealment of truth. Logicians and moralists have a term for it: *suppressio veri*, or suppression of the truth, referring to concealment of facts that ought to be made known. They also thought up another concept for something more than "mere" concealment although still short of a direct lie: the *suggestio falsi*. Here the misrepresentation is more (so to speak) positive. In the first case, the lobbyist would be withholding facts from the decision makers that they ought to have in order to make a correct judgment. In the second case, the lobbyist would be telling the decision makers something that, although not actually false, manages to convey a false impression and allows the listeners to believe what is untrue. Since the statement conveys a suggestion of falsehood (*suggestio falsi*), it comes closer than the *suppressio veri* to constituting a direct lie.

In short, some political scientists take comfort too readily in the belief that what they simply identify as lies will, sooner or later, recoil on the heads of the perpetrators. Anyone who makes, as above, some of the classical distinctions, is unlikely to be so complacent. There are degrees of falsehood. And we must never forget that a lobbyist's presentation is almost always *ex parte*, one-sided in the literal sense that the other side is not present. Some policy makers (e.g., former Senator Paul Tsongas of Massachusetts) attempted to transcend the "limits of the form" by seeing rivals or antagonists at the same time, staging a kind of minidebate. Others may summon up a kind of surrogate adversary by inviting a lobbyist to state the principal *opposing* arguments and how he or she responds to these, much as an aggressive TV interviewer will report some damaging characterization or statement and ask: "What do you say to that?" Generally, however, a lobbying "transaction" is tantamount to an *ex parte* proceeding, with all its limitations.

No doubt it is true, as a lobbyist told Ornstein and Elder, the relationship or interaction is "all built on confidence. It really is, it's just amazing, it's credibility and confidence."[95] One can accept that and yet, bearing in mind degrees of falsehood, wonder whether such confidence can ever be fully justified, the credibility ever be fully deserved. Objectively well founded or not, however, such credibility and confidence no doubt constitute a necessary condition for retaining access. No doubt, too, the supply of what recipients perceive and accept as broadly accurate information is central to the credibility and confidence.

So much, in outline, for the various modes of gaining and retaining access. But, of course, gaining access is no more than "the end of the beginning" (in the Churchillian phrase). Somehow the privilege of access has to be turned to good account—securing, sooner or later, some authoritative decision. Thus we reach the edge of the crucial topic but pause at the brink in order to inquire into the other main approach, the roundabout (or indirect).

ROUNDABOUT LOBBYING

Recalling that the distinction between direct and roundabout is a matter of degree, we may first identify the "write-in" campaign, categorizing it (if we wish) as more roundabout than the techniques discussed above but less so than p.r. ventures of the broad, relatively unfocused kind. If it were taken to be the lineal descendant of the petition to Parliament, institutionalized in England during the seventeenth century, the "write-in" would rank as one of the most venerable techniques of its kind. In any case, it is still much used. The late V. O. Key, Jr., culled one example from the American Medical Association's 1950 campaign against national health insurance. At the outset the mail received by one hundred members of the House of Representatives ran five to two *in favor*. Nine months after the campaign had got under way, the mail ran eight to two *against*.[96] Returning from a visit to the Middle East in the 1970s, Senator Charles Percy (Rep.-Illinois) was quoted as saying that Israel could no longer count on the United States "just to write a blank check," adding that Israel had missed some opportunities to negotiate with the Palestine Liberation Organization. Mobilized by the American Israel Public Affairs Committee (eleven thousand members then), a small army reached for their pens, typewriters or telephones. Within about a week, twenty-two hundred telegrams and four thousand letters piled up in the senator's office. Of that mail, 95 percent was hostile to the senator and his views. Most of it came from Jewish groups in Chicago: "They threaten" (an aide wrote for the senator's eye) "to withhold their votes and support for any future endeavors."[97]

One of the classic efforts of that decade concerned federal "no-fault" automobile insurance and lawyers, 16 percent of whose "gross legal product" derived from crash litigation (Mark Green calculated). Originating in the states, the policy reached the federal domain in the late sixties and early seventies. It crystallized in 1972 as the (Philip) Hart-Magnuson Bill (named of course for the two Democratic senators). States would have been required to enact, within a specified time, no-fault laws meeting minimum federal standards. Despite the reservations of its then president, Mr. Robert W. Meserve, himself a distinguished Boston trial lawyer, the American Bar Association came out against the bill. But the great fight was fought by the American Trial Lawyers Association (ATLA), whose twenty-five thousand members then stood to lose $1 billion a year in fees according to *Washington Post* reporter Morton Mintz, writing with Washington lawyer Jerry S. Cohen. One of the techniques employed by the ATLA was a "write-in." Its San Francisco chapter thoughtfully provided stamped addressed envelopes for writing to California's two democratic senators. The Utah group was even more considerate. The Democratic senator there (Frank E. Moss) received letters from six constituents opposing the bill. "Each letter was typed, apparently on the same machine, on a sheet of plain white paper; each was mailed in a similar envelope; and each text was identical to one or another of the 'suggested letters' that the Utah Trial Lawyers Association had circulated to its members."[98]

Whether or not as cause and effect, the bill was effectively killed in the Senate by the very narrow margin of three votes. When, in another version, it came up again in 1974, the Los Angeles Trial Lawyers Association excelled themselves. They dispatched Western Union mailgrams to their nearly three thousand members asking them to call a toll-free Western Union number with a list of people, including not only associates but "secretaries, clients, relatives, friends," who wished to be on record as opposing "no-fault." The operators would then choose one of thirty messages, already prepared by the Los Angeles chapter, for transmission to President Nixon and nine senators, including of course both of California's. That meant ten messages for each name supplied. As a result of that maneuver, forty-three hundred telegrams quickly went off to the favored ten. An "elaborate and devious lobbying system," John Gardner of Common Cause called it.[99] Senator Frank Moss characterized it as employing the "methodology of deception," referring to "electronic techniques to disguise a highly organized lobby effort against the national no-fault legislation as a groundswell of opinion from ordinary citizens."

By all accounts, the master manipulator of this technique is the National Rifle Association (NRA). It does not hesitate to take on such media institutions as CBS. One occasion was the screening in 1975 of a news documentary, Irv Drasnin's "The Guns of Autumn," described (by journalist Les Brown) as containing "graphic scenes of the killing of animals" in the context of "hunting as a recreational activity." Soon after its announcement, CBS News began receiving "acrimonious mail from gun advocates." For the screening two months or so later, more than half-a-dozen advertisers withdrew their commercials. They were responding to calls from the NRA (and some gun and hunting groups).[100]

As for the still bigger guns, the NRA has claimed to be able to generate 500,000 letters to Congress within seventy-two hours, which would be hard to swallow if journalist Robert Sherrill, who researched and wrote about the subject of gun control, did not take it seriously.[101] The linking mechanism in the midseventies was an IBM 370 computer, programmed to send telegrams to five hundred "influentials" in each of the home states of (relevant) senators. The five hundred Joves—Jove (or Jupiter) being the god of the sky whose thunderbolts destroyed his enemies—would then let loose their thunderbolts of letters, telegrams and telephone calls. Whether these have ever totalled half-a-million on a particular issue is uncertain. One has heard of twelve thousand to Congress within a month in 1965, and, within a shorter period, thirty-six thousand in 1975. But it may well be true that the precise total hardly matters. According to Sherrill's Law: "The practical objective of letter-writing campaigns is not to actually get a majority of the people behind a position and to express themselves on it . . . but to get such a heavy, sudden outpouring of sentiment that lawmakers *feel* they are being beseiged by a majority."[102] That's plausible. If it's also true, then the NRA has to be accounted one of the most effective groups of recent times insofar as effectiveness is a function of letterwriting and other such communications.

MOBILIZING CONSTITUTENTS

Those who write may or may not be constituents of the addressee. But there is no doubt that the more the writers (or callers) are constituents, the more effective (all other things being equal) will their communication be. Refocus on the NRA. Early in 1975 the Crime Subcommittee of the House Judiciary Committee began to consider gun control legislation. On February 24, an amendment by Representative Martin A. Russo (Dem.-Illinois) to ban *new* concealable weapons (defined by size) passed 18–14. On February 26 the NRA dispatched thousands of mailgrams to its members calling on them to "contact your congressmen" before the meeting of the parent committee on March 2. As a result "committee members were deluged with calls and letters from constituents." The New York Democrat Edward Pattison received about four hundred communications; the California Democrat, George E. Danielson, 150 telegrams and 150 phone calls.[103] By 17–16 the House Judiciary Committee did do what was expected of it, recommitting the whole bill to the subcommittee, "a move" (wrote journalist Nancy Hicks) "that will probably kill any chance of firearms control in this Congress."[104] What had mainly happened was that four representatives, including Pattison and Danielson, switched from support for the Russo amendment to voting for recommittal. (The other two were Henry J. Hyde [Rep.-Illinois] and Walter Flowers [Dem.-Alabama].) All that remained was for the *Washington Post* to "wish the good soldiers of the gun lobby a restful night's sleep."[105] Its "push," agreed committee Democrat John F. Seiberling (Ohio) and Peter Shields (National Council to Control Handguns), had proved "insurmountable."

No wonder that, among the lobbyists interviewed by political scientist Abraham Holtzman in 1962–63, one promoting the cause of conservation spoke "with envy and admiration" of another who "was far more familiar than he was with the hunting and fishing habits of congressmen and their families—data vital to the conservationists lobbying in Congress."[106] That brings us to a general point. The success of the NRA partly reflects a cultural phenomenon—the propensity of good, red-blooded Americans to take to the woods in the fall and shoot whatever is incautious enough to move—including a considerable number of fellow-Americans. That is also why the corporations take such trouble to set up hunting camps and lodges, where important decision makers are accommodated and cared for free of charge—except of course to the taxpayer, the cost of what appears to be corporate generosity commonly finding its way into the bill submitted to some government department, above all defense, as part of a procurement contract (if indeed the cost were not simply tax-deductible).

However, we should not put too much weight on a cultural trait—there is also at work an institutional variable of general application. Granted a representative system of government, the mobilization of constituents obviously is as "natural" a ploy as anyone can imagine. This leads to the point that just as (a) letter writing (and the like) and (b) mobilizing constituents are closely related, so are (b) and (c)—bringing influence to bear during the course of an election.

ELECTORAL ACTIVITY

This is a compound of many elements. The most important one—the campaign contribution—has already come under scrutiny in our examination of access. What was said there belongs here too but need not be repeated. In addition, of course, numbers may be brought to bear. This technique is naturally much used by labor unions. Alexander E. Barkan, the retiring head of the Committee on Political Education, AFL-CIO, pointed out in 1981 that the computer center at its Washington headquarters could summon up the names of 15 million union members and their families organized by congressional district.[107]

The implications of the claim are at least twofold. To begin with, it signifies a capacity to identify potential support for COPE-endorsed candidates and to make it probable that a high proportion of such would-be (or hoped-for) voters have their names on the electoral registers. Thus for 1976, the computer system has been credited with bringing about 6 million *new* registrations.[108] That is plausible. By midsummer 1973, COPE already had close to 9 million names in its computer memory bank. Lists of names had been coming in from the three out of four affiliated unions participating in the project. After verification of the listings, printouts were made and dispatched to the state AFL-CIOs. Details of ward, precinct, party affiliation, whether or not registered, and telephone number were then incorporated. Passed back to the Washington computer, such information became available for printouts in whatever form—mail labels, for example, or three-by-five cards—a state or local COPE requested, organized by various characteristics, notably (for this discussion) by unregistered voters. At that time, the computer could turn out, in one hour, seventy-five thousand mail labels, or thirty-thousand of the three-by-five cards.[109]

Since registration is obviously a necessary but not a sufficient step, the registered supporters or "leaners" have to be persuaded to vote and even conveyed to the polling booths. Here again the computer serves the cause well by identifying not only voters (of the right kind) but also helpers. These, combined with the full-time union officials, given leave for the duration of the war, make up a formidable force. In his 1981 valedictory, Mr. Barkan put the total at "literally hundreds of thousands." Whether that should be taken literally is doubtful. Looking back in February 1973 on the 1972 election, an AFL-CIO spokesman, Al Zack, claimed: "On election day, we had more than 100,000 COPE volunteers ringing doorbells, running car pools, baby-sitting for voters . . . by far the largest numbers we ever had on an election day."[110] For the 1976 election, journalist A. H. Raskin reported a total of 120,000 " 'volunteers'."[111]

So *"hundreds of* thousands" would seem to be hyperbole. Nevertheless, the truth is impressive enough, especially taken in conjunction with the registration drive and many related services, all, of course, serving to top up the campaign contributions, by member unions as well as COPE. Think only of some facets of COPE's efforts for and during the 1980 election—bearing in mind that comprehensive, up-to-date accounts of the AFL-CIO, etc., as an interest group are hard to come by. Start with COPE's campaign contributions: a little less than three-quarters of a million dollars (January 1 1979 to October 15 1980). That was "hard money," disbursed in packages of up to $5000—the legal limit—for any one candidate. But "soft money" was also spent, e.g., about $1 million on various "nonpartisan black, Hispanic, elderly and youth groups affiliated with the federation, whose only function is to register people and persuade them to vote," remarked Mr. Barkan.[112] The group leaders would of course be guided by the computer.

Refocus now on a state COPE, Pennsylvania. The Washington computer supplied it with "several sets of labels addressed to 1.2 million federation members in the state." There, at the beginning of October, officials not only of AFL-CIO but other unions (Teamsters, Mine Workers, etc.) "were assigned to work in every race in which the outcome was in doubt. These officials will work until election day." On that day "many thousands" of union volunteers (said Jim Mahoney, director of the state COPE) would service telephone banks and canvass door-to-door, having previously helped with large mailings of campaign literature to union members and their families. Again, "soft money" would be drawn upon for conveying political information to union members: probably some $450,000.[113]

To mention (as above) some individual unions is to be reminded that they cut a swath of their own distinct from COPE's. Consider, for instance, the United Automobile Workers. Through its Voluntary Community Action Program (a political action committee) in the period 1976–80, it spent over two million dollars, earning sixth place among the top twelve PAC spenders in that stage of the electoral cycle (see Table 8–8).[114]

In addition, the UAW released its own officials to work in the campaign: for instance, in Pennsylvania it stood "shoulder-to-shoulder" with the Mine Workers and the Teamsters (and the State Education Association) "until election day." There and elsewhere it rendered many other valuable services (although neither these nor the officials' time were "chargeable" as political contributions). If what other big unions contributed, *de facto* and *de jure*, apart from COPE, is counted as well, the grand total must have been enormous.

This emphasis on large numbers must not be allowed to obscure the possibility that even small numbers may be effectively applied to particular election campaigns where intensity of view on the part of certain activists

TABLE 8–8   Expenditures and Receipts of the Top Twelve Political Action Committees in 1979–80

	EXPENDITURES	RECEIPTS
National Conservative Political Action Committee	$7,463,833	$7,600,637
Congressional Club	$7,212,745	$7,873,974
Fund for a Conservative Majority	$3,046,454	$3,093,544
Realtors Political Action Committee	$2,576,077	$2,753,139
Citizens for the Republic	$2,384,710	$2,356,751
United Automobile Workers		
Voluntary Community Action Program	$2,024,437	$1,792,406
Americans for an Effective Presidency	$1,874,312	$1,920,377
American Medical Political Action Committee	$1,812,021	$1,728,392
Committee for the Survival of a Free Congress	$1,623,750	$1,647,556
National Committee for an Effective Congress	$1,420,238	$1,406,788
Gun Owners of America Campaign Committee	$1,396,670	$1,414,951
Automobile and Truck Dealers Election Action Committee	$1,390,245	$1,271,857

serves, so to speak, as a multiplier. The antiabortion, or prolife, movement has often been cited in this connection, and with reason. By the time of the presidential primaries in early 1976, the "prolifers" (wrote journalist Judy Klemesrud) had "succeeded the antiwar pickets of 1968 and 1972 as the loud and angry protestors at almost every gathering of presidential candidates. A favorite tactic is drowning out a campaign speech by playing *Taps* on a trumpet."[115] "Dedication," a Boston leader called it.[116] But to another journalist following the story it was "political rage."[117] Both terms, evidently, are related, if in varying degrees, to what the political scientist commonly calls "intensity."

Such intensity may find violent expression, as in the firebombing of a Planned Parenthood or abortion clinic. But throughout the seventies and into the eighties it continued to be "released" with a metaphorical bang during elections. As Eleanor Randolph of the *Los Angeles Times* summed it up in November 1979: "Those antiabortion organizations have become one of the most politically advanced of the new single-issue combat brigades, dispatching squads of protesters to greet candidates whenever they appear in public. The groups have learned how to make a small minority of voters swing, or at least sway, an election."[118] Swinging and even swaying are hard to judge. Swaying could plausibly be attributed to the antiabortion forces in the 1978 senatorial election in Iowa, in which Democratic Senator Dick Clark was displaced. True, from his liberal voting record, he had to expect trouble of more than one kind. But observers thought at the time that the abortion issue, which was prominent in the campaign, cost him ten thousand votes.[119] The margin of defeat was only some twenty-six thousand. Later Michael Barone and Grant Ujifusa would report that right-to-life opposition eroded his majorities to virtually nothing in the Catholic counties and neighborhoods.[120]

In all such judgments, there are almost insuperable difficulties. This applies even more strongly to the defeat in 1980 of four distinguished Democratic senators: Bayh, Church, Culver and McGovern. For instance, Senator Frank Church (Idaho) was "targeted" by two antiabortion groups, Stop the Baby Killers, and the National Right to Life Committee. But he was also marked down for destruction by the ABC Committee, or Anyone But Church, offspring of the National Conservative Political Action Committee[121] (look back at Table 8–8). Idaho was one of the six states where NCPAC spent in all over $1.2 million to dislodge the six Democratic senators up for reelection.[122] (Not one cent was "chargeable" to—so to speak—the Federal Election Commission—another loophole). In the event, four of the senators went down to defeat: The relieved survivors were Senators Alan Cranston (California) and Thomas Eagleton (Missouri).

No mere mortal can allocate the praise—or blame. Here, however, it is sufficient to be aware that relatively small numbers may be greatly enhanced by the intensity of beliefs. One index of that intensity in 1980 was supplied by the letter that Stop the Baby Killers circulated in South Dakota and elsewhere saying that Mr. McGovern and his liberal colleagues were "political baby killers" who "apparently think that it's perfectly OK to slaughter unborn infants by abortion."[123] An even more telling instance dates from 1977, "when a tall, gaunt man started following [Senator Dick Clark] as he traveled the state on weekends, greeting constituents. . . . The tight-lipped protester dragged a huge black cross made mobile by a small wheel attached to its base. The cross had antiabortion slogans attached to it."[124] To what extent he contributed to Senator Clark's defeat the following year, no one can ever know. But it seems as certain as anything can be that he contributed something and that in so contributing he should be counted, not as one man, but many men. There could hardly be a more striking (probable) example of the multiplication of numbers by way of intensity. Similarly, those who took the trouble on the Sunday before the election to distribute leaflets at church parking lots are believed by *some* observers to have tipped the scales against Senator Clark.[125]

The point need not be labored, but observe in passing the significance of "marrying" intensity to *large* numbers as well as to wealth. That describes the happy lot of the NRA:

1 large numbers (1.8 million in 1980)
2 membership x annual dues of $15 (or variants, such as lifetime payment) = about $13.26 million (1979), 62 percent of budget (then $21.4 million)
3 intensity. Possible indices: (a) willingness of members to make voluntary payments amounting to $2.2 million, or 10 percent of budget (1979), to support the Institute for Legislative Action, the NRA's lobbying instrument;[126] (b) passionate concentration on a small number of election campaigns, e.g., South Dakota, 1980, when for a time the NRA ran daily advertisements claiming that "George McGovern wants to take your guns away." Columnist Mary McGrory called it a

single-issue group "of singular ferocity." She went on to recall the New Hampshire candidates' forum in February, 1980, when the American public "got its first taste of the rampaging gun owners." Presidential candidate John Anderson had remarked that it was not unreasonable to require gun owners to register their purchases, just as car owners do. "From the expletives and obscenities hurled at him, you might have thought he had proposed to divest the audience of its wives or homes."[127] John Herbers, too, had reported at the time from Concord, New Hampshire that "a few nights ago the gun lobby demonstrated its fire power with a noisy rally of outdoorsmen in which most of the Republican candidates came out strongly for an armed citizenry."[128]

So one could go on. It is enough here to realize that the techniques adopted by a group may be reinforcing, also that the resources accruing to a group may be cumulative. Therein lies part of the explanation of the power of the NRA.

Under this subheading of electoral activity, other ploys and strivings might be catalogued, but the main things have been touched upon, enabling us to proceed to the next consideration.

PUBLIC RELATIONS

"Public relations covers a lot of acreage—blurring out into advertising, slopping over into selling, dipping down into publicity, and touching—or at least aspiring to—the 'making' of public opinion itself." That was the voice of Professor Robert Heilbroner in 1957.[129] In political-science circles, at least, the concept is still a little blurred, judging by the attention given to political advertising. One clarifying step is to distinguish the forms or modes of p.r. from p.r. itself. In addition to the familiar whole- or half-page "ads" in newspapers, the forms may include op-ed statements (really a species of political advertising) as well as TV and radio spots; entertainment and press junkets; "canned" material used by the media without attribution; lectures, seminars, and public meetings; exhibitions, shows and "stunts." The common thread—and so p.r. itself—may then be seen as its broadest as the systematic action taken by an organization to influence public opinion, including "pictures in the head" (a Walter Lippman phrase) favorable to the organization itself. For a more specifically political definition, we may turn back to a noted p.r. practitioner, Edward L. Bernays: "Public relations is the attempt, by information, persuasion, and adjustment, to engineer public support for an activity, cause, movement, or institution."[130] In a nutshell, it is "the engineering of consent." The phrase was much too candid to suit many people in p.r. business, although it was not essentially different from the one he had used—"molding public opinion"—a decade or so earlier.[131] Here, in any case, the objective is less a favorable image than a favorable policy decision.

In attempting to adapt the broader concept to interest-group politics, one is hampered by the paucity of systematic data relating, in particular, to the groups and issues that have already come our way. But some illustrations can be provided, starting with activities apparently intended to provide no more, at least in the short run, than a pleasing "picture in the head" *of* the initiating organization.

"PICTURES IN THE HEAD." Here one is at first inclined to think of carefully calculated large-scale efforts to reach a mass public, but the attempt may be made vicariously, i.e., by means of a gradual build-up through a specialized public. Buttering up the press is an example. You know that free entertainment—liquor, accommodation, and various facilities—has often been provided by defense contractors for the delectation of gentlemen in the Pentagon and Congress. Entertaining the press extends the idea and good cheer. Take the 1975 National Governors' Conference, a third of the cost of which was kindly borne by a number of large corporations. The entertainment included "a lavishly appointed riverboat ride"[132] not only for staff but also reporters. The Mid-Continent Oil and Gas Association was the generous host, "lavishly appointed" almost certainly being in part a euphemism for a well-stocked bar. The expectation must surely have been that, combined with other exercises in calculated hospitality, the "riverboat ride" would leave a favorable impression that, one way or another, would sooner or later find its way into the papers.

The cultivation of the public at large (or *mass* public), however, calls for more systematic and continuous effort. This is preeminently the manipulation of symbols through the so-called mass media. The group's objective is to present itself in an attractive light by claiming to be the author of good works or at least to have in abundance the virtues relevant to the context and hour. The types of virtues claimed include being ecologically aware or sensitive, caring for the environment, caring for people, social responsibility, guarding and promoting of the arts, being innovative, resourceful, and productive. If it proves necessary to ring the changes, the group always has patriotism to fall back on, as in "keeping America great" (or strong, safe, clean, beautiful, etc.). Evidently, the intention is to make the group attractive in the eyes of the general public through an association (if only in the mind) with good deeds and/or good qualities.

Examples of this kind of thing as embodied in advertisements include the following:

1. *caring for people* (a) Pharmaceutical Manufacturers Association (PMA), 1967–69: "The yearly drug profit: 25 lives. . . . Drug companies produce a long list of products that lose money but save lives. . . . but like everyone, drug makers must realize a profit to survive and grow."[133] (b) Mobil Oil, 1974: reminding America that children should be immunized against various diseases, including polio.

2. *caring for the environment* Chemical Manufacturers Association: how the chemical industry is helping to clean up the nation's lakes and waterways, investing

more than any other U.S. industry in fighting pollution—which seems fair enough: which industry poisoned the nation's lakes and waterways in the first place?

3. *innovative* PMA, 1978: said to be spending $900 million a year to improve old medicines and create new ones.

4. *guardian and promoter of the Arts* (a) Allied Chemical Corporation, 1976: "The road to culture is paved with profits." The business community was said to have donated over $600 million in the previous five years to "preserve and enhance" the nation's cultural assets. (b) Mobil Oil's celebrated "Masterpiece Theatre" series on PBS "Upstairs, Downstairs" was the classic. Its identification with the company was kept up for some years, e.g., in 1976, when noting the death (in real life) of Angela Baddeley, who played the cook, the p.r. person coyly added that the series was one "with which we've long been associated on public broadcasting stations."[134] By 1982, however, the connection did not have to be specifically made, e.g., "The Flame Trees of Thika" (about an English family "starting over" before World War I in what became Kenya). The series itself, as well as the link between it and the oil corporation, was by then so well established that the ad did not even mention Mobil funding, merely concluding: "It's high adventure, brought to you in the high style that you've come to expect from 'Masterpiece Theatre'."

Not so, however, with its ad three days later announcing the start of a special TV series (also on PBS and imported from England), "Life on Earth" (which happily married the environment/ecology theme to culture and the arts): "The Mobil-funded production portrays animal behavior rarely observed and sometimes never before filmed."[135]

Here, obviously, we have been making a transition from political advertising as such to the sponsorship of TV programs, to which advertising is hooked, before and after. But this, too, is quite consciously political. As a leading Mobil official once explained in a burst of candor: "A reader sees a Mobil message, and associates it with Big Oil. So he may be wary. But he also associates it with the company that brings him 'Upstairs Downstairs,' so maybe he's a little more open-minded and a little more receptive."[136] In line with that, notice that these linking ads did not mention the word *oil:* it was not even contained in the title of the company. In the midseventies the company's print series, *Observations* (to be noticed below) had mentioned the dreaded word—Mobil Oil Corporation.

If there remains any doubt in anyone's mind about the political significance of it all, turn again to *The Nation* (and Robert Sherrill). Another Mobil official was even blunter than the person quoted above: "The programs build enough acceptance to allow us to get tough on substantive issues."

That was reported in 1979. By 1980 such sponsorship had become very fashionable: 115 public broadcasting corporate underwriters whose donations came to $30 million. But four dominated: Mobil, Exxon, ARCO ("the best seats in the house are free"—for its PBS concerts), and Gulf. These contributed more than half of the $30 million. During February 1981, an analysis of prime-time programming on PBS (by *Boston Globe's* Robert A. McLean) revealed that the big four sponsored 72 percent of the shows seen weeknights between 8 and 10 p.m. But a decision the following May by the Federal Communications Commission seemed likely to stimulate some serious competition in sponsorship. The FCC then agreed to allow such PBS stations as Boston's WGBH-TV (Channel 2) to present more prominently the name of the generous corporate donors, which, it was locally hoped, would "attract new underwriters, as well as please the old ones—and relax their check-writing hands." Chevron U.S.A. (Standard Oil, California) promptly made "a grant of undisclosed size" (but put at $1.5 million) to public TV in New York (WNET-TV).[137]

Analytically, Mobil Oil's *Observations* series, placed in the Sunday supplements of about a hundred newspapers (1979), marked the transition from pleasing "pictures in the head" to out-and-out advocacy. The columns carried cartoons with snippets and tidbits of information presumably designed for readers spending a somnolent Sunday afternoon at home. Some of the material was innocuous, but much that appeared so was in fact politically tinged. Take an item like "Wild Goose Place" (which caught the eye in part because it echoed the familiar phrase). It drew attention to Maryland's sanctuary for wood ducks and Canada geese—$325,000 (45 percent) of the cost of which "came via the federal government from offshore gas and oil drilling revenues." The writer continued: "All told, the offshore search for oil and gas has generated $1.4 billion since 1969 for conservation and recreation. That's one of the best uses we could imagine for the dollars we send to Washington."[138] Other items did not hook on to something agreeable, like a bird sanctuary, but got straight to the political point. From that to advocacy advertising is only a short step.

ADVOCACY ADVERTISING. Its increase during the 1970s has been called "dramatic." Again, the oil companies have been prominent. A study by the Boston political consulting firm, Gens, Valley and Associates, determined that in 1977 seven of the top advocacy advertisers were oil companies. In the first half of 1977 alone, oil companies spent for this purpose $1.1 million in just four newspapers: *Washington Post, Washington Star, New York Times* and the *Wall Street Journal*.[139] This was apart from what the American Petroleum Institute and the American Gas Association put out.

As we have come to expect, Mobil Oil has again been far out in front, virtually having its own spot in several of the most distinguished newspapers in the country, especially the lower right-hand corner of the op-ed page of the *New York Times* on Thursdays. The practice started in October 1970 on the inspiration (it was thought) of Herbert Schmertz[140] although he himself explains that credit should also be given to the chairman, president and other leading executives of the company. In any case, the idea was inspired in the other sense: "Just buying any old ad space wouldn't get the job done. They didn't want their stuff buried back among the truss ads and real estate blurbs. They wanted it framed and set apart and treated with journalistic reverence, and they wanted this to happen in the most prestigious newspapers."[141]

But would the *Times* really sell space regularly on one of its two opinion pages, the only one in fact open to articles from outside contributors? That seemed unlikely because it would be tantamount to letting Mobil buy its way into the role of a *Times* columnist (as many have pointed out, including Michael Gerrard of the NYU Law School). But the *Times* management approved. Appearing only irregularly to begin with, the pieces were published more or less weekly after January 1972, being only occasionally intruded upon. By fall 1979, after some seven years or so had elapsed, four hundred such op-ed pieces had appeared at a cost of $5000 each. That was apart from publication in the *Wall Street Journal, Washington Post, Chicago Tribune, Los Angeles Times*, and the *Boston Globe* ($2550 for the quarter page, in 1979). In critical periods, as during the time (1976) of the proposed divestiture of the big oil companies, material would be placed in a hundred papers across the land.

No content analysis of the series appears to have been published by a political scientist. Some sense of the content is conveyed by the *New York Times'* own columnist, Russell Baker, who characterized the pieces as "quarter-page lectures of freshman's economics." But they have been both less innocuous and more interesting than that implies. *More interesting* because written gracefully and quite often wittily. *Less innocuous* because the authors showed themselves masters of the *suppressio veri* as distinct (you will recall) from the simple lie. Thus, the miniessays on the company's own profitability neglected to tell the reader about those glaring loopholes and concessions that will be remarked upon in chapter nine. In other words, they did not tell the public that the "reasonable" profits they were citing were struck *after* the intangibles, the depletion allowance (in the good old days that lasted a generation), and the rest had been deducted.

Mobil's op-ed series is almost invariably featured in textbooks, in itself a kind of triumph of public relations. Another kind of advocacy is seldom, if ever, dealt with—televised "special reports" on such current policy issues as oil exploration, the price of gasoline, and energy policy in general. From 1976 to 1980 eleven such special reports were produced. These half-hour programs had TV journalists interviewing Mobil executives and other experts who spoke up for the company's positions on energy. Distributed free to local TV stations, the reports were then aired at weekends and late at night. A 1980 special, "Energy at the Crossroads," was shown by sixty-two stations before the year was out. Again, as with the op-ed series, all this had perturbing features. The programs lacked balance: no environmentalists or other potential critics. Far from being identified as hired by Mobil, the interviewers were presented (or at least viewers were left to conclude) that they were above the battle. Indeed, Mobil's own involvement was barely acknowledged—just a lightning flash on the screen at the very end: "Produced for Mobil Oil by DWJ Associates." Mobil's media manager even confessed to A. Kent MacDougall of the *Los Angeles Times:* "In most cases, viewers get the impression that the interview is the station's own. We make certain everything we send out is identified. But what stations do then is their own business."[142] Maybe, although it is also Democracy's. The point, in any case, is that there are TV stations all over America only too delighted to fill in with free footage.

In winding down, one ought to dispel any impression that Mobil Oil has for some reason been given excessive attention here. Certainly other examples abound. Take the Sugar Association, which, in 1981, prepared "special reports" picked up by sixty-five radio stations. Questions were put to this trade association's president by a man who was not identified but who actually was a p.r. man it retained. The questions "enabled the president to defend sugary foods against proposed federal restrictions on TV advertising to children."[143] Consider also the international p.r. firm, Burson-Marsteller.[144] It prepared a videotape for a pharmaceutical client in the form of a news report which managed to bring in the client's name. Sent out (free of course) to "several hundred-TV stations, it was used by more than half of them. Not surprising, commented the vice-chairman of the company's Washington office, "when you look at the amount of time stations are filling up on the early evening news."[145]

So one could go on. This kind of thing is certainly not practiced by Mobil Oil only, nor by oil corporations only, not even by corporations only. Nor is "canned" material picked up only by TV and radio stations with more air time on their hands than they know what to do with. Thus, the AFL-CIO has claimed that, during the 1978 battle for labor law reform, it inspired three hundred favorable editorials in newspapers based on material it had supplied through a syndicate. This outfit, in fact, specialized in distributing prepared *editorial* matter to newspapers, claiming that clients could be "guaranteed 10 percent use of canned materials."[146]

Nevertheless, the focus on the techniques and methods used by Big Oil and especially Mobil Oil is justifiable, partly because it complements the material in chapters 9, 10 and 12. Moreover, the big oil companies almost certainly spend more on p.r. and associated activities than any other class of corporations. And in their company Mobil is acknowledged to be the most "pushy" and intransigent. It may not deserve President Carter's description as "perhaps" the most irresponsible corporation in America. But it certainly spends lavishly on p.r.: in 1981, $21 million was budgeted for that alone, quite apart from direct lobbying and other related activities, not to mention campaign contributions.

This rounds off what one is able to say here about advocacy advertising and brings us to another transitional zone. Just as Mobil's *Observations* series could be taken, analytically, to mark the transition from simple "pictures in the head" to advocacy advertising, so the latter naturally brings us close to p.r. for clearly demarcated policy campaigns.

P.R. IN POLICY CAMPAIGNS

Here again we must distinguish the *thing* p.r. from its several forms or modes, which means in particular resisting the tendency to think only of political advertising. In 1977, for example, on the deregulation of natural gas, Gulf Oil took the trouble to bring to the capital newspaper writers from as far afield as Baytown, Texas; Casper, Wyoming; Grants, New Mexico; and Joplin, Missouri. The purpose was described, of course, as "educational . . . a chance for writers from outside Washington to find out what the issues are." These were essentially the decontrol of oil and natural gas prices, with special reference to a windfall profits tax (chapters 10 and 12). Put up at the Hyatt-Regency, these out-of town writers took breakfast with Senator Gary Hart (Dem.-Colorado), who had introduced an amendment to a natural-gas pricing bill that was pleasing to the smaller, independent companies at least. There followed a seminar featuring three senators, seven representatives, several aides and officials, and a vice-president of the U.S. Chamber of Commerce. In diversity of view, the seminar was far from being hopelessly biased, but the "weight of the presentations" (according to Jerry Ackerman of the *Boston Globe*) tilted toward the industry's policy of deregulation.[147]

"About half" of those writers let Gulf pay all or part of their air fares and hotel bills. Some papers took care to protect their virtue, e.g., the editors of the *Joplin Globe*, who got an assurance in writing from Gulf that the company "would not expect us to write anything at all." Others, like the *Boston Globe*, played it safe, attending but declining to accept "hospitality." No such hospitality seems to have been offered for the seminar put on a week earlier (at the Marriott Inn, on the Pike near Boston) for New England papers. Organized by the Georgia-Pacific Corporation, a leading manufacturer of newsprint, this seminar turned into "an out-and-out appeal for natural-gas pricing deregulation." The argument was advanced not so much by the sponsoring company as by Bruce Melaas, chairman of the Petrochemical Energy Group, representing twenty-one firms that use natural gas to make plastics and chemicals. The twenty-one included Dow Chemicals, DuPont, Dart Industries and Monsanto.

Meanwhile, oil company executives were flying around the country in a series of orchestrated visits to newspaper editors in 150 cities. The purpose is obvious enough but received authoritative expression from the mouth of H. H. Hardy, vice-president for p.r. at the American Petroleum Institute: "It has been our perception that guys on the Hill tend to look at the editorials in their (district) newspapers as indicative of the attitudes of the people in their district."[148]

That p.r. takes many forms was demonstrated earlier in the same policy area. After the Supreme Court's Phillips decision in 1954 (chapter 10, section 2), an industry group hired Hill and Knowlton to persuade public opinion that it should be reversed. As in the other cases just noted, H. and K. entertained the press (luncheon at New York's Savoy-Plaza), then for some weeks briefed editors at their place of work; organized a great network of local volunteers to exert local and regional influence; printed booklets; produced a film; obtained editorial comment and placed news items; reached radio and TV—all in addition to political advertising. What is true, however, is that political advertising ran away with most of the money—it cost $800,000 out of a total of about $1,680,000 (over seventeen months). Almost $400,000 of that accrued to H. and K. to cover its retainer and staff charges (sixteen were busy at the peak of the campaign).[149]

Even from that incomplete sketch, we perceive a great barrage being "laid down" for Oil and Gas. But again we must remind ourselves that other interest groups are likely to be engaging the enemy (indirectly) at more or less the same time, if not with such heavy guns. Turn back to the illustrations drawn just above from the 1977 energy battle. Bethlehem Steel was taking space to urge readers to write to their congresspersons saying that coal should be "one answer" to future energy problems.[150] In 1978 the same corporation was advertising in another policy area but no doubt with the same end in mind (survival): "Vigorous enforcement of existing trade laws can save jobs for steelworkers—and for a lot of other Americans, too." And so: "Washington must help" to prevent unfair trade practices such as "dumping." Write to "your representatives in Washington and tell them so."[151]

Many other examples could be cited. Even so it is not misleading to round off with yet another reference to Oil and Gas, whose companies are so fabulously rich and politically active. Early in 1981 Mr. John E. Swearingen, chairman of the board of Standard Oil, Indiana, wrote to stockholders saying that the management "wholeheartedly endorses the president's program . . . the package President Reagan has proposed must be enacted." But it may not be enacted "unless the members of the House and Senate are reminded that Mr. Reagan's program represents the will of the people. I urge you, therefore, to write promptly to your representative and to your senators to express your support for his proposals. The future of our nation is at stake."

Columnist David Broder, who published this missive, poked a little fun at "the will of the people": he could not "recall an oil company president being quite so sure that the election represented the will of the people when the president was Jimmy Carter, and the program involved a windfall profits tax." But here we are mainly interested in two things: writing to stockholders as another roundabout technique, but above all in Mr. Broder's own comment that the S.O. Indiana chairman was "simply trying to revive the tradition of public persuasion that has been part of Standard Oil's history since the days when that fabled public relations man, Ivy Lee, undertook to improve the image of its Rockefeller founders." Lee once told a group of executives that "crowds are led by symbols and phrases. Success in dealing with crowds . . . rests upon the art of getting believed in."[152] That, from the early years of this century, still illuminates what p.r. is all about.

WITHHOLDING SUPPLIES

Every author of this kind of book deals with the techniques sketched above (even if resorting to different terminology). Few, if any, bring in what, if true, ought to be accounted a technique—the withholding of supplies from the market in order to influence public policy. This, it has been asserted, is what was done in order to build up pressure for the deregulation of natural-gas prices. It seems to be common ground that during the natural-gas shortage of 1976–77, Texaco had in the Gulf of Mexico "rights over one-half trillion cubic feet of retrievable natural gas in proved reserves that it did not attempt to tap." Responding to the charge (but not denying the numbers), a company spokesman declared that they were bound by contracts of one kind or another and so had to choose between "a shortfall on some consumer today versus a larger shortfall on some consumer tomorrow. It's an ethical judgment." A congressional staff study also criticized Gulf Oil for having violated the Natural Gas Act by failing to deliver the contracted daily amount to a major pipeline company serving sixteen states. Gulf denied "deliberate withholding of gas," arguing that they were doing everything "humanly possible" to fulfill the contract. [153]

Nevertheless, a private report commissioned by some of the major gas utilities did indeed conclude that natural-gas producers had failed to bring to market proven reserves that could have offset "much of this winter's cutbacks to consumers." As summarized for members of the Associated Gas Distributors, the report (David Bird noted) "added to the growing controversy over whether the gas companies were deliberately withholding supplies in the hope of selling at much higher prices in the future."[154] Looking back at all this the following year, Representative Harley O. Staggers (Dem.-West Virginia) used some startling language. With the industry in his sights rather than a company, he warned that he would consider it "treason against the interests of America if you withhold gas from the marketplace *in the future*."[155] (Emphasis added.) Later congressional investigators did find hundreds of wells capped in the Gulf of Mexico. Even some energy experts thought that the whole thing had been "a hoax."[156]

That the oil companies as such "were holding back supplies of crude oil to cash in on higher prices that will come from decontrol" was the charge levied in 1979, among others by Representative Benjamin S. Rosenthal, (Dem.-New York), chairman of a relevant subcommittee. That spring there occurred the notorious panic at the pumps, with gas lines "sometimes miles long" and enraged truckers revealing a violent streak. Was crude oil deliberately stockpiled? Were refining runs deliberately cut back? Yes, wrote Fred J. Cook in *The Nation*, making the so-called shortage "one of the greatest frauds ever perpetrated on a helpless people."

All such charges are difficult for the outsider to assess. Studies released by two federal departments in 1980 tended, on the face of it, to exonerate the industry of causing the 1979 panic at the pumps. The Justice Department found that 62 percent of the shortage was attributable to a shortfall in imports; 16 percent to lower production in the U.S.A.; and the rest to lower yields from refineries. The Department of Energy report apparently said much the same thing.[157] One's confidence in that report, however, is dimmed by the disclosure that it was prepared by consultants to oil companies. And in rebuttal of the former report, Mr. Cook might have quoted himself on oil tankers dawdling at sea, speed reduced to 10 knots from 16–17; an unexplained increase in the turnaround time in port; and the diversion of supplies to the lucrative "spot" market in Europe as later revealed about Exxon, for example, by Brian Ross in a series on the NBC "Nightly News."[158] An investigation by Donald Bartlett and James Steele (Knight Ridder Service) based on interviews and a study of "hundreds" of industry and government documents, also concluded that the "slash in imports by oil companies" in 1978 had been deliberate.[159] Curiously enough, a report emanating from the White House could also be cited in rebuttal. This had been prepared by the energy adviser (Terence O'Rourke) to Alfred Kahn, the White House anti-inflation economist from Cornell. Said to have been "exhaustively documented," it found that U.S. companies had indeed been diverting relatively low-priced crude from the American market to the spot market in Rotterdam.[160]

We also know, reverting to natural gas, that no sooner had the president signed the new legislation authorizing gradual deregulation of prices than there appeared an "unexpected" glut, which the administration tried to explain away as a "gas bubble," i.e., a short-term phenomenon. The industry took the same tack, hoping to "rescue its own faltering credibility," as political scientist Walter Rosenbaum put it.[161] Whatever had happened to those dwindling reserves? Part of the answer may be that the dwindling was only like doodling—on paper. Some companies, the then director of FTC's Bureau of Competition disclosed, "fudged" their reports to the federal government: "Gas reserves in some areas were underreported by 1000 per cent."[162]

On balance, one is inclined to believe that the main charges were well founded. But that would not be the end of the debate. President Carter expressed the view that, obviously, some natural gas was being withheld from the market. But this, he added, was "understandable." What he had in mind could be called the logic of the market economy, a theme which Mobil in 1980 developed in an op-ed piece under: "It's all 'ho hum' to Adam Smith." They were answering a front page story in the New York Times (December 1980) about the sudden disappearance of the natural-gas shortage. It would have been no surprise to Adam Smith, replied the company. He would have expected a boost in natural-gas production following even the degree of deregulation of prices already accomplished: "Congress passed legislation raising the price ceilings on newly discovered gas, and the economy's natural gyroscope started functioning again." That was "democratic capitalism" at work.[163]

With those words, Mobil, in explaining the resumption of supplies seemed, by the same token, to be explaining their restriction, tantamount to endorsing or accepting the "withholding" charge. However, if both types of action—the cutting back and the surge forward—are merely responses to the economic gyroscope, is it proper to treat the cutting back as a technique (as it is *not* in the literature on interest groups)? On balance, yes. To believe in a gyroscope is tempting. It would explain why, as Bartlett and Steele pointed out, the major oil companies "simultaneously reduced imports" in 1978 and then "suddenly began increasing them" early in 1979. Otherwise one would be in danger of thinking the unthinkable—that the majors, defying the antitrust laws, were "in cahoots" together. Alas, "the economy's natural gyroscope" is only a metaphor. Even if reached independently, the decisions were, of course, taken by managements who doubtless well understood their political significance. Thus, "withholding," although reflective of a market economy, is properly treated as a technique for influencing public policy.

LITIGATION

Unlike "withholding," litigation is almost invariably touched upon in books of this kind. The subject has indeed its landmark article, Clement Vose's "Litigation as a Form of Pressure Group Activity," although other authors, cited by Professor Vose, had already cut a swath to the site. His principal example was drawn from the experience of the NAACP, which "frankly admits the deliberate and conscious use of litigation to secure economic, social, and political gains for Negroes."[164] (That was written in 1958, before Negro turned *black*). Resurveying the field in September 1981, Professor Vose still gave NAACP/ NAACP Legal Defense Fund, Inc.,[165] "a prime place among organizations engaged in litigation."[166] A case from that period concerned tax exemption for educational institutions practicing racial discrimination—immediately; these included the Bob Jones University of Greenville, South Carolina, and Goldsboro Christian Schools of Goldsboro, North Carolina, although the brief pointed to over one hundred racially segregated private educational institutions. Repudiating the brief it had filed as recently as that September, the Justice Department in January 1982 made it plain that the administration was prepared to grant such tax exemption. The NAACP filed papers in the Supreme Court to stop that (although it was not quite as quick off the mark as the Lawyers Committee for Civil Rights Under Law, which had gone for an injunction two days before).[167]

Evidently, "litigation is speech *plus*," as Mr. Justice Harlan said (for the minority) in a celebrated NAACP case in 1963. Evidently, too, it is "a form of political expression," as Mr. Justice Brennan remarked (for the majority) in that same case.[168] But is it an important form of political expression? In our language here, is it an important technique? From early on some authors cast doubt on the usefulness of the concept. Thus in 1966

Nathan Hakman, consigned the notion, specifically with the NAACP Legal Defense Fund, Inc. in mind, to the "folklore" of political science. His research demonstrated that interest groups had until then acted as friends of the court (*amici curiae*) in a relatively small proportion of the cases decided by the Supreme Court. Several points may be made in rebuttal. First, acceptance of his findings does not rule out the significance of the *amicus* brief. This is the "functional equivalent" of the lobbyist's technique of supplying information to members of Congress and bureaucrats. And several types of groups can be shown to have made fruitful use of it. Karen O'Connor, for example, recalled in 1977 that the Women's Rights Project (WRP) of the American Civil Liberties Union had got into sex (or gender) discrimination cases by resorting to the *amicus* approach.[169]

Secondly, the *amicus* procedure entails an intervention by a third party in a two-sided battle already in progress. But who got the battle going: where did the original initiative come from? As a noted authority, Henry J. Abraham, has remarked, a litigant may well "act as a front or a foil" for some organization.[170] But that is not easy to establish.

Thirdly, an *amicus* brief is only one way into "the system": there is also what Frank Sorauf called "direct representation" by attorneys. Here the previous question reappears: whom do the attorneys really represent?

All in all, it would seem that counting *amici* briefs in an earlier period hardly provides a firm basis for the characterization "folklore." On the other hand, if, for the sake of argument, such briefs are taken as an index, then they increased during the 1970s, certainly in specific issue areas. Thus Karen O'Connor and Lee Epstein found that among the noncommercial cases decided by the Supreme Court in that decade or so, interest groups submitted *amici* briefs in over three out of four cases involving sex (or gender) discrimination.[171]

Parallel to that there would seem to have been greater use of the litigation technique generally in the same decade. Mr. Justice Brennan had focused on relief for minorities: "Groups which find themselves unable to achieve their objectives through the ballot frequently turn to the courts . . . under conditions of modern government, litigation may well be the sole practicable avenue open to a minority to petition for redress of grievances."[172] Blacks and Jehovah's Witnesses are among those invariably cited. But, as Professor Abraham pointed out, the use of litigation has extended beyond minorities to "almost every segment of the body politic," parts of which Professor Vose identified in 1981:

1. unions and employers' associations
2. church organizations
3. women's organizations
4. American Indians
5. the disadvantaged (e.g., physically handicapped; mentally ill).

To that, at least one other category should be added: environmental groups. The Sierra Club's suit (with others) to stop construction of the Peripheral Canal in California provides a good example. The canal was to carry fresh water from the moist north to the drier south. The effect, argued the club, would be to pollute northern California fresh water with salt water.[173]

Here the most striking phenomenon is what might be called the institutionalization of the public-policy lawsuit. One is thinking of those relatively new entities, the public-interest law firms, deliberately created to pursue certain public-policy objectives, environmental included, by means of litigation. That is their *raison d'être*.

PROTEST AS A POLITICAL RESOURCE

The abortion issue may be used to draw attention to the only other technique that need be touched upon in this book: the "demonstration," possibly preceded by a march, and, contingently, violence. The March for Life from the White House to the Capitol in January 1979 is one example. On the Capitol steps, a great crowd of sixty thousand abortion opponents, or "prolife" proponents, heard their leaders denounce "the baby killers." The action was countered in Washington by the National Abortion Rights Action League, and in New York by a march on St. Patrick's Cathedral by several hundred men and women with a vanguard of some three dozen Jewish and Protestant clergy "to protest the antiabortion statements and actions of Roman Catholic Church leaders."[174]

Harassment and violence have marked the relations between the respective forces, although, it would appear, in one direction only. In February 1979 a man entered the Bill Baird abortion clinic in Hempstead, Long Island, carrying a lighted torch and a can of gasoline. He set fire to the clinic and made off: later a suspect was arrested. Fifty patients, counselors, doctors and nurses escaped unharmed, but the building—a clinic from 1967—was destroyed. Mr. Baird placed the ultimate, not direct, responsibility for the outrage on the antiabortion interest groups, such as Right to Life, as well as on "the Roman Catholic Church," for applying such epithets as "baby killers" and "murderers" to those who operated his clinic and others of the kind. Proabortion supporters promptly called him with proposals for retaliation by firebombing the Right to Life headquarters or even a Roman Catholic church. Naturally, he put them off.

Such attacks had been getting disturbingly common for some years. In 1977, for example, the Planned Parenthood Clinic in St. Paul was set on fire ($250,000 damage and suspension of work for six months). So was the Vermont Women's Health Center in Burlington (service out for a month longer), and most of the Ladies Clinic in Omaha after at least four bottles of gasoline sailed through its windows. Ohio at first fared better: neither the firebomb aimed at the Margaret Sanger Clinic in Cincinnati nor the chemical bomb thrown through a window of the Women's Center there actually exploded. But early in the new year a fire started in ten different locations at a Columbus abortion clinic caused damage put at $200,000. In February a woman worker at the Concerned Women's Clinic in Cleveland suffered chemical burns when a man caught her in the face with a plastic bag containing gasoline. He also started a fire (damage $30,000) that sent a young woman scurrying from the operating table through the smoke to safety (and put the clinic out of commission—damage $30,000). At the Chicago Loop Mediclinic, on the day before Mother's Day 1978, some adults and children from Friends for Life broke into the waiting room: the adults regaled a patient with a Mother's Day message as the children stood with flowers and a crucified doll. The patient was rather moved. At an Anchorage, Alaska, clinic, some militants chained themselves to a bed in the operating room until the police took them away. In a warmer spot (Phoenix, Arizona), a physician who undertook abortions had his children harassed and his dog dispatched, by poison, to some canine destination.[175]

As the eighties unfolded, however, such violence seemed to be giving way to harassment. This was said to have included "threatening phone calls to employees and clients" of a private abortion clinic on Staten Island, New York, and the "gluing shut of the locks on the building." Some artists painted "abortion mill" on the front door. Twice, at least, pickets took the license-plate numbers of clients' cars and informed their families by phone. In October 1981 the clinic gave up the ghost, closing its doors.[176]

Reflecting on these illustrations, you might well object: isn't this group v. group not group v. government, so should it count as technqiue? This is indeed an instance of what James Q. Wilson called organizational opposition as distinct from organizational competition. Such opposition is characterized by incompatible goals, the struggle over which amounts to an attempt by one side to raise the cost to the other side of continuing a given course of action. This is a general phenomenon stipulatively defined by Professor Wilson as *protest;* the other mode of handling organizational opposition is conceived of as an exchange of compensations, defined by Professor Wilson as *bargaining.*[177]

Now, protest in this sense may be engaged in for several reasons, but one is "to activate third parties," or what Michael Lipsky had earlier designated "reference publics." These are publics *of* some authoritative body such as Congress or an agency/bureau, *to* which it *refers* (i.e., which it has in its mind's eye)—constituents, say, campaign contributors, clienteles or the media.[178] Thus the process is indeed "highly indirect," which is congruent with the notion of roundaboutness used here. (It also makes *protest* a more restrictive term than in everyday usage. But its very limitation to indirectness suits our purpose here very well.) In other words, if the antiabortion militants intended not merely to damage or destroy some abortion clinics but also to communicate *through* the media *to* government, they were using a (roundabout) technique.

In the Lipskyite conception, protest is not protest unless it is indirect. However, indirectness, would seem to be a matter of degree. One might propose a convention that the greater the physical proximity to an (authoritative) target, the *less* indirect the "demo" may be deemed to be. At one end of the spectrum in the early 1980s we would find the New England Conference on Women and Life on Earth, coordinating about thirty women's groups. Starting at daybreak at Arlington National Cemetery, they moved on to the Pentagon bearing such signs as "No Nukes" and "Stop the Arms Race." There they numbered about thirteen hundred, of whom perhaps one hundred fifty were arrested for trying to block the entrances to the building. The Atlantic Life Community was more broadly based, responsible (between Christmas 1980 and New Year's) for a three-day confrontation between a daily gathering of three hundred people and the Pentagon authorities. On one occasion Gerald Berrigan, of the famous (some would say, notorious) family of militants, spilled blood and ashes on a Pentagon wall.

The religious symbolism is obvious, reminding us that issues other than abortion and gun control may be charged with intense emotion. The blood symbol (not necessarily religious in each case, however) was again resorted to on successive days in April 1981. Ten persons threw "red paint or blood," which had been carried in baby bottles, on the North Portico pillars of the White House. One of the signs they displayed carried the pun—"We cannot hug our kids with nuclear arms."[179] On the following day, five protesters (two of them men) somehow penetrated into the heart of the State Department, three to within several feet of Secretary of State Haig's office, where they poured what they described as blood and ashes on the carpet and on the Chippendale furniture. The "blood," one of them said, stood for "the blood of all those who died in Vietnam."

By contrast, the antinuclear warfare drive resumed in the summer of 1978 used techniques that were more indirect, or roundabout. One striking event was what *Newsweek* called a "half-mile-long human chain [of people] five abreast," converging on the U.S. Naval Base in Bangor, Washington, where the Trident nuclear-missile submarines were to be placed. Another was Survival Sunday, a Hollywood Bowl rally of ten thousand people, many of whom marched at the special United Nations session on disarmament. On the anniversary of the dropping of the atomic bomb on Hiroshima, there were many demonstrations in New England, including one by Boston Mobilization for Survival "demanding zero nuclear weapons."[180]

Across the nation Mobilization for Survival embodied the antinuclear power forces as well, i.e., the environmentalists. They had been fighting the development of nuclear power since 1958 at least, thinking of the (successful) struggle against the Pacific Gas and Electric Company's proposed nuclear reactor at Bodega Head, north of San Francisco.[181] But they had used the law and local politics to prevail. In the East some two decades later, although the legal approach was still pursued (as by the New England Coalition on Nuclear Pollution), the struggle was taking an increasingly radical form. At Montague, Massachusetts, site of a proposed reactor, militants toppled the weather-testing tower. Formed in 1976, the Clamshell Alliance mounted a major attack the following May on the plant under construction at Seabrook, New Hampshire. Ignoring an injunction, about two thousand penetrated on to the site: over fourteen hundred were arrested.[182] That, up to a point could be considered direct, but it was essentially roundabout in that the real targets were in Washington—immediately the Nuclear Regulatory Commission and the White House. The roundaboutness was even clearer in June 1978, when nine thousand or more occupied a site conveniently provided (it was far too expensive to arrest them if they refused bail, as they did in 1977, and of course there had been no room at the inn—they had overflowed the jails into the armories). By contrast, 1978 was more fun: music and speeches, as if staged for the media. The 1980 turnout (eleven hundred over the Memorial Day weekend) also passed without incident.

By 1980, however, the movement had started to show another face. The Campaign for Safe Energy, started in Boston, deliberately kept their distance from "the counterculture people associated with"[183] the Seabrook demonstrations. Intervening in the presidential primary in New Hampshire, they managed to make nuclear power a major issue there, as one candidate, Senator Howard Baker, Jr., remarked. With that, however, we have come almost full circle, back to more traditional and direct forms of action.

Obviously, a great deal more could be written. To think of the Clamshell Alliance is to be reminded of Greenpeace, the save-the-whales group of twenty to thirty thousand members worldwide. Its efforts from 1976 to stop the seal hunts in Newfoundland attracted international attention for its basic goal. The (intellectual) connection with Clamshell is that in 1979 the Boston chapter was divided on whether to tackle nuclear energy (as well as off-shore oil drilling). One view was: "Greenpeace is not like Clamshell. . . . If we get into that we'll use more scientific people. We're not twits"[184]—which suggests one of the constraints upon "goal succession."

In the latter part of the seventies there was little protest by blacks either in Professor Lipsky's sense or the commoner one, compared with the outbursts of the tumultuous sixties. But some took part (February–July 1978) in the long march of twenty-five hundred American Indians from San Francisco to Washington, D.C., where a weeklong demonstration was mounted to preserve their "endangered rights." The spectacular march, if not the demonstration, was roundabout. So in a way was the specific complaint of media bias: "They remember the Jewish Holocaust, but we should ask the media why they have forgotten the massacres of the Indians."[185]

The "mass march itself," reporter Marcia Kunstel has remarked, is a technique "made essentially safe and acceptable by activists of the fifties and sixties."[186] Thus one kind of group may learn from the techniques developed by others. In this instance, as she pointed out, the learners included, at

labama, in 1979, marching men in white robes with peaked hoods,
/hite power! White power!"

ᴕᴏ ᴏne could go on, from (in the same year) the sporadic violence of truckers, some of it caught on television, during the gasoline shortage, and the highly visual invasion of the capital by the American Agriculture Movement, using two thousand tractors instead of tanks (but still inflicting a great deal of damage to grass and ground), to the burning of two effigies in Lafayette Park across from the White House in January 1982. The protestors were a group of women backers of the Equal Rights Amendment. One of the effigies represented President Reagan, the other the judge who had recently ruled that Congress had acted illegally in extending the period for ratification of the amendment. Charged with an interesting offense, "incommoding the sidewalk," twenty women were each fined $50.

However, not attempting to be encyclopedic, one has reached one's limit on the subject of techniques.

CHAPTER NINE
DISTRIBUTIVE POLICY:
Taxation and the Oil
Depletion Allowance

INTRODUCTION TO PART 3

A catalogue of methods and techniques is as useful as any other catalogue. The one just presented does disclose a good deal about the resources that interest groups bring to bear upon the federal government in the hope of influencing public policy as well as something about the paths they mark out and follow. It also casts some light upon our basic framework: the interaction of society and state (end, chapter 1), of social power and political authority (beginning, chapter 2). Now one would like to throw more light on the character of that interaction in the course of placing interest groups in the context of some actual public policies.

One of the boldest generalizations relating interest groups to the federal government is still Theodore Lowi's *policies determine politics*, or, as Ira Sharkansky would elucidate: "Different kinds of policy are likely *to stimulate* different kinds of interactions among other features of politics,"[1] which, of course, include interest groups. So, here, the focus becomes: as the policy or issue changes, so does the role of interest groups in the political process (the "politics" in Professor Lowi's cryptic proposition).

These are deep waters, still not properly plumbed, at least to the satisfaction of all mariners; the ideas remain controversial even in the early eighties, two decades after they were first advanced in Professor Lowi's "seminal" article (as several scholars characterized it early on). Yet even here, in an introductory book, we can hardly avoid giving his work some consideration. It crops up in many political-science contexts, and in any case it bears directly on the subject in hand, notably the attempt to relate patterns of interest-group activity to patterns of policy.

Think back, then, to the end of chapter 5, where there appeared the (original) Lowian division of (domestic) policy into distributive, regulatory, and redistributive. There the first was defined by direct quotation, *in extenso*, with examples. As its name suggests, regulatory policy constrains behavior according to rule. Unlike distributive policy, it cannot be "cut" into small units and distributed widely, making everyone a beneficiary: some are consciously "indulged" by the policy maker, others "deprived," according to some broadly formulated principle. Examples included the allocation of an overseas air route or a TV channel, and the prohibition of a labor practice, deemed to be unfair. This implies that the area to which the policy applies will be comparatively broad, such as an industry or occupation.

Broader still in expected impact is the redistributive, impinging on something like "social classes," or "haves and have-nots." Income tax, if steeply progressive, affords a characteristic example. On the other hand, this type of policy resembles the regulatory in "indulging" one set of people at the expense of others, although the numbers will be greater, the lines of cleavage more distinct and permanent and, with that, the contending coalitions more persistent.[2]

This scheme was in itself intriguing but doubly so for the study of interest groups. As James Q. Wilson, author of a major work on political organizations, would put it, acknowledging "Lowi's fundamental insight": "The substance of a policy influences the role of organizations in its adoption."[3] Thus policy (substance/content) was cast as the independent variable, whereas the dominant paradigms, or models, had represented policy as a dependent variable. In other words, in the shorthand of everyday conversation, policy was cast as a cause of the political roles and relationships, not as a result of these, including, over a certain range, the actions of interest groups.

Modified by Professor Lowi himself and others, this scheme found its way into some standard texts, as, burnished and much extended, in the work of Randall B. Ripley and Grace A. Franklin (1976).[4] Yet, in that very year, a foreign scholar, Francesco Kjellberg, was asking: "Do policies (really) determine politics.?"[5] Two years later, Michael Hayes, in a notable article signalling a revival in the academic study of interest groups, obliquely answered, "No," arguing that "what makes an issue fall within a given (political) arena" is something other than the characteristics of the policy.[6]

Thus, two years after the Lowian scheme had apparently entered the mainstream of American political science (e.g., via Ripley-Franklin), its central proposition (*policies determine policies*)—the "point" of the typology—was being rejected. Meanwhile, the typology itself, which had been dismissed by some as early as 1970, now came under the hammer blows of Greenberg, Miller, Mohr, and Vladeck, writing in the leading political-science journal: "No single theoretical construct has been more important to the development of public policy studies than Lowi's categorization scheme, yet . . ."[7] And they proceeded swiftly and forcefully to undermine that scheme, arguing (among other things) that the categories provided cannot be "operationalized" (say, made precise enough to be measured), so that researchers cannot be sure of putting any particular policy into the right "box" and the prediction (*policies determine politics*) cannot be tested.

As the eighties advanced, the debate continued, including a rather sharp exchange in *Social Science Quarterly*,[8] a prize-winning book by Michael Hayes,[9] and a paper read by Eric Uslaner at the 1982 meeting of the American Political Science Association.[10] Of this debate, all one can report here is that Professor Hayes now specifically repudiated *policies determine politics* as a proposition that "comes dangerously close to being circular," i.e., ostensibly making policy outcome the independent variable accounting for policy process only to proceed to employ "policy process to explain outcomes." Professor Uslaner, too, set his face against the proposition. But then he also attacked "the other" proposition: *politics determines policies*, which he attributed to Robert Salisbury, an early "consumer" of the Lowian typology who had nonetheless written: "The active political system continues to be decisive in determining the kind of policy."[11] "Active political system" had then been reduced to *demand patterns* (interest groups, individuals, etc.) and *decisional systems* (the authoritative institutions, such as president or Congress), whereupon the argument became "that the interactions of demand patterns and the decisional system . . . are systematically associated with the differentiated *types* of policy." This meant, within political science (narrowly defined) as distinct from political sociology,[12] that *demand patterns* and *decisional system* are the determinants of the types of policy, now totaling four if one accepted Professor Salisbury's addition of another species—the self-regulatory. This is the foundation on which Michael Hayes had built his revision version, so that Professor Uslaner was at odds with him, too, *via* "the Salisbury connection." (He did not actually discuss Professor Hayes's work in either his 1982 APSA paper or his 1981 unpublished MS, *Shale Barrel Politics: Energy Politics and Institutional Decentralization in the Congress.*)

Evidently, it would be imprudent at present, particularly in an introductory work, to put one's shirt on any of these conceptualizations. Yet we do need help, i.e., some simplifying classification. The compromise reached here is as follows. Neglecting the exciting but unsettled questions of causal relationship and typology, we shall simply draw our categories from the record of American experience. Often under the name of "promotional" (recall chapter 6), distributive policy has long been a feature of American public life. So, too, with regulatory policy and the self-regulatory tacked on by Robert Salisbury, still denoting constraints on behavior but self-imposed and thus perceived as increasing, not decreasing, "the beneficial options to the group."[13] Historically, these three categories have been as "real" and common as anything in American government, as anyone may confirm from the standard texts, such as Fainsod, Gordon and Palamountain's *Government and the American Economy* (1959), or Martin Schnitzer's *Contemporary Government and Business Relations* (1983).[14] Since such policy types have been predominant for something like a century, our examples will be weighted in their favor. As Professor Hayes reminds us, genuinely redistributive policies have been conspicuous by their rarity (if not quite absence).[15] Still, redistributive policy (much discussed in the study of public finance) deserves some attention, which it will receive here through the case of the so-called windfall profits tax. This was the equitable face of the deregulation of oil prices, which may be regarded as a self-regulatory policy, enabling one to revive a point that critics of the Lowian scheme have made many times: the categories are not mutually exclusive.

In order to illuminate the distributive arena we shall turn to taxation policy, which needs illustrating all the more because political scientists as such, and interest-group specialists in particular, have generally failed to take their cue from an economist writing over half-a-century ago: "Modern taxation or tax making in its most characteristic aspect is a group contest in which powerful interests vigorously endeavor to rid themselves of present or proposed tax burdens."[16] In fact, the celebrated case studies have taken quite a different tack, being about the Anti-Saloon League (to promote Prohibition), tariffs, the Employment Act of 1946, and the like (or drawn from the field of foreign policy and defense, outside our range here). Here we shall take a tax case from the important energy field: oil depletion allowance, which can teach us a good deal about public policy in America in the period 1926–1984.

The energy field will also be tapped to yield a self-regulatory case: deregulation of natural gas. Within the realm of the regulatory, the newer, social kind will be drawn upon under "setting environmental standards," which also provides a bonus—it brings out the problem of implementing public policy even after victory has apparently been secured (by the president over the heads of the commercial interests). The regulation of personal behavior will also be introduced.

Despite the caution expressed only three paragraphs back, this (essentially teaching) procedure may make it seem that, after all, we shall be following in the post-1964 footsteps of Lowi and others. Not so: what follows is without commitment, at present, to any particular scheme, about which one will remain agnostic until conclusive research makes one a true believer. Rather, we shall be drawing upon well-documented features of the American political experience, the actual *kinds* of public policy produced over several generations if not necessarily under the names adopted here. (Of course, anyone is free to revert to the older terminology, notably *promotional* instead of *distributive*.). Meanwhile, you have been made aware of a seminal tendency in the literature, also that the acquisition of knowledge is more controversial and "hazardous," the current fabric of knowledge more frayed at the edges, than the confident reconstructions of many standard texts would lead you to suppose.

TAXATION: OIL DEPLETION ALLOWANCE

At the conclusion of the 1981 budget bargaining, a House of Representatives aide who had worked on the tax bill remarked that, all things considered, the "oil language" had come out pretty well: "We only started out with $2500 for royalty owners and we came out with $11.8 billion over five years." That masterly understatement, referring of course to $11.8 billion in unexpected tax breaks for the oil interests, was reported in chapter 1, where, however, his final sentence was omitted (to avoid having to provide an explanation at that stage): "By giving up on depletion, we were able to keep everything else."[17]

What happened during the budget preparation and proceedings demonstrates once again how special a special privilege the oil depletion allowance has been and how far Washington would go even in the early eighties in order to preserve it and please the oil interests (if not the general body of taxpayers). Supposedly, the issue had been settled in 1975, when the majors were at last deprived of the allowance and the independents were to have the level very gradually reduced from 22 percent to 15 percent by 1984 (and thereafter). In 1981, budget director David Stockman gallantly proposed to President Reagan that this sacred cow should be slaughtered then and there only to have the president reject that out of hand. Congresspersons even tried to go one better and freeze the depletion allowance (due to drop to 20 percent that year) at 22 percent. That was put into a bill by the Oklahoma Democrat, Representative James R. Jones, and from there it passed into the Conable-Hance (or administration) bill (recall chapter 1). That provision alone would cost the taxpayer $4.2 billion (through fiscal 1986). The total House package of concessions to the oil interests would cost $16 billion (over the same period). Despite that, when the House and Senate conferred, Assistant Secretary of the Treasury John E. Chapoton (before that a Houston lawyer) "was urging the conferees to adopt the House language on oil."[18] For the Senate, no less a person than Kansas Republican Senator Dole, "along with other Senate conferees, likewise is trying to get the House's depletion language into the report." But among the conferees four House Democrats, led by Representative Sam Gibbons (Florida), dug in their heels. Supporting him were Dan Rostenkowski (Illinois), "Pete" Stark (California), and Charles Rangel (New York). A Senate Republican aide commented later: "We tried about six or eight different packages with less and less depletion. It just wouldn't sell." Eventually, Senator Dole, after "clearing" with White House chief of staff James Baker and the other Baker, majority leader of the Senate, threw in the towel, fearful that if he kept trying to save the depletion language, the whole conference might unravel. That, of course, would have been unbearable. After all, 16 minus 4.2 equals 11.8. When it's literally in billions, and unexpected, what's left makes for a fairly acceptable consolation prize even by the standards of the oil world. One lobbyist for the independents (the principal beneficiaries) did have the grace to acknowledge that, saying (recall chapter 1): "It's a real bonanza, there's no getting around it."[19] But the independents generally went away dissatisfied. They had been treated with great tenderness. Senator Dole arranged for them to meet Treasury Secretary Donald Regan to talk things over. Later (July 9), six of them, representing the Independent Petroleum Association of America, were received at the White House by President Reagan and Vice-President Bush. This was the kind of treatment that plain citizens of the democracy might well envy (since they are never likely to receive it). Still, the IPAA delegation did not walk away from the White House with the biggest prize of all—exemption from the windfall profits tax—despite President's Reagan's campaign promise to abolish it entirely. But no wonder: that would have cost the taxpayer $25 billion over the five-year period. So on that issue the independents had to make do with the 50 percent cut in the windfall profit rate for newly discovered oil, a concession estimated to be worth $3.2 billion over five years, mainly accruing to them. Altogether they stood to benefit to the extent of more than $6 billion over the five years, out of a total package worth $11.8 billion to the industry as a whole. A bonanza indeed, especially considering that, as recently as June 4, Treasury Secretary Regan had assured reporters that, in the administration bill, the only oil provision contemplated was the $2500 exclusion for royalty owners from the windfall profits tax.[20]

Bearing that episode in mind, you will be less surprised than you might otherwise have been by the oil interests' penetration of important congressional committees in order to establish (percentage) depletion allowance, and their capacity to hold their ground against all attackers for half-a-century or more. Since these included the formidable senators Robert La Follette and Huey Long; President Franklin D. Roosevelt ("a device for dodging taxes"); President Truman; distinguished Republican senators such as John J. Williams (Delaware) and Ohio's Robert A. Taft ("a gift," a "special privilege beyond what anyone else can get"); and Democratic senators Hubert Humphrey, Paul Douglas, and William Proxmire, that survival over the half-century was no mean achievement. Just as illuminating in its way is the (ostensible) fact that for a quarter of a century the congressional critics (if they existed) were silent.

The story starts in 1913 (the age of Woodrow Wilson and Robert La Follette) with the introduction of the first (permanent) income tax in the United States. It was then decreed that those in certain extractive industries could, in calculating their taxable income, deduct up to 5 percent of their gross income, subject to ceilings—original cost of the property or its market value on a particular date in 1913. Up to a point (original cost), that was something like depreciation and so not unreasonable (restoring the capital that produces the income that is about to be taxed). But the history of the policy from then onward is the history of a rapid retreat from the depreciation principle. In 1918 Congress extended the depletion idea to the value of all new discoveries (*discovery value depletion*). The administrative definition of what constituted *new* was so generous (to the interests) that discovery depletion came to be widely permitted in the tax calculations. In fact, in the early 1920s, a Senate Select Committee would discover that out of some 13,600 claims for that allowance, only 35 related to actual discoveries of new oil. It followed that wildcatters, whom some congresspersons may have originally intended to help, benefited but little. Not more than 3–4 percent of discovery depletion allowances went to them, according to an expert who had headed up a division of the Income Tax Unit. The real beneficiaries were the large established companies. One of these was a Texas company, which enjoyed a discovery value of $38.9 million on property it had bought for $250,000.

One way or another the Treasury tax official who (in 1921) characterized discovery depletion as "really a gift in the form of tax-free income" was surely justified. For that was not the only special treatment accorded the special interests. As the Senate Select Committee reported, "the large oil-producing companies" not only received most of the discovery-depletion exemption but could also "deduct the prospecting and developing expense, intended to be offset by discovery depletion, from income as operating expense." This must have been a reference to the so-called intangible drilling expenses provision, first introduced in 1916, not by Congress, but by regulations of the Internal Revenue. Since these seemed to encroach upon the power of the purse, their constitutionality was always in doubt, but conveniently for the interests, the issue was left dangling for over half-a-century—until resolved, happily still in their favor, by Congress, which substituted its wishes for a court's opinion.

The issue excited controversy because it was no minor working rule that the Internal Revenue had issued but a major policy decision. For "intangible drilling expenses" did constitute a kind of depreciation, but a specially privileged kind. The expenses of drilling for oil were conceived as divisible into two parts: (a), for putting up the derrick, pipes and other such equipment, and (b), for wages and salaries, fuel, rental of tools and machines, etc.

Now (a) takes (or took) one-tenth to one-quarter of these outlays, and (b) nine-tenths to three-quarters. Suppose you spent $100,000 on drilling an oil well. In other industries, that would be treated as a capital outlay to produce an income-generating property to be depreciated over a term of years, depending on its useful life. The Internal Revenue, however, would allow you, the oil driller, to write off $90,000 or $75,000 from (b) for the year in which these outlays were incurred, the foundation for an excellent "tax shelter." As to (a) you would write that off in the normal way in accordance with one of the standard methods of depreciation.

Now the beauty of all this was that you, the oil driller, could get two big bites at the cherry. First, exceptionally rapid depreciation on your outlays (treated not as capital outlays, really, but as if they were current or running expenses appropriately chargeable to the current year). Secondly, when the income began to flow, you took the depletion allowance right off the top.

What that amounted to was determined by Congress in 1925 after the criticisms advanced by the Senate Select Committee and various economists had prompted an overhaul of the system. This could have meant a return to the concept of original cost, as the Treasury proposed. But no; Congress retained the novel but rewarding idea of mythical costs, ones not actually incurred. However, it changed the method of calculation, abandoning, just for oil and gas among the extractive industries, "fair market value" in favor of a fixed percentage of *gross* income. The percentage established was a curious 27.5 percent. This was not determined in the cool light of reason. Oil company supporters in the Senate had made a play for 35 percent, but they lost by a single vote. So the senate came down to 30 percent. The House wanted 25 percent, a figure that may have originated with the president of the Mid-Continental Oil and Gas Association. Apparently the conferees simply split the difference. From then on, in any case, until 1969, you could have deducted 27.5 percent from your gross income from oil production (subject to a ceiling in any one year of 50 percent of your net income).

So it worked out this way: you immediately wrote off (b) above for the year in which the expenses were incurred, and gradually wrote off (a) by one of the standard methods of depreciation. Then, from the resulting gross income, you deducted 27.5 percent off the top.

Moreover, Congress at this time cut the already tenuous connection of this allowance with *discovery*, allowing the 27.5 percent to apply even to old wells. All this embodied an astonishing series of concessions. Remember that with depreciation (or amortization) you have to stop (naturally) when the original cost has been written off. Not so with percentage depletion, which could continue to be applied so long as the oil well was yielding income. This reveals its true nature, if any demonstration was needed, as a special kind of subsidy.

Obviously, the strong tendency of a depletion allowance of indefinite duration ("world without end, amen" as Senator Paul Douglas, a former professor of economics, liked to say) was to enable the oil companies to recover far more than they had invested. Equally obviously, the "intangibles" concession—(b) above—so valuable in itself,[21] accentuated that tendency. Taken together, they go a long way to explain why the oil companies have paid so little tax compared with other industrial corporations. One says "a long way" because at least one other factor was at work—the foreign tax credit. This, too, goes back to the World War I era (the Revenue Act of 1918), although it was made use of by the oil companies only from the 1950s. The companies were then permitted by the Treasury to count the royalty payments to Saudi Arabia *as if they were taxes*, which meant that such foreign "taxation" could be set off as a *credit* against the companies' tax liability in the U.S. That was obviously far more beneficial than simply deducting royalties as business expenses in the normal way.

However, that episode raises quite different issues from the ones pursued here because the change of definition served the cause of American foreign economic policy and American diplomacy in ways that inevitably involved the State Department. In other words, even *if* the foreign-tax issue were to be counted as distributive, it was not handled by the congressional committee system in the "regular" way. (This serves to remind us that Professor Lowi's schema touched only domestic policy. In practice, of course, the foreign and domestic are often mixed up.)

Why, then, bring in the foreign-tax issue at this point? It needs to be mentioned here because it greatly compounded one of the principal consequences of the distributive policies. For the "intangibles" rule was applied to American oil companies overseas (the multinationals). So was the percentage depletion allowance. It was the combination of these three concessions that so greatly favored the oil companies. When corporate tax rate was 40 percent, the oil companies in 1971 were paying as shown in Table 9–1.

That works out as 5 percent overall; it was 5.3 percent for the ten years 1962 through 1971 (taking the same companies). In 1974 the top nineteen oil companies averaged 7.6 percent, but by then the corporate rate was 48 percent. It is true that to cite official corporate rates of 40 percent and 48 percent grossly exaggerates the favorable treatment received by the oil companies. Other industrial corporations also keep their chartered accountants hard at work, so the effective rate is far less than the official one; just under 24 percent (for 143 companies studied) when the apparent rate was 48 percent.[22]

Still, even putting aside the special feature of foreign tax credit and refocusing on the domestic oil and gas industry and the truly distributive, the broad contrast remains. As the Petroleum Industry Research Foundation (funded by the industry) remarked after studying the five years ending 1972: "As in previous years, the oil industry's federal income tax payments per dollar of revenue were smaller than those [of other corporations], particularly when compared to mining and manufacturing industries."[23] And it explained:

TABLE 9–1

COMPANY	PRE-TAX PROFIT ($ BILLION)	PERCENTAGE PAID IN U.S. TAXES
Gulf	1324	2.3
Mobil	1153	7.4
Standard, Calif.	856	1.6
Standard, N.J.	2737	7.7
Texaco	1319	2.3

"The reason for the difference lies primarily in percentage depletion and . . . intangible drilling and development costs."

Now that was three years after the so-called Tax Reform Act of 1969 had reduced percentage depletion from 27.5 to 22. Evidently, the reduction had not proved too painful. Therein lies another reason for suspecting, with Bruce Oppenheimer, and Ruskay-Osserman, that the change was more symbolic than real,[24] i.e., less a genuine reform than a sop to the general public, much agitated to learn that some millionaires, and some oil companies, paid not one cent in federal tax, not as a freak result but for years on end. Also, as Washington-based journalist Erwin Knoll put it in 1970: "Some congressional critics suspect that the oilmen were not entirely displeased when Congress voted to reduce the depletion allowance, since they hope that this action will ease the pressures against other oil privileges now under attack."[25] Hence the title of his article: "The Oil Lobby Is Not Depleted." The reason was brought into the light of day by Senator Fred Harris of Oklahoma: even under current law, most of the larger companies had an *effective* depletion rate of about 23 percent and so would barely be touched by the so-called reform.[26] Intriguingly, that was precisely the figure fought for in the Senate by Democratic senator Russell Long of Louisiana after the House Ways and Means Committee had done the unthinkable—voted to reduce the percentage to 20. Having failed by a whisker to restore the full 27.5 percent, the senator (rich in oil stocks himself)[27] appealed for 23 percent, "to give us something to bargain with" (in the House-Senate conference).[28] The maneuver worked well, yielding the 22 percent compromise.

For genuine reform, the nation had to wait until 1975. Once again, the House Ways and Means Committee led the way, although almost in spite of itself. In 1974, for the first time ever, that committee had voted to end the allowance (by 1977, with some exceptions). But the more ardent reformers wanted to abolish it immediately. Led by the Philadelphia Democrat, William J. Green, they made an end run around the committee chairman, Wilbur D. Mills, by getting the Democratic Caucus to instruct that the issue be brought to the floor of the House. But the chairman prevented a score: he just refused to act. By 1975, however, he had fled the congressional scene, having become embroiled all too publicly with an Argentinian dancer, a disaster for him but an opportunity for the reformers, since he had been a chairman of exceptional ability and power. They played the same card again, and, overcoming the new chairman, Al Ullman (Oregon), who kept urging caution, they triumphed. In the first House vote on the issue since 1926 (a classic reflection of a distributive policy), members voted about three-to-two in favor of including repeal of the allowance in the Tax Reduction Bill, which they then passed by rather more than three-to-one. Of course, Senator Long, as chairman of Senate Finance, promptly threatened that the depletion amendment "will be taken off this bill." Taken off it was in early March, when Republican senator Robert Dole of Kansas marked out a fall-back position for the oil interests by suggesting a study of "some alternatives for depletion, perhaps a tax credit for intangible drilling expenses." This special privilege of deducting capital expenditure as current expenses had already attracted much criticism (as noted earlier). But a tax credit would have been more valuable still, coming dollar for dollar off the presumptive tax liability.

In the end, however, the praetorian guard of oil-state Democrats and Republicans who had so successfully defended the oil companies for so long suffered a rare defeat. Congress proceeded to eliminate the 22 percent allowance as applied to the major oil companies as such.[29] But, as so often in House-Senate conferences, Senator Long rode in to the rescue, holding out (Tom Arrandale wrote) "for a permanent independent producer exemption." Since most natural gas production was also exempted, even the big companies were not entirely bereft. But no doubt the relatively small oil producers as such came off best. Scheduled to be very gradually cut to 15 percent by 1984, this exemption for independents saved them, in 1975 alone, some $500 million in taxes that they would have paid if the House of Representatives had got its way on this issue. In conference the reformers had agreed to that exemption in order to grasp the greater prize—the undermining of what journalist Eileen Shanahan had earlier called "possibly the most controversial section of the entire tax code, the 22 percent depletion allowance for producers of oil and natural gas."[30]

Whatever had gone wrong, from the point of view of the major oil companies? In order to answer that even in outline one needs to ask: what had gone *right* for them all the way from 1926 to 1975, with only a little upset in 1969? In the early eighties, the most comprehensive treatment of this particular topic was still the work of Bruce Ian Oppenheimer, who analyzed in considerable depth and from many vantage points the modest reform of 1969. His ultimate purpose was to portray policy as an independent variable (to that extent following Lowi, whose policy categories, however, he declined to adopt). But, in building up to that climax, he credited three variables (or "variable groups") with considerable explanatory force: (a) constituency ties, (b) rules, procedures, and processes, and (c) nature of the opposition. In appropriating the Oppenheimer scheme, one will modify it a little to emphasize points that its author himself advances but cannot easily accommodate within the tripartite structure, e.g., the "packing" of the crucial tax committees with members sympathetic, or at least not hostile, to percentage depletion, a variable placed under (a) even though said to vary independently of it. What follows can be no more than the bare bones, so the work itself should be consulted.[31]

CONSTITUENCY TIES

The proposition is "that much of the industry's success comes from simple constituency relationships." These are broadly conceived to include not only the form one thinks of first—constituency/Congress—but also ties with the executive, notably with the Treasury among departments as well as with the president from time to time. For the period he covered (1950–69), Professor Oppenheimer cited two secretaries of the Treasury drawn from the oil world: George Humphrey and his successor, Robert B. Anderson, (not to be confused with Robert O. Anderson, of Arco). Mr. Robert B. had been director of both the API and the IPAA, from which one would deduce that percentage depletion would be safe so long as he was at the Treasury. In fact, as president of the Texas Mid-Continent Oil and Gas Association, he had already testified in support of it. While serving at the Treasury he retained an exceptionally close relationship to the industry, being scheduled (as Bernard Nossiter disclosed in the *Washington Post*) to receive some very large sums of money under arrangements made just before he took office.

This "Treasury connection" can be extended backward and forward from the first modification of the depletion allowance in 1969. In 1971 John Connally, the Democrat reborn a Republican, took over as secretary. Close to the oil interests of his native Texas, he was quick to assert that the depletion allowance was no loophole (although the Treasury itself had determined that, in 1948 and 1949 for example, oil and gas producers were annually deducting as depletion more than nineteen times the actual cost). Looking the other way to the very beginnings of this very special tax deduction, one perceives Andrew Mellon as secretary of the Treasury all the way from 1921 to 1932. That straddled the period of transition from cost depletion to percentage depletion and the extension of this (also in 1926) to income from all oil and gas production, not merely what had been discovered by the claimant. This meant it could be applied to income from properties that had been purchased, thus losing its purported rationale as an incentive to exploration.[32] Now, it appears (Ronnie Dugger reported) that Secretary Mellon took no public position on the depletion policy, but as a member of the banking family that dominated Gulf Oil, he probably did not regard it with disfavor. In fact, the 1926 Revenue Act, which included the two fundamental "reforms" mentioned above, "was widely regarded as his triumph."[33] When President Coolidge signed it into law, Mellon was standing beside him.[34]

Taking constituency in its commoner, congressional sense, one finds that there were (at the relevant time) 15 states with significant oil production, hence 30 senators, buttressed by 117 representatives from the districts. Analyzing the serious attacks on percentage depletion that began after World War II, when President Truman declared there was no tax loophole so inequitable, Professor Oppenheimer discovered that in only three out of ten reform votes on the floor did oil-state senators fail to furnish less than 90 percent support for keeping the 27.5 percent allowance. The lowest support recorded was 77 percent. Virtually all the fluctuations occurred among senators based outside the oil-producing states.[35]

In the House, too, over forty years or more, support for percentage depletion remained firm and even unquestioned. After President Truman's disparaging remarks in 1950, and his modest proposal for reform (reduce the allowance to 15 percent) thirty-three members descended on the Ways and Means Committee to reaffirm their faith in the sanctity of 27.5 percent (that compromise, you will recall, between figures originally plucked out of the sky). Twenty-eight members went on the same errand the following year after the president again pressed his case.[36]

That was the stage at which the defenders of the faith went in for some reinsurance, making abundantly clear one reason why the faith had been so little questioned. From the discussion of congressional norms in chapter 5, you will easily identify the instrument—logrolling. Already, in the then recent past (1942), Senator Elmer Thomas of Utah had forced through an extension of the allowance to rock asphalt and ball-and-sagger clay. Other minerals were favored the following year. Now, in 1951, the National Sand and Gravel Association demanded fair play: didn't sand and gravel also get used up in the course of production? Who could deny it? Discrimination, cried a spokesman. Congress threw Sand and Gravel 5 percent. But having carried off the bone, the association came to realize that its rival in some respects, limestone, was getting 15 percent. Surely, the 10 percent differential was unfair? But, then, why had limestone been so favored? Because *its* rival for road-building, rock asphalt, had been accorded 15 percent, thanks to the persuasive powers of that senator from Utah. So, following a crazy logic, it went on until even clams and oysters were included, or rather their shells. The point of no return was reached when Congress had to say that "soil, sod, dirt, turf, water or mosses, minerals from sea water, the air or similar inexhaustible sources" did *not* qualify for the depletion allowance.[37] But about a hundred minerals had been "logged" through. The total cost was enormous: from $880 million in 1946 to some $3.2 billion in 1956, to nearly $5.5 billion in 1967. What that meant in terms of *net* loss to the Treasury was not easily determined. Prodded by Senator Paul Douglas, the Treasury put the annual loss in the early sixties at about $1.5 billion.[38] He thought that would increase, but toward the end of the decade it was reported by Erwin Knoll to be about $1.3 billion, annually. Even that, of course, was quite a lot of money, which we, the ordinary taxpayers, had to make up, all other things remaining equal. Mr. Knoll made the point very tellingly: President Nixon vetoed an appropriations bill (fiscal 1970) for HEW and the Department of Labor, because some part of it was deemed inflationary. How much of it? About $1.3 billion.[39] The implication is that those cutbacks need not even have been proposed if oil, sand and gravel, limestone, rock asphalt, oyster and clam shells, and the like, had not been accorded such special privilege.

So the scathing term used by journalists Drew Pearson and Jack Anderson in this very context—*loophole legislators*—was certainly not unjustified. Neither was Senator Paul Douglas's statement: "The depletion allowance for oil and gas has spread like a great disease."[40] But we must keep reminding ourselves that when congresspersons extended percentage depletion allowance to limestone, rock asphalt, flowerpot clay, and (the grand climacteric) clam and oyster shells, etc., etc., they were not merely legislating loopholes as such but executing tactical maneuvers characteristic of the distributive-policy arena. Moreover, although the result might well be likened to a disease (or blight), the spread was carefully calculated: it was not just "catching."

Thus bargains in the classic mode reinforced the constituency connection in supporting the centerpiece of the whole structure: the percentage depletion for oil and gas. It formed the centerpiece in several respects (a) no other beneficiary received as much as 27.5 percent; the other minerals were given 5 percent, 7.5 percent, 10 percent, 14 percent, 15 percent, 22 percent, etc. These numbers, too, were plucked from the sky (e.g., 5 percent for clam and oyster shells, even more obviously arbitrary when suddenly increased to 15 percent in 1966). But they cost the taxpayer less; (b) out of every $5 claimed in percentage depletion, $4 related to the oil and gas industry, although toward the end of the 1960s, research initiated by government disclosed that for the $1.3 billion that the oil depletion allowance was costing the Treasury annually, the industry was spending only $150 million on additional new exploration;[41] and (c) the departures from tax equity were the most striking. It was not simply that the companies paid such a low rate compared with other industrial companies: in some years they paid no federal taxes at all. According to Jack Anderson, that applied to five oil companies in 1964.[42] Atlantic-Richfield (included in Mr. Anderson's list) was later reported by Erwin Knoll to have paid no federal taxes from 1964 to 1967. Texas Gulf was similarly blessed in 1973, and Occidental Petroleum in 1979.[43] An oil and gas operator who over twelve years had sold some $50 million worth of oil, with an income in some years of $5.5 million, was reported (in a Treasury study) to have paid no federal tax for the whole of that period[44] (truly, for him, a "gilded age"). Whoever said that Dallas, among other cities, is a monument to the 27.5 percent oil depletion allowance[45] was not, perhaps, entirely correct. The "intangibles" allowance also contributed, and was believed by some, such as oilman George E. Allen, to have been an even more valuable concession: "He said, chuckling: 'Almost no one outside the industry knows about the intangible allowance.'"[46]

But the whole history of these policies confirms that the author of the Dallas-as-a-monument remark had penetrated to the heart of the matter. Special privilege in taxation helped to make Dallas what it is, here using Dallas as a symbol for the industry and for the fabulous fortunes it engendered (with a little help from the Treasury, Internal Revenue Service, and Congress).

Logrolling in Congress, then, buttressed the constituency variable in defense of percentage depletion. To this, one would oneself wish to add the dispensation of money, including campaign contributions, which Professor Oppenheimer mentioned only to set aside in order to highlight "simple constituency relationships" arising from the distribution of the industry. To the general question, we shall return, but for the time being we follow the Oppenheimer line.

COMPOSITION OF KEY COMMITTEES

If the oil interests enjoyed constituency-related connections to some 25–30 percent of the House/Senate membership, that was an excellent foundation for influencing public policy, but of course the "right" people had to be on the key committees, which, for percentage depletion and other tax issues, meant Ways and Means and Senate Finance. The "right" people did get on. As an oil lobbyist remarked: "You had people on Finance that represented oil states." These, in fact, were *over*represented on that committee in the period 1950–69 (in terms of their membership in the Senate as a whole). On Ways and Means, they were somewhat underrepresented (on a similar basis), having but five (not a mirrorlike seven), i.e., 20 percent of the committee, conveniently divided between the two parties (e.g., three Democrats and two Republicans, in 1969).[47]

Of course, not even Senate Finance with its 40 percent oil-state representation over the period could be considered "safe for depletion." What helped to make it safe was, again, logrolling in the form that Lewis Froman called "simple," i.e., specific "swaps" and supports of the type: You continue to support depletion for oil and gas and I'll support it for oyster and clam shells, or cement and lime. But there is of course some limit to Nature's bounty and even congresspersons' imaginations, so the interests had to exert themselves still more in order to preserve their tax privilege.

In the Senate, the relationship of oil-and-gas policy to committee membership generally was probably well represented (in the era when depletion policy flourished) by the report about Senator Olin Johnson's deep desire to become a member of the Democratic Steering Committee. Despite being a southerner (South Carolina), he was kept off by Lyndon Johnson and Robert Kerr "because he might harm the cause of oil." It is true that, in several ways, he was atypical, even a bit of a liberal. But "aching in his bones" to get on the Steering Committee, he approached Johnson's protégé, Bobby Baker, who told him what he evidently already knew—that he was not considered reliable on oil policy. Out of this came an arrangement: tell Lyndon and Bob that he would "vote for their natural gas bill and anything else oil wants, short of hanging all the poor folks. Hell, if it'll do any good, I'll comb my hair with crude oil."[48] He got his place on the committee, and presumably was not called upon to do anything more undignified than "vote right."

What that committee did, formally, was to steer members into the standing and other committees. In other words, it was the committee on committees. In reality, Lyndon Johnson ruled the roost. He served the oil interests in two ways, negative and positive. First, he ensured that critics and "unreliables" (in terms of oil policy) were kept off the Finance Committee. As Senator Paul Douglas put it: "I sometimes suspected that the major qualification for most aspirants for membership on the Finance Committee was a secret pledge or agreement to defend the depletion allowance against all attacks. I suspected, also, that campaign funds reinforced these pledges."[49]

Was his suspicion reasonable? Certainly, in making the assignment, Johnson did not follow the rule of seniority where Douglas was concerned, passing him over in favor of George Smathers for example (elected two years after Douglas). The latter was again being sidetracked in 1955 when the columnist Doris Fleeson came to his rescue, charging that Johnson was acting at the behest of the Texas oil and gas interests. After some months Johnson gave way and put him on.

Senator Douglas's version of events is independently confirmed by other observers, such as columnists Rowland Evans and Robert Novak, but they also generalize the point: "The extraordinary treatment of Douglas also reflected Johnson's desire to keep the Finance Committee free of northern liberals opposing special tax advantages for the oil and gas industry."[50]

Of course, as they noted, Johnson was running no great risk because "the Finance Committee was already so stacked in favor of the oil and gas industry." Douglas himself would make the same point, but more politely.[51] Another senator, however, was just as blunt as the journalists: "Johnson stacked the committee. Probably Rayburn did the same thing in the House but not so easily. . . . That committee (Finance) has been loaded on oil for years."[52]

If Johnson stacked a committee, or anything else, it probably stayed stacked. But it seems that similar influence was brought to bear in Republican assignments to the Finance Committee. Someone well versed in Republican committee assignments recalled that he had never experienced interest-group activity in relation to Appropriations, but "they become extremely active when selections for Commerce or Finance are under consideration." He explained: "Where one vote might tip the scales for or against revising the oil depletion allowance . . . an assignment becomes a 'life or death' matter, and lobbyists actively seek assignments for 'friendly' senators."[53]

What of the House of Representatives? The other senator was right: Speaker Rayburn, another Texan who had learned the hard way what he had to do if he wished to continue his political career, "did the same thing." One of his closest colleagues told John Manley, an authority on the Ways and Means Committee in the period under discussion, "Rayburn had two things. One was trade. He was 100 percent for international trade. And the second was depletion allowance for oil and gas. These were the two."[54] Of course, those who had got on to the committee in the Rayburn era could not remember being asked what their views were on depletion policy ("of course," because it is obvious that politicians, in Boston and elsewhere as well as in Washington, have such bad memories that it is hard to understand how they can function at all). But the evidence is overwhelming: if you didn't support depletion allowance, or at least couldn't keep your mouth shut, you couldn't be assigned to the committee. So this committee, too, was stacked.

In short, both key committees were utterly unrepresentative of the nation, by design, not chance. On top of everything else, the oil interests were "built-in": the nation was not. That might well be regarded as a manifestation of "special-interest democracy."

RULES AND PROCEDURES

These are never neutral, but make a difference to policy. A principal example is that closed rule in the House, whose effect over the years, as it impinged on the Ways and Means Committee, was to help the oil interests retain percentage depletion. On bills for raising revenue, Ways and Means is privileged to report directly to the House floor, but traditionally it sought from the Rules Committee a closed rule, i.e., one prohibiting on the floor all amendments other than committee amendments. Part of the reason for the tradition (explained Lewis Froman) was to prevent "excessive logrolling on the floor of the House,"[55] with which judgment John Manley and Representative Spark M. Matsunaga, a member of the Rules Committee, agreed (although these two also stressed the technicality and complexity of tax measures).[56]

The significance for interest-group methods is obvious. A closed rule for Ways and Means enhanced its power and so its attractiveness for supplicants of all kinds. This adds a dimension to the discussion just concluded about stacking the membership of the committee. Hold the line there on depletion and you would almost certainly be safe on the floor. There would be a bonus, too: very few would understand what was going on, which is characteristic of distributive policy, and, arguably, of special-interest democracy.

OPPOSING FORCES

It must suffice to record this: several groups (AF of L, National Grange, American Bureau Federation) were from time to time mildly critical of percentage depletion, but systematic and sustained opposition was lacking. One reason may occur to you from chapter 3: the difficulty of organizing diffuse interests despite a common base. There were other reasons that cannot be elucidated here. In any case, the sad fact remained "that almost no one now speaks for the general public . . . on tax matters,"[57] i.e., there was little or no serious opposition on the particular tax matter under review, percentage depletion.

Put all these variables together (à la Oppenheimer) and you can explain a great deal of what had gone right for the oil interests over the years, which should contain much of the explanation of what went wrong toward the end of the sixties. As you would expect, basic constituency ties, reflecting oil and gas production, had not weakened. But the Ways and Means Committee could not be stacked and managed, or at least it was not, after the death of Speaker Rayburn in 1961. So, during the sixties, the oil companies' grip on the committee weakened. Whereas in 1960 not a single member had spoken up against percentage depletion, seven voted in 1969 for a more severe cut (to 16.5 percent) than the 20 percent that eventually obtained a majority. Six of the seven had joined the committee after Rayburn's death; one, a few months before. The closed rule still applied, but arguably then worked to the disadvantage of the interests, in the judgment of an oil lobbyist. Had it not applied, the 27.5 percent "might have been logrolled back into the bill," i.e., bargains might have been struck on the floor of the House.[58] The rule, in any case, had not changed.[59] Nor had the lack of systematic opposition to percentage depletion (and other tax privileges) been made good. On the other hand, pressure for tax reform had been growing since 1967, stimulated by President Johnson's request for a 10 percent income-tax surcharge, by Senator Robert Kennedy's disclosure that some millionaires escaped paying any income tax at all, and by other developments. How, indeed, as Senator Paul Douglas had asked in 1963, could sixty-six members of the Congress face the taxpayers—the workman or small farmer who, on an income of $5200, pays $456 in taxes, when these tremendous holes exist in the tax structure, such as "$3 billion of depletion allowances completely free from taxation"; and "$2 billion of intangible drilling and development costs written off virtually in the first year"? The former professor of economics (at Chicago) perhaps underrated the capacity of congresspersons to look taxpayers in the face and still do unkind things to their rear. But, one way or another, "a taxpayers' revolt" (as it was called) did crystallize, which even the Ways and Means Committee evidently found it imprudent to ignore.

The upshot, of course, was the Tax Reform Act of 1969, which, thanks to the oil companies' second line of defense, the Senate Finance Committee, did not prove intolerably painful. In fact, insofar as it impinged on them, the so-called reform was token, the policy indeed symbolic (in the language and judgment of Bruce Oppenheimer, taking from Murray Edelman the celebrated distinction between symbol and substance). Still, symbols may be hostages to the future, convertible, in the right circumstances, into substance. One direct consequence of the 1969 act was the founding of Taxation with Representation (1970), authoritatively described as "a companion nonprofit organization" to Tax Analysts and Advocates (TAA), which legally served "charitable and education purposes" but ones "grounded in the assumption that special interests have over time unjustifiably reduced their tax liabilities, resulting in a transfer of income from underrepresented taxpayers to members of the special-interest group."[60] Its offshoot is clearly a lobbying instrument. In 1971 Ralph Nader followed suit with his Tax Reform Research Group, to whose Robert Brandon, a well-placed observer—James Byrne, editor of *Tax Notes* (published by TAA)—would give credit as the man most responsible for undermining the depletion allowance in 1975.[61] Mr. Brandon organized the winning coalition that included the AFL-CIO and such public interest groups as Common Cause. That points to a profound development of one of the Oppenheimer variables: "If there's anything new in taxes in 1975, it's the existence of a sophisticated public interest lobby on tax questions."[62]

Summoning up the other Oppenheimer variables in a preliminary attempt to understand 1975 rather than 1969, one would not expect constituency ties to have weakened. These may even have been becoming a little more extensive with the prospect of Alaska's joining the oil states near the top of the league (the pipeline would open in 1977). Certainly the oil industry remained entrenched in the Senate Finance Committee. On the other hand, the composition of Congress as a whole "was changing drastically." Walter Oleszek calculated (in 1978) that "roughly two-thirds of the House and more than half the Senate changed hands from the 1964 elections on." Since "many [he thought] came to Congress determined to revitalize the institution," one may plausibly attribute intensity as well as extension (or numbers). Dr. Oleszek went on: "By the start of the 96th Congress in 1979, almost half the House will have begun their service in 1975 or since."[63]

Within the general trend, the character of the very first of that crop (i.e., elected in 1974) was of crucial importance for percentage depletion. It was not only the post-Watergate election but the one after the startling increase in oil prices by the OPEC cartel, from which the majors profited spectacularly only to incur unpopularity almost of the same order. So the election brought "dozens of new liberal Democrats to the House." And as a tax lobbyist for Gulf Oil remarked: "A lot of these new members ran against the oil companies." Once again, one may plausibly hypothesize intensity as well as extension (or an increase in numbers) from that lobbyists's next sentence: "You've got an emotional Congress, and some emotional issues, and we are the whipping boy for the 94th Congress."[64]

In the formulation preferred here, composition of the Ways and Means Committee was treated separately from constituency ties (because, as Professor Oppenheimer acknowledged, it could vary independently). What happened after the 1974 election, in time for the 94th Congress (1975–76), was that the House Democratic Caucus, continuing to grow in power, expanded Ways and Means from twenty-five to what Alan Ehrenhalt (*Congressional Quarterly*) called "a noisy and diffuse thirty-seven."[65] That "liberalized" the composition, which meant, as members and lobbyists agreed, a fundamental change in attitudes (or group norms). "Most" Democratic members of the committee now received oil-company representations with skepticism; indeed, were gently reproached by Frank Ikard, the API president,[66] with not really listening. Fortuitously, as noted earlier, the strong man of the committee, chairman Wilbur Mills, would soon leave Congress for more tranquil surroundings. He had done his best to preserve percentage depletion by defying the Democratic Caucus in 1974 when they mandated a floor vote on the reformers' amendment to stop it there and then.[67] He not only failed to ask for a rule from the Rules Committee (as a member of it would recall) but kept the whole bill off the floor.[68] In late February 1975, the Democratic Caucus voted 153–98 to get the depletion issue on to the House floor, where the repeal amendment was attached to another (tax-cutting) measure by a clearcut 248–163. The whole bill was then promptly approved (317–97) without further modification.[69]

All this is interrelated with the third variable (or variable group): rules and procedures, which, in flux for something like a decade and a half, reached a climax in 1974–75. Some of these developments were identified in chapter 5. All we can add here are the following: (a) "more willingness on the part of the Committee on Ways and Means to forgo requesting a closed rule on every measure" (as a member of the Rules Committee, Spark M. Matsunaga, and Professor Ping Chen would put it);[70] (b) increase in the size of Ways and Means to thirty-seven, with "liberalization," also transfer of its authority as committee on committees to the Democratic Steering and Policy Committee; (c) further successful assertion of the authority of the Democratic Caucus, which had been revived in 1969 after about half-a-century of disuse (had it been alive and effective, Speaker Rayburn might not have been able to stack the Ways and Means Committee with the defenders of percentage depletion, while keeping off its critics). Against the grain of the generally decentralizing tendencies of the reformist seventies (recall chapter 5), (c) tended to centralize or consolidate *some* of the dispersed power of the majority party in the House. These and the other tendencies came to a head in 1973–75, almost as if timed for the 94th Congress in general and the undermining of percentage depletion in particular.

The fourth variable—the emergence of systematic opposition—brings us back full circle to the start of this brief examination, where the crystallization of a new phenomenon—a "sophisticated public interest lobby on tax questions"— was remarked upon. Put these four variables together and you have some preliminary idea of where to look for a more thorough explanation of the conditions under which even long entrenched interests may be challenged and cut back if not entirely rooted out. Recall, too, the cargo-preference case as outlined in chapter 1, where a brief attempt was made to suggest the conditions under which the interests were held at bay. These, obviously, are no more than illustrations, from which no one perturbed about America's becoming a special-interest democracy could extract great comfort. Still, in the right circumstances, which up to a point may be reproducible, it does seem that even classic distributive policy, so piecemeal as almost not to be perceived as policy and in any case artfully screened from public view, can be challenged and substantially (not just symbolically) modified if not entirely destroyed. From that, even the more cautious among us may be encouraged—if only to undertake further research in the hope of generalizing more confidently about the conditions of successful reform in the distributive arena.

CHAPTER TEN
REGULATORY AND SELF-REGULATORY POLICIES:
Setting Environmental Standards and Deregulating Natural Gas Prices

The concept of self-regulatory policy (you will recall from the introduction to this part, set out at the opening of chapter 9) was Robert Salisbury's gift to Theodore Lowi. It was widely accepted (by those who found the original scheme to their taste) as a necessary addition. One form of it universally acknowledged turns upon delegation of authority to the professions, notably physicians and lawyers. But here one prefers an illustration from the field of energy policy. No doubt, as Eric Uslaner remarked in 1982, the deregulation of natural gas prices fits the bill,[1] and it will be drawn upon here. But one has to enter a caveat. The story of the deregulation of natural gas prices is but one phase—the *dénouement*—of their regulation, which was embarked upon as far back as 1938. If political scientists seriously studied regulatory and self-regulatory policy, they might find that, over a certain range, the umbilical cord could not be cut without damage to our understanding of events and analysis of their meaning. In other words, over a certain policy range, regulation and self-regulation may go hand in hand and have to be studied together. Here, in any case, it is convenient for teaching purposes, to illustrate both types side by side (i.e., in the same chapter) before turning to the regulation of personal behavior deemed, by traditional community standards, to have a *moral* component. That, surely, is different from the regulation of market prices, and the like.

However, in the original Lowian framework (which one is still making use of as a teaching device even if it eventually proves expendable, like a scaffolding that has served its purpose), regulatory policy was broadly conceived, at least by implication. For in Professor Lowi's celebrated article, despite the promise of a cross-head, "Areas of Policy Defined,"[2] there is no formal definition of "regulatory policy," possibly because this was deemed to be intuitively obvious. But other scholars, acknowledging Lowian inspiration, have filled the gap. For example:

> Regulatory policies are those that limit peoples' freedom to engage in certain kinds of conduct. (Robert S. Friedman)
> Regulatory policies are governmental actions that extend governmental control over particular behavior of private individuals or businesses. (Randall Ripley and Grace Franklin)[3]

As illustration, one selects from the newer, social form of regulation as well as from the older, economic species. The former (highway beautification) will, as a bonus, convey a good deal about the conflict between amenity values and corporate values as well as something about the problem of implementing federal policy. The second case starts out as traditional regulatory but turns into a kind of self-regulatory.

HIGHWAY BEAUTIFICATION

This is shorthand for clearing billboards and junkyards from the sides of highways or from within sight of drivers and passengers, thus adding to the total beauty of the scene, derived from a subtle blending of engineering skill and the art of landscaping in what undoubtedly is the greatest national highway system in the world.

Concern for roadside beautification already had a long if discontinuous history, going back to the early years of the environmental movement before World War I. But the particular history is linked to the interstate highway program launched in 1956. Two years later the federal government tried to tempt the states to ensure that there would be no billboards nearer than 660 feet of the right-of-way. The inducement was a bonus of 0.5 percent. In other words, the federal government would pay altogether 90.5 percent of the construction costs of the new interstate system.

The temptation was resisted, not necessarily on grounds of Christian conviction. By 1965 some forty-one thousand miles of "interstates" had been built—but bonuses had been claimed for no more than two hundred miles. Only half the states had "signed on," making themselves eligible. Only ten had received the bonus. Some states had not legislated; some had legislated but failed to secure compliance.

In 1958, too, an act had enabled states to buy up strips of land alongside the highways the better to preserve the scenery and general amenities. For this purpose they were authorized to take 3 percent from the Highway Trust Fund. Until 1965 the states never touched (or even bit) the hand that would have fed them. In that year three states did collect small amounts covering all of fifty miles. Car junkyards remained prominent: about fourteen thousand of them graced the borders of more than a quarter of a million miles of federal-aid primary roads.[4]

The official report on junkyards appeared in May 1965. That was when the White House Conference on Beauty was held, attended by some eight hundred dignitaries and activists. It followed what is believed to have been, in February, the first-ever presidential message declaring beauty to be a national objective: in cities, parks, and rivers as well as on the borders of highways, or, in short, the environment in general. Then, after the White House Conference, the fundamental idea crystallized:

> The economy, and the roads that serve it, are not ends in themselves. They are meant to serve the real needs of the people of this country. And those needs include the opportunity to touch nature and see beauty, as well as rising income and swifter travel.
>
> Therefore, we must make sure that the massive resources we now devote to roads also serve to improve and broaden the quality of American life.

That presidential letter accompanied a bill designed to translate those noble sentiments into concrete rules covering, in relation to the interstates, (i) what outdoor advertising would be permissible, and (ii) the locating, or siting, of billboards and junkyards. One of the things allowed under (i) would be the signs that we four-wheeled nomads have come to recognize as welcome invitations to telephone, fill up, stop the night, and take food and other nourishment. As for (ii), billboards and junkyards were to be pushed back about a thousand feet from the highways, or at least screened.

And who was to see to it that all this (and more) would actually happen? The states, resorting to their police power, that omnibus concept enabling provision to be made and enforced for the safety, health, and general welfare of the people. If that did not work, then states were authorized to buy out the owners of the billboards and junkyards, compensating them with federal money drawn from the Highway Trust Fund. But suppose the states failed to act? They would lose the highway funds supplied by the federal government.

This novel regulatory proposal promptly produced the only too predictable coalitions. The possibility—danger—of drawing on the Highway Trust Fund aroused the ire not only of the American Road Builders' Association and the Associated General Contractors but also of the National Association of Counties and the American Association of State Highway officials. Each feared that amenity, or scenic beauty, would be purchased at the expense of road construction: first things ought to be put first. The Institute of Scrap Iron and Steel, the National Auto and Truck Wreckers Association, and the National

Association of Secondary Material Industries joined hands in opposing the junkyards proposals. The American Motor Hotel Association and the Roadside Business Association came out against the billboard-control proposals. Surprisingly, these as a whole did find favor with the Outdoor Advertising Association of America, Inc., the only serious gap among the predictable groups of opponents. The reason for this "defection" appears to have been that the business of its members was concentrated in the industrial and commercial zones. If (a) it could take a hand in determining the contours of the zones, not leaving it wholly to the Commerce Department, and (b) such jointly-shaped zones could be exempted from the billboards provision, the association's interests would be well served. Before the battle was over, both (a) and (b) were conceded.

That was something specifically opposed by the loose coalition supporting the administration measure: the National Wildlife Federation, Izaak Walton League, and Garden Club of America. But they lost. Should one have predicted anything else? Must David always be expected to defeat Goliath? In this instance the odds seemed to favor David because the bill had the strong backing of Lady Bird Johnson and, accordingly, of her even more formidable husband in the White House. Justly celebrated as a great twister of arms, President Johnson was then at the height of his powers. That summer found the bill safely contained within a House committee (Public Works); and in September the president got it out of there and on to the House floor. After the Senate had passed it, the House followed suit in early October, but to the accompaniment of much groaning, wailing and gnashing of teeth. The ranking Republican on the committee, for example, professed to have "never before seen such pressures and arm twisting from the executive branch."[5] A certain Representative Gerald Ford also complained of it.

Whether that should count as grist to the Lowian mill is not entirely clear. Did the type of policy—regulatory—really *determine* the process? Evidently, the issue *was* lifted out of the subcommittee and committee realm into the congressional. But would that have happened without not just the president but an unusual combination of president-and-wife? It seems doubtful, although of course no one can be sure. In any event, the upshot of the admittedly higher-level process, entailing indeed a widening of the scope of the conflict, was far from what the administration wanted. The president got *a* bill, not his or hers. Operating mainly through the Roads Subcommittee of the Senate's Committee on Public Works, opponents secured many amendments, some of them fundamental:

1. billboards control: only 660 feet off, not 1000
2. junkyards provision: industrial and commercial zones exempted
3. use of police power, which in some 46 percent of the states was already being used to enforce zoning rules—implying that the owners would bear the cost of removal gave way to full compensation, mostly by the federal government, e.g., 75 percent for interstates, 50 percent on other roads.

4. funding: from the U.S. Treasury *not* the Highway Trust Fund
5. sanctions: disobedient states would lose not 100 percent of their federal highway funds, but only 10 percent.

Even without reckoning other changes, we can see that, despite all the trumpeting with which it was greeted, the bill had been well and truly emasculated. The feeble sanctions made it unlikely that the ever-lethargic states would act. If they did, full compensation would be paid. But that would be outrageous. As the *New York Times* remarked, the private rights in billboards (supposedly worth $180 million) were essentially a social (or public) creation: no interstates, etc., at a (planned) cost to the taxpayers of some $26 *billion*, no private rights to be compensated.[6] How absurd—how stupid—to allow the billboard advertisers to double-dip, skim the cream, getting compensation for what the American people had created by their own (financial) sweat! Moreover, (4) above implied that road construction was to be regarded as sacrosanct: beauty or amenity must not be allowed to detract from it. That reminds one of what Lewis Mumford wrote in 1958, looking back at the recently inaugurated highway-building program and the responsibility for it of the American people:

> The most charitable thing to assume about this action (the highway program) is that they hadn't the faintest notion of what they were doing. Within the next fifteen years they will doubtless find out; but by that time it will be too late to correct all the damage to our cities and our countryside, not least to the efficient organization of industry and transportation, that this ill-conceived and preposterously unbalanced program will have wrought.[7]

So it turned out: among other things, the railroads and most local transit systems were ruined, some deliberately as a result of the connivance of the highway lobby, the automobile manufacturers, and elements of the oil industry. But in the 1950s Lewis Mumford's was a voice crying in the wilderness. The immediate point for this discussion, however, is that the defense of the Highway Trust Fund in 1965 was resoundingly successful even when president-and-first-lady led the attack.

Did both the Johnsons understand what had happened to their bill? The resulting act, in any case, was little more than *symbolic*.[8] That is the term to which Murray Edelman, in the midsixties, gave currency for acts (or any other policy outputs) that do no more than *appear to* meet the problem or satisfy the claimants. The implied contrast, of course, is with substantive acts and other policies, genuinely designed to get to grips with the problem and genuinely satisfy.

The extent of the symbolism may be gauged not only by the amendments specified above but also by the provision that the transportation secretary, working with the state highway departments (those opponents of the measure), were required, in the first instance, *not* to implement the act but to *study* the implications of implementation and report to Congress by January 1967 (the bill had been passed in October 1965). Among the questions to be researched were: what would be the economic impact? What would implementation cost? To ensure that the department did not rush wildly into anything, Congress instructed the secretary to hold public hearings before promulgating regulations, and then to present these, elucidating the criteria, for congressional review (also by January 1967). As if that were not enough of a brake, Congress took care to provide no funds for implementation.

By agreement with eight states, some minor progress was achieved in the latter part of 1967. But fundamentally the money was not forthcoming. The Senate obliged but the House did not, in what some political scientists would regard as a nondecision. Its Public Works Committee approved an appropriate measure but only on a strict party vote (18–14). Smelling defeat on the House floor, the Democratic leadership declined to put the bill to the test.

Thus it came about that, after June 30, 1967, no funds at all were available to carry out the highways beautification authorized in 1965. As a spokesman for the Bureau of Public Roads (within the department) put it, presumably with a straight face: all the provisions of the 1965 act remained in force except the authorization of the funds.[9]

Whether by design or chance, denial of funds turned out to be the principal method by which the billboard and associated interests, working through congresspersons, stifled the 1965 act: not death by a thousand cuts so much as death by slow starvation. Thus in 1968, one of those (superficially) unnatural alliances of Republicans and conservative (mostly southern) Democrats succeeded in removing all such beautification funds from the Federal Aid Highway Act of that year (covering fiscal 1970). The Senate rectified that, or tried to, but settled in the end for a mere $25 million (a tenth of what they had put back in, admittedly for three years, not one).

So one could go on. But how the interests can block implementation of an act is not the subject of this chapter. The main purpose is to illustrate the establishment of a regulatory policy (in this instance, social) and the general nature of the political activity (or process) which it engendered.

Our provisional conclusion is that, as predicted by the Lowian paradigm or schema, variation in the type of policy did induce variation in the political process. In addition, we have learned something about the formulation of regulatory policy of a certain kind, the social (in this instance, environmental), and the corresponding role of interest groups.

DEREGULATION OF NATURAL-GAS PRICES

Here we set out to illustrate regulatory policy in the economic sphere, with special reference to its serious modification or even abandonment, attempted if not attained. In sketching this minicase, we look "both ways," backward from

1956 to the beginning of this policy (one can hardly understand *dis*-establishment without establishment), and then forward to the present day.

The regulation of natural-gas prices was of course one aspect of the regulation of the industry in some larger sense. It had started, in a way, with the Public Utility Holding Company Act of 1935, commonly known as the Wheeler-Rayburn Act. This touched natural gas by circumscribing resort to the holding-company device practiced in particular by the electric-power industry (thirteen such companies controlled 75 percent of the whole privately owned electric utilities).[10] But natural gas? It came into the picture because natural-gas companies had often been drawn into the imperial domain of the holding companies.

With the mode of regulation imposed in 1935 we need not concern ourselves, although we may note in passing that the establishment of that extremely important regulatory policy did indeed precipitate passionate debate and broad coalitions of the expected (Lowian) kind. The point for us is rather that natural gas was very gradually becoming more significant. Originally a troublesome joint-product of oil drilling, having to be burned off or released into the air, it grew in importance after the development, in the late 1920s, of the electrically welded, seamless pipe. What that did, as Ralph Huitt well said, was to "make a natural resource of a nuisance."[11]

The politicoeconomic significance of natural-gas transmission by pipeline is clear. It bore the seeds of a monopolistic tendency because (a) there was no practicable alternative and (b) the cost of installation was so great, apart from the analytically separable tendency of the companies toward vertical integration. Moreover, components of the energy industry, including oil, naturally tended toward "combination" to share burdens and neutralize risks. The holding company was a popular contemporary form of it.

Such developments and potentialities created a presumption in favor of some sort of federal regulation. The quasi-monopolistic advantages of the pipeline companies, some of which were oil and gas producers, tended to put the cities and states at their mercy. The former in particular fought back through the U.S. Conference of Mayors and the Detroit-launched Cities Alliance. More broadly, geology and geography (or climate) had conspired to make the Southwest the center of production but the North and Northeast the principal markets. Transmission would extend for a thousand or even two thousand miles (e.g., Houston-Boston), and of course entail the crossing of many state lines.

In 1938 Congress attempted to deal with the issue by way of the Natural Gas Act, which conferred on the Federal Power Commission (FPC)[12] authority to regulate interstate transportation, sale and pricing of natural gas. But it did so in words that lacked the clarity of crystal. One might almost say that the history of public policy in this area for the next forty years turned upon conflicting interpretations of the 1938 act, for that reason even more of a landmark than it otherwise would have been.

The key text turned out to be Section 1(b), which defined the FPC's jurisdiction as applying

> to the transportation of natural gas in interstate commerce, to the sale in inter-state commerce of natural gas for resale for ultimate public consumption for domestic, commercial, industrial, or any other use, and to natural-gas companies engaged in such transportation or sale, but shall not apply to any other transpor-tation or sale of natural gas or to the local distribution of natural gas or to the facilities used for such distribution or to the production or gathering of natural gas.

Gathering means collecting from wells in several areas, which might be in different states, and passing into a common pipeline before sale.

But where did production and gathering end and sale begin? A natural gas company might produce its own, buy in from others, mix the two, then convey the mixture through its own lines to a point within the state where a sale was made to pipeline companies that transported and sold the gas out of state. Such a company was Louisiana's Interstate Natural Gas Company.[13] It claimed that what was alleged to be a sale was really "in" the gathering. But the Supreme Court in 1947 disagreed, adding that the production or gather-ing clause was to be "strictly construed," as with control of *physical* produc-tion for conservation, etc. Sales of natural gas entering into *inter*state com-merce were subject to FPC jurisdiction, and, accordingly, to regulation.[14]

But where exactly did that leave the so-called independents, those pro-ducers *un*connected with any pipeline company? Were they exempt? Appar-ently not, judging by *Interstate Natural Gas Co. v. FPC* (1947). Yet to the outside observer at least, the distinction between their production/gathering and sale ought to be less difficult to draw. They at least would be able to make "arm's length" sales to the pipeline companies. However, the FPC had vacil-lated, first disclaiming responsibility and then reversing itself, partly in re-sponse to changes in the composition of the commissioners.

As we would expect from other cases, the locus of activity then changed from Supreme Court to Congress and beyond. As Ralph Huitt would put it, the interstate case "spurred the industry to apply the kind of unremitting pressure to the agencies of government which can be maintained by a single-minded interest group with concentrated leadership and great resources."[15] The moves, in fact, were already under way, taking essentially two forms:

I   a bill (from Oklahoma congresspersons) to exempt the sales of *all* producers from FPC regulation, i.e., integrateds as well as independents,

II   a bill to exempt only independents.

The early proposals were variations on those two themes, but the real issue became (II). This proposal is sometimes represented in the literature as "more modest" or "more moderate." The truth is, however, that by 1947 the independents were supplying the pipeline companies with almost 62 percent of their gas. The dominance of the independents at a later stage may be judged from *Fortune's* calculation in 1959 that the top two hundred independents produced over 90 percent of the supply of natural gas.[16] So the battles might include (I), but the outcome of the war really turned on (II).

Whether in recognition of that, or in response to pressure on individual commissioners, or some combination of both, the FPC initially set its face against (I) while supporting (II). It not only backed the (II) bill but also issued the same year a celebrated (some would say, notorious) order of self-denial, saying that the 1938 act did *not* give it authority over the sales of the independents to the pipeline companies (Order no. 139, 1947).

That Commission "line," already foreshadowed, had already been disputed by Representative Ross Rizley (Rep.-Oklahoma), whose name was on the principal (I) bill: "no such sectionalizing of the Commission's jurisdiction and of the act's application can be fairly read into or out of section 1 (b) as it now stands."[17] He persuaded the committee[18] and then the whole House, only to be blocked by the Senate in 1947 and 1948. This meant that his bill expired as that (80th) Congress expired.

However, when the legislative drive was resumed in the 81st Congress (which lacked the services of Representative Rizley), the proponents (from Oklahoma and Arkansas, of whom the best known was Senator Robert Kerr, himself an oil-and-gas millionaire) concentrated upon exempting "only" the independents. One writes "only" because these were increasingly the sources of interstate gas. One calculation in May 1949 put the proportion as over 75 percent.[19] In any case, exempt the independents and you have essentially won the game.

All went well in the House, where the principal bill passed by a majority of over fifty. But in the Senate the committee (also called the Interstate and Foreign Commerce Committee) held back partly under the influence of Leland Olds, a commissioner (and former chairman) of the FPC. Recall here that the FPC was on record as being in favor of exempting the independents—that 1947 order, from which only one commissioner had dissented, and he was Claude E. Draper—not Leland Olds. But by now the latter had changed his mind, presumably in recognition of the boom in natural gas and the increasingly important role of the independents.

Later the committee did report out the Kerr bill, but the Senate made no progress because it proceeded to turn on Leland Olds himself. For Olds was up for reappointment, or rather, he had served ten years and wanted another five-year term. But there was a new power in the land—the oil-and-gas industry—and they wanted to get rid of Olds. As columnists Evans and Novak would write: "The industry refused to tolerate an FPC dedicated to tough regulation of natural gas prices. The reappointment of Leland Olds for another term of the FPC would have ensured an anti-industry majority on the commission. Olds was a marked man"[20] (*anti-industry* could also be rendered *proconsumer*). And so "the Senate pack" was let loose on Olds. Well to the front were Edwin C. Johnson (Dem.-Colorado), chairman of the Commerce Committee, and Lyndon B. Johnson. The latter, although a freshman, got himself the chairmanship of the *ad hoc* subcommittee on the nomination of Olds, whom he accused of almost everything, virtually including sympathy with communism.

That was McCarthyism before McCarthy. In fact, Lyndon Johnson's diatribe revealed more about himself than about Olds—that he was indeed moving to the Right and (assuming the location were different) toward Big Oil and Gas. No doubt his attack went down well in Texas. It certainly succeeded in the Senate. Despite an attempt at rescue by Senator Paul Douglas, the "senatorial lynching" (the Evans/Novak term) went ahead as planned. By 15–53, New Dealer Leland Olds was out. Republicans voted against him almost to a man. But so did twenty-one Democrats, defying a Democratic president: Rep., 2–32; Dem., 13–21. These Democrats were from the South and Southwest (something like the old Confederacy).

With Olds left "twisting in the wind," the two Johnsons, Kerr himself of course, and others such as Russell Long (Dem.-Louisiana) pressed on with the bill, which passed the Senate without difficulty in March 1950. As usual, the division was very much Southwest *v*. North and Northeast (although New England did not present a united front). In the House two days later it was a close call, the Senate version passing by only two votes. Speaker Sam Rayburn, another Texan, took to the floor to urge its passage. He had already learned to accommodate himself to the new oil-and-gas interests of Texas.

That, it must have seemed, was that. But providence moves in mysterious ways. In place of Olds, Monrad C. Wallgren, a former Democratic governor, won easy confirmation, although at least one senator considered him a man of the Left. If that were even partly true, wouldn't he be likely to take the same side as Olds most recently had? That, in any case, was the stance he adopted *vis-à-vis* the Kerr bill. Olds's departure had left the commission evenly divided. Wallgren's arrival tipped the balance in favor of the opponents of the basic principle of the bill. They recommended its veto, and President Truman duly obliged, declaring authority to regulate to be in the public interest. His reason was the peculiar nature of the industry. By this he meant "the inherent characteristics of the process of moving gas from the field to the consumer. Buyers of natural gas cannot easily move from one producer to another in search of lower prices." Competition was unlikely to be effective in keeping prices at reasonable levels. Notice the president's words, "authority to. . ." Despite price increases, he quietly remarked, the FPC had not *in fact* regulated arm's length sales by independents to pipeline companies. But it ought, the president added, to retain the authority.[21]

Was that a hint? As if to prepare the way for the exercise of such authority, the FPC proceeded to rescind its 1947 order. Now it was more or less in line with the Supreme Court (*Interstate Natural Gas*), and not out of line with Congress, if not exactly in, so far as actual legislation went. But 1951 saw yet another switch—in relation to Phillips Petroleum. Technically an independent (because unconnected with a pipeline company), Phillips was already a giant in oil and gas, busying itself at virtually every operating stage and no doubt transporting gas into interstate commerce. Did the FPC have jurisdiction? No, answered three of the five commissioners in 1951, including the sole dissenter from the 1947 order (disclaiming jurisdiction), Claude Draper. (In other words, in 1947, when the majority had said no to jurisdiction, he had said yes.) Yes, said a court of appeals. And yes, said the U.S. Supreme Court in 1954, 5–3, Mr. Justice Jackson taking no part: *Phillips Petroleum Co. v. State of Wisconsin*, 347 U.S. 672 (1954).

Here again the contours of the rival coalitions can be discerned. It was a northern state, Wisconsin, that took the stand on behalf of the ultimate consumers. It had the support of Wayne County, Michigan, and several cities, including Detroit (instrumental in bringing about the 1938 act), Milwaukee and Kansas City, Missouri. Ranged against them were not only the company but also the FPC, the Texas Railroad Commission, the Corporation Counsel of Oklahoma, and the State and Oil Conservation Commission of New Mexico.

What next? The oil and gas interests could have let the matter rest: they were already a long way from the poor house. But potentially there were millions of dollars at stake in annual income, billions counting the reserves (*potentially* implies: if the FPC ever got around to taking rate (or price) regulation seriously). So, predictably, the struggle continued. Equally predictably, the strategy was two-pronged: work on Congress and on the FPC.

CONGRESS

The congressional drive was the most ambitious the industry had so far mounted. Preparations started at a breakfast meeting in November 1953, i.e., after the court-of-appeals decision but before the Supreme Court's. The occasion was the Chicago convention of the American Petroleum Institute (API). It led to the launching in October 1954 of the General Gas Committee (GGC), Washington-based from the beginning of the following year. Its members that spring were individual producers, representatives of pipeline companies and of the trade associations, oil company executives and employees, and, inevitably, attorneys. That base was soon broadened to include not only drilling companies but banks and steel companies. Funding was provided by corporate members.[22]

With its six or seven hundred members, the GGC obviously had to divide up the work, which was allocated to five committees. The legislative sported five registered lobbyists representing two oil companies and three of the trade associations. This looked all the more formidable because the representation of natural-gas consumers was so weak. The problem of course is, as

Edith Carper would write, that "the 'consumer' is a stock character with diffuse interests."[23] Defense against price-gouging (feared in the absence of regulation) fell upon two existing, and two *ad hoc* bodies. These comprised the United Auto Workers and the National Institute of Municipal Law Officers. The first of the *ad hoc* bodies was the Mayors' Committee based on cities in the East. The second, although not unprecedented, was comparatively new in this line-up: a group of local utility companies selling to the ultimate consumers. It took organizational form as the Council of Local Gas Companies, based, like the Mayors' Committee, on eastern cities. Formed at a breakfast meeting in October 1955, during the course of the Los Angeles convention of the American Public Gas Association (which had the utilities at its core), the council soon reached Washington, where it registered as a lobby. Funding came from the companies. The Municipal Law Officers had no money of their own. Presumably the Auto Workers drew on union funds.

What the contest came to be about was the Harris bill, named for Representative Oren Harris (Dem.-Arkansas), who may have been approached, not by the GGC as such, but by oil company executives back home. His measure addressed not exactly the jurisdictional issue as such but rather the mode or form of regulation. Essentially, this was not to be the utility-type (a standardized mark-up on costs) but "reasonable market price." In June the (revised) Harris bill produced a tie in the House Commerce Committee, but it got out the following day by just one vote (16–15). In July one vote also cleared the bill from the House Rules Committee, with thanks due to Speaker Sam Rayburn, who also helped on the floor of the House, where the margin of victory was six votes, 209–203. The 209 contained 86 Democrats; the 203, 136. In the Rules Committee it had been 6–5 for a rule, one member abstaining.

The chairman of the GGC (otherwise president of an independent oil and gas company) could smell success. He wrote:

> I think the industry owes a debt of gratitude to the Speaker. Without his solid support, the Harris bill could have been killed on the rules vote, and certainly I feel sure that he was good for more than the six-vote majority. Quite frankly, I am terrifically pleased that the Harris bill has passed the House. With Lyndon's improvement in health and with only ninety-six Senators to hold the pulse and discuss the logic of the Fulbright bill, I feel our task in the Senate is not so tough. This work in the Senate can be done bodily, without a lot of fanfare and notoriety and with Lyndon's leadership, we should be able to send the gas legislation to the White House in the first month of the next session.[24]

("Lyndon" of course was the Senate majority leader, Lyndon Johnson. Senator Fulbright's bill was identical with the one presented by his Arkansas colleague, Representative Oren Harris.)

Naturally, the interests did not go into hibernation until the following session. All year long what the *Wall Street Journal* called a "king-sized publicity campaign" had been running in order to favor the industry and so the legislation toward which the GGC was driving. This work was the responsibility of the Natural Gas and Oil Resources Committee, launched in October 1954 on a sea of money—close to $2 million, about four-fifths of it from twenty-six gas and oil corporations. On the publicity $1.5 million was to be spent according to a plan conceived by the New York p.r. firm, Hill and Knowlton. Nearly all the money allocated was spent: up to March 1956, about $1.4 million, of which some $798,000 (56 percent) went on advertising in, for example, the three national news magazines, in *Business Week*, and the like. Although the committee did not register as a lobby,[25] some of the ads actually came out for the Harris bill, including this masterpiece of Orwellian doubletalk:[26] "A handful of utilities, led by big Eastern interests" was advocating utility-type controls for natural gas producers. In a box there was this punch-line: "The Harris bill protects consumers." *A handful of* suggests, if not monopolists, then oligopolists—*Big* Business interests in the *East* (the focus of the advertising campaign) threatening the consumer, whom Congress was trying to protect.

This, and very much more, was going on in the background. The specific effort to win over senators was taking place in the states. Thus, a GGC officer and chairman, at the time, of Gulf Oil spoke to one of Pennsylvania's two Republican senators, James Duff. In Montana, the then head of the legal department of Shell Oil, who happened to have been the state's (Democratic) attorney general, was invited to approach the state's (Democratic) senator, Mike Mansfield. There was a great deal more of the kind on behalf of the GGC. It was supplemented by individual company initiatives. For example, a Texas-based attorney for Shell Oil attempted to influence Senator Prescott Bush of Connecticut, a gas-consuming state certainly, but he himself had been an investment banker and so might be "sympathetic" to corporations. The attorney tried to "reach" the senator through his son, Mr. George Bush, the attorney's neighbor in Texas, where he had come to seek his own fortune, in, as it happened, oil. The attorney met the senator twice.

Others tried something less orthodox. In January 1956, the future vice-president of the United States received a midnight telephone call from a Fort Worth man who said he worked for a well-known oil firm. Senator Bush, the caller expostulated, was helping to ruin the oil business. If Mr. Bush did not rein in his father, his new oil enterprise in Texas would be boycotted. Mr. Bush was not intimidated. He complained to a senior partner in the firm—as luck would have it, a personal friend—and received apologies from him as well as a withdrawal of the threat by its perpetrator.

At about this time, an oil company lobbyist offered Senator Francis Case (Rep.-South Dakota) a *de facto* bribe to support the measure.[27] Despite the senator's startling disclosure, the Senate proceeded to pass the bill by a majority of twenty[28] only to have it vetoed by President Eisenhower. This was all the more galling to proponents because he was well known to be in favor of the principle it embodied. He acted on good-government grounds, arguing that the disclosure tended to create doubt on the part of the American people as to the "integrity" of their system of government.

Within twelve months, however, the president tried to make amends in his budget message. A new bill sailed through the House in 1957; early the following year, its prospects looked good. But then, in February, the whole sky clouded over. The *Washington Post* disclosed that a Republican national committeeman from Texas had asked oil and gas men to attend a dinner in Houston for House minority leader, Joseph Martin (Massachusetts). Through this dinner $100,000 was raised (tickets @ $100). But the real issue was that the organizer referred to Representative Martin, who had voted for exemption, in this way:

> Joe Martin . . . has always been a friend of Texas, especially of the oil and gas producing industries. He mustered two-thirds of the Republican votes in the House each time the gas bill passed.[29]

and:

> It will be up to Joe Martin to muster at least 65 percent of the Republican votes in order to pass the gas bill this year. . . . He has to put Republican members from northern and eastern consuming areas on the spot politically because the bill is not popular.[30]

"A flagrant exchange of money for votes," claimed the Democratic national chairman. In the subsequent hue and cry, the bill vanished.

That was that in Congress for many a long day—virtually for two decades. Now the only hope of undermining the *Phillips* decision lay inside the FPC. If only the commissioners would learn to go slow in the application of the law, the interests might yet win a victory of sorts. And they did. It is true that applying the law meant attempting to apply the "rate base cost-of-service method"—the traditional formula for regulating public utilities, i.e., cost plus a fair rate of return—to the thousands of independent producers, accordingly creating a great administrative burden. On the other hand, the commissioners seemed content to make haste slowly: certainly they did not make a fuss, or propose a suitable alternative. The truth almost certainly is, as someone who had served on the staff of the FPC told Daniel Fiorino, the largely Republican commission (of that Eisenhower era) really "did not want to regulate." And so, as special assistant James M. Landis, former dean of the Harvard Law School, and highly experienced in the work of regulatory agencies, would tell President Kennedy in 1960, the FPC constituted "the outstanding example in the federal government of the breakdown of the administrative process." The FPC, he concluded, had virtually refused to "obey the mandates of the Supreme Court of the United States and other federal courts."[31]

At that point—1960—the FPC sought salvation through scrapping its old "system" in favor of prices (or rates) determined by geographical areas, in each of which there would be two price levels depending on whether the output was (a) old (pre-January 1961) or "associated," i.e., produced in conjunction with oil, or (b) new. In other words, the FPC went wholesale rather than retail, with a higher price for (b) than for (a). The rationale was predictable: stimulate producers to deliver more gas to the *inter*state market. In 1963, the Supreme Court seemed ready to digest the new policy—*Wisconsin v. Federal Power Commission* (373 U.S. 294)—which was formalized in 1965 in relation to the Permian Basin area (New Mexico/West Texas). After that, or if you wish after 1960, there was dual pricing for natural gas even in *inter*state transactions (there already was dual pricing as between intrastate and interstate).

Three years later the Supreme Court endorsed the practice as well as the principle of area pricing—*Permian Basin Area Rate Cases*, 390 U.S. 747 (1968)—thus putting its seal of approval on the FPC's Permian Basin direction. In that sense, the commissioners and the justices seemed to be enjoying a meeting of minds as the sixties drew to a close. The work on area pricing continued and was virtually complete before the decade ended.[32]

The respite was brief. Even before OPEC startled the world in 1973, an ostensible shortage of natural gas upset the delicate equilibrium. One writes *ostensible* because many were those who believed that the shortage was contrived by the natural-gas interests in order to force the hands of the policy makers. Others argued that the shortage was genuine and only to be expected because the FPC had set the prices (or rates) too low to encourage the producers. Whatever the objective truth, the commissioners began to veer toward deregulation, attempting, for example, to exempt small producers, but they were thwarted by the Supreme Court. However, they did succeed in abandoning adjudicative hearings (something like trials) in favor of rule-making proceedings. One of the earliest applications of that was the proposal, made known in June 1974, to abandon area pricing in favor of a national uniform rate for all "new" gas (produced after a certain date).

This "party line" was vigorously advocated in the Senate in 1975 in what looked like yet another tactical switch from one policy-making location to another. The coalitions called into play were for the most part the expected ones: labor unions, e.g., Auto Workers (not then back in the AFL-CIO), Steelworkers, Communication Workers and United Mine Workers; with their peak organization, the AFL-CIO; Congress Watch (a Naderite creation); and the Consumer Federation of America against almost all components of the industry, although the Independent Gasoline Marketers Council threw in its lot with opponents (including the Rural Electric Cooperatives). What is more intriguing is the *de facto* role of the newly established Federal Energy Administration (FEA)[33] in the camp of the proponents. What it took on (at the taxpayers' expense) was in effect a p.r. campaign for the deregulation policy. It took the form of a radio advertisement denouncing those who claimed there would be no natural-gas shortage during the 1975–76 winter, but mainly of three pamphlets and booklets. The first (August 1975) listed states where shortages were to be expected that winter. Written by a consultant under contract, the pamphlet was actually reviewed before publication by several members of the American Gas Association, representing the producers. A booklet, introduced by no less a person than the FEA Administrator, Frank G. Zarb, explained the (postulated) shortage solely in terms of federal price controls. Hence, Congress should deregulate the price of natural gas.[34]

At that stage, then, the line of cleavage between the contending forces lost its simplicity of outline. The gas and associated interests were arrayed not only with the FPC but also with the FEA, which even busied itself pamphleteering in the constituencies. Behind the FEA stood President Ford, who had brought in Mr. Zarb to replace Mr. John C. Sawhill, the first administrator. In other words, it was a coalition of private and public entities that confronted the labor unions and the other private defenders of price control. Such an alliance of private and public forces is by no means uncommon, but the public contribution is not always as clearly displayed as it was in that case.

In October the Senate in effect matched the FPC's policy of the previous year by voting for deregulation of "new" natural gas. But the House, attempting to go farther (with the help of the House leadership, notably Speaker Carl Albert, from a gas-producing section of Oklahoma), just failed by four votes (February 1976). Independents were exempted but price controls on the major (oil) companies producing gas were in fact tightened. Resisting that measure, the Senate through the Commerce Committee made a fresh start in May, voting 18–1 to permit a trebling of the price of "new" onshore natural gas. According to one economist's estimate, that would increase consumers' costs by $8.9 billion to $12.5 billion a year.[35]

Once again, the scene changed swiftly to the FPC. As if determined to carry the ball for a slow-running Congress, the commissioners, by now mostly Republicans appointed after President Nixon's arrival in the White House in 1969, went ahead with their own version of price decontrol. For interstate gas produced in 1973–74, a doubling of the current price would be permissible. After 1974 the ceiling would be higher again, although not as high as in the recent Senate bill. Since "old" gas was untouched, the FPC had constructed a three-tier system. The policy was tantamount to deregulation by easy stages.

It was not, however, what the oil and gas interests wanted—they wanted complete deregulation, now. This was something presidential candidate Jimmy Carter found it expedient to promise. Its cause seemed certain to prosper as a result of the icy winter that followed his election, when snow fell in Miami and natural-gas supplies fell off alarmingly across the frozen land. For, apart from anything else, after a private report commissioned by Associated Gas Distributors (a trade organization of utilities) concluded that reserves had been withheld from the market during the crisis, President Carter commented: "I think it's obvious to all of us that there are some instances where natural gas is withheld from the market."[36] It was, however, "understandable" that producers of natural gas would withhold it "to wait for higher prices." The implication of that, in the light of the campaign promise, was (one would have thought) deregulation. This, however, the president side-stepped not only in his emergency measure (Emergency Natural Gas Bill, 1977, which passed within a week)—which was understandable—but also in his comprehensive proposals that April. These called for a sharp increase in the price of *new* gas from all sources, eliminating the distinction between *intra-* and *inter*state supplies. But there would still be regulation, even of intrastate prices, until then the prerogative of the states.

Determined on deregulation, the interests now mobilized their forces in Congress. In the first step of "a long acrimonious battle," the Energy and Power Subcommittee of the House Commerce Committee in early June actually voted (12–10) for deregulation, five Democrats, headed by Representative Robert Krueger (Texas), joining hands with seven Republicans. Three weeks later, however, by a "razor-thin margin," the parent committee reversed its subcommittee (22–21). President Carter commended the committee for "their courage in the face of strong lobbying pressure," which had indeed been intense, particularly for the votes of six of them.[37]

The comment by James Flug, director of the Energy Action Committee, one of the newer consumers' groups, was more somber: "Today's vote was just the first step in a long, treacherous road. The fact that industry came so close to removing price controls should be a warning to the public about the power and the greed of the oil lobby."[38]

The second step was taken about two weeks later in mid-July, when the issue again came before the House Commerce Committee and Mr. Flug found himself ranged against David Foster, executive vice-president of the Natural Gas Supply Committee, the principal lobbying instrument for achieving deregulation. Mr. Foster had previously practiced his art on behalf of cable-TV interests. After a hard-fought battle, analyzed in remarkable detail by Al Hunt of the *Wall Street Journal*,[39] the defenders of price control just held their ground: 23–20. That embodied a turnover of one vote as compared with the end of June. It belonged to another of the Carters, Representative Tim Lee Carter of Kentucky, Republican but from a low-income district. As Mr. Flug accompanied him from the House floor on the committee room, he again stressed what deregulation would cost the poor, saying that "someone as conservative as James Schlesinger has come to that conclusion."[40] (Mr. Schlesinger was secretary of the Department of Energy.) Whether or not as cause and effect, the congressman "voted right"—from Mr. Flug's more leftish perspective.

In the House itself in early August, after yet another "tense, close battle fought on two fronts—one on the House floor by oratory, the other in the halls outside by lobbyists—the administration forces beat back deregulation, 199–277."[41] Moreover, regulation would now apply intrastate as well as interstate, thus eroding the long-standing distinction. On the other hand, the price of *new* gas could rise some thirty cents per thousand cubic feet, even higher in appropriate circumstances.

For the Natural Gas Supply Committee, it was back to square one. But of course they weren't about to go into liquidation, if only because they had an annual budget of $500,000 to $750,000.[42] They sweated out that summer. As Carl Suchocki of the Committee recalled: "Word went out: we have to get out to the grassroots, and we have one month to do it."[43] David Foster added: "Few of our people went to the beach in August. They stayed at their desks through the smog and heat."

What they set out to do was stimulate a ground swell from the constituencies, reasoning that the larger users, anxious to pay more if that would ensure supplies, had to make their voices heard in addition to those of the natural-gas producers. Workers and shareholders were invited to write or wire their senators on the assumption that, even if they had to pay higher gas bills, they would be preserving their pensions and dividends. Their response to that "pitch" is unknown. But leading employers in various states telephoned their senators to warn of plant shutdowns and layoffs if adequate supplies could not be guaranteed. Meanwhile twenty-eight p.r. specialists met in Washington to coordinate arguments for deregulation, packages of which were then dispatched to "wholesale" points throughout the country.

Then, as congresspersons, especially senators, returned after Labor Day to the scene of their travail, they found the lobbyists waiting. These, of course, had been busy all year long. As Bob Rankin of *Congressional Quarterly* would report: "The Capitol was crawling with lobbyists of every shape, stripe and persuasion from the day Carter sent his energy package to Congress." But now came what Nick Laird, vice-president for government relations at the American Gas Association, would characterize as "one of the most intensive, all-out efforts I've ever witnessed." As *Time* reported:

> In traditional fashion, some camped out in alcoves just off the Senate floor, where they propagandized senators with an array of computer studies and charts. So many executives of major firms swarmed to Washington to make personal pitches that an aide to energy czar James Schlesinger groused, "the sky was black with Learjets."

Roundabout approaches still continued, however. Thus Chris Farrand, the U.S. Chamber of Commerce's director of energy and environment, called up senators from the comfort of his own office. Pointing out that he never visited Capitol Hill, he remarked: "I generate three or four calls to a senator. He'll take those calls while three or four lobbyists are waiting outside his office."[44]

As for the other side, made up of union lobbyists and consumer groups, including Energy Watch, they, in the opinion of one obsever were only "loosely allied, often unorganized."[45] If true, it would have mattered less earlier on in the House, where the Commerce Committee had a proconsumer majority, enabling it as the parent committee to reverse the narrow producers' victory in the subcommittee. In the Senate, however, the measure was taken straight to the parent committee, on which there was no consumer majority. The committee (Energy) split 9–9, two Democrats, from Louisiana and Kentucky, joining the seven Republicans. That was a kind of victory for the proponents of deregulation because it enabled the measure to go forward to the floor. But there, in early October, the most striking effort came from opponents, who filibustered for nine days and stalled, altogether, for thirteen, led by two Democrats, Senators Abourezk (South Dakota) and Metzenbaum (Ohio).

The filibuster was broken, not by proponents of deregulation (i.e., opponents of the Democratic president's policy), but, of all things, by the Democratic majority leader, Senator Robert Byrd, and the vice-president of the United States, Walter Mondale, who actually turned up to preside; both, it was said, were hand-in-glove with President Carter. In what Senator Gary Hart (Dem.-Colorado) called "a sophisticated steamroller" but which was really rather brutal,[46] the leaders prevailed, breaking the filibuster. The cries of wounded senators could almost have been heard in Alexandria. Despite that, the upshot the following day was a victory, by four votes, for deregulation, in particular for new natural gas found onshore.

What the breaking of the filibuster meant tactically is hard to determine. There was "strong evidence"[47] that even three days later the White House thought the Senate tables could be turned. Soon, in any case, the president was breaking a lance with, at one remove, those very forces that he had apparently just rescued in the Senate. In a nationally televised press conference, arguing that the energy crisis was still tantamount to, in the famous borrowed phrase he had already used, "the moral equivalent of war," the president warned that "as in time of war, there is potential war profiteering in the impending energy crisis." If that potential "war profiteering" were actualized, it would produce "the biggest rip-off in history." Expressing his approval of the free market system, he argued that the oil-and-gas industry was not part of it. The prices set were not determined competitively but by a cartel.[48]

Good, straight-from-the shoulder stuff, but it came a little late in the day. The Senate—or the gas interests—had spoken: the president himself, in high summer, had not. Now the battleground would become the House-Senate conference, as to which Senator Abourezk warned: "If you want to talk about lobbying, wait until the oil and gas boys zero in on the conference committee members."[49] If the "zeroing in" occurred (which no one doubts), it left no public trace. What is known is that the conferees went about their business at a very leisurely pace, seldom exerting themselves "more than five hours a day" and "often" enjoying "three-day weekends."[50] The principal issue—natural gas regulation—was not even reached until the beginning of December. In three weeks not an inch of ground was gained. Until the major issue was settled, nothing else could be, or at least *would* be. As chairman of the Finance Committee, Senator Russell Long, speaking for the oil and gas interests of Louisiana in which he himself had substantial holdings, declined to proceed with the tax part of the energy package until the conferees reached agreement on the deregulation, and so the pricing, of natural gas.[51] Failing to reach agreement, the conferees went home for Christmas.

The new year brought no relief. After months of inconclusive discussions behind closed doors, the leading conferees were called to the White House where the president himself hoped to break the deadlock. Out of that came what was hailed as the April 21 compromise, reached after negotiations that had lasted into the small hours of the morning and in which, as in the final session during daylight hours, Energy Secretary James Schlesinger played a notable part as go-between.

The principal feature of the so-called compromise (some might say, surrender), was the abolition of federal price controls on "new" natural gas as from January 1, 1985. Meanwhile the base price of "new" gas would be hiked to $1.75 *per thousand cubic feet* (from rather less than $1.50), and increased each year by about 10 percent until 1981. The small rate of increase permitted from 1981 to 1985 was expected to produce a price of about $4.05 in 1985. Under the 1977 Carter proposals the corresponding figure would have been some $3.44. That meant a total of $25–31 *billion more* in higher gas prices than under the House bill passed in August 1977.[52]

The most subtle concession in the whole so-called compromise turned on the definition of *new* in "new gas." As to time, the price hike was to be backdated to April 1977 when the president had submitted his energy package. That was neat: evidently there *had* been delay since then, but who had caused it? Essentially, the Senate. By August 1977 Speaker "Tip" O'Neill had "delivered" the House for the president's natural-gas policy. But the Senate proceeded to drag its feet.

Even neater was the definition of *new* in the sense of place or location. It would, for example, include gas from new wells 2.5 miles or more from an existing well. That *might* serve the national interest, but it might also simply provide nothing more than a new *way* of tapping an existing supply. No one who has read even a little about the "hot oil war" in East Texas in the early thirties will ever underestimate the ingenuity and resourcefulness of oil-and-gas men. *Hot* was to oil as (more or less) *bootleg* was to liquor during the Prohibition years, or, in other words, production over the amount legally permitted. One "favorite device" was the by-pass carrying the oil into a secret pipeline. As double insurance, one such operator had the well's control valve set up in his house at the side of the toilet. When the state or federal inspectors came looking, his wife would scurry into the bathroom, lock the door and turn off the valve. Some wells proved to be dummies. Given ten wells, the operator would be entitled to ten "allowable" amounts: so much more convenient, and less expensive, to set up nine "stage-set" wells and produce the total amount from the real one. There was simple theft, too: what looked like a well turned out to be a hook-up into the Humble Company's pipeline. Some theft was rather more complicated. One small refiner paid off a company's employee for the privilege of tapping their pipeline, only to have someone surreptitiously tap his, and, in the cold light of morning, cheekily offer *him* a deal in "hot oil."[53]

In the light of all that and much else, including the Teapot Dome scandal of the early twenties, the attempt to bribe Senator Case in the fifties, and, in the sixties and early seventies, some of the events later denoted by "corporate Watergate," one fancies that much of the "old" gas was destined to be passed and sold off as "new," receiving, if not earning, the higher price.

That is a personal view: how in fact did the competing interest groups read the compromise as a whole? In assessing that, we need to remind ourselves that with such a complex set of proposals as the energy package, the line of cleavage is not likely to be easily discerned, at least initially. In the twelve months from April 1977 (launching of the policy) to April 1978 (achievement of the compromise by the élite conferees), observers had first noted "scores of narrowly focused lobbies. Small oil refiners worked their own angles." Among the larger forces, the "nation's major utilities were scrambling all over," while car manufacturers exerted themselves to beat off the proposed tax on their gas-guzzling dinosaurs. But the main focus of the oil-and-gas interests was the same as ours in this sketch: deregulation. On that issue the battle lines were fairly clearly drawn: unions, consumers and environmentalists in general and the Energy Action Committee in particular *v*. the Natural Gas Supply Committee, with help from the API, the Independent Petroleum Association of America (IPAA), the American Gas Association, and, transcending the sector, the National Council of Farmer Co-operatives and the U.S. Chamber of Commerce. The last two were speaking for the larger users, many of whom would be found among the chamber's seventy thousand member businesses, and among the National Council's 3.5 million farmers and 118 farm and marketing co-ops.[54] That, by the way, underlines the significance of the coalition's title: Natural Gas Supply Committee (look back and compare the titles used by the corresponding associations in the 1950s). It was a Republican representative, Tom Railsback (Illinois), who pointed out in this period that the "Supply Committee" was "supported by the major oil companies."[55] So presumably, it was to serve their interests. Even so, some large users, aka consumers in one sense, joined hands with producers.

Then the compromise of April 1978 was reached. It quickly sliced into the array of forces. The Consumer Federation of America opposed it. So did the AFL-CIO and Americans for Democratic Action. But the opposing camp also harbored such original proponents as the Chamber of Commerce and IPAA. Lines were blurred within Congress, too, even among the conferees. In the House particularly, the question posed was: would conferees *not* included in that magic circle of joint conferees[56] which had reached the compromise go along with it? The Connecticut Democrat, Toby Moffett, declined, arguing that the House conferees had gone "against the will of the House," and that the measure would line the pockets of the gas industry without giving the public much in return.[57] In late May, however, the compromise was narrowly endorsed (one vote) by the House conferees and a little more easily (three votes) by their Senate counterparts.

That settled one thing: the struggle would be transferred to the floor of Congress. But not for some months. Its outcome remained quite unpredictable. Outside Congress, as the weeks passed, almost the only clear thing was the confusion. For the AFL-CIO, George Meany (as well as Douglas Fraser for the UAW) wrote to all senators advocating defeat of the bill on the ground that it would hurt consumers. But one hardly expected their lobbyists to meet regularly with those of the Chamber of Commerce in order to coordinate tactics. The steel industry was divided. The car manufacturers were divided (Chrysler came out in favor). Agriculture was divided, not for the first time.[58] Even the oil industry itself was divided. Atlantic-Richfield (ARCO) backed the compromise. Others, like EXXON, agreed to stay on the sidelines. But Standard Oil, Indiana (AMOCO) fought the compromise, and coordinated tactics with James Flug, of Energy Action.

Most of these lines of stress converged on the Senate in August. There adversity had also been making strange bedfellows: Senator Kennedy with Senator John Tower (Rep.-Texas), and Senator Russell Long with the perpetrators of the 1977 filibuster, Senators Abourezk and Metzenbaum, all united against the compromise and accordingly against the president. What *he* was doing was mounting "the most extensive administration lobbying on a piece of domestic legislation"[59] since he had taken office. The upshot, in late September, was a comfortable victory for the compromise (57–42).

Would the House follow suit, however? The leaders' strategy was still to have the whole measure voted upon as a single package. What opponents of the compromise wanted was to detach the gas-pricing section from the whole measure, the better to destroy it. In the Senate, even at that late stage, Senator Abourezk helped the cause by first attacking the tax section of the bill, which delayed the House's consideration of the measure as a whole, and then using a related tax *credit* bill to mount a filibuster. The first maneuver produced a couple of days' delay; the second kept the Senate up until after midnight one Saturday (i.e., Sunday morning) and the House (or some two dozen staunch members) all through that night.

The graver threat had arisen in the House Rules Committee, which declined (8–8) to grant a rule permitting a single vote on the whole package. Under pressure, however, three Democrats changed their minds the following day, or at least their votes. Even then the House endorsed the procedure (on Friday the 13th) by only one vote (207–206). That, really, was it: the substantive vote (231–168) came almost as an anticlimax at 7:30 a.m. on the Sunday morning. (In the Senate, James Abourezk had fired his last shot seven hours earlier.)[60] It was time for breakfast or early church, according to taste and stamina.

Clearly, a very long night in more senses than one. It could be said, as to regulation of natural gas prices, to have lasted forty years—1938 to 1978.

CHAPTER 11
REGULATORY POLICY:
Going to Pot

When we learn about the lengths to which the dairy lobby (reflecting one kind of agribusiness) will go in order to increase its income, and, other things being equal, reduce ours as we pay more for milk products in the supermarket, it is difficult not to wax indignant. Suppose, however, that the agribusiness is not only in milk but also marijuana? It has already happened in California, where by 1980 the cultivation of this sort of grass was estimated to earn more than $1 billion a year, "more than any other agribusiness" except cattle, milk and cotton.[1] The center of production was to be found in the north in Humboldt and Mendocino counties (the latter's crop in 1979 appears to have sold for $1.2 million on the streets). But it seemed to be a poor county that failed to produce a million dollars' worth. Cultivation being a felony, growers were understandably shy about reporting such income, but the Internal Revenue Service, ever alert to the challenge embodied in its title, was doing its enterprising best to make some collections. Whether it would collect and tell was not altogether clear.

So far as one knows at present, the Californian growers have not made their way to the White House. But signs of interest-group development there have been. In one town in Humboldt County, "the growers have made political allies and gained financial clout." Enforcement of the law has been weak. Less than 10 percent of the crop seems to have been destroyed in 1979. The country district attorney (as of 1980) said openly that "the stiffest penalty" he would seek "for a large grower—one in the $300,000 cash crop bracket—is a year in the county jail."[2] Not very severe for a felony, supposedly a major crime. But then of course, in the United States, no one can pick up a political scent faster than a district attorney.

With so much at stake, this particular political tendency in California will surely grow. Suppose it reaches the point where the growers' (not to mention yet the users') lobby becomes significant, like the milk producers', in cooperation with kindred souls. Now this is an agribusiness, also like milk production, that generates a great deal of free-floating cash (up to $200 for an ounce in 1980, compared with a mere $40 for regular grass). The (putative) lobby will surely float some of it in the direction of both Sacramento and Washington, D.C. Whether a PAC could be established is not such an absurd question as it might seem because one county actually does "report marijuana in its agricultural statistics."[3] Assume in any case that a legal method of making political contributions can be found. The underlying activity, from which the funds are derived, however, would (for the moment at least) remain illegal, even criminal. Would you be as harsh in your criticism of the political actions of *this* form of agribusiness as you may well be of the milk producers and their dairy lobby? These acted illegally but on the basis of an activity as innocent as milking a cow.

Californian growers are believed, by 1980, to have got 30 percent of the market within the state. So the American market as a whole (say, 16 million regular users in 1977) must still depend upon imports. Thus there is another Big Business originating beyond these shores. How big is suggested by the "busts" even though these doubtless represent only a small fraction of the flow. In October 1978, for example, at the Oakland-Pontiac airport, state police confiscated 5.5 tons of marijuana that had been packed, probably with much tender loving care, in five-gallon pails and flown in by a four-engine cargo plane. A couple of fellows sat in a truck for its arrival waiting unaware that the police were also part of the reception committee.

If that was the biggest "bust" in the history of the Wolverine State, it was not the biggest in the history of the traffic. In March 1973, a combined Mexican-United States police team got their hands on more than twenty-four tons that were ready for shipment north of the border where (in a different sense) the grass was believed to be greener. The record up to that year was the forty-two tons discovered in Jamaica, all *en route* for the United States. Within its own boundaries at that time, the laurel wreath would have to be bestowed upon Florida for the twenty tons discovered there just before Christmas, 1973 (appropriately enough, at that time, on Mexico Beach). Florida's achievement was enhanced the following March when nearly two tons of hashish were brought to light in Miami.[4]

As the decade was drawing to a close, however, all such records were broken. At Port Arthur, Texas, in late November 1978, Customs Service agents stopped the unloading of twenty-five to thirty tons from a shrimp boat on to trailer trucks. That, it is thought, would have been worth $12 million on the street. In the month following, an unregistered Colombian fishing trawler bound for Gloucester, Massachusetts, was seized off Cape Cod. In late January 1979 the eleven crew members, all from Colombia, were indicted for attempting to take thirty-four tons of marijuana into the United States. One could not help wondering how this haul would be guarded until the case came to trial. Early in the previous month thirteen hundred pounds of Colombian marijuana held as evidence in federal drug prosecutions had been stolen from a Brooklyn warehouse. That was the largest amount of marijuana to have slipped out of law enforcement hands in the northeastern part of the country.[5]

Are you critical of Big Business in this sense as you may be in other contexts? Naturally, much depends on who *you* are. Among high-school seniors, class of 1979, more than six out of ten had tried smoking pot at least once (the "ever used" category). Something like one in ten were more or less daily users. Among the population as a whole, the "ever useds" came to 43 million in an earlier year (1977), when the current users were of the order of 16 million. But to be consistent, wouldn't you have to be as critical of Big Business in this sense as of the milk producers and of the corporations unmasked in their own special Watergate? And so the question arises: are your—our—interests somehow closely bound up with the special interests?

Any interest you might have in the fate of the growers would of course be no more than derivative. Actual users (such as 55 percent of college students in the midseventies) have a much more direct interest in modification or repeal of the law. In order to understand what would be involved in that, and what the prospects are, we need to know something about how and why the public policy emerged and developed.

OPIATES AND COCAINE

The first legislative attack on narcotics, specifically on opium use and possession and on the existence of opium dens, was launched rather more than a hundred years ago, in San Francisco in 1875. That resulted in a new phenomenon, the criminalization of narcotics use and possession, as that San Francisco ordinance was partly copied by four western states. Fifteen or sixteen others were moved to train their guns on the opium dens.[6] A special case of this general phenomenon was constituted by morphine, an extract from opium dating back to 1803 but coming to be more used during the Civil War, when it was injected to relieve pain (the hypodermic needle having been recently invented). Some soldiers became addicted, their withdrawal symptoms being identified as "the army disease." After the war, overprescribing by doctors combined with the marketing of proprietary medicines containing morphine to produce *morphinomania*. By the early years of this century, morphine had replaced opium as the no. 1 opiate of the streets.[7]

By then, heroin, a derivative of morphine but (it was belatedly realized) far more addictive, had been available for a few years (since 1898). For some time, however, its use was licit (for example, as a cough suppressant) rather than illicit. The rival to morphine on the streets in those years was cocaine, derived from the leaves of the coca-tree, which is to be found in many tropical countries but especially South America, where the chewing of the leaves to produce a "high" was a well-established custom. The value of cocaine as a local anesthetic had been discovered in 1884, but it also began to be sniffed. By the end of the century *cocainomania* had been officially identified as a problem among southern blacks, and as a source of violent crime. Once again the states bestirred themselves. By 1912 the number of states in which a doctor's prescription was required for cocaine was forty-four, more than for opiates.[8]

In response to growing public concern, Congress itself had acted six years earlier by way of the Pure Food and Drug Act. Until then federal laws for the protection of the public against impure food and dangerous drugs had applied essentially to imports and exports. General pure food bills had been introduced from 1890 onward but failed to make progress. Opposition had come partly from the "strict constitutionalists" of those days, notably in the South, arguing that such a measure usurped the police power[9] of the states, supposedly guaranteed by the Tenth Amendment. The main obstacle, however, had been the business interests, particularly the Proprietary Association of America. They were overcome by a combination of popular forces, including journalistic writings, but above all by the efforts of one of America's great public servants, Dr. Harvey W. Wiley, principal chemist at the Department of Agriculture from 1883 to 1912. Insofar as the act concerned drugs, it required conformity with the United States Pharmacopoeia as to standards and proper labeling of the contents, especially (in this context) if the mixture contained more than prescribed amounts of opiates. Three years later an act prohibited the import of opium except for medicinal purposes and even then only through designated ports.

THE HARRISON ACT, 1914

That early trend was sustained by the Harrison Act of 1914 and by precisely the same device—the resort to an asserted federal police power, ostensibly in the form of a tax measure, to attack a particular social evil. The act required that, with certain exceptions,[10] anyone who imported or in any other way dealt with opium or coca leaves should register with the collectors of internal revenue and pay a special tax. That included the sale and transfer of the two drugs, and even giving them away. Generally an unregistered person found in possession would be presumed to be in violation of the law unless he or she could produce a doctor's prescription. The sanction would be a fine of up to $2000 or five years in prison, at the discretion of the court.[11] The states followed suit. Before 1914, few had prohibited mere possession: by 1931 some seven out of ten forbade possession of cocaine and/or opiates. One in six forbade possession of a hypodermic syringe.[12]

CANNABIS

Up to that point, cannabis had hardly appeared on the scene except as hemp cultivated for its fiber or seed.[13] In the nineteenth century a few writers and artists on both sides of the Atlantic put it to the other use, but essentially hemp remained an agricultural crop. In the United States, however, it had lost ground before the century was out to southern cotton and to jute imported from India, although what had been cultivated naturally continued to flourish wild. Curiously enough (was it a coincidence?), marijuana use began in the United States at the turn of the century after the plant had lost much of its value as a cash crop in the usual sense. The demand came from Mexican immigrants to the United States, especially to New Mexico and above all Texas: the practice in towns along the Mexican border has been dated from about 1900. A decade later the Gulf Coast was also a center for it, especially New Orleans, the supplies coming in, not by land but by sea, from Cuba as well as the Mexican ports of Vera Cruz and Tampico. From New Orleans the habit was carried upriver and then from Mississippi ports to the great urban centers.

By the 1930s it seems the users of marijuana belonged to two broad social categories: poor Spanish-American communities in the Southwest, probably immigrants by origin, and black communities in the South. Occupationally, jazz musicians are believed to have been particularly inclined to "turn on," which suggests that New Orleans and New York City stood out as places where the practice grew.[14] But we have to keep a sense of proportion: all told, marijuana smokers are believed not to have exceeded fifty thousand at a time when the total population age 15–49 amounted to some sixty-five million (1930 Census).

Nevertheless, it was now that the federal authorities, more the bureaucracy than any other part of government, made their successful move against marijuana, having failed to get cannabis into the Harrison Act of 1914. After that, with one exception—in 1915 the Treasury, relying on the Food and Drug Act, decided that Mexicans crossing the border with the "locoweed" on their person should henceforward be guilty of smuggling—the matter had been left to the states, six out of ten of which, by 1931, prohibited the use of the drug for nonmedical purposes. Louisiana had led the way in 1911 (no refills of prescriptions containing cannabis), followed by four New England States (no such sales without a prescription). Federalization had been hampered in part by the common constitutional obstacle—in this case: did not the Harrison Act invade "the reserved police power of the states"? In addition, unlike opium, hemp was grown commercially in the United States, so that a successfully asserted police power would impinge upon cultivation in various states, including Kentucky, Wisconsin and Illinois.

From 1932 onward the Treasury, in particular its newly formed Bureau of Narcotics headed by Commissioner Anslinger, grasped the nettle and found a way out of the dilemma—a new act quietly drafted without consultation of the interests. This, the Marihuana Tax Act of 1937, excluded hemp cultivation proper. Anyone who imported marijuana, including the resin (the source of hashish), or manufactured, dispensed or otherwise dealt with it, was required (again, with certain exceptions) to register and pay a tax both on the role— importer, manufacturer, etc.—and on subsequent transfers, which were unlawful except on the basis of written orders made on government forms. Transfer to someone who had registered and paid the occupational tax attracted only a nominal "extra," but to anyone else (with authorized exceptions) it would be a stiff $100 an ounce or fraction thereof.[15] The intention, obviously, was to stamp on marijuana use, not to raise revenue, although the format chosen might well enable the act to survive a challenge in the courts. Violations of any section of the act could be punished by a fine of up to $2000 or by a prison term of up to five years, or both, according to the judgment of the courts.

For about twenty years after that, the official treatment of marijuana continued to be hostile, even increasing in severity. In 1951 the Boggs Act, referring back to the Harrison Act of 1914 and the Marihuana Tax Act of 1937, distinguished between first offenses and repeated ones, making the former a "two-to-five" rather than an "up-to-five." Third and subsequent offenses could draw "ten-to-twenty" (though, curiously enough, the $2000 fine set by the Harrison Act remained intact despite the erosion of the value of the dollar). That was put right, however, by the Narcotic Control Act of 1956, several sections of which were specifically concerned with marijuana. Thus, for example, a violation of the rule about "sale or other transfer without written order" could draw a fine of up to $20,000, in addition, for a first offense, to a "five-to-twenty" prison term ("ten-to-forty" for second and subsequent offenses).[16] By then about a third of the states had legislated "little Boggs acts," and one or two drew away from the rest of the field. Louisiana, for example, provided a "five-to-ninety-nine" year prison term even for possession of a narcotic drug.

As it turned out, with the legislation of the midfifties, the high-water mark was reach. Soon the tide was on the ebb.

THE SIXTIES

One sign of it was the Drug Abuse Control Amendments of 1965, which extended federal control of "pep pills" and hallucinogens, but did not prohibit possession for personal use or by a member of one's own household (or, intriguingly, for administration to an animal owned by the possessor), even though the hallucinogens covered L.S.D. (lysergic acid diethylamide), widely believed to be dangerous. That was modified in 1968, when possession of such drugs other than by prescription was made illegal. Even so, possession would not be a felony, in line with the earlier legislation, but a misdemeanor, sanctioned by a $1000 fine and/or up to a year in jail for a first offense.

In the following year the Marihuana Tax Act of 1937 was undermined. Dr. Timothy Leary, who had become nationally known for his L.S.D. experiments at Harvard, then got himself tangled in the marijuana laws, and was actually convicted in a federal district court in Texas of being a transferee of marijuana who had failed to pay the transfer tax required by the 1937 Act. He appealed to the Supreme Court on the ground that such a requirement violated his Fifth Amendment rights against self-incrimination. He was obviously well advised, since there were several recent cases to build on, including *Marchetti v. United States* (1968). This concerned wagering (or gambling), the general point being that even though it was a crime in most states of the Union, if you actually indulged in it, then, under federal law (a 1951 revenue act), you had to register, pay a gambling stamp and an excise tax (10 percent) on your gross wagers. Since the IRS was entitled to pass the word to the local prosecutors, you were damned if you did and damned if you didn't. In *Marchetti* the Supreme Court accepted the Fifth Amendment privilege as a complete defense to a prosecution for having failed to register and pay the occupational tax on wagers. On the same lines, the Court decided in 1969 that Dr. Leary would have exposed himself to a serious risk of self-incrimination under state law had he filled out the written order form and paid the $100 an ounce transfer fee under the federal law.[17] So Congress's long-term strategy for controlling conduct that the Constitution left to the states—wrapping the legislation, as Mr. Justice Frankfurter put it, "in the verbal cellophane of a revenue measure"[18]—had received a distinct setback.

In the same year, President Nixon asked Congress for a comprehensive treatment of the drug problem. He still intended to retain minimum sentences for possession of drugs, while possession of marijuana (untouched by the 1965 and 1968 amendments) was still to be a felony. Finding Congress in no mood to follow suit, he beat a retreat. Hence the Comprehensive Drug Abuse Prevention and Control Act of 1970, which classified marijuana with heroin, L.S.D., mescaline and peyote as substances with a high potential for abuse and no medical use recognized in the United States, jettisoned mandatory minimum sentences except for professional criminals, and made possession, if for one's own use, a misdemeanor. The distribution of a small amount of "grass" for no profit would be the equivalent of possession. On the other hand, of course, a misdemeanor is a crime, and it would attract, for first offenders, up to a year in prison and up to $5000 as a fine, or both.[19]

THE POT LOBBY

It was somewhere about this time that the interest groups came on the scene. Obviously, two lines of reform presented themselves: you could decriminalize or you could go the whole hog and legalize. As early as 1967 a group at the University of Buffalo was advocating legalization, which was being discussed in the newspapers before the decade was out.[20] In the early seventies Amorphia, a California group, campaigned to the tune of "free backyard grass," the right to grow it yourself. They showed imagination and innovative skill in launching such parallel groups as Grannies for Grass, Mothers for Marijuana, and Jocks for Joints. In the finest sporting tradition, the Jocks for Joints once challenged some nonsmokers to a game of softball, offering to play "stoned" in order to demonstrate that the use of grass is not physically debilitating. A somewhat more orthodox group, the Consumers' Union also called for legalization (November 1972).[21]

The main drive, however, until December 1978, was in the direction of decriminalization, the vehicle for it being the National Organization for the Reform of Marijuana Laws (NORML). This was created by Keith Stroup in 1970 after he—a lawyer—had been called by a friend who had been "busted" in Washington, D.C. An incensed Mr. Stroup, by then a smoker himself, passed the hat around the foundations: ten of them declined, but then the Playboy Foundation came up with $5000, on the strength of which he gave up his job and launched NORML. Some months later the Playboy Foundation gave another $5000 and *Playboy* (that ornament of Judaeo-Christian civilization) supplied a free advertisement that brought in some but not enough. Once again the begging bowl was passed to the Playboy Foundation, which graciously agreed to contribute $100,000 a year: NORML was in business. Within about three years Mr. Stroup was its $18,000 a year executive director and registered lobbyist, supported by paid staff of seven, four of whom were based in Washington.[22] By 1978 the number of paid employees had reached twelve, most of them of course in the capital, in what *Rolling Stone* described as "a narrow, three-story townhouse in a slightly seedy neighborhood."[23] Membership stood at about twenty thousand, and the budget ran to $450,000 a year. *Playboy* still remained the group's "primary angel," supplying $40,000 of the total, but Stewart Mott, heir to a General Motors fortune, was chipping in with $30,000 annually, and cartoonist Garry Trudeau was contributing the originals of his *Doonesbury* strip for auction. Thus backed, Mr. Stroup had indeed, in Eileen Brennan's phrase, "transformed the U.S. pot lobby from a scruffy high-by-night operation into a twenty-thousand-member pressure group with five lawyers on its national payroll."[24]

By then, moreover, a distinguished team had been recruited for the advisory board of the organization. Some of them were "angels," such as Stewart Mott and Hugh Hefner (of *Playboy*). Others belonged to or touched Academe: Lester Grinspoon and Norman Zinberg (Harvard Medical School),

Howard S. Becker (Northwestern), and Neil Chayet, a Boston lawyer and trustee of Tufts University. There were two U.S. senators and Dr. Benjamin Spock. But in one way at least the most significant name was Ramsey Clark's. Mr. Clark had been one of the first approached for help by Keith Stroup to get NORML under way. "I wanted to use his name, to have him on our board or something." Although Mr. Clark supplied ideas and "suggested sources of money" he declined to have his name used.[25] Since then, evidently, much water has flowed under the bridge.

Within that flow two currents may be distinguished. The first turned simple possession of less than one ounce from a felony (pre-1969) to a misdemeanor (end of 1972) in all but eight of the fifty states, matching the 1970 federal act. In most jurisdictions that left sale (not necessarily for remuneration) a felony (two years to life, maximum), although about a third of them (by November 1977) had enacted "accommodation" rules, that is, permitting a small amount to be handed over to a friend as a favor. Cultivation and manufacture remained on a par with sale (of considerable quantities).[26]

Oregon started the other current in 1973 as the first state to decriminalize possession of small quantities of marijuana, the sanction being a civil fine of up to a maximum of $100. For other violations criminal penalties were retained. Between the summer of 1975 and spring 1977, seven other states took more or less[27] the same path. In June New York became the ninth state to join in, making possession of up to twenty-five grams (less than one ounce but enough for twenty to thirty cigarettes) punishable, first time around, by a fine of up to $100. Possession of more than twenty-five grams, as well as public use and display, or handing over a cigarette to someone, remained a misdemeanor, albeit class B, that might draw up to three months in jail.[28]

Nationally, however, the wagon was not rolling along. In April 1975 Senator Javits (one of the two senators mentioned above) introduced the Marijuana Control Act to provide that possession of not more than one ounce for private use (or transfer of such if not for profit) "shall not constitute a crime against the United States." Such actions would attract a civil penalty of up to $100. Congressman Koch, destined to become Mayor of New York City, introduced an identical measure in the House.[29] NORML supported their efforts, writing: "The next time you light up a joint, let your senator know how you feel." The injunction continued: "Get off your butt and do something about getting the use of marijuana decriminalized. Let someone know how you feel about the issue. Write your Senator or Congressman now! . . . Write the letter. The pen has power."

Not invariably, however. That legislation seems to have disappeared with hardly a ripple (it passed unreported at the time even by the lynx-eyed *Congressional Quarterly*). In August 1977 President Carter, trying to keep a promise given during his election campaign, put his authority behind decriminalization (for an ounce or less). Violators would simply be fined. Federal penalties for trafficking would remain intact, while the states would remain free to follow their bent.[30] Despite that appeal, the goal seemed some way off still in 1978. The NORML leadership, however, remained confident in the arena where it mattered most—within the states. In June, Mr. Stroup anticipated that after the fall elections a dozen states might decriminalize: he hoped that the decriminalization battle would be won within three years. Two months later the then eastern regional coordinator, Frank Fioramonti, forecast that "ten to twelve states would go decrim next year, after elections are over."[31]

Before the year was out, however, the NORML strategy changed from "decrim" to legalization. This had been advocated by some of the organization's advisers for many years, by Dr. Grinspoon, for example, since 1971 and possibly earlier.[32] But Mr. Stroup had invariably described NORML as a "a nonprofit, citizen-action lobby whose only purpose is to decriminalize the marijuana smoker."[33] At the end of 1978 he gave up the leadership of the organization, for which he had made great sacrifices (abandoning his career, "losing" his marriage, and living in the offices for five years). He had also developed a cough, which he denied (to Edwin Newman of NBC and the *New York Times*) was a symptom of chronic bronchitis, though he did say to Mr. Newman: "I think marijuana smoking on a daily basis is almost bound to cause some complications in your lungs because you are bringing in smoke into your lungs and I doubt that that is healthy."[34]

In any event, he stepped down and was replaced by Mr. Fioramonti, the eastern regional coordinator, who had previously served the Ad Hoc Lawyers' Committee to Legalize Marijuana. He had already told *Rolling Stone* that summer that "decriminalization is certain," and that "already one-third of the people, and one-third of the land area of the U.S.—though not one-third of the states—is decriminalized territory."

If so, what sociologists know as the problem of goal succession was readily solved: on to legalization. At that stage, however (August 1978), Mr. Fioramonti saw legalization as ten to fifteen years away.[35] The tactics of it became a little clearer in late December just after NORML had changed its strategy:

> We won the first half of the war when President Carter advocated decriminalization in 1977, but we have to be one step ahead of everyone else now. By the 1980 campaign, either we'll have made some serious inroads toward legalization with politicians and candidates, or the movement may be in serious trouble.[36]

But President Carter had specifically turned his face against legalization. And Peter Bensinger, of the Federal Drug Enforcement Administration, was determined to do battle, exclaiming: "Legalization is a completely unrealistic proposal." He went on to deny that the federal authorities "can't interdict the marijuana trade . . . if someone had said that we could get Turkey to wipe out its poppy fields ten years ago, who would have believed it?"[37] So by early

1979, the battle lines were drawn. Oddly enough, opposition to legalization was then developing "in an unforeseen place—among drug traders and users themselves." As an importer from Tampa, Florida, told Barnard L. Collier, who was writing about "Operation Stopgap": "It's part of the American tax revolt. Pot and coke prices have been about the same for years. Thousands of organizations are making a living from it. The feds can't stop it. So who needs it legal so we can pay a dope tax?"[38]

NORML nonetheless has continued to fight the good fight. Its goal from mid-1975 to the end of 1976 has been described as "seeking a noncriminal approach to the private use and possession of marijuana." on which about $20,000 was spent (in California) in that period in order to influence state policy. But in 1977–78 the goal was transformed into "legalizing personal use of marijuana," in pursuit of which some $39,000 (two full years) was expended. In 1979 the goal remained the same and the total was about $16,000.[39] The precise grand total was $76,369. About three-quarters of it went for the services of the same person, Mr. Gordon S. Brownell.

In 1980, however, legalization remained an elusive goal. (That was, *de jure*, the official goal. *De facto*, the goal had been approximated.) A bill introduced by Assemblyman Willie Brown, Jr. (Democrat, San Francisco) to permit adults to grow for personal use had recently failed and an initiative proposition backed by NORML had failed to reach the ballot the previous November.

This sketch is interesting if only because it brings out the relative weakness of the pot lobby as such and accordingly the relationship between cultural change and modification of public policy, as occurred with marijuana use in the sixties (when for example "joints" began to be smoked by "a better class of people" compared with those dubious fellows who rolled reefers thirty years before). For the moment you need reflect only upon this. Suppose you want the law modified—decriminalization, or, even what is empirically (if curiously) untrue of most users, legalization[40]: You send NORML a couple of bucks, or you support some other group, financially or in the flesh. That makes you part of the pot lobby (as Patrick Anderson called it in the *New York Times*).[41] That is your right, but presumably the foundation for it may also be used to support lobbies of a very different kind—on the face of it, of any kind. Whatever you claim for yourself in terms of pot, must (it would seem) be conceded to others in terms of milk.

The point can be made in terms of free speech. One version of this appeared in late 1979 as federal officials were circulating a model law to prohibit the sale, display and advertisement of "drug paraphernalia," the pipes, clips, spoons, bowls, blenders and other such (to some of us, mysterious) accoutrements of the new way of taking one's pleasure. This would mean (it was asserted) that to sell a mirror with the word *cocaine* imprinted on it would become illegal. But that, a writer argued, would sweep away "the most basic of American institutions—free speech."[42] Grant and extend that and you have a defense of the pot lobby. But this is also the defense often advanced on behalf of lobbies in general (as indeed of wealthy individuals), in relation, for example, to campaign contributions. To be able to give one's own money, it is claimed, is a form of speech. This apparently means not only "freedom for fat cats" as individuals[43] but as associations, e.g., the milk producers. Does it follow, then, that the milk lobby cannot be "disciplined" without inflicting serious damage upon the pot lobby (or of course any other that you might wish to join or support)? In the ancient phrase revived for this somewhat different context: Is freedom indivisible?

CHAPTER 12
REDISTRIBUTIVE POLICY:
Taxing Windfall Profits

In the Lowian scheme, redistributive policy resembles the regulatory in *not* being capable of division into small units or items, and so in laying bare the stakes (in making manifest winners and losers); but *what* is at stake is greater. That is because it impinges on broader categories of people: rich *v.* poor, privileged *v.* underprivileged, or, where social stratification is politically significant, upper class *v.* lower class, and the like. The core idea (in the study of public finance, of left-wing movements, etc., as well as in the Lowian formulation) is of transferring some value—some *thing* that people want (wealth, income, rights, etc.)—from one "level" to another. Because there is so much at stake, the conflict is likely to be extensive as well as intensive and quite possibly cast in "ideological" terms, reaching beyond Congress to the president in the White House. It may even reach the U.S. Supreme Court, as in the present case. In October 1980 the Independent Petroleum Association of America, supported by other oil interests and some oil states, filed suit in federal court to challenge the legality of the so called profits tax. This, they argued, undermined property ownership, which they declared to be the foundation of personal freedom: "The tax legitimizes the confiscation of a politically unpopular minority's property and rights by a majority."[1] There could hardly be a clearer statement of a particular policy's being perceived by one set of actors as a confrontation between *have* and *have-nots,* which was also very much in the minds of many of their antagonists in Congress.

So, in this instance at least, recalling the controversy about the Lowian typology (start of chapter 9), it would be easy to show that the characterization of this issue as redistributive does follow from the dominant perceptions of the actors. On the other hand, the so-called windfall profits tax[2] was a political "return" for the gradual decontrol of oil prices, a conscious "reimbursement" to the nation, which surely means that this apparently self-regulatory policy itself has a redistributive dimension.

That, arguably, is also true of the original policy of control (a regulatory policy in the Lowian scheme), even though it was imposed not by some socialistically inclined liberal but by President Nixon, summoning the authority of an act he had denounced almost to the point of veto and declared he would not use. Exactly a year after he had signed it—the Economic Stabilization Act, signed August 15, 1970—he imposed a 90-day wage-price-rents freeze in order to damp down the inflation that President Johnson had bequeathed to the American people. Promising that there would be neither a "permanent straitjacket" on the free enterprise system nor "a huge price-control bureaucracy," the president proceeded, after the ninety-day period was up, not only to extend controls but to make these mandatory by way of a bureaucracy (though not a huge one)—a Pay Board and a Price Commission. That phase lasted until January 1973, when Mr. Nixon suddenly reverted to voluntary guidelines for most of the economy. After a relapse—June 1973 to April 1974—during which another freeze was imposed, mandatory controls were jettisoned in the spring of 1974—but not for oil because by then the OPEC cartel had quadrupled its prices.

The voluntary system of January 1973 was placed in the hands of a Cost of Living Council (CLC), replacing the Board and Commission. One of the things it promptly did was to introduce a two-tier price system for crude oil (and refined products, here neglected). As with natural gas, "old" oil was to be differentiated from "new," and its price controlled. "New"[3] would go free (as would imports of crude). Its price soon shot up to something like double that of "old"—$5.25 for a barrel of "old" as against $10 plus for "new." As a result of such dual pricing, by about mid-1974 almost 40 percent of all domestic oil in the United States had been deregulated.[4] This policy, you will observe, was the handiwork of a bureaucratic body before it was adopted by Congress, just as the Federal Power Commission had blazed the trail with the dual pricing of natural gas.

Even so, the incoming president (Ford) wanted to go the whole hog. Declaring his faith in the principle of "conservation-by-price," he proposed in his 1975 State of the Union message that all oil prices should be decontrolled. After a year-long battle, however, he was obliged to compromise on this and related issues, and even accepted *de facto* control of the price of "new" oil that had previously been free. There were some crumbs of comfort for the president (if not for industry, which was furious). Prices would gradually rise.

Although now controlled, "new" oil would still be over twice as expensive as "old." As the latter was depleted, the average market price (a composite of the two categories) would gradually rise. This would also happen because an annual increase of 10 percent was "legislated in."

Some comfort may also have extracted from the provision that these mandatory controls would lapse in May 1979. True, the president would then have the option of extending them, on the old basis or some new one. But two and a half years after that all such price controls were to be abandoned. The glorious dawn would be October 1, 1981—unless some president persuaded Congress to change its mind.

Providence ensured that there would be no such change. In April 1979 came the second oil shock (as Robert Stobaugh and Daniel Yergin would call it)[5]: the fall of the shah of Iran, this time never to be reinstated. In a televised address to the nation at the beginning of April, President Carter announced not only that he would permit the price-control system to lapse in 1981 but also that decontrol was to start almost immediately on June 1 (i.e., as soon as legally possible). The objective, of course, was to reduce the nation's dependence on foreign oil. In the latter half of the 1970s, oil imports into the United States had increased spectacularly, up to very nearly half of all domestic consumption. To be dependent upon "a thin line of tankers stretching halfway around the earth" to the Persian Gulf was dangerous.

Obviously true, but of course the oilmen, who would soon be able to start charging something approaching OPEC prices, stood to gain extra profits of a magnitude hard to calculate but evidently in billions rather than millions. Before such listeners could open the champagne, the president pulled the joker out of his sleeve. Those extra, or "windfall," profits would be heavily taxed and the proceeds put in a trust fund for (a) the poor, (b) mass transit, but above all (c) a "security fund" for the development of other sources of energy. Thus came about what was promptly called the *windfall* profits tax, although no doubt the oilmen invented their own, more arresting epithets.

It would certainly be complex in execution. The windfall tax would be (the president proposed) 50 percent of what was earned by way of the new, gradually decontrolled prices (which were intended eventually to reach the OPEC level). The foundation for this was the distinction already encountered between "old" (pre-1973) oil and "new," also known, respectively, as "lower-tier" and "upper-tier." But the waters were muddied by proposing to permit some of that "old" to be sold as "new." Thus, for example, some producers would be able to sell four-fifths of their "old" as "new," an increase then of over $7 a barrel.

In time the gain would be greater. For "new" (post-1973) oil would be permitted to increase its price every month until it reached the OPEC level[6] on October 1, 1981. That part of the "old" *treated* as "new" would of course rise with the rising tide, although 50 percent of it all would be taxed away.

Looking ahead the planners naturally exempted future discoveries, and specifically Alaskan crude, so one has to remember to distinguish between "new" and "newly discovered." However, with the exception of Alaskan crude, the percent would apply, over and above a base agreed with the Treasury, to *all* future price increases attributable to OPEC decisions. This component of the windfall tax was commonly referred to as the "OPEC tax."

All that—and there was much more—would seem to have many of the ingredients of an administrator's nightmare. But for us—students of interest groups and public policy—the question that arises has more to do with the lines of cleavage and the coalitions. As a *New York Times* writer remarked, "the sides are by no means tidy or predictable."[7] Like a hunting dog, the president himself immediately "pointed" to the prey, or opposition. As to the distribution of the yield from the windfall tax, he predicted an "inevitable scrambling by interest groups for a larger share of these revenues," which could "leave the Congress divided, bogged down and unable to act."[8] But of course if the oil lobby had its way there would be no yield to distribute because no such tax would have been imposed. Two days later, at the annual Jefferson-Jackson dinner in Richmond, Virginia, the president said: "We must face the facts. The oil lobby does not like the idea of this energy security fund for the American people. They are going to be all over Capitol Hill like a chicken on a June bug." (This security fund is the one mentioned in (c), above.) Already (he went on) some people were "saying that the windfall profits tax and energy security fund will never pass. They say that the oil lobby has more influence on Congress than the American people. I say—let's prove them wrong."[9]

That "proving wrong" was made all the more difficult to achieve by the president's own strategic decision *not* to link the windfall tax to decontrol: no tax, no decontrol. He had considered that, only to reject it.[10] One consequence of the decision was obvious—the oil companies were strengthened (some analysts would say, made more intransigent) in their opposition to the tax. For, granted decontrol "without strings," what did they have to lose by such opposition? President Carter had made it, gamblers say, "odds to nothing."

The companies' view was of course represented in Washington by congresspersons from oil-producing states, notably by such senators as Russell Long of Louisiana, chairman of the Finance Committee. But congresspersons were at sixes and sevens, in part reflecting the divisions in the ranks of those who might have been expected to be the president's natural allies:

For decontrol plus a tax	Senator Abraham Ribicoff (Dem.-Connecticut), a member of the Finance Committee
Against decontrol	Representative Toby Moffett (Dem.-Connecticut), Senator Edward Kennedy but also Senator Henry Jackson (despite his friendship with James Schlesinger, reputed to be the author of the Carter proposals)[11]

| Against decontrol | labor unions, public interest groups |
| For decontrol but with a stronger tax | League of Women Voters (Some in the previous category might have been prepared to adopt this position, swallowing decontrol with a more powerful sweetener.) |

Such divisions were far from being "merely" intellectual. Addressing the American Society of Newspaper Editors in New York on the subject theme of the growing power of special interest groups, Senator Kennedy argued:

> And now the overbearing power of the oil lobby has exerted its influence in two new and unacceptable ways. First, it has intimidated the administration into throwing in the towel without even entering the ring on the issue of oil price decontrol. And second, it has also intimidated the administration into submitting a token windfall tax that is no more than a transparent fig leaf over the vast new profits the industry will reap.

The president's reply was succinct: "Baloney." Whether it was also valid, however, is disputable. His main point was that price controls would lapse as from October 1, 1981: "This is not a decision I made. I am complying with the existing law, and in order to minimize the impact of decontrol we're carefully and slowly phasing out control."[12] Not exactly. He did make a decision (unless it should be accounted a nondecision) *not* to ask Congress to extend controls between May 1979 and September 1981, either on the existing basis or a new one. For that he had authority. He could also have sought some continuation after September 1981: the expiration due then was not necessarily written in tablets of stone for all time. That he had not made the decision is true; that it was irrevocable or irreversible is not. What may have been true is that the votes for *any* extension were "not there" in the spring of 1979. Certainly House Democrats themselves were deeply divided. In the other place many a senator could be expected to be more oily than Democratic: as Representative Thomas Downey (Dem.-New York) remarked, referring to the oil interests: "That's where they have their horses."[13]

Before the issue reached Congress, however, the president had himself mounted a white charger and ridden off in the direction of the American people. In other words, he was appealing in classic fashion, over the heads of congresspersons to the general public, attempting to define the terms of the debate. At a special Oval Office ceremony on April 26, he focused, not on decontrol, but on the windfall tax. Grasping the reports of staggering increases in first-quarter profits by the oil companies,[14] he could safely claim that these were "already awash with their greatest profits" since OPEC had unleashed its thunderbolt in 1973. From that it was an easy transition to this characterization of the terms of the debate in Congress: "The congressional battle over the windfall profits tax and the energy security trust fund will be a classic confrontation pitting the common and public good against the enormous power of a well-organized special interest."[15]

So far, so good. But many considered that the president made a tactical error in asking for only 50 percent, and then dropping broad hints that he would be not displeased to see a higher rate imposed. Calling that a "dreadful mistake," Representative Charles Vanik (Dem.-Ohio) added: "To start off with the position you want to end up with is a mistake." As if to rectify it, the Ways and Means Committee in mid-June raised the rate to 70 percent. Two oil-state Democrats, James J. Jones (Oklahoma) and J. J. Pickle (Texas), went down to defeat with all twelve Republicans (22–14).

In the full House, however, they made a remarkable recovery. Ways and Means asked for a closed rule, admitting of no revisions on the floor, but the Rules Committee declined. A substitute measure put up by Democrat James Jones in alliance with Louisiana Republican W. Henson Moore not only reduced the tax to 60 percent but cut off its whole application in 1990, whereas the president sought a permanent tax to recapture for the general public a large part of all future price increases by the OPEC cartel. Although opposed by no less a person than the chairman of Ways and Means, Al Ullman (Dem.-Oregon), the substitute passed easily (236–183). Southern Democrats (in the proportion of three to one) went a long way toward making that victory possible by joining hands with all but ten of the Republicans.

Even so, the House version, in the eyes of Senator Robert Dole (Rep.-Kansas), remained "punitive." Anticipating difficulty even with senators of his own party, President Carter invited the whole Finance Committee to the White House in late July to discuss the tax and plead for swift action. The committee's chairman, Russell Long, yet another oil-state Democrat, promised that Congress would complete the business in October, and held out hope of a bill that the president would be "pleased to sign." Possibly doubting that, Mr. Carter held a news conference the following day, and predicted a "massive struggle" in the Senate, where "the oil lobby" would focus its attention. He appealed to the people to speak up, especially to senators, saying he did not think he could "prevail alone here in Washington with an oil lobby working quietly unless the American people let their voices be heard."[16]

A "massive struggle" there may have been behind the scenes, but overtly, "massive inaction" would have been the apter term. Little was achieved by early October. But then came a stunning victory—for the oil lobby. By 12–8, the Senate Finance Committe destroyed the link between the windfall tax and future OPEC price increases. It did so by putting a cap on the total amount of revenue to be secured by the tax: once that was reached, it would signal the end of play. Needless to say, this amendment was offered by a senator from an oil-producing state—Malcolm Wallop (Rep.-Wyoming).

Still not satisfied, the Finance Committee soon proceeded, by various other devices, to cut down the proportion of the windall profits to be "recaptured" for the public. That would be about half if the president had his way (rather more than half if the House had its). Now the Senate reduced the "cut" to rather more than one quarter. Thus roles were tending to be reversed. The House Ways and Means Committee had "gone strong," only to be weakened on the floor. The Senate Finance Committee, predictably, "went weak": could they be strengthened on the floor? Appreciating the possibility, the president, in late October, appealed to the whole Senate to improve the committee version of the bill. If not, he warned, the administration would "shift our combat zone" to the House-Senate conference committee. If the final result were not satisfactory, then: "We'll move toward additional proposals to the Congress which could be quite punitive to the oil industry."[17]

What were the chances of success on the floor of the Senate? Virtually every senator was approached (an administration spokesman revealed). On the other hand, the tax was an "extremely intensely lobbied piece of legislation."[18] So as late as mid-November, about half the senators were still reckoned to be uncommitted. Toward the end of the month, however, some commitments began to be made, notably an exemption from the tax of the first thousand barrels a day of independent companies' production. This privilege was secured by Lloyd Bentsen, the Texas Democrat, but with the support of Democrats of a very different hue, such as Alan Cranston (California), Gary Hart (Colorado), John Culver (Iowa), George McGovern (South Dakota), and Frank Church (Idaho). One hypothesis for their unusual vote, advanced by political analyst Ann Pelham,[19] is that they (and the others) were up for reelection in 1980 and had no wish to attract the attention of some out-of-state oil company PAC. If so, it was not enough to save the last three named, who went down to defeat in 1980, victims in part of intervention by conservative political action committees.

The roving Senators returned to the fold, however, on the question of raising the tax rate to 75 percent (from 60 percent) on oil discovered between 1973 and 1978, an amendment put up by two members of the Finance Committee, Bill Bradley (Dem.-New Jersey) and John Chaffee (Rep-Rhode Island). "Confiscatory," cried their chairman Russell Long (who, as columnist Mary McGrory had written earlier in the year, "never met with an oil company he didn't like," and who, according to another journalist, Jack Newfield, "personally owns $1.2 million in oil and gas property").[20] But, taking a national as distinct from a parochial (or special interest) view, the proposal was not unreasonable. The oil at issue (or risk) was upper-tier, or "new" oil (after 1972, before 1979). In May 1979 it had been selling for about $13 a barrel. Decontrolled, it would be rising toward the OPEC price, which was about $18 in that same month. Moreover, by administrative juggling and redefinition, much lower-tier (or "old") oil was to be *treated as* "new," and *it* was then selling at $5.85.[21] From that "cumulative" windfall, the American public (or taxpayers) surely deserved a very large cut.

Even the Senate could hardly deny that, especially as, by November, the OPEC price was more like $25.[22] By a majority of nineteen, the Senate late that month backed Bradley-Chaffee. But Robert Dole (Rep.-Kansas) and other oil-state senators then threatened a filibuster, which, however, was not mounted at that time, and the Senate went on in early December to give positive approval of Bradley-Chafee by an even more comfortable majority of twenty-three.

Like a dark cloud overhead, the filibuster eventually "burst," descending on those who, like Abraham Ribicoff (Dem.-Connecticut), wanted to extend the windfall tax even to newly discovered oil (i.e., post-1978), but only at 20 percent (of the windfall component).[23] "Ludicrous" was Senator Long's characterization this time. The filibuster worked. In private negotiations held mainly in the office of majority leader Senator Robert Byrd, it was agreed to cut that rate to 10 percent—20 percent being kept for two other, less significant types of oil—and narrow the application (by raising the base price to $20. See note 23 again).

On these and other matters the Senate put its seal of approval (about three to one) in mid-December (so much for Senator Long's promise to President Carter to have it done with in October). The upshot was that the Senate representatives went into conference with windfall "items" expected to bring in $178 billion by 1990. But the House's total stood at $277 billion. Whether because the senators at least must have been tired, even exhausted, or more generally because the inescapable Christmas vacation was looming up, the conferees promptly split the difference, taking the midpoint of $227 billion. But where, from the Senate's standpoint, would the extra $49 billion ($227 − $178) be coming from? Senator Dole was justified in his complaint: setting a revenue total without settling the details was like "getting your dinner before you read the menu." Consistently, he was one of three Senate conferees to vote against the compromise, which had the backing, however, of Russell Long and Lloyd Bentsen, and, with them, a majority.

So the position by Christmas 1979 was that the Senate had indeed, of its own volition, strengthened its Finance Committee's decisions, going into Conference with $40 billion more than the committee had proposed ($178 − $138). But then the "ante" had been raised by $49 billion ($178 + $49 = $227). The House, on the other hand, had "lost" about the same amount: what would they drop or cut? Everyone must have dispersed for the festivities having no real inkling of the answers to those perplexing questions.

A few days before Christmas the president took action that was intended to stimulate an early resolution of those perplexities. "In a move to twist the arm of Congress" (wrote Helen Thomas, of United Press International), he announced on December 22 that he would hold up one part of the decontrol scheme due to come into effect on January 1. This concerned marginal, mainly "old" (pre-1973) oil, four-fifths of which had been decontrolled since the previous June, enabling the price to rise from some $6 a barrel to $13. It was the remaining fifth (about 1 percent of total domestic production) that was due to be "let go" in January. That meant about a hundred thousand barrels a day, so the postponement would cost some producers about $700,000 a day.

Ms. Thomas identified the owners of these marginal wells as the independents. But on the same day Ernest Holsendolph of the *Times* reported that majors were also among the owners, and that, except for Alaska, all oil-producing states would be affected. If so, the presidental "message" could be interpreted as extending to the industry as a whole and from them to Congress generally and the conferees in particular. Either way, the president made it clear (if only to Ms. Thomas) that he now considered that "the windfall profits tax was an essential companion to decontrol."[24]

By late January 1980 it was clear that, despite their successful lobbying of the Senate, the independents were going to have to bear the burden of about 46 percent of the "extra" $49 billion.[25] Virtually exempted by the Senate, the independents would now have to pay the tax even on newly discovered oil. The fact that this would be at a special low rate would hardly have comforted them.

For the oil interests as a whole, a crucial issue, with billions of dollars at stake, turned on the question of whether to stop applying the windfall tax on a certain date (1990, the House had decreed) or after a certain sum of money had been reached (the Senate's position). Obviously, if OPEC kept on jacking up world prices, the second method would bring the tax to an end comparatively soon, and the percentage recovered for the nation would fall. That the House would not countenance: As Ways and Means chairman, Al Ullman, put it: "We are not willing to put the oil companies on the side of oil price increases."[26] Ultimately, the idea of a date was retained: a three-year tapering off starting at the beginning of 1988, provided that the $227 billion had been recovered by then. If not, the tax would be retained, but the rundown would start in any case at the beginning of 1991.

As for the open conflict between the majors and the independents, which was reflected in and through Congress, the independents' loss of exemption for newly discovered (post-1978) oil (and some other categories) was all the more painful because the rate settled upon was, at 30 percent, higher than Senator Ribicoff had originally proposed. On the other hand, they would pay only 50 percent on the first thousand barrels a day of production from pre-1979 wells as against the general rate of 70 percent (of the *windfall* component). They also received other special treatment of the kind. Moreover, in calculating the amount of windall tax due, they were to get a special concession on top of a special concession. From chapter 9 you will recall that, among oil companies, only the independents in 1975 were left in possession of the oil depletion allowance. But surely the 22 percent deduction from gross income would *not* be permitted when it came to calculating the windfall profits tax? Would such a deduction not go against the objective of the tax, which was to recover for the nation some considerable part of the $1 trillion (thousand billion) windfall profits expected to accrue to the oil companies over a decade as a consequence of decontrol? The White House thought so. But a move (by the Vermont Democrat, Senator Patrick J. Leahy) to stop the independents from "charging" depletion allowance had already been made in the Senate and failed by twenty votes. Now it survived the conference. This concession was estimated to be worth $13 billion to the independents.[27] Little wonder that Representative Sam Gibbons (Dem.-Florida) should comment: "If the House conferees can be criticized for anything, it is for being far too generous to the independent producers."[28]

Even so, friends of the independents fought on in both the House and Senate after the conference reports had been sent there. What they wanted, still, was exemption (up to a certain level), a battle seemingly won at the end of 1979. Senator Henry Bellmon (Rep.-Oklahoma) even encouraged such producers from his state to demonstrate in Washington before the Senate vote. They came, camping out on the Mall below Capitol Hill. They may have watched him, with other senators such as David Boren (a Democrat but from the same state) and Robert Dole, the Kansas Republican, hold up the vote for a few days. The two last-named even wanted the issue to go back to the Finance Committee for fifteen days, which the majority leader, Robert Byrd, resisted, saying it would just give "the lobbyists the opportunity to work everybody over." In the end it was about two to one for approving the conference report (it had been more like three to one in the House).

Despite all the sound and fury, the companies, majors and independents, had come out of the year-long struggle rather well. As Senator Long put it: "Those who have to pay the tax can afford it. You're not going to see anybody applying for welfare because he has to pay this tax." Or, as William Winpisinger, head of the Machinists Union, had remarked about a year earlier, there would be no windfall profits tax without a windfall.[29] A few months after that "a longtime Washington oilwatcher" also hit the nail squarely on the head. Commenting on what had happened in Ways and Means and in the full House, he said, "When you consider that any windfall tax under 100 percent means a profit, they made out like bandits on the floor. But don't expect them to let on they're happy. That's part of the game."[30]

CHAPTER 13
AMERICA:
"A Special-Interest
Democracy"?

Now we have come full circle and there has to be a reckoning. What, in the end, are we to make of Mr. Magruder's rueful reflections that served as a text for this inquiry? How should we evaluate the sharp criticisms and gloomy foreboding of those distinguished Americans in different walks of life who later wrote or spoke much as he had on that occasion, although not otherwise of his way of thinking, nor "driven" by having played a part in the Greek tragedy that was Watergate? In short, to what extent is America a special-interest democracy?

Even to pose such questions is to realize that this part is the hard part. In groping for answers, you (and, in the last resort, the burden of judgment *is* on you) should be in no doubt as to what a book of this kind can and cannot accomplish. It is essentially a teaching book, in more senses than one. Without emulating an encyclopedia, it conveys a substantial amount of basic information, as in the long chapters about the groups themselves and the methods and techniques they employ. But it is also designed to teach in a general liberal-arts sense by replaying the remarks of various persons of distinction, several of whom apparently spoke with authority, and proceeding to place those remarks in a proper context. When that was done, the clear blue sky of plausible commentary clouded over, simplicity turned into complexity, and some relevant facts even became questionable or at least hard to determine.

With that you should have been emancipated in some degree from the tyranny of Authority, from allowing the social status of the judge (eminent journalist, head of a famous university, experienced public official, etc.) to carry too much weight in your acceptance of the judgment. This is not to say that the views of those who were quoted in the opening chapter were wrong, only (it was and will be suggested) incomplete—as they, hemmed in at the time by the usual constraints of occasion and purpose, might well agree.

More specifically, this book is designed to teach about interest groups in other than the obvious sense. One inference to be drawn from part 3 is that interest groups do not constitute a political sun around which some planets revolve. In other words, in this book one is not projecting an interest-group theory of politics in which "everything" is (or appears to be) reducible to groups, including explanations of public policy. On the contrary, if the analysis of the type presented in part 1 were carried further, we could be travelling in the direction of a theory of interest-group politics. Readily acknowledging that interest groups constitute only part of the political universe, the propounder of a theory of interest-group politics attempts to explain that part. Thus, in the first section of this book, five umbrella categories containing "variables" were said to explain in very broad terms the pattern of interest-group activity, i.e., a part of the whole. Whether or not such a structure of explanation holds up, it is clearly directed toward a phenomenon that is partial and limited and in that sense is both partial and limited itself. By contrast, an interest-group theory of politics, as in the landmark book by Arthur F. Bentley (1908) and in the derivative work of such moderns as Earl Latham's *The Group Basis of Politics,* is (or would like to be) holistic and all-embracing.[1]

In focusing upon interest-group activity, one chose to deal with a relatively small number of instances in some depth rather than follow the standard textbook format of a larger number of instances briefly introduced then quickly banished. The in-depth procedure would seem to have some advantages, revealing more of the forces at work and inserting time into our perceptions and judgments. For the study of issues, especially their resolution, on a particular date may easily distort our assessment of America as a special-interest democracy. For example: the study of percentage depletion conveys one impression in the period 1926–69, another in 1969–75, yet another 1975 into the mideighties. Focusing on the earliest period, we fear that the characterization is true. Focusing on the most recent period, we are encouraged to believe that the system is not beyond redemption and may yet be reclaimed for "real" democracy. At least it weakens the first impression and prompts us to ask under what conditions an appropriate change may be secured.

That part of the book is of course exploratory: the case studies as such can *prove* nothing.[2] Here one simply selected some cases to fit the provisionally agreed-upon types of policy, using politically significant issues, or ones that had points for this analysis, to illuminate the play of forces generally and of interest groups in particular. Recall, too, that distributive and regulatory policies were stressed ("weighted") to match, roughly, what is commonly believed to be their frequency. That might prove to be another source of bias. Altogether, one's selection, although defensible in an introductory work, could not avoid being arbitrary. So the case studies are not conclusive, only suggestive.

Still, the book has to be taken as a whole. Looking back over the ground we have covered, you would surely find reason to agree that some part of the indictment of America (at least in the form reported in our epigraph) lacks merit:

> We don't have a democracy of the people now. We have a special-interest democracy. We have the auto lobby, the oil lobby. The individual has no way of appealing to the government.
> The true democracy is where the individual is able to affect his own situation. That is not true in this country anymore. The big lobbies can do it, but the individual can't.

Whether that referred to individuals who attempt to organize but are defeated (unlike the "big lobbies"), or to truly unattached or unaffiliated individuals is not clear. But even these can and do "do something" about their own situation, according to indications in the case studies. Those well placed to judge saw a taxpayers' revolt behind the Tax Reform Act of 1969, which "dented" the oil depletion allowance for the first time in over forty years. Even if this, and perhaps the whole act, was symbolic in the Edelman (and Oppenheimer) sense, it had been stimulated "from outside." This, unlike the later revolts (such as Proposition 13 in California and Proposition 2½ in Massachusetts) appears not to have been organized but rather reflected a changing public mood, picked up on the sensitive antennae of President Nixon and especially of Wilbur Mills as chairman of the Ways and Means Committee. Perhaps we may say that individuals "did something" by speaking up—critical comments in public and angry remarks to congresspersons.

The 1975 Act (which, you will recall, chopped off the majors' depletion allowance) is even more germane. In 1974, the individual as voter had sent altogether seventy-five freshmen Democrats to the House, many of them distinctly liberal. One general consequence was that the 94th Congress turned into "the most partisan in recent years" (David W. Brady would write in 1980).[3] What the voter had had in mind doubtless included "Watergate, campaign finance reform, Vietnam."[4] But since many of the freshman Democrats had run against the oil companies, their election may be thought of as preparing the ground for the assault on oil depletion. In the usual roundabout way of elections, the individual as voter had "done something."

These are only straws in the wind, but they point us in the right direction, as contemporary scholarship covering elections and public opinion confirm. As against the helpless individual, Gerald Pomper and Susan Lederman pose *the protective meddler*—the individual who, "stimulated by external events," is from time to time moved "to meddle" in elections, voting for his or her specific interests. As they summed up the literature in 1980: "The evidence of electoral studies, then, is that the voters, by their meddling in elections, can protect themselves."[5] Even more apt for our discussion of special-interest democracy and the place of the individual is this earlier summing up by Alan Monroe, who has researched questions of public opinion and public policy: "The electoral process is a meaningful mechanism for increasing the degree of democracy in the political system."[6]

In this there is a lesson for all of us. To a very considerable degree the study of interest groups is the study of what James Rosenau called *citizenship between elections*.[7] The division of intellectual labor is convenient and defensible, especially when one wishes to relate interest groups to public policy (since the impact of elections on policy is indirect). But, by the same token, such limits to inquiry tend to distort *some* perceptions and judgments. This is no more a problem for us than for those who focus upon Congress, or the bureaucracy or even the presidency, but it is something to carry in our mind.

As to the individual's being able, between elections, to affect his or her own situation or to find an organizational way of "appealing to the government," the case studies provide instances: NORML, and the Energy Action Committee opposing the deregulation of natural gas. A great many other instances cropped up in chapter 7, supporting an observation made long ago by Nelson Polsby about America's being "fractured into a congeries of hundreds of small special-interest groups."[8] Even in the realm of organizations-*of*, dominated by interest groups that enjoy a "natural" functional base, individuals were seen to have found a way: elderly ones, females, and blacks, most obviously. Individuals pursuing causes (organizations-*for*) have produced a rich harvest, ranging from the Campaign to Stop Government Lying, and Action for Children's Television, to the National Gun Control Center and the National Coalition for the Homeless.

Think in particular of the groups that have come to cast exceptionally long shadows over the national landscape, e.g., the ten associations ranged around the law governing abortion. "Dissenting" individuals set out to defy or change the law and change it they did. They included:

1. *The referrers*, who referred women to doctors who would perform abortions. One woman stood on busy streetcorners in San Francisco handing out mimeograph sheets bearing the appropriate information. In New York City a man started a referral service. There, too, Protestant clergymen and Jewish rabbis established (May 1967) the Clergy Consultation Service on Abortion. This was a referral service, the need for which had been earlier remarked upon by a Baptist minister and two Episcopalian clergymen.

2. *The militants,* including some men (e.g., Mr. William Baird, in Boston and Long Island) but mainly women. A representative figure was Mrs. Patricia Maginnis, active in California from 1961 and a great seeker after confrontation with the authorities.

3. *The Benthamites*, named (for this context) after Jeremy Bentham (1748–1832), the Oxford-educated philosopher, a lawyer by profession who devoted most of his life, however, to the reform of the English legal and political system, in which he and his followers were immensely successful. Here the name may be applied to those who cast a cool, sceptical eye at contemporary social institutions and arrangements, who write about these in a critical vein and produce practical reform proposals for which they may actively campaign. A representative figure was Mr. Lawrence Lader of New York City, a prolific writer advocationg reform (as well as an activist). But there were also those individuals who founded the Association for the Study of Abortion (at the pure research end of this continuum), the Society for Humane Abortion, and the California Committee on Therapeutic Abortion, all creations of the midsixties. Above all, perhaps, there were those who used the good offices of the old-established (1923) American Law Institute (ALI) to produce a model law (a very Benthamite thing to do). According to their plan, the main criterion for an abortion would be serious impairment of the woman's physical and mental health, as distinct from saving her life (the rule in almost all states). Grave physical deformity or mental retardation in the baby would be another criterion, as would conception from rape or incest.

It was this ALI plan that served as a battering-ram to break down the walls of the states,[9] starting in Colorado in 1967, when what Mr. Lader has called an "inside" strategy proved effective, i.e., winning over a small number of state legislators.[10] That worked in North Carolina too. California quickly followed. In 1968 and 1969 seven more states reformed along the same ALI pattern. This happened so swiftly (and three other states would "fall" the ALI way in 1970–73) that it can hardly be attributed simply to interest groups along conventional lines. The development looks more like a great wave. Even so, much of its energy may be fairly traced to the efforts of individuals who organized themselves to change their situation, one test (according to Mr. Magruder) of "a true democracy."

Remarkable as the advance had been, it failed to satisfy some individuals, who set out to transcend the ALI model and secure total repeal (i.e., remove all restrictions), which opponents would later characterize as "abortion on demand." Their vehicle was the National Association for Repeal of Abortion Laws (NARAL, an acronym that now means National Abortion Rights Action League), which got under way in Chicago in February 1969. The first meeting of its steering committee took place in New York about a week later in the Madison Avenue office of Mr. Stewart Mott, heir to a General Motors fortune, which he drew on to get the movement started.[11] (Note, recalling chapter 3, how the Olsonian problem—if indeed perceived as a problem—was in part overcome.) This far more ambitious drive gained some legislative ground at the beginning of the seventies but soon faltered. The legislative highwater mark was reached in 1972.

Under the American system, however, as one door closes, another can usually be made to open: at least, it offers far more opportunities and alternatives than any other western system. A perceptive contemporary observer,

Professor Judith Blake, had already remarked in 1971 that the Supreme Court might then provide "the only road to rapid change" in abortion policy.[12] And so it proved. After a meandering journey (1971–72) through several federal and state supreme courts, whose judges overturned a number of state abortion laws, the destination was reached on January 22, 1973, with *Roe v. Wade*, buttressed by *Doe v. Bolton*. These two rulings legalized abortion by invalidating state laws either prohibiting it or restricting it to specific circumstances—fundamentally, to save the life of the woman. "Jane Roe" masked the identity of a single but pregnant woman who had brought suit against Texas because she could not get a legal abortion there. "Mary Doe" was a married woman living with another man after being abandoned by her husband. She had challenged the relatively liberal Georgia statute.[13]

The role of energetic individuals may also be seen in the aftermath of the Supreme Court decision. This shocked opponents into creating the National Right to Life Committee (NRLC) out of the antiabortion organizations in the states. More germane for our theme here is the founding in 1977 of the Life Amendment Political Action Committee. Dissatisfied with the NRLC, Mr. Paul Brown (who, with his wife Judie, had long been active in opposition) gave up his job as manager of a K-Mart store to launch this more ambitious and uncompromising body. Then aged forty, he would recall: "For the first nine months, the organization consisted of me, and for three of those months I got no pay."[14] Intervening in the 1978 elections, such organizations were widely believed to have contributed to the defeat of some well-known U.S. senators.

Many other instances of individual initiative may be gleaned by glancing back to chapter 7, but perhaps the most remarkable example of all is afforded by the *consumerism* of about the midsixties to the late seventies. That this was something new is suggested by the fact that the term did not find a place in Webster's dictionary until 1971 (report Anderson, Brady and Bullock).[15] What that newness consisted in, we need not stop to consider. The point is that consumerism, as the world knows, was the handiwork very largely of one man, Mr. Ralph Nader. Others prepared the way, notably Senator Paul Douglas, who had labored long for his truth-in-lending bill, so that borrowers should be told the true rate of interest they would be paying.[16] Others contributed at the time, including adjutants who proved worthy of the captain. But that he was the captain who picked the terrain and led the attack is hardly open to doubt. Or, changing to journalist Linda Charlton's metaphor in 1978: "He is the unchallenged 'father' of the consumer movement."[17]

In any case, the number of individuals "who made a difference" was as small as the resulting "conglomerate" was large. By 1978 the Naderite peak, Public Citizen, claiming 1.1 million supporters, embraced six major components, including a lobbying unit, a litigation group, an aviation consumer action project (baggage liability and overbooking, with consequent "bumping"), an energy project, and two groups handling research into health questions and tax reform. In addition, there were a number of spin-offs that might be regarded as satellites.

Beyond all this, other signs of individual initiative could easily be discerned—the public interest groupings, which, even as late as 1978, were "often . . . popularly thought of as 'Nader' "[18] but were in fact more extensive, including (David Vogel would say that year)

> a variety of law firms, research centers, lobbying groups and membership organizations that are distinguished by their commitment to public policies that do not selectively or materially benefit those who support them.[19]

Of these there may have then been as many as 150, about half of them specializing in public interest law. Even if the total reached "only" one hundred (another estimate), that represented a most luxuriant flowering. Surely, the president of Columbia University (William J. McGill) had reason for saying (in 1979):

> We are living through one of the most remarkable periods in our history. This bewildering struggle of advocacy groups in the United States is producing amazement elsewhere in the world. The amazement is partly admiration for the creativity of our political system and partly apprehension that we may one day tear ourselves apart in the enthusiasm of our contentiousness.[20]

In the last part of the second sentence, President McGill sounded a bit like President Bok of Harvard and some others quoted in the opening chapter. But the immediate point is that those advocacy groups that caused amazement, and the great many other interest groups for which the term "advocacy" is less apt, were created by a small number of persons excited by an idea and imbued with the energy, skill and determination to make something of it. So we are tempted to conclude, as against Mr. Magruder, that the individual can (a) appeal to the government, and (b) affect his or her situation by organizing between elections (as well as by voting).

However, it is now clearer than it was to begin with that (a) and (b) are not interchangeable, but rather make up two criteria: interest groups might enjoy (a) without achieving (b). In other words, the "bewildering stuggle of advocacy groups" might achieve catharsis (relief of tension) rather than the substance of policy. The evidence so far presented bears principally upon (a); what about (b)? Thus we are led into questions of responsiveness and of the influence of interest groups. For, as J. Roland Pennock wrote a generation ago, the idea of responsiveness "is central to any study of politics. It is the counterpart of influence. The person or group that exerts influence is influential; the person or group on whom it is exerted is responsive."[21]

As a word or term (the concept is trickier), *responsiveness* hardly requires a formal definition. But *influence* had better be defined as that "relation among actors in which one actor induces other actors to act in some way they would not otherwise act."[22] Note well that that is what many writers would designate as "power." Indeed, its author, Robert Dahl, had earlier (1957) defined power in just that way, but in later work he equated "power" with *coercive* influence and "attached" it (so to speak) to the state, in the tradition of the English philosopher, John Locke.[23] In keeping with the provisional distinction (opening chapter) between society and state, one is here reserving "influence" for what interest groups *exert* on the authorities. But be aware that usage varies from one writer to another.

Note also that this concept of power (the term favored by the critics about to be mentioned) is at bottom interpersonal, and that a rival concept has been proposed. This, if it gained acceptance, would enable the critics to make an "end run" around assessments of power in America based upon policy making or decision making, and to offer a different interpretation. For example: the big banks of America had, in 1981, "an effective U.S. income tax rate of 2.3 percent" (*Fortune* and others reported).[24] The critics would like to be able to say that the big banks enjoyed power (influence in the usage to be followed here) even if it could not be readily traced on the screen of policy making, or decision making. The idea does have a certain attraction. But here one intends to cling to the traditional, and still the commoner, conception.

CHAPTER 14
INFLUENCE AND
RESPONSIVENESS

These are dauntingly large subjects even for the limited purpose in hand. In the hope of gaining one or two insights, we shall "walk around" each in turn, bearing in mind (from Professor Pennock) that they are reciprocals. No doubt, even as late as 1982, Charles Wiggins and William Browne were right to say that "systematic inquiry" into the "influence of interest groups is long on theory and short on data." They themselves had studied a state legislature in the tradition of Wilder Crane; Wahlke, Eulau, Buchanan, and Ferguson; and Harmon Zeigler and Michael Baer, among others.[1] The Wiggins-Browne research catches the eye all the more because it makes use of a Lowian typology—if this is dead, as many critics say, it evidently refuses to lie down—modified by Salisbury-Ripley-Hayes. They found, for example, that interest groups (in Iowa) were particularly active in the area of regulatory policy, where their influence matched their degree of activity, or involvement.[2] But interesting as this research tradition is, it is of no immediate assistance to us because we have committed ourselves to a broad judgment of the character of American democracy as seen through the prism of the special interests.

There is another research tradition, sociological in origin, that offers us the broad characterization we should like to possess. C. Wright Mills was its leader, and G. William Domhoff and Michael Parenti are among its practitioners. Representative titles include *The Power Elite, The Higher Circles,* and *Democracy for the Few*. As expressed by Mills in 1956, probably *the* central theme has been:

> America is now in considerable part more a formal political democracy than a democratic social structure, and even the formal political mechanics are weak.[3]

That sounds like something Mr. Magruder might have said. In fact Mills cared little about special interests in our sense. These, interacting especially with Congress—itself (he said) "a tangle of interests"—occupied only the middle reaches of power: the "big decisions" were made elsewhere, as in the executive, one component of an interrelated power elite encompassing the corporations, the military and the great law firms of Washington and New York City.[4]

One's own view is that "the middle level" of power does not deserve to be so quickly ejected from consideration. Indeed, one goes much of the way with sociologist-social philosopher Daniel Bell in commenting on this dismissal of "middle level" policy making and policies as rather unimportant, hardly worth the effort of studying: "*Yet are these not the stuff of politics*, the issues which divide men and create the interest conflicts that involve people in a sense of ongoing reality: labor issues, race problems, tax policy, and the like? Is this not the meaning of power to people as it touches their lives?"[5] Adding women to the men (who are divided), one would answer, "yes." However, one has no intention of taking part in this long-drawn-out controversy. It is enough to say that since the Wright Millsian tradition mainly focuses on "big decisions," particularly in foreign policy and defense, it cannot be of any direct assistance here, where one has concentrated on domestic policy and for the most part at a less rarefied level.

In the absence of general research directly usable as a check on the impressions gained from this relatively limited inquiry, we would do well to get back to basics. As economist Carl Kaysen, Robert Dahl, and Grant McConnell (among others) explained a long time ago, influence is typically influence over a certain range, or scope. The oil industry could "pull off" percentage depletion, and other tax privileges that indeed helped to make Dallas what it is today. But did it count in abortion law reform? Does it count on the issue of whether abortions should be on Medicaid, or whether parents should be informed when their pregnant teenage daughters go looking for an abortion? Did it count in the marijuana issue? The trend during the seventies was toward decriminalization in the states, eleven of which "replaced criminal penalties for personal use" by "minor citations and small fines, which are often not enforced." The trend was arrested in 1978, after which no state decriminalized. In 1982 possession remained an offence under federal law as well of course as in the remaining thirty-nine states.[6] Did the oil companies have anything to do with any of that?

If such issues are considered too remote from the oil companies' interests, what about federal elementary and secondary education policy? Here the influential core, among interest groups, has been said (by Norman C. Thomas and others)[7] to be the "big six"—the National Education Association and its five affiliates (school administrators, state school officers, school boards, state boards of education, congress of parents and teachers). Having grown very rapidly in the 1970s (and changed its character in the process from an association—essentially run by administrators and supervisors—to a union of teachers),[8] the NEA in the early 1980s was a massive body of about 1.75 million members looked after by some fourteen hundred full-time organizers across the land. A large annual budget supported a battalion of six hundred on Sixteenth Street in the fashionable northwest section of Washington,[9] including a government relations department of about two dozen, six of whom were lobbyists.[10] In addition, there were about thirty other, more specialized bodies based in Washington, not forgetting the NEA's rival, the half-million strong American Federation of Teachers (AFT).

Those cited were academic observers of federal education policy. For the view of an important public official, Mayor Koch of New York City (where the AFT is strong) may be quoted: "The education lobby is the strongest in the country. They are the most educated."[11]

Turning abruptly to federal health policy, one may again ask: what influence do the oil companies have on that? Take one component of it of enormous importance in the mideighties: the cost of Medicare. In the early eighties, Medicare hospital expenditures had been increasing at a rate of 18–20 percent annually.[12] By 1988 (the Congressional Budget Office estimated) the Medicare Hospital Insurance Trust Fund (financed from payroll taxes) would be bankrupt.[13] Now, in 1978–79 President Carter had tried to introduce mandatory controls on hospital costs. He was held up, and ultimately defeated, by what he called "the opposition of powerful lobbying groups." Everyone who followed health issues "knew exactly whom he was talking about," including at the head of the column the American Hospital Association (public and community hospitals) and the Federation of American Hospitals (proprietary, or profit-making, hospitals), with powerful back-up from the American Medical Association.[14] The help of the AMA, one hospital leader remarked, was "absolutely critical."[15]

Following that failure, hospital costs soared. By 1982 the Reagan administration was sufficiently perturbed to propose "prospective payment" in place of the current system of retrospective, or cost-based, reimbursement, by which the hospitals recover reasonable costs "after the event." The plan would entail a standard fee for each of the 467 diagnostic categories.[16] But once again the interest groups blocked the administration's path.

Conversely, neither the health lobby nor the education lobby ("strongest in the country") had anything whatever to do with percentage depletion, intangible drilling expenses, the foreign tax credit, the quota system that kept out foreign oil (and kept home prices up), deregulation of natural gas prices, synfuels policy, and so on and so forth. If you exclaim, "Of course not!" you will be showing your awareness of something that is not obvious to everyone, at least not "the other way around," i.e., when discussing the influence (power, such critics would say) of business generally and the corporations in particular over public policy. It was in just that context in 1959, even addressing distinguished scholars, that economist Carl Kaysen posed his questions: "The corporation: how much power? What scope?"[17]

The larger and still highly controversial question of "business as a system of power," as it was once comprehensively called, cannot be pursued. But *scope* as applied to interest groups generally has to be dealt with now. That scope, or policy range, would *tend* to be limited is something that the interrelated themes of chapter 2 should have led us to expect: differentiation of function, specialized knowledge and resources, the supporting values and beliefs ("bargaining," professionalism, etc.) and the like. Knowing that, we would surely hypothesize:

A.   function *tends* to determine scope
B.   scope *tends* to circumscribe influence.

For hypothesis A there is a great deal of evidence in the literature, but an elucidation and a qualification are necessary. First, *scope* has to be properly identified for the proposition to work. The "natural" scope of a corporation would include tax policy, monetary policy, labor law, occupational safety and so on. But some corporations took a stand on the hospital-cost-containment issue, a component of health policy. Did scope there "slip the leash" of (economic) function? No, because the policy concern derived from corporate payments of Blue Cross and other such insurance for their employees. Other policy ramifications (i.e., ostensible extensions of scope) may be less easy to identify but still derive from function. So: scope *does tend* to follow the contours of function, but the contours have to be traced correctly.

The qualification is that scope may truly (i.e., in fact) transcend function, being lifted over the normal boundary fence by ideals or commitment to some interest broader than the functional (or immediate group) interest. The concern of both United Auto Workers and AFL-CIO (among others in the labor field) for an array of consumer issues might be considered of that nature. So might some of the efforts (e.g., to influence school education) undertaken in the early eighties by the U.S. Chamber of Commerce, although that characterization would no doubt be still more controversial. Whether these are good examples or not, the point remains that scope is not invariably anchored to, and so restrained by, function.

In thinking about hypothesis B we can no longer afford to gloss over the distinction between being busy and being effective, or influential. To echo Shakespeare's *Macbeth:* does the strutting and fretting really get results, or does it amount to little more than "sound and fury, signifying nothing"? It is seldom easy to answer. But even if activity is converted fairly consistently into influence, this will not usually exceed scope. From that we may extract some comfort. For it would mean that influence is unlikely to extend far beyond function (recall A and B above). Since, in the *gesellschaft*-type society, function is highly differentiated, i.e., divided, influence is likely to be also. This tends to eliminate one of the most perturbing meanings that might be attached to "special-interest democracy." For wide-ranging influence exerted by a relatively small number of interest groups would, on the face of it, threaten to subvert the democratic order.

If that affords some comfort, it must not be allowed to induce complacency. Even a single, relatively narrow function may provide a basis for disproportionate influence on policy by the derivative interest groups. Should there be many such disportionately influential groups, then, even if each kept to a relatively narrow scope, we would still have the makings, but in a different sense, of a "special-interest democracy." Here, of course, we badly need to separate the wheat of influence from the chaff of mere activity. Research on that has yet to be done in the form and on the scale required for a broad judgment of American democracy. But something has been done on influence's counterpart, responsiveness (that component, or dimension, of democracy). So let us reflect a little on responsiveness in the hope of gaining a few insights that might sharpen our judgment.

RESPONSIVENESS

Responsiveness to *what*, exactly? One traditional answer was "the will of the people," a notion easy to make fun of because "the people" seemed to have no will worth talking about. However, with the invention of scientific polling, it became possible to point to something that might be passed off as the will of the people, or at least to identify opinions of a sort. One puts it that way because the "operation" is plagued by uncertainty. For example: did government respond to a will of the people for liberalization of the abortion law, and if so, on what terms? In June 1972 a Gallup poll asked respondents whether they agreed with the statement that "the decision to have an abortion should be made solely by a woman and her physician." The answers came:

AGREE	DISAGREE	NO OPINION
64%	31%	5%

Of the 31 percent, two out of three would have made an exception for a woman whose mental health was being put at risk.[18]

Whether respondents realized it or not, the principal finding meant abortion-on-request ("solely" by woman and doctor). Proponents were naturally elated, but was that the will of the people? Demographer Judith Blake would later report, from her review of the surveys conducted over twelve years (1965–77), that support for abortion-on-request never exceeded 31 percent.[19]

Contrast that with another Gallup poll taken in early December 1972, which turned upon this question:

> Would you favor or oppose a law which would permit a woman to go to a doctor to end pregnancy at any time during the first three months?

The answers were:[20]

	FAVOR	OPPOSE	NO OPINION
Nov. 1969	40%	50%	10%
Dec. 1972	46%	45%	9%

Was December's will the "same" as June's, only differently expressed? Or what?

There is another related problem: the will of the people (or public opinion) to which government is expected to respond presumably has to be "autonomous," or authentic. A Harris poll published in April 1973 asked a question on the legalization of abortion that had been asked twice in 1972 and once "recently," with these results:

	FAVOR	OPPOSE	
June 1972	48%	43%	(Compare
August 1972	42%	46%	Gallup poll of
Spring 1973	52%	41%	June 1972, above)

What may have happened here is a phenomenon that the Harris survey itself called the "crystallizing of public opinion" *after* the Supreme Court decision had been reached and publicized in late January 1973.[21] To the extent that, *as a direct result of the decision,* public opinion hardened, it lost part of its "autonomous" nature.[22]

To say all this is not to cast doubt on the reality of a trend in public opinion toward *some* liberalization (see the Gallup poll of December 1972, above). It was also broadly based in the sense of including substantial proportions of American Catholics, members of a church most adamant in its opposition to abortion under any circumstances whatever. Thus 31 percent of Catholics had been in favor in 1969; 36 percent in 1972. (Catholic opinion on legalization also appears to have moved after the Supreme Court decision: 36 percent in favor of legalization in August 1972; 40 percent, spring 1973. See Harris poll of April 1973 above.) But did government respond to that apparent change in public opinion? Some state legislatures did. Congress did not, and surely would not have dreamed of doing so, at least in the short run. As we know, it was the Supreme Court, often said to be the most unrepresentative part of the federal system, that broke "the cake of custom." But was it *responding* as distinct from *acting?* To answer affirmatively we should have to assume that the Supreme Court not only reads the election returns but studies the polls. In any case, it was the so-called unrepresentative, certainly unelected, branch of the federal government that apparently responded to a very gradual shift in the national structure of values and beliefs.

GUN CONTROL

The issue of gun control is well known to be one in which public opinion has been firmly established for a generation or more but without evoking a matching response by the federal government. As far back as 1938 Gallup reported that 79 percent supported mandatory registration of firearms, a result more or less repeated the following year. The data then vanish but are complete and consistent for more recent years (see Table 14-1).

That, surely, is as unambiguous an expression of public opinion as we can hope to elicit. The question of responsiveness is less easy to pursue. As Robert Weissberg pointed out in his lucid discussion, firearms control is, by tradition, a matter for state (or local) government. As with marijuana and abortion, the federal government comes on the scene rather late in the day (critics of the trend might retort that even then it was "too early"). The first federal landmark is the Gun Control Act of 1968, which among other things required interstate shipments to be licensed, serial numbers imprinted on firearms and a record kept of every ammunition sale. Attempts in the Senate in 1972 to have all guns registered and all owners licensed were "overwhelmingly defeated."[24] Three such drives between 1975 and 1980 were "aborted." In the meantime nine million new handguns had been produced (for a total in private hands of possibly fifty million), and thirty-five thousand of "our fellow Americans" had died in handgun murders.[25]

TABLE 14-1   Would You Favor or Oppose a Law Which Would Require a Person to Obtain a Police Permit Before He or She Could Buy a Gun?

	FAVOR	OPPOSE	NO OPINION
1959	75	21	4
1964	78	17	5
1965	73	23	4
1966	68	29	3
1967	73	24	3
1971	71	25	4
1972	71	25	4
1974*	72	28	—

When the question was in the form of agree/disagree with this: "Registration of all firearms should be required."

The attempt by the Treasury Department early in 1978 to introduce new regulations for tracing firearms is particularly instructive. These would have required uniform serial numbers on American-made guns and quarterly reports on sales from manufacturers and dealers, but not registration or personal information about purchasers. Some two hundred thousand letters landed on congresspersons' desks, eighteen to one against the proposed regulations. The House voted to cut $4.2 million from the budget of the Treasury unless it saw the error of its ways. It did, withdrawing the regulations.

Of the thwarting of the American people on this issue or, in other words, the utter lack of responsiveness of American government, there can be surely no doubt. But who or what is responsible? Commentators have often stressed the subcultural component, a form of *machismo*, or, since it might be female, assertiveness. As journalist Alistair Cooke once wrote about Texas, "possession of a gun is almost a token of virility or family pride."[26] That there is such a regional phenomenon, no one doubts, but too much can be made of it: the views of the American public as a whole are as unmistakable as Congress in particular has been unresponsive to them.

Here, unquestionably, special interests *have* got in the way, although their exact nature has been commonly misunderstood even by scholars, most of whom single out the National Rifle Association (NRA) as the perpetrator. Formed in the early 1870s, the NRA claim a following of three million, whose inner core is a dues-paying membership of about a third of that total. They certainly are an influential lobby, making a "massive effort" against the gun control bill of 1968 (when Robert Kennedy and Martin Luther King were assassinated, the former by a "Saturday night special"), and managing to keep it from being strong. After it was passed, they made a weak bill weaker by getting an exemption for ammunition for shotguns and most long rifles. The decision they won "exempting rimfire cartridges wipes out that section of the 1968 act." Their hand was behind the defeat of the proposed Treasury regulations in 1978 as well as the various congressional initiatives in the late seventies. As a senator justly remarked in 1965, the NRA is "one of the most formidable and effective lobbies in legislative history."[27]

The source of the NRA's power in Congress is partly subcultural or regional ("good liberals" from hunting states tend, on that issue, to march to a different drummer on their home ground), but once again campaign contributions come into it. In 1978 no fewer than 142 Representatives and 21 Senators took about half-a-million dollars from the NRA's Political Action Committee.[28] The NRA is clearly a very wealthy organization with assets of some $19 million and an annual budget of about $8 million.

What is commonly overlooked, however, is that the NRA is only a part of the relevant "special interest," the sporting tip to the iceberg of economic interests that benefit enormously from *the lack* of gun control. Alistair Cooke pointed this out back in 1965. The NRA had been urging members not to lose "the battle" against a would-be regulatory bill. Attorney General Katzenbach commented: "It is impossible for me to understand the NRA's view of what battle is being fought and what the stakes are." Mr. Cooke enlightened him: "Nobody has been tasteless enough to tell him, yet, that the battle is for the money orders of 35 million gun-owners; and the stakes are nothing less than a multimillion dollar business."[29]

Representative Michael Harrington (Dem.-Massachusetts) got it exactly right in 1974 when he pointed out that the NRA

> is not the sum of the gun lobby armada, however, but rather its highly visible and imposing flagship. Central to the lobby's unapparent economic power are the country's gun manufacturers (Remington Arms, Winchester, Browning Arms, Colt Industries, Smith and Wesson, Savage Arms, Sturn-Ruger, Daisy) and gun dealers (New York's dignified Abercrombie & Fitch, Interarmco in Virginia), which do an estimated annual business of $1.5 billion.

Nor did he fail to remark upon the organic connection between the two entities: "22 percent of the NRA's annual income flows from manufacturer and dealer advertising in *American Rifleman*."[30] Thus some portion of what is passed on to congresspersons by the NRA can be properly imputed to the manufacturers and dealers of firearms.

Nor does that exhaust the economic interests involved. Revealing the civic courage that might partly explain why he later found it more comfortable to go back home to practice law, Representative Harrington pointed out (in the "environmental decade") that conservation and wildlife preservation groups also formed part of the gun lobby, the National Wildlife Federation, the Wildlife Institute, and the Isaac Walton League among them. How to explain this "improbable environmental link"?

> Firearms hunters spend about $72 million a year on hunting licenses and $27 million a year in federal excise taxes on guns and ammunition, most of which is committed by state laws to conservation and wildlife programs.

So the gun lobby is broader and more of a hybrid than it has often been represented to be. Even so, its "kingpin" (as Stanford N. Sesser reported in 1972) is indeed the NRA. One can hardly dispute the characterization of Carl Perian, the former professor of criminology turned Senate staffer, who had much to do with the drafting of the 1968 Gun Control Act: "The NRA is a very efficient minority. Look at their new headquarters building and the money they spread around. If the NRA didn't exist, this country would be equal with all the civilized nations in the world in sharply restricting the use of ammunition and firearms."

And, he could have added, an American president might have escaped assassination. For Lee Harvey Oswald, presumptive assassin of President Kennedy, "purchased his rifle by mail order from an ad in *The American Rifleman*," the NRA magazine "financed largely through advertising by gun and ammunition makers" (according to the *Wall Street Journal*).[31]

In this policy area, then, Congress *is* indeed responsive, but *not* to the general public, the great majority in fact only to some very special interests. If this were a paradigm of the political process in America, we would indeed have a special-interest democracy. But is it generally true and if so why? This book, although reasonably reflective of the literature, does not assemble enough evidence for you to reach a final conclusion, so you are advised to read and discuss further. One's own judgment, based on wider reading than is reflected here, is that Leroy N. Reiselbach's proposition of long ago is essentially correct when we are focusing on policy making between elections. In a work devoted to the responsiveness of American institutions generally, Professor Rieselbach, an authority on Congress, wrote: "Congress is responsive, at least to organized interests."[32] Add in the undoubted ability of interest groups to gain access to, and the required result from, the higher levels of the administration, even the White House (dairy co-operatives, ITT etc.) and, cumulatively, there does appear to be a *prima facie* case for the charge that America is (to say the least) on the way to becoming a special-interest democracy. That case is surely stronger in the mideighties than it was when Professor Rieselbach and his colleagues at Indiana made their assessment in the late sixties.

In trying to puzzle out the other question—why?—let us keep focusing on Congress and confront the issue touched upon earlier: the comparative importance of the constituency variable and interest-group (and other) influence in the determination of congresspersons' specific voting decisions. It is far from easy to deal with. One authority on Congress, William J. Keefe, tells us that the evidence is "mixed"; another, Randall B. Ripley, that the patterns disclosed by the research "are less than crystal clear." That evidence may be reviewed in their work. Here one will simply draw on a notable piece of original research in the hope of helping that discussion along. One of the most distinguished attempts to determine the relative weight of the variables governing voting in fifteen "big votes" in the House of Representatives, reflecting some of the major issues of the sixties, was made in 1969 by John W. Kingdon. He presented constituency as "setting the general policy boundaries" within which the representative "must operate." One facet of that concerned industries important in the district. Thus a tobacco-state representative explained that many families in his district made a living on tobacco:

> If you could show me some way my people are going to eat if I vote against cigarettes, I'll do it.[33]

Professor Kingdon: "So you start with this constituency factor."

> It starts there and it ends there. That's all there is to it. If you don't, you aren't going to be around here very long. Not on something like this, where their livelihood is involved.

However, since the constituencies do not always speak so clearly, or just remain resoundingly silent, it turned out that fellow congresspersons had even more significance in influencing the votes (according to what Professor Kingdon was told in interviews). This did not leave much of a place for interest groups. Although spontaneously mentioned with considerable frequency, these were of major or determinative importance in the voting decision only about a quarter of the time (26 percent), compared with 47 percent for fellow congresspersons and 38 percent for constituency. Even then the groups had to be tied to the constituencies if they were to count, so the interviewees "repeatedly" asserted.[34]

So, in 1969 John Kingdon pointed us in the same direction as had, among others, Bauer and colleagues, whom, even in the 1981 edition of his book, he quotes with approval as to the "disadvantages and weaknesses of lobbying organizations." However, Professor Kingdon "tries out" the conclusions of Bauer et al., and others, including himself, on a high-level civil servant in Washington, who "snorts": "They don't know what they're talking about. Lobbies are really thick with congressmen. You better believe it."

That sounds more like the journalists and some economists, reinforcing the division line-up. So what *are* we to believe? Professor Kingdon did draw a sample of "big issues," thus revealing his interest in politics, not merely statistics. Still there might have been something odd about his fifteen "big votes." One notes, too, that he writes campaign contributions into the constituency variable, enhancing its value. Updating his work for the 1981 edition, he continues that treatment and even writes the single-issue groups of the seventies into the constituency variable. Thus the "four or five important contributors" activated by a lobbyist he interviewed are related to "a strong connection to members' constituencies." But, in the eighties at least, campaign contributions via PACs (and single-issue groups insofar as they contribute) are surely to be treated as an exogenous force, partly independent of constituency. Consider the implications of Table 14–2.[35]

TABLE 14–2 **The Ten Members of the U.S. House of Representatives and Senate Who Received Most in Contributions from 94 Oil Industry PACs During 1979–80**

SENATE		HOUSE	
Charles Grassley (R-Iowa)	$144,639	Jack Fields (R-Texas)	$77,354
Steven Symms (R-Idaho)	$142,330	Marge Roukema (R.-N.J.)	$47,500
James Abdnor (R.-S.D.)	$119,699	Denny Smith (R.-Ore.)	$46,381
Dan Quayle (R-Ind.)	$101,169	Frank Wold (R.-Va.)	$44,480
Frank Murkowski (R-Alaska)	$84,999	Cleve Benedict (R-W.VA.)	$41,981
Robert Kasten (R-Wisc.)	$67,681	Bobbi Fiedler (R-Calif.)	$37,981
Russell Long (D-La.)	$64,750	Gregory Carman (R-N.Y.)	$37,280
Arlen Specter (R-Penn.)	$57,481	Hal Daub (R-Neb.)	$34,480
Robert Dole (R-Kan.)	$51,020	James Coyne (R-Penn.)	$30,930
John P. East (R-N.C.)	$40,262	John Hiler (R-Ind.)	$29,531

One would of course be disappointed if Russell Long's name failed to appear there, or Robert Dole's; after all, they belong, respectively, to Louisiana and Kansas. But what is Iowa (in the person of Charles Grassley) doing at the top of the list? The "constituency" is corn and hogs, not oil and gas. As you see, Senator Grassley was closely followed by Senator Symms of Idaho, a state which historically is redolent of silver, and nowadays, of paper and lumber with potatoes. For this and related reasons it would seem that campaign contributions can no longer be treated simply as part of the constituency variable, a practice that Professor Kingdon continued even in 1981.[36] By then, surely, the historical connection had been broken. In the seventies, the spectacular growth of PACs alone has meant that, breaking their territorial bounds or bonds, interest groups now range far and wide.[37] Accordingly, they should be counted in part as a variable distinct from constituency, tending to restore the importance traditionally ascribed to them.

Take another bearing: for the same election, 241 congressional candidates each received $5000 or more from the oil and gas industry. At the outside (Bruce Oppenheimer had calculated) the total industry base was some 147 (117 Representatives plus 30 Senators). So what was going on? According to the National Committee for an Effective Congress, of the House incumbents who received $5000+ from industry PACs, 40 percent had committee or subcommittee assignments of great importance to the industry (such as Commerce and Energy; Ways and Means). Another 20 percent had committee assignments of lesser, but still considerable importance (Merchant Marine; Public Works; Science and Technology).[38]

Or narrow down to the Ways and Means Committee, once packed with to-the-death-defenders of the true faith in the oil depletion allowance. Of its thirty-five members, twenty-four received more than $280,000 from corporate PACS in the first half of 1981. This was not a period when substantial campaign contributions were to be expected, as Congress Watch pointed out. The five main beneficiaries had had no primary opposition and had sailed home in the general election with two-thirds of the vote. The leading beneficiary was Representative James Jones, Democrat of Oklahoma and chairman of the Budget Committee.[39] At least he hailed from a major oil-producing state, but only one of the other four was sitting on oil (in Illinois). Altogether, what counted was committee role, not constituency.

Confirmation of the tendency may be derived not only from what interest groups and lobbyists do but from what they say. In explaining to the Securities and Exchange Commission in 1975 their contribution to a congressman, the president and CEO of Ashland Oil stated flatly: "There would have been no contribution had he not been a member of the House of Representatives and ranking member of the Ways and Means Committee."[40]

In 1981 a former government official turned lobbyist was talking to journalist Rudy Abramson about the Washington lobbying establishment. He was anxious to dispel the notion, popular (he believed) outside Washington, "that Republicans never talk to Democrats, and Democrats never talk to Republicans, that it's striped pants against baggy pants."[41] In fact, the Washington lobbying establishment is tightly knit, enabling "Republican insiders" to prosper during periods of Democratic dominance, and vice versa:

> The good lobbyists know that party lines don't count for much anymore. Their stock-in-trade is raising money for members of the Senate Finance Committee plus the Banking Committee and the Ways and Means Committee in the House.

So, in the seventies and eighties if not before, campaign contributions *by interest groups* surely ought to be treated in some degree as "detached" from the constituency variable. To *what* degree one is not in a position to say, but it seems likely to be substantial, given modern direct-mail, computerized solicitation and the "mobility" of PACs. As to effectiveness, we should surely stop accepting without question the conventional wisdom (put about by congresspersons, interest groups and lobbyists as well as too many political scientists) that all a campaign contribution secures is access. Never very plausible, it is far less so today, following the astonishing disclosures of "corporate Watergate," supported obliquely by the "Koreagate" and ABSCAM revelations. Consider the nature of oil-company contributions to the reelection of President Nixon in 1972[42] (see Table 14–3).

Think of what was entailed: bogus subsidiaries created, sending money (over $5000) to a foreign country without reporting it, slipping the money back into the county illegally, the mislabeling of accounts, false bookkeeping, etc., as well, of course, as "simple" breaches of the law on campaign contributions. Would corporate executives have gone to such lengths by such devious means, breaking the law every step of the way, to contribute such large sums of money *just for access?*

Think, too, of the new legalized trend. For the 1980 elections, the oil industry alone (counting 190 PACs) contributed $6 million to House and Senate candidates. If that was just for access, the corporate executives and lobbyists should surely be sued by their stockholders. For the 1978 elections, the maritime unions alone contributed about $1,150,000: *just for access?* Recall the issue of cargo-preference legislation (chapter 1): what are reasonable people to

TABLE 14–3

COMPANY	TOTAL CONTRIBUTION	SECRET CONTRIBUTION
Gulf Oil	$1,176,500	$1,132,000
Getty Oil	179,292	77,500
Standard Oil of California	166,000	102,000
Sun Oil	157,798	60,000
Phillips Petroleum	137,000	100,000
Exxon	127,747	100,672
Ashland Oil	103,500	100,000

conclude? Consider, too, the case of hospital-cost containment, which President Carter attempted to secure as the no. 1 priority in the 1979 battle against inflation. In November of that year, an amendment backed by the American Medical Association to the president's proposal passed the House 234–166. It simply called for more research, a harmless provision. Was it coincidence that 202 of the 234 had recently received altogether some $1,640,000 in campaign contributions from the AMA? Was it a coincidence that all but two of the top 50 House beneficiaries of AMA money (1976 and 1978)—the ingrates were Representatives Gladys Spellman of Maryland and Carroll Hubbard, Jr. of Kentucky—voted for the AMA-backed amendment (in effect, side-tracking cost containment)? Was it coincidence that of the 48 freshman representatives who voted for the amendment, 27 had been well supplied for their campaign by the AMA? It can also be shown that, of the 166 opposers, 44 had received no AMA money and the rest "substantially smaller" sums as compared with those who voted *for*.[43]

Occasionally, a member of Congress is bold enough to pierce the "rhetorical smoke" (George Thayer), to confess to "the dirty little secret that everyone knows" (John Gardner, the Republican who created Common Cause).[44] One such congressional maverick was also Republican, former representative Millicent Fenwick (New Jersey). Her axiom, announced on television, is that "of course" there is a link between campaign contributions and congressional votes. She recalled asking for a vote from colleagues only to be told: I get so much money from such-and-such a group and so cannot vote along with you. (*Not* the sort of thing that congresspersons told John Kingdon in accounting for their votes). As she put it in 1982, referring to PACs: "We cannot produce the votes and legislation we should under the pressure that results from this kind of giving."[45]

In the Senate, the former Republican minority leader, Hugh Scott, once put it another way. Every senator, according to him, realizes that every contribution implies an obligation: "Some sort of obligation is very often felt by the recipient, some sort of obligation may be in the mind of the donor. The obligation may be slight . . . some minor favor. On the other hand, the donor may expect benefits which he has no right to expect." If that is ambiguous, as Gary Jacobson characterizes it,[46] the reason may have been that when Senator Scott spoke (in 1973), he had been receiving $10,000 a year from Gulf Oil for well over a decade. A Gulf lobbyist eventually pointed out that these sums were not political contributions but for the senator's personal use (an explanation that hardly explained). In any case, the senator's remark that "every time a contribution is made, some sort of obligation is implied" may be assumed to have come from the heart.

Where is all this leading us? Insofar as campaign contributions by interest groups and their lobbyists are directed outside constituency boundaries, groups cannot be "collapsed" into the constituency variable (as Professor Kingdon argued for the sixties), but should be accorded some independent force. If such campaign contributions are also effective (as argued here), then the influence of groups has, after all, to be reckoned with, and the tendency to discount them, noticeable from the midsixties, has to be itself discounted.

One gains courage for this judgment as soon as one realizes that most of the research bearing on the question has focused on Congress: it's how congresspersons decide; congresspersons' voting decisions; money in congressional elections; Congress: the electoral connection; and so on. Yet campaign contributions have also been effective in influencing presidential decisions. The dairy lobby stands as the type-case. While not neglecting Congress, from 1968 onward it sets its sights on presidential elections because the price-support levels for milk that could not be cleared by the market were determined within the executive branch. It started in earnest with President Johnson and would-be president Hubert Humphrey in 1968. The former withdrew from the presidential race on March 21, but a week or so later increased milk price-supports by 7 percent (compared to a cost-of-living increase over the year of 2.8 percent). Some $90,000 of his campaign expenses were then picked up by the dairy co-ops out of corporate funds (they had not yet established PACs).[47] Are you being tempted here into the *post hoc, ergo propter hoc* fallacy? It is true that one cannot prove as in a court of law a connection then between the increase in milk price-supports and the picking up of the tab. But, not long afterward, such a connection is as well established as anything of the kind can be. Mr. Humphrey having been demolished, the dairy lobby turned toward his conqueror, President Nixon, starting promptly *in 1969* with a useful $100,000 hand-delivered to his own personal lawyer. Some eighteen months later the lobby excelled itself with the promise of $2 million for President Nixon's reelection campaign, after which he graciously reversed the price-support decision already taken by his secretary of agriculture. As a result the industry got a higher parity that translated into perhaps $300 million *more* on the milk checks sent out by the government in 1971 alone. Obviously, the decision was worth far more than what one may reasonably call the purchase price—the campaign contribution.

In judging the ostensible connection between the dairy interest and President Johnson in 1968, one should also have in mind the attitudes of their leaders. The comment one of them made on their 1971 triumph is revealing: "We dairymen cannot afford to overlook this kind of benefit. Whether we like it or not, this is the way the system works." We also have the evidence of journalist Frank Wright, who investigated the lobby's campaign contributions at the time. He has recalled the episode as "a classic case of special interest trying to buy its way to power. What made it so different from so many others was that the dairy guys were so new at it, so naive and so gross. They really were up front about it; you sell, we buy."[48]

The dairy lobby had only itself to blame if that's how it appeared to experienced observers. *Spend* it certainly did. Apart from the $100,000 in 1969 to President Nixon's personal lawyer, it lavished (1969–70) more than

$500,000 on a clutch of congresspersons, including $185,000 on Wilbur Mills, chairman of the House Ways and Means Committee. Along the way there were, by its standards, more modest disbursements to be followed, in 1971, by the ace of trumps—the promise of $2 million for the great reentry of the gladiators in 1972.

The point for us now (apart from partly understanding why a carton of milk costs as much as it does in the supermarket) is that, in judging the effectiveness of campaign contributions, we should not have allowed ourselves to be confined, by various political scientists, to the congressional experience. There is much more to be brought into the calculation. Bear in mind, too, that *all* this (and of course much more) was happening in a period when the 1960s revision about interest groups was turning into orthodox opinion. Groups and their attendant lobbies were deemed to be disorganized, dithering, lacking in financial resources, and evidently rather "dumb." Note, too, that just when John Kingdon was stressing the constituency variable as a major determinant of congresspersons' voting decisions, interest groups were spreading a great deal of money around on terms that had nothing to do with the constituency relationship. The case of the ubiquitous Wilbur Mills has already been mentioned. Another instance may be culled from David Mayhew. In the 1970 campaigns, Representative George H. Fallon (Dem.-Maryland) received 167 donations from the highway-construction interests in thirty-seven states *other than his own*. He happened to be chairman of the House Public Works Committee.[49]

What's left for the constituency variable remains "less than crystal clear" (in Professor Ripley's words). One is inclined to the view expressed by a legislator of distinction, former U.S. Senator William Fulbright, that "the modern legislator" does not "really [serve] constituents as a community, but the best-organized, best-funded, and most politically active interest groups within the constituency."[50] Here, obviously, there are conceptual as well as factual difficulties. But one's own conclusion, for the seventies and eighties at least, is that Congress is indeed mainly responsive to the organized interests (Leroy Rieselbach), is indeed "a tangle of interests" (Wright Mills). Bearing in mind that the executive branch, even the White House, is also responsive in the same sense, one can hardly dispute that America does *tend* to be a special-interest democracy.

In the last resort, however, one would not wish to attribute this "tilting" of American democracy to any particular method employed by the special interests, such as campaign contributions, "musical chairs" or the $1 billion a year that the corporations were estimated to have been spending in the late seventies on propaganda (or public relations).[51] Or rather, one would prefer to place all these within the framework we have been using: the interaction of the social order and political authority. At least until the perhaps distant day when methods and techniques can be measured, these may be more fruitfully seen as "symptoms" of the growing tension between two systems of representation, the functional and the territorial. If indeed the organized interests are consistently predominant in contemporary America, it means that the *de facto* system of functional representation is swamping the territorial (or geographical) arrangements provided by the Constitution. To the elucidation of this point we now turn.

CHAPTER 15
A DUAL SYSTEM OF REPRESENTATION

One of the perennial questions about representation is, of course: *what* is or should be represented? In the original mode of representation, more or less invented during the course of the Middle Ages, the answer was: some collectivity. In England, for example, during the thirteenth century, Dominican friars came to be represented in assemblies of their own by priors and others whom they had elected (that is, just *chosen*); towns and boroughs were represented at local courts; the shires (or counties)—by "four discreet knights"—at various national councils. Before the century was out the idea had been extended to the convocations (or assemblies) of the regular clergy, and above all to the gradually emergent Parliament. The knights and townsfolk represented local communities, *comunaultés, communes* in what eventually took shape under the name of the House of Commons. Into it the lower clergy were later drawn, again through representatives (called proctors).[1] Since the higher clergy (the archbishops and bishops) were already being "consulted" along with the barons,[2] the units of representation in Parliament came to be the "estates" of the realm, or, more loosely put, collectivities or groups of one sort or another.

By contrast, during the course of the nineteenth century, in the United States as well as Britain, various reforms tended increasingly to make the unit of representation the individual, treated more or less in abstraction from his or her social context, hence Samuel Beer's label for it, *liberal individualism*.[3] Concretely, it revealed itself in the principle of *one person, one vote*, and, in the striving for equal electoral districts, *one vote, one value*. So the foundation of the official system of representation became, ideally, the independent person, a distant cousin, perhaps, of Olsonian man and woman (chapter 3). Exercising the right of private judgment, this person chooses a representative who is also expected (on some variants of this theory) to exercise his or her independent judgment. The responsibility of the representative to the elector is ensured, in principle, by regular elections at reasonably short intervals, possibly supplemented by such special devices as a recall procedure. In parliamentary systems of government, the line of responsibility extends to the cabinet, the supreme executive body, because it has come to be drawn from (although not as a committee of) Parliament. In the British case, entirely the product of unplanned historical development, the "linkage" came to be individual-Parliament-cabinet.

The American Constitution was, of course, planned: such application of reason to the political order was indeed one of the startling novelties it embodied. In that planning, the "accountability line" was originally made to follow some devious paths, including:

A. individual—state legislatures—U.S. Senate
B. individual—presidential electors—president

The relationship at A lasted right up to 1913, when direct elections were instituted by constitutional amendment. Technically, relationship B still exists, but a crucial change in political practice occurred in the first decade of the nineteenth century, when, under pressure from the rising democratic forces, most states conceded popular election of the presidential electors. Since they have hardly ever deviated from their marching orders, or instructions, the change made the accountability line less devious.

In such ways as these the role of the individual as the unit of representation was enhanced. That tendency was sustained by the modification of the state rules for choosing presidential electors. When their popular election was first conceded by the states, the method prescribed was the district plan. Districts were local communities, parallel to but not identical with congressional districts. But that could mean a split vote within a state, inevitably regarded as an unpardonable sin by the new breed of party organizers. In the language that Lassalle would later use (he mobilized a section of the German working class), they wanted a united force to use as a "hammer" against their opponents. Gradually states switched to the unit rule, which in a sense embodies a head-count principle, or numbers as against communities. By 1840 the district plan was a fading memory.

Much else had to be accomplished before one could claim that the individual had been fully built into the system of representation. Thus, in the

United States as in Britain, the historic connection between the ownership of property and the suffrage (or right to vote) had to be severed, which in the U.S. was the work of the period 1820–40. After that, the concept of the "unencumbered" individual had to be universalized to include women and blacks, which, one way or another, was a long time a-coming in a meaningful, or usable form. In the United States the end of that road was not reached until the 1960s, with not simply the civil rights legislation, but also at least one landmark decision by the Supreme Court, *Baker v. Carr* (1962). In that case it was held that the courts could judge the fairness of legislative apportionments and see to it that serious inequalities are removed. One argument particularly relevant to our theme was that a single vote in one county of Tennessee was worth eight in another, and even nineteen elsewhere in the state.[4] As Chief Justice Warren would say in a related case (*Reynolds v. Sims*) two years later: "Legislators represent people, not trees or acres. Legislators are elected by voters, not farms or cities or economic interests." He went on to make the same point (as to Alabama) that had already been made about Tennessee: "It would appear extraordinary" to propose that some of a state's voters could (in effect) "vote two, five, or ten times for their legislative representatives, while voters living elsewhere could vote only once."[5] "Extraordinary" the idea had indeed become, but that is because the nation had gradually adopted what Charles Beard and John D. Lewis called the "Euclidian theory of representative democracy," the representation of "free and equal heads—abstract political persons."[6]

Long before that happened, however, political parties had been invented,[7] blurring the bold lines drawn in the last five paragraphs. Dating from the 1790s, the parties—Federalist and Republican—obviously cut across the individualistic tendencies of the system of representation constitutionally established or implied. As everyone knows, the parties came to play a very important (if unprescribed) role in the practical working of the political system. But for various reasons that cannot even be hinted at now, the parties did not "grow" in the sense most relevant to the subject of this book. As E. Pendleton Herring would one day write: "Parties have a definite and strategic position in the functioning of the governmental machine, but their position as a prompter of policy and opinion is becoming of less and less significance."

In the half-century or so since that was written, the position of the parties as prompters of policy has deteriorated considerably. Even the "strategic" position of the parties in the functioning of the governmental machines has been eroded "at the edges," where party organization has weakened and party loyalty (or partisan identification) has declined. The significance of all this for our particular theme is that, as senator-to-be Daniel Patrick Moynihan put it in 1972, "we are getting an atomized electorate, by definition an unstable one." This implies a tendency to return to the *status quo ante*—the more individualistic system of representation that prevailed before, say, 1800.

The trend toward a dual system of representation, however, has not been arrested because, up to a point and within a certain range, the party has been replaced by the group. Writing in 1928, Mr. Pendleton Herring placed this development as having become important "within comparatively recent years." As a result:

> Today when the voter becomes fired with an overpowering conviction as to the truth or falsity of a particular matter of political, social, or economic importance, he does not immediately look to the party as the vehicle to give support and expression to his doctrine. He finds about him numerous organized groups built around certain definite interests. It is to them that he turns for support and cooperation.

Of course, "fraternal, religious, social, and economic" groups were hardly new. The newness consisted in their hybrid nature—part societies, part minority parties. The Pendleton Herring "societies" are our organizations, with dues-paying members, elected officers, and "a continuous existence." They were like minority parties in having "a direct interest in certain phases of politics, a policy toward the government, and often a definite program to be obtained at the hands of the legislators." Exemplified not only by the Anti-Saloon League but also by the Chamber of Commerce of the United States, such organizations had "within very recent years . . . increased and multiplied. More important still, they have become highly organized and are today conducted by shrewd and capable leaders."[8]

How recent this all was is open to argument. Over a quarter-of-a-century earlier the Russian-born, French-educated writer Moisei Ostrogorski had observed that the method of "temporary combinations," such as citizens' movements, civic federations and "leagues," that is, "free associations of men brought together for a particular cause," was "coming into more and more regular use in the United States."[9] Looking back from the 1970s, constitutional historian Loren Beth remarked: "The growth in number, scope, and level of organization of pressure groups was a major fact of the politics of the closing years of the nineteenth century."[10]

Obviously everything would depend on the meaning of *recent*, on whether all three writers were using the same concept (Herring's, including for example the U.S. Chamber of Commerce, was certainly broader than Ostrogorski's), and so on. For us the more interesting question is the tendency for group to replace party as a source of effective policy representations, and why that was happening (which may throw light upon our situation today). Ostrogorski was in no doubt about it (or anything else much): the parties were at fault.[11] It was not only that their organizations ("the machines") were stiflingly powerful: the rank and file were also dogmatically partisan, revealing a "devotion" to party almost religious in character. Proud of his "immaculateness," the "humble party follower" adheres to a "creed" of voting the straight party ticket, whatever it may be. "The sins against the religion of the party are sins against the ticket."[12]

Professor Beth, however, saw it another way. Immediately following the sentence from him quoted above came his assessment of some of the consequences of the proliferation of groups late in the century. Tending more and more "to exist outside, and independent of, the major parties," the groups made it "even more difficult for the party organizations to maintain an intelligent concern with policy issues, especially at the local level. This seems to have been a factor in the attrition of local interest and participation in politics which was so marked a feature of the new century."[13] On this reading the parties were, up to a point, victims of the depredations of the groups, possibly (to continue the Ostrogorski metaphor) more sinned against than sinning insofar as their policy role was concerned.

This reading fits the organizational revolution theme better than the alternative interpretation does. Instead of perceiving group growth (in that period) simply as a corrective to the policy-forming deficiencies of the party system, groups are seen (for reasons sketched in chapter 2) as riding a great wave that inundates or touches many a distant shore. Whatever the truth about the original relationship, we do know that with the great development of groups we acquired another system of representation, obviously unplanned and unofficial. To commentators in more than one country this emergent social structure seemed something like feudalism, or at least contained elements reminiscent of the medieval period. What they seized upon, however, and what they thought of it all, varied widely. In the United States, the Irish-born editor E. L. Godkin characterized Cornelius Vanderbilt (the shipowner turned financier who got control of the New York Central and other railroads) as "a lineal successor of the medieval baron that we read about, who . . . had the heart and hand to levy contributions on all who passed his way."[14] That was written in 1869, eight years or so before Commodore Vanderbilt died worth an estimated $100 million or thereabouts. Others, possibly taking their cue from Godkin, talked about the "robber barons."[15] By 1902 journalist W.J. Ghent was noting a "seignorial" relationship between the great industrial magnates and the rest of the nation. The captains and lieutenants of industry were daily increasing their power—political as well as socioeconomic—and becoming "the ranking order in a vast series of gradations." At the bottom stood the "lower orders," not just a proletariat but also including farmers, middlemen, teachers, and ministers of religion, all essentially subordinate, having to "make their peace with those who have the disposition of the livings. The result is a renascent feudalism, which, though it differs in many forms from that of the time of Edward I,[16] is yet based upon the same status of lord, agent and underling."[17]

As to "the ranking order," they were "considerate," even benevolent (hence the title of Ghent's book, *Our Benevolent Feudalism*). That was partly prudence. "The new barons" sought public support through "conspicuous giving": though large, however, their beneficence is "rarely prodigal." The beneficiaries are hospitals; also colleges and churches "which teach reverence for the existing regime"; libraries, too, where the unemployed could pass the time "in relative contentment." By contrast, the barons "avoid a too obvious exercise of their power upon political institutions," which in any case (so the author asserted) is never used, even by accident to correct "what reformers term injustice."

In England the feudal or medieval experience was then being drawn upon in more significant ways, tending to transmute both the theory of representation and the relationship of groups to the state (in the European sense of the nation politically organized). The new group theory eventually came to be called pluralism. Its inspiration was partly sociological (a burgeoning of groups in Britain too) and partly intellectual.[18] The main source of intellectual influence was Otto von Gierke, who had uncovered, or rediscovered, the quasi-independent role of groups in medieval Germany. A part of his encyclopedic work was translated into English in 1900 under the title *Political Theories of the Middle Age*.[19] Before very long the pluralists were making themselves felt, arguing for an autonomous role for associations largely independent of the state, which was deemed to be, in the last resort, only one association among many, with no overriding claims upon the loyalty and obedience of members of private associations, such as churches and labor unions.[20] This could be represented as a decentralization of power from the state to private organizations, not unlike feudalism proper.

One subgroup within this pluralistic tendency looked back to the craft guilds of the medieval period (if not to feudalism as such): these were the guild socialists. Guilds would be the recipients of decentralized economic power within a broadly socialized economy: transcending the customary division between employer and employee, each guild would "cover" an industry or sector and operate more or less autonomously within (as we should now say) a national plan. That is, they would be the functional equivalent within industry of another medieval institution, the "liberty," an independent territory such as a town granted a charter by the king.[21] Parliament would survive but the more thoroughgoing writers in this genre were out to transform even *its* representational base, as indicated in the title of a work published in 1910, *The Reform of the Electorate Based Upon the Professions and Trades in Place of Local Constituencies*. The unit of representation for Parliament would be the occupational guild.[22] Just after World War I, the argument was generalized by political theorist G. D. H. Cole who claimed, as against liberal individualism, that persons as such cannot be represented, only groups of persons engaged in some common task, true representation being always specific and functional. "Parliament professes to represent all citizens in all things, and therefore as a rule represents none of them in anything." The principle of the alternative system of representation would be this: a person should count "as many times over as there are functions in which" he or she is interested. Instead of " 'One man, one vote,' we must say 'One man, as many votes as interests, but only one vote in relation to each interest.' "[23]

What the organizational revolution tended to do, then, was to provide a basis for arguments favoring (in effect) the reintroduction of an older system of representation—the one historically supplanted by liberal individualism. Some, like Douglas Cole, seemed ready to reverse the historical process by letting liberal individualism go—be itself supplanted. As it turned out, pluralism in its English form, and guild socialism too, spluttered and went out, extinguished (as a contemporary remarked) by the Defense of the Realm Acts, that is, by the expansion of state power during World War I (1914–18). However, organizational development itself resumed, tending to introduce functional representation in a looser, less systematic form than had been advocated.

In the United States after World War I some observers were almost lyrical in their praise of the extra dimension accorded by the multiplicity of groups. Thus the Kansas editor, William Allen White, noted (in 1924) that, in response to the necessities of "a complicated civilization," America had developed two kinds of government, one official and visible, the other unofficial and "invisible." In high-school civics classes the "fiction of one vote for one person is still maintained," but those well versed in practical politics "know that men, and women now may have as many votes in government as they have interests [compare G.D.H. Cole's wording, text to note 23] for which they are willing to sacrifice time and thought and money." And such sacrifice would not be unbearable: "A few hours' time, a few dollars in money, and a little thought devoted to the purpose in his heart will find a way to thrust that purpose with terrific force into the agencies of government, under splendidly organized minorities." Again, "it takes time and intelligence, and a little money, but not much. For $50 a year the average family ought to be able to buy half-a-dozen powerful votes in government, each vote ten times as powerful as the vote guaranteed by the Constitution."[24]

That "buy" is not to be taken in a pejorative sense: it simply meant the influence that a family could expect to get through joining in and paying dues. White did go on to acknowledge that "these extra-constitutional groups are not perfect," some in fact being "desperately wicked," others occasionally manipulated by "unscrupulous and greedy" men, while some of the money spent to maintain this "invisible government" went into "waste and bribery." But on the whole, clearly, he warmly approved of the rival system of representation that he had identified.

Evidently, White had voluntary associations—membership organizations—mainly in mind. That in America, only two generations ago, such an experienced political observer should have regarded these as "extra-constitutional groups"[25] is arresting. However, it is his recognition of "two kinds of government" that one wishes to recall. NORML and the various groups *pro* and *con* the abortion laws fit his bill (as, of course, do many other idea or cause groups). But in our day at least (and even in his, probably, but he was too close to it to see), the really effective "other government" consists in the professional organizations (such as the AMA), and in the economic ones:

business; agriculture; that hybrid, agribusiness; and labor, all facets of the organizational revolution.

Within that, the rise of the big corporation is the most striking feature. It principally reflects the astonishing growth of industry after the Civil War. By the midnineties the value of the output of American industry equalled that of Britain, France and Germany *all combined*. By the start of World War I, the U.S. was producing over a third of the world's industrial goods.[26] Already the first billion-dollar corporation had been put together (U.S. Steel, 1901, with assets of some $1,400,000,000). A count in 1909 revealed fifty giants. By 1930 the top two hundred corporations had assets of $81 *billion*, about half of all the corporate wealth in the land. The other half was widely diffused among some three hundred thousand corporations. In 1980, the five hundred largest U.S. industrial corporations had assets of $1175 billion, sales of $1650 billion. Exxon alone became (as Ford S. Worthy reported) the Fortune 500's "first twelve-digit revenue collector in 1980, ringing up"[27] sales worth more than $103 billion. For 1979, business reporter Anthony J. Parisi (chapter 7) put Exxon just ahead of Sweden and only a bit behind Spain. In fact, the revenues of many another giant American corporation exceed those of many governmental units, such as American states and a number of smaller European nations.

The great corporations may also be matched against labor. No less a person than the distinguished business historian, Alfred D. Chandler, Jr., has pointed out that, looking back over the twentieth century as a whole, even (organized) Labor, despite political clout, "has been able to impress its will on corporate managers only in a limited way."[28] The argument cannot be elaborated here but seems indisputable taking the century as a whole.

By this and other paths one may reach, with Professor Chandler, this conclusion:

> From the beginning, it seems, businessmen have run the American economy. . . . They, more than any other group in the economy, have managed the production, transportation, and distribution of goods and services. No other group—farmers, blue-collar workers, or white collar workers—has ever had much to do with the overall coordination of the economic system or its adaptation to basic changes in population and technology.[29]

Granted such a crucial role, and armed with such vast resources, *American* corporations have naturally *tended* to burst the bonds of the traditional representative order. The words are italicized in order to stress that one is pointing to strong tendencies, not inevitabilities. It was the truly fabulous nature of so many corporations in the U.S. (and, perhaps, at so early a date) that, combined with the comparative weakness of government in the U.S., tended to pervert the representative system, which was never designed to accommodate such "elemental forces."

Of course, the organizational revolution extends far beyond that. The agricultural experience is particularly apt. The broad-gauge farmers' organizations were built in the period 1867 (the Grange) to 1920 (Farm Bureau Federation). "Lack of representation in the councils of the nation" (essentially in Congress)[30] was precisely what farmers complained of "constitutionally," i.e., apart from their various grievances of the other kind (falling prices for farm products, railroad rates, etc.). The complaint was expressed, in the mid-1870s, in terms of occupational representation: that great army of lawyers in Congress (six out of ten) but only seven in a hundred who had farmed, although the 1870 Census revealed that 47 percent of the working population was still employed in agriculture. But in time the farmers' organizations came to be a central element in a dual system of representation. The agricultural component was expanded after World War II by the entry of the National Farmers' Organization. Since then the corporations have penetrated the agricultural world, producing the phenomenon of agribusiness. This may be counted as part of its immediate context, or it might be held to reinforce the point just made about corporations in general. Either way, agribusiness clearly makes the dual system of representation "more so." Labor in the blue-collar sense is obviously part of it, as are many professional associations such as the AMA and the National Education Association (preparing, spring 1982, to lay out $2 million and deploy two hundred experienced campaign workers in the fall elections, mainly in the hope of stopping the introduction of tuition tax credits and—if not too late—the destruction of the Department of Education). Thus, despite the constitutional doctrine that legislators represent neither "trees or acres" nor "economic interests," a place has had to be found, *de facto*, for the more significant of these.

Even within that complex the corporations stand put like great trees in a forest. The reason is that they are the operating units of the economy, uniquely responsible, as Professor Chandler remarked, for its overall coordination. The peaks have their distinctive uses, the NAM and the like, but even without them, the corporations count, and have to count, for a great deal in the making of public policy. The launching of the Business Roundtable, made up of the corporate CEOs, and its easy entry into the corridors of official power, reflects that reality as well as a new or renewed determination on their part to be heard.

REPRESENTATION AS RESPONSIVENESS

In sum, the United States has come to be endowed with an exceptionally strong system of functional representation vis-à-vis the traditional or constitutional arrangements. What light does this cast on the responsiveness of government? The literature on representation and responsiveness (as of their cousin, participation) is large and often perplexing. It may be enough here to report that, according to one treatment, representation "translates" into responsiveness. Thus political philosopher Hannah Pitkin wrote (followed by such others as Eulau and Prewitt): "We show a government to be representative not by demonstrating its control over its subjects but just the reverse, by demonstrating that its subjects have control over what it does. . . . [It] must also be responsive to the people."[31]

As it turned out, she meant not so much policy responsiveness ("a constant activity of responding") as "a constant condition of responsive*ness*, of potential readiness to respond." But this illuminates very well one facet of the complex reality in the U.S. where government "tilts" toward the functional order in general and the corporate in particular. In addition to the material already presented, think also of the advisory committee system. The term *advisory committee* is broader than it seems, being defined in Executive Order 11007 (February 1962) to include

> any committee, board, commission, council, conference, panel, task force, or other similar group, or any subcommittee, or other subgroup thereof, that is formed by a department or agency of the government in the interest of obtaining advice or recommendations, or for any other purpose, and that is not composed wholly of officers or employees of the government. . . . The term 'industry advisory committee' means an advisory committee composed predominantly of members or representatives of a single industry or group of related industries, or of any subdivision of a single industry made on a geographic, service or product basis.[32]

Of these industry and public advisory committees in 1971, there were 1166, about three out of ten (354) attached to the old giant, the Department of Health, Education and Welfare. More germane to our theme are the attachments to such Departments as Agriculture (198, or 17–18 percent) and Interior (58, or 5 percent):[33]

Among Agriculture's 26, one notices the National Tobacco Industry Advisory Committee; among Interior's 20, the National Petroleum Council. The NPC is intriguing. Formed in 1946, it originally consisted of "85 men prominently identified with all phases of the petroleum and natural gas industries," deemed to represent the whole, not their companies. Thus its function was to be "a composite spokesman for the oil and gas industries to the Department of Interior" on "energy matters . . . as requested." By the early 1970s the council had grown to 118 members, most of whom were CEOs or principal officers of industry associations. They provided between them an operating budget of some $700,000 (fiscal 1972).[34]

TABLE 15–1   Advisory Committees in the Executive Branch (1971)

AGRICULTURE		INTERIOR	
PUBLIC	INDUSTRY	PUBLIC	INDUSTRY
172	26	48	10
Total 198			58

Now, great care was taken to secure balance within the industry, geographically, but also as between interests. Oil corporations to gas corporations were as three to one. There were two dozen small oil and gas companies said (surprisingly) to be for the most part unincorporated; and eighteen trade associations, including the API, the American Gas Association, the Independent Natural Gas Association of America, and the regional and more specialized bodies. Twenty-one places were even found for corporations described as "closely allied" with industry, which brought in the chairman of Monsanto, the chairman and president of duPont de Nemours, and a vice-president of the Chase Manhattan Bank.

Thus one may fairly conclude that the terms of Executive Order 11007 (Section 4) requiring industry committees to be "reasonably representative" were complied with; the provision for banker, etc., among the "closely allied" may be construed as generous. However, there was no place for the ultimate consumer or even the intermediate consumer, represented by the American *Public* Gas Association (speaking for 225 municipally owned and other utilities). It was left to the old Montana liberal Senator Lee Metcalf to ask the awkward question during some Senate Hearings in 1971. Addressing the executive director of the NPC, he asked: "Why do you brag about having a well-balanced council within industry but you do not want it well-balanced without the industry?" Witness answered: "We can take care of this advice to the secretary much better if we do not have the consumer included in the council," which, in a way, seems only too probable. But it did not prevent Senator Metcalf from asking the other awkward question—about the absence from all these deliberations and proceedings of the American Public Gas Association as representative of the *public* utilities: "Why cannot we then have a member of the APGA as a part of the National Petroleum Council? Why are not representatives of these retail consumers included on the membership of the council?" By contrast, as special counsel E. Winslow Turner remarked, a *private* utility, the Pacific Gas & Electric, had the chairman of its executive committee as a "full-fledged member" of the council.[35]

Evidently, the Department of the Interior, responsible for the composition of the NPC, had gone out of its way to provide for "a constant condition of responsive*ness*"—to the oil and gas corporations and their allies. The then president of the APGA put it in terms familiar to us:[36]

> The exclusion of representation of gas consumers' interests from the National Petroleum Council is not in the public interest because it restricts the major, effective lobbying effort on the Department of Interior's Office of Oil and Gas to a proindustry group.

The American Public Power Association could have made the same complaint. That sort of exclusion still prevailed in the midseventies, Mark Nadel reported.[37] So Senator Metcalf's 1971 question about the usefulness of the NPC seems not unreasonable: "The only advantage is that this [the NPC] gives a prime opportunity for the heads of large oil companies of America to have special access to the secretary of interior or the president that they would not have had had this council not been created?"[38]

Put all this in the context of "musical chairs" (between the oil companies and, for example, the Oil and Gas Office of the Interior Department); of the lavish campaign contributions, so carefully distributed to occupants of key positions in the legislative arena; of successful influence upon the very composition of the Ways and Means and Finance Committees; of sustained p.r. campaigns, etc.; and one has to agree with Robert Engler, an authority on the subject, that "the industry has permeated the entire body politic."[39]

Functional representation, however, is far from being limited to "a constant condition of responsive*ness*" (situational responsiveness, it might be called). From chapter 1 and part 3 alone, we see that this mode of representation also induces "a constant activity of responding," i.e., policy responsiveness. Many more examples could be adduced, amounting to some confirmation of a strong tendency for the functional to encroach upon the constitutional at various points (at least) in the structure of representation. That does seem to be the most fundamental interpretation one may offer of the concept (and epithet) "special-interest democracy."

This brings us full circle to where this discussion began and to a problem rather more intractable than it appeared at the outset. In the most notable analysis of the relevant kind in recent years, Charles Lindblom agreed with historian Alfred Chandler in stressing the role of businessmen in the overall coordination of the economic system. Professor Lindblom concluded: "The large private corporation fits oddly into democratic theory and vision. Indeed, it does not fit."[40] Here one has argued for a broad view of the functional, which he approaches (acknowledging physicians and farmers) only to dismiss.[41] But, echoing him, one might propose that functional representation fits oddly into democratic theory, whose traditional basis has been communal or at least territorial. If the "fit" is indeed odd, the question arises whether the encroachment of functional representation upon the territorial system can be arrested.

To pursue such a fundamental question—to bring out and advocate the reforms that would be entailed—is no part of the purpose of this book. Its point of view is no doubt as plain as its presentation and style are frequently provocative. But what one wishes to provoke is thought and discussion—a way of thinking, not, immediately, a way of doing. Even so, the description and analysis do provide, within the "conservative" limits implied in Part 1, some "reformist" signposts. Clearly, the grand strategy of reform would be to favor and foster the territorial "side" of representation at the expense of the functional. That would entail, among other things, strengthening the federal government as a policy-making system (as distinct from extending its policy-making range or reach). Thus, in Congress, for example, the self-imposed impediments to effective leadership—such as those derived from the decentralization "drive" of the seventies—could be in part removed. As often advocated in the past by Austin Ranney and others, a reform strategy would also entail responsible party government. By the early eighties, the goal seemed more remote than ever. But in explaining in 1980 "how to tame the special-interest groups," Everett Carll Ladd added a practicable reform to the traditional case in calling for a constitutional amendment to limit spending.[42] This, he thought, would subject Congresspersons to intense pressure from the special interests, making the former only too glad to surrender "some of their independence to strong parties" in exchange for protection. The reasoning of course is that, all other things being equal, the power of interest groups varies inversely with the power of the parties.

So long as there is functional differentiation, there will be functional representation of some kind. But its instruments could be limited. Thus the whole system of campaign financing, PAC-money, and honorariums could be undermined by public financing, free air-time for candidates, and the like. A Denver boot should be put on the "revolving door" (or "musical chairs"). And paradoxically we could encourage one kind of differentiation as a counter to the other. This is an old dream and practice, going back to the National Consumers' League of 1899 (it is still at work) and the People's Lobby of 1906, which gave up the ghost in 1950. Its "lobbyist for the people," Ben Marsh, was an early, if less sophisticated, Ralph Nader. Common Cause, the Naderite conglomerate, and the public-interest law firms have provided valuable counterweights to the occupationally-based interest groups. For although embodying functional differentiation themselves, and certainly not impeccable or above reproach, they have fairly consistently taken a broad view of the common good.

The purpose of this book, however, is not to offer precise prescriptions nor sovereign remedies. As planned at least, it has embodied a learning *process,* starting with authoritative simplicities and proceeding to bring out the complexities and complications that lurk in most subjects of consequence. Of course, it was also intended to provide information, guide analysis and provoke discussion of an important subject. It is, after all, your democracy. Or it was.

FOOTNOTES

CHAPTER 1: AMERICA: "A SPECIAL-INTEREST DEMOCRACY"?

1. Studs Terkel, in conversation with Jeb Stuart Magruder and William Sloane Coffin, Jr., "Reflections on a Course in Ethics," *Harper's*, October 1973, p. 72.

2. James Reston, *New York Times*, September 5, 1979.

3. *New York Times*, December 26, 1979.

4. Archibald Cox, *Boston Sunday Globe*, February 17, 1980.

5. *New York Times*, May 15, 1979.

6. Steven V. Roberts, *New York Times*, October 18, 1979.

7. *New York Times*, January 11, 1981.

8. *New York Times*, July 17, 1979. In the second paragraph "balance" should probably be "balanced," as in *Boston Globe* (from Associated Press), July 16, 1979. There are other minor differences between the two reports, settled here by following the *Times* throughout.

9. *Boston Globe*, January 15, 1981.

10. *New York Times*, November 8, 1980.

11. *New York Times*, April 29, 1981.

12. *New York Times*, March 17, 1981.

13. *Boston Globe*, June 25, 1981.

14. Barbara R. Bergmann, *New York Times*, April 4, 1982.

15. Adam Clymer, *New York Times*, January 19, 1983.

16. Albert R. Hunt, *Wall Street Journal*, July 26, 1982.

17. Bruce L. R. Smith and James D. Carroll, "Reagan and the New Deal: Repeal or Replay?", *PS*, XIV (fall 1981), 759.

18. *National Journal*, July 14, 1979.

19. William Greider, "The Education of David Stockman," *The Atlantic Monthly*, December 1981, p. 36.

20. *New York Times*, June 7, 1981.

21. Karen W. Arenson, *New York Times*, July 5, 1981.

22. Phil Gailey, *New York Times*, May 17, 1982.

23. Fred Barnes, "Uncontrolled Greed: The Making of a Tax Bill," *Reader's Digest*, September 1982, p. 98.

24. Robert Lenzner, *Boston Globe*, July 26, 1981.

25. Barnes, "Uncontrolled Greed."

26. Lenzner, *Boston Globe*.

27. Dale Tate, *Congressional Quarterly*, June 6, 1981

28. Steven V. Roberts, *New York Times*, July 18, 1981.

29. Bill Keller, *Congressional Quarterly*, June 27, 1981.

30. Richard Corrigan, *National Journal*, August 15, 1981.

31. Fred Barnes, *Reader's Digest*, September 1982, p. 99. See also Steven V. Roberts, *New York Times*, July 18, 1981.

32. Ibid. The $9 billion was said to be in *new* write-offs. David Rogers, Washington Bureau of the *Boston Globe* (August 7, 1981), put the *total* gain for the industry at $11.8 billion.

33. Richard Corrigan, *National Journal*, August 15, 1981.

34. Barnes, *Reader's Digest*, pp. 99–100.

35. *National Journal*, August 15, 1981.

36. Ibid. Rep. Wilson later admitted he had miscalculated.

37. Rogers, *Boston Globe*, August 7, 1981.

38. Ibid.

39. Ibid.

40. *National Journal*, August 15, 1981.

41. William Greider, *The Atlantic Monthly*, December 1981, p. 51.

42. Robert Healy, *Boston Globe*, July 28, 1982.

43. David Rogers, *Boston Globe*, July 23, 1982.

44. Healy, *Boston Globe*.

45. Stanley S. Surrey, quoted in Robert H. Haveman and Robert D. Hamrin, *The Political Economy of Federal Policy* (New York: Harper & Row, Publishers, 1973), p. 83.

46. Robert R. Reischauer, in Aaron Wildavsky and Michael J. Boskin, eds., *The Federal Budget: Economics and Politics* (New Brunswick, N.J.: Transaction Books, 1982), p. 245.

47. E.g., The Marine Firemen's Union PAC., sponsored by the Seafarers' International Union.

48. *Congressional Quarterly*, December 21, 1974

49. George Will, quoted by Charles Peters, in Charles Peters and James Fallows, eds., *The System* (New York: Praeger Publishers, Inc., 1976), p. 166.

50. *Congressional Quarterly*, December 21, 1974. The Republican senator was Dewey F. Bartlett.

51. George A. Smathers had been a U.S. Senator from Florida (1951–69), and before that a representative. Like many others, he did not go home again.

52. Peters and Fallows, *The System*, p. 167.

53. Morton Mintz and Jerry S. Cohen, *Power, Inc.* (New York: The Viking Press, 1976), p. 130.

54. Rep. David Stockman, *Time*, May 18, 1981, p. 23.

55. Founded in 1972, it focused on the environmental implications of federal energy

policy. Enjoying no members but with a budget of $200,000 from contributions (1975), it kept ten lobbyists busy at this time.

56. *Congressional Quarterly,* October 1, 1977.

57. *New York Times,* July 29, 1977.

58. *Washington Post,* September 1 and 2, 1977.

59. Ann Cooper, *Congressional Quarterly,* October 22, 1977. For examples of one newspaper's use of Common Cause press releases on this subject, see *New York Times,.* August 18, 1977, and August 6, 1976.

60. Bruce Ian Oppenheimer, *Oil and the Congressional Process* (Lexington, Mass.: Lexington Books, Inc., 1974), Ch. 3.

61. *Boston Globe,* October 17, 1977.

62. *Congressional Quarterly,* October 22, 1977, p. 2223.

63. *New York Times,* April 23, 1982.

64. Ibid., July 14, 1982.

65. Hugh Heclo, "Issue Networks and the Executive Establishment," in Anthony King, ed., *The New American Political System* (Washington, D.C.: American Enterprise Institute, 1978), esp. p. 102. See also the article by the Scottish political scientist, A. Grant Jordan, "Iron Triangles, Woolly Corporatism and Elastic Nets: Images of the Policy Process," *Journal of Public Policy,* I (February, 1981) pp. 95–123.

66. Arthur Selwyn Miller, "The Constitution and the Voluntary Association: Some Notes Toward a Theory," in J. Roland Pennock and John W. Chapman, eds., *Voluntary Associations* (New York: Atherton Press, 1969), p. 235.

CHAPTER 2: ORGANIZATIONAL REVOLUTION: VALUES AND BELIEFS

1. Richard Robinson, *Definition* (Oxford: Clarendon Press, 1950), pp. 117–126.

2. Robert H. Salisbury, "Interest Groups," in Fred I. Greenstein and Nelson W. Polsby, eds., *Handbook of Political Science,* Vol. 4, (Reading, Mass.: Addison-Wesley Publishing Company, 1975), p. 175.

3. "An interest group," according to de Grazia, "may be defined as a privately organized aggregation which attempts to influence public policy" [From Alfred de Grazia, "Nature and Prospects of Political Interest Groups," in Donald C. Blaisdell, ed., *Unofficial Government: Pressure Groups and Lobbies* (Philadelphia: *The Annals* of the American Academy of Political and Social Science, September 1958), p. 113.]

4. Oxford English Dictionary; The American Heritage Dictionary of the English Language.

5. Robert Presthus, *Elites in the Policy Process* (New York: Cambridge University Press, 1974), pp. 65–66.

6. Ibid., p. 118.

7. Joseph LaPalombara, *Interest Groups in Italian Politics* (Princeton, N.J.: Princeton University Press, 1964), p. 16.

8. Harwood L. Childs, ed., "Pressure Groups and Propaganda," (Philadelphia: *The Annals* of the American Academy of Political and Social Science, May, 1935), foreword.

9. Allen Potter, *Organized Groups in British National Politics* (London: Faber and Faber, 1961), Ch. 1.

10. *New York Times,* November 16, 1977.

11. Harwood L. Childs, *Labor and Capital in National Politics* (Columbus, Ohio: Ohio State University Press, 1930); V. O, Key, Jr., *Politics, Parties and Pressure Groups* (New York: Thomas Y. Crowell Company, 1958); David B. Truman, *The Governmental Process* (New York: Alfred A. Knopf, 1951).

12. Kenneth E. Boulding, *The Organizational Revolution* (New York: Harper & Brothers, Publishers, 1953).

13. S. N. Eisenstadt, ed., *Political Sociology: A Reader* (New York: Basic Books Inc., Publishers, 1971), p. 317.

14. Neil J. Smelser, "Mechanisms of Change and Adjustment to Change," in Bert F. Hoselitz and Wilbert E. Moore, eds., *Industrialization and Society*, (UNESCO: Mouton, 1963), pp. 35–41.

15. Eisenstadt, *Political Sociology*, introduction to chapters 9–12, and "Social Change, Differentiation, and Evolution," *American Sociological Review* 29 (1964), 376.

16. Raymond Aron, "Social Class, Political Class, Ruling Class," *European Journal of Sociology*, I (1960), as reproduced in Eisenstadt, ed., *Political Sociology*, p. 209.

17. Ibid., p. 320.

18. Samuel P. Hays, "The New Organizational Society," in Jerry ısrael, ed., *Building the Organizational Society* (New York: The Free Press, 1972), introduction, pp. 1–3.

19. Ibid.

20. Eric Woolf, "They Divide And Subdivide, And Call It Anthropology," *New York Times*, November 30, 1980.

21. A. L. Kroeber and C. Kluckhohn, "The Study of Culture," in Daniel Lerner and Harold D. Lasswell, eds., *The Policy Sciences* (Stanford, Calif.: Stanford University Press, 1951), p. 86, n.5.

22. Gabriel A. Almond, "Comparative Political Systems," *Journal of Politics*, 18 (August 1956); Gabriel A. Almond and Sidney Verba, *The Civic Culture* (Boston: Little Brown and Company, Inc., 1965); Gabriel A. Almond and G. Bingham Powell, *Comparative Politics* (Boston: Little Brown and Company, Inc. 1966); Samuel H. Beer and Adam Ulam, eds., *Patterns of Government* (New York: Random House, 1958).

23. Gabriel A. Almond and Sidney Verba, eds., *The Civic Culture Revisited* (Boston: Little Brown and Company, Inc., 1980), p. 26.

24. Arend Lijphart in Almond and Verba, *Civic Culture Revisited*, pp. 47–49.

25. Ibid.

26. Robert H. Wiebe, *The Search for Order, 1877–1920* (New York: Hill and Wang, 1967), pp. 152–53.

27. Norman H. Nie, G. Bingham Powell, Jr., and Kenneth Prewitt, "Social Structure and Political Participation: Developmental Relationships, II," *American Political Science Review*, 63 (1969), 808.

28. Sidney Verba and Norman H. Nie, *Political Participation in America: Political Democracy and Social Equality* (New York: Harper & Row, Publishers, 1972), p. 83, n. 3.

29. Lester W. Milbrath and M. L. Goel, *Political Participation*, 2nd ed. (Chicago: Rand McNally College Publishing Company, 1977).

30. Gabriel A. Almond and Sidney Verba, *The Civic Culture* (Boston: Little Brown and Company, Inc. 1965), pp. 142–43.

31. Ibid., p. 171.

32. Ibid., p. 151.

33. Ibid., p. 153.

34. Dale C. Nelson, "Ethnicity and Socioeconomic Status as Sources of Participation," *American Political Science Review*, 73 (1979), 1027.

35. Almond and Verba, *The Civic Culture*, p. 127.

36. Beer and Ulam, eds., *Patterns*.

37. Presthus, *Elites*, p. 4.

38. Michael T. Hayes, "Interest Groups and Political Culture: A Revision of Elazar's Typology," paper presented at annual meeting of the American Political Science Association, New York, 1981.

CHAPTER 3: ORGANIZATIONS INTO INTEREST GROUPS

1. Mancur Olson, Jr., *The Logic of Collective Action*, paperback ed. (New York: Schocken Books, 1968), pp. 20–21, 122–27. Originally published in 1965 by Harvard University Press.

2. Mancur Olson, Jr., in Thomas Wilson and Andrew S. Skinner, eds., *The Market and the State* (Oxford, Eng.: Clarendon Press, 1976), p. 108, and Olson, *Logic*, p. 21.

3. Olson, *Logic*, pp. 3, 34–35.

4. Ibid., pp. 6, 159–62.

5. One feels that Mr. Olson would very much like to include the humanitarian and philosophic, etc., groups in his theory, but his move to do so is only tentative, even half-hearted. His restraint, however, was probably prudent: any extension of the argument would have entailed discussion of altruistic behavior in general; psychological egoism (people pursue their own good— that is how they are made); ethical egoism (anyway they *ought* to . . .); and other such problems with which moral philosophers and others have grappled. That in turn would have required re-examination of the concept of the rational individual in economic organizations, the very basis of the Olson book. The original foundation of economics as it cut itself off from philosophy, etc., was psychological hedonism, a species of psychological egoism making pleasure/happiness "the good." Even today, one feels, economists are still psychological egoists/hedonists at heart.

6. See Paul Lutzker, *The Politics of Public Interest Groups: Common Cause in Action* (Ann Arbor, Michigan: Xerox University Microfilms, 1974) for a different interpretation.

7. Graham Wootton, *Pressure Groups in Britain, 1720–1970.* (Hamden, Conn.: Archon Books, 1975), p. 69

8. Robert H. Salisbury, "Interest Groups," in Fred I. Greenstein and Nelson W. Polsby, eds., *Handbook of Political Science*, vol. 4 (Reading, Mass.: Addison-Wesley, 1975), p. 193.

9. J. David Greenstone, "Group Theories," in *Handbook*, vol. 2, p. 288.

10. James A. Bill and Robert L. Hardgrave, Jr., *Comparative Politics: The Quest for Theory* (Columbus, Ohio: Charles E. Merrill Publishing Company, 1973), p. 132 and n. 50.

11. Mancur Olson, "The Political Economy of Comparative Growth Rates," p. 23, paper read at American Political Science Association annual meeting, 1978.

12. William Allen White, *Politics: The Citizen's Business* (New York: The Macmillan Company, 1924), pp. 16–17.

13. James Q. Wilson, *Political Organizations* (New York: Basic Books, Inc., Publishers, 1973), pp. 120–21.

14. Ibid., p. 28, n.10, citing Dr. Roberts's Ph.D. dissertation at Ohio State University, 1971.

15. Brian Barry, *Sociologists, Economists and Democracy* (London: Collier-Macmillan Ltd., the Macmillan Company, 1970), p. 29.

16. William A. Gamson, *The Strategy of Social Protest* (Homewood, Ill.: the Dorsey Press, 1973), pp. 19–23, 68–71.

17. David Marsh, "More on Joining Interest Groups," *British Journal of Political Science*, 8, Part 3 (July 1978), 383–84. For a criticism of the article, see ibid., article by J. R. Shackleton, 375–380.

18. Olson, *Logic*, p. 123, n.50.

19. If one were seriously dealing with dislocation/disturbance in relation to labor unions in Britain, one would have to go back beyond the Industrial Revolution's conventional starting date, 1760. During that period, the break-up of the medieval craft gilds "released" journeymen against masters once the opportunities for such advancement were reduced, as apparently happened during the eighteenth century when the "trade societies," or early unions, got under way.

20. Greenstone, "Group Theories," in *Handbook*, vol. 2, p. 288–9.

21. William A. Gamson, *The Strategy*, pp. 64–66.

22. Robert H. Salisbury, *Interest Group Politics in America* (New York: Harper & Row, Publishers), pp. 38–41.

23. White, *Politics,* pp. 10–11

24. Charles B. Hagan, review, *American Political Science Review,* 60 no. 1 (March 1966), 130.

25. Robert T. Golembiewski, review, *American Sociological Review,* 31 no. 1 (Feb., 1966), 117. Emphasis added.

26. David Marsh, "More on Joining Interest Groups," *British Journal of Political Science,* 8, Part 3 (July 1978), 381.

CHAPTER 4: THE CONSTITUTION

1. Analysis up to June 1972 of Supreme Court interpretations alone produced a volume of almost two thousand pages. See Congressional Research Service, Library of Congress, *The Constitution of the United States of America* (Washington, D.C.: Government Printing Office, 1973).

2. W. L. Newman, *The Politics of Aristotle,* vol. I (Oxford, Eng.: Clarendon Press, 1887), p. 243.

3. International Labour Office, *Freedom of Association,* vol. II (Geneva: I.L.O., 1927), pp. 88–90; Jean-Daniel Reynaud, *Les Syndicats en France* (Paris: Librairie Armand Colin, 1963), pp. 9–10; Jean Montreuil, *Histoire du Movement Ouvrier en France* (Paris: Aubier, Editions Montaigne, 1946), pp. 40–45.

4. I.L.O., ibid., p. 91; Louis Rolland, *Droit Administratif* (Paris: Dalloz, 1957), p. 240.

5. Reynaud, *Les Syndicats,* p. 10.

6. I.L.O., *Freedom of Association,* p. 95, n.1.

7. Charles E. Wyzanski, Jr., "The Open Window and the Open Door," *California Law Rev.,* 35 (1947), 341, 336–37.

8. Perry Miller, *Nature's Nation* (Cambridge, Mass.: The Belknap Press of Harvard University Press, 1967), pp. 155–56.

9. Crandall v. Nevada, 6 Wall. 73 U.S. 35 (1868).

10. Congressional Research Service, *The Constitution,* p. 1033, n.10, and Robert F. Cushman, *Cases in Constitutional Law,* 5th ed. (Englewood Cliffs, N.J.: Prentice-Hall Inc., 1979), p. 254.

11. United States v. Cruikshank, 92 U.S. 542, 552–553 (1876), cited in *The Constitution,* ibid., and Cushman, *Cases,* p. 648.

12. Slaughter-House, 16 Wall.36 (1873), cited in Cushman, *Cases,* pp. 250–51.

13. Bannon v. Baltimore, 7 Pet. 243 (1833), cited in Cushman, *Cases,* p. 248.

14. Congressional Research Service, *The Constitution,* p. 1031.

15. Gitlow v. New York, 268 U.S. 652 (1925), cited in Cushman, *Cases,* p. 447.

16. Stanley I. Kutler, ed., *The Supreme Court and the Constitution,* 2nd. ed., (New York: W. W. Norton & Company), 1977, p. 331. Professor Kutler is one of those who calls the holding "casual" (ibid., p. 330).

17. Near v. Minnesota, 283 U.S. 697 (1931), cited in Cushman, *Cases,* pp. 472–76, 280.

18. De Jonge v. Oregon 299 U.S. 353 (1937), cited in Stanley I. Kutler, *Supreme Court,* pp. 429–31.

19. Congressional Research Service, *The Constitution,* pp. 1031–32.

20. Ibid., pp. 1485; David Fellman, *The Constitutional Right of Association* (Chicago: University of Chicago Press, 1963), pp. 71–72.

21. Fellman, ibid., p. 73.

22. NAACP v. Alabama, 357 U.S. 449 (1958), cited by Stanley I. Kutler, *Supreme Court,* p. 459.

23. Ibid., p. 458.

24. Fellman, *Constitutional Right,* p. 65.

25. Congressional Research Service, *The Constitution*, p. 967. 361 U.S. 516 (1960).

26. 377 U.S. 288 (1964), cited by C. Herman Pritchett, *The Federal System in Constitutional Law* (Englewood Cliffs, N.J.: Prentice-Hall Inc., 1978), p. 309.

27. Cushman, *Cases*, p. 459

28. Congressional Research Service, *The Constitution*, p. 966.

29. Ibid., pp. 990, 966 and n.2; Thomas G. Walker, *American Politics and the Constitution* (North Scituate, Mass.: Duxbury Press, 1978), p. 122.

30. Griswold v. Connecticut, 381 U.S. 479 (1965), cited in Cushman, *Cases*, p. 303.

31. Congressional Research Service, *The Constitution*, p. 966, and n.3.

32. Kusper v. Pontikes, 414 U.S. 51 (1973), cited in Congressional Research Service, *The Constitution of the United States of America*, 1976 Supplement (Washington, D.C.: Government Printing Office, 1977), pp. S63–64.

33. Martin Diamond, "Conservatives, Liberals and the Constitution," reproduced in L. Earl Shaw and John C. Pierce, eds., *Readings on the American Political System* (Lexington, Mass.: D. C. Heath and Company, 1970), p. 70.

34. Arthur W. MacMahon, in E.R.A. Seligman, ed., *Encyclopedia of the Social Sciences*, vol. VI (New York: The Macmillan Company, 1931), p. 173.

35. *The Federalist*, no. 45.

36. Ibid., no. 46.

37. Herbert Wechsler, "The Political Safeguards of Federalism," as reproduced in Daniel J. Elazar, *The Politics of American Federalism* (Lexington, Mass.: D. C. Heath and Company, 1969), p. 33.

38. *Oeuvres Complètes*, ed. by Roger Caillois (Paris: Librairie Gallimard, 1951), pp. 397–98.

39. Joseph Dedieu, *Montesquieu* (Paris: Matier, 1966), p. 215.

40. *The Federalist* 47. Madison had studied Montesquieu under President Witherspoon at Princeton.

41. Ibid. Yet the point had to be made all over again in the 1930s even in France. See citations in Louis Althusser, *Montesquieu: La Politique et l'Histoire* (Paris: Presses Universitaires de France, 1964), p. 93, n.2. M. Althusser himself felt obliged even a generation later to write a chapter headed "the myth of the separation of powers." Evidently some myths take a long time to die.

42. Diamond, *Readings* (note 33), pp. 69–70.

43. *The Federalist* 46.

44. Spark M. Matsunaga and Ping Chen, *Rulemakers of the House* (Urbana, Ill.: University of Illinois Press, (1976), p. 15, quoting Clem R. McSpadden (Okla.).

45. Said to Rachelle Patterson of the *Boston Globe*, July 27, 1979. See also *New York Times*, July 26, 1979.

46. Morton Grodzins, "American Political Parties and the American System," *Western Political Quarterly*, XIII (December 1960), as reproduced in Stephen V. Monsma and Jack R. Van Der Slik, eds., *American Politics* (New York: Holt, Rinehart and Winston, 1970), p. 593.

47. Grodzins, in L. Earl Shaw and John C. Pierce, *Readings*, p. 83.

CHAPTER 5: CONGRESS

1. William J. Keefe and Morris S. Ogul, *The American Legislative Process: Congress and the States*, 4th ed. (Englewood Cliffs, N.J.: Prentice-Hall Inc., 1977) p. 313. They refer to "political interest groups" in Trumanian fashion, but in these pages that translates into "interest groups," as explained in chapter 2.

2. J. E. Neale, *The Elizabethan House of Commons* (London: Jonathan Cape, 1949), pp. 336, 337 and n.2.

3. Ibid., pp. 390–91.

4. Ibid., pp. 276, 384.

5. *The Economist,* August 12, 1899.

6. See the pioneering book by J. D. Stewart, *British Pressure Groups: Their Role in Relation to the House of Commons* (Oxford, Eng.: The Clarendon Press, 1958).

7. Richard H. Leach, *American Federalism* (New York: W. W. Norton & Company, Inc., 1970), pp. 28–29.

8. C. Herman Pritchett, *The Federal System in Consitutional Law* (Englewood Cliffs, N.J.: Prentice-Hall Inc., 1978), pp. 202–203; Leach, ibid., p. 27.

9. Robert F. Cushman, *Cases in Constitutional Law,* 5th ed. (Englewood Cliffs, N.J.: Prentice-Hall Inc., 1979), p. 127.

10. Leach, *American Federalism,* p. 30

11. *The Federalist,* no. 51

12. Congressional Quarterly, *Guide to the Congress of the United States* (Washington, D.C.: Congressional Quarterly Service, 1971), p. 155.

13. Ibid., p. 158.

14. Ibid., p. 134.

15. Ibid., p. 135. Reed's successor, Cannon's predecessor, was Charles F. Crisp.

16. Quoted in Paul S. Reinsch, ed., *Readings on American Federal Government* (Boston: Ginn and Company, 1909), p. 249.

17. Nelson F. Polsby, "The Institutionalization of the U.S. House of Representatives," *American Political Science Review,* 62 (1968), 156.

18. Woodrow Wilson, *Congressional Government,* 11th ed. (Boston, Mass.: Houghton, Mifflin and Company, 1895), p. 69. Originally published in 1885.

19. Congressional Quarterly, *Guide,* pp. 41, 87, 105.

20. George B. Galloway, *The Legislative Process in Congress* (New York: Thomas Y. Crowell Company, 1953), p. 288

21. Polsby, *Institutionalization* (n.17).

22. The speaker was made a member of the Rules Committee just before the Civil War but was cast out following the great turnabout of 1909–10. That exclusion was revoked as a result of the post-World War II reforms, but in practice the Speaker still does not attend.

23. Roger H. Davidson, "Representation and Congressional Committees," in Norman J. Ornstein, ed., Changing Congress: The Committee System, *The Annals* of the American Academy of Political and Social Science, 411 (January 1974), 55.

24. Ibid.

25. Cited in William J. Keefe, *Congress and the American People* (Englewood Cliffs, N.J.: Prentice-Hall, Inc., 1980), p. 66.

26. Richard F. Fenno, Jr., *Home Style: House Members in Their Districts* (Boston: Little, Brown and Company, 1978), p. 222. See Ch. 7 generally.

27. Davidson, *Representation,* p. 51

28. Ibid.

29. David R. Mayhew, *Congress: The Electoral Connection* (New Haven, Conn.: Yale University Press, 1974), pp. 14–15.

30. Common Cause, *The Government Subsidy Squeeze* (Washington, D.C.: Common Cause, 1980), pp. 27, 52.

31. Woodrow Wilson, *Congressional Government,* p. 113.

32. Davidson, *Representation,* p. 49

33. George F. Goodwin, Jr., "Subcommittees: The Miniature Legislatures of Congress," *American Political Science Review,* 56 (1962), 597.

34. These were only the *progeny* of the *standing subject* committees, the most relevant concept here. In addition there were in (1970) thirty-three select/special committees in the House; sixteen such in the Senate, making 268 subcommittees in all (49 + 219). The total had been 180 after the 1946 reforms. That later number (250–260) remains the order of magnitude.

35. Congressional Quarterly, *Guide*, p. 151

36. *Boston Sunday Globe*, Nov. 23, 1980.

37. After only one full term in the House, he was put on Ways and Means by John Nance Garner of Texas, the incoming Speaker, with the support of Sam Rayburn, also of Texas and a future Speaker. Despite his lack of seniority, the Texas delegation voted unanimously for him. In grooming him for leadership, what did Texas want, and what did Texas get, especially after he took over the Speakership from Rayburn? Or did his unusually rapid preferment merely reflect his playing poker with Garner?

38. Ibid. See also Congressional Quarterly, *Guide*, pp. 136–37; John F. Manley, *The Politics of Finance* (Boston: Little, Brown and Company, 1970), pp. 22–24; and the account by ex-lobbyist Robert N. Winter-Berger, *The Washington Pay-Off* (New York: Dell Publishing Co., Inc., 1972) chapters 1 and 2.

39. Bruce F. Freed, *Congressional Quarterly*, Nov. 8, 1975.

40. Richard F. Fenno, Jr., *Congressmen in Committees* (Boston: Little, Brown and Company, 1973), p. 94.

41. Ibid., p. 95, Table 4.3.

42. See David W. Rohde, *The Annals*, January 1974, pp. 39–47.

43. Leroy N. Rieselbach, *Congressional Reform in the Seventies* (Morristown, N.J.: General Learning Press, 1977), p. 48.

44. *Congressional Quarterly*, January 24, 1976.

45. Ibid.

46. William J. Keefe and Morris S. Ogul, *American Legislative Process*, p. 172.

47. Davidson, *Representation*, (note 23), p. 57.

48. The idea was merely put up for discussion by Professor Davidson; he is not responsible for its transfer to this argument.

49. Quoted in Carol S. Greenwald, *Group Power: Lobbying and Public Policy* (New York: Praeger Publishers, 1977), p. 195.

50. Norman J. Ornstein and Shirley Elder, *Interest Groups, Lobbying and Policymaking* (Washington, D.C.: Congressional Quarterly Press, 1978), pp. 81–83.

51. Walter J. Oleszek, *Congressional Procedures and the Policy Process* (Washington, D.C.: Congressional Quarterly Press, 1978), p. 41.

52. Catherine Rudder, in Leroy N. Rieselbach, ed., *Legislative Reform* (Lexington, Mass.: Lexington Books, 1978), p. 76.

53. In Lawrence C. Dodd and Bruce I. Oppenheimer, eds., *Congress Reconsidered* (New York: Praeger Publishers, 1977), pp. 256–57.

54. A reform was legislated in 1946, but after a show of trying to make it work, Congress chose to ignore its own creation.

55. Ibid., p. 262.

56. Joel Havemann, *Congress and the Budget* (Bloomington, Indiana: Indiana University Press, 1978), pp. 40–41, 33. James A. Thurber, in Rieselbach, *Legislative Reform*, p. 163.

57. James A. Thurber, *Legislative Reform*, p. 166.

58. Havemann, *Congress*, p. 39.

59. Aaron Wildavsky, *The Politics of the Budgetary Process*, 3rd ed., (Boston, Mass.: Little Brown and Company, 1979), pp. 258–9.

60. Oil companies operating overseas were allowed by the IRS to treat royalty payments not as ordinary business expenses to be deducted but as tax credits, a far more profitable procedure.

61. Christopher R. Conte, *Congressional Quarterly*, May 12, 1979.

62. *New York Times,* May 30, 1979. The speaker was Rep. Jim Mattox (Dem.-Texas), a member of the House Budget Committee.

63. *Congressional Quarterly,* June 30, 1979, p. 1317; Common Cause, *The Government Subsidy Squeeze* (Washington, D.C.: Common Cause, 1980), pp. 64–65 and Appendix III.

64. Havemann, *Congress,* pp. 124, 132–3, 64–5. For earlier analyses of his, see *National Journal,* September 18 and 25, 1976.

65. Havemann, *Congress,* 132–3.

66. Judy Gardner, *Congressional Quarterly, April 3, 1976.*

67. Havemann, *Congress,* p. 64.

68. Gardner, ibid.

69. Ibid.

70. Havemann, *Congress,* p. 64.

71. James R. Wagner with Harrison H. Donnelly, *Congressional Quarterly,* Feb. 26, 1977.

72. Judy Gardner, *Congressional Quarterly,* April 2, 1977.

73. Wagner with Donnelly, *Congressional Quarterly.*

74. The term was used in the nineteenth century in the context of *distributing* the public lands. It "matches" what, following today's historians, will be called "promotional" in chapter 6.

75. Theodore J. Lowi, "American Business, Public Policy, Case-Studies and Political Theory," *World Politics,* 16 (1964), 690.

76. Ibid, p. 713 Table 2, note**.

77. "Matching" and "match" are used in the hope of avoiding here the important question of which entity constitutes the independent variable. For Professor Lowi the nature of the policy, in this case distributive, is the independent variable determing the "play"—the level or location of the "institutional unit" ("in most cases" the committee or sub-committee) and the nature of the process. This formulation has been widely discussed in the profession. However, longitudinal (say, historical) study makes one wonder whether, at the outset, it was not the existence of standing committees as the *initial* points of entry and then of virtual decision that *called forth* policy in disaggregated form. See chapter 9 below.

CHAPTER 6: THE POSITIVE STATE

1. Francis W. Coker, *Recent Political Thought* (New York: D. Appleton-Century Company Inc., 1934), ch. XX.

2. Carter Goodrich, ed., *The Government and the Economy,* 1783–1861 (Indianapolis: The Bobbs-Merrill Company Inc., 1967.

3. William Letwin, ed., *A Documentary History of American Economic Policy Since 1789* (Chicago: Aldine Publishing Company, 1962), p. xix. That land alone "may easily have been worth" $500 million at the time.

4. J. R. T. Hughes, "Transference and Development of Institutional Constraints Upon Economic Activity," in Paul Uselding, ed., *Research in Economic History* (Greenwich, Conn.: JAI Press, 1976), p. 52.

5. Originally headed by the Bureau of Indian Affairs, which was set up in 1824 as a part of the War Department, this function was eventually transferred to the Department of the Interior when it was set up in 1849. Its scope broadened to include the Indians of Alaska after the purchase of that territory from Russia in 1867.

6. Franklin Roosevelt won a sweeping victory in the Electoral College (472:59) after the 1932 election. But if the popular vote gave any indication of popular attitudes on the federalization of relief, remember that Hoover received 15 votes to Roosevelt's 22.

7. James Q. Wilson, "The Rise of the Bureaucratic State," *The Public Interest,* fall 1975, pp. 96, 98.

8. Lloyd D. Musolf, *Government and the Economy* (Chicago: Scott, Foresman and Company, 1965), ch. 5.

9. James Clotfelter, *The Military in American Politics* (New York: Harper & Row, Publishers, 1973), p. 55.

10. William Lilley and James C. Miller, "The New 'Social Regulation'," *The Public Interest* (spring 1977), p. 49.

11. James Sterling Young, *The Washington Community, 1800–1828* (New York: Columbia University Press, 1966), Tables 1 and 2.

12. U.S. Bureau of the Census, *Statistical Abstract of the United States*, 102d. ed., (Washington, D.C.: Government Printing Office, 1981), Table 459.

13. Peter Woll, *American Bureaucracy*, 2nd ed. (New York: W. W. Norton & Company Inc., 1977), p. 36, n.2; Louis M. Kohlmeier, Jr., *The Regulators* (New York: Harper & Row, Publishers, 1969), p. 307.

14. *Statistical Abstract*, 102 d. ed., Table 506.

15. J. M. Peirce, *Tax Digest* (August 1936), cited in Ray F. Harvey and others, eds., *Government in American Society* (New York: William Sloane Associates, 1950), p. 126.

16. E. Pendleton Herring, *Public Administration and the Public Interest* (New York: McGraw-Hill Book Company, Inc., 1936), p. 259.

17. Quoted in Leonard D. White, *The Republican Era: 1869–1901*, (New York: The Macmillan Company, 1958), p. 234. Emphasis added.

18. Robert S. Page, in Dwight Waldo, ed., *Public Administration in a Time of Turbulence* (Scranton: Chandler Publishing Company, 1971), p. 63.

19. Eugene B. McGregor, Jr., "Politics and Career Mobility of Bureaucrats," *American Political Science Review*, 68 (1974), 24; Hugh Heclo, *A Government of Strangers* (Washington, D.C.: The Brookings Institution, 1977), p. 118.

20. Hedrick Smith, *New York Times*, Nov. 8, 1980.

21. Frederic C. Mosher, *Democracy and the Public Service* (New York: Oxford University Press, 1968), pp. 103–106.

22. George J. Gordon, *Public Administration in America* (New York: St. Martin's Press, 1978), pp. 241–2.

23. In theory, professionals could be recruited other than by the merit system: for instance, their professional bodies could be invited to nominate. It is also conceivable that they could be retained on some other basis. But of course this is empirically quite improbable. In any case, the Federal Service Entrance Examination started in 1955 joins the two concepts together: a common entrance examination and then a test of specific professional skills.

24. Ibid., p. 242.

25. Mosher, *Democracy*, p. 112.

26. James Q. Wilson, "The Rise of the Bureaucratic State," p. 95.

27. Theodore J. Lowi, *The End of Liberalism*, 2nd ed. (New York: W. W. Norton & Company, 1979), p. 101.

28. Francis E. Rourke, ed., *Bureaucratic Power in National Politics* (Boston: Little Brown and Company, 1965), vii.

29. Ibid., 3rd ed., 1978, ix–x.

30. John Bibby and Roger Davidson, *On Capitol Hill* (New York: Holt, Rinehart and Winston, Inc., 1967), p. 6.

31. Randall B. Ripley, *Congress: Process and Policy* (New York: W. W. Norton & Company, 1975), p. 22.

32. Lester W. Milbrath, *The Washington Lobbyists* (Chicago: Rand McNally & Company, 1963), pp. 121, 152.

33. Donald R. Fusfeld, "The Rise of the Corporate State in America," *Journal of Social Issues*, 6 (March 1972).

34. Louis Hartz, *The Liberal Tradition in America* (New York: Harcourt, Brace & Co.,

1955). Samuel P. Huntington, *American Politics: the Promise of Disharmony* (Cambridge, Mass.: The Belknap Press of Harvard University Press, 1981), pp. 39–40, and "Paradigms of American Politics," *Political Science Quarterly* 89, (1974), 16.

35. Richard E. Neustadt, *Presidential Power* (New York: John Wiley & Sons, Inc., 1960), pp. 33, 39.

CHAPTER 7: THE UNIVERSE OF GROUPS

1. Graham Wootton, *Pressure Groups in Britain, 1720–1970* (London: Allen Lane/Penguin Books, and Hamden, Conn.: Archon Books, 1975).

2. W. Lloyd Warner, Darab B. Unwalla, and John H. Trimm, *The Emergent American Society*, vol. 1 (New Haven, Conn.: Yale University Press, 1967), p. 280. "Basic annuals" include Gale's *Encyclopedia of Associations* (Detroit: Gale Reference Service) and *National Trade & Professional Associations of the United States* (Washington, D.C.: Columbia Books, Inc.).

3. Editors of *Fortune* with Russell W. Davenport, *U.S.A.: The Permanent Revolution* (New York: Prentice-Hall, 1951), pp. 131–6.

4. Robert Presthus, *Elites in the Policy Process* (New York: Cambridge University Press, 1974), Methodological Appendix-1, p. 470, and Table 3–1, p. 80.

5. Kay Lehman Schlozman and John T. Tierney, "More of the Same: Washington Pressure Group Activity in a Decade of Change," paper presented at annual meeting of the American Political Science Association, Denver, 1982, p. 11.

6. Jack L. Walker, "The Origin and Maintenance of Interest Groups in America," paper presented to annual meeting of American Political Science Association, New York, 1981; Thomas L. Gais, Mark A. Peterson and Jack L. Walker, "Interest Groups, Iron Triangles and the Presidency in American National Government," paper presented to annual meeting of the Midwest Political Science Association, Milwaukee, 1982.

7. U.S. Bureau of the Census, *Statistical Abstract of the United States*, 1982 (Washington, D.C.: Government Printing Office), Table 876, p. 528.

8. Anthony J. Parisi, *New York Times Magazine*, August 3, 1980.

9. Ford S. Worthy, *Fortune*, May 5, 1980.

10. Walter S. Measday, in Walter Adams, ed., *The Structure of American Industry*, 6th ed. (New York: Macmillan Publishing Co., Inc., 1982), p. 64.

11. Edward S. Herman, *Corporate Control, Corporate Power* (New York: Cambridge University Press, 1981), pp. 1, 190.

12. *Wall Street Journal*, January 11, 1978.

13. Edwin M. Epstein, *The Corporation in American Politics* (Englewood Cliffs, N.J.: Prentice-Hall, Inc., 1969), ch. 3.

14. Douglas Martin, *New York Times*, May 9, 1982.

15. Douglas N. Dickson, "Corpacs," *Across the Board*, 18 (November 1981), p. 20.

16. Hugh P. Baker, "Practical Problems of Trade Associations," in William M. Ransom and Parker Thomas Moon, eds., *Proceedings*, vol. XI, no. 3, (Columbia University: Academy of Political Science, April 1925), p. 83.

17. Clarence E. Bonnett, *Employers' Associations in the United States* (New York: The Macmillan Company, 1922), p. 13; Charles A. Pearce, *Trade Association Survey*, 1941, as quoted by Ray Harvey and others, *Government in American Society* (New York: William Sloane Associates, 1950), pp. 363–4.

18. The great constitutional historian F. W. Maitland called it a "most powerful instrument of social experimentation." Who could have dreamed, though, that it would serve the cause of market capitalism in faraway America, Standard Oil in particular?

19. The Writing Paper Manufacturers Association has been claimed as the first (1861). But much depends on whether we "allow for" a change of name consummating a continuous history.

On such a basis the National Association of Cotton Manufacturerers has been accounted the oldest. It was renamed in 1906; it had been the New England Cotton Manufacturers' Association since 1865, and before that the Hampton County Cotton Spinners' Association (1854). Similarly, the American Iron and Steel Association is often dated to 1864. But it originated in the American Iron Association (Philadelphia, 1855).

20. Merle Fainsod, Lincoln Gordon and Joseph C. Palamountain, 3rd ed., *Government and the American Economy* (New York: W.W. Norton & Company, Inc., 1959), pp. 467–8.

21. Joseph Henry Foth, *Trade Associations* (New York: The Ronald Press Company, 1930), pp. 16–17.

22. Government wanted business organized at least "for the duration," preferably in a single representative body. That was exactly the British experience, too, in both World Wars.

23. Fainsod et al., *Government*, p. 468.

24. Arthur Robert Burns, *The Decline of Competition* (New York: McGraw-Hill Company, Inc., 1936), p. 45.

25. These terms themselves remind us of the similar "centralizing" tendencies at work among corporations as such, culminating in the first great merger movement at the turn of the century.

26. Robert H. Wiebe, *The Search for Order, 1877–1920* (New York: Hill and Wang, 1967).

27. Joseph F. Bradley, *The Role of Trade Associations and Professional Societies in America* (University Park, Pa.: The Pennsylvania State University Press, 1965), p. 25.

28. Clair Wilcox, quoted in H. H. Liebhafsky, *American Government and Business* (New York: John Wiley & Sons Inc., 1971), p. 171.

29. Lester Milbrath, *The Washington Lobbyists* (Chicago: Rand McNally & Company, 1963), pp. 30 and 149.

30. Sandra Bower, *National Journal*, June 9, 1979.

31. Robert Pear, *New York Times*, January 14, 1983.

32. Ibid.

33. e.g., Boston 1832: an association of merchants and shipowners was formed to confront their laborers, who were showing a perturbing disposition toward "unlawful combination."

34. Bonnett, *Employers' Associations*, pp. 15–17; George Gorham Groat, *An Introduction to the Study of Organized Labor in America* (New York: The Macmillan Company, 1922).

35. International Labour Office, *Freedom of Association*, vol. V (Geneva, Switzerland: I.L.O., 1930), p. 13.

36. Groat, *An Introduction*, p. 35.

37. Albert Fried, *Socialism in America* (Garden City, New York: Doubleday & Company, Inc., 1970), p. 75.

38. Groat, *An Introduction*, p. 32, and in *The Annals* of the American Academy of Political and Social Science, 179 (May 1935), 9.

39. Fried, *Socialism*, 82.

40. Groat, *An Introduction*, p. 80.

41. Albert Fried, *Except to Walk Free: Documents and Notes in the History of American Labor* (Garden City, New York; Doubleday & Company, Inc., 1974), p. 138.

42. National Board of Trade, *Proceedings*, 1868, pp. v and vi.

43. Albert Kleckner Steigerwalt, *The National Association of Manufacturers 1895–1914* (Grand Rapids: University of Michigan, 1964), p. 97.

44. International Labour Office, *Freedom of Association*, p. 22.

45. Steigerwalt, *The National Association*, p. 105.

46. Bonnett, *Employers' Associations*, pp. 295, 310–11, 396.

47. Ibid., p. 98.

48. International Labour Office, *Freedom of Association*, p. 18.

49. *National Journal,* January 5, 1974, pp. 19–23.

50. It did not rejoice in it for long. In 1784 the New York State Legislature, confirming the charter, called it "The Corporation of the Chamber of Commerce in the State of New York," a less "romantic" as well as a less accurate title.

51. Wootton, *Pressure Groups in Britain,* p. 44. The first body in England to bear the title *Chamber of Commerce* was started in Leeds, Yorkshire, in 1785. There were bodies of the kind in Glasgow, Belfast and Edinburgh.

52. Kenneth Sturges, *American Chambers of Commerce* (New York: Moffat, Bard and Company, 1915, for Williams College, Mass.), pp. 45–49.

53. Wiebe, *The Search,* p. 33.

54. David B. Truman, *The Governmental Process,* 2nd ed. (New York: Alfred A. Knopf, 1971), pp. 85–6.

55. Sturges, *American Chambers,* p. 63 (for 750); Bradley, *Trade Associations,* p. 42 (for 700). Earlier the chamber itself had put the total at 500.

56. Bonnett, *Employers' Associations* pp. 323–353. On horizontal/vertical, see *National Journal,* April 1, 1972.

57. On the Colorado coalfield (fall 1913–spring 1914), it was open warfare. At Ludlow alone, in 1914, twenty-one were killed in ten days. Altogether, in that brief period, fifty people lost their lives.

58. Philip Taft and Philip Rose, pp. 320–321, 330–332, 281.

59. Robert Sobel, *The Age of Giant Corporations* (Westport, Conn.: Greenwood Press, 1972), p. 73.

60. *Congressional Quarterly,* March 1, 1980.

61. Congressional Quarterly Service, *The Washington Lobby,* 4th ed. (Washington, D.C.: Congressional Quarterly Inc., 1982), p. 115.

62. Richard E. Cohen, *National Journal,* June 11, 1977.

63. Ibid.

64. Congressional Quarterly Service, *The Washington Lobby.*

65. James W. Singer, *National Journal,* February 24, 1979.

66. Congressional Quarterly Service.

67. Singer, *National Journal*

68. Ibid.

69. Donald Roots Hall, "Intergroup and Cooperative Lobbying," *Capitol Studies* (Washington, D.C.: The United States Capitol Historical Society, 1972), p. 19.

70. Ibid., p. 21.

71. James Deakin, *The Lobbyists* (Washington, D.C.: Public Affairs Press, 1966), pp. 222–23; Wesley McCune, *Who's Behind Our Farm Policy?* (New York: Frederick A. Praeger, 1956), pp. 94–6.

72. Bernard D. Nossiter, *Washington Post,* September 10, 1959, as quoted by Donald Roots Hall, ibid., 18–19. The McClellan Committee was the Select Committee on Improper Activities in the Labor or Management Field (1957–59), chaired by Senator McClellan. The focus was on six or seven unions, principally the Teamsters.

73. *National Journal,* April 1, 1972.

74. Mark Green and Andrew Buchsbaum, *The Corporate Lobbies: Political Profiles of the Business Roundtable & The Chamber of Commerce* (Washington, D.C.: Public Citizen Inc., 1980), p. 22.

75. E. Pendleton Herring, *Public Administration and the Public Interest* (New York: McGraw-Hill Book Company, Inc., 1936), p. 308.

76. Quoted in Grant McConnell, *Private Power and American Democracy* (New York: Alfred A. Knopf, 1966), p. 277.

77. Kim McQuaid, *Big Business and Presidential Power* (New York: William Morrow and Company, Inc., 1982), p. 31.

78. Quoted in Herring, ibid., p. 309

79. McQuaid, *Big Business*.

80. Herring, *Public Administration*.

81. Modelled on Toynbee Hall in the East End of London (1884), these "settlements" were centers of voluntary service for the urban poor. Jane Addams's Hull House, Chicago (1889) and Lillian Wald's "The House on Henry Street" (1895) are among the best remembered.

82. Forrest McDonald, *The Phaeton Ride* (Garden City, New York: Doubleday & Company, Inc., 1974), pp. 88.

83. e.g., Myron C. Taylor (U.S. Steel), Alfred Sloan (General Motors), Pierre S. du Pont, Thomas J. Watson (IBM), W. Averell Harriman (Union Pacific Railroad), Winthrop W. Aldrich (Chase National Bank), and Robert E. Wood (Sears, Roebuck).

84. Herring, *Public Administration*, p. 308.

85. McConnell, *Private Power*, p. 276.

86. Ibid., p. 276.

87. McQuaid, *Big Business*, pp. 30–31.

88. Hobart Rowen, "America's Most Powerful Private Club," *Harper's* Magazine, September 1960, p. 80.

89. McQuaid, *Big Business*, p. 31.

90. McConnell, *Private Power*, p. 277; Rowen, ibid., p. 82.

91. Beatson Wallace, *Boston Globe*, May 18, 1982.

92. Ibid.

93. McConnell, ibid., pp. 277–8.

94. Hobart Rowen, *The Free Enterprisers* (New York: Putnam, 1964), pp. 63, 66.

95. Ibid.

96. Ibid., p. 77.

97. Ibid.

98. Beatson Wallace, *Boston Globe*, May 18, 1982.

99. Boston Globe, May 10, 1980.

100. The top ten *Fortune* companies consisted of six oils, two autos, IBM, and General Electric (not in that order); the banks were Citibank, Bank of America, and Morgan Guaranty Trust; and the life insurance companies were Prudential and Metropolitan Life.

101. Congressional Quarterly, *The Washington Lobby*, 3rd ed. (Washington, D.C.: Congressional Quarterly, Inc., 1979).

102. Green and Buchsbaum, *The Corporate Lobbies*, p. 68.

103. Congressional Quarterly, *Lobby* (n. 101), p. 123.

104. McQuaid, *Big Business*, p. 285.

105. Ibid., p. 289.

106. Ellis W. Hawley, *The New Deal and the Problem of Monopoly* (Princeton, N.J.: Princeton University Press, 1968), p. 163.

107. *Business Week*, December 20, 1976. Ronald L. Soble, *Los Angeles Times*, carried in *Boston Sunday Globe*, September 14, 1975.

108. McQuaid, *Big Business*, p. 290.

109. Soble, *Los Angeles Times*.

110. Thomas Ferguson and Joel Rogers, *The Nation*, December 15, 1979, p. 625.

111. Gilbert Burck, *Fortune*, June 4, 1979, p. 88.

112. Green and Buchsbaum, *The Corporate Lobbies*, p. 77. This is not the impression one gets from Ferguson and Rogers in *The Nation*, p. 622, col. 2.

113. *Fortune*, June 4, 1979.

114. Green and Buchsbaum, *The Corporate Lobbies*, pp. 93–5.

115. Beatson Wallace, *Boston Globe*, May 18, 1982.

116. Green and Buchsbaum, *The Corporate Lobbies*, p. 73.

117. The three words italicized are used because, using different sources, one cannot always be absolutely certain of contemporaneous service. But the dates of service *are* close together, and the general point is unassailable.

118. Between Roundtable and Council there is also virtual representation of companies (e.g., Alcoa, General Electric and many others). This may extend even to privately held corporations such as Bechtel: George P. Shultz, future secretary of state (roundtable, policy) and S.D. Bechtel, Jr. (council, executive). Note Bechtel as the source of another recruit to the Reagan Administration: Caspar W. Weinberger, to Defense. Note also, in passing, that Donald T. Regan (Merrill Lynch), at Reagan's Treasury, had been a member of the roundtable's policy committee.

119. *Business Week*, March 7, 1983.

120. David Brody, in Stephen E. Ambrose, ed., *Institutions in Modern America* (Baltimore: The John Hopkins Press, 1967), p. 15.

121. Alfred D. Chandler, Jr., *The Visible Hand* (Cambridge, Mass.: The Belknap Press, 1977), p. 286.

122. It is, however, not true, as some assert, that the unions made no progress at all in organizing the unskilled and semiskilled. These were picked up in some degree in 1918–20, when textile, clothing and food unions tended to become industrial, i.e., to embody vertical integration. Essentially, it was the new breed within the "real" mass-production industries that the AF of L failed to come to terms with.

123. *Boston Globe*, June 13, 1981.

124. Stephen Brill, *The Teamsters* (New York: Simon & Schuster, 1978), pp. 281–2.

125. Wilfrid C. Rodgers, *Boston Globe*, February 23, 1983.

126. U.S. Bureau of the Census, *Statistical Abstract of the United States*, 102nd ed., (Washington, D.C.: Government Printing Office, 1981), Table 689, p. 411.

127. U.S. Department of Labor, Bureau of Labor Statistics, *Directory of National Unions and Employee Associations*, 1979 (Washington, D.C.: Government Printing Office, 1980), App. E.

128. Ibid., p. 56.

129. The other two unions were the Machinists and the International Union of Electrical, Radio and Machine Workers (IUE). "Primary" means agriculture and mining; "secondary" means manufacturing.

130. Department of Labor, *Directory*, p. 57.

131. Ibid., p. 59.

132. Wilfrid C. Rodgers, *Boston Globe*, February 23, 1983.

133. Named the Hotel and Restaurant Employees and Bartenders International Union until 1982. Both membership totals are for 1983.

134. Rodgers, *Boston Globe*.

135. Corinne Lathrop Gilb, *Hidden Hierarchies: The Professions and Government* (New York: Harper & Row, Publishers, 1966), p. 27.

136. Seymour Martin Lipset and Mildred A. Schwartz, *The Politics of Professionals* as reprinted by the Institute of Industrial Relations, University of California, Berkeley, from Howard Vollmar and Donald L. Mills, *Professionalization* (Englewood Cliffs, N.J.: Prentice-Hall, Inc., 1966), p. 300.

137. Walter Shapiro, *Washington Monthly*, December 1972.

138. Robert Reinhold, *New York Times*, July 25, 1980.

139. Marshall O. Donley, Jr., *Power to the Teacher* (Bloomington, Indiana: Indiana University Press, 1976), p. 30.

140. James D. Koerner, *Who Controls American Education?* (Boston, Mass.: Beacon Press, 1968), pp. 26 and 96.

141. Donley, *Power*, p. 203.

142. Congressional Quarterly, *The Washington Lobby*, 3rd ed. (Washington, D.C.: Congressional Quarterly Inc., 1979), p. 209.

143. R. Joseph Monsen, Jr., and Mark W. Cannon, *The Makers of Public Opinion* (New York: McGraw-Hill Book Company, 1965), p. 155.

144. Stephen K. Bailey, *Education Interest Groups in the Nation's Capital* (Washington, D.C.: American Council on Education, 1975), p. 17.

145. Ibid., p. 129, and Donley, *Power*, p. 203.

146. Bailey, *Education*, p. 11.

147. Based on (a) an "impressionistic questionnaire" submitted to "most" of the top policy makers in the education division of HEW and on the staffs of congressional committees, and (b) subsequent interviews with them; (c) interviews with representatives of the associations whose performance was being judged. Source: Same as for note 148.

148. Bailey, *Education*, pp. 28–9.

149. Norman C. Thomas, *Education in National Politics* (New York: David McKay Company, Inc., 1975), pp. 137–41, 153.

150. Ibid., p. 139, and Koerner, *Who Controls*, p. 31. The term *establishment* to denote a perennial, but unofficial, governing group dates back to England in the early 1950s, when it was used by historian A.J.P. Taylor and then by journalist Henry Fairlie (who has long practiced his trade in the United States). But the *concept* goes back at least to William Cobbett, a crusading, yet conservative, English author and activist early in the nineteenth century. His name for it was "The Thing." Koerner may have been the first to adapt the *term* to decision making in American education.

151. Linda E. Demkovich, *National Journal*, December 1, 1979.

152. Robert Reinhold, *New York Times*, July 25, 1980.

153. Demkovich, *National Journal*.

154. Stanley Kelley, *Professional Public Relations and Political Power* (Baltimore: The Johns Hopkins Press, 1956), chapter II.

155. Demkovich, *National Journal*.

156. Patricia Theiler, *Common Cause*, January/February, 1983.

157. Timothy D. Schellhardt, *Wall Street Journal*, October 28, 1982.

158. *Boston Globe*, March 7, 1979.

159. Two years earlier the AMA had blocked his appointment as assistant secretary for health and scientific affairs in the Nixon administration.

160. *Boston Globe*, March 7, 1979.

161. Tamar Lewin, *New York Times*, January 16, 1983.

162. Ibid.; Thomas C. Hayes, *New York Times*, May 16, 1980.

163. Bryce Nelson, *Los Angeles Times*, carried in *Boston Globe*, December 8, 1980.

164. Sheldon Zalaznick, *Fortune*, September 1969.

165. Edward Wiest, *Agricultural Organization in the United States* (New York: Arno Press Inc., 1975) (first published 1923), p. 147.

166. He also mentioned the American Society of Equity (1902). By about 1918 it had some 40,000 members, mainly in Wisconsin. At that time, and on the same arithmetical basis, the National Farmers Union had 140,000. These statistics are not consistent with those supplied elsewhere. Some sources use individual membership; others, family.

167. Wiest, *Agricultural Organization*, p. 506.

168. Donald Holley, *Uncle Sam's Farmers* (Urbana: University of Illinois Press, 1975), p. 196.

169. Half a dozen state granges critical of the conservative stances of the National Grange. Their movement dated from 1910.

170. Gilbert C. Fite, "The Changing Political Role of the Farmer," as reproduced in H. R. Mahood, *Pressure Groups in American Politics* (New York: Charles Scribner's Sons, 1967), p. 170.

171. Denton E. Morrison and Allan D. Steeves, "Deprivation, Discontent, and Social Movement Participation," *Rural Sociology* 32 (1967), 415.

172. Murray R. Benedict, *Farm Policies of the United States*, 1790–1950 (New York: The Twentieth Century Fund, 1953), p. 190.

173. Robert L. Tontz, "Membership of General Farmers' Organizations, United States, 1874–1960," *Agricultural History*, 35–38 (1961–64), 144–45.

174. Ibid., pp. 145–6 and Table 1.

175. Brad Pokorny, *Boston Globe*, April 25, 1982.

176. United States Department of Agriculture, *A Time to Choose* (Washington, D.C.: USDA, 1981), pp. 34, 44.

177. Michael McMenamin and Walter McNamara, *Milking the Public: Political Scandals of the Dairy Lobby from LBJ to Jimmy Carter* (Chicago: Nelson-Hall, 1980), p. 25.

178. *New York Times*, May 27, 1974.

179. McMenamin, *Milking the Public*, pp. 38–9, 43–4.

180. Ibid., p. 105.

181. Don Paarlberg, *American Farm Policy* (New York: John Wiley & Sons, Inc., 1964), p. 116.

182. Ross B. Talbot, "Farm Organizations and the National Interest," in Charles M. Hardin, ed., *The Annals of the American Academy of Political and Social Science*, September 1960, p. 112.

183. *New York Times*, March 2, 1978.

184. William Robbins, *New York Times*, December 14, 1977.

185. *New York Times*, March 22, 1979.

186. Ben Bradlee, Jr., *Boston Globe*, February 10, 1983.

187. Harry C. Boyte, *The Backyard Revolution* (Philadelphia: Temple University Press, 1980).

188. Benjamin Horace Hibbard, "Legislative Pressure Groups Among Farmers," in Harold L. Childs, ed., *The Annals*, May 1935, p. 19.

189. The McNary-Haugen Bill, named for Senator Charles L. McNary (Rep.-Oregon), and Rep. Gilbert N. Haugen (Rep.-Iowa). It passed twice (1927, 1928), only to be vetoed by President Coolidge.

190. Fite in Mahood, *Pressure Groups*, p. 171.

191. Ibid.

192. A significant amendment to the Agriculture Marketing Act of 1929. This, during the Hoover Administration, marks the beginning of a federal government commitment to obtain higher prices for farm products.

193. Fite in Mahood, *Pressure Groups*.

194. Talbot, *Farm Organizations*, p. 112.

195. Paarlberg, *Farm Policy*, p. 117.

196. USDA, *A Time to Choose*, pp. 42–7.

197. Graham K. Wilson, *Special Interests and Policymaking* (New York: John Wiley & Sons, 1977), pp. 5–6.

198. John D. Black, "The McNary-Haugen Movement," *American Economic Review*, XVIII (1928), 405.

199. Janet F. Boles, *The Politics of the Equal Rights Amendment* (New York: Longman, 1979), p. 14.

200. Charles A. Selden, "The Most Powerful Lobby in Washington," *The Ladies' Home Journal*, April 1922.

201. This doesn't count the Woman's Party, which "works alone." The fourteen were League of Women Voters, General Federation of Women's Clubs, Women's Christian Temperance Union, National Congress of Mothers and Parent-Teachers Association, National Women's Trade Union League, Daughters of the American Revolution, American Home Economics Association, National Consumers' League, American Association of University Women, National

Council of Jewish Women, Girls' Friendly Society, Young Women's Christian Association, National Federation of Business and Professional Women, Women's League for Peace and Freedom.

202. Barbara Sinclair Deckard, *The Women's Movement* (New York: Harper & Row, Publishers, 1975), p. 287.

203. Ibid., p. 320.

204. Ibid., pp. 341, 343, 352; Karen O'Connor, "Litigation as a Form of Political Activity," paper presented at annual meeting of APSA, 1977.

205. In the late seventies, its leader and ERA-orginator, Alice Paul (b. 1885), was still sitting in a Connecticut nursing home waiting for her "impossible dream" to come true. For sentimentalists within the American political-science profession, that was in itself almost enough to make us want her amendment ratified. She had sacrificed so much to make America a more just society.

206. Meanwhile, several states had rescinded their ratification. But the constitutionality of such rescissions remained doubtful. If states can rescind, how can the federal amendment process be expected to work?

207. Janet F. Boles, *Political Studies*, fall 1982.

208. Leslie Bennetts, *New York Times*, February 6, 1981; Susan Jaffee, *Boston Sunday Globe*, February 8, 1981.

209. *Political Studies*, fall 1982.

210. Ibid.

211. Enid Nemy, *New York Times*, February 7, 1982.

212. Anne N. Costain, "The Struggle for a National Women's Lobby: Organizing a Diffuse Interest," *Western Political Quarterly*, 33 (1980), 476.

213. Pam Conover, Steve Coombs, and Virginia Gray, "The Attitudinal Roots of Single-Issue Politics: The Case of 'Women's Issues,'" paper presented at annual meeting of APSA, 1980), pp. 13–14.

214. Kathleen Beatty, *Political Studies*, fall 1982. David W. Brady and Kent L. Tedin, "Ladies in Pink: Religion and Political Ideology in the Anti-ERA Movement," *Social Science Quarterly*, 56, (March 1976).

215. Boles, *Political Studies*, fall 1982; Anastasia Toufexis, *Time*, July 12, 1982.

216. Joyce Gelb and Marian Lief Palley, *Political Studies*, fall 1982.

217. Nadine Brozan, *New York Times*, October 11, 1982.

218. Herbert J. Gans, "Symbolic Ethnicity: The Future of Ethnic Groups and Cultures in America," in *Ethnic and Racial Studies*, 2 (1979), pp. 1–2.

219. *Wall Street Journal*, November 17, 1982.

220. John M. Crewsdon, *New York Times*, June 18, 1979.

221. James Stuart Olson, *The Ethnic Dimension in American History* (New York: St. Martin's Press, 1979), *passim*.

222. *New York Times*, April 10, 1983.

223. *New Republic*, June 25, 1978.

224. William J. Lanouette, *National Journal*, March 13, 1978.

225. Not including in 1978 the American Jewish Committee, whose Washington representative, Mr. Hyman Bookbinder, wished to avoid the impression of "a unified, monolithic-seeming Jewish community." Also, "we wanted to have freedom of action."

226. Ibid.; *New York Times Magazine*, November 7, 1982.

227. *New York Times*, April 21, 1983.

228. *Boston Globe*, April 23, 1983.

229. He was actually born in Germany, but that was accidental (his parents were visiting). His father was a German immigrant to the U.S. (the celebrated Henry Villard). His mother was a daughter of the abolitionist, William Lloyd Garrison (Massachusetts-born, like Dr. Du Bois).

230. *The Kerner Report* (New York: Bantam Books, 1968), p. 223. (Report of the National Advisory Commission on Civil Disorders).

231. Leslie W. Dunbar, "The Southern Regional Council", *The Annals* of the American Academy of Political and Social Science, January 1965, pp. 110–11.

232. Kerner Report, pp. 228–9.

233. William H. Harris, *The Harder We Run: Black Workers Since the Civil War* (New York: Oxford University Press, 1982), pp. 170–72.

234. Harvard Sitcoff, *The Struggle for Black Equality, 1953–1980* (New York: Hill and Wang, 1981), pp. 228–9.

235. Michael B. Preston, Lenneal J. Henderson, Jr., and Paul Puryear, *The New Black Politics* (New York: Longman, 1982), p. 75.

236. Richard J. Meislin, *New York Times*, December 31, 1981.

237. *Boston Globe*, December 16, 1973.

238. Henry J. Pratt, *The Gray Lobby* (Chicago: University of Chicago Press, 1976), p. 92.

239. *Boston Globe*, December 27, 1978.

240. Ibid.

241. Judy Klemesrud, *New York Times*, June 22, 1981.

242. Irene L. Evans, *Denver Post*, September 1, 1982.

243. Warren Weaver, Jr., *New York Times*, October 17, 1981.

244. Warren Weaver, Jr., *New York Times*, December 6, 1981.

245. Carol S. Greenwald, *Group Power: Lobbying and Public Policy* (New York: Praeger Publishers, 1977), pp. 18–19.

246. Pratt, *The Gray Lobby*, p. 39.

247. Angus Campbell, quoted in Pratt, *The Gray Lobby*.

248. Henry J. Pratt, "Old Age Associations in National Politics," in Frederick R. Eisele, ed., *The Annals* of the American Academy of Political and Social Science, September 1974, pp. 116–17.

249. Abraham Holtzman, *The Townsend Movement: A Political Study* (New York: Bookman Associates, Inc. 1963), chapter ix.

250. Pratt, "Old Age," p. 116.

251. Steven Roberts, *New York Times*, October 24, 1977.

252. *U.S. News and World Report*, November 22, 1971.

253. Quoted in James L. Adams, *The Growing Church Lobby in Washington* (Grand Rapids, Michigan: William B. Eerdmans Publishing Company, 1970), p. 2.

254. Luke Eugene Ebersole, *Church Lobbying in the Nation's Capital* (New York: The Macmillan Company, 1951), chapter II and pp. 51, 58–59.

255. Adams, *Church Lobby*, p. xi.

256. Ibid., p. 273.

257. Murray S. Stedman, Jr., *Religion and Politics in America* (Harcourt, Brace & World, 1964), p. 94.

258. Frances Fox Piven and Richard A. Cloward, *Regulating the Poor: the Functions of Public Welfare* (New York: Vintage Books, 1971), pp. 206–10.

259. Ibid., p. 321.

260. Ibid., p. 322.

261. Ibid., p. 330–31.

262. Lawrence Neil Bailis, *Bread or Justice: Grassroots Organizing in the Welfare Rights Movement* (Lexington, Mass.: Lexington Books, 1974). pp. 36–7.

263. Richard A. Cloward and Francis Fox Piven, *The Politics of Turmoil* (New York: Vintage Books, 1975), pp. 134–5.

264. Frances Fox Piven and Richard A. Cloward, *Poor People's Movements* (New York: Vintage Books, 1979), p. 317.

265. Their concept of such a triangle is curiously limited. It was never confined to "government and capital." On the contrary, the concept works just as well for the Seafarers and the

Marine Engineers; the Maritime Administration; and the Merchant Marine Subcommittee of the House. Another well known example: traditional veterans' interest groups; Veterans Administration; House and Senate Veterans' Affairs Committees.

266. Frances Fox Piven and Richard A. Cloward, *The New Class War* (New York: Pantheon Books, 1982), pp. 120–21.

267. Hugh Heclo, "Issue Networks and the Executive Establishment," in Anthony King, ed., *The New American Political System* (Washington, D.C.: American Enterprise Institute, 1978), p. 102.

268. Congressional Quarterly, *The Washington Lobby*, 4th ed. (Washington, D.C.: Congressional Quarterly Inc., 1982), p. 139.

269. Ibid., p. 138.

270. *Business Week*, May 9, 1983.

271. Ladies' Association for Soldiers' Relief, 1st Annual Report (Philadelphia, 1863), p. 8.

272. Well over 600,000 dead (from all causes, both sides). Wounded (both sides): say, 375,000. Call it a million dead or wounded.

273. Mary R. Dearing, *Veterans in Politics*, (Baton Rouge: Louisiana State University Press, 1952).

274. Martha Derthick, *The National Guard in Politics* (Cambridge, Mass.: Harvard University Press, 1965); Vincent Davis, *The Admirals Lobby* (Chapel Hill: The University Press of North Carolina, 1967).

275. Bill Keller, *Congressional Quarterly*, June 14, 1980.

276. It came out for the Employment Bill of 1946, making the federal government responsible for maintaining income and employment. The VFW did not back the bill, neither did the Legion (whose support had been sought).

277. Douglass Cater, *The Reporter*, May 14, 1959.

278. V. O. Key, Jr., *Journal of Politics* 5 (1943), 27–40, and *Politics, Parties and Pressure Groups* 2nd ed., (New York: Thomas Y. Crowell, 1950), pp. 127–8.

279. Marcus Duffield, *King Legion* (New York: Harrison Smith, 1931), p. 49.

280. Bill Keller, *Congressional Quarterly*, June 14, 1980.

281. Ian Menzies, *Boston Globe*, December 23, 1982.

282. The alliance joined four performing-arts groups (dance, symphony, opera and theater communications) with one visual-arts organization, the arts museums. It was meant to be integrative: "A clear solo voice for the arts instead of a choral cacophony." Grace Glueck, *New York Times*, Nov. 16, 1977.

283. *Boston Globe* (from Associated Press), February 22, 1983.

284. *National Journal*, January 17, 1976.

285. Council on Environmental Quality, 4th Annual Report, 1973, pp. 396–7.

286. Congressional Quarterly, *The Washington Lobby*, 4th ed., p. 144.

287. Ibid.

288. Congressional Quarterly, *The Washington Lobby*, pp. 143–44.

289. Philip Shabecoff, *New York Times*, August 6, 1979.

290. Philip Shabecoff, *New York Times*, April 19, 1981.

291. Michael McCloskey, Sierra Club mail solicitation, n.d., p. 3.

292. Shabecoff, *New York Times*, April 19, 1981.

293. Council on Environmental Quality, 4th Annual Report, 1973.

294. *National Journal*, February 19, 1972.

295. Council on Environmental Quality, Report, p. 390.

296. Marion Edey in Garrett de Bell, ed., *The Environmental Handbook* (New York: Ballantine Books, 1970), pp. 312–13.

297. Andrew S. McFarland, *Public Interest Lobbies: Decision Making on Energy* (Washington, D.C.: American Enterprise Institute 1976), p. 45.

298. Merrill Sheils, William J. Cook and Frank Maier, *Newsweek*, October 1, 1979.

299. Energy Coalition circular, n.d. (probably late November 1979).

300. *Fortune*, May 30, 1983.

301. Lynton K. Caldwell, Lynton R. Hayes, and Isabel M. MacWhirter, *Citizens and the Environment* (Bloomington, Indiana: Indiana University Press, 1976) p. 197.

302. Professor Caldwell et al. also reported that the California Democratic Council (seventy thousand) made the question a campaign issue, and also appealed to the Democratic president in the White House (Kennedy) to have the project stopped. But it is not clear what effect all this had.

303. Ibid. pp. 196–204.

304. *New York Times*, October 11, 1976.

305. Donald W. Stever, Jr., *Seabrook and the Nuclear Regulatory Commission* (Hanover, N.H.: University Press of New England, 1980), p. 14.

306. *Boston Sunday Globe*, May 18, 1977, which, as against Stever, made the year 1974, not 1975.

307. David Howard Davis, *Energy Politics*, 3rd ed. (New York: St. Martin's Press, 1982), p. 234.

308. For the industry in a broader sense—mining, manufacturing, engineering contracting, etc.—there is the American Nuclear Energy Council (1975). It seems to be essentially a lobbying mechanism.

309. Harry C. Boyte, *The Backyard Revolution: Understanding the New Citizen Movement* (Philadelphia: Temple University Press, 1980), p. 85.

310. Davis, *Energy Politics*.

311. Ibid.

312. *New Hampshire Times*, April 14, 1976, cited in Stever, *Seabrook*, pp. 165 and 234.

313. *Boston Globe*, May 8, 1977.

314. Seacoast area residents of New Hampshire and northern Massachusetts formed specifically to fight off Seabrook. Always small, it partly made up for that by its intensity and readiness to spend. It even retained a public-interest law firm (Berlin, Roisman and Kessler, of Washington).

315. *Boston Globe*, May 8, 1977.

316. Stever, *Seabrook*, pp. 166 and 235–6.

317. Ibid., pp. 235–6.

318. *Boston Globe*, June 13, 1978.

319. Michael Kenney and Richard Higgins, *Boston Globe*, June 13, 1978.

320. *New York Times*, August 8, 1978.

321. Their subsequent convictions were overturned by the New Hampshire Supreme Court in December 1980 on the ground that the state's disorderly-conduct law conflicted with the right of free speech.

322. *Boston Globe*, December 18, 1980.

323. Davis, *Energy Politics, p. 235.*

324. *Boston Globe*, September 23, 1981.

325. Walter A. Rosenbaum, *Energy, Politics and Public Policy* (Washington, D.C.: Congressional Quarterly Press, 1981), p. 107.

326. *New York Times*, October 11, 1976.

327. Boyte, *Backyard Revolution*

328. Strategic Arms Limitation Agreement between the U.S.A. and the Soviet Union. SALT I started in 1969, with agreement reached in 1972.

329. *American Legion Magazine*, November 1978, p. 40.

330. *Newsweek*, June 5, 1978; Andrew Cherlin, *New York Times*, June 22, 1978.

331. *Boston Globe* (from Associated Press), June 26, 1978.

332. *Boston Globe,* August 7, 1978.

333. In 1983, the Nuclear Free Cambridge Campaign, an offshoot of Mobilization for Survival, was working for a nuclear-free zone in the adjoining city of Cambridge, where so much nuclear weaponry had been developed. Its method was to get a city ordinance, embodied in a binding referendum, on the ballot.

334. *Boston Globe,* August 7, 1978.

335. Congressional Quarterly, *The Washington Lobby,* 3rd ed. (Washington, D.C.: Congressional Quarterly, Inc., 1979), pp. 27–49.

336. *New York Times,* December 19, 1982.

337. *U.S. News and World Report,* April 15, 1983.

338. *New York Times,* June 5, 1982.

339. *U.S. New and World Report,* April 15, 1983.

340. *New York Times,* May 6, 1983.

341. In March, Senator Edward Kennedy had predicted "an uphill battle" in 1983 but that the freeze resolution "would pass within the next couple of years." He likened it to Medicare, which "went through a similar fight and eventually passed." *Boston Globe,* March 15, 1983.

342. *Boston Globe,* March 15, 1983.

343. Arthur S. Link, *Woodrow Wilson and the Progressive Era, 1910–1917* (New York: Harper & Row Publishers, Torchbooks, 1963), p. 54, n. 1.

CHAPTER 8: METHODS AND TECHNIQUES OF INFLUENCE

1. Henry J. Tasca, quoted in John M. Dobson, *Two Centuries of Tariffs* (Washington, D.C.: United States International Trade Commission, 1976), p. 10.

2. Harold Underwood Faulkner, *American Economic History,* 4th ed. (New York: Harper & Row Publishers, 1938), p. 590.

3. David J. Rothman, *Politics and Power: The United States Senate, 1869–1901* (Cambridge, Mass., Harvard University Press, 1966), p. 195.

4. Peter H. Odegard, "Lobbies and American Legislation," *Current History,* 31 (1930), p. 694. *New York Times,* May 4, 1983.

5. Odegard, *Lobbies,* p. 696.

6. Stanley J. Kelley, Jr., *Professional Public Relations and Political Power* (Baltimore: The Johns Hopkins Press, 1956), chapter 1.

7. A. R. Spofford, "Lobby," in John J. Lalor, ed., *Cyclopaedia of Political Science,* II (New York: Charles E. Merrill & Co., 1888).

8. *Literary Digest,* July 6, 1913.

9. *Metonymy:* Substitution of the name of an attribute of a thing, or of an associated feature of it, for the thing, e.g., *crown* for *queen* or the royal function; *sword* for *the military* or military function.

10. It made no attempt to bring in the administration, or bureaucracy, as a target, although precedents for that had existed since the midthirties, e.g., the Public Utilities Holding Company Act of 1935, which required one to register and report if appearing before the Federal Power Commission or the Securities and Exchange Commission.

11. Congressional Quarterly, *Guide to the U.S. Congress* (Washington, D.C.: Congressional Quarterly, Inc., 1971), pp. 304a–305a.

12. *United States v. Rumely,* 345 U.S. 1953, 44–45, 47. They already knew that "merely" appearing before a congressional committee "in support of or opposition to legislation" was exempt under #308(a) of the act.

13. *United States v. Harriss,* 347 U.S. 1954, 620. One of the justices took no part. The court divided five-to-three.

14. Ibid., 623.

15. Appropriately for an increasingly *gesellschaft* social order, "person" had been defined at the beginning of the act to include "association, corporation, and any other organization or group of persons" (#302).

16. *Congressional Quarterly* Supplement, January 24, 1981, for 1980 Lobby Registrations.

17. Tamar Lewin, "The Invisible Lobbyists," *The Nation*, June 10, 1978. Carol S. Greenwald, *Group Power: Lobbying and Public Policy* (New York: Praeger Publishers, 1977), p. 201.

18. Bill Keller, *Congressional Quarterly*, July 26, 1980.

19. *Boston Globe* (from Associated Press), March 31, 1983.

20. Lewin, *Invisible Lobbyists*.

21. Jimmy D. Johnson, quoted in *Business Week*, March 18, 1972.

22. *Time*, August 7, 1978. See also *Business Week*, April 17, 1978.

23. *Time*, August 7, 1978.

24. J. Wade Miller (B. F. Goodrich Co.) quoted in *Business Week*, March 18, 1972.

25. *U. S. News and World Report*, May 7, 1979.

26. David Sheridan, *Saturday Review*, April 8, 1972.

27. *Time*, August 7, 1978.

28. Ibid.

29. Lynn Rosellini, *New York Times*, July 24, 1981.

30. Spofford, *Lalor's Cycopledia*. Charles B. Lipsen and Stephan Lesher, *Vested Interest* (Garden City, New York: Doubleday & Co.), 1977, chapter 2.

31. "Ms. Lobbyist Goes to Washington," *Business Week*, May 7, 1979.

32. Jeffrey M. Berry, *Lobbying for the People* (Princeton, N.J.: Princeton University Press, 1977), p. 34, Table II–3.

33. David Vogel, "Promoting Pluralism: The Public Interest Movement and the American Reform Tradition," paper delivered at APSA annual meeting, 1978. Clement Vose, "Litigation as a Form of Pressure Group Activity," *The Annals* 319 (1958).

34. Lester W. Milbrath, *The Washington Lobbyists* (Chicago: Rand McNally & Company, 1963) p. 148, Table VII–2.

35. Mark J. Green, *The Other Government: The Unseen Power of Washington Lawyers*, rev. ed. (New York: W. W. Norton & Company, Inc., 1978), p. 60 and note.

36. *Congressional Quarterly* Supplement, January 24, 1981.

37. *National Journal*, October 4, 1975.

38. Jeff Garth, *New York Times*, October 29, 1980.

39. Here again the correct unit of analysis would seem to be the firm rather than the individual. It included James E. Smith, a former comptroller of the currency, and other distinguished ex-Treasury officials.

40. Mr. Korologos had also been a Congressional aide, to a Republican senator. Another partner, Michael Reed, however, had served a Democrat, Carl Albert, when he was Speaker of the House. The fourth partner, Stanley Ebner, had been general counsel for the Office of Management and Budget in the Nixon administration.

41. Steven V. Roberts, *New York Times*, October 10, 1977.

42. *Congressional Quarterly* Supplement, ibid.

43. Rudy Abramson, *Los Angeles Times*, carried in *Boston Globe*, March 1, 1981.

44. Ibid.

45. Robert M. Kaus, *Harper's*, August 1982; William J. Lanouette, *National Journal*, February 28, 1981.

46. James F. Clarity and Phil Gailey, *New York Times*, June 15, 1983; Lanouette, *National Journal*.

47. Charles Peters, *How Washington Really Works* (Reading, Mass.: Addison-Wesley

Publishing Company, 1980), p. 7. David Truman, *The Governmental Process* (New York: Alfred A. Knopf, 1971), pp. 264–5.

48. Ibid. See also James Deakin, *The Lobbyists* (Washington, D.C.: Public Affairs Press, 1966), pp. 100–102.

49. Abraham Holtzman, *Interest Groups and Lobbying* (New York: The Macmillan Company, 1966), p. 88.

50. Truman, *Governmental Process*.

51. Ibid., pp. 268–70.

52. Ibid., p. 251.

53. Ibid., p. 251.

54. Peters, *How Washington Really Works*, p. 11.

55. Common Cause, *Money, Power and Politics* (Washington, D.C.: Common Cause, 1981), p. ii.

56. Jack Newfield, *The Village Voice*, November 5, 1979.

57. Common Cause, *Money, Power*, pp. 74–80.

58. Michael R. Gordon, *National Journal*, July 11, 1981.

59. Two hundred PACs sponsored by corporations and trade associations "with a substantial interest in oil and gas production" were studied by the New York-based National Committee for an Effective Congress (national director: Russell D. Hemenway). The top ten integrated domestic and international companies were covered as well as many smaller enterprises.

60. Russell D. Hemenway, National Committee for an Effective Congress, press release March 29, 1981.

61. David Nyhan, *Boston Globe*, September 29, 1976.

62. Ibid., October 1, 1976.

63. James Deakin, *New York Times*, November 17, 1974.

64. Rachelle Patterson, *Boston Globe*, April 23, 1979.

65. Drew Pearson and Jack Anderson, *The Case Against Congress* (New York: Pocket Books, 1969), p. 314; *Parade*, May 6, 1973.

66. Dan Rapaport, *Inside the House* (Chicago: Follett Publishing Company, 1975), p. 187.

67. *Newsweek*, March 16, 1981.

68. *Business Week*, May 7, 1979.

69. Charles B. Lipsen with Stephan Lesher, *Vested Interest*, chapter 2.

70. Milbrath, *Washington Lobbyists*, preface and appendix A.

71. Jack Anderson, *Parade*, March 16, 1980.

72. Michael C. Jensen, *New York Times*, November 12, 1972.

73. Ibid.

74. Robert Engler, *The Brotherhood of Oil* (Chicago: University of Chicago Press, 1977), p. 171.

75. Jensen, *New York Times*.

76. *Congressional Quarterly*, December 27, 1980, p. 3647.

77. Ibid., p. 3643.

78. Michael J. Malbin, *Unelected Representatives* (New York: Basic Books, Inc., Publishers, 1980).

79. Ibid., p. 19, quoting Harrison Fox and Susan Hammond.

80. Stuart Taylor, *New York Times*, May 10, 1981. They were to be helped by Thomas L. Ashley, the Ohio Democrat defeated in 1980 after thirteen terms in the House. Mr. Curtis had been his choice. Mr. Ashley had been chosen by Speaker O'Neill in 1977 to chair an *ad hoc* committee to steer the Carter energy program through the House. That was one source of his attraction for General Public Utilities.

81. William Keefe and Morris Ogul, *The American Legislative Process*, 5th ed. (Englewood Cliffs, N.J.: Prentice-Hall Inc., 1981), p. 317.

82. Carol S. Greenwald, *Group Power: Lobbying and Public Policy* (New York: Praeger Publishers, 1977), p. 64.

83. Peters, *How Washington Really Works*, p. 5.

84. Bill Keller, *Congressional Quarterly*, December 27, 1980, p. 3643.

85. Truman, *Governmental Process*, p. 269.

86. Keller, *Congressional Quarterly*, p. 3646.

87. Truman, *Governmental Process*, pp. 333–34.

88. Norman J. Ornstein and Shirley Elder, *Interest Groups, Lobbying and Policymaking* (Washington, D.C.: Congressional Quarterly, 1978), pp. 84–86 (*cf*, pp. 75–76).

89. Lewis Anthony Dexter, *How Organizations Are Represented in Washington* (Indianapolis: The Bobbs-Merrill Company, Inc., 1969), pp. 131–132; Truman, *Governmental Process*, pp. 334–35.

90. Ibid., p. 131.

91. Ornstein and Elder, *Interest Groups*, p. 77.

92. *New York Times*, November 22, 1981.

93. Ibid., December 3, 1981.

94. Ibid., November 22, 1981.

95. Ornstein and Elder, *Interest Groups*, p. 77.

96. V. O, Key, Jr., *Politics, Parties and Pressure Groups* 5th ed., (New York: Thomas Y. Crowell, 1964), pp. 131–32.

97. Peters, *How Washington Really Works*, pp. 13–14.

98. Morton Mintz and Jerry S. Cohen, *Power, Inc.* (New York: The Viking Press, 1976), p. 287.

99. Quoted in Mintz and Cohen, *ibid.*, p. 69.

100. *New York Times*, September 6, 1975.

101. Robert Sherrill, *Why They Call It Politics*, 3rd ed. (New York: Harcourt Brace Jovanovich, 1979), p. 262.

102. Ibid., pp. 261–62.

103. Mary Link, *Congressional Quarterly*, March 6, 1976.

104. Nancy Hicks, *New York Times*, March 3, 1976.

105. Quoted in *The Guardian* (London), March 21, 1976.

106. Holtzman, *Interest Groups*, p. 106.

107. Philip Shabecoff, *New York Times*, April 19, 1981.

108. Graham K. Wilson, *Interest Groups in America* (New York: Oxford University Press, 1981), pp. 19–20.

109. Rex Hardesty, *The American Federationist*, May, 1975.

110. *Boston Globe*, February 22, 1973.

111. *New York Times*, December 20, 1976.

112. Shabecoff, *New York Times*.

113. Ibid.

114. *New York Times*, May 31, 1981.

115. Judy Klemesrud, *New York Times*, March 1, 1976.

116. Ibid., Dr. Mildred Jefferson.

117. Ibid., Lesley Oelsner.

118. Eleanor Randolph, *Los Angeles Times*, November 13, 1979.

119. Ibid.

120. Michael Barone and Grant Ujifusa, *The Almanac of American Politics* (Washington, D.C.: Barone & Company, 1982), p. 372.

121. Bernard Weinraub, *New York Times*, May 11, 1980.

122. Mark Shields, *Washington Post*, April 17, 1981.

123. Bernard Weinraub, *New York Times*, March 24, 1980.

124. Eleanor Randolph, *Los Angeles Times*, November 13, 1979.

125. Larry Light, *Congressional Quarterly*, June 14, 1980.

126. Jim Mann, *Los Angeles Times* (carried in *Boston Globe*, April 26, 1981).

127. Mary McGrory, *Boston Globe*, July 28, 1980.

128. John Herbers, *New York Times*, February 24, 1980.

129. Robert Heilbroner, *Harper's*, June, 1957.

130. Edward L. Bernays, *The Annals*, March 1947, pp. 113–120.

131. *The Annals*, 179 (May, 1935), p. 82.

132. Mark V. Nadel, *Corporations and Political Accountability* (Lexington, Mass.: D. C. Heath and Company, 1976), p. 51.

133. The Kefauver hearings had by then disclosed that one American company bought a drug from a French manufacturer and sold sixty of the tablets worth 11.7 cents for $8.40. A markup of 7,079%, exclaimed the *New York Times* and others. According to the First National City Bank, N.Y.C. (c. 1970), the industry had earned every year after 1955 a net income after taxes of 9.6 to 11.9% of sales as against the average of 5.2 to 6.7% for forty-one other manufacturing industries. Or 17.8 to 24% of net worth as against 9.8 to 15% of net worth in the forty-one.

134. "Observations," *Parade*, March 28, 1976.

135. *Boston Globe*, January 4, 1982 and *New York Times*, January 7, 1982.

136. Robert Sherrill, in Robert Engler, ed., *America's Energy* (New York: Pantheon Books, 1980), p. 294.

137. *Boston Globe*, July 1, 1981.

138. *Parade*, March 28, 1976.

139. Common Cause, *The Power Persuaders* (Washington, D.C.: 1978), p. 26.

140. A Kennedy Democrat, he had found a comfortable niche working for Mobil. By 1981 he had risen to be vice-president and director of public relations. The company allowed him to take leave in 1980 to work for Senator Edward Kennedy's ill-starred campaign. This is known as working both ends of the street.

141. Robert Sherrill, in Robert Engler, ed., *America's Energy* (New York: Pantheon Books, 1980), p. 295.

142. A. Kent MacDougall, *Los Angeles Times*, carried in *Boston Globe*, January 11, 1981.

143. Ibid.

144. Active also in British politics, e.g., in defeating the location of a third London airport in North Buckinghamshire. See Graham Wootton, *Pressure Politics in Contemporary Britain* (Lexington, Mass.: Lexington Books, 1978), chapter 6.

145. *National Journal*, May 31, 1980.

146. Ibid.

147. Jerry Ackerman, *Boston Globe*, September 16, 1977.

148. Ibid.

149. Irwin Ross, *The Image Merchants* (Garden City, N.Y.: Doubleday & Company, Inc., 1959), *passim*.

150. Coal was costing from one-third to one-half as much as oil. And the U.S.A. held about a third of the world's economically recoverable coal reserves.

151. *Newsweek*, February 28, 1977 and *National Journal*, May 27, 1978.

152. David S. Broder, *Boston Globe*, March 15, 1981.

153. James Wagner with Harrison H. Donnelly, *Congressional Quarterly*, February 26, 1977.

154. David Bird, *New York Times*, February 26, 1977.

155. Ann Pelham, *Congressional Quarterly*, May 27, 1978.

156. Robert Sherrill, *New York Times Magazine*, October 14, 1979.

157. Robert D. Hershey, Jr., *New York Times*, July 18, 1980.

158. Fred J. Cook, in Robert Engler, ed., *America's Energy* (New York: Pantheon Books, 1980), p. 291.

159. Donald L. Bartlett and James B. Steele (Knight Ridder Service), carried in *Boston Globe*, June 17, 1979.

160. Cook, in *Energy*.

161. Walter A. Rosenbaum, *Energy, Politics and Public Policy* (Washington, D.C.: Congressional Quarterly Inc., 1981), p. 159.

162. Robert Sherrill, *New York Times Magazine*, October 14, 1979.

163. *Boston Globe*, December 22, 1980.

164. Clement E. Vose, *The Annals*, September 1958, p. 31.

165. Separated for tax purposes from NAACP proper in 1938, this is not a membership organization. The board and staff are all lawyers.

166. Clement E. Vose, "Interest Groups and Litigation," paper presented at APSA annual meeting, 1981, p. 3.

167. Stuart Taylor, *New York Times*, January 16, 1982. *Washington Post*, carried in *Boston Globe*, January 14, 1982.

168. *NAACP v. Button* (Attorney General of Virginia, et al.), 371 U.S. 415, 1963.

169. Karen O'Connor, "Litigation as a form of political activity: how women's groups have used the courts," paper presented at annual APSA meeting, 1977, pp. 19–21.

170. Henry J. Abraham, *The Judicial Process*, 3rd ed. (New York: Oxford University Press, 1975), p. 233.

171. Karen O'Connor and Lee Epstein, "Amicus Curiae Participation in U.S. Supreme Court Litigation: An Appraisal of 'Hakman's Folklore'," *Law and Society Review*, 16 (1981–82), Table 1.

172. *NAACP v. Button*, 371 U.S. 415, 1963.

173. Fred Barbash, *Washington Post* (carried in *Boston Globe*, April 29, 1981).

174. *New York Times*, January 23, 1979.

175. *Newsweek*, June 5, 1978.

176. Associated Press, carried in *New York Times*, October 6, 1981.

177. James Q. Wilson, *Political Organizations* (New York: Basic Books, Inc., Publishers, 1973), pp. 263–82.

178. Michael Lipsky, "Protest as a Political Resource", 62 *American Political Science Review* (December 1968), pp.1144–1158.

179. Another sign read; "Why work and pay for mass suicide?" It being April 15, the last day for the annual rite of filing income tax returns, the happy band also hurled tax forms at the pillars (as one has often been tempted to do).

180. *Newsweek*, June 5, 1978. *Boston Globe*, August 17, 1978.

181. Lynton Caldwell and others, eds., *Citizens and the Environment* (Bloomington, Indiana: Indiana University Press, 1976), pp. 195–204.

182. *Boston Sunday Globe*, May 8, 1977.

183. John Herbers, *New York Times*, February 21, 1980.

184. *Boston Globe*, January 23, 1979.

185. *Boston Sunday Globe*, July 16, 1978.

186. Marcia Kunstel (*Atlanta Journal*) in *New York Times*, August 25, 1979.

CHAPTER 9: DISTRIBUTIVE POLICY: OIL DEPLETION ALLOWANCE

1. Ira Sharkansky, in Sharkansky, ed., *Policy Analysis in Political Science* (Chicago: Markham Publishing Company, 1970), p. 6.

2. Theodore J. Lowi, "American Business, Public Policy, Case-Studies, and Political The-

ory," *World Politics*, 16,(July 1964), 688–695; "Four Systems of Policy, Politics and Choice," Inter-University Case Program Inc., November 1971, p. 3.

3. James Q. Wilson, *Political Organizations* (New York: Basic Books Inc., Publishers, 1973), p. 330.

4. Randall B. Ripley and Grace A. Franklin, *Congress, The Bureaucracy and Public Policy* (Homewood, Ill.: The Dorsey Press, 1976).

5. Francesco Kjellberg, "Do Politics (Really) Determine Politics? And Eventually How?" *Policy Studies Journal*, 5 (Autumn 1976).

6. Michael Hayes, *Journal of Politics*, 40 (1978), 160.

7. George D. Greenberg, Jeffrey A. Miller, Lawrence B. Mohr, and Bruce C. Vladeck, "Developing Public Policy Theory," *American Political Science Review*, 71 (1977), 1534.

8. Peter J. Steinberger, "Typologies of Public Policy," *Social Science Quarterly*, 61 (September 1980), challenged by Elinor Ostrom and Ira Sharkansky, same issue.

9. Michael Hayes, *Lobbyists and Legislators* (New Brunswick, N.J.: Rutgers University Press, 1981), p. 25.

10. Eric M. Uslaner, "Energy, Issue Agendas, and Policy Typologies," paper read at APSA annual meeting, 1982.

11. Robert Salisbury, in Austin Ranney, ed., *Political Science and Public Policy* (Chicago: Markham Publishing company, 1968), p. 165.

12. In political sociology, the ultimate independent variable had been represented (in this context) as *system resources*, e.g., wealth. Accepting that, Professor Salisbury was out to show that political variables (his *demand patterns* and *decisional system*)—intervening variables in this broader framework—still "made a difference" (to the *type* of policy). This was all part of a debate about socioeconomic conditions, political processes and public policies in the American states. For the state of the art at the time he was writing, consult the bibliographical essay by John H. Fenton and Donald W. Chamberlayne, *Polity* 1 (spring, 1969), pp. 388–405.

13. Salisbury, in *Political Science*, p. 158.

14. Merle Fainsod, Lincoln Gordon and Joseph C. Palamountain, Jr., 3rd. ed. *Government and the American Economy* (New York: W. W. Norton & Company, Inc., 1959). Martin Schnitzer, *Contemporary Government and Business Relations* (Boston, Mass.: Houghton Mifflin Company, 1983).

15. One's own view is that truly redistributive policy is rare in America not so much because of the demand patterns and decisional system (Salisbury) or demand and supply (Hayes) but, fundamentally, because the Left in the U.S. has been so weak and ineffective.

16. T. S. Adams, "Ideals and Idealism in Taxation," *American Economic Review*, XVIII (March, 1928), p. 1.

17. Richard Corrigan, *National Journal*, August 15, 1981.

18. Ibid.

19. David Rogers, *Boston Globe*, August 7, 1981.

20. Corrigan, *National Journal*, Thomas B. Edsall, *Washington Post*, carried in *Boston Globe*, May 1, 1983, Barnes, *Reader's Digest*, September 1982.

21. As noted, the immediate write-off provided a splendid tax shelter against non-oil income if nothing else. Or you could think of it as economist Alfred E. Kahn did—as an interest-free loan to those who could take the accelerated first-year deduction.

22. Philip M. Stern, *The Rape of the Taxpayer* (New York: Vintage Books, 1974). p. 229. *Boston Globe*, December 19, 1974. Table 9-1 also came from this book.

23. Petroleum Institute Research Foundation, *New York Times*, May 28, 1974.

24. Bruce Ian Oppenheimer, *Oil and the Congressional Process* (Lexington, Mass.: Lexington Books, Inc., 1975), ch. 5; Joseph A. Ruskay and Richard A. Osserman, *Halfway to Tax Reform* (Bloomington, Indiana: Indiana University Press, 1970), pp. 2, 94, 1246.

25. Erwin Knoll, "The Oil Lobby is Not Depleted," *New York Times Magazine*, March 8, 1970.

26. Russkay and Osserman, ibid., p. 94.

27. According to Jack Newfield in 1979, the senator then owned $1.2 million in oil and gas property, and had earned over $100,000 in 1978 from his oil interests. *Village Voice* (N.Y.), Nov. 5, 1979.

28. Oppenheimer, *Oil*, p. 125.

29. Tom Arrandale, *Congressional Quarterly*, October 18, 1975.

30. Eileen Shanahan, *New York Times*, May 28, 1974. *Congressional Quarterly*, March 29, 1975.

31. Oppenheimer, *Oil*, pp. 10, 15, 74.

32. Stephen L. McDonald, *Federal Treatment of Income From Oil and Gas* (Washington, D.C.: The Brookings Institution, 1963), p. 14.

33. Ronnie Dugger, "Oil and Politics," *Atlantic Monthly*, September 1969.

34. Too much should not be made of that. Even under the earlier form of depletion, Gulf Oil had come off well, receiving $4 million from it in two years, according 'to Senator James Couzens (Rep.-Michigan). A multimillionaire businessman from Detroit, he was a scourge of the depletion principle, failing to see (he would say) why Gulf, Standard and the other majors should not pay their taxes as other companies had to.

35. Oppenheimer, *Oil*, p. 23.

36. That path had been well beaten for almost a century. In 1866 the Pennsylvania oil producers descended on Ways and Means to have a federal tax on crude oil repealed. The committee obliged.

37. Stern, *The Rape* p. 243.

38. Paul Douglas, *In Our Time* (New York: Harcourt, Brace & World, Inc., 1967), p. 11.

39. Erwin Knoll, *The Oil Lobby;* Stern, *The Rape*, p. 298, note*.

40. Drew Pearson and Jack Anderson, *The Case Against Congress* (New York: Pocket Books, Inc., 1969), ch. 5 and p. 124 quoting Senator Douglas.

41. Stern, *The Rape*, p. 238.

42. Jack Anderson, *Washington Exposé* (Washington, D.C.: Public Affairs Press, 1967), p. 209.

43. *New York Times*, June 30. 1980.

44. Stern, *The Rape*, p. 229.

45. Anderson, *Exposé*, p. 208.

46. Ibid., p. 209.

47. Oppenheimer, *Oil*, p. 33.

48. Bobby (Robert G.) Baker with Larry L. King, *Wheeling And Dealing* (New York: W. W. Norton & Company, 1978), pp. 99–100.

49. Paul Douglas, *In Our Time* (Harcourt, Brace & World Inc., 1967), p. 12.

50. Rowland Evans and Robert Novak, *Lyndon B. Johnson: The Exercise of Power* (New York: New American Library, 1968), p. 113, note.

51. Paul Douglas, *In the Fullness of Time* (New York: Harcourt Brace Jovanovich Inc., 1971), p. 427.

52. Oppenheimer, *Oil*, p. 74.

53. Ibid., p. 95.

54. John F. Manley, *The Politics of Finance* (Boston, Mass.: Little Brown and Co., 1970), p. 27.

55. Lewis A. Froman, Jr., *The Congressional Process* (Boston, Mass.: Little Brown and Co., 1967), p. 51.

56. Manley, ibid. Spark M. Matsunaga and Ping Chen, *Rulemakers of the House* (Urbana, Ill.: University Illinois Press, 1976), p. 21.

57. Tom Field of Taxation with Representation, a public interest group, quoted in Oppenheimer, *Oil*, p. 102.

58. Oppenheimer, pp. 72, 90.

59. Other rules and procedures, including informal norms (chapter 5), might have changed, however. Here we are simply using the special case of the closed rule to illustrate one element in an explanatory framework.

60. Thomas C. Heller, "Public Interest Law and Federal Income Taxes," in Burton A. Weisrod and others, eds., *Public Interest Law* (Berkeley, Ca.: University of California Press, 1978), p. 447.

61. James Byrne, quoted in *Congressional Quarterly*, May 3, 1975.

62. Oppenheimer, *Oil*, ch. 4.

63. Walter J. Oleszek, *Congressional Procedures and the Policy Process* (Washington, D.C.: Congressional Quarterly Press, 1978), pp. 40, 43.

64. Alan Ehrenhalt, *Congressional Quarterly*, May 3, 1975.

65. Ibid.

66. Another example of musical chairs (or revolving door): not just a former congressman (from Texas) but a member of Ways and Means himself from 1955 to 1961.

67. Also to convert the existing tax credit into a simple business deduction. This was an amendment in the name of an antidepletion fighter, Charles Vanik (Ohio).

68. Matsunaga and Chen, *Rulemakers*, p. 41.

69. *Congressional Quarterly*, March 1, 1979.

70. Matsunaga and Chen, *Rulemakers*, p. 22.

CHAPTER 10: REGULATORY AND SELF-REGULATORY POLICIES

1. Eric M. Uslaner, "Energy, Issue Agendas, and Policy Typologies," paper presented at annual meeting of APSA, 1982.

2. Theodore J. Lowi, "American Business, Public Policy, Case-Studies, and Political Theory," *World Politics*, 16 (1964), 690.

3. Robert S. Friedman, "Professionalism: Expertise and Policy Making," (N.Y.C.: General Learning Press, 1971), p. 5. Randall B. Ripley and Grace A. Franklin, *Congress, The Bureaucracy, and Public Policy* (Homewood, Ill.: The Dorsey Press, 1976), p. 18.

4. Among the federally aided roads, there were class A or primary (main highways), class B or secondary (farm-to-market and feeder roads), and class C, or urban. Those primaries connecting up the great cities and industrial areas were designated interstates.

5. Congressional Quarterly, *Congress and the Nation*, II (Washington, D.C.: Congressional Quarterly, Inc., 1969, p. 476–480.

6. *New York Times*, September 14, 1965. Lewis Mumford, "The Highway and the City," in Garrett de Bell, *The Environmental Handbook* (New York: Ballantine Books, 1970), p. 182.

7. Mumford, *The Highway*.

8. Murray Edelman, *The Symbolic Uses of Politics* (Urbana, Ill.: University of Illinois Press, 1967).

9. Congressional Quarterly, *Congress and the Nation*, II, pp. 486–87.

10. Background: Industry's energy revolution in that era had been from steam power to cheap electricity. In 1914 about a third of American industry had relied upon electricity for its power. By 1929 the proportion was three-quarters.

11. Ralph K. Huitt, in Emmette Redford, ed., *Public Administration and Policy Formation* (Austin: University of Texas Press, 1956), p. 55.

12. Established in 1920. Its original focus was water-power but also, derivatively, electricity. In 1930 it was reorganized as an independent regulatory agency with five commissioners appointed by the president. The Wheeler-Rayburn Act gave it authority over interstate electricity.

13. A boomerang of a title. The company would one day argue, even before the U.S. Supreme Court, that it was not engaged in interstate commerce. This would have been more

convincing if it had not previously argued, successfully, that it should be free of state regulation precisely because it was engaged in interstate commerce.

14. Congressional Research Service, Library of Congress, *The Constitution of the United States of America* (G.P.O., 1973), p. 276, citing 331 U.S. 682 (1947).

15. Ibid.

16. Richard Austin Smith, "The Unnatural Problems of Natural Gas," *Fortune*, September, 1959.

17. Rep. Ross Rizley (Oklahoma), Hearings before the Committee on Interstate and Foreign Commerce, House of Representatives, "Amendments to the Natural Gas Act," April-May, 1947, p. 17.

18. The Interstate and Foreign Commerce Committee. The House vote was by voice.

19. Ibid., 1949, p. 112.

20. Rowland Evans and Robert Novak, *Lyndon B. Johnson: The Exercise of Power* (New York: The New American Library, Inc., 1968), pp. 44–5.

21. Huitt, ibid., pp. 96–97.

22. Edith T. Carper, *Lobbying and the Natural Gas Bill* (Inter-University Case Program, no. 72, 1962), p. 9.

23. Ibid., p. 7.

24. Ibid., p. 13.

25. One of the incidental advantages of that may be illustrated as follows. Humble Oil gave the Committee $175,000, which it set off against income tax as an operating expense. But the $3855 to the GGC, a registered lobby, was treated as a lobbying expense.

26. Ibid., pp. 14–18, 22.

27. Ibid., pp. 24, 26.

28. Republican senators Prescott Bush and James Duff voted against exemption. Whether or not as the effect of indirect influence, Democratic senator Mike Mansfield voted *for*. So did 21 other Democratic senators, who split 22–24.

29. Ibid., p. 39.

30. Congressional Quarterly, *Congress and the Nation*, II, p. 983.

31. Daniel J. Fiorino, in James E. Anderson, ed., *Economic Regulatory Policies* (Lexington, Mass.: Lexington Books Inc., 1976), pp. 90, 92.

32. Fiorino, ibid., pp. 93–94.

33. Formed in July 1974, it replaced what was meant to be temporary, the Federal Energy Office, set up the previous December in the wake of the OPEC embargo and quadrupling of oil prices.

34. *Congressional Quarterly*, May 22, 1976.

35. Ibid., June 5, 1976.

36. *New York Times*, February 26, 1977.

37. Ibid., June 30, 1977; *Congressional Quarterly*, June 11, 1977.

38. *New York Times*, February 26, 1977.

39. Albert R. Hunt, *Wall Street Journal*, July 15, 1977.

40. Ibid.

41. Bob Rankin, *Congressional Quarterly*, August 6, 1977.

42. *Time*, October 17, 1977.

43. Ibid.

44. Ibid.

45. Ibid.

46. With the connivance of Vice-President Mondale, Majority Leader Byrd flattened thirty-three amendments in ten minutes, nine according to another source. In any case, very quickly.

47. Bob Rankin, *Congressional Quarterly*, December 24, 1977.

48. Ibid., October 15, 1977.

49. *Time*, October 17, 1977.

50. Rankin, *Congressional Quarterly*, December 24, 1977.

51. Congressional Quarterly, *Energy Policy* (Washington, D.C.: Congressional Quarterly Inc., 1979), p. 13.

52. Bob Rankin, *Congressional Quarterly*, April 22, 1978.

53. James Presley, *A Saga of Wealth: The Rise of the Texas Oilmen* (New York: G. P. Putnam's Sons, 1978), ch. VII, especially 172–193. Even this trade description was wrong. Such a mixture of the criminal and the merely illegal was known as "boiling hot oil." Outraged at the "rustling," the mere "hot oiler" wanted his lawyer to complain to the supervising authority. The lawyer did not seem to think that a good idea. This reminds one of the distinction between "honest graft" (e.g., the state legislator using inside knowledge for private profit) and "graft" (e.g., a payoff).

54. *Time*, October 17, 1977.

55. *Congressional Quarterly*, April 22, 1978.

56. Technically it was a magic circle of individual congresspersons who happened to be conferees. In other words, the meetings were informal, as Senator Jackson made plain.

57. Ann Pelham, *Congressional Quarterly*, May 27, 1978.

58. National Grange (for), American Farm Bureau Federation (against). In 1977 it had been Farm Bureau *v*. National Farmers Union.

59. David E. Rosenbaum, *Congressional Quarterly*, September 16, 1978.

60. Ann Pelham, *Congressional Quarterly*, October 21, 1978.

CHAPTER 11: REGULATORY POLICY : GOING TO POT

1. Pamela G. Hollie, *New York Times*, July 13, 1980.

2. Ibid.

3. Ibid.

4. Andred C. Tartaglino, acting deputy administrator, Drug Enforcement Administration, in *Marihuana-Hashish Epidemic and Its Impact on United States Security* (Subcommittee of the Committee on the Judiciary, United States Senate, 93rd Congress, May-June, 1974), p. 9.

5. Of course, it did not begin to rival in street value the 398 pounds of heroin and cocaine stolen from the New York Police Department's property clerk's office in 1972. That was valued at $70 million. *New York Times*, December 8, 1978.

6. Richard J. Bonnie and Charles H. Whitebread II, *The Marihuana Conviction* (Charlottesville: University of Virginia Press, 1974), p. 310, n. 19.

7. Ibid., pp. 8 and 14.

8. Ibid., p. 15.

9. The power to regulate for the sake of health, morals, safety or welfare.

10. Such as employees of properly registered employers, and designated public officials.

11. H.R. 6282, December 17, 1914 and 38. Stat. 785 (1914).

12. Bonnie and Whitebread, *Marihuana*, p. 20.

13. Whether the genus *cannabis*, originally from Asia, has but one species, *sativa*, or three may be safely left to the botanists. For us *cannabis* is just hemp. Suitably beaten, the stem provides a fiber from which rope and twine, canvas and oakum are made. The seed is for the birds (literally), but may be crushed as a foundation for soap, paint and varnishes. Asians have long extracted a beverage by boiling the leaves (reminding one of the European practice of brewing beer from the hop plant, which is part of the hemp family). Hemp also secretes a dark brown resin (a viscous fluid), mainly in the flowering heads. If you press a lot of these together, the resin aggregates and you have *hashish*. This is an Arabic word, meaning "dried herb" or

"dried grass." Dried and ground for use, the plant becomes marijuana (or marihuana), a term derived from Mexican-Spanish, but known colloquially as "Mary Jane," "pot," "grass," "the weed" and even "tea." Verbal forms include "toking" and "smoking a joint."

14. This was the era that introduced the *reefer*, marijuana in cigarette form. A movie of the time bore the title, *Reefer Madness*, the consequence attributed to such smoking. The etymology of *reefer* is uncertain: it might be derived from the action of rolling the stuff into a cigarette on the analogy of sailors reefing a sail.

15. H.R. 6906, August 2, 1937, Sec. 2(a), Sec. 7(a) (1) and (2).

16. Sections 101, 102, and 106 deal with marijuana alone. The "sale or transfer without written order" covered narcotics as well as marijuana (Sec. 103, amending Section 7237 of the Internal Revenue Code of 1954).

17. *Leary v. United States* (1969).

18. In *United States v. Kahriger* (1953), in which, however, the Supreme Court upheld, by a majority, the 1951 Revenue Act requiring gamblers to register, etc. At that stage, the Court had rejected self-incrimination as a defense, a holding reversed in *Marchetti*.

19. H.R. 18583. A second category (Schedule II) embraced substances with a high potential for abuse but some medical use, e.g., methadone. Schedule III, including "speed," covered substances with recognized medical use and lower physical dependence (though potentially high psychological dependence). Schedule 4 covered substances with low potential for abuse, recognized medical use, and limited danger of dependence.

20. Cited in Laurence A. Gooberman, *Operation Intecept*, (New York : Pergamon Press, Inc., 1974), pp. 121–23 and 171, n. 50 and 67.

21. Patrick Anderson, "The Pot Lobby," *New York Times Magazine*, January 21, 1973.

22. Ibid. Also two in New York and one in Boston.

23. Charles Perry, *Rolling Stone*, August 10, 1978, by which time there were offices in New York, Chicago and San Francisco.

24. *People*, June 19, 1978. Financial support, unspecified, also came from *High Times* (*Rolling Stone*, August 10, 1978).

25. Anderson, *Pot*.

26. *Marijuana: A Study of State Policies and Penalties* (Washington, D.C. National Institute of Law Enforcement and Criminal Justice, 1977), part 1, pp. 86–89, part 2, pp. 5–7.

27. Andrew C. Tartaglino, *Decriminalization of Marijuana* (House Select Committee on Narcotics Abuse and Control, 95th Congress, March 1977), p. 362.

28. *New York Times*, June 30, 1977.

29. S. 1450 (Judiciary) and H.R. 6108 (Interstate and Foreign Commerce), April 17, 1975.

30. *Boston Globe*, August 3, 1977 from Knight News Service.

31. *People*, June 19, 1978; *Rolling Stone*, August 10, 1978.

32. Lester Grinspoon *Marihuana Reconsidered*, 1st ed., (Cambridge, Mass.: Harvard University Press, 1971), cited in Gooberman, *Operation Intercept*, p. 121.

33. E.g., *Decriminalization of Marijuana*, p. 340; also U.S. Senate, Subcommittee on Alcoholism and Narcotics, Hearings, November 1974, p. 100.

34. *New York Times*, December 28, 1978; N.B.C., *Reading, Writing and Reefer*, December 10, 1978, p. 41 (see also p. 43). The *Times* had followed up a *New York Post* story saying that Mr. Stroup was retiring because of chronic bronchitis caused by smoking marijuana.

35. *Rolling Stone*, August 10, 1978.

36. *New York Times*, December 28, 1978.

37. Ibid.

38. *Parade*, Sept. 17, 1978.

39. State of California, Fair Political Practices Commission, *A Report on Lobbying*, 1975–76 (August 17, 1977), 1977–78 (Sept. 20, 1979), and 1979 (April 2, 1980).

40. In every age category in 1979, "substantial proportions" wanted to keep marijuana use illegal or even make the law stricter. This was true of youths (12–17) and older adults (26 and

over). Even among the 18–25s (the most susceptible or the most daring, according to your point of view), about 40 percent agreed. Two out of three high-school seniors disapproved of regular use. Secretary of Health, Education and Welfare, National Institute of Drug Abuse: *Marijuana and Health* (G.P.O., Washington, D.C., 1980), p. 5.

41. Anderson, *Pot*.

42. Michael Antonoff, *New York Times*, Nov. 16, 1979.

43. In his essay of that title, columnist William Safire wrote, "even richies" have rights. *New York Times*, July 7, 1980.

CHAPTER 12: REDISTRIBUTIVE POLICY: TAXING WINDFALL PROFITS

1. *Boston Globe*, October 14, 1980.

2. Despite the title of the measure (Crude Oil Windfall Profit Tax, 1980) and the universal use of the term at the time, this was in fact an excise tax. It tapped the increased *revenue* that the oil companies would earn once controls were removed. Was the use of the misnomer, *windfall profit* a subconscious, or even conscious, acknowledgment of redistributive intentions?

3. Roughly, from 1973 onward. More technically, production from a leasehold above the level reached during 1972. Later: in production as of May 15, 1973.

4. William A. Johnson, in Gary Eppen, ed., *Energy: The Policy Issues* (Chicago: University of Chicago Press, 1975), p. 109.

5. Robert Stobaugh and Daniel Yergin, *Boston Globe*, January 18, 1981, and *Energy Future* (New York: Vintage Books, 1983), p. 6.

6. In the spring of 1979, the OPEC price was $16 a barrel at one point, $18 a little later.

7. *New York Times*, May 9, 1979.

8. Ann Pelham, *Congressional Quarterly*, April 7, 1979.

9. Terence Smith, *New York Times*, April 8, 1979.

10. Ibid.

11. Curtis Wilkie, *Boston Globe*, April 15, 1979.

12. *Boston Globe*, May 1, 1979.

13. Pelham, *Congressional Quarterly*, June 2, 1979.

14. *Mobil and Texaco* were up 81 percent. Texaco excelled itself in the second quarter: up 132 percent on the corresponding period in 1978.

15. Kathryn Waters Gest, *Congressional Quarterly*, April 28, 1979.

16. Pelham, *Congressional Quarterly*, July 28, 1979.

17. Ibid., October 27, 1979.

18. Ibid., November 17, 1979.

19. Ibid., December 1, 1979.

20. Jack Newfield, *Village Voice*, November 5, 1979.

21. *New York Times*, May 9, 1979.

22. Pelham, *Congressional Quarterly*, December 1, 1979.

23. Meaning then the difference between $16–17 a barrel (the base price), plus inflation, and the selling price. This would be the main element in what was being then called the "minimum tax."

24. Helen Thomas (U.P.I.), carried in *Boston Globe*, December 23, 1979. Ernest Holsendolph, *New York Times*, December 23, 1979.

25. A. O. Sulzberger, Jr., *New York Times*, January 23, 1980.

26. *Congressional Quarterly*, January 26, 1980.

27. Sulzberger, *New York Times*, February 25, 1980. Earlier (December 9, 1979) the paper had reported estimated relevant savings of $18 billion.

28. Martin Tolchin, *New York Times*, March 14, 1980.

29. Pelham, *Congressional Quarterly*, March 29, 1980. Helen Dewar, *Washington Post*, carried in *Boston Globe*, March 28, 1980.

30. Said to Warren Weaver, Jr., *New York Times*, July 2, 1979.

CHAPTER 13: AMERICA: "A SPECIAL-INTEREST DEMOCRACY?"

1. Arthur F. Bentley, *The Process of Government* (Chicago: University of Chicago Press, 1908). Earl Latham, *The Group Basis of Politics* (Ithaca: Cornell University Press, 1952).

2. That is their nature. Scholars use the case-study method for various purposes: to generate hypotheses, to check some existing proposition, and so on. Always ask: what is this case study *for*?

3. David W. Brady, in Bruce A. Campbell and Richard J. Trilling, eds., *Realignment in American Politics* (Austin: University of Texas Press, 1980), p. 200; Michael Barone and others, *The Almanac of American Politics* (New York: E. P. Dutton & Co., Inc., 1976), introduction, v.

4. Barone, *Almanac*.

5. Gerald M. Pomper with Susan S. Lederman, *Elections in America*, 2nd ed., New York: Longman, Inc., 1980), pp. 73–78.

6. Alan D. Monroe, *Public Opinion in America* (New York: Dodd, Mead & Company, 1975), ch. 14.

7. James N. Rosenau, *Citizenship Between Elections* (New York: The Free Press, 1974).

8. Nelson W. Polsby, *Community Power and Political Theory*, 2nd ed. (New Haven: Yale University Press, 1980), p. 118.

9. The federal government had little to do with the issue. One exception was the Comstock Act of 1873, which sought to suppress the trade in and circulation of obscene literature and articles for immoral use. This provision was interpreted to include instruments and articles for inducing abortion.

10. Lawrence Lader, *Abortion II: Making the Revolution* (Boston, Mass.: Beacon Press, 1973), p. 62.

11. Bernard N. Nathanson with Richard N. Ostling, *Aborting America* (Garden City, New York: Doubleday & Company, Inc., 1979), p. 47 and ch. 7.

12. Judith Blake, *Science*, 191 (January–March 1971), p. 548.

13. See John Brigham, ed., *Making Public Policy* (Lexington, Mass.: D.C. Heath and Company, 1977) for a valuable collection of documents on this and other issues.

14. Roger M. Williams, in Carl Lowe, ed., *New Alignments in American Politics* (New York: The H. W. Wilson Company, 1980), p. 138.

15. James E. Anderson, David W. Brady and Charles Bullock III, *Public Policy and Politics in America* (North Scituate, Mass.: Duxbury Press, 1978), p. 244.

16. Mark V. Nadel, *The Politics of Consumer Protection* (Indianapolis: Bobbs-Merrill, 1971). He had more luck with that than with his attacks on oil depletion allowance. Even so, his truth-in-lending measure was locked up in committee for eight years. By the time it passed (1968), he had been knocked out of office. This means he was not in the Senate for the first ever "dent" in percentage depletion.

17. Linda Charlton, *New York Times*, January 29, 1978.

18. Ibid.

19. David Vogel, Promoting Pluralism: The Public Interest Movement and the American Reform Tradition, paper delivered at the annual meeting of the APSA 1978. p. 1.

20. William J. McGill, quoted by Carl Lowe, *New Alignments*, preface.

21. J. Roland Pennock, "Responsiveness, Responsibility, and Majority Rule," *American Political Science Review*, 46 (1952), 790.

22. Robert A. Dahl, *Modern Political Analysis* (Englewood Cliffs, N.J.: Prentice-Hall., 1963) and "The Concept of Power," Behavioral Science, 2 (1957), 201–215.

23. "Political power, then, I take to be a right of making laws with penalties of death, and consequently all less penalties, for the regulating and preserving of property, and of employing the force of the community, in the execution of such laws. . . ."

24. *Fortune,* July 11, 1983.

CHAPTER 14: INFLUENCE AND RESPONSIVENESS

1. Charles W. Wiggins and William P. Browne, "Interest Groups and Public Policy Within a State Legislative Setting," *Polity,* 14 (1982), 548.

2. Ibid., Table VII.

3. C. Wright Mills, *The Power Elite* (New York: Oxford University Press, 1959), p. 274.

4. Ibid., p. 251.

5. Daniel Bell, in G. William Domhoff and Hoyt B. Ballard, eds., *C. Wright Mills and the Power Elite* (Boston, Mass.: Beacon Press, 1969), p. 211.

6. Philip M. Boffey, *New York Times,* July 8, 1982.

7. Norman C. Thomas, *Education in National Politics* (New York: David McKay Company, Inc., 1975), p. 137.

8. Stephen K. Bailey, *Education Interest Groups in the Nation's Capital* (Washington, D.C.: American Council on Education, 1975), p. 15.

9. *U.S. News and World Report,* June 11, 1979.

10. Ibid. In 1983 the NEA President earned over $61,000, *New York Times,* November 8, 1983.

11. Mayor Koch, *New York Times,* January 30, 1980.

12. The supplementary medical part of Medicare (physicians' bills) were also expected to rise by 18 percent annually 1980–85. About a quarter would be paid for by beneficiaries in the form of premiums. The rest was scheduled to come out of federal general tax revenues.

13. Dr. Karen Davis, *New York Times,* August 24, 1983.

14. Philip Shabecoff, *New York Times,* April 16, 1978.

15. Linda E. Demkovich, *National Journal,* December 1, 1979.

16. Robert Pear, *New York Times,* November 21, 1982.

17. Carl Kaysen, in Edward S. Mason, *The Corporation in Modern Society* (Cambridge, Mass.: Harvard University Press, 1959), ch. 5.

18. George Gallup, reported in *Boston Globe,* August 25, 1972.

19. Judith Blake, cited in Bernard N. Nathanson with Richard N. Ostling, *Aborting America,* (Garden City, N.Y.: Doubleday & Company, Inc., 1979), pp. 265–66.

20. *Boston Sunday Globe,* January 28, 1973.

21. *Boston Globe,* April 19, 1973.

22. Such crystalizing is not uncommon, the Harris survey reported. What, in the 1950s, had been "narrow divisions on education, jobs, and housing rights turned into decisive majorities following the landmark decisions of the Warren Court." (*Brown v. Board of Education,* 1954, would no doubt be one of these.) Similarly, the act of Congress in 1971 giving eighteen-year-olds the right to vote in federal elections, about which there had been "a close to even public opinion," was followed by a clear majority, *Boston Globe,* April 19, 1973.

23. Robert Weissberg, *Public Opinion and Popular Government* (Englewood Cliffs, N.J.: Prentice-Hall, Inc., 1976), p. 127, Table 6–17.

24. These were amendments to a Senate bill banning the sale of the cheap "Saturday night specials." Their import had been prohibited by the 1968 act, which did not however apply to parts, an invitation to bring in and assemble in the U.S. This was done on a large scale. The Senate passed the bill but it was allowed to die in the House.

25. Richard Higgins, *Boston Globe Magazine,* March 9, 1980.

26. Alistair Cooke, *The Guardian* (London), May 22, 1965.

27. Ibid. The immediately preceding quotation is from Ronald P. Kriss, *Saturday Review,* August 26, 1972.

28. Richard Higgins, *Boston Globe Magazine,* March 9, 1980.

29. Cooke, *Guardian.*

30. *Boston Sunday Globe,* February 3, 1974.

31. *Wall Street Journal,* May 24, 1972.

32. Leroy N. Rieselbach, ed. *People v. Government: The Responsiveness of American Institutions* (Bloomington, Indiana: Indiana University Press, 1975), p. 80.

33. John W. Kingdon, *Congressmen's Voting Decisions,* 2nd ed. (New York: Harper & Row, Publishers, 1981), p. 37.

34. Ibid., p. 146. Bauer's work is Raymond A. Bauer, Ithiel de Sola Pool, and Lewis Anthony Dexter, *American Business and Public Policy,* 2nd ed., (New York : Atherton Press, 1972).

35. *Boston Globe,* September 10, 1981.

36. Kingdon, *Congressmen's,* p. 157.

37. As well, of course, as individuals. In 1982, Thomas P. O'Neill III (son of the Speaker of the U.S. House of Representatives) was campaigning for governor in Massachusetts. In February, seven of the seventeen who contributed the legal maximum of $1000 had Louisiana addresses. In all, ten were from out of state. *Boston Globe,* April 11, 1982.

38. National Committee for an Effective Congress, press release, March 29, 1981.

39. *New York Times,* October 14, 1981.

40. Marshall B. Clinard and Peter C. Yeager, *Corporate Crime* (New York: The Free Press, 1980), p. 158, n. 1.

41. Quoted by Ruby Abramson, *Los Angeles Times,* carried in *Boston Globe,* March 1, 1981.

42. William J. Crotty, *Political Reform and the American Experiment* (New York: Thomas Y. Crowell Company, 1977), p. 147.

43. Common Cause, *The Government Subsidy Squeeze* (Washington, D.C.: Common Cause, 1980), appendices I and Ia.

44. George Thayer, *Who Shakes the Money Tree?: American Campaign Financing from 1789 to the Present* (New York: Simon & Simon & Schuster, 1973), p. 273.

45. *New York Times,* January 15, 1982.

46. Gary C. Jacobson, *Money in Congressional Elections* (New Haven: Yale University Press, 1980), pp. 67 and 171.

47. Michael McMenamin and Walter McNamara, *Milking the Public: Political Scandals of the Dairy Lobby from LBJ to Jimmy Carter* (Chicago: Nelson-Hall, Inc., Publishers, 1980), pp. 45–46, 52–61.

48. Ibid., p. 5, quoting Frank Wright.

49. David R. Mayhew, *Congress: The Electoral Connection* (New Haven: Yale University Press, 1974), p. 93.

50. Senator William Fulbright, *New York Times,* May 26, 1979.

51. Dr. S. Prakash Sethi, Hearings before a Subcommittee on Government Operations, House of Representatives, May and July 1978, p. 383.

CHAPTER 15: A DUAL SYSTEM OF REPRESENTATION

1. Tasswell-Langmead's *English Constitutional History,* 11th ed. by Theodore F. T. Plucknett, (London: Sweet & Maxwell Limited, 1960), Chap. 6.

2. These "lords spiritual and temporal" eventually formed the House of Lords. The lower clergy "took off" from the House of Commons in the fourteenth century and have never returned.

That applies to what became the Anglican clergy. Other ministers of religion—Methodists, Baptists, etc.—are eligible to be Members of Parliament.

3. Samuel H. Beer, *Modern British Politics* (New York: W. W. Norton & Company, 1982), ch. II (rev. ed. of *British Politics in the Collectivist Age,* 1969).

4. *Baker v. Carr,* 369 U.S. 186 (1962).

5. *Reynolds v. Sims,* 377 U.S. 833 (1964).

6. Charles A. Beard and John D. Lewis, "Representative Government by Evolution", *American Political Science Review,* XXVI (April 1932), p. 235.

7. See, to begin with, Roy F. Nichols, *The Invention of the American Political Parties* (New York: The Free Press, 1967).

8. E. Pendleton Herring, *Group Representative Before Congress* (Baltimore: The Johns Hopkins Press, 1929), pp. 2–3.

9. Moisei Ostrogorski, *Democracy and the Organization of Political Parties* (Garden City, New York: Doubleday & Company, Inc., 1964), pp. 365–66.

10. Loren P. Beth, *The Development of the American Constitution* (New York: Harper & Row, Publishers, 1971), p. 132.

11. Ostrogorski, *Democracy,* pp. 353–55.

12. Ibid., p. 173.

13. Beth, *Development,* pp. 132–33.

14. Quoted in John A. Garraty, *The New Commonwealth, 1877–1890* (New York: Harper Torchbooks, 1968), p. 28.

15. The term was invented by Matthew Josephson, *The Robber Barons* (New York: Harcourt, Brace, Jovanovich, 1934).

16. The English king under whom the Parliamentary development touched upon above was achieved. He also distinguished himself by conquering Wales and annexing it. But the principle of Welsh representation in the House of Commons was not conceded until the time of Henry VIII, who was of Welsh descent, early in the sixteenth century, i.e., some 250 years later. So the representative system was originally English.

17. W. J. Ghent, *Our Benevolent Feudalism,* (New York: The Macmillan Company, 1902), p. 9.

18. The interaction of the sociological and the intellectual constitutes a problem in "the sociology of knowledge." It is here neglected, as are other influences and variables.

19. Otto von Gierke, *Political Theories of the Middle Age* (Cambridge, Eng.: Cambridge University Press, 1900).

20. J. N. Figgis, *Churches in the Modern State* (London: Longmans, 1913). H. J. Laski, *Authority in the Modern State* (New Haven: Yale University Press, 1919).

21. Place or area in which certain rights and privileges are exercised.

22. For an attempt to relate guild socialism to A. H. Maslow's theory of motivation, see Graham Wootton, *Workers, Unions, and the State* (New York: Schocken Books, 1967), ch. 10.

23. G. D. H. Cole, *Social Theory* (London: Methuen & Co., Ltd., 1920), pp. 106–108, 115.

24. William Allen White, *Politics: The Citizen's Business* (New York: The Macmillan Company, 1924), pp. 16–17.

25. This reminds one of the British political historian, Ramsay Muir, who referred a little later (1930) to "organized special interests outside of the regular machinery of the Constitution."

26. Alfred D. Chandler, Jr., "The Role of Business in the United States: A Historical Survey," in Eli Goldston and others, *The American Business Corporation* (Cambridge: M.I.T. Press, 1972), p. 43.

27. *Fortune,* May 4, 1981.

28. Chandler, *The Role,* p. 53.

29. Ibid., p. 55.

30. John D. Black, "The McNary-Haugen Movement," *American Economic Review,* XVIII (1928), p. 405.

31. Hannah Pitkin, *The Concept of Representation* (Berkeley: University of California Press, 1967), pp. 232–33. Heinz Eulau and Kenneth Prewitt, *Labyrinths of Democracy* (Indianapolis: The Bobbs-Merrill Company, Inc., 1973), chap. 21.

32. Hearings before the Subcommittee on Intergovernmental Relations, Senate Committee on Government Operations, *Advisory Committees,* 1971, Part 1, p. 102.

33. Ibid., Part 2, pp. 702–736.

34. Ibid., Part 2, pp. 557–58.

35. Ibid., pp. 567–70.

36. Ibid., p. 538.

37. Mark V. Nadel, *Corporations and Political Accountability* (Lexington, Mass.: D. C. Heath and Company, 1976), pp. 33–34, 70.

38. Hearings before the Subcommittee on Intergovernmental Relations, *Advisory Committees,* 1971, Part 2, p. 485.

39. Ibid., p. 483.

40. Charles E. Lindblom, *Politics and Markets* (New York: Basic Books, Inc., Publishers, 1977), p. 356.

41. Ibid., pp. 176–77, 356.

42. Everett Carll Ladd, *Fortune,* October 20, 1980.

ACKNOWLEDGMENTS

The statement by Jeb Magruder, quoted on page 1, and repeated on page 305, is reprinted from the October 1973 issue of *Harper's* magazine by special permission. Copyright © 1973 by *Harper's* magazine. All Rights Reserved.

The excerpted portion of James Reston's column which appears on page 1 is reprinted by permission of the The New York Times. Copyright © 1973 by The New York Times Company.

The excerpted portion of Barbara Bergman's essay which appears on page 4 is reprinted by permission of The New York Times. Copyright © 1982 by The New York Times Company.

Robert Dole's statement, as quoted in the excerpted portion of Albert Hunt's *Wall Street Journal* column which appears on page 5, is reprinted by permission of *The Wall Street Journal*, © Dow Jones & Company, Inc., 1982. All Rights Reserved.

Richard Corrigan's account of the fate of the Conable-Hance bill, which appears on page 9, is reprinted with permission from the *National Journal*, © 1981.

The portions of *The Washington Post* editorial which appear on pages 16–17 are reprinted by permission of *The Washington Post*. Copyright *The Washington Post*.

James Wilson's critique of Charles Lindblom, which appears on page 95, is reprinted by permission of *The Wall Street Journal*, © Dow Jones & Company, Inc., 1978. All Rights Reserved.

The excerpted portion of Frances Fox Piven's/Richard Cloward's book, which appears on page 156, is used by permission. Copyright Pantheon Books, a Division of Random House, Inc.

The excerpted portion of Marion Edey's essay, which appears on page 165, is reprinted by permission of Viking Penguin Inc. and Ralph Nadar. Copyright © 1975 by Ralph Nadar.

The Charles Peters quotation, which appears on page 198, is reprinted with permission. © 1980, Addison-Wesley, Reading, Massachusetts.

Table 8-6, which was compiled by Michael Gordon (see footnote 58, Chapter 8) and appears on page 204, is reprinted with permission from the *National Journal*.

Table 8-7, which was compiled by Michael Milbin (see footnote 78, Chapter 8) and appears on page 210, is reprinted by permission of Basic Books. © 1980 Basic Books, Inc., Publishers.

INDEX

SUBJECT INDEX